# About this Book

Genocide and war crimes are increasingly the focus of scholarly and activist attention. Much controversy exists over how, precisely, these grim phenomena should be defined and conceptualized. *Genocide, War Crimes and the West* tackles this controversy, and clarifies our understanding of an important but under-researched dimension: the involvement of the US and other liberal democracies in actions that are conventionally depicted as the exclusive province of totalitarian and authoritarian regimes.

Many of the authors are eminent scholars and/or renowned activists; in most cases, their contributions are specifically written for this volume. In the opening and closing sections of the book, analytical issues are considered, including questions of responsibility for genocide and war crimes, and institutional responses at both the domestic and international levels. The central section is devoted to an unprecedentedly broad range of original case studies of Western involvement, or alleged involvement, in war crimes and genocide.

At a moment in history when terrorism has become a near universal focus of public attention, this volume makes clear why the West – as a result of both its historical legacy and its contemporary actions – so often excites widespread resentment and opposition throughout the rest of the world.

# Genocide, War Crimes and the West

*History and Complicity*

**Edited by Adam Jones**

ZED BOOKS
*London & New York*

*Genocide, War Crimes and the West* was first published in 2004 by
Zed Books Ltd, 7 Cynthia Street, London N1 9JF, UK,
and Room 400, 175 Fifth Avenue, New York, NY 10010, USA

www.zedbooks.co.uk

Designed and typeset in Monotype Bembo by Illuminati, Grosmont
Cover designed by Andrew Corbett
Printed and bound in Malaysia

Distributed in the USA exclusively by Palgrave Macmillan, a division of
St Martin's Press, LLC, 175 Fifth Avenue, New York, NY 10010

A catalogue record for this book is available from the British Library
Library of Congress Cataloging-in-Publication Data available

ISBN 1 84277 190 6 (Hb)
ISBN 1 84277 191 4 (Pb)

# Contents

# PART I

# Overview

# I

# Introduction:
# History and Complicity

## Adam Jones

In April 2001, convicted mass murderer Timothy McVeigh – about to die in the first US federal execution in 150 years – sent a letter to a Fox News correspondent seeking 'to explain ... why I bombed the Murrah Federal Building in Oklahoma City,' killing 168 people. He referred to his terrorist action as 'a retaliatory strike' and 'counterattack' for the FBI attack against the Branch Davidians at Waco, Texas. But McVeigh then took a surprising analytical leap, turning to 'identifiable pattern[s] of conduct' by the US government in the international sphere:

> borrowing a page from US foreign policy, I decided to send a message to a government that was becoming increasingly hostile, by bombing a government building and the government employees within that building who represent that government. Bombing the Murrah Federal Building was morally and strategically equivalent to the US hitting a government building in Serbia, Iraq, or other nations.... Based on observations of the policies of my own government, I viewed this action as an acceptable option. From this perspective, what occurred in Oklahoma City was no different than what Americans rain on the heads of others all the time, and subsequently, my mindset was and is one of clinical detachment.[1]

There is no reason, of course, to question depictions of McVeigh as a murderous thug. His letter nonetheless raised some pertinent questions. Why was McVeigh's murderous thuggery and 'free-lance fanaticism' (Morrow, 2001) viewed as egregious and indefensible, indeed meriting the death penalty, while wholesale thuggery by his government tends to be seen as politics as usual? And was McVeigh's 'mindset ... of clinical detachment' any worse than the criminality and amorality that had turned the United States into the world's leading 'rogue state'? (See Huntington, 1999; Blum, 2001.[2])

Around the time McVeigh's letter was released, one long-buried, state-sponsored crime was making global headlines. Bob Kerrey, a former US senator and Democratic presidential candidate who later headed the New School University in New York, acknowledged that on 25 February 1969 he had led a commando unit of Navy Seals in an attack on the South Vietnamese coastal village of Thanh Phong. The Seals' primary task was 'kidnap or assassination missions, looking to eliminate Vietcong leaders from among the local population' (Vistica, 2001). Accounts differ as to what happened when the team arrived in the hamlet. According to Kerrey, the Seals came across a 'hooch' (house) that had not appeared in intelligence reports. 'We've got some men here, we have to take care of them,' Kerrey said he was told by members of his team. That meant collective killing: 'Standard operating procedure was to dispose of the people we made contact with. Kill the people we made contact with, or we have to abort the mission.' Kerrey said he took no part in these initial killings. The team moved on to another cluster of dwellings, where, according to Kerrey, it came under fire, which was returned. Twelve hundred rounds of US ammunition later, Kerrey said he made a terrible discovery. In the 'hooches,' 'I was expecting to find Vietcong soldiers with weapons, dead. Instead I found women and children.'

Other testimony, though, suggested an even more grisly, and systematic, slaughter of civilians. Kerrey's Navy Seal comrade Gerhard Klann claimed that Kerrey had been fully aware that the unit's eventual victims were civilian women and children, and had given the order anyway to mow them down in cold blood. 'Klann says that Kerrey gave the order and the team, standing between 6 and 10 feet away, started shooting – raking the group with automatic-weapons fire for about 30 seconds. They heard moans, Klann says, and began firing again, for another 30 seconds. There was one final cry, from a baby.' In response, Kerrey claimed that even if Klann's account were true, the actions were defensible. 'Under the un-written rules of Vietnam, we would have been justified [in killing civilians even] had we not been fired upon. You were authorized to kill if you thought that it would be better.... We were instructed not to take prisoners' (Vistica, 2001).

The US media and public response to Kerrey's confession was striking: 'many Americans seem[ed] quicker to sympathize with the former war hero [Kerrey] and to lament the "horror of war" rather than focus on the real issues of crime and justice' (Goldhagen and Power, 2001). *Time* magazine emphasized not the victims of the US attack, but the 'private agonies' and 'aching experience' of 'physically and psychically scarred veterans like Kerrey,' for whom 'the war is never quite over' (McGeary and Tumulty, 2001).

Amidst the conservative bluster and liberal commiseration, a few commentators and organizations did call for a thorough investigation of Kerrey's alleged crimes, and the backdrop of US-sponsored atrocities — perhaps genocide — against which they occurred. For Human Rights Watch, Kerrey's revelations suggested that US military units 'may have directly violated the Fourth Geneva Convention of 1949 and resulted in "grave breaches" of that Convention, or war crimes.' The organization called for US Defense Secretary Donald Rumsfeld 'to initiate without delay a full and independent investigation to establish whether during the Vietnam War certain U.S. military policies, orders and practices ... constituted or led directly to the commission of war crimes by U.S. forces' (Human Rights Watch, 2001). Bruce Shapiro, writing in *Salon* (Shapiro, 2001), called for the establishment of a South African-style 'truth commission' to investigate US war crimes in Vietnam. 'Suppressed atrocity,' Shapiro wrote, 'haunts not just its victims and shadows not just its perpetrators, but distorts the political life of entire societies.'

The broader debate over Vietnam, after a decade or more of jingoistic posturing, re-crystallized around the figure of former US Secretary of State Henry Kissinger (see the chapters in this volume by Mario Aguilar, Steven Jacobs, and Suhail Islam and Syed Hassan). Kissinger, and the administrations he served, were directly or indirectly responsible for some of the bloodiest crimes of the post-World War II era. They included the sustained US bombing campaigns against peasant societies in Vietnam, Cambodia, and Laos; the Indonesian invasion of East Timor in December 1975, which rapidly assumed genocidal dimensions; and the West Pakistani assault on what was shortly to become independent Bangladesh, in 1970–71, a more gigantic slaughter still. On a smaller scale, but at a cost of thousands more lives, Kissinger encouraged, aided, and abetted the military coup that overthrew the democratically elected government of Salvador Allende in Chile in 1973.

Kissinger has retained a considerable cachet within the United States, as evidenced by his appointment to head the commission struck to investigate the events of 11 September 2001. (Kissinger accepted but subsequently withdrew, citing possible conflicts of interest.) A growing number of voices, however, have called for him to play a very different role: that of prisoner in the dock. The case for arraigning Kissinger for war crimes and crimes against humanity was made most prominently, and pithily, by the British journalist Christopher Hitchens, whose two-part series for *Harper's* magazine was subsequently published as a slender book, *The Trial of Henry Kissinger* (Hitchens, 2001). In the present work, three authors take diverse approaches to the Kissinger case, and consider its implications for the volume's central themes.

The United States was not the only Western country to play host to such controversies as a new century began.

In France, Paul Aussaresses, a former general in the Algerian war (1954–62), brazenly acknowledged that during the war 'he and his "death squad" tortured and killed twenty-four prisoners with the full knowledge and backing of the French government.' That government, said Aussaresses, 'was regularly informed about, and tolerated the use of, torture, summary executions and forced displacements of people' (Agence France-Presse, 2001; see Raphaëlle Branche's chapter in this volume). Aussaresses was unrepentant about his involvement in the crimes. French President Jacques Chirac, who served in the army in Algeria, declared himself 'horrified' by the revelations; Chirac called for the general to be stripped of his Légion d'honneur and face military sanctions. Observers noted that the general's account, 'and [his] insistence that he is unrepentant, have reopened deep wounds from the most painful chapter of France's colonial past and revived a divisive debate over whether those responsible should or can be brought to trial' (Agence France-Presse, 2001).

In the end, Aussaresses *was* put on trial – but for 'complicity in justifying war crimes,' not for the crimes themselves, which were covered by a 1962 amnesty. In January 2002, Aussaresses was found guilty, and fined $6,500 – 'a sentence so trivial that it served only to underline the fact that his deeds were exempt from punishment, and that France had little interest in revisiting the past' (Shatz, 2002). Nonetheless, the public re-examination of a past grown stale was surely preferable to a blanket of silence – not least for those who had been on the receiving end, or their survivors, as Mariner notes:

> Without a doubt, relatives of the thousands of suspects who were 'disappeared' during Algeria's independence conflict must take some satisfaction in seeing a French court formally condemn the French army's abusive practices, even if, from their perspective, the judgment is more than forty years late. The court's official acknowledgment that the abuses committed by the French in Algeria were war crimes and, as such, unjustifiable in any circumstances, marks an important step forward. Although much has been written about the systematic use of torture during the war, France has never apologized for its army's conduct, nor have French officials shown much interest in sanctioning an official reexamination of the period. (Mariner, 2002)

In Belgium, government authorities and intellectuals finally began to reckon with the country's often tawdry, sometimes genocidal, colonial past. The empire's 'heart of darkness' was in Congo, where independence in 1960 was followed by the murder of the country's leading nationalist figure, Patrice Lumumba. In February 2002 the Belgian government, which had 'steadfastly denied any involvement until new evidence collected by a parliamentary commission confirmed the direct role of Belgian agents in carrying out and covering up the murder,' admitted its participation in Lumumba's assassination, and formally apologized (Riding, 2002; see Thomas Turner's chapter in this volume).

According to the *New York Times*, 'the motivation for the crime was to avoid losing control over Congo's resources.' Decades earlier, a similar preoccupation with the vast territory – seventy-five times larger than Belgium itself – had prompted Belgian King Leopold to seize Congo as his personal property, turning it into the grotesquely misnamed 'Congo Free State.' Between 1885 and 1908, millions of Congolese males were conscripted into forced labor, and driven deep into the jungle to gather rubber for export. The 'rubber terror' inflicted a staggering death toll on the laborers, and their protracted – or permanent – separation from wives and families exacerbated the demographic holocaust. Adam Hochschild's 1997 book *King Leopold's Ghost* exposed for a global public the astonishing scale and savagery of the killing; he estimated the overall toll (direct deaths plus demographic decline owing to the lowered birth rate) as approaching *ten million* Congolese (Hochschild, 1998).

In response to the furor that Hochschild's work generated in Belgium, the Royal Museum for Central Africa announced 'the first far-reaching review of Belgium's colonial past.' The initiative 'raises the broader question of a country's continuing responsibility for unsavory [!] actions carried out in its name generations or even centuries earlier. These range from promotion of the slave trade and annexation of territories to colonial repression and ransacking of natural resources' (Riding, 2002). Stated museum director Guida Gryseels: 'It is a reality which touches the deepest part of the Belgian soul. We really haven't coped with it, and the revelations came as a real shock. We were brought up knowing that we brought civilisation and good to Africa. [Allegations of brutality] weren't taught in schools' (quoted in Osborn, 2002).

Across the Channel in the United Kingdom, a penetrating re-examination of Britain's imperial role was also under way – one facet of the movement for reparations for Western exploitation of slave labor (see Francis Njubi Nesbitt's chapter in this book). The issue came to a head at the United Nations conference on racism in Durban in 2001, at which British representatives fought against declaring slavery a 'crime against humanity' (McGreal, 2001).[3] Activists increasingly targeted municipal authorities, building on the success achieved in December 1999, when the municipal council of Liverpool, a city that had boomed during the slaving era, made 'an unreserved apology for the city's involvement in the slave trade,' acknowledging the 'untold misery' and its legacy for 'Black people in Liverpool today' (Nelson, 2002).

## 'Democrisy' and the dissident strand

'The standard of justice,' wrote Thucydides more than two thousand years ago, 'depends on the equality of power to compel and that in fact the strong do what they have the power to do and the weak accept what they have to accept' (cited in Bass, 2000, frontispiece). A profusion of modern-day examples in international politics reminds us that Thucydides' observation has legs. But today it also seems to require revision. The strong *are* sometimes constrained from doing what they have the power to do – or at least from doing it as and when they wish to. The end of settler colonialism and transoceanic slavery as 'acceptable' international conduct provide two examples. The US *non*-invasion of Central American countries in the 1980s, contrasted with an earlier uninhibited reliance on sending in the Marines, offers another.

Meanwhile, the 'weak' – the majority of the world's population and the governments that claim to represent them – have in recent decades shown less willingness to 'accept what they have to accept', at least without protracted and voluble struggle.[4] Among other things, they have virtually eliminated (formal) colonialism from the face of the earth – an epochal and under-recognized achievement, even though the vanquished beast appears to be making a comeback with the US occupation and administration of Iraq (Hartung et al., 2002; Sanger and Schmitt, 2002).[5] Conceptions and institutions of international justice; national and international human rights movements; campaigns for truth and restitution – all these are now well-established features of international relations and domestic politics. Henry Kissinger, for one, could hardly disagree, despite his preference for Thucydidean realpolitik. The very factors that constrain Kissinger's foreign travel itinerary are those that, more and more, may be constraining the actions of the powerful around the world.

So this book forms part of a wider contemporary trend, in which the actions and atrocities of the powerful are under examination and public criticism as never before in history. But why the focus on crimes, or alleged crimes, of *Western* states? After all, they are hardly unique in their adherence to Thucydides' maxim. Genocide, war crimes, and crimes against humanity blight societies throughout the underdeveloped world, and domestic leaders and elites must often shoulder a large or dominant portion of the blame.

In my view, allegations of Western involvement in genocide and other crimes carry, and *should* carry, a special bite and resonance, especially for the Western citizens who will predominate as readers of this book. Such readers confront the phenomenon of *democrisy*, which I define as the stain of hypocrisy that attaches to regimes that are avowedly democratic in character, that allow comparative freedom and immunity from naked state violence domestically, but that initiate or participate in atrocious actions beyond their borders.[6] This contradiction between domestic and international practice is far less stark in reality, as indigenous inhabitants and minority groups within Western states can attest. But the disparity between democratic ideals, *comparatively* well respected at home, and blatant depravity abroad clearly forms a foundation for most contemporary critiques of the West's role in atrocity. Consider, for example, this passage from Edward S. Herman's 1982 study, *The Real Terror Network*:

> It is difficult to avoid a sense of outrage not only at the realities of this real terror network but also at western hypocrisy. An important element in that hypocrisy is the pretense of western non-involvement [in terror]. Thus, while the killings and torture in the NSSs [National Security States] are sometimes mentioned in the news media – as inexplicable background facts, like cosmic radiation, and for some reason not deserving indignation remotely proportional to the crimes in question – the U.S. role in establishing and maintaining the NSSs in power is generally suppressed altogether. This pattern of hypocrisy, aversion of the eyes, and absence of indignation at extensive and serious crimes can be rationally explained only in terms of a structure of [domestic] interests. … A systematic dichotomous treatment can be found across the board, whereby huge crimes by state terrorists within the U.S. sphere of influence are either suppressed or given brief and muted treatment, [while] abuses attributable to enemies are attended to repeatedly and with indignation and sarcasm. (Herman, 1982: 8, 16)

Evident here is Herman's outrage at the *despoliation of democracy* implied by the state's criminal connivance. References to the 'pattern of hypocrisy' (a specifically *Western* hypocrisy), to 'pretense,' media blackout, 'absence of [public] indignation' – all these criticisms would make little sense outside a context of democratic freedoms. I am reminded, too, of the 'Letter to America' by South African writer Breyten Breytenbach, which closes this volume. For me it is one of the most thoughtful and impassioned denunciations of the US global role issued after 11 September 2001. And anger at *democrisy* pervades it. Breytenbach demands to know in what way US 'priorities [are] any different from those of the defunct Soviet Union or other totalitarian regimes' – implying that they should be different, dramatically so – and then confesses in a revealing way the 'difficulty' he encounters in critiquing US actions:

Why is it difficult? Because the United States is a complex entity despite the gung-ho slogans and simplistic posturing in moments of national hysteria. Your political system is resilient and well tested; it has always harbored counterforces; it allows quite effectively for alternation: for a swing-back of the pendulum whenever policies have strayed too far from middle-class interests – with the result that you have a large middle ground of acceptable political practices. Why, through the role of elected representatives, the people who vote even have a rudimentary democratic control over public affairs! Except maybe in Florida. Better still – your history has shown how powerful a moral catharsis expressed through popular resistance to injustice can sometimes be…. And all along there was no dearth of strong voices speaking firm convictions and enunciating sure ethical standards. (Breytenbach, 2002)

'Where are [the strong voices] now?' Breytenbach asks plaintively. Again, it is not a question that could easily be directed to citizens of an authoritarian or dictatorial state. Breytenbach is acknowledging that plurality and possibility for change exist under democracy, even in the world's most imperial democratic state. That recognition both fuels and shapes his anger against the 'cracker fundamentalists, desk warriors … warmed up Dr. Strangeloves and oil-greedy conservative capitalists' who, in his view, have hijacked US democracy since 9/11. But even the corrupted democracy allows polemics like Breytenbach's to appear, and in a non-trivial, relatively mainstream forum (his letter was originally published in *The Nation*). This is broadly true of countries where *democrisy* obtains. They allow a searchlight to be trained upon the state's actions; domestic critics, at least, rarely need to fear a visit from a death squad or professional torturer. As a result, citizens, too, are in danger of bolstering *democrisy* through their quiescence. Breytenbach implies that they – we – have a special capacity and thus a special obligation to speak out and to intervene.

Such interventions have been part of the 'Western' tradition since long before a modern (or post-modern) phenomenon like *democrisy* could arise. Think of Bartolomé de las Casas' denunciations of Spanish depredations in the Americas, for example. But interventionism took a momentous step forward with the rise of mass democracy, education, urbanization, and communication in the West. These social upheavals spawned, as early as the nineteenth century, 'a range of popular organizations and movements [that] sought to condemn war, to temper its severity when it occurred and, even more ambitiously, to create international dispute mechanisms that might obviate it entirely' (Reisman and Antoniou, 1994: xviii). Such mobilized opinion had a profound impact on legislation drafted to govern crimes of war (notably with the Hague and Geneva Conventions). It underpinned two of the most large-scale and successful international social movements in history: the anti-slavery movement, and the later campaign against Belgian forced labor in Congo, led by the Irishman Roger Casement. Aroused publics and non-governmental organizations contributed seminally to key pieces of post-World War II legislation, such as the Universal Declaration of Human Rights and the Convention on the Prevention and Punishment of the Crime of Genocide, both passed by the United Nations in 1948. And the interventions continue today, on a still greater scale, as chapter after chapter in this book makes clear.

The interventions are more necessary than ever, in part because *democrisy* has always been in the eye of the beholder. For proponents and defenders of Western states, for those who buttress the idea of the West's exceptional role as a civilizing force, no hypocrisy enters the equation – because there is no systematic deviation from the democratic norm, whether internally or outside Western states' boundaries. Democratic states *'wouldn't* do' something atrocious; therefore they 'don't.' Any suggestion that they regularly have done it, and continue to do it, is viewed as intemperate or ungrateful at best, dangerous or extremist at worst. The result is an effective 'culture of impunity,' in which the atrocities committed by Western states and their allies are systematically ignored, explained away, defined out of existence, or openly celebrated – anything to preserve them from serious and objective criticism.

*Genocide, War Crimes and the West* can be seen as an attempt to erode, in some small way, this culture of impunity. As such, it forms part of a 'dissident strand' in analyses of Western foreign and domestic policy. I do not mean to say that the contributors' approaches and conclusions are uniform. A significant proportion, for example, do not condemn in blanket fashion the actions of a given Western state or states. But none, I think, would support the idea that the behavior of Western democratic states, abroad or at home, is purely benevolent, and therefore exempt from systemic critique.

The emergence of the dissident strand took a somewhat different path in each Western country, strongly influenced by events in the decolonizing countries and their independent successors in the 'Third World.' I do not intend to provide a detailed multinational history here, but will limit myself to exploring the dissident strand as it took shape in the most powerful Western country and the leading focus of such critiques, the United States, with passing references to parallel developments elsewhere.

The dissident literature on US foreign and domestic policy has deep roots in populist and socialist traditions that extend far back into the nineteenth century. One need only consult the record of the spirited debates over US intervention in the Philippines and Cuba at the turn of the twentieth century, for example, to see that skepticism towards proclaimed policy goals is nothing new in the American body politic. In its post-World War II incarnation, dissidence was connected closely with the US's emergence as the dominant global power. The 'grand strategy' implemented after the war to organize international relations according to US ambitions led naturally to interventions, both overt and covert, on a scale unprecedented in US (indeed world) history. This prompted, beginning in the late 1950s, the rise of a 'revisionist' school of historians led by William Appleman Williams with his 1959 work *The Tragedy of American Diplomacy*.

Williams was less radical than many of his successors, but his appears to have been the first prominent academic voice of the postwar era to point out the basic expansionist continuity in American policy, at home and abroad. The closing of the 'frontier' at the end of the nineteenth century brought an end to the continental drive that had placed much of North America under US control and exterminated the majority of its native inhabitants. For Williams, the imperial campaign that took over, continuing into the post-World War II era, was founded on a desire for new international markets and favorable economic arrangements to bolster prosperity domestically, and to compensate for the loss of an ever-expanding *Lebensraum* on the North American continent itself.

The primacy of economic considerations in Williams's model was duplicated in the more detailed dissident analyses that proliferated in the 1960s, with the United States turning large parts of Indochina into wastelands cratered by high explosives. David Horowitz led the way with his *Free World Colossus* (Horowitz, 1965), a book that the author eventually disowned and withdrew from sale after his conversion to hardline neo-conservatism.[7] With the international New Left reaching its apogee, the years 1966–69 saw the publication of a succession of core dissident texts: Edward S. Herman's *America's Vietnam Policy: The Strategy of Deception* (1966); Franz Schurmann et al.'s *The Politics of Escalation in Vietnam* (1966, co-authored by a contributor to this volume, Peter Dale Scott); Howard Zinn's *Vietnam: The Logic of Withdrawal* (1967; see also Zinn, 1980); Gabriel Kolko's *The Politics of War* (1968; see also Kolko, 1988); Richard J. Barnet's *Intervention and Revolution* (1968); and Noam Chomsky's first collection of essays, *American Power and the New Mandarins* (1969, gratifyingly reissued by the New Press in 2002). More or less concurrently, soul-searching on the domestic issue of race produced the first 'Black Power' texts (see, e.g., Malcolm X, 1965; Cleaver, 1968), as well as Dee Brown's majestic revisionist account of the 'settling' of the American West, *Bury My Heart at Wounded Knee* (Brown, 1972).[8]

Congressional revelations, in the mid-1970s, of Central Intelligence Agency (CIA) interventionism throughout the Third World were buttressed by the memoirs of former CIA operatives, notably Philip Agee (*Inside the Company: CIA Diary*, 1975) and John Stockwell (*In Search of Enemies: A CIA Story*, 1978). These taboo-breakers paved the way for more mainstream authors to contribute well-documented dissident critiques, such as William Shawcross's *Sideshow: Kissinger, Nixon, and the Destruction of Cambodia* (1979); Seymour M. Hersh's ruthless dissection of the Kissinger myth, *The Price of Power* (1983); Stephen Schlesinger and Stephen Kinzer's history of the US-sponsored coup in Guatemala in 1954, *Bitter Fruit* (1983; see also Immerman, 1982); and *New York Times* journalist Raymond Bonner's chilling study of US policy in El Salvador, *Weakness and Deceit* (1984).

It is vital to acknowledge the contributions of a number of 'Third World' writers whose critiques of Western imperialism penetrated the Western consciousness from the 1960s to the 1980s. These included Frantz Fanon's studies of the psychology of colonial oppression (*The Wretched of the Earth*, 1963; *Black Skin, White Masks*, 1968); Che Guevara's *Guerrilla Warfare* (1961) and *Reminiscences of the Cuban Revolutionary War* (1968); Paulo Freire's *Pedagogy of the Oppressed* (1970); Walter Rodney's *How Europe Underdeveloped Africa* (1972); Eduardo Galeano's *Open Veins of Latin America* (1973); Edward Said's *Orientalism* (1979); and Rigoberta Menchú's *I, Rigoberta Menchú* (Burgos-Debray, 1983). Perhaps for the first time, a broad and multifaceted dialogue was initiated between Third World critics and activists and their First World sympathizers – a process mirrored by the rise of numerous solidarity committees in Western communities and on Western university campuses.

The wave of US-supported and -inspired coups in Latin America and elsewhere during the 1960s and 1970s led to the establishment of 'National Security States' (NSS), in which selective or blanket terror was used to crush popular mobilization and reduce citizens to a state of fear and passivity. Roughly contemporaneously, a neoconservative critique was gestating within US political and academic life, built on the Rambo-esque conviction that victory in Vietnam had been sabotaged by domestic interests (including pusillanimous politicians and hyper-critical mass media). From this interpretation of the recent past, it followed that waging the Cold War with the Soviets required not the squeamishness of the 'Vietnam Syndrome,' but unabashed militarism and interventionism.

With the ascent to power of Ronald Reagan in 1981, this strand found its most potent expression. The result was a renewed campaign of US support for terrorist states and movements around the world, accompanied by large-scale but usually 'covert' violence in Central America, southern Africa, and elsewhere. This could all be presented as the result of a staunch commitment to *fighting* terrorism – a trope that was possible only if the term 'terrorism' was strictly limited in its practical application, designating movements and regimes deemed hostile to the United States.[9] Some of the most terror-fueled regimes of the twentieth century – in Guatemala, El Salvador, and Indonesia, to cite just three – were thus redefined as *progressive*, as 'embattled democrats,' as 'caught between extremes' of left (the popular and guerrilla opposition) and right (the paramilitaries and death squads, somehow divorced from the regimes that constituted and directed them). Meanwhile, 'retail' terrorist movements, whose power was minuscule in comparison with the 'wholesale' state terror that predominated in the Western sphere of influence, were depicted as nothing more than cogs in a communist machine. Their origins lay not in local grievances but in the Soviet Union's attempt to undermine Western democracy and establish Red supremacy worldwide.

This frankly Orwellian framing of terrorism was enthusiastically adopted by the school of 'terrorology' that crested around this time, with contributions from scholars like Walter Laqueur (*Terrorism*, 1977; *The Age of Terrorism*, 1987), Jeane Kirkpatrick (*Dictatorships and Double Standards*, 1982), and Paul Wilkinson (*Terrorism and the Liberal State*, 1977; *Terrorism: Theory and Practice*, 1979); the diplomat and future Israeli Minister Benjamin Netanyahu (*Terrorism: How the West Can Win*, 1986); and journalistic hacks such as Claire Sterling (*The Terror Network*, 1981) and Arnauld de Borchgrave and Robert Moss (*The Spike*, 1980).

The generally reactionary thrust of US politics, academics, and mass media in the 1980s spawned a reaction, in turn, from proponents of the dissident strand. An important and perhaps unique exception in the academic study of 'terrorology' was Michael Stohl, whose edited volume *The Politics of Terrorism* (1988) remains one of the field's enduring classics.[10] The broader dissident strand produced a range of seminal studies of 'counter-terrorism' and 'counter-subversion' (which amounted, in the dissident view, to large-scale terrorism and subversion). Edward S. Herman led the way with a 1982 work, the title of which, *The Real Terror Network*, aimed squarely at confronting Claire Sterling's influential thesis (Herman, 1982; see also Herman and O'Sullivan, 1990). Building on seminal 1970s works co-authored with Noam Chomsky (Herman and Chomsky, 1979a; 1979b), Herman analyzed the politics of the emerging school of 'terrorology,' the terroristic underpinnings of US client-state networks throughout the Third World, and the role of mass media in establishing 'acceptable' parameters of thought and analysis. He was also one of the first to emphasize the role of 'sub-fascist' client states in imposing terror that Western countries could support without having to micro-administer.

During the same period, Noam Chomsky continued his forceful evaluations of US policies in *Towards a New Cold War* (1982), *Turning the*

*Tide* (1985) and *The Culture of Terrorism* (1988). Herman and Chomsky collaborated again on *Manufacturing Consent: The Political Economy of the Mass Media* (1988). Michael McClintock published his devastating two-volume indictment of *The American Connection* to despotic regimes world-wide (1985).[11] Michael Parenti weighed in with *Inventing Reality: The Politics of the News Media* (1986) and *The Sword and the Dollar: Imperialism, Revolution and the Arms Race* (1989; see also Parenti, 2000). The focus on 'covert' and 'low-intensity' warfare in US strategy produced some significant dissident analyses of these phenomena (e.g. Klare and Kornbluh, 1988). Notable critical voices in the mass media throughout the decade included the British critics Alexander Cockburn (1987) and Christopher Hitchens (1990), as well as the Australian John Pilger (1989; 1994).

The dissident literature on terrorism and counter-terrorism achieved something of a summation with the publication of Alexander George's edited volume *Western State Terrorism* in 1990. This book, perhaps the most obvious forebear of *Genocide, War Crimes and the West*, deserves closer consideration here, and comparison with the present work.

An omnibus approach links *Western State Terrorism* to *Genocide, War Crimes and the West*. George's book drew together and summarized the dissident literature of the 1970s and 1980s that had turned accepted conventions of 'terrorism' on their head, though its contribution was largely ignored in public and academic discourse. A number of pivotal figures of that litera-ture (Noam Chomsky, Edward Herman, Michael McClintock, Richard Falk) were represented. The book was a seminal contribution, published by a major press (Polity). That it is virtually unknown today – though it is still, fortunately, in print – perhaps attests to the enduring hegemony of the mainstream discourse on terrorism.

George and his contributors produced a powerful, wide-ranging volume with a strikingly consistent tone and methodology. The contribu-tors rejected the facile equation of terror with small-scale, 'retail' terror-ism directed against Western states. Through their (and Michael Stohl's) explicit focus on Western support for *state* terrorism, the conceptual playing field was substantially broadened. State terror was also brought up against its conceptual limits – that is to say, attention was paid to the points at which terrorism spills over into aggressive war and genocide. George's edited book thus shares with this one a skeptical approach towards Western claims of moral righteousness and impunity from criticism. However, fewer contributors to the present volume adopt as forthrightly dissident a stance as that of the luminaries assembled for *Western State Terrorism*. Indeed, several of them argue for a more nuanced evaluation of Western complicity in genocide and war crimes. A few – like Steven Jacobs, Eric Langenbacher, and David Bruce MacDonald –

bring in qualified verdicts in the particular cases they examine. (Thomas Turner's consideration of Western involvement in the murder of Patrice Lumumba, meanwhile, can perhaps be viewed as a motion for retrial!) Nonetheless, by their simple (and complex) presence in this volume, they demonstrate a conviction that Western countries cannot claim impunity from the investigative searchlight that they routinely turn on 'the Other' worldwide. When the analytical terrain broadens to allow cases for both the prosecution and defence to be presented, *even if an exculpatory verdict is eventually passed*, we are far from a mainstream framing that relies upon nipping any such debate in the bud.

In addition to a somewhat broader range of approaches and conclusions, there are other differences between *Genocide, War Crimes and the West* and George's edited work. One is the scale of the project: Zed has generously granted the present set of contributors much greater space with which to work. The result is a book that contains nearly two dozen chapters and document excerpts, compared to the nine in *Western State Terrorism*. The available space is, moreover, devoted to themes that are in many ways substantially different from George's. The present book does not situate itself in the 'terrorism' literature per se, focusing more (as the subtitle suggests) on war crimes and genocide. The landmark contributions to the study of terrorism and 'terrorology' in *Western State Terrorism* can therefore stand, and be supplemented here by related but distinct lines of investigation.

George's volume contained just three case studies of Western involvement in large-scale terrorism or other criminal activity (Britain and Northern Ireland; Indonesia during the epic massacres of 1965–66; and southern Africa during the Reagan era of the 1980s). A key ambition of *Genocide, War Crimes and the West*, on the other hand, is to present the most geographically and historically comprehensive survey yet of Western involvement in war crimes and other atrocities. Treatment is accorded to subjects as diverse as the German extermination, early in the twentieth century, of the Herero and Nama peoples of Namibia (then South West Africa); US maraudings in Southeast Asia and Latin America; residential schools for Native Americans in Canada and the US; France's coming to terms with its past of torture and atrocity in Algeria; and the structural violence that underpins more visible forms of oppression and brutality.

A difficulty with much of the dissident writing on terrorism, war crimes, and genocide is that it is frankly depressing to read. William Blum's *Rogue State* (Blum, 2000), surely the most encyclopedic popular compendium of US criminality and mendacity yet assembled, suffers somewhat from its overwhelming accumulation of grim detail. Noam Chomsky has often grappled with the concerns of his large audience that his work is so unremittingly bleak as to almost rule out possibilities for constructive (or even peaceful) change. Chomsky has responded by stressing the huge accomplishments of progressive movements over the last two hundred years – ending slavery and colonialism, securing rights for women and workers, gradually opening up the range of permissible thought in authoritarian and democratic societies alike, and so on. Fortunately, the list is not a short one. But the overriding and indispensable focus of this literature, greatly assisted by the work of non-governmental human rights organizations, has been on cataloguing the crimes in which Western democracies have been complicit – and frequently cataloguing them in stomach-churning detail. Such wrenching data are then deployed as evidence for the broader case: that *democrisy* must be exposed; that Western states must be placed under the moral microscope along with the designated Other.

There is no shortage of contributions in *Genocide, War Crimes and the West* that follow something of the same strategy, and readers will be moved at many points by empathy for suffering peoples beyond our borders or (*pace* Churchill's study of residential schools and Prontzos's examination of structural violence) on our doorsteps. But contributors have also been asked to adopt a constructive approach as far as possible: to explore issues of justice, restitution, truth and reconciliation. So it is that Jan-Bart Gewald, while pulling no punches in his depiction of the German genocide in Namibia, devotes much of his chapter to an analysis of how Herero national consciousness gradually led to a powerful and partially successful campaign for compensation from the present-day German government. Brian Willson's passionate evocation of war crimes in Vietnam likewise issues a heartfelt call for reconciliation through painful acknowledgment of past wrongs, and commitment to peaceful and constructive relations in the future. Mario Aguilar casts his own study of Chile in the context of the growing impetus for a legal process against Henry Kissinger and surviving co-conspirators in the Nixon administration.

A separate section groups together essays that adopt a broad comparative approach to these themes. Ernesto Verdeja provides a wide-ranging and highly readable overview of 'Institutional Responses to Genocide and Mass Atrocity,' exploring the profusion of truth-and-reconciliation campaigns in countries such as Chile and El Salvador, and the complex trade-offs with which they must deal. Building on the research carried out for his groundbreaking book on the subject, Arthur Jay Klinghoffer provides a fascinating overview of the evolution of 'citizens' tribunals,' beginning with the Reichstag fire of 1933 and continuing into the contemporary era with tribunals examining US policies in Vietnam and Central America, the destruction of indigenous peoples, the worldwide oppression of women, and much else besides. (The activities of the citizens' tribunals are also reflected in two documents: Jean-Paul Sartre's 1967 address to the Vietnam tribunal, and the 'criminal complaint' filed by Ramsey Clark, who has overseen a similar process in the case of UN sanctions and US/British military actions against Iraq.)

## Genocide and the West

Over the past two decades, building on the systematic attention devoted to the Jewish holocaust from the 1960s onwards, the multidisciplinary field of comparative genocide studies has established itself in the social sciences. Its contributors hail from an impressive range of disciplines and pursuits, including political science and international relations, sociology, anthropology, criminology and international law, gender and queer studies, and (last but not least) human rights investigation and activism. At the same time as our book draws on dissident analyses of state terror in the 1970s and 1980s, it should be seen explicitly as a contribution to the important and still emerging field of comparative genocide studies.[12]

The mainstream of this field in many ways represents a notable improvement over the narrow-minded and jingoistic 'terrorism' literature of the 1970s and 1980s. From the start – that is to say, from the publication of Leo Kuper's *Genocide: Its Political Use in the Twentieth Century* in 1981 – the literature has been more attentive to the Western role in international crime and atrocity, including 'the crime of crimes' – genocide. (One might link this to the school's foundation in study of the Jewish holocaust. That event surely and forever put paid to notions that 'civilized' Western states were immune to outbursts of unfathomable violence, or that 'civilized' democratic states would not stand by and wash their hands of responsibility as the horror mounted.)

The title of Kuper's book indicated its author's preoccupation with the state as guiding force, in both the committing and the obfuscating of acts of genocide. In a chapter of almost biblical resonance, Kuper bitterly declaimed against the 'right of the sovereign state' to wage genocide within its own borders. Genocide was a crime intimately bound up with the Westphalian state system and the United Nations institutions which, with their foundation in national governments and Westphalian notions of sovereignty, were a contemporary offshoot of that system. Kuper was ruthless in condemning the complicity of states, *including Western states*, in practical and political support for genocide (as with the kid-glove treatment accorded the Khmer Rouge's representatives to the General Assembly, after their genocidal reign had been ended by the Vietnamese). His global-historical survey of genocide included the trampling of indigenous civilization by Western colonialists worldwide. And Kuper recognized the intimate link between genocide and war, as with his controversial claim that the US destruction of Hiroshima and Nagasaki, among other acts of 'strategic bombing,' constituted genocide.

Since Kuper, numerous other writers have expanded our understanding of Western involvement in genocide. Chroniclers of the destruction of indigenous civilizations in North America and Australasia have been among the most prominent; Ward Churchill's *A Little Matter of Genocide* (1997) and David Stannard's *American Holocaust* (1992) are both indispensable to an understanding of themes addressed in this volume by Peter Dale Scott and by Churchill himself.[13] The Guatemalan case has been widely accepted as a contemporary genocide against an indigenous population, and is prominent in many studies, although the dimension of Western complicity – the overthrow of the democratic Arbenz regime in 1954; subsequent counterinsurgency aid and training; the funnelling of arms through Israel and South Korea at the height of the genocide in the late 1970s and 1980s – remains underexplored. East Timor was also absorbed into the literature as a paradigmatic case of genocide – somewhat unevenly, but a little ahead of public and political opinion galvanized by the international Timor solidarity movement.

Adam Hochschild's prizewinning study of the Congo under Belgian rule, *King Leopold's Ghost*, brought to light a holocaust in the heart of Africa that seemed comparable, in its scale and savagery, to the Nazis' attempted extermination of the Jews decades later. A number of useful anthologies have emerged, almost all featuring attention to cases of Western involvement in genocide beyond the Nazi case. Historically distant events like the Herero genocide, explored here by the expert pen of Jan-Bart Gewald, have been rescued from obscurity, at roughly the same time as social movements have rendered them pressing political concerns.

Kuper's original dissection of the failures and hypocrisies of the Western state system has inspired a rapidly growing substrand of the genocide literature that focuses on state response, or tragic lack of response, to mass atrocity. Studies of the Jewish Holocaust, beginning with Arthur Morse's *While Six Million Died* (Morse, 1968; see also Wyman, 1984) have highlighted Western passivity as Hitler's machinery of extermination was developed and deployed. US support for the Indonesian invasion of East Timor, leading directly to genocide and to one of the highest death tolls, relative to population, since the Jewish holocaust, received sustained attention in works like Mathew Jardine's *East Timor: Genocide in Paradise* (Jardine, 1999). Linda Melvern's *A People Betrayed: The Role of the West in*

*Rwanda's Genocide* lambasted Security Council inaction in the face of the mass killings of Rwandan Tutsis and moderate Hutus; Melvern's core thesis is on display in her chapter for this book. Samantha Power's recent, compulsively readable study, *'A Problem from Hell': America and the Age of Genocide* marks the apotheosis of this literature to date. Power surveys the inability and unwillingness of the US and other Western powers to confront genocides effectively – sometimes because they were too busy supporting them or (*post facto*) their perpetrators, as with Saddam Hussein's Anfal campaign against the Kurds and the Khmer Rouge's post-1978 diplomatic trajectory. A parallel literature in human rights, exemplified by Des Forges (1999), has been similarly blunt in its condemnations, while internal UN investigations have directed strong self-criticisms against the international organization that crumbled before the *génocidaires* in the Balkans and Rwanda.

Theoretical probes have been made into subjects such as 'conventional' warfare, structural and gendered violence, and the natural environment, with the corresponding proliferation of terms such as 'omnicide,' 'ecocide,' and 'gendercide.' Eric Markusen, in separate collaborations with Robert Jay Lifton (1990) and David Kopf (1995), has worked to explore the omnicidal rationale at the heart of both the 'nuclear mentality' and the strategic bombing campaigns of the Second World War. (The issue is explored in Eric Langenbacher's impressively nuanced chapter in this volume.) Other studies of 'conventional' warfare sought to emphasize its genocidal logic and dimensions, as with Omer Bartov's studies of the 'barbarization' of the Eastern Front in World War II (e.g. Bartov, 1985) and John Dower's comparison of exterminatory ideology and rhetoric in the Pacific War (Dower, 1986). The analysis is highly relevant to cases like Namibia, Algeria, the Philippines, and Vietnam, all of which receive consideration in this book as case studies of Western complicity in genocide and war crimes.

Denunciations of global environmental destruction and calls for protection and preservation have been issued by such writers as Vandana Shiva, who explicitly, and for me persuasively, considers these to be issues of genocide and genocide prevention. Mike Davis, meanwhile, has turned his sights from pre-apocalypse Los Angeles (subject of his *City of Quartz* and *Ecology of Fear*) to the role of state-assisted famines in producing the modern Third World. His imposing *Late Victorian Holocausts* (2001) alleges Western complicity in megadeath, as colonizing powers and their local surrogates exacerbated some of the worst 'natural' disasters and human catastrophes of the nineteenth and early twentieth centuries. Such critiques, with their focus on the destructive and imperialist strategies of the Western path to modernity, point to another important thread in the skein of

Western complicity in genocide and mass atrocity. They are echoed here in the chapters by Brian Willson and Peter Prontzos.

## Definitions, caveats and acknowledgments

The term 'the West' is notoriously amorphous and ambiguous. For the purposes of our volume, it is defined as the industrialized democracies of Western Europe, North America (excluding Mexico), and Australasia. Japan is not considered; nor are complexly positioned actors like the Soviet Union/Russia, Israel, and South Africa.

Key terms deployed throughout this book are likewise open to extensive debate – and are in fact extensively debated. One could fill a volume with the definitional debate over 'genocide' alone. I have not sought to impose uniform definitions of these terms on contributors. However, I believe that the definitions of 'war crimes' and 'crimes against humanity' enshrined in the Rome Statute of the International Criminal Court (ICC) are not at odds with any of the essays offered here. The ICC defines 'war crimes' as

> Grave breaches of the Geneva Conventions of 12 August 1949, namely, any of the following acts against persons or property protected under the provisions of the relevant Geneva Convention: (i) Wilful killing; (ii) Torture or inhuman treatment, including biological experiments; (iii) Wilfully causing great suffering, or serious injury to body or health; (iv) Extensive destruction and appropriation of property, not justified by military necessity and carried out unlawfully and wantonly; (v) Compelling a prisoner of war or other protected person to serve in the forces of a hostile Power; (vi) Wilfully depriving a prisoner of war or other protected person of the rights of fair and regular trial; (vii) Unlawful deportation or transfer or unlawful confinement; (viii) Taking of hostages.

Of relevance is the list of 'other serious violations of the laws and customs applicable in international armed conflict,' specifically:

> Intentionally directing attacks against the civilian population ... [or] civilian objects; ... Intentionally launching an attack in the knowledge that such attack will cause incidental loss of life or injury to civilians or damage to civilian objects or widespread, long-term and severe damage to the natural environment which would be clearly excessive in relation to the concrete and direct overall military advantage expected; ... Attacking or bombarding, by whatever means, towns, villages, dwellings or buildings which are undefended and which are not military objectives; ... Killing or wounding a combatant who, having laid down his arms or having no longer means of defence, has surrendered at discretion; ... Employing asphyxiating, poisonous or other gases, and all analogous liquids, materials or devices; ... Committing outrages upon personal dignity, in particular humiliating and degrading treatment; ... Intentionally using starvation

of civilians as a method of warfare by depriving them of objects indispensable to their survival, including wilfully impeding relief supplies...

'Crimes against humanity,' meanwhile, are defined as:

> any of the following acts when committed as part of a widespread or systematic attack directed against any civilian population, with knowledge of the attack: (a) Murder; (b) Extermination; (c) Enslavement; (d) Deportation or forcible transfer of population; (e) Imprisonment or other severe deprivation of physical liberty in violation of fundamental rules of international law; (f) Torture; (g) Rape, sexual slavery, enforced prostitution, forced pregnancy, enforced sterilization, or any other form of sexual violence of comparable gravity; (h) Persecution against any identifiable group or collectivity on political, racial, national, ethnic, cultural, religious, gender ... or other grounds that are universally recognized as impermissible under international law ...; (i) Enforced disappearance of persons; (j) The crime of apartheid; (k) Other inhumane acts of a similar character intentionally causing great suffering, or serious injury to body or to mental or physical health.

'Genocide' is perhaps the most extreme crime against humanity; as used throughout this volume, the term refers to destruction of human groups and their members, by murder and possibly other means (this is a shading on the UN Convention/ICC definition of genocide).[14]

*Genocide, War Crimes and the West* aims to be the most comprehensive collection of its kind ever published. But it is far from exhaustive. Most obviously, there is nothing on Germany and the Nazi Holocaust, no less a 'Western' phenomenon than any other examined in these pages (see Lindqvist, 1997). In partial compensation, Jan-Bart Gewald's rich and learned study of the Herero/Nama genocide in Namibia provides one of the most concise yet wide-ranging analyses in English of a key predecessor of Nazi rule. Likewise, Western involvement in the Southern African wars of the 1970s and 1980s,[15] Western support for Israel in its war against the Palestinians,[16] and British actions in Northern Ireland pass unexamined. We offer no chapter on the ideology and practice of nuclearism, and the implications of a possible 'omnicide' of humanity as a result of the machinations of nuclear states, including Western states.[17]

I hope, instead, that this book will be seen for what it is: a contribution, perhaps the most wide-ranging one, to the literature on crimes and atrocities committed by or with the active complicity of the Western countries. The justifications for such a focus have already been explored. We do not pretend to offer a systematic comparison of Western crimes set against those variously classed as communist, socialist, totalitarian, autocratic/ dictatorial, and so on. Such comparisons are not an empty exercise, as works like Rummel's *Death by Government* (1994) and some of the recent 'democratic peace' literature in International Relations have demonstrated

(Henderson, 2002). But they are secondary to the contention that, regardless of how other state crimes compare with those of the West, Western citizens – the primary audience for this book – should have a special concern for atrocities committed at the behest of their own leaders, ostensibly in their name. *Genocide, War Crimes and the West* exploits the freedom that still exists in democratic societies to unveil the darkest state abuses, and to ask core questions about state policy – even if approaches and conclusions differ, as they should under democracy.

I offer my sincere thanks to all the authors represented in this volume. I am also most grateful to Zed Books for taking on the project despite its formidable bulk, and for shepherding it through to publication. Special thanks to Zed editor Robert Molteno for his unfailing support and guidance. Thanks also to Rosemary Taylorson, Julian Hosie and Anne Rodford.

I am sure contributors will join me in expressing our appreciation to family, friends, and colleagues for the sustenance they have provided throughout the preparation of this book, and beyond.

## Notes

1. For the text of McVeigh's letter, see Fox News, 2001.
2. Harvard scholar Samuel Huntington's contribution makes it clear that the depiction of the US as a rogue state – or at least the recognition that a good part of the world supports that depiction – is not limited to the radical end of the spectrum. Huntington – a member of the Trilateral Commission of the 1970s, and author of the 'clash of civilizations' thesis – published his article in *Foreign Affairs* in 1999. It is worth quoting at length:

> While the United States regularly denounces various countries as 'rogue states,' in the eyes of many countries it is becoming the rogue superpower.... On issue after issue, the United States has found itself increasingly alone, with one or a few partners, opposing most of the rest of the world's states and peoples. These issues include UN dues; sanctions against Cuba, Iran, Iraq, and Libya; the land mines treaty; global warming; an international war crimes tribunal; the Middle East; the use of force against Iraq and Yugoslavia; and the targeting of 35 countries with new economic sanctions between 1993 and 1996. On these and other issues, much of the international community is on one side and the United States is on the other. The circle of governments who see their interests coinciding with American interests is shrinking.... In the past few years the United States has, among other things, attempted or been perceived as attempting more or less unilaterally to do the following: pressure other countries to adopt American values and practices regarding human rights and democracy; prevent other countries from acquiring military capabilities that could counter American conventional superiority; enforce American law extraterritorially in other societies; grade countries according to their adherence to American standards on human rights, drugs, terrorism, nuclear proliferation, missile proliferation,

and now religious freedom; apply sanctions against countries that do not meet American standards on these issues; promote American corporate interests under the slogans of free trade and open markets; shape World Bank and International Monetary Fund policies to serve those same corporate interests; intervene in local conflicts in which it has relatively little direct interest; bludgeon other countries to adopt economic policies and social policies that will benefit American economic interests; promote American arms sales abroad while attempting to prevent comparable sales by other countries; force out one U.N. secretary-general and dictate the appointment of his successor; expand NATO initially to include Poland, Hungary, and the Czech Republic and no one else; undertake military action against Iraq and later maintain harsh economic sanctions against the regime; and categorize certain countries as 'rogue states,' excluding them from global institutions because they refuse to kowtow to American wishes.... At a 1997 Harvard conference, scholars reported that the elites of countries comprising at least two-thirds of the world's people – Chinese, Russians, Indians, Arabs, Muslims, and Africans – see the United States as the single greatest external threat to their societies. They do not regard America as a military threat but as a menace to their integrity, autonomy, prosperity, and freedom of action. They view the United States as intrusive, interventionist, exploitative, unilateralist, hegemonic, hypocritical, and applying double standards, engaging in what they label 'financial imperialism' and 'intellectual colonialism,' with a foreign policy driven overwhelmingly by domestic politics. (Huntington, 1999)

3. A draft of a proposed resolution for the Durban conference, intended for submission by European Union delegates, reads: 'The European Union profoundly deplores the human suffering, individual and collective, caused by slavery and the slave trade. They are among the most dishonourable and abhorrent chapters in the history of humanity. The EU condemns these practices, in the past and present, and regrets the suffering they have caused' – though without acknowledging Europe's central role in the slave trade.

4. In purely military terms, the shock to the West of successful wars of national independence was duplicated by the events of September 2001, in which the West's own technologies were turned against it. This has sharply transformed the 'playing field' of war and terrorism. In the First World–Third World relationship, terror-bombing that kills thousands on the other side is no longer a Western monopoly.

5. There is much to Alexander Cockburn's assertion that the post-11 September world has witnessed 'an imperial onslaught as brazen and lawless as any colonizing sortie of the nineteenth century' (Cockburn, 2002).

6. The radically different levels of domestic 'protection' available to elites versus minorities deserve much greater exposition, but are generally outside the boundaries of the present study, with the exceptions of Ward Churchill's examination of the residential school system for Native Americans, and Peter Prontzos's analysis of the costs of structural violence both within and beyond the countries of the developed West.

7. The ideological journey was described in Horowitz's memoir, *Radical Son: A Generational Odyssey* (Horowitz, 1997).

8. Important works of revisionist cinema, notably Ralph Nelson's *Soldier Blue* and Arthur Hill's *Little Big Man* (both 1970), also contributed to the resurgence of Native American issues. A fuller examination of the dissident stream should attend to such popular-culture artefacts, including some of the fiction and protest music that asked searching questions about US policies at home and abroad.

9. A reasonably objective definition of terrorism is offered by the US Congress: '[An] act of terrorism, means any activity that (A) involves a violent act or an act

dangerous to human life that is a violation of the criminal laws of the United States or any State, or that would be a criminal violation if committed within the jurisdiction of the United States or of any State; and (B) appears to be intended (i) to intimidate or coerce a civilian population; (ii) to influence the policy of a government by intimidation or coercion; or (iii) to affect the conduct of a government by assassination or kidnapping.' United States Congressional Code, 1984, quoted in Chomsky (2001: 16n).

10.  Stohl's work places state terrorism, including in Western countries and throughout the Western sphere of influence, alongside terrorism by minorities, insurgent groups, and other 'retail' actors. Indeed, in the third edition of the book, published in the late 1980s, Stohl cited as 'Myth 1' of the study of terrorism that 'political terrorism is exclusively the activity of nongovernmental forces,' and included as a parallel myth 'that terrorism is not something practiced by the governments of liberal Western democracies' (Stohl, 1988: 7–8). He stressed as the 'major requirement' of the study of terrorism 'an analysis, rather than an assumption, of the historical and political sources of the terrorism within a conflict situation'.

11.  The work by Herman, Chomsky, and McClintock has exerted significant influence over a new generation of scholars of state terror. See, e.g, Sluka, 2000, esp. pp. 7–10.

12.  For a sampling of key texts in the literature on comparative genocide (which is not to imply that all these scholars would self-identify as primarily concerned with the subject), see, in alphabetical order: Alvarez, 2001; Andreopoulous, 1999; Bell-Fialkoff, 1999; Chalk and Jonassohn, 1990; Charny et al., 1999; Chorbajian and Shirinian, 1999; Churchill, 1997; Dadrian, 1975; Glover, 1999; Hinton, 2000, 2002; Jonassohn with Björnson, 1998; Katz, 1994; Kuper, 1981; Levene and Roberts, 1999; Markusen and Kopf, 1995; Power, 2002; Rosenbaum, 1996; Rummel, 1994; Schabas, 2000; Stannard, 1992; Staub, 1989; Totten et al., 1997; Wallimann and Dobkowski, 2000.

13.  Churchill's volume is more explicitly positioned in the genocide studies literature. It includes a thorough overview of the field's evolution and some of its central concerns and debates.

14.  The legal definition of genocide, enshrined in the 1948 Convention on the Prevention and Punishment of the Crime of Genocide and the statutes of the new International Criminal Court (ICC) is: 'any of the following acts committed with intent to destroy, in whole or in part, a national ethnical, racial or religious group, as such; (a) Killing members of the group; (b) Causing serious bodily or mental harm to members of the group; (c) Deliberately inflicting on the group conditions of life calculated to bring about its physical destruction in whole or in part; (d) Imposing measures intended to prevent births within the group; (e) Forcibly transferring children of the group to another group' (Articles I and II). Article III specifically makes 'conspiracy to commit genocide,' 'incitement to commit genocide,' and 'complicity in genocide' as punishable, regardless of 'whether they are [carried out by] constitutionally responsible rulers, public officials or private individuals.'

My own preferred definition of genocide, adapting (with the italicized phrase) that of Steven Katz, is: 'the actualization of the intent, however successfully carried out, to murder *in whole or in substantial part* any national, ethnic, racial, religious, political, social, gender or economic group, as these groups are defined by the perpetrator, by whatever means.'

15.  Concise case-study treatments are available in George's edited volume *Western State Terrorism* (see Rolston, 1990; Gervasi and Wong, 1990).

16.  The seminal indictments include Chomsky, 1984; Hirst, 1984; and Beit-Hallahmi, 1987.

17.  For an overview, see Lifton and Markusen, 1990.

# References

Agee, P. (1975). *Inside the Company: CIA diary*. London: Allen Lane.

Agence France-Presse (2001). Chirac wants sanctions against Algeria torture general. Agence France-Presse dispatch, 4 May.

Alvarez, A. (2001). *Governments, citizens, and genocide: A comparative and interdisciplinary perspective*. Bloomington: Indiana University Press.

Andreopolous, G.J. (1999). *Genocide: Conceptual and historical dimensions*. Philadelphia: University of Pennsylvania Press.

Authers, J., and Wolffe, R. (2002). *The victim's fortune: Inside the epic battle over the debts of the Holocaust*. New York: HarperCollins.

Barnet, R.J. (1968). *Intervention and revolution: America's confrontation with insurgent movements around the world*. New York: Meridian Books.

Bartov, O. (1985). *The eastern front, 1941–45: German troops and the barbarisation of warfare*. London: Macmillan.

Bass, G.J. (2000). *Stay the hand of vengeance: The politics of war crimes tribunals*. Princeton, NJ: Princeton University Press.

Bauman, Z. (1989). *Modernity and the Holocaust*. Ithaca, NY: Cornell University Press.

Beit-Hallahmi, B. (1987). *The Israel connection: Who Israel arms and why*. New York: Pantheon.

Bell-Fialkoff, A. (1999). *Ethnic cleansing*. New York: St. Martin's Griffin.

Blum, W. (2001). *Rogue state: A guide to the world's only superpower*. London: Zed Books.

Bonner, R. (1984). *Weakness and deceit: U.S. policy and El Salvador*. New York: Times Books.

de Borchgrave, A., and R. Moss (1980). *The spike: A novel*. New York: Crown Publishers.

Breytenbach, B. (2002). Letter to America. *The Nation*, 23 September.

Brown, D. (1972). *Bury my heart at wounded knee: An Indian history of the American West*. New York: Bantam.

Burgos-Debray, E., ed. (1983). *I, Rigoberta Menchú: An Indian woman in Guatemala*. London: Verso.

Chalk, F. and Jonassohn, K. (1990). *The history and sociology of genocide: Analyses and case studies*. New Haven: Yale University Press.

Charny, I., et al., eds (1999). *Encyclopedia of genocide*. Santa Barbara, CA: ABC-CLIO.

Chomsky, N. (2001). *9–11*. New York: Seven Stories Press.

——— (1988). *The culture of terrorism*. Boston: South End Press.

——— (1985). *Turning the tide: U.S. intervention in Central America and the struggle for peace*. Boston: South End Press.

——— (1984). *The fateful triangle: Israel, the U.S., and the Palestinians*. Montreal: Black Rose Books.

——— (1982). *Towards a new cold war: Essays on the current crisis and how we got there*. New York: Pantheon Books.

——— (1969). *American power and the new mandarins*. New York: Pantheon Books.

Chomsky, N., and Herman, E.S. (1979a). *The political economy of human rights*. Vol. 1, *The Washington connection and Third World fascism*. Montreal: Black Rose Books.

——— (1979b). *The political economy of human rights*. Vol. 2, *Postwar Indochina and the reconstruction of imperial ideology*. Montreal: Black Rose Books.

Chorbajian, L., and Shirinian, G., eds (1999). *Studies in comparative genocide*. New York: St. Martin's Press.

Churchill, W. (1997). *A little matter of genocide: Holocaust and denial in the Americas, 1492* to the present. San Francisco: City Lights Books.

Cleaver, E. (1968). Soul on ice. New York: McGraw-Hill.

Cockburn, A. (2002). American journal. Counterpunch, 5 December. www.counterpunch. org/cockburn1205.html.

———— (1987). Corruptions of empire: Life studies and the Reagan era. London and New York: Verso.

Dadrian, V. (1975) A typology of genocide. International Review of Modern Sociology 5, Fall.

Davis, M. (2001). Late Victorian holocausts: El Niño famines and the making of the Third World. London and New York: Verso.

De Brie, C. (2001). Slaves to the past. Le Monde diplomatique, October.

Des Forges, A. (1999). 'Leave none to tell the story': Genocide in Rwanda. New York: Human Rights Watch.

Dower, J. (1986). War without mercy: Race and power in the Pacific War. New York: Pantheon Books.

Fanon, F. (1967). Black skin, white masks. New York: Grove Press.

———— (1963). The wretched of the earth. New York: Grove Press.

Fox News [2001]. McVeigh's letter to Fox News. http://foxnews.com/story/0,2933, 17500,00.html.

Freire, P. (1970). Pedagogy of the oppressed. New York: The Seabury Press.

Galeano, E. (1973). Open veins of Latin America: Five centuries of the pillage of a continent. New York: Monthly Review Press.

George, A., ed. (1990). Western state terrorism. London: Polity Press.

Gervasi, S., and Wong, S. (1990). The Reagan Doctrine and the destabilization of Southern Africa. In A. George, ed., Western state terrorism, 212–52. Oxford: Polity Press, 1991.

Glover, J. (1999). Humanity: A moral history of the twentieth century. New Haven and London: Yale University Press.

Goldhagen, D.J., and Power, S. (2001). Kerrey should be investigated. The Boston Globe, 3 May.

Guevara, C. (1968). Reminiscences of the Cuban revolutionary war. New York: Monthly Review Press.

———— (1961). Guerrilla warfare. New York: Monthly Review Press.

Hartung, W.D., Berrigan, F., and Ciarrocca, M. (2002). Operation endless deployment. The Nation, 21 October. www.thenation.com/doc.mhtml?i=20021021&s=hartung.

Henderson, E.A. (2002). Democracy and war: The end of an illusion? Boulder and London: Lynne Rienner.

Herman, E.S. (1982). The real terror network: Terrorism in fact and propaganda. Boston: South End Press.

———— (1966). America's Vietnam policy: The strategy of deception. Washington, DC: Public Affairs Press.

Herman, E.S. and Chomsky, N. (1988). Manufacturing consent: The political economy of the mass media. New York: Pantheon.

Herman, E.S., and O'Sullivan, G. (1990). The terrorism industry: The experts and institutions that shape our view of terror. New York: Random House.

Hersh, S.M. (1983). The price of power: Kissinger in the Nixon White House. New York: Summit Books.

Hinton, A.L., ed. (2002). Annihilating difference: The anthropology of genocide. Berkeley: University of California Press.

————, ed. (2000). Genocide: An anthropological reader. Malden, MA: Blackwell Publishers.

Hirst, D. (1984). *The gun and the olive branch: The roots of violence in the Middle East.* London and Boston: Faber & Faber.

Hitchens, C. (2001). *The trial of Henry Kissinger.* London: Verso.

———— (1990). *Prepared for the worst: Selected essays and minority reports.* London: The Hogarth Press.

Hochschild, A. (1998). *King Leopold's ghost: A story of greed, terror, and heroism in Central Africa.* Boston: Houghton Mifflin.

Horowitz, D. (1997). *Radical son: A journey through our times.* New York: The Free Press.

———— (1965). *Free world colossus.* London: Macgibbon & Kee.

Human Rights Watch (2001). U.S.: Urgent need for Vietnam investigation: Human Rights Watch letter to U.S. Secretary of Defense Donald H. Rumsfeld. Press release, 7 May. www.hrw.org/press/2001/05/rumsleto507.htm.

Huntington, S. (1999). The lonely superpower. *Foreign Affairs* 78, no. 2 (March/April).

Immerman, R.H. (1982). *The CIA in Guatemala: The foreign policy of intervention.* Austin: University of Texas Press.

Jardine, M. (1999). *East Timor: Genocide in paradise.* Monroe, ME: Odonian Press.

Jonassohn, K., with Björnson, K.S. (1998). *Genocide and gross human rights violations in comparative perspective.* New Brunswick, NJ: Transaction Publishers.

Katz, S.T. (1994). *The Holocaust in historical context.* Vol. 1, *The Holocaust and mass death before the modern age.* New York: Oxford University Press.

Kirkpatrick, J. (1982). *Dictatorships and double standards: Rationalism and reason in politics.* New York: Simon & Schuster.

Klare, M.T., and Kornbluh, P. (1988). *Low-intensity warfare: Counterinsurgency, proinsurgency, and antiterrorism in the eighties.* New York: Pantheon Books.

Klinghoffer, A.J., and Klinghoffer, J.A. (2002). *International citizens' tribunals: Mobilizing public opinion to advance human rights.* New York: Palgrave.

Kolko, G. (1988). *Confronting the Third World: United States foreign policy, 1945–1980.* New York: Pantheon.

———— (1968). *The politics of war: The world and United States foreign policy, 1943–1945.* New York: Pantheon.

Kuper, L. (1981). *Genocide: Its political use in the twentieth century.* Harmondsworth: Penguin.

Laqueur, W. (1987). *The age of terrorism.* Boston: Little, Brown.

———— (1977). *Terrorism.* Boston: Little, Brown.

Levene, M., and Roberts, P. (1999). *The massacre in history.* New York: Berghahn Books.

Lifton, R.J., and Markusen, E. (1990). *The genocidal mentality: Nazi Holocaust and nuclear threat.* New York: Basic Books.

Lindqvist, S. (1997). *'Exterminate all the brutes': One man's odyssey into the heart of darkness and the origins of European genocide.* New York: New Press.

McClintock, M. (1985). *The American connection.* 2 vols. London: Zed Books.

McGeary, J. and Tumulty, K. (2001). The fog of war. *Time* Magazine, 30 May.

McGreal, C. (2001). Africans angry at refusal to debate slavery reparations. *Guardian,* 1 September.

Mariner, J. (2002). Torture: Don't ask, don't tell. *FindLaw's Legal Commentary,* 4 February. http://writ.news.findlaw.com/mariner/20020204.html.

Markusen, E., and Kopf, D. (1995). *The Holocaust and strategic bombing: Genocide and total war in the twentieth century.* Boulder, CO: Westview Press.

Melvern, L. (2000). *A people betrayed: The role of the West in Randa's genocide.* London: Zed Books.

Minow, M. (1998). *Between vengeance and forgiveness: Facing history after genocide and mass violence.* Boston: Beacon Press.

Morse, A. (1968). *While six million died: A chronicle of American apathy.* Corner House Publishers.

Morrow, L. (2001). Bob Kerrey and collateral damage. *Time*, 30 April. www.time.com/time/nation/article/0,8599,108054,00.html.

Na'Allah, A.-R. (2000). Thoughts on the Atlantic slave trade: The roles of Africans and the issue of apology for slavery. *West Africa Review* 1, no. 2.

Nelson, D. (2002). Pressure mounts on Britain to remember its slave trade past. *OneWorld UK*, 26 August.

Netanyahu, B. (1986). *Terrorism: How the West can win.* New York: Farrar, Straus & Giroux.

Osborn, A. (2002). Belgium exhumes its colonial demons. *Guardian*, 13 July.

Parenti, M. (1989). *The sword and the dollar: Imperialism, revolution and the arms race.* New York: St. Martin's Press.

——— (1986). *Inventing reality: The politics of the mass media.* New York: St. Martin's Press.

——— (1995). *Against empire.* San Francisco: City Lights.

Pilger, J. (1994). *Distant voices.* London: Vintage.

——— (1989). *A distant country.* London: Cape.

Power, S. (2002). *'A problem from hell': America and the age of genocide.* New York: Basic Books.

Reisman, W.M., and Antoniou, C.T. (1994). *The laws of war: A comprehensive collection of primary documents on international laws governing armed conflict.* New York: Vintage.

Riding, A. (2002). Belgium confronts its heart of darkness. *New York Times*, 21 September.

Robinson, R. (2000). *The debt: What America owes to blacks.* New York: Plume.

Rodney, W. (1972). *How Europe underdeveloped Africa.* London: Bogle Ouverture.

Rolston, B. (1991). Containment and its failure: The British state and the control of conflict in North Ireland. In A. George, ed., *Western state terrorism*, 155–79. Cambridge: Polity Press.

Rosenbaum, A., ed. (1996). *Is the Holocaust unique? Perspectives on comparative genocide.* Boulder, CO: Westview Press.

Rummel, R.J. (1994). *Death by government.* New Brunswick: Transaction Publishers.

Russell, B. (1967). *War crimes in Vietnam.* London: Allen & Unwin.

——— (1965). *War and atrocity in Vietnam.* London: Allen & Unwin.

Said, E. (1979). *Orientalism.* New York: Vintage.

Sanger, D.E., and Schmitt, E. (2002). U.S. has a plan to occupy Iraq, official report. *New York Times*, 11 October.

Schabas, W. (2000). *Genocide in international law: The crime of crimes.* Cambridge: Cambridge University Press.

Schlesinger, S., and Kinzer, S. (1983). *Bitter fruit: The untold story of the American coup in Guatemala.* New York: Anchor Press.

Schurmann, F., et al. (1966). *The politics of escalation in Vietnam.* Boston: Beacon Press.

Shapiro, B. (2001). Is it time for a Vietnamese truth commission? *Salon*, 2 May. www.salon.com/news/feature/2001/05/02/kerrey/index.html.

Shatz, A. (2002). The torture of Algiers. *New York Review of Books*, 21 November.

Shawcross, W.M. (1979). *Sideshow: Kissinger, Nixon, and the destruction of Cambodia.* New York: Simon & Schuster.

Sluka, J.A., ed. (2000). *Death squad: The anthropology of state terror.* Philadelphia: University of Pennsylvania Press.

Stannard, D.E. (1992). *American holocaust: The conquest of the new world*. New York: Oxford University Press.

Staub, E. (1989). *The roots of evil: The origins of genocide and other group violence*. New York: Cambridge University Press.

Stohl, M., ed. (1988). *The politics of terrorism*, 3rd edn. New York: Marcel Dekker.

Sterling, C. (1981). *The terror network: The secret war of international terrorism*. New York: Holt, Rinehart, & Winston.

Stockwell, J. (1978). *In search of enemies: A CIA story*. New York: W.W. Norton.

Totten, S., et al., eds (1997). *Century of genocide: Eyewitness accounts and critical views*. New York and London: Garland Publishing.

Vistica, G.L. (2001). One awful night in Phanh Phong. *New York Times* Magazine, 25 April.

Wallimann, I., and Dobkowski, M.N., eds (2000). *Genocide in the modern age: Etiology and case studies of mass death*. Syracuse, NY: Syracuse University Press.

Wilkinson, P. (1979). *Terrorism: Theory and practice*. Boulder, CO: Westview Press.

——— (1977). *Terrorism and the liberal state*. London: Macmillan.

Williams, W.A. (1959). *The tragedy of American diplomacy*. New York: Dell.

Wyman, D.S. (1984). *The abandonment of the Jews: America and the Holocaust, 1941–1945*. New York: Pantheon Books.

X, Malcolm (1965). *The autobiography of Malcolm X*. New York: Grove Press.

Zinn, H. (1980). *A people's history of the United States*. New York: Harper & Row.

——— (1967). *Vietnam: The logic of withdrawal*. Boston: Beacon Press.

# 2

# Shades of Complicity:
# Towards a Typology of Transnational
# Crimes against Humanity

## Peter Stoett

My title is immediately puzzling, perhaps, since this volume takes the more concise terms 'genocide' and 'war crimes' as central themes, and because of the inclusion of that rather imprecise word, 'transnational.' But in an effort to avoid the definitional debates so often surrounding genocide analyses, and to embrace without conceit all of the instances of violence that form the empirical basis for this volume, I opt to use the much more encompassing *crimes against humanity*, which I apply to mass human rights violations in or out of 'wartime.'[1] Further, since our central meeting point is Western complicity, I include the adjective *transnational* to suggest that we are dealing, ultimately, with the impact and guilt of actors and structures external to the immediate vicinity of atrocity, whether they be distanced by space and time, or are purposeful visitors. It would be unnecessarily limiting to discuss an interstate context only, for the inclusion of nonstate actors, and of the 'transnational harm' of which they are capable (Linklater, 1999: 474–5), is central to international justice.

Mass murder and/or genocide are, of course, the principal and most outrageous crimes against humanity, and there are others, such as torture and/or systemic rape campaigns, that elicit similar repugnance. Some nation-building processes, at certain times, have involved these policies – whether or not we suggest they were also intrinsic to the prevalent ideologies at the time. Separating atrocious policies for analysis is viewed as unnecessarily reductionist by some, and as integral to the legal pursuit of justice to others. Undeniably, it opens the door to an extensive discussion of what meaning we ascribe to such terminology. But I suspect this is not the space for rehashed arguments over meaning, my own exhausted patience for such debates aside. Rather, we seek here to open a much-needed discussion of complicity in crimes against humanity, a topic often under-analyzed, and a research agenda that receives comparatively little attention in literature on massive human rights violations.

This dearth reflects an unwillingness to examine critically the foreign policies of Western states, and a conscious effort to avoid accusations of engaging in conspiracy theorizing. However, it is essential to the broader effort of promoting human rights and the avoidance of crimes against humanity that it be given due attention. Beyond the extended debate between universalism and cultural relativism – a debate often framed on a false dichotomy – one of the principal complaints leveled against the formal human rights approach emanating from the West is that it is pervaded by hypocrisy. Open discussions of Western complicity can sustain a more genuine and reflective debate, even if they open terrible wounds in the process. There is, to be sure, an element of anger in the analysis of Western involvement in atrocities that have disfigured the development of many peoples and states, and reparations movements have sought material recompense for past actions. But ending the culture of impunity is a forward-looking enterprise. It is one fraught with analytic dilemmas, however; and, beyond the demand that some form of intentionality can be discovered, we lack a clear typology of complicity.

Lest I be accused of generating false expectations, I should state immediately that this chapter will not provide a *clear* typology, because to do so would require acrobatic feats of the imagination. Precise, mutually exclusive, categories will elude us, and I seek only to furnish several useful generalizations.

## Complicity as a theme

Curiously, despite repeated cases of Western complicity, only limited formal efforts have been made to conceptualize compliance in crimes against humanity, especially in the mainstream international relations literature. I will return to this disturbing silence in my conclusion. However, it would be remiss to argue that such efforts have been absent from genocide studies, a field where, it would seem, they are a more natural fit. This results, perhaps, from efforts to ascertain the extent of public participation in the Holocaust, and related debates about the extent of civilian knowledge and the failure of the Allies to reroute part of their war effort towards halting the Final Solution. The anguished effort to understand the collective and individual mentality of the 'bystander' to large-scale atrocity is an older theme, but it reached new heights of academic interest with the Holocaust, owing to the links between atrocity and normality (see Horwitz, 2000; Goldhagen, 1996).

There are at least two methods by which we can arrive at a typology of complicity in crimes against humanity. One the one hand, we can struggle with the question of intentionality, mirroring the more specific debate that surfaced with regard to the Holocaust. Here we are concerned with the ongoing ontological debate concerning agents and structures: can we ascribe intention to individual actors, or are crimes against humanity the consequence of structural demands translated into psychotic behavior? In the case of the Holocaust, the intentionalists emphasize the anti-Semitic motives of Hitler himself at the apex of Nazism (see Evans, 1989, for discussion). In contrast, the functionalist school sees a largely unsystematic policy unfolding in the wake of bureaucratic competition to implement the Final Solution (see Burrin, 1994).[2] An uneasy compromise can be reached with Frank Chalk's reminder that 'systemic variables facilitate genocide, but it is people who kill' (1994: 56).

This debate has preoccupied international relations theorists as well, but they have yet to apply it to the question of complicity in crimes against humanity committed 'abroad.' Alexander Wendt has modified his social constructivist views by adopting the term 'supervenience,' referring to a 'nonreductive relationship of dependency [between structure and agent], in which properties at one level are fixed or constituted by those at another, but are not reducible to them' (1996: 49). Unless one denies this compromise, it is indeed difficult to cast a typological mold based on intentionality or structure as the central organizing theme. While it would be plausible to argue that some theories about political violence favor structure over agency, it is equally demonstrable that political theorists such as Foucault (1977) reject such dichotomies and stress the inter-relationships between the two. We will return to this theme in the discussion of the globalization thesis near the end of this chapter, but we put it aside for now.

The second approach, adopted here, emphasizes distance as the central organizing concept. This can be done through both time and space, or, in more structural and constructivist explanations, as a collapse of time and space producing a historicized moment. Though the measurement of either time or space is perhaps best left to physicists, we can categorize acts of complicity with reference to the distance between the accomplice and the atrocity committed. This allows us to categorize cases where contributions to crimes against humanity are direct, indirect, in the past, and in the present. In some cases criminality may be alleged, but in others the distance involved will preclude such a charge. (However, these cases leave open the route toward reparation payments and other forms of institutional redress.)

If this sounds vague, it is. More precise attempts at defining complicity leave us with equal room for interpretation, however. For example, Israel

Charny establishes a subcategory for 'Accomplices' in his broader effort to establish a generic definition of genocide. These are described as: 'Persons, institutions, companies, or governments who knowingly or negligently assist individuals, organisations, or governments who are known murderers or potential murderers to gain access to mega-weapons of destruction, or otherwise to organise and execute a plan of mass murders.' Further, if this exhaustive list is deemed insufficient, one can establish first-, second-, or third-degree complicity in genocide by evaluating the extent of pre-meditation, totality or singlemindedness of purpose, resoluteness to execute policy, efforts to overcome resistance, devotion to bar escape of victims, and persecutory cruelty (Charny, 1994: 89). The line between assisting and committing the act remains unclear, and the degree-of-complicity typology poses insurmountable obstacles for the kind of information-gathering necessary to operationalize formal criminal investigations, leaving aside the ethical and judicial dilemmas associated with a definition that includes both 'potential murderers' and 'resoluteness to execute policy.' Charny does, however, offer a path toward the transnational understanding that I argue is necessary, including the role of non-state actors, and his framework does take us beyond the problematic inclusion of all acts of war.

I now proceed to discuss the categories of complicity that may help to facilitate a discussion of the responsibility for, and obligations of, external actors involved in crimes against humanity. These are arranged to reflect degrees of distance from the acts themselves. *Resonant complicity* rises from historical abuses, distant in time but still present in implication. *Indifference and selective intervention* refer to ethical claims that, even when physical proximity to the acts existed, actors neglected their obligation to intervene to stop them. Another category is most useful for describing *material contributions*, by way of technical and financial assistance or collusion. And the shortest distance, in time and space, is of course reserved for the category of *direct participation*, when external actors have pulled triggers, dropped bombs, and performed other acts of murder. In conceptual terms, this category is the least interesting, and will receive short shrift here; but it is certainly well represented in other chapters in this volume.

A final category, which does not depend on a scale of distance and assumes a long-term process as well as normative proximity to structural violence, opens the debate about whether we should declare *globalization as a destructive process*. I argue that this is less valuable as a category than as an area for heuristic discussion. Finally, I turn the question away from complicity and toward obligations, briefly introducing the themes of inter-vention and reparations.

*Resonant complicity*

Inayatullah and Blaney, based on a prior assessment by Todorov, write of the Spanish explorer Cortés and the 'unquestioned sense of superiority that limits his understanding of the other and permits their destruction' (Inayatullah and Blaney, 1996: 75; Todorov, 1984; for a similar treatment of contact between the British and Indians, see Nandy, 1983). The conditions for eliminationist polices are established with an ontological basis, and such expansionist and imperialistic thinking resonates well into the contemporary era. Charny defines genocide in the course of colonization or consolidation of power as something that is 'undertaken or even allowed in the course of or incidental to the purposes of achieving a goal of colonisation or development of a territory belonging to an indigenous people, or any other consolidation of political or economic power through mass killing of those perceived to be standing in the way' (1994: 80). The last words are the most suggestive; their resonance is heard in the reparations debates of today.

I do not intend here to suggest that the ethnocidal destruction of indigenous peoples is not currently a problem. On the contrary, such destruction continues with alarming speed; Helen Fein refers to it as developmental genocide (1990: 30, 82–83), a theme to which I return in the section on globalization below. The case of the Yanomami of Brazil and Venezuela is especially striking. Between 1987 and 1991, roughly 12 to 13 per cent of the population was lost, due primarily to predatory mining practices on traditional lands (American Anthropological Association, 1991). But this can be related to a broader historical practice of conquering the Amazon and its people. Similarly, the contemporary plight of aboriginals in Australia and North America, Russia, and elsewhere, can be linked to colonial policies which resonate in today's understanding of their condition.

It is of course more contentious to argue, as does Ward Churchill, that such policies are best labeled genocidal. Churchill's work may be seen a double indictment: he takes some genocide scholars to task for promoting the refrain of so-called Holocaust uniqueness, and condemns recent policies towards North American First Nations (1997). As usual, the application of the term 'genocide' raises some eyebrows. As Moses writes in the case of Australia's Aborigines:

> the difficulty in applying the UN definition of genocide to colonial cases of mass death rests on the fact that most of the indigenous fatalities were not usually the direct consequence of an intended policy of extermination. Disease, malnutrition, alcohol, a decreased birth-rate, and increased intertribal warfare accounted, in the main, for the catastrophic decline in the Aboriginal population in colonial Australia. (2000: 90)

Similarly, Bartrop (1997) does not find the destruction of the Powhatans of Virginia to be a case of genocide. Chalk and Jonassohn insist on the phrase 'intentional physical destruction'; cultural suppression may be ethnocide, but is not genocide (1990: 23).

Moses does conclude, however, that European policies and attitudes evolved in an 'exterminatory direction' and, in an equation similar to the Wendtian understanding of supervenience outlined above, 'the structure of the process became consciously incarnated in its agents, and this is the moment when we can observe the development of the specific genocidal intention that satisfies the UN definition' (2000: 92). Mark Levene describes pre-genocidal policies 'creeping' up to the more robust variety (1999a). Russell Thornton's book *American Indian Holocaust and Survival: A Population History since 1492* provides a quantitative assessment of the native American population collapse following first contact, and the recent resurgence of that same population. He argues that, 'while warfare and genocide were not very significant overall in the American Indian population decline, they were important causes of decline for particular tribes. Some American Indian peoples were even brought to the point of extinction by warfare and genocide, or perhaps it is more accurate to say, by genocide in the name of warfare' (1987: 47). David Stannard, in his book *American Holocaust: Columbus and the Conquest of the New World*, concludes that 'firestorms of microbial pestilence *and* purposeful genocide began laying waste the American natives' almost immediately following first contact with Europeans. The two operated in an interdependent dynamic, within the overarching context of a European/Christian racist ideology, and this trend is no relic: 'The murder and destruction continue, with the aid of and assistance of the United States.... And many of the detailed accounts from contemporary observers read much like those recorded by the conquistadors' chroniclers nearly 500 years earlier' (Stannard, 1992: xiii; see also Jonas, 1991).

Elsewhere, Levene (1999b) links genocide to a crisis-mode of nation-building, while Astourian (1999) connects the drive toward modern Turkish statehood with a racist nationalism, and Barta (1987) contends that Australians live in objective 'relations of genocide' with Aborigines: European settlement sealed the fate of those who previously occupied land taken for pastoral purposes. The last-mentioned case has, perhaps, led to the most blatant form of official denial, with the possible exception of the Armenian massacres. The Human Rights and Equal Opportunity Commission's 1997 *Bringing Them Home* report alleged that the forcible removal of 100,000 children of mixed Aboriginal and white descent between 1910 and 1970 constituted a case of genocide, according to Article II(e) of the United Nations Genocide Convention (Wilson,

1997). The Australian government flatly rejected this condemnation, though a modest compensation package was proffered (see Innes, 2001; Reynolds, 2001) In Canada, the Report of the Royal Commission on Aboriginal Issues (Indian and Northern Affairs Canada, 1996) has acknowledged past governments' policies of forced assimilation, producing some measure of transparency in dealing with cases still ongoing (Indian and Northern Affairs Canada, n.d.).

This category of complicity is receiving increasing attention. Mark Cocker provides one of the more comprehensive accounts in *Rivers of Blood, Rivers of Gold: Europe's Conflict with Tribal Peoples*. He deploys several case studies, including the Spanish conquest of Mexico, the British treatment of Tasmanian Aborigines, Euro-American dispossession of the Apaches, and the German annihilation of the Herero and Nama in South West Africa (see also Gewald's chapter in this volume). Technological superiority facilitated eliminationist policies, in both the material and ideational sense: '[t]echnological inferiority equaled moral inferiority and, at times, moral worthlessness' (1998: 364). Adam Hochschild's critically acclaimed *King Leopold's Ghost* (1999) contributes further to an appreciation of the ruthless policies of colonial expansion in southern Africa. No doubt more top-quality work on this theme will emerge as more historians become engaged with the issues. The resonance of historical injustice, meanwhile, will continue to galvanize activists as well.

## Indifference and selective intervention

This category follows the resonant complicity category in terms of chronological distance only, and by its very nature is the most difficult category to define. The core suggestion here is that the West is often guilty by negligence: that by maintaining indifference as a policy preference, and limiting the cases where the West intervenes to stop crimes against humanity, it becomes complicit in the acts of violence themselves. Thus such a category is generally presupposed by a counterfactual claim that, had the West intervened and sent sufficient troops or aid, it would have made a substantial and positive difference to the genocidal outcome. Surprisingly, and despite the traditional fixation on national-interest concerns, this category has emerged as a viable one due largely to analyses and rhetorical treatments of human security (see Hampson, 2001), as well as the outcome of two tragic recent events where the response of the international community was widely viewed as inadequate: Bosnia and Rwanda.[3]

Again, the theme of what 'should have been done' is an old one: the Allies neglecting to bomb railway tracks leading to Auschwitz comes to mind. But concern over lost opportunities in Rwanda struck an especially disconcerting chord, and inspired serious debate over the limitations of peacekeeping and humanitarian intervention. I return to the latter theme in the section on obligations, below, but maintain a focus here on the retrospection that the Rwanda debacle encouraged. This was clearly a case in which the Western world, with the possible and self-interested exception of France, decided to do next to nothing, despite evidence that an un-paralleled African genocide was unfolding. The blame is apportioned widely here, from individuals intrinsic to the decision-making process, to the pathologies of bureaucracies in international organizations, to socially constructed understandings that can lead to dysfunctional behavior (on the latter, see Barnett and Finnemore, 1999; on constraints imposed by norms, see Jones, 1992). According to Barnett, himself involved in the decision-making process, UN Secretary-General Boutros-Ghali initially 'emanated indecision to the point of paralysis, if not complacency … a disturbingly distant stance from the unfolding tragedy and … a troubling abdication of responsibility and leadership' (Barnett, 1997a: 559).[4] Barnett and others believe that an unspoken consensus had emerged post-Somalia: put bluntly, that 'the UN had more to lose by taking action and being associated with another failure than it did by not taking action and allowing the genocide in Rwanda' (1997a: 561). The Americans, meanwhile, were reluctant to send troops into a war zone, resenting the suspicion that 'the international community seemed willing to fight down to the last US citizen' (1997a: 562).[5]

As Holly Bukhalter points out, the US did become quite engaged, through non-UN channels, in what she terms the fifth phase of the Rwandan genocide (July 1994) – deploying soldiers in (the former) Zaire and even Rwanda itself to aid with relief efforts among refugee populations (1994). But its initial reluctance has led to much condemnation. As Samantha Power notes, though, the saga of US response to the genocide 'is not a story of wilful complicity with evil. U.S. officials did not sit around and conspire to allow genocide to happen. But whatever their convictions about "never again," many of them did sit around, and they most certainly did allow genocide to happen' (Power, 2001: 86).

The fall of Srebrenica and other tragedies that facilitated perpetration of crimes against humanity in the former Yugoslavia have also generated a concern that, while not necessarily reflecting indifference, international commitment is weak and unacceptably selective. Dutch peacekeepers at Srebrenica, for example, have been criticized for failing to protect civilians or quickly pass on information that could have led to the suppression of the Serb drive, although it should be remembered that the peacekeepers were outnumbered twelve to one by advancing Serb troops:

Although [the peacekeepers] did not witness mass killing, they were aware of some sinister indications. It is possible that if the members of the battalion had immediately reported in detail those sinister indications to the United Nations chain of command, the international community might have been compelled to respond more robustly and more quickly, and that some lives might have been saved. This failure of intelligence-sharing was also not limited to the fall of Srebrenica, but an endemic weakness throughout the conflict, both within the peacekeeping mission, and between the mission and Member States. (United Nations General Assembly, 1999: 105–6)

It is, of course, difficult to demonstrate that the troops *could* have made a difference, even had they acted or reported immediately. One can expect too much of the UN and the Security Council, which is, after all, based on a unit-veto system that explicitly recognizes national interest as the guiding foreign policy theme, albeit within the overall context of collective security. In cases of selective exclusion – where the great powers avoid overt intervention – some form of great-power interest in the region in question can usually be found. These cases of neglect, therefore, may overlap with our next category of complicity.

A final, and still more controversial, inclusion in this category is the case of economic sanctions imposed through bilateral or multilateral mechanisms that have exceeded the norm of proportionality and are perceived as excessively punitive. This goes beyond the silent genocides of neglect discussed by Henry Shue (1980) and others concerned with the impact of structural adjustment programs. It could refer, as an ICJ judge once suggested, to an arms embargo that limits a persecuted people's ability to resist crimes against humanity (in this case, the Muslims in Bosnia).[6] The most publicized current case is, of course, the recent sanctions regime against Iraq, which according to some estimates resulted in over a million deaths (see Halliday's contribution to the present volume). While I would not be prepared to label this an act of genocide, it can be plausibly argued that the policy denied the material needs of a population already struggling with postwar economic dislocation and the enduring dictatorship of a leader who, had the West demonstrated the necessary resolve during the Gulf War of 1990–91, would no longer have been in power – and therefore could not be used as a reason to justify continuation of the sanctions.

## Material contributions

Many crimes against humanity are committed by governments and/or opposition forces that benefit from direct assistance from the West. Here we enter again the thorny debate over intentionality. It is clear, however, that support for genocidal regimes appears in many guises, regardless of whether we ascribe to Western actors an intention to commit such crimes. While it would be remiss to allege that Western powers were directly involved in the Rwandan genocide, analysts critical of both the aid and the foreign policy communities have contended that, prior to the large-scale massacres of 1994, 'even though the Rwandan government was implicated in racist and genocidal violence against Tutsis, the international community, while pushing for peace and democratisation, also continued and even stepped up its military collaboration with the regime' (Uvin, 1998: 96). Others point to American assistance to Israel and Egypt as cases in which regimes that use torture and commit other rights violations receive large chunks of the aid budget.

In the Rwandan case the figures do, perhaps, speak for themselves: Melvern cites an arms deal between Egypt and Rwanda in March 1992 for US$6 million of light weapons and arms, including 450 Kalashnikov rifles, 2,000 rocket-propelled grenades, 16,000 mortar shells and more than 3 million rounds of small-arms ammunition. The French state-owned bank Crédit Lyonnais acted as guarantor for the deal, which involved the transfer of $1 million in cash instalments in London; again, the trans-national character of complicity is evident (Melvern, 2000: 66). On one level, then, we can look to trade and aid statistics for the period preceding large-scale massacres – though in the Rwandan case the claim was made that such armaments were necessary to defend the state from further invasion by rebels of the Rwandan Popular Front (RPF). It may be prudent to limit our charges here to such cases, lest this category become in-distinguishable from the complaint that many governments have relations with states with dubious human rights records.

Another possible complication is that governments themselves do not always control what their nationals do in the international capitalist marketplace. Shell's involvement with the Nigerian military in oppressing the Ogani and other Niger Delta peoples has become infamous, but it would be difficult to charge either the British or the Dutch with com-plicity in this case. In the case of Talisman, the Canadian firm that helped to perpetuate the government of Sudan's genocidal policies in the south of that country, the Canadian government, though it stopped short of demanding Talisman refrain from further investment, did condemn the investment in a report. But the company refused to pull out of Sudan until their status on the New York stock exchange was challenged, which was related to American anti-terrorist initiatives and not Canadian human rights concerns.

One can argue also that, beyond governments and multinational firms, even aid agencies and other non-governmental actors can contribute

indirectly to exploitative situations in which crimes against humanity are
common. This can extend beyond the case of refugee camps hosting
murderers after genocidal outbreaks. Here the Sudan may again prove
illustrative. Mark Duffield argues that the problem in this case is not the
rush to cope with emergency situations, or complicity in perpetuating the
civil war in Sudan, but rather the fact that efforts to obtain peace can
result in the continuation of prior relations of exploitation and, by
extension, genocidal policies not directly linked to the civil war effort. As
he puts it,

> goal-oriented humanitarianism in the transition zone can be argued to have
> reinforced those everyday relations that denote 'peace.' In other words, aid
> agencies have strengthened and tacitly supported those economic and political
> relations of desocialisation, subordination and exploitation that constitute normal
> life. In the transition zone, since the Dinka are enmeshed in such relations, aid
> policy has been complicit in their oppression. (Duffield, 2001: 205)

Similarly, Uvin charges the development community with a greater
concern for continuing with a predetermined aid process than for heeding
the stormclouds brewing prior to the genocide in Rwanda.[7]

In a more immediate sense, it is evident that aid efforts can increase
oppression and the opportunity for combatants to engage in war crimes
and crimes against humanity. Aid commodities are often

> stolen, diverted and manipulated to the interests of those at war. Warriors also
> use aid in indirect ways. By controlling the locations where they may be delivered,
> commanders manipulate population movements. By negotiating with aid agencies
> for the safe delivery of goods, commanders gain legitimacy in the eyes of those
> who depend on aid for survival and, sometimes, in the eyes of the international
> community. (Anderson, 1998: 141)

It may seem churlish to accuse Western aid agencies of complicity in
crimes against humanity, and such a charge must be made with great care,
since aid organizations are indispensable in many emergency situations.
Nonetheless, a critical perspective might strengthen their effectiveness and
reduce their potential level of complicity in the long term.

Yet another transnational actor must be taken into account, further
complicating the analytical landscape. The privatization of security forces
has become an increasingly pertinent theme, both in the old-style sense of
mercenaries involved in local conflicts with murderous outcomes (Sierre
Leone, for example), and in the sense that such forces are gradually attain-
ing the status of state agents. There may be cases where such forces can,
in fact, offer fruitful paths toward the cessation of crimes against humanity;
but this is a double-edged sword. Private firms such as Executive Outcomes, the Control Risks Group, Defence Services Limited, Sandline

International, and Saladin Security are expanding their markets and deepening the remarkable transition toward privatized security, with British and American firms leading the way. In Colombia, in the mid-1990s, DSL was involved in coordinating the defence of BP's oil infrastructure and personnel with the Colombian army and police, resulting in charges of complicity in human rights abuses by Colombian authorities (see Duffield, 2001: 66; Vines, 1999). (DSL also provided security and logistics personnel to the UN mission in the former Yugoslavia in 1992.) An aggressive external expansion program has been launched by the primary American firm, Virginia-based Military Professional Resources Incorporated (MPRI); MPRI assisted the modernization of the Croatian military in 1994 (Cilliers and Douglas, 1999: 115). Such forces will generally be only one step removed from governmental oversight, and if they are involved in crimes against humanity in the future it will be difficult to claim they have acted in the interests of 'the West,' or its governments.

## Direct participation

The inclusion of this category is the easiest to defend. Here we confront a wide array of possible strategies of complicity, from the acts of occupying forces during wartime to the aerial bombardment campaigns conducted by NATO forces in Serbia (see MacDonald's chapter in this volume), or American forces in Afghanistan (see Jones's Conclusion in the Introduction to this volume). A 1993 decision by the International Court of Justice ordered Serbia and Montenegro to abstain from allowing their troops to commit genocide in Bosnia and Herzegovina (see Chalk, 1994: 61). However, this was an unusual case. It is more common for the international community to accept the premiss that 'war is war' and that civilian casualties are part of the inevitable price of victory.

The remaining articles in this volume deal, at some length, with cases where direct participation of Western governments in crimes against humanity have been alleged. These can take the form of active participation in coups which give rise to genocidal regimes, supply of soldiers and/or military advice, supply and delivery of arms, and, at the extreme, the military application of force resulting in large-scale death and destruction. It should be clear that this category is concerned above all with war crimes.

The issue is also a controversial one, since war efforts tend (with prominent exceptions) to generate patriotic fervor and, especially in cases where such campaigns are directed against genocidal expansionism, it becomes easier to dismiss their harsher consequences (see Langenbacher's chapter this volume, for a treatment of the Allies' bombing of German cities). Journalist Christopher Hitchens has focused on the role of American policymakers like Henry Kissinger in decisions that may have contributed to genocidal consequences in Vietnam, Cambodia, Bangladesh, and East Timor (Hitchens, 2001; see Jacobs's and Aguilar's chapters in this volume). Others, such as Daniel Goldhagen, author of the controversial bestseller *Hitler's Willing Executioners: Ordinary Germans and the Holocaust* (1996), and Samantha Power, a former International Crisis Group consultant and currently Executive Director of Harvard University's Carr Center for Human Rights, have called for an investigation into atrocities that US Senator Bob Kerrey is alleged to have ordered while on combat operations during the Vietnam War (Goldhagen and Power, 2001; see also Jones's introduction to this volume). It is highly unlikely that either Kissinger or Kerrey is under any real threat of investigation by the US government, of course; but such paper indictments do challenge the 'culture of impunity' considered in this volume.

There is room for considerable debate here concerning the actual conditions of direct intervention: whether contributions are coordinated with foreign states or are unilateral in nature; whether they precede the dispatching of an occupation force; and whether they extend beyond physical attack to policies of cultural and/or political assimilation, which would return us to the first category presented in this chapter. In ethical terms, the debate over *jus ad bellum* continues.

### Globalization as a destructive process

Finally, a general theme linking all the above types of complicity, and yet one with the least attractive analytic rewards, is that globalization is akin to murderous imperialism (see Prontzos's chapter in this volume). Before briefly exploring this theme, I would like to make my own position clear. I would accept the inclusion, given my limited understanding of the negative impact of imperialism, but would decline to advocate its adoption by analysts concerned with the more formal criminality aspect of complicity in crimes against humanity. Further, globalization does create conditions for enhanced communication and international organization which can contribute to the *mitigation* of crimes against humanity. But it can also be seen as a process of homogenization, and as a context that encourages eliminationist solutions to the 'problem' of difference.

More than the others, then, this category is closer to an ideological position than an analytical tool, and it requires us to move beyond immediate intentionality and engage with a more structural level of analysis. Though pockets of opposition to globalization are eliminated by a combination of proactive acts of atrocity, these occur within the context of structural violence: historical and entrenched conditions which favor Western states and corporations. An ideology that seeks to eliminate 'inefficiency' and opposition to a market-value system, as philosopher John McMurtry (1998) argues, is both ruthless and self-perpetuating. The process began in the industrial core, as Marx described it in his chapter in *Capital* on the 'Bloody Legislation against the Expropriated from the End of the 15th Century' (1967: 717–44). It continued with colonization, imperialism, market-induced structural adjustment programs in the wake of the Third World debt crisis, the marginalizing of protest groups, and so on.[8] One can, of course, argue that the nation-building exercise has been fueled by eliminationist impulses, and the 'mobilization of predatory identities' (Appadurai, 2000: 132)[9] toward this end. Why, then, would the global polity-building exercise, stripped of its liberal veneer, be any different?

This line of thinking has much in common with the 'pathology of modernity' argument in the literature on the Holocaust and the 'totalitarian potential of modernisation' (Welch, 1999: 2). Mass murder can thus be seen as a product, not a failure, of modern society (Bauman, 1989). This can be viewed from a materialist perspective as well, in the work of Aly and Heim (1988). The authors consider the implementation of the Final Solution in Poland to have been a rational by-product of capitalist organisation. To move from here to a blanket condemnation of globalization, however, is a big leap indeed. It can be argued that the violence accompanying the process of globalization is indicative of an inhumane approach to governance, but to make a further argument of Western complicity would be provocative at best.

To conclude this section: it is not enough merely to disentangle the many threads binding Western governments to agents of genocide and crimes against humanity elsewhere. There are common, socially constructed, and quite persistent conceptual linkages as well. These include myths based on race, nation, rationality and science (see Peukert, 1993), state security, progress, and the aggressive globalization of norms and value systems. The myths may advance human rights on the one hand, but justify the marginalization and neglect of entire populations on the other.

## Obligations: ending the culture of impunity?

In each of the categories presented above we can see points of entry to the issue of transnational complicity, whether in the policy of colonial eliminationism; in the decision to do nothing or to ignore the suffering caused by policies based on national interest; in the material contribution to regimes and opposition forces committing atrocities; or in the outright application of military force (in the 'national interest'), which can be said to constitute crimes against humanity. The chapters to follow capture case studies of each, but they go further, suggesting justice can be restored through a variety of means, including citizens' tribunals, reparations, and truth and reconciliation commissions (on the latter, see Deegan, 2001: 136–64). A broader question is that of obligation: what responsibilities do Western states and citizens have in the battle against the culture of impunity? This question can be broken down into the twin themes of intervention and reparations.

It might seem obvious to argue that the West has an obligation *not* to intervene when doing so will only worsen the situation for civilians and combatants. As early as 1758, Emmerich de Vattel wrote:

> To give help to a brave people who are defending their liberties against an oppressor by force of arms is only the part of justice and generosity. Hence, whenever such dissension reaches the state of civil war, foreign nations may assist that one of the two parties, which seems to have justice on its side. But to assist a detestable tyrant … would certainly be a violation of duty. (quoted in Moynihan, 1990: 175)

Beyond this, the duty to intervene is a hotly contested subject in international legal and policy circles. It is at best perceived as a diffuse duty, as described by international relations ethicist Michael Walzer, 'which is to say, no one's duty in particular, so in fact the brutalities and oppression of international society are more often denounced than interdicted' (1997: 107; see also Tamir, 2000: 262). Despite the claim advanced by Wheeler (2000) that a norm of humanitarian intervention is emerging, there is considerable dissension on this subject (Vincent, 1986; see also International Commission on Intervention and State Sovereignty, 2000).

We can suggest, however, that an obligation exists, when intervention to confront crimes against humanity is the chosen course, to pursue the project humanely and in a well-coordinated fashion, though the latter is obviously difficult given time constraints. Harold Adelman suggests a complementary second-order norm is the obligation on the part of the international community to strive for coherence in its interventionist policies: 'it is incumbent upon all parties to make their best efforts to arrive at a coherent policy when attacking the issue. Just as in an operating room, so in international interventions: You cannot have each of the parties pursuing different goals and following different procedures' (2001: 199). More to the point, one can argue an obligation exists to avoid duplicity – that arguing for peace in civilian conflicts and selling arms to warring parties,

**Table 2.1**    Sources of reparations claims

| World War II | 'Transition to democracy' | Colonialism |
| --- | --- | --- |
| State-sponsored mass killing, forced labor, sexual exploitation (Axis powers: Germany, Japan, Austria) | State terrorism, other authoritarian practices (in Latin America, Eastern Europe, South Africa) | Classical European colonialism (claims from formerly colonized against former colonial powers, e.g. Africa, and from indigenous groups against states 'dominated by the descendants of their European conquerors') |
| Wartime incarceration of Japanese populations (Allied powers: US, Canada) | | |
| Economic collaboration with Nazi crimes ('putatively neutral' states: Switzerland, France, Netherlands) | | Internal colonialism (slavery, Jim Crow, apartheid) |
| | | Neo-colonialism (claims against international lending agencies – e.g. World Bank, IMF – seen as partial cause of Third World poverty, population displacement and environmental destruction – e.g. funding dam construction) |

*Source*: Based on Torpey, 2001: 335–6, constructed by Michael Innes.

for example, represent not only a breach of ethics, but expensively counter-productive behavior.

Beyond the question of intervention lies that of institutional responses. Since these are dealt with at length in the next chapter, I will proceed quickly here, suggesting only that the issue of reparations for past atrocities poses the greatest analytical and policy challenge (see Verdeja's and Njubi Nesbitt's chapters in this volume). Perhaps the most enlightening treatment of the reparations issue is that offered by John Torpey. He sees reparation demands rooted in racial identity as the most promising in terms of galvanizing claimants (class-based demands, he suggests, present a much more complicated process of victimization). Torpey lists three sources of reparations demands, beginning with the relatively straightforward claims related to World War II, and continuing with the therapeutic process of sorting out claims related to regime transition and 'clarifying the circumstances under which the victims of the regime suffered' (Torpey, 2001: 335). Finally, there are claims related to colonialism (classical European expan-

**Table 2.2** Types of reparations claims

| Symbolic/commemorative | Antisystemic/transformative |
| --- | --- |
| 1. Typically World War II-centered claims.<br><br>2. 'Backward looking,' intended to cultivate awareness of the victims' suffering, explicitly involving the mobilization of ethnocultural consciousness.<br><br>3. Material compensation secondary. Although some of the claimants – Holocaust survivors, comfort women – bear the physical scars of their torment, the benefits accrued to symbolic/commemorative claims are more of a psychological sort. | 1. Typically colonialism-centered claims.<br><br>2. 'Forward looking,' often connected to broader programs of social progress. Intended to address injustice of past systems of domination (colonialism, apartheid, slavery, segregation) seen as contributing to ongoing economic imbalance and deprivation.<br><br>3. Mobilization of ethnocultural victimhood of some claimants. (Aboriginals, black Americans) indicates a symbolic/commemorative element. |

*Source*: Based on Torpey, 2001: 336–7, constructed by Michael Innes.

sionism, internal colonialism, and neocolonialism). These can be further separated into symbolic/commemorative and antisystemic/transformative claims (see Table 2.2).

For our purposes, it is noteworthy that many of the reparations claims involve a transnational element. This is evident in the case of the slave-trader, or the economic collaborator with Nazi crimes, or the neo-colonialist. A discussion of the value of such claims as socializing agents is beyond the scope of this chapter, but Torpey's claim that, for many victimized groups, 'the road to the future runs through the prolonged disasters of the past' (2001: 337) suggests that this could be one means of avoiding the homogeneity fostered by the West's globalizing strategies, and should be taken seriously as part of a violence-avoidance campaign. At the same time, admitting the legitimacy of such claims (beyond the patchwork of reparations agreements) opens a door most state leaders, including finance ministers, would rather leave firmly closed, or only slightly ajar.

In terms of other obligations, a recent decision by the International Court of Justice suggests there is an obligation to refrain from committing genocide by using nuclear weapons, and that the continuation of global warming, largely the result of Western states' economic activities, threatens the very existence of millions of inhabitants of small island states and coastal regions.[10] In both cases, however, we would have to expand the array of perpetrators beyond 'the West,' to include states such as Russia, India, and China.

Much has been written of the importance of political identity, generated by social constructions of difference, which create the contextual preconditions for genocidal behavior.[11] Institutions do have the ability to construct and even structure knowledge (see Foucault, 1977); and this process might in itself give the green light for the perpetration of atrocities. Barnett writes of 'an intimate connection between the discourse of acting in the best interests of the international community, the bureaucratisation of peacekeeping, and the production of indifference' (Barnett, 1997a; see also Rieff, 1995, on Bosnia). Perhaps the more demanding obligation, then, is to avoid the reflexive turn to what Herzfeld (1993), borrowing from Weber (1963), refers to as 'secular theodicy': the tendency to overlook evil in some places for the greater good of a collective identity, in this case that of the international community itself. Put another way, it cautions against the acceptance of constructed images of order that mask structural violence.

At the very least, Western scholarship has an obligation to avoid oversimplifying events. As Rene Lemarchand poignantly reminds us, the 'Manichean dichotomy simply does not does not apply' in the Rwandan case (1998: 42). Casting foreign crimes against humanity as examples of good guys versus bad guys is more than inaccurate; it is self-rationalization, and precludes a deeper understanding of both the causes of atrocious events and the extent of our own complicity.

## Conclusion

Accusations of complicity in crimes against humanity are, to some degree, contingent on the adoption of a legal approach. Events are seen largely as 'crimes,' rather than as historical processes. Therefore they are even further from constituting, in a material or ideational sense, a structure that prompts future generations to continue such practices. Though some would prefer this latter view, the former (that is, the assumption of criminality) enables us to be more specific with our admonitions and, perhaps, criminal prosecutions and calls for recompense. One path leads us to a greater operational understanding, while the other offers greater conceptual and historical breadth.

Arguing for the latter strategy, Ward Churchill believes that the 'reproduction, evolution, and perfection of any hegemonic structure is inevitable, left to its own devices' (1997: 3). Accordingly, he seeks to forge a 'viable countergenocidal praxis' (1997: 8), much as Foucault and others write of counter-hegemonic understandings and readings of power. In the case of crimes against humanity, such a strategy must begin with an understanding of the extent of Western complicity, since the West's own narrative is essential to the modern project of state construction. It is as important to challenge seriously the accuracy and legitimacy of claims that Western involvement necessarily denotes intentionality, or for that matter carries with it an obligation to provide reparations. This critical examination of critical theory, as it were, can be fruitful for the fields of international and transnational studies, genocide studies, and legal approaches to conflict deterrence. But it can also lead the observer to ask some fundamental questions.

For example, if we accept Uvin's troubling analysis that (at least in the Rwandan case) development assistance contributes to structural violence, it follows that we need to rethink the entire Westernization project, and seek studiously and systematically to avoid involvement where it can lead to complicity in mass violence. The primary agenda for social scientists working in this area may well be to identify those moments when such complicity becomes possible, and to integrate this recognition into the range of policymaking options. The alternative is simply to wish away Western involvement, which is hardly likely to succeed; or to succumb to despair, accepting the inevitability of Western collusion in crimes against humanity in the name of national interest or the pursuit of profit.

Sporadic cases of 'spontaneous communal violence' aside (Holsti, 2000: 169), most instances of mass killing before and since the larger inter-state wars have been cases of 'death by government' (Rummel, 1994). This should lead us to analyze more closely the complex links between such murderous states and their Western allies. The more entrenched historically these links are, and the less geographically and chronologically distant, the stronger is the case of Western complicity. The case-study chapters in this volume will explore these linkages in much greater detail.

## Notes

I am especially grateful for the research assistance of Michael Innes, M.A. candidate in the Department of History, Concordia University, and for a paper he prepared in this context: 'Genocide and the West: A Survey of Recent Literature.' I also appreciate helpful comments from members of the Montreal Institute for Genocide Studies (MIGS) seminar at Concordia University, led by history professor and genocide scholar Frank Chalk. I assume full responsibility for the content of the chapter, however.

1. We could cover several volumes discussing the 'proper' definitions of genocide, war crimes, crimes against humanity, 'war time,' and other concepts. Space precludes elaboration, as we have more than enough conceptual complexity to manage. For

relevant definitional discussions see Chalk and Jonassohn, 1990; Charny, 1994; Chalk, 1994; Stoett, 1995; Melson, 1992; Katz, 1996; and Palmer, 2000; for a social constructivist approach see Berger, 1993.

2. Balfour offers a succinct summary of the functionalist school: 'Functional processes formed the foundation for the vast and systematic mass killing that defined the Holocaust and it cannot be understood apart from the role played by such relatively mundane operations … bureaucratic procedures carried out by regular civil servants were essential to both the formulation and implementation of the Holocaust…. Existing organizations adapted themselves and contributed to the evolving task of separating Jews from the society of the Third Reich to the point where their destruction became the logical and efficient solution to an administrative problem' (1997: 137).

3. Note the evocative title of the volume edited by Cushman and Mestrovic, *This Time We Knew: Western Response to Genocide in Bosnia* (1996).

4. However, it can be suggested that the Secretary-General's special envoy to Rwanda downplayed the crisis, suggesting it was evidence of a traditional war between the RPF and the army more than a genocide proper. See Bukhalter, 1994: 46.

5. On this theme see also Kuperman, 2001; Des Forges, 1999; Klinghoffer, 1998.

6. The judge found that the Security Council resolution establishing the arms embargo on the former Yugoslavia 'in effect called on Members of the United Nations, albeit unknowingly and assuredly unwillingly, to become in some degree supporters of the genocidal activity of the Serbs and in this manner and to that extent to act contrary to a rule of jus cogens.' In Bosnia v. Serbia II, ICJ Reports 1993, quoted in C. Scott et al. (1994: 14–15). Special thanks to Carol McQueen for bringing this to my attention.

7. 'Up to 1994, with few exceptions, projects in the pipeline were executed without change; no human rights conditionalities were added to overall aid disbursements or specific projects' (Uvin, 1998: 99).

8. McMurtry cites an analysis by Chase Manhattan Bank of the Chiapas rebellion in southern Mexico, and quotes as follows: 'While Chiapas, in our opinion, does not pose a fundamental threat to Mexican political stability, it is perceived to be so by many in the investment community. The government will need to eliminate the Zapatistas' (1998: 231). This is a fascinating quotation, given the starkness of the language; even if taken as benevolently as possible, elimination would require the destruction of a political organization with non-military means, and of course the Mexican government's initial approach to the rebellion was anything but non-military. Problematically, however, the only source McMurtry offers is a newspaper article written by himself (1995).

9. Appadurai: 'Most nations achieve their sense of their cultural homogeneity in the face of remarkable and known diversities and fierce micro-attachments that have to be erased, marginalized or transformed…. Whether it is peasants being transformed into Frenchmen, Scots being turned into Britons, Hindus into Indians, for some nations to be imagined, others have to be deemed "unimaginable"' (2000: 132). This is a troubled statement at best, and not because of the determinism creeping in at the end; it also overlooks the possibility of multiple political identities, and the resilience of traditional associations.

10. The Court was asked for two opinions, one concerning whether the use of nuclear weapons would be a violation of the World Health Organization's constitution (this was rejected); the second asked whether or not the use of nuclear weapons would be a violation of international law. The Court declared that nuclear weapons are generally illegal, but did not conclude definitely on whether the threat or use of nuclear weapons would be lawful or unlawful in the 'extreme circumstance of self-defence.' This ambiguous declaration has inspired disarmament activists, even though it is clear

that the Court was divided over the issue of whether the right to self-defense or the principles of international law should prevail. See Grisdale, 1997.

11. For example, Uvin discusses the debate about distinguishing Tutsi from Hutu: 'Do the differences in stature ... reflect the fact that they are from very different genetic stock ... differences in diet, with Tutsi cattle herders living on an almost exclusive diet of milk products? Or are they the result of biased sampling (everyone who was tall was categorized as Tutsi, thus "proving" that all Tutsi are tall)?' (Uvin: 2001). Uvin cites chapter 2 of Taylor, 1999, as an interesting discussion of this debate.

# References

Adelman, H. (2001). Humanitarian intervention in Zaire: A case study of humanitarian realism. In R. Irwin, ed., *Ethics and security in Canadian foreign policy*, 181–207. Vancouver: UBC Press.

Adelman, H. and Suhrke, A., eds (1999). *The path of a genocide: The Rwanda crisis from Uganda to Zaire*. New Brunswick, NJ: Transaction.

Aly, G, and Heim, S. (1988). The economics of the Final Solution: A case study from the General Government. In *Simon Weisenthal Center Annual*, 5, 3–48.

American Anthropological Association (1991). *Report of the special commission to investigate the situation of the Brazilian Yanomami*. www.aaanet.org/committees/cfhr/docshist.htm.

Anderson, M. (1998). Some moral dilemmas of humanitarian aid. In J. Moore, ed., *Hard choices: Moral dilemmas in humanitarian intervention*. New York: Rowman & Littlefield.

Appadurai, A. (2000). The grounds of the nation-state: Identity, violence, and territory. In K. Goldmann, U. Hannerz, and C. Westin, eds, *Nationalism and internationalism in the post-Cold War era*, 127–42. London: Routledge.

Astourian, S. (1999). Modern Turkish identity and the Armenian genocide. In R. Hovannisian, ed., *Remembrance and denial: The case of the Armenian genocide*. Detroit: Wayne State University Press.

Balfour, D. (1997). Historiography of the Holocaust: A cautionary tale for public administration. *American Review of Public Administration* 27, no. 2: 133–44.

Barnett, M. (1997a). The U.N. Security Council, indifference, and the genocide in Rwanda. *Cultural Anthropology* 12, no. 4.

——— (1997b). Bringing in the New World Order: Liberalism, legitimacy, and the United Nations. *World Politics* 49, no. 4: 526–51.

Barnett, M. and Finnemore, M. (1999). The politics, power, and pathologies of international organizations. *International Organization* 53, no. 4: 699–732.

Barta, T. (1987). Relations of genocide: Land and lives in the colonization of Australia. In I. Wallimann and M. Dobkowski, eds, *Genocide and the modern age*, 237–51. New York: Greenwood Press.

Bartrop, P. (1997). The Powhatans of Virginia and the English invasion of America: Destruction without genocide. In C. Tatz, ed., *Genocide perspectives I*, 66–108. Sydney: Centre for Comparative Genocide Studies.

Bauman, Z. (1989). *Modernity and the Holocaust*. New York: Polity Press.

Beigbeder, Y. (1999). *Judging war criminals: The politics of international justice*. New York: St. Martin's Press.

Berger, R. (1993). The 'banality of evil' reframed: The social construction of the 'Final

Solution' to the 'Jewish Problem.' *Sociological Quarterly* 34, no. 4: 594–618.

Bukhalter, H. (1994). The question of genocide: The Clinton administration and Rwanda. *World Policy Journal* 11, no. 4.

Bull, H., ed. (1984). *Intervention in world politics*. Oxford: Clarendon Press.

Burrin, P. (1994). *Hitler and the Jews: The genesis of the Holocaust*. London: Edward Arnold.

Chalk, F. (1999). Radio broadcasting in the incitement and interdiction of gross violations of human rights including genocide. In R. Smith, ed., *Genocide: Essays toward understanding, early warning, and prevention*. Williamsburg, VA: Association of Genocide Scholars, 185–203.

——— (1994). Redefining genocide. In G. Andreopoulos, ed., *Genocide: Conceptual and historical dimensions*, 47–63. Philadelphia: University of Pennsylvania Press.

Chalk, F., and Jonassohn, K. (1990). *The history and sociology of genocide: Analyses and case studies*. New Haven: Yale University Press.

Charny, I. (1994). Toward a generic definition of genocide. In G. Andreopoulos, ed., *Genocide: Conceptual and historical dimensions*, 64–94. Philadelphia: University of Pennsylvania Press.

Churchill, W. (1997). *A little matter of genocide: Holocaust and denial in the Americas, 1492 to the present*. San Francisco: City Lights Books.

Cilliers, J., and Douglas, I. (1999). The military as business. In J. Cilliers and P. Mason, eds, *Peace, profit or plunder? The privatisation of security in war-torn Africa*, 111–22. South Africa: Institute for Security Studies.

Cocker, M. (1998). *Rivers of blood, rivers of gold: Europe's conflict with tribal peoples*. London: Jonathan Cape.

Craig, S., et al. (1994). A memorial for Bosnia: Framework of legal arguments concerning the lawfulness of the maintenance of the U.N. Security Council's arms embargo on Bosnia and Herzegovina. *Michigan Journal of International Law* 16: 14–15.

Cushman, T., and Mestrovic, S., eds (1996). *This time we knew: Western responses to genocide in Bosnia*. New York: New York University Press.

Deegan, H. (2001). *The politics of the new South Africa: Apartheid and after*. London: Longman.

Des Forges, A. (1999). *Leave none to tell the story: Genocide in Rwanda*. New York: Human Rights Watch.

Duffield, M. (2001). *Global governance and the new wars: The merging of development and security*. London: Zed Books.

Ericksen, R., and Heschel, S., eds (1999). *Betrayal: German churches and the Holocaust*. Minneapolis: Fortress Press.

Evans, R. (1989). *In Hitler's shadow: West German historians and the attempt to escape from the Nazi past*. New York: Pantheon.

Fein, H. (1993). *Genocide: A sociological perspective*. London: Sage Publications.

Feldman, A. (1991). *Formations of violence*. Chicago: Chicago University Press.

Foucault, M. (1977). *Discipline and punish*. New York: Vintage.

Galtung, J. (1969). Violence, peace, and peace research. *Journal of Peace Research*, 6, no. 1: 167–91.

Giddens, A. (1996). *In defence of sociology: Essays, interpretations and rejoinders*. Cambridge: Polity Press.

Goldhagen, D.J. (1996). *Hitler's willing executioners: Ordinary Germans and the Holocaust*. New York: Alfred A. Knopf.

Goldhagen, D.J. and Power, S.J. (2001). Kerrey should be investigated. *The Boston Globe*, 3 May.

Gourevitch, P. (1998). *We wish to inform you that tomorrow we will be killed with our families: Stories from Rwanda.* New York: Farrar Straus & Giroux.

Grisdale, D. (1997). The International Court of Justice opinion on nuclear weapons: Implications for Canadian policy.' *Canadian Foreign Policy* 5, no. 1: 153–67.

Hampson, F.O., et al. (2001). *Madness in the multitude: Human security and world disorder.* Toronto: Oxford University Press.

Heidenrich, J. (2001). *How to prevent genocide: A guide for policy makers, scholars, and the concerned citizen.* New York: Praeger.

Herzfeld, M. (1993). *The social production of indifference: Exploring the symbolic roots of Western bureaucracy.* Chicago: University of Chicago Press.

Hitchens, C. (2001). *The trial of Henry Kissinger.* London, New York: Verso.

Hochschild, A. (1999). *King Leopold's ghost: A story of greed, terror, and heroism in colonial Africa.* Boston and New York: Houghton Mifflin.

Holsti, K. (2000). From Khartoum to Quebec: Internationalism and nationalism within the multi-community state. In K. Goldmann et al., eds, *Nationalism and internationalism in the post-Cold War era,* 143–69. London: Routledge.

Horwitz, G.J. (2000). Places far away, places very near: Mauthausen, the camps of the Shoah, and the bystanders. In O. Bartov, ed., *The Holocaust: Origins, implementation, aftermath,* 204–18. London: Routledge.

Inayatullah, N., and Blaney, D. (1996). Knowing encounters. In Y. Lapid and F. Kratochwil, eds, *The return of culture and identity in international relations theory,* 65–84. Boulder: Lynne Rienner.

Indian and Northern Affairs Canada (1996). *People to people, nation to nation: Report of the Royal Commission on Aboriginal Peoples.* Ottawa: Indian and Northern Affairs Canada. www.ainc-inac.gc.ca/ch/rcap/index_e.html.

———— (n.d.). Backgrounder: The residential school system. www.ainc-inac.gc.ca/gs/schl_e.html.

Innes, M.A. (2001). Genocide, ethnocide, or hyperbole? Australia's 'stolen generation' and Canada's 'hidden holocaust.' *Cultural Survival Quarterly,* Fall.

International Commission on Intervention and State Sovereignty (2000). *The responsibility to protect.* Ottawa: Department of Foreign Affairs and International Trade. www.icissciise.gc.ca/pdfs/Commission-Report.pdf.

Jones, D. (1992). The declaratory tradition in modern international law. In T. Nardin and D. Marpel, eds, *Traditions of international ethics.* New York: Cambridge University Press.

Jonas, S. (1991). *The battle for Guatemala: Rebels, death squads, and US power.* Boulder: Westview Press.

Katz, S. (1996). The uniqueness of the Holocaust: The historical dimension. In A. Rosenbaum, ed., *Is the Holocaust unique? Perspectives on comparative genocide,* 19–38. Boulder: Westview Press.

Klinghoffer, A. (1998). *The international dimension of genocide in Rwanda.* London: Macmillan.

Kuperman, A.J. (2001). *The limits of humanitarian intervention: Genocide in Rwanda.* Washington, DC: Brookings Institution Press.

Lemarchand, R. (1998). US policy in the Great Lakes: A critical perspective. *Issue: A Journal of Opinion* 26, no. 1.

Levene, M. (1999a). The Chittagong Hill tracts: A case study in the political economy of 'creeping' genocide. *Third World Review* 20, no. 2: 339–69.

———— (1999b). Connecting threads: Rwanda, the Holocaust, and the pattern of contemporary genocide. In R. Smith, ed., *Genocide: Essays toward understanding, early warning, and prevention.* Williambsurg, VA: Association of Genocide Scholars.

Linklater, A. (1999). The evolving spheres of international justice. *International Affairs* 75, no. 3: 473–82.

McMurtry, J. (1998). *Unequal freedoms: The global market as an ethical system.* Toronto: Garamond Press.

McMurtry, J. (1995). A day in the life of the New World Order. *The Globe and Mail,* 1 April.

Marx, K. (1967). *Capital.* New York: Progress Publishers.

Melson, R. (1992). *Revolution and genocide: On the origins of the Armenian genocide and the Holocaust.* Chicago and London: University of Chicago Press.

Melvern, L. (2000). *A people betrayed: The role of the West in Rwanda's genocide.* London: Zed Books.

Moses, D. (2000). An antipodean genocide? The origins of the genocidal moment in the colonization of Australia. *Journal of Genocide Research* 2, no. 1: 89–106.

———— (1998). Structure and agency in the Holocaust: Daniel Goldhagen and his critics.' *History and Theory* 37, no. 2: 194–219.

Moynihan, D. (1990). *On the law of nations.* Cambridge, MA: Harvard University Press.

Nandy, A. (1983). *The intimate enemy: Loss and recovery of self under colonialism.* Oxford: Oxford University Press.

Novick, P. (2000). *The Holocaust in American life.* Boston and New York: Houghton Mifflin.

Palmer, A. (2000). *Colonial genocide.* Adelaide: Crawford House Publishing.

Peukert, D. (1993). The genesis of the 'Final Solution' from the spirit of science. In T. Childers and J. Caplan, eds, *Reevaluating the Third Reich,* 234–252. New York: Holmes & Meier.

Power, S. (2001). Bystanders to genocide: Why the United States let the Rwandan tragedy happen. *The Atlantic Monthly,* September: 84–108.

Prunier, G. (1995). *The Rwanda crisis, 1959–1994: History of a genocide.* London: Hurst.

Reynolds, H. (2001). *An indelible stain: The question of genocide in Australia's history.* Victoria: Penguin Books Australia.

Rieff, D. (1995). *Slaughterhouse: Bosnia and the failure of the West.* New York: Simon & Schuster.

Rummel, R.J. (1994). *Death by government.* New Brunswick, NJ: Transaction Books.

Scharfe, S. (1996). *Complicity, human rights and Canadian foreign policy.* Montreal: Black Rose Books.

Shue, H. (1980). *Basic rights: Subsistence, affluence, and U.S. foreign policy.* Princeton: Princeton University Press.

Stannard, D.E. (1992). *American holocaust: Columbus and the conquest of the New World.* New York: Oxford University Press.

Stoett, P. (1995). This age of genocide: Conceptual and institutional implications. *International Journal* 50, no. 3: 594–618.

Tamir, Y. (2000). Who's afraid of a global state? In K. Goldmann et al., eds, *Nationalism and internationalism in the post-Cold War era,* 244–67. London: Routledge.

Taylor, C. (1999). *Sacrifice as terror: The Rwandan genocide of 1994.* Oxford: Berg.

Thornton, R. (1987). *American Indian holocaust and survival: A population history since 1492.* Norman and London: University of Oklahoma Press.

Todorov, T. (1984). *The conquest of America: The question of the Other.* New York: Harper & Row.

Torpey, J. (2001). 'Making whole what has been smashed': Reflections on reparations. *Journal of Modern History* 73: 333–58.

United Nations General Assembly (1999). *Report of the Secretary General pursuant to General Assembly resolution 53/35: The fall of Srebrenica*. U.N. doc A/54/549, 15 December: 105–06.

Uvin, P. (1998). *Aiding violence: The development enterprise in Rwanda*. New York: Kumarian.

Vincent, R.J. (1986). *Human rights and international relations*. Cambridge: Cambridge University Press.

Vines, A. (1999). Mercenaries and the privatisation of security in Africa in the 1990s. In G. Mills and J. Stemlau, eds, *The privatisation of security in Africa*, 47–80. Johannesburg: South African Institute of International Affairs.

Walzer, M. (1997). Responses to Kukathus. In I. Shapiro and W. Kymlicka, eds, *Ethnicity and group rights*, 105–11. New York: New York University Press.

Weber, M. (1963). Theodicy, salvation, and rebirth. In *Sociology of religion*, trans. E. Fischoff. Boston: Beacon Press.

Welch, S. (1999). A survey of interpretive paradigms in Holocaust studies and a comment on the dimensions of the Holocaust. Paper presented to the seminar, 'Famine and political killings: Causation, scale, and state responsibility.' University of Melbourne, 13 August. www.edu/gsp/conference papers.html.

Wendt, A. (1996). Identity and structural change in international politics. In Y. Lapid and F. Kratochwil, eds, *The return of culture and identity in international relations theory*, 47–64. Boulder: Lynne Rienner.

Wheeler, N. (2000). *Saving strangers: Humanitarian intervention in international society*. Oxford: Oxford University Press.

Wilson, Sir R. (1997). *Bringing them home: Report of the National Inquiry into the Separation of Aboriginal and Torres Strait Islander Children from Their Families*. Sydney: Human Rights and Equal Opportunity Commission. www.austlii.edu.au/au/special/rsj project/rsjlibrary/hreoc.

# PART II

# Genocide, War Crimes and the West

# 3

# Imperial Germany and the Herero of Southern Africa: Genocide and the Quest for Recompense

## Jan-Bart Gewald

On 9 September 2001, the Herero People's Reparations Corporation lodged a claim in a civil court in the US District of Columbia. The claim was directed against the Federal Republic of Germany, in the person of the German foreign minister, Joschka Fischer, for crimes against humanity, slavery, forced labor, violations of international law, and genocide.

Ninety-seven years earlier, on 11 January 1904, in a small and dusty town in central Namibia, the first genocide of the twentieth century began with the eruption of the Herero–German war.[1] By the time hostilities ended, the majority of the Herero had been killed, driven off their land, robbed of their cattle, and banished to near-certain death in the sandy wastes of the Omaheke desert. The survivors, mostly women and children, were incarcerated in concentration camps and put to work as forced laborers (Gewald, 1995; 1999: 141–91). Throughout the twentieth century, Herero survivors and their descendants have struggled to gain recognition and compensation for the crime committed against them.

Following a brief description of the Herero genocide, this chapter provides a chronological overview of the way in which the Herero have sought to draw the world's attention to the crimes committed by Imperial Germany in Namibia. Calls for compensation will in the end revolve around the issue of German government responsibility. That is, to what extent were the Herero genocide and related atrocities the product of official German policy? To what extent were the criminal acts not merely the actions of individuals? Material presented here will show that the Herero genocide and associated atrocities were indeed officially sanctioned. In the war, the German settlers and soldiers carried out a shoot-to-kill policy, conducted extrajudicial killings, established concentration camps, employed forced labor, and in at least two cases established death camps. After the war, the loss of Herero liberty, land, and stock was officially sanctioned in legislation. At no stage after 1904 were any German settlers or soldiers brought to justice for genocidal acts committed in Namibia between 1904 and 1908.

## The Herero–German War

In 1904, a war characterized by extreme brutality and deliberate genocide broke out in the central Namibian settlement of Okahandja. It arose from a series of misunderstandings and the self-fulfilling prophecies of the paranoid settler class.[2] As the war steadily spread across central Namibia, it grew in intensity and viciousness, as fresh contingents of German troops despatched from Imperial Germany poured into the country and attempted to impose their vision of 'order' on the territory and its inhabitants. The personal involvement of the German Kaiser, Wilhelm II, in deciding how the war was to be fought in German South West Africa signalled the highest authorization and endorsement for acts committed in the name of Imperial Germany. In a conscious policy of genocide, German soldiers and settlers sought, shot, beat, hanged, starved, and raped Herero men, women, and children. When the war finally ended, no fewer than 80 per cent of the Herero had lost their lives. Those who remained in Namibia, primarily women and children, survived in concentration camps as forced laborers employed on state, military, and civilian projects (Gewald, 1999: 141–230). In short, the war and its aftermath were characterized by extreme acts of violence and cruelty on the part of German soldiers and settlers.

The diaries, letters, and photographs of contemporaries graphically portray the indiscriminate shootings, hangings, and beatings which were the order of the day. Missionary Elger, stationed in the settlement of Karibib, described the manner in which Herero prisoners were treated:

> Things proceeded in a particularly brutal manner. Herero prisoners were terribly maltreated, whether they were guilty or not guilty. About 4 Herero were taken prisoner, because they were supposed to have killed a railway worker (Lehmann, Habis). The court martial ordered them to be freed and declared them to be not guilty. However one could not release them as they bore too many marks of shameful abuse [*Schandlicher Misshandlung*] on their bodies. For example, people had beaten an eye out of one. After the court martial had declared them to be innocent, some of the Germans outside immediately resumed the abuse with the words, 'the court has declared you to be innocent, we however want to string you up.'[3]

After the initial battles, the civilian governor was relieved of his command and replaced by the Kaiser's own candidate, Lieutenant-General Lothar von Trotha.[4] Under the command of von Trotha, the German army sought to engineer a crushing defeat of the Herero in the vicinity of the Waterberg (Pool, 1979: 210–11). In keeping with von Moltke's principles of separate deployment and encirclement, von Trotha sent his armies to annihilate the Herero at the Waterberg. Or, as he put it in his own words:

> My initial plan for the operation, which I always adhered to, was to encircle the masses of Hereros at Waterberg, and to annihilate these masses with a simultaneous blow, then to establish various stations to hunt down and disarm the splinter groups who escaped, later to lay hands on the captains by putting prize money on their heads and finally to sentence them to death. (von Trotha's diaries cited in Pool, 1991: 251)

On 11 August, the battle of Hamakari at the Waterberg took place. The Herero were defeated and fled in a southeasterly direction into the dry desert sands of the Kalahari, known to the Herero as the Omaheke.[5] On Sunday, 2 October 1904, after holding a field service, General von Trotha addressed his officers (Rust, 1905: 384). He declared that the war against the Herero would be pursued in all earnestness, and read a proclamation that stated, among other things:

> The Herero people must … leave the land. If the populace does not do this I will force them with the *Groot Rohr* [cannon]. Within the German borders every Herero, with or without a gun, with or without cattle, will be shot. I will no longer accept women and children, I will drive them back to their people or I will let them be shot at.
> These are my words to the Herero people.
> [Signed] The great General of the mighty German Kaiser.[6]

A number of authors have sought to deny or at least downplay the existence and implications of Trotha's proclamation, which has become known as the extermination order (*Vernichtungsbefehl*).[7] However, Trotha's own words, in his diary and elsewhere, indicate that he understood the implications of his proclamation full well. On the day the proclamation was issued, Trotha wrote in a letter:

> I believe that the nation as such should be annihilated, or, if this was not possible by tactical measures, have to be expelled from the country by operative means and further detailed treatment. This will be possible if the water-holes from Grootfontein to Gobabis are occupied. The constant movement of our troops will enable us to find the small groups of the nation who have moved back westwards and destroy them gradually....

My intimate knowledge of many central African tribes (Bantu and others) has everywhere convinced me of the necessity that the Negro does not respect treaties but only brute force. (Pool, 1991: 272–4)

From 1904 and into 1905, one of von Trotha's officers, Major von Estorff, 'had the thankless task of chasing after the refugees in the Sandveld and preventing their return'. Estorff's own words clearly describe both his own actions and the intentions of his commanding officer, Trotha:

I followed their spoor and found numerous wells which presented a terrifying sight. Cattle which had died of thirst lay scattered around the wells. These cattle had reached the wells but there had not been enough time to water them. The Herero fled ahead of us into the Sandveld. Again and again this terrible scene kept repeating itself. With feverish energy the men had worked at opening the wells; however the water became ever sparser, and wells ever more rare. They fled from one well to the next and lost virtually all their cattle and a large number of their people. The people shrank into small remnants who continually fell into our hands [*unsere Gewalt kamen*]; sections of the people escaped now and later through the Sandveld into English territory [present-day Botswana]. It was a policy as gruesome as it was senseless, to hammer the people so much; we could have still saved many of them and their rich herds, if we had pardoned and taken them up again; they had been punished enough. I suggested this to General von Trotha, but he wanted their total extermination. (von Estorff, 1979: 117; author's translation)

In early 1905, the German parliament rescinded von Trotha's extermination order, after which time captured Herero were placed into concentration camps (*Konzentrationslager*) and put to work as forced laborers. By late 1905, an estimated 8,800 Herero were confined in camps, working on various military and civilian projects scattered across German South West Africa (*Berichte der Rheinischen Missions-Gesellschaft*, 1906: 10). Missionary sources provide us with eyewitness accounts of conditions in the camps. Missionaries stationed in the Herero *Konzentrationslager* reported to their superiors in Germany on the extensive and unchecked rape, beatings and execution of surrendered Herero by German soldiers (Gewald, 1999: 184–204). Missionary Kuhlmann spoke of the delight of settler women witnessing the drawn-out public hangings of captured Herero in Windhoek. At one such hanging, a drooling Herero fighting for his life was berated: 'You swine, wipe your muzzle' (Oermann, 1998: 113–14). In Karibib, missionary Elger wrote:

And then the scattered Herero returned from the Sandfeld. Everywhere they popped up – not in their original areas – to submit themselves as prisoners. What did the wretched people look like?! Some of them had been starved to skeletons with hollow eyes, powerless and hopeless, afflicted by serious diseases, particularly with dysentery. In the settlements they were placed in big *kraals*, and there they lay, without blankets and some without clothing, in the tropical rain on the marshlike ground. Here death reaped a harvest! Those who had some semblance of energy naturally had to work....

It was a terrible misery with the people; they died in droves. Once 24 came together, some of them carried. In the next hour one died, in the evening the second, in the first week a total of ten – all [lost] to dysentery – the people had lost all their energy and all their will to live....

Hardly cheering cases were those where people were handed in to be healed from the effects of extreme mistreatment [*schwerer Misshandlungen*]: there were bad cases amongst these.[8]

In the settlement of Windhoek, missionary Meier described the condition of Herero who came to the sickbay run by the mission. His words provide some idea of what occurred in the Windhoek camp:

How often these poorest, those who deserved pity, came staggering! Many of them, who could no longer move, were brought on stretchers, most of them unconscious; however, those who could still think were glad that the hard supervision of the ... guards in the Kraal and their Shambok [rawhide whip] ... had for the time being been left behind.[9]

The Herero camps were finally abolished in 1908. Thereafter, the Herero were confined within a tangled web of legislation that sought to control every aspect of the lives of all black people living in German South West Africa (GSWA). Within the areas of German control, all Africans over the age of 8 were ordered to wear metal passes. These passes, which were embossed with imperial crown, magisterial district, and labor number, were used to facilitate German control of labor. In addition, Herero were prohibited from owning land and cattle, the two foundations of what had been a society based on pastoralism.[10]

## The 'Blue Book'

At the outbreak of the First World War, South African forces under British command invaded GSWA and successfully defeated the much-vaunted German army. As the war progressed, it became clear that the victorious parties had no intention of allowing Germany to retain its colonies. To this end, from at least 1915 onwards British colonial officials were instructed to gather materials which would strengthen the British Empire's claims to Germany's colonies.[11] In Namibia, this task was made much easier by the existence of an extremely well-organized and detailed government archive which awaited the incoming military administration in Windhoek. It contained chillingly detailed accounts and reports on the manner in which GSWA settlers, and the colony's administration, had

dealt with the country's original inhabitants. Apart from files dealing with
the incarceration of Herero in concentration camps and their distribution
among settlers and private companies, the archives also contained a series
of files on the excesses of settlers who had flogged Herero and Nama[12]
workers. Glass-plate negatives detailed the torn and rotting backs of women
flogged for alleged insubordination, and pages upon pages of court transcripts detailed the brutal lashing of laborers.[13]

The combination of dry testimony taken from the German archives in
Windhoek, along with a series of painstakingly detailed statements given
under oath by surviving Namibians, formed the basis of one of the most
shocking documents of colonial history. The *Report on the Natives of South-
West Africa and their Treatment by Germany* (London, 1918), generally referred
to as the 'Blue Book,' remains an indispensable source document on the
nature of German colonial rule in Namibia. It is beyond question that
these materials effectively scuttled any attempts by Germany to retain
control over its former colonies, and Namibia in particular.[14] In Article
119 of the Versailles Treaty, Germany was declared unfit to govern colonies,
and was forced to renounce 'in favor of the Principal Allied and Associated
Powers all her rights and titles over her oversea possessions.' In addition,
under Article 22 of the new League of Nations charter, Namibia was held
to be 'inhabited by peoples not yet able to stand by themselves under the
strenuous conditions of the modern world,' and thus was deemed a territory that could 'be best administered under the laws of the Mandatory
[the Union of South Africa] as integral portions of its territory.' Accordingly, Namibia was placed under the jurisdiction of South Africa (see du
Pisani, 1985: 76).

Though the 'Blue Book' is one of the primary documents detailing the
injustices perpetrated against the Herero and Nama peoples of Namibia,
it was not used to ensure that Herero would receive compensation. Instead,
the 'Blue Book' served to ensure that Namibian territory would be granted
to South Africa to administer as a mandated territory. Far from the Herero
receiving their land back, the new South African administration forced
them to settle on marginal lands in reserves established on the fringes of
the Omaheke, the desert into which they had been driven in the past.
The new South African administration continued the policies initiated by
its German predecessor. The lands previously occupied by the Herero
continued to be reserved for white settlement, and in the years after
World War I the South African administration pursued an aggressive policy
of land settlement for white Afrikaans-speaking immigrants from Angola
and South Africa. In short, the injustices described with stark clarity in
the 'Blue Book' were dismissed in the interests of white settler unity.

## White settler unity and the 'Blue Book'

Nonetheless, the existence of the 'Blue Book' came to bedevil settler politics under the South African mandate. German settlers called for the 'Blue Book' to be banned and all extant copies destroyed. In 1925, the first all-white election for a legislative assembly took place. Representatives of the German settler party, the Deutsche Bund in Südwestafrika, opposed settler parties allied to the Union of South Africa. Anxious to maintain a working relationship with the settler bloc in the legislative assembly, the South African administrator, A.J. Werth, acceded to settler demands for the abolition of the 'Blue Book.' Thus, in 1926, one Mr Strauch, a member of the legislative assembly, tabled a motion stating that the 'Blue Book' 'only has the meaning of a war-instrument[15] and that the time has come to put this instrument out of operation and to impound and destroy all copies of this Blue Book, which may be found in the official records and in public libraries of this Territory.'[16]

The motion passed, and legislation came into effect in all territories administered by the Union of South Africa banning distribution of the 'Blue Book.' Copies were no longer made available to the public, were removed from libraries, and were destroyed. In the rest of the British Empire, copies of the 'Blue Book' were transferred to the Foreign Office. Even in wartime Britain as late as 1941, in response to a request from the Ministry of Information, it was noted that 'no copy may be issued without authority of the librarian.'[17]

Strauch, and his fellow members of the Deutscher Bund, consciously used the Herero genocide – or rather the recorded role of German settlers and soldiers in it – to put pressure on the South African administration. As Strauch noted, passing the motion he had proposed 'would … remove one of the most serious obstacles to mutual trust and cooperation in this country [Namibia].' In his view, 'the honour of Germany had been attacked in the most public manner and it was right that the attack should be repudiated in an equally public fashion…. The defence of the honour of one's country was a solemn duty imposed upon all sons of that country.' The validity of Strauch's claims went unquestioned by the assembly, and certainly no Herero view of the events was allowed an airing. The subjective arguments of Strauch and his compatriots thus sought to obscure the past in the interest of preserving their own privileged position as settlers. The promise of peaceful cooperation with the German settler community was uppermost in the minds of South Africa's administrators. Strauch's claim that 'the Germans were ready and anxious to cooperate in the building up of South West but they could not do so fully until the stigma imposed by the publication of the Bluebook ... had been removed from their name' was considered a more powerful consideration than either historical veracity or the views of Namibia's African inhabitants.

## Seeking to deny the past

In the run-up to Namibian independence in 1990, Brigitte Lau, a historian well known for her uncompromising stand against South African colonial rule in Namibia, published an article that shocked and surprised many of her colleagues. In her article, she stated: 'There is absolutely no evidence ... that the Herero perished or were used on a large scale as "slave laborers"' (Lau, 1989: 5). Furthermore, Lau argued that the *Vernichtungsbefehl* issued by General Lothar von Trotha, commanding officer of German forces in Namibia at the time, 'was a successful attempt at psychological warfare never followed in deed' (Lau, 1989: 5). In addition, Lau sought to problematize the term *Vernichtung* by arguing that it did not imply extermination.[18] Finally, she argued that the basis for much of the allegations of genocide by German soldiers in Namibia, the 1904 '*Report of the Treatment of Natives by Germany*' (*sic*), was 'an English piece of war propaganda with no credibility whatsoever' (Lau, 1989: 5).[19] Needless to say, Lau's article exploded like a bombshell among the small community of scholars specializing in Namibian history (Lau, 1989: 4–8).[20]

With hindsight, and on the basis of later conversations, it became clear that Lau wished to move the academic community away from what she saw as its unjust fascination with the Herero–German war. Instead, she argued, historians should concentrate on what she considered to be the more destructive colonial rule of South Africa in Namibia. Yet again, the genocide that Imperial Germany perpretrated upon the Herero was being negated and denied in the interests of contemporary politics. Nevertheless, Lau's article, recently republished in German, continues to have repercussions that extend far beyond Namibian history. On the electronic website of the Traditionsverband ehemaliger Schutz und Überseetruppen (Traditional association of the former protectorate and overseas forces), an organization that seeks to preserve and glorify the memory of Germany's colonial armies, Lau's article is predictably acclaimed.[21] In addition, the Traditionsverband directs readers to 'Wiedergutmachung am der Volk der Herero?' (Restitution for the Herero People?), an article that denies von Trotha harboured any genocidal intentions, and seeks to dismiss Herero claims for reparations.[22]

## Michael Scott and Herero representations to the UN

To the members of the white settler community, it may have looked as if the attempt to destroy and rewrite the past according to their own preferences had succeeded. For a number of years after 1926, nothing was heard of the Herero genocide. Within the territory, Herero had been forced to withdraw to the newly established Native reserves, where they refrained from directly articulating demands that related to the genocide (Gewald, 2001). This is not to say that the genocide was no longer of any importance to Herero society – far from it. Instead, Herero society turned in upon itself, seeking as far as possible to refrain from any interaction with the colonial state. References to the genocide perpetrated against the Herero surfaced from time to time in unexpected places, yet the subject was no longer part and parcel of the colonial discourse.[23]

In the aftermath of World War II, the South African government undertook steps to incorporate Namibia as the fifth province of the Union of South Africa. To this end, in 1946 a series of carefully structured meetings were held with the African population of the territory. As the newly formed United Nations had taken over from the League of Nations, Namibia, as a mandated territory, fell again under South African jurisdiction, with UN oversight. It was widely hoped that the colonially appointed and recognized leaders of Namibia's African populations would give their sanction to South Africa's plan to incorporate Namibia. However, this was not to be. The events of 1904–08 again became central to the concerns of settlers and the colonial administration with the arrival of the Rev. Michael Scott in Windhoek in 1947.[24] In conjunction with Herero leaders, Scott used the atrocities perpetrated in the Herero genocide as a weapon against the incorporation of Namibia into South Africa. In the immediate aftermath of the Holocaust, the full extent of which was still only just beginning to be understood, an earlier genocide inflicted by the fathers of the Nazi perpetrators made for powerful political ammunition (Emmett, 1999: 253).

Throughout most of 1948, Michael Scott lived in a tent along the Gammans river, just beyond the old location of Windhoek. Here he met and entertained township residents, many of whom had experienced the horrors of German rule firsthand (Troup, 1950: 173–80). Scott could not fail to have his attention drawn to the Herero genocide. Here, in a nutshell, Scott held, were the core inequities of colonial rule: a people had been driven off their land, slaughtered, banished to live in barren homelands – and still they held no rights. This concise presentation of history served to detail the injustice suffered by the Herero, at the hands not only of Imperial Germany, but of the mandated power, South Africa.

An article entitled 'Michael Scott and the Hereros,' published in *The New Statesman and Nation* in 1949, aptly summarized Scott's view of Namibian history:

> Then came the German colonists, hungry for land; and finally von Trotha, a general whom Hitler would have delighted to honour.... In 1904 he issued the 'Extermination Order.' All Hereros whether man, woman or child were to be killed. An orgy of looting, torture, and massacre followed. To read the records is exactly like reading the accounts of the obliteration of Poland, except that the Germans had not gas chambers then, but killed babies with their own hands, or burned sick old women in their huts. The tribe broke and fled.... The majority, all but fifteen thousand out of ninety thousand, were hacked to pieces by the Germans or died of thirst.[25]

The mention of von Trotha's 'extermination order' clearly indicates that Scott had managed to gain access to a copy of the 'Blue Book.' Scott's history also made explicit the link between the horrors perpetrated by the Nazis and the activities of Imperial Germany's forces in Namibia, a link that continues to generate considerable academic interest.[26] In addition, Scott explored how the South Africans had betrayed the Herero:

> In the 1914 war, lured by British promises that native lands would be returned, the desert remnant trekked back. But in 1918 they met not the British as the Mandatory Power, but the South Africans, who never for a moment considered giving them back their tribal lands. Some pastures were left to the German settlers who remained. More went to the Afrikaner settlers.[27]

Throughout 1948 and 1949, in the face of constant harassment, Scott sought to bring conditions in Namibia to the attention of the world. Eventually, in November 1949, the United Nations granted Scott an official hearing. Clearly, this did not stand him in good stead with South African officialdom. In the months following Scott's hearing, a campaign was initiated by the colonial authorities in Namibia, seeking to cast aspersions on Scott's statements.[28] Vilified in the press, Scott continued to be supported by Herero, many of whom recalled the events of 1904–08 to justify their faith in the reverend. One such Herero, who signed his letter 'A Native who has been deprived of his land from 1904–1950,' noted: 'I want to emphasise that the information given by the Rev. Michael Scott at UNO is what actually happened in S.W.A. and was obtained from the best reliable sources' (*Windhoek Advertiser*, 1950). Shortly after, Scott, already the victim of constant harassment, was declared a prohibited immigrant and prevented from ever returning to Namibia.

## Genocide and the establishment of nationalist parties

In the Namibia of the 1950s, the events of 1904–08 continued to live in the memory of many Africans, and led directly to the establishment of the South West African National Union (SWANU) and the South West African Peoples Organization (SWAPO). Particularly within SWANU, which came to be dominated by Herero ideologues, the loss of land incurred in the Herero genocide proved a major mobilizing factor (Ngavirue, 1997: 214n; Emmett, 1999: 283n). However, the political mobilization which had begun in earnest in Namibia in the years after World War II was brutally terminated by the shootings of December 1959. The shootings, by the South African authorities, were a response to African protests against the apartheid Group Areas Act (Dierks, 1999: 124). In the aftermath of the killings, there was a substantial South African government clampdown on nationalist political organizations in Namibia. This resulted in a massive flight into exile by many of Namibia's most highly skilled and articulate Herero.[29] It was in the context of these events that some Herero leaders who had remained in the territory sought to play down the conflict and tension engendered by the commemoration of the Herero genocide. Instead, they sought to pursue a policy of appeasement, and urged leaders of the German community to do the same. As Herero chief Hosea Kutako stated in response to German commemorations of the battle of Hamakari:

> We do not want to cling to the past or to have old war grudges. Our aim is to forget the past and to look forward rather than backward and to have good relations with all sections of the population; but good relations cannot exist if some people try to remind us of the bad past. (*Windhoek Advertiser*, 1964a)

In contrast, younger Herero – men such as Clemens Kapuuo, Hosea Kutako's eventual successor – were far less conciliatory. When German settlers wished to commemorate the Herero–German war, Kapuuo reminded them of the terror wrought in the genocide, and its links to the Holocaust:

> To our minds there is little difference between the extermination order of General von Trotha and the extermination of Jews by Adolf Hitler. The members of the *Alte Kameraden* are today a free people whereas the Hereros are not and are under a foreign Government which was elected partly by members of the *Alte Kameraden*. It is natural that the Hereros would be opposed to the celebration of a battle which placed them under foreign domination up to this day. (*Windhoek Advertiser*, 1964b)

As might have been expected, Carl Schrader, spokesman for the Alte Kameraden, denied that the Herero had been 'exterminated.'

## The Herero genocide and nationalist struggle

Given the gravity of the Herero genocide, it seems remarkable that until the 1970s the only published account of the genocide in English was the 'Blue Book.' The revisionist academic theses of the German historians Horst Drechsler and Helmut Bley first appeared in German in 1966 and 1968, in East and West Germany respectively. Bley's work, *South West Africa under German Rule, 1894–1914*, appeared in English in 1971, whilst Drechsler's *'Let us Die Fighting': The Struggle of the Herero and Nama against German Imperialism (1884–1915)* was only published in English in 1980. These two excellent studies were primarily concerned with a debate over the nature of German imperialism and the development of totalitarian societies. In particular, both books sought – and located – the roots of National Socialism in Germany's colonial past in Namibia. For both historians, the genocide committed against the inhabitants of Namibia between 1904 and 1908 foreshadowed later events in Western Europe between 1939 and 1945. As Bley noted in the conclusion to his work: 'In SWA conditions crossed over into totalitarianism. This confirms, perhaps even reinforces, Hannah Arendt's contention that in African colonialism one may find the seeds of modern totalitarian rule' (Bley, 1971: 282, referring to Arendt, 1967: 185–222). These two books had a tremendous impact upon the manner in which the outside world perceived Namibia and South Africa's occupation of the territory.

In exile, the genocide against the Herero and Nama came to be one of the pillars of anti-colonial propaganda, deployed by those who wished to rid Namibia of its South African occupiers. Initially, this propaganda was based primarily on the works of Bley and Drechsler. The publication of *To be Born a Nation* by the SWAPO publicity bureau in London (SWAPO, 1981) owed much to these two works.

In the early 1980s, shortly after completing his Ph.D. in history at Oxford University, Peter Katjavivi (now vice-chancellor of the University of Namibia) became the highly articulate spokesman for SWAPO in London. Well-versed in Namibian history, Katjavivi, in condemning the attacks of South African forces, did not hesitate to liken them to those perpetrated by von Trotha seventy-five years earlier. The anti-colonial struggles of the Herero and Nama came to be applied to all of Namibia, as if the nationalist struggle had begun with the wars undertaken by Imperial Germany against the two groups. The published version of Katjavivi's thesis, *A History of Resistance in Namibia*, clearly adopted this framework. In addition, it argued that Namibia's colonial governments were part of a continuum, with South African soldiers and police in the 1980s merely continuing the work begun by the German colonial *Schutztruppe* in the 1890s (Katjavivi, 1984).[30]

## Namibian independence, Herero genocide and Herero unity

Whereas in the years leading up to Namibian independence (1990) the Herero genocide had been successfully appropriated by nationalist forces allied to SWAPO, immediately after Namibian independence the genocide became the preserve of Herero elites opposed to the new government. In the run-up to independence, Herero activists began seeking a formal apology from the German government for the events of 1904–08. In the late 1980s, SWANU activists living in Germany approached the anti-apartheid movement in the Netherlands for assistance in bringing a case against the West German government.[31]

Since independence, the SWAPO government of Namibia has gone out of its way to ensure that Herero claims for reparation remain muted, or are nestled within the demands of the nation-state that SWAPO controls. The last time government ministers referred directly to the issue was during the visit of the then chancellor of Germany, Helmut Kohl, to Namibia in 1995. At the time, the Namibian foreign affairs minister, Theo-Ben Gurirab, noted in an interview that the injustices committed against the Namibian people by the former German colonial power would always remain a 'pestering [sic] sore.' The two countries needed to discuss war reparations 'at some stage,' but the issue was not a current priority for government, though Gurirab did add: 'We must have the courage and frankness to discuss this when the time is right' (Fild, 1995). The current Namibian government is well aware of the benefits that accrue to the state from continued close cooperation with Germany. No less than 46 per cent of the country's development budget is paid for by Germany (*The Namibian*, 1996). German military advisors and technicians are stationed in Namibia, where they teach and assist Namibian Defence Force personnel (Weidlich, 1995). In addition, direct flights from Germany bring europacking tourists, many of whom do not want to be troubled by thoughts of a terrible past. When the legal successors to the mighty German Kaiser visited Namibia and enjoyed the hospitality of its government, Chancellor Helmut Kohl and Bundes-President Herzog refused to meet Herero representatives, and were unwilling to offer an apology to the people of Namibia for what had happened in the past. Instead, Herzog referred to the war as 'a dark chapter in our bilateral relations' and made the extravagant claim that the massacres constituted 'a burden on the conscience of every German' (McNeil, 1998). At the time of writing, the government of Germany has made no official statement with regard to Herero claims. Nonetheless, while still in opposition, Germany's current governing parties did agree that what had occurred in Namibia constituted genocide (*The Namibian*, 1990).

## Regaining the international stage

It is in the context of the above events that on 22 August 1999, Dr Kuaima Riaruako, the self-appointed paramount chief and king of all of the Herero, proclaimed that the 'Herero nation' as a whole had decided to approach the International Court of Justice (ICJ) in The Hague in order to lay a charge of genocide against the German state, calling for reparations for the slaughter and other atrocities inflicted on the Herero. At the time, Riaruako's statement ruffled a few feathers in Namibia itself. German diplomats in Windhoek emailed colleagues in Bonn/Berlin to look into the issue. Two days later, a clinically worded statement by a spokesperson of the World Court put everyone, with the exception of Riaruako, at ease: 'Only states may be parties in contentious cases before the ICJ and hence submit cases to it against other states.'[32]

In the absence of a formal apology, the call for war reparations from the Federal Republic of Germany has become more vociferous. Government inaction, the continued extensive presence of German tourists, settlers, businesses and farms, and continued marginalization of the Herero lend increasing legitimacy to the Herero claims. This new visibility was evident with the launch of two court cases in the US District of Columbia. With the support of Afro-American organizations, the 'Herero People's Reparations Corporation' (HPRC) was established as a corporation, in keeping with the laws of the District of Columbia, and the court cases were launched in its name. Three German companies, Deutsche Bank AG, Terex Corporation (Orenstein und Koppel), and Woermann Line (Deutsch Afrika Linien), were charged, along with the Federal Republic of Germany (in the person of its foreign minister, Joschka Fischer). The introductory paragraph of the charge reads as follows:

> the Federal Republic of Germany ('Defendant' or 'Germany'), in a brutal alliance with German multi-national corporations, relentlessly pursued the enslavement and the genocidal destruction of the Herero Tribe in Southwest Africa, now Namibia. Foreshadowing with chilling precision the irredeemable horror of the European Holocaust only decades later, the Defendant formed a German commercial enterprise which cold-bloodedly employed explicitly sanctioned extermination, the destruction of tribal culture and social organization, concentration camps, forced labor, medical experimentation and the exploitation of women and children in order to advance their common financial interests.[33]

## Conclusion

At various stages in the past hundred years, the Herero genocide has leapt onto or fallen off the international stage. Every so often, a group of researchers, activists, or spokespeople stumbles upon this allegedly 'forgotten' genocide. Attempts are made to draw attention, once again, to the horrors of the past, whilst governments in power consistently attempt to sideline the issue or exploit it for their own ends. The 'Blue Book' thus was not used to ensure that Herero regained their lands or received compensation for the wrongs done to them. Instead, documentation of the genocide was used to prevent Germany from regaining control of its colonies, and ensure that these would instead be granted as mandated territories to the victorious allies. At later stages, in the interests of white-settler unity, the 'Blue Book' was dismissed as a propaganda tract. The denial of the wrongs inflicted upon the Herero has continued to the present. In Namibia, a postcolonial government, anxious to retain the support of its German financial and trading partner, has sought to mute demands for war reparations, claiming that all Namibians, irrespective of ethnicity, suffered under colonial rule. However, German administration – and hence genocide – never extended into northern Namibia, the area from which the current government derives its ethnic base of support.

The Federal Republic of Germany, as the legal successor to Imperial Germany, is responsible for what happened in the name of the Kaiser in Namibia. Genocide was perpetrated; thousands of people were put to work as forced laborers; thousands were subjected to all manner of abuse. People were robbed of their land, possessions, and livestock, and driven forever from their ancestral lands. It is hard to say what form recompense in this egregious case should take; but a simple apology would be a beginning.

## Notes

This chapter builds upon a series of papers that the author presented in the course of 2001 and 2002, of which the most notable are: 'Anticipating the Kaiser German soldiers and the Herero Genocide,' presented at 'Die koloniale Begegnung: Afrikanerinnen in Deutschland (1880–1945): Deutsche in Afrika (1880–1918),' Bad Godesberg, 5–8 September 2001; and 'Presenting the Past to Fight the Present: An Overview of the Manner in which the Herero Genocide Has Been Used for Political Purposes in the Course of the 20th Century,' Afrika Studie Centrum, Leiden, 2001.

1. Throughout this chapter, I use the term 'Namibia' to refer to the territory that used to be known as German South West Africa.

2. Regarding the concept of self-fulfilling settler prophecies, see Marks, 1970.

3. Evangelical Lutheran Church in the Republic of Namibia (ELCRN), V12 Karibib, author's translation.

4. See Bley, 1971: 158–63, for a discussion of the appointment of von Trotha.

5. See Pool, 1979: 219–40. Omaheke is the Otjiherero name for the sandveld area east of the Waterberg.

6. Namibian National Archives Windhoek (NNAW), ZBU D.1.a Band 3–4, leaf

165. With thanks to Mr. W. Hillebrecht for finding it at such short notice. Author's translation.

7. See Lau, 1989; Poewe, 1986; Spraul, 1988; and Sudholt, 1975.

8. ELCRN, V. 12, Missions Chronieken, Karibib 1906, written by Missionary Elger. See also *Berichte der Rheinischen Missions-Gesellschaft,* 1906: 11–12. That this mistreatment of Herero was not merely incidental but structural, is indicated by a circular letter from military headquarters in Windhoek to the German officer commanding Karibib in late 1906. The letter noted: 'due to the mishandling of Herero prisoners, who act as carriers, it is advisable to recruit Ovambo labor as carriers.' NNAW, STR 19 *1. und 4. Kompagnie Karibib*, Letter Windhuk 16/11/06.

9. ELCRN, V. 37, Missions Chronieken, Windhoek (Herero/Ovambo).

10. For an overview of German legislation regarding Africans in Namibia, see Zimmerer, 2001.

11. Public Records Office (PRO) CO 537/1–17, Telegram from Mr Long, to Australia, New Zealand and South Africa, 4 January 1918, quoted in 'Memo for War Cabinet,' 15 October 1918.

12. Prior to the colonization of Namibia, Khoe speakers dominated southern and central Namibia. These people, the majority of whom were pastoralists, were derogatorily referred to in the past as Hottentots, and are presently known as Nama. In the wars of 1904–08, the Nama lost virtually all of their land and at least 30 per cent of their population. For a detailed, and as yet unsurpassed, overview of the German Nama wars, see Drechsler, 1980: 176–217.

13. The glass plate negatives and files – in fact most of the original source material used to compile the 'Blue Book' – have been sought out by J. Silvester and J.-B. Gewald in the National Archives of Namibia. Silvester and Gewald are currently preparing an edited and annotated edition of the 'Blue Book.'

14. Mayer (1967) provides a detailed and authoritative account of the Versailles Treaty negotiations. Carnegie Endowment for International Peace (1924) contains a complete text of the 1919 Treaty.

15. Note the remarkable similarity in language used by Brigitte Lau (1989: 5), who stated, nearly seventy years later, that the 'Blue Book' was 'an English piece of war propaganda with no credibility whatsoever.'

16. NNAW, ADM 225, Memorandum on the Blue Book, Annexure A. In addition, the administration was 'requested to make representations to the Union Government and to the British Government to have this Bluebook expunged from the official records of those Governments.' Furthermore, Strauch's motion requested that the Administration 'take into consideration the advisability of making representations to the Union Government and the British Government to impound and destroy all copies of the Bluebook, which may be found in the public libraries in the respective Countries and with the official booksellers mentioned on the title-sheet of the Bluebook.'

17. PRO F0371/26574 Minute, 20 June 1941.

18. Regarding the term *Vernichten*, Lau took her lead from Karla Poewe, who stated: 'The use of the word "vernichten," which unknowledgeable people translate as *extermination*, in fact meant, in the usage of the times, breaking of military, national, or economic resistance' (Poewe, 1985: 60). For a response to this debate over meaning, see Jonassohn and Doerr, 1999.

19. Research into the origins and compilation of the *Report on the Natives of South-West Africa and their Treatment by Germany* (London 1918), which is being edited and annotated for publication in 2002 by J.-B. Gewald and J. Silvester, indicates the report was based on sound evidence.

20. A slightly reworked copy of this chapter was published in Heywood, 1995: 39–52. Lau's article elicited responses from Randolph Vigne and Henning Melber (1990); Tilman Dedering (1993); and J.-B. Gewald (1994: 67–76). Lau's piece followed on a series of articles and books that have sought to deny the genocide, or, at the very least, called for a revision of histories dealing with the war. See, in this regard, Kühne, 1979; Nuhn, 1989; Poewe, 1986; Spraul, 1988; and Sudholt, 1975.

21. See www.traditionsverband.de/; author's translation.

22. Nordbruch is a German citizen who, upon completing his German national service, moved to South Africa in 1986. He continues to live in South Africa, yet travels widely lecturing to right-wing audiences. He is closely linked to the German National Partei Deutschland (NPD), being one of their foremost speech writers.

23. Thus, while searching for waterholes in the newly established Herero reserves in the eastern reaches of South West Africa, British administrators stumbled across the site of the German massacre of Herero at Ombakaha. See Gewald, 1999: 182.

24. Scott is one of the more remarkable figures of southern African history. Having encountered Gandhi in India, he became actively involved in the anticolonial struggle, first in India and later in southern Africa. Initially Scott campaigned amongst the Indian community in Natal, and later became active in drawing attention to and improving the shameful living conditions in Bethel, one of Johannesburg's 'native locations.' Following his lobbying for Namibian independence, Scott was declared a prohibited immigrant and prevented from ever returning to Namibia and South Africa. In exile, he founded the Africa Bureau in London, and continued campaigning for Namibia's independence, even going so far as to drop his initial nonviolent approach. In 1958, while attending the All African People's Conference in Accra, Scott delivered a speech to the delegates on behalf of the Herero people living in Namibia, who had been prevented from sending their own representatives. In his speech, Scott called for the creation of an African Freedom Army, saying: 'Africa needs such a freedom army urgently if it is to be saved from inhumanity.' Scott continues to be fondly remembered by many in Namibia. His activities brought the injustices of colonial rule in Namibia to the attention of the wider world. For an overview of this remarkable man's life, see Troup, 1950.

25. NNAW, SWAA 1981, A 427/48, Rev. M. Scott, typed copy of article that appeared in the *New Statesman and Nation*, 5 March 1949.

26. Hannah Arendt was the first academic to alert the world to the linkages that exist between Germany's colonial past and the later development of the National Socialist state (see Arendt, 1967). The work of East and West German historians Horst Drechsler and Helmut Bley further developed this theme, and recently a new generation of historians has once again taken it up. A sampling of some of the papers presented at the annual meeting of the African Studies Association in Houston, Texas, in November 2001 shows the current prominence of the trend. They included Jan-Bart Gewald, 'Anticipating the Kaiser: German Soldiers and the Herero Genocide'; Jeff Gaydish, '"Die Lösung der Eingeborenenfrage": The Role of the Swakopmund Concentration Camp in the Development of German "Native Policy" in Southwest Africa'; and Casper Erischsen, 'Shark Island: Forgotten Concentration Camps and History in Colonial Namibia, 1904–1908.'

27. See note 26.

28. See, for example, NNAW, SWAA 1981, A 427/48, M. Scott, draft letters of Bowker written to the *Windhoek Advertiser* and published 1 March 1950.

29. These included Moses Katjiongua, Mburumba Kerina, Fanuel Kozonguizi, Zedekia Ngavirue and many more.

30. Katjavivi's 1984 thesis formed the basis for Katjavivi, 1988. Similar to Katjavivi's work was that of fellow Herero exile, Kaire Mbuende (1986).

31. Author's personal observation regarding meetings held in Amsterdam in 1988 and 1989.

32. Published accounts in *The Namibian* newspaper, 25 August 1999 and 8 September 1999.

33. Case papers in the possession of the author.

# References

Arendt, H. (1967). *Origins of totalitarianism*. New York: Harcourt, Brace & World.

*Berichte der Rheinischen Missions-Gesellschaft (BRMG)* (1906). Wuppertal, Germany.

Bley, H. (1971). *South West Africa under German rule, 1894–1914*. Evanston: Northwestern University Press.

Carnegie Endowment for International Peace (1924). *The Treaties of Peace 1919–1923*. New York: Doubleday, Page.

Dedering, T. (1993). The German–Herero War of 1904: Revisionism of genocide or imaginary historiography? *Journal of Southern African Studies* 19, no. 1: 80–88.

Dierks, K. (1999). *Chronology of Namibian history: From pre-historical times to independent Namibia*. Windhoek: Namibian Scientific Society.

Drechsler, H. (1980). *'Let us die fighting': The struggle of the Herero and Nama against German imperialism*. London: Zed Books.

Du Pisani, A. (1985). *South West Africa/Namibia: The politics of continuity and change*. Johannesburg: J. Ball Publishers.

Emmett, T. (1999). *Popular resistance and the roots of nationalism in Namibia, 1915–1966*. Basel: P. Schlettwein Publishing.

Fild, L. (1995). War reparations on govt agenda. *The Namibian*, 21 September.

Gewald, J.-B. (2001). *'We thought we would be free': Socio-cultural aspects of Herero history in Namibia, 1915–1940*. Cologne: Rüdiger Küppe Verlag.

——— (1999). *Herero Heroes: A socio-political history of the Herero of Namibia, 1890–1923*. Oxford: James Currey.

——— (1995). Forced labour in the *Onjembo*: the Herero-German war of 1904–1908. *Itinirario* 19, no. 1: 97–104.

——— (1994). The great general of the Kaiser. *Botswana Notes and Records* 26: 67–76.

Heywood, A., ed. (1995). *History and historiography*. Windhoek: Discourse/MSORP.

Jonassohn, K., and Doerr, K. (1999). The persistence of Nazi Germany. MIGS occasional paper. Montreal: Montreal Institute for Genocide Studies.

Katjavivi, P. (1988). *A history of resistance in Namibia*. London: Zed Books.

——— (1984). The rise of nationalism in Namibia and its international dimensions. D.Phil. thesis, Oxford University.

Kühne, H. (1979). Die Ausrottungsfeldzüge der 'Kaiserlichen Schutztruppen in Afrika' und die sozialdemokratische Reichstagsfraktion. *Militärgeschichte* 18: 208–16.

Lau, B. (1989). Uncertain certainties: The Herero–German war of 1904. *Mibagus*, no. 2, April: 4–8.

McNeil Jr., D.G. (1998). Its past on its sleeve, tribe seeks Bonn's apology. *New York Times*, 31 May.

Marks, S. (1970). *Reluctant rebellion: The 1906–8 disturbances in Natal*. Oxford: Clarendon Press.

Mayer, A.J. (1967). *Politics and diplomacy of peacemaking: Containment and counterrevolution at Versailles, 1918–1919*. London: Weidenfeld & Nicolson.

Mbuende, K. (1986). *Namibia: The broken shield*. Lund: Liber.

*The Namibian* (1996). German visit is a 'total success.' 24 June.

———— (1990). Major German parties agree on 'genocide.' 5 November.

Ngavirue, Z. (1997). *Political parties and interest groups in South West Africa (Namibia): A study of a plural society*. Basel: P. Schlettwein Publishing.

Nuhn, W. (1989). *Sturm über Südwest: Der Hereroaufstande von 1904 – Ein düsteres Kapitel der deutschen kolonialen Vergangenheit Namibias*. Koblenz: Bernhard Graefe Verlag.

Oermann, N.O. (1998). Mission, church and state relations in South West Africa under German rule (1884–1915). D.Phil. thesis, Oxford University.

Poewe, K. (1986). *The Namibian Herero: A history of their psychosocial disintegration and survival*. Lewiston: Edwin Mellen Press.

Pool, G. (1991). *Samuel Maharero*. Windhoek: Gamsberg Macmillan.

———— (1979). *Die Herero-opstand 1904–1907*. Pretoria: Haum.

Rust, C. (1905). *Krieg und Frieden im Hererolande. Aufzeichnungen aus dem Kriegsjahre 1904*. Berlin: Ernst Siegfried Mittler und Sohn.

Spraul, G. (1988). Der 'Völkermord' an den Herero: Untersuchungen zu einer neuen Kontinuitätsthese. *Geschichte in Wissenschaft und Unterricht*, December: 713–39.

Sudholt, G. (1975). *Die deutsche Eingeborenenpolitik in Südwestafrika. Von den Anfängen bis 1904*. Hildesheim: Georg Olms Verlag.

SWAPO (1981). *To be born a nation: The liberation struggle for Namibia*. London: SWAPO Dept of Information and Publicity.

Troup, F. (1950). *In face of fear: Michael Scott's challenge to South Africa*. London: Faber & Faber.

Vigne, R. and Melber, H. (1990). Shark Island revisited. *South African Review of Books*, February–March, June–July, August–October.

von Estorff, L. (1979). *Wanderungen und Kämpfe in Südwestafrika, Ostafrika und Südafrika: 1894–1910*. Windhoek: John Meinert.

Weidlich, B. (1995). Helmut Bistri: Offizier und Gentleman. *Allgemeine Zeitung*, 1 December.

*Windhoek Advertiser* (1964a). 'Forget the past': Improve race relations, Kapuuo urges Kameraden. 7 August.

———— (1964b). Hereros oppose Waterberg celebrations: Alter Kamerad denies 'extermination.' 29 July.

———— (1950). Letter to the editor. 18 March.

Zimmerer, J. (2001). *Deutsche Herrschaft Über Afrikaner: Staatlicher Machtanspruch und Wirklichkeit im kolonialen Namibia*. Hamburg: Lit Verlag.

# 4

# Genocide by Any Other Name: North American Indian Residential Schools in Context

## Ward Churchill

> We must begin with the misrepresentation and transform it into what is true. That is, we must uncover the source of the misrepresentation; otherwise, hearing what is true won't help us. The truth cannot penetrate when something is taking its place.
>
> *Ludwig Wittgenstein*

'Genocide' is among the more profoundly misunderstood words in the English language. Most often, the term has been cast as no more than a synonym for mass murder – albeit mass murder of the most extreme sort – and considerable scholarly energy has been expended in debating the scale of killing or proportionality of its impact upon victim groups necessary for one or another slaughter to qualify as 'truly' genocidal rather than simply blending into history's vast panorama of butchery. More refined – or tedious – lines of analysis have devolved upon such questions as whether certain modes or methods of killing must be present if a given 'exterminatory phenomenon' is to be considered 'genuinely' genocidal. Still others have delved into the function(s) served by mass murder in what are taken to be genocidal settings and, most ambiguously, the nature of the intentions which must guide perpetrator groups if their actions are to be construed as genocidal.

While it has been argued that such inquiries are undertaken for purposes of making our understanding of genocide more 'rigorous,' they have for the most part had a decisively exclusionary effect, establishing definitional and conceptual threshold criteria for what has been aptly described as the 'incomparable crime' so narrow that supposedly reputable researchers were asserting by the mid-1990s that the nazi-perpetrated judeocide of World War II was 'phenomenologically unique.' The conclusion embodied in such contentions is that 'real' genocide 'has happened [only] once, to the Jews under Nazism' (Bauer, 1978: 38). Not even the fate of the Sinti and Romani (Gypsies), simultaneously exterminated by the nazis in a proportion entirely comparable to that of the Jews – and in the same camps, by the same methods and under the same official decrees – is accorded equal footing. Similar absurdities abound.

The motives underlying imposition of such radical constraints upon the meaning of genocide have been anything but pure. On the one hand, as Edward Alexander has approvingly observed, their development has been a key element in a conscious strategy designed to invest the Jewish people with a monopoly on the sort of 'high-grade moral capital' attending genocidal victimization, a matter translating into certain of the political advantages enjoyed by the State of Israel (Alexander, 1994: 195). On the other hand, the result is plainly exculpatory, allowing virtually every perpetrator regime or society other than the Germans under Hitler to dodge not only the stigma of their history but other potential consequences of their crime(s). Small wonder that such a truncation and deformation of the definition of genocide has long been a practice embraced enthusiastically and all but universally by the world's ruling elites and the 'responsible' intellectual establishments they sponsor. Indeed, in many quarters, it amounts to official policy.

That the policy at issue involves the 'routine denial' of a plethora of genocides – not least in countries such as France and Canada, where comparable denials of the nazi judeocide constitute a statutory offense – should be self-evident. The implications, as Roger Smith, Eric Markusen, and Robert Jay Lifton have pointed out in connection with the much-denied 1915–18 Turkish genocide of Armenians, are exceedingly grim.

> Where scholars [and other ostensibly reliable commentators] deny genocide, in the face of decisive evidence that it has occurred, they contribute to a false consciousness that can have the most dire reverberations. Their message is: [genocide] requires no confrontation, no reflection, but should be ignored, glossed over. In this way, scholars lend their considerable authority to the acceptance of this ultimate human crime. More than that, they encourage – indeed invite – a repetition of the crime from virtually any source in the immediate or distant future. By closing their minds to the truth, that is, scholars contribute to the deadly psychohistorical dynamic in which unopposed genocide begets new genocides. (Smith et al., 1995)

Clearly, such denial is diametrically opposed to the openness described as essential by Leo Kuper, Israel Charny, and others, who have devoted themselves to the task of conceiving ways and means of preventing the recurrence of 'the human cancer.' Because, as Irving Louis Horowitz has noted, 'genocide is always and everywhere an essentially political decision,' and since, following Huey P. Newton, politics itself must be seen as an 'ability to define a phenomenon and cause it to act in a desired manner,' the need to approach eradication of genocide from the vantage point of definitional viability – thence precision – is of cardinal importance (Horowitz, 1976: 39; Newton quoted in Cleaver, 1969: 10). Hence, we would do well to review the actual meaning of the term as it was set forth by Raphael Lemkin, the man who coined it in 1944 (Lemkin, 1944: 79–95). From there, it will be possible to apply Lemkin's concept in analyzing a process that lies well beyond the parameters of what has become the norm of genocide scholarship, thereby restoring to his formulation something of its original efficacy and promise.

## Form and scope of the crime

The first and most striking of aspect of Lemkin's explanation of the neologism he created by combining 'the ancient Greek word *genos* (race, tribe) and the Latin *cide* (killing)' was the care he took to distinguish it from literal murder (irrespective of the scale on which the murder was committed) (Lemkin, 1944: 79). Rather, he was at pains to emphasize that he was addressing virtually *any* policy undertaken with the intention of bringing about the dissolution and ultimate disappearance of a targeted human group, *as such*.

> Generally speaking, genocide does not necessarily mean the immediate destruction of a nation, *except* when accomplished by mass killing ... It is intended rather to signify a coordinated plan of different actions aiming at the destruction of the essential foundations of the life of national groups, with the aim of annihilating the groups themselves. The objectives of such a plan would be disintegration of the political and social institutions, of culture, language, national feelings, religion, and the economic existence of national groups, and the destruction of personal security, liberty, health, dignity, and even the lives of the individuals belonging to such groups. Genocide is directed against the national group as an entity, and the actions involved are directed against individuals, not in their individual capacity, but as members of the national group. (Lemkin, 1944: 79, emphasis added)

Thus, while Lemkin acknowledged that outright physical extermination was one means by which genocide might be perpetrated, he was quite unequivocal in his insistence that it was not a necessary ingredient of the crime, far less that it was the 'essential' feature. What was essential in Lemkin's conception was that extinguishing the existence of a target group be undertaken as a matter of policy. Insofar as such a process was evident, it fell within the rubric of genocide, 'even though the individual members survived' the process of group liquidation (Lebanese delegate to

UN ad hoc committee, quoted in Davis and Zannis, 1973: 20). There is in fact every indication that Lemkin saw the physical survival of all or most members of groups subjected to genocide as being normative, their physical extermination exceptional. Consider what may be taken as the very core of his definition:

> Genocide has two phases: one, destruction of the national pattern of the oppressed group; the other, the imposition of the national pattern of the oppressor. This imposition, in turn, may be made on the oppressed population which is allowed to remain, or upon the territory alone, after the removal of the population and colonization of the area by the oppressor's own nationals. (Lemkin, 1944: 79)

Hence, as Zygmunt Bauman has noted, Lemkin was primarily concerned with depicting the essential ingredients of what might be termed 'ordinary genocide,' a process which is 'rarely, if at all, aimed at the total annihilation of the group' in physical terms (Bauman, 1989: 119). So decisive was the nonlethal dimension of ordinary genocide in Lemkin's estimation that he observed how the term 'denationalization' might have sufficed to encompass what he meant were it not for the fact that 'in connoting the destruction of one national pattern, it does not connote the imposition of the national pattern of the oppressor' (Lemkin, 1944: 79–80). Similarly, he observed that 'denationalization,' sometimes taken to connote a mere deprivation of citizenship, failed to encompass the fact that genocide, in some instances at least, involved 'destruction of the biological structure' of the target group (79–80). Much more than killing is at issue in this last connection. Involuntary sterilization and other measures designed to prevent births among the target group falls within the scope of 'biological genocide' (86–7). Not all of these are even physical in any literal sense. Lemkin held the nazi refusal to permit marriage between Poles to be genocidal, for example (86).

Such understandings from the outset informed the international legal discourse on genocide. In 1947, the Secretary-General of the newly formed United Nations, pursuant to Economic and Social Council (ECOSOC) Resolution 47(IV), retained Lemkin to head up a committee of experts charged with drafting a law to define, prevent, and punish the crime of genocide (this was the so-called Secretariat's Draft of the present Genocide Convention). Here, Lemkin offered substantial clarification of what is entailed, elaborating the nature of the protected classes involved – which he'd earlier referred to simply as 'national' or 'oppressed' groups – by listing 'racial, national, linguistic, religious [and] political groups' as falling under the law's rubric (by implication, economic aggregates were included as well). Genocide itself is defined in a twofold way, encompassing all policies intended to precipitate '1) the destruction of [such] a group' and '2) preventing its preservation and development.' The modes through which such policy objectives might be attained are then delineated in tripartite fashion and in considerable detail.

1. *Physical genocide* includes both direct/immediate extermination (*à la* Auschwitz and the Nazis' *Einsatzgruppen* operations in the USSR) and what are referred to as 'slow death measures': i.e. 'subjection to conditions of life which, owing to lack of proper housing, clothing, food, hygiene and medical care or excessive work or physical exertion are likely to result in the debilitation [and] death of individuals; mutilations and biological experiments imposed for other than curative purposes; deprivation of [the] means of livelihood by confiscation, looting, curtailment of work, and the denial of housing and of supplies otherwise available to the other inhabitants of the territory concerned' (Davis and Zannis, 1973: 18–20; Arad et al., eds., 1989).

2. *Biological genocide* includes involuntary 'sterilization, compulsory abortion, segregation of the sexes and obstacles to marriage,' as well as any other policies intended to prevent births within a target group' (Davis and Zannis, 1973: 20).

3. *Cultural genocide* – which encompasses the schema of denationalization and imposition of an alien national pattern that Lemkin had described as being the central feature of the crime in 1944 – includes all policies aimed at destroying the specific characteristics by which a target group is defined, or defines itself, thereby forcing them to become something else. Among the acts specified are the 'forced transfer of children … forced and systematic exile of individuals representing the culture of the group … prohibition of the use of the national language … systematic destruction of books printed in the national language, or religious works, or the prohibition of new publications … systematic destruction of national or religious monuments, or their diversion to alien uses [and] destruction or dispersion of objects of historical, artistic, or religious value and of objects used in religious worship' (Davis and Zannis, 1973: 20).

Significantly, no hierarchy is attached to these classifications. The perpetration of cultural genocide is presented as an offense every bit as serious – and subject to exactly the same penalties – as perpetration of physical or biological genocide. This was so in part because Lemkin held that the crux of what others would later call 'the genocidal mentality' (Lifton and Markusen, 1988) resides squarely within the cultural domain, and because he understood that there is ultimately no way of segregating the effects of cultural genocide from its physical and biological counterparts. For Lemkin, the deliberate destruction of cultures kills individuals just as surely as do guns and poison gas, especially when combined with imposition of the sorts of slow death measures which all but invariably attend such undertakings. There is thus no way in which cultural genocide may be reasonably set apart from physical and biological genocide as a 'lesser' sort of crime.

Lemkin's draft was submitted to ECOSOC in November 1947, and, in turn, the Council subjected it to review by a seven-member ad hoc committee chaired by the US representative. The revised draft convention, which was unanimously adopted by the UN General Assembly on 9 December 1948, retained just enough of Lemkin's thinking to be (barely) workable. The second article of the 1948 Convention on Prevention and Punishment of the Crime of Genocide defines the crime as being 'any of the following acts committed with intent to destroy, in whole or in part, a national, ethnical, racial or religious group, as such,' by:

(a) killing members of the group;
(b) causing serious bodily or mental harm to members of the group;
(c) deliberately inflicting on the group conditions of life calculated to bring about its physical destruction in whole or in part;
(d) imposing measures intended to prevent births within the group;
(e) forcibly transferring children of the group to another group.

It is worth noting the obvious at this juncture: killing is only one of five criteria, or 20 percent of the total. The other four – 80 percent of the entire definition of genocide posited in international law – consist of or devolve upon explicitly nonlethal lines of action, although (b) and (c) overlap with Lemkin's 'slow death measures.' Note, too, that not only perpetration of these acts, but *attempting* to commit any of them, conspiring to do so, inciting them, or any other complicity in their commission are all criminal offenses under the convention's third article. Under Article IV, it is specified that 'persons committing genocide or any of the other acts enumerated in Article III shall be punished, whether they are constitutionally responsible rulers, public officials or private individuals.'

## Genocide in North America

Both the United States and Canada have dodged implementation of the Genocide Convention from the outset, albeit in somewhat different ways. In Canada, the strategy was to foster an illusion of acceptance – Parliament voted to ratify the convention on 21 May 1952 – while quietly redefining the crime in the country's domestic enforcement statute so as to omit any mention of policies and actions in which Canada was and is engaged. Thus, the convention's prohibitions of policies causing serious bodily or mental harm to members of a target group and/or effecting the forcible transfer of their children were from the first moment expunged from Canada's 'legal understanding' (Davis and Zannis, 1973: 24). In 1985, the Canadian statute was further 'revised' to delete measures intended to prevent births within a target group from the list of proscribed policies and activities. In its present form, Canadian law admits only items (a) and (c) among the criteria posited under the Convention's second article as being constitutive of the crime of genocide. At least one Canadian court, moreover, has recently entered a decree making it a criminal offense for anyone to employ the term in any other way (*Daishowa Inc.* v. *Friends of the Lubicon*, 1998; for analysis, see Churchill, 2003: 247–61).

The sheer disingenuousness embedded in this definitional distortion is abundantly reflected in the parliamentary debates leading up to the 1952 'ratification.' Although the official position was that only those provisions of the genocide convention 'intended to cover certain historical incidents in Europe that have little essential relevance in Canada' were being excised (House of Commons, 1952: 61), it was clearly noted that then-current 'proposals to impose integrated education upon [American] Indian children, for example, might fall within [the Convention's] prohibition' against forced transfer of children (Canadian Civil Liberties Association, 1952: 6). Since the government had in fact been doing far more than entertaining proposals in this regard for the better part of a century – and would continue to do so for another 30 years – its claim that 'mass transfers of children to another group are unknown … in Canada' can only be seen as a bald-faced lie (House of Commons, 1952: 61). In effect, the Canadian statute was knowingly crafted not as an instrument of prevention or punishment, but rather as a mask for the fact that Canada was consciously committing genocide, and had every intention of continuing to do so.

As for the US, having led the way in watering down the convention during the UN revision process, it refused even to pretend to accept the resulting instrument for forty years. When the Senate did finally vote for ratification on 19 February 1986 – the ratifying instrument was not deposited with the United Nations Secretariat until November 1988 – it did so on the basis of an attached set of reservations, referred to as the 'Sovereignty Package,' which purported to set the US Constitution above international law and to render the country exempt from compliance.

The record of preratification debates conducted by US senators from 1950 onward is even more illuminating than that of their Canadian counterparts. A major sticking point for two successive generations was whether the Convention's stipulation that killing members of a target group solely on the basis of their group membership is a genocidal act, irrespective of the numbers involved. This meant that the thousands of lynchings of African Americans carried out by the Ku Klux Klan constituted genocide, and would thus require the US to declare the Klan a criminal organization in the same sense the nazi SS had been declared such at Nuremberg. Another question was whether the entire corpus of US race law and policy might not be construed as genocidal.

Less discussed, but equally or more to the point, was the relationship of the US to American Indians. Here, the country was in violation of every one of the criteria posited in the Convention's second article. While direct killing of the sort evidenced in scalp bounties and military extermination campaigns had mostly ended by the early twentieth century, the US imposition of slow death measures upon Native North Americans was quite clear-cut in 1950, and to a considerable extent remains so today.

The policy basis for this situation rests in the unilateral extension of federal 'trust authority' over what remained of Indians' lands pursuant to a 1903 Supreme Court opinion, a maneuver through which the government empowered itself to license the exploitation of indigenous resources by preferred corporations at a small fraction – usually no more than 10 per cent – of the royalty rates prevailing on the open market. Even this pittance did not go to the Indians themselves, but was placed instead in 'trust accounts' administered 'in behalf of' their native owners by the US Interior Department's Bureau of Indian Affairs (BIA). From there, some 90 per cent of it – nearly $140 *billion*, by current estimates – has been 'lost' (that is, expended for purposes other than the well-being of the Indians whose money it was and is) (see Kennedy, 2002; Brinkley, 2003).

The upshot of this has been that as the US economy bloated itself on the wealth of native people, the people themselves have been driven into the depths of a destitution resembling that prevailing in the Third World. To take but one example, it was recently estimated that nearly 90 per cent of the dwellings on the Pine Ridge Reservation in South Dakota, the poorest in the country for more than fifty years, were effectively uninhabitable. Basic sanitation and water purification facilities were all but nonexistent, as was anything resembling adequate nutrition or medical care. Such conditions are by no means atypical of reservation settings throughout the US, and the impact upon the health and longevity of native people has been predictably severe.

> The Indian health level is the lowest and disease rates the highest of all major population groups in the United States. The incidence of tuberculosis is 400 percent higher than the national average. Similar statistics show that the incidence of strep infections is 1,000 percent, meningitis 2,000 percent, and dysentery 10,000 percent higher. Death rates are shocking when Indian and non-Indian

populations are compared. Influenza and pneumonia are 300 percent greater killers among Indians. Diseases such as hepatitis are in epidemic proportions, with an 800 percent higher chance of death. Diabetes is almost a plague. Overall, according to official census data, reservation-based American Indians experience an average lifespan one-third shorter than the general US population, with a marginally better ratio prevailing in Canada. (Strickland, 1997: 53)

Clearer examples of the 'deliberate infliction of conditions of life calculated to bring about [a target group's partial] physical destruction' and the imposition of policies 'causing serious bodily and mental harm' to the rest are difficult to imagine. In sum, all the hallmarks of what Lemkin described as 'a coordinated plan of different actions aimed at destroying the essential foundations of [existence] of national groups, with the aim of [eliminating] the groups themselves,' remain ongoing realities in both of the settler states asserting contemporary hegemony over the North American continent.[1]

## 'To kill the Indian...'

Since the end of the 'Indian Wars' in 1890, by which point the indigenous population of North America had been reduced to 5 per cent or less of its pre-invasion total, the weight of policy in the US and Canada alike has been placed on 'assimilating' – 'digesting' might be a better word – the residue of survivors. Described in 1910 by one of its chief practitioners, US Indian Commissioner Francis Leupp, as 'a mighty pulverizing engine for breaking up [the last vestiges of] the tribal mass' (Leupp, 1910: 93), the objective of assimilation policy was from the outset to eliminate all American Indians culturally recognizable as such by some point in the mid-twentieth century. That its proponents failed to completely achieve this goal, despite sustained and concerted effort, is due to a number of mediating factors, not least the depth and degree of resistance mounted by the victims themselves.

Beginning with the unilateral extension of US jurisdiction over Indian Country in 1885 – actually, the process commenced much earlier in Canada – several components have featured prominently in giving assimilation policy its shape and substance. These include a comprehensive program to abolish the traditional indigenous practice of holding land in common, imposing in its stead an Anglicized system of individual property titles which undermined the cohesiveness of native societies, laid the groundwork for expropriation of more than two-thirds of the territory remaining in Indian hands at the turn of the century, and spawned an intractable 'heirship problem' precluding effective use by the nominal owners of what little was left. Concomitantly, programs were adopted to supplant the traditional mode of defining group members by genealogy (kinship) with 'blood quantum' (racial) criteria, to prohibit traditional spiritual practices and virtually compel the adoption of Christianity, to reshape traditional modes of governance along the lines of corporate boards, to disperse the native population as widely as possible, and, mostly during the 1950s, to 'terminate' the existence of more than a hundred distinct 'bands' and 'tribes' (i.e. they were simply declared 'extinct'). All of this was undertaken on the basis of a self-ordained 'plenary' – that is to say, unlimited and absolute – power held by federal authorities over American Indian lands and lives.

So, too, was the program that served as the linchpin of assimilationist aspirations. This was an initiative begun both north and south of the border during the 1870s, and lasting over a century, in which it was ideally intended that every single aboriginal child would be removed from his or her home, family, community, and culture at the earliest possible age and held for years in state-sponsored 'educational' facilities, systematically deculturated, and simultaneously indoctrinated to see her/his own heritage – and him/herself as well – in terms deemed appropriate by a society that despised both to the point of seeking as a matter of policy their utter eradication. That some native children escaped such processing had far less to do with the ambitions of those administering the system than with the fact that the US–Canadian settler states ultimately proved unwilling to allot sufficient resources to the task. Still, at its peak, the complex of Indian residential schools – 'boarding schools,' as they were called in the US – was large enough to accommodate about half of all Native North American children at any given moment, and something in the order of 80 per cent of several succeeding generations of native youngsters underwent some portion of their schooling therein.

The nature of the crime bound up in this coldly calculated 'education for extinction' was put quite bluntly by Captain Richard Henry Pratt, the army officer selected by the US to create and supervise its system in 1879. The objective, Pratt publicly declaimed in 1895, was to 'kill the Indian, save the man' in every pupil (Pratt, 1895: 761–2). Or, to rephrase it as US Indian Commissioner William A. Jones did in 1903, the goal was to 'exterminate the Indian but develop a man' (quoted in Coleman, 1993: 46). The core thinking of those running the system could not have been framed more clearly: to be discernibly Indian was to be other than human; to be human, one could not be discernibly Indian. The formulation, and the mentality it reflects, is identical at base to that displayed in General Phil Sheridan's earlier and much-celebrated observation that 'the only good Indian is a dead one,'[2] an enunciation but a step removed from Colonel

John Chivington's infamous order, issued just prior to the Sand Creek Massacre of 1864, that his troops should slaughter Indian babies right along with their parents and other adults because, after all, 'nits make lice' (see Hoig, 1961; Svaldi, 1989).

Canada in most respects modeled its system on that of the US. Proceeding first under the mantle of the 1857 Act to Encourage the Gradual Civilization of the Indian Tribes in the Province, and then under the 1884 Indian Advancement Act, the Indian Department took as its goal 'tribal dissolution, to be pursued mainly through the corridors of residential schools' (Milloy, 1999: 19). Pratt's notion of killing Indians to save men was frequently voiced within the circles of those charged with 'educating' Indians, while Commissioner Jones's Canadian counterpart, Duncan Campbell Scott, announced that the goal was 'to be rid of the Indian question. That is [the] whole point. Our objective is to continue until there is not a single Indian in Canada that has not been absorbed into the body politic, and there *is* no Indian problem' (quoted in Titley, 1986: 50, emphasis added). Such endeavors, he explained at another point, were quite consistent with the fact that 'progress' – that is, consolidation of the Canadian state – would be unnecessarily difficult 'so long as the Indians remain a distinct people and live as separate communities' (quoted in Miller, 1996: 121).

Given the overtly genocidal character of such pronouncements, and the absolute centrality of the residential school system to Indian policy implementation in both the US and Canada for a sustained period, it is important to delve more deeply into the details of the system's functioning. Only in this way, can their implications be properly understood. And only in such understanding can there be hope that some of the residential schools' lingering effects might be redressed.

### Forcing the transfer of children

There can be no question that the transfer of children upon which the residential school system depended was coercive, that it was resisted by indigenous parents and other adults – and often, to the extent they were able, by the youngsters themselves – and that physical force was used to overcome that resistance. In 1893, legislators authorized the BIA to 'withhold rations, clothing and other annuities from Indian parents or guardians who refuse or neglect to send and keep their children of proper school age in school' (*Statutes at Large of the United States*, Vol. 27: 635). Canada followed suit with an amendment to its Indian Act in 1894 that authorized the cabinet to 'make regulations, which shall have the force of law, for the commitment by justices or Indian agents of children of Indian blood under age of sixteen years to [an] industrial school or boarding school, there to be kept … for a period not extending beyond the time at which such children shall reach the age of eighteen years' (*An Act to Further Amend the Indian Act*, c. 32, 57–8 Vict.).

In some cases, the basic elements of coercion built into such legislation were sufficient to produce compliance. Where resistance was concerted, however – or threatened to be – direct applications of force were not infrequent. A typical scene was recorded by the agent of the Mescalero Apache Reservation in 1886.

> Everything in the way of persuasion and argument having failed, it became necessary to visit the [Indians'] camps with a detachment of police, and seize such children as were proper, and take them away to school, willing or un-willing. Some hurried their children off to the mountains or hid them away in camp, and the police had to chase and capture them like so many wild rabbits. This proceeding created quite an outcry. The men were sullen and muttering, the women loud in their lamentations, and the children almost out of their wits with fright. (*Annual Report of the Commissioner of Indian Affairs*, 49th Cong., 1st Sess., 1886: 417)

Virtually every memoir produced by a former boarding school student contains a section recounting the official use of force to compel enrollment (see, e.g., Sekaquaptewa as told to Udall, 1962: 8–12; Kaywaykla, 1970: 199–200; Kabotie, 1977: 8–10).

Although the military was not used to impound native children in Canada, the history there is otherwise quite similar. In 1893, for example, the Cree leader Star Blanket was deposed from his position as chief of his band and informed by the Indian Department that he would be reinstated only if he helped secure students for the residential schools. Officials routinely 'withheld food rations from parents who resisted the removal of their children,' and there are numerous accounts of the Royal Canadian Mounted Police (RCMP) 'herd[ing] children onto … trains like cattle' in the process of transporting them to institutions that 'none of [them] wanted to go to … any more than [they] wanted to go to hell or a concentration camp' (Fournier and Grey, 1997: 56; Johnson, 1989: 6). So pervasive was the use of force and coercion that in 1908 the recruitment methods employed by the Red Deer Industrial School in Alberta, which consisted of 'coaxing and persuading instead of bribery and kidnapping,' were offi-cially highlighted as a marked exception to the rule (Milloy, 1999: 69–70).

Aside from the emotional trauma afflicting any family or community whose children are being 'stolen from [their] embrace' (paraphrasing Fournier and Grey, 1997), the resistance mounted by Native North Americans to the removal of their children for 'education' in residential facilities was usually based on a firm understanding that the process was consciously genocidal. Analyst John Milloy has observed that 'reaction to [residential schooling] from First Nations governments across the southern part of [Canada] was resolutely negative. They recognized immediately its implications for continued tribal existence' (Milloy, 1999: 19). As a now anonymous native leader put it as early as 1858, the purpose of the whole procedure was self-evidently to 'break [indigenous societies] to pieces' (quoted in Milloy, 1999: 19).

### Destroying the national pattern of the oppressed group

In psychological terms, the regimen of residential schools was deliberately and relentlessly brutal. From the moment the terrified and bewildered youngsters arrived at the schools, designed as they were to function as 'total institutions' (Goffman in Etzioni, 1961: 313–14), a comprehensive and carefully calibrated assault on their cultural identity commenced. For boys and girls alike, this began with a thorough scrubbing and 'disinfection' – alcohol and kerosene were among the astringents used for the latter purpose – often accompanied by staff commentary about 'dirty Indians.' For boys, the next step was to undergo the humiliating experience of having their heads shorn, military-style. 'At the heart of the policy was the belief that the [boys'] long hair was symbolic of savagism; removing it was central' to destroying their sense of themselves as Indians (Adams, 1995: 101).

The same was true of the children's clothing and other personal items, all of which were taken from them. In exchange, they were issued uniforms expressly intended to separate them from the 'excessive individualism' of their own traditions by reducing them 'to sameness, to regularity, to order' (Milloy, 1999: 124). Then came their names. Those with 'savage' or 'unpronounceable' identifiers like Chesegesbega or Sitahpetale, which included the great majority of new arrivals, quickly found themselves saddled with Anglicized replacements like 'Smith' and 'Miller.' A consistent theme running through autobiographical material written by former students is how this procedure in particular engendered an abiding sense that they had 'lost' themselves and were thus 'stranger[s] with no possibilities' for the future.

Such despair was perfectly in keeping with the desires of those in charge, in that it rendered the already malleable children still more so. The schools operated under the mandate of effecting a 'complete change' in their charges (Inspector of Indian Schools J.A. Macrae in 1886, quoted in Milloy, 1999: 38), a matter described in Canada – under the premise that 'true civilization must be based on moral law, which Christian religion alone can give' – as the 'building and developing character on the foundation of Christian morality, making Christian faith and love the wellspring and motive of conduct' (Convention of the Catholic Principals of Indian Residential Schools, 1924, quoted in Milloy, 1999: 38; Presbyterian Women's Missionary Society, quoted in Coleman, 1993: 42). In the US, more secular objectives were additionally set forth.

> It is of prime importance that a fervent patriotism be awakened in [the children's] minds.... They should be taught to look upon America as their home and the United States government as their friend and benefactor. They should be made familiar with the lives of great and good men and women in American history, and be taught to feel pride in all their great achievements. They should hear little or nothing of the 'wrongs [done] the Indians,' and of the injustice of the white race. If their unhappy history is alluded to it should be to contrast it with the better future that is within their grasp. (Indian Commissioner Thomas J. Morgan, quoted in Coleman, 1993: 42)

All of this was calculated to take considerable time, even under optimal conditions. Hence, from the outset, it was standard practice that the students be kept in the schools year-round and for as long as a decade, with neither visits to their homes nor visits from their families – even letters were sometimes withheld – because of the 'deleterious ... influences' such interaction might exert (Superintendent General for Indian Affairs Edgar Dewdney in 1891, quoted in Department of Indian Affairs, 1889: xi). As early as 1863, US Indian Commissioner William P. Dole complained that any other course led to repeated 'infection' of the youngsters with 'the filthy habits and loose morals of their parents' (*Annual Report of the Commissioner of Indian Affairs*, 37th Cong., 3rd Sess., 1863: 172). By 1888, the message was being framed even more bluntly: 'Children leaving even the best of training schools for their homes [are] like swine return[ing] to their wallowing filth, and barbarism' ('Report of the School at Lawrence, Kansas,' attached to *Annual Report of Commissioner of Indian Affairs*, 37th Cong., 3rd Sess., 1863: 172).

With the youngsters thus isolated, and otherwise stripped of the most immediate links to their cultural identity, a deeper and more comprehensive demolition was undertaken. This devolved upon absolute prohibitions on the speaking of indigenous languages and the knowledge and practice of native spirituality. Although instruction was already delivered exclusively in that language, the BIA promulgated a regulation in 1890 requiring that 'pupils be compelled to converse with each other in English, and should be properly rebuked or punished for persistent violation of this rule' (cited in Adams, 1995: 140). Canada, which followed suit in 1896, was even more explicit, positing not only the inculcation of English and/or French but destruction of students' ability to speak their own languages as goals. Almost universally, 'school staff in addition to their other responsibilities were assigned the duty of preventing pupils from "using their own languages",' even in private conversations or prayer (Milloy, 1999: 39). Doing so, of course, meant that the children had to be placed under virtually continuous surveillance. The resulting stew of fear, loneliness and obliterated self-esteem, sustained for most students over periods of years, was quite literally devastating to all who underwent it.

### Imposing the national pattern of the oppressor

The resemblance of residential schools to military facilities extended far beyond haircuts and uniforms. Captain Pratt's prototypical Carlisle Indian Industrial School, which opened its doors in November 1879 and in many respects served as the template for what followed, was actually established in an unused army barracks in Pennsylvania, as were a number of others. Although less conspicuous there, the situation in Canada was similar. 'Dormitories' were typically built along the lines of barracks bays, and children were regimented in military fashion. As every newcomer quickly discovered, 'nearly every aspect of his [or her] daily existence – eating, sleeping, working, learning, praying – would be rigidly scheduled, the hours of the day intermittently punctuated by a seemingly endless number of bugles and bells demanding this or that response' (Adams, 1995: 117).

Pratt and his superiors sought to justify their imposition of a 'Prussian' regime with glowing descriptions of the 'health benefits, ability to concentrate, and self-confidence' supposedly imparted thereby (*Annual Report of the Commissioner of Indian Affairs*, 55th Cong., 2nd Sess., 1898: 541). More candid – or honest – observers extolled the 'virtues' of 'patriotism' and 'obedience' being systematically hammered into previously 'wild' youngsters (see, e.g., Grinstead, 1914: 153). As might be expected, these mindsets structured the roughly two hours per day devoted in most schools to 'academic' instruction. Here, first emphasis was on the 'Three Rs' – reading, 'riting and 'rithmetic – with the goal of bringing all students up to the rudimentary levels of proficiency necessary to allow them to meet the needs of potential employers in the 'real world.' As the children progressed, increasing weight was placed on what were called the 'lessons of citizenship' or 'civilization.' The children came to identify far more with the mythic legions of noble white men populating their textbooks and classroom lectures than they did with the grotesquely distorted caricatures of their own ancestors and traditions presented therein.

The second half of the instructional day was explicitly devoted to the proselytizing of Christianity. Implanting the 'true faith' was integral to the overseers' mandate to 'impose the national pattern' they represented (indeed, the churches had established Indian residential schools as part of their missionary programs long before governments of either the US or Canada set out to do so). In both countries – partly to acquire the benefit of their experience, partly as a cost-constraining expedient – these pre-existing institutions and their staffs/faculties were simply incorporated, usually on a contract basis, into the official system, with the result that the churches were in this sense made responsible for the fulfillment of official policy. Conversely, church representatives were positioned to exert decisive influence in the formation of educational policy as it pertained to Indians.

In Canada, 'the residential school system was a creature of the federal government even though the children in the schools were, in most cases, in the care of the churches' (Milloy, 1999: xiii), while in the US, the reverse may ultimately have been the case. 'Even as the government edged the mission societies to the margin' in the US, however, 'its teachers also sought to imbue pupils with some form of Christianity. For most secular as well as missionary educators, "civilization" was inconceivable unless grounded in Christian ... values' (Coleman, 1993: 115). Consequently, and regardless of whether church or state was ascendant in operating the schools at any given moment or location, the result was the same. Even as they underwent a harsh and thoroughgoing process of deculturation (or 'denationalization'), the children were systematically 're-enculturated' to function in psychointellectual terms as 'little white people.' Given the virulently racialist constructions of role and place by which the US and Canadian settler societies were and are defined, of course, 'white' was and is something an American Indian child could never become.

### The 'slow death measure' of starvation

In the boarding schools, 'hunger was a continual and symptomatic problem.' A 1944 report submitted to Canada's Department of Indian Affairs by Dr. A.B. Simes, medical superintendent of the Qu'Appelle Indian Hospital, concluded that '28% of the girls and 69% of the boys [were] underweight' in the nearby Elkhorn School (Manitoba) (Simes, 1944). The same or worse was true of virtually every Indian residential facility in the country. The reason is not hard to find. Having forced thousands of native youngsters into the schools, the government was willing to spend almost nothing to feed them: the department's per capita allocation for Indian residential school support – all support, that is, not just food – at the time of Simes's report was 49 cents per day (and in many schools, only a fraction of that meager sum was actually being spent on students) (Milloy, 1999: 118, 332 n101).

It has since been argued that, given its overall economic situation during most of the period in question, this was 'the best Canada could do.'
At the time, however, even Indian Department officials acknowledged
that the rates applied to supporting native residential students were 'exceptionally low' (quoted in Milloy, 1999: 103). The truth of this admission is
revealed in a comparison of annual allocations made to sustain white
children in residential facilities in 1938, the year the all-time high rate of
$180 was applied to Indians. A per-capita rate of $550 was allotted to the
Manitoba School for Boys, to name one example, while the provincial
School for the Deaf received a governmental subsidy of $642 per student
(about *three-and-a-half times* the rate paid to support a native child). Church-
sponsored facilities serving white children also did far better than those to
which Indian youngsters were consigned: St. Norbert's Orphanage in
Winnipeg received $294 per student, St Joseph's $320 (R.A. Hoey to Dir.
of Indian Affairs H. McGill, 4 November 1938).

In the US, things were even worse. Although the Child Welfare League
of America reported that the average expenditure per white child in a
residential institution ranged from $313 to $541 annually, the 1928 Meriam
Report concluded that as little as 9 cents per day ($32.85 per year) was
being expended on the feeding of a native child in a government boarding
school (Meriam, 1928: 12, 327–31, 348–50). Even assuming that triple this
amount was involved by the time a child's clothing, medical care and the
like were added in – a wildly optimistic expectation, under the circumstances – the annual per capita expenditure on a native youngster was still
less than $100, or about one-quarter the amount expended on the average
white child in a residential facility (Wilbur and DuPuy, 1931: 126). In
1929, moreover, Representative Louis C. Cramton, chair of the House
Subcommittee on Appropriations for the Department of Interior, argued
vociferously – and unopposed by Indian Commissioner Charles Burke –
that even this meager sum was 'extravagant' (quoted in Szasz, 1999: 19).

The results of such governmental 'frugality' were as grim as they were
predictable. As Dr Simes discovered at the Elkhorn School, 'there was not
enough milk, no potatoes or other vegetables on stock, and ... the children never received eggs' (quoted in Milloy, 1999: 115). If anything, Simes's
findings understated the case. But Indian Affairs Director Duncan Campbell
Scott dismissed claims about such dire conditions as 'exaggerations,' even
'libels,' claiming in the face of all evidence that 'ninety-nine per cent of
the Indian children at these schools are too fat' (D.C. Scott to F. Mears,
11 January 1924). Hence, no departmental action was taken. Year after
year, school by school, the situation remained the same.

The quality of such food as the children received was also a serious
issue. Accounts of bug-ridden and spoiled foodstuffs abound, as when

most of the students at Shubenacadie became violently ill after being served liver so tainted that it had taken on a greenish cast. The children's inability to stomach such fare sometimes had dire consequences. A young girl at Shubenacadie who, 'unable to swallow some soggy bread,' vomited in her plate, found her face pushed into the mess by a nun supervising the dining room and was forced to eat what she'd regurgitated (Millward, 1992: 11). Nor was this the only report of such methods being used to prevent 'food wastage.'

The number of American Indian children who actually died of starvation during their time in the residential schools is unknown. Probably, from that cause alone, it was not many. However, the 'link between poor diets and poor health' was well known to officials in both the US and Canada from a point long before either had imposed its residential education system upon native children. The implications tend to speak for themselves, not only in view of the staggering disease-driven mortality rates within the schools (discussed in the next section), but also with respect to the sharply reduced life expectancy afflicting survivors from start to finish. It is also worth noting that the effects of chronic malnutrition would unquestionably have been far worse had the children in most schools not devised ways of supplementing their diets by foraging and/or 'stealing' from institutional larders.

## 'Indirect killing' by disease

Since at least as early as 1763, when Lord Jeffrey Amherst ordered smallpox-infected blankets to be distributed to the Ottawas as a means of 'extirpat[ing] this execrable race,' the spread of disease has been a conscious part of the Euroamerican/Eurocanadian approach to facilitate the 'vanishing' of Native North America (see, e.g., Stearn and Stearn, 1945: 44–50). Probably not the first time, and certainly not the last, that epidemics were deliberately unleashed, Amherst's gambit serves as an especially crystalline example of a larger whole. Most often, the methods employed were less direct, as when the US Army interned the entire Navajo population at the Bosque Redondo for four years (1864–68) under conditions that left half their number dead of malnutrition, exposure and, above all, disease. The residential schools must take their unfortunate place in this latter category.

Mortality rates in the schools were appalling from the outset. While comprehensive data for the US are sketchy – partly because of a policy of sending terminally ill children home to die, their deaths thus lumped in with reservation statistics – no less an authority than Duncan Campbell Scott observed that, in Canada, 'fifty percent of the children who passed through these schools did not live to benefit from the education they received therein' (Scott, 1913: 615). To place this startling proportion in proper perspective, it should be borne in mind that the death rate at the infamous nazi concentration camp of Dachau was 36 per cent, mostly from disease. At Buchenwald, another notorious example, the rate was 19 per cent. At Mauthausen, described by historian Michael Burleigh as exhibiting 'the harshest regime of all the concentration camps,' the death rate was 58 per cent (again, mostly from malnutrition and attendant disease) (Burleigh, 1997: 211). What is known of the US experience suggests that conditions and outcomes there were, at best, only marginally better than those pertaining under Scott's regime in the north.

The vast majority of fatalities among youngsters in the schools were caused by the rampant spread of contagious diseases, primarily tuberculosis (although influenza had its moments as a major killer, and smallpox made an occasional appearance). At the Crow Creek School (South Dakota), for instance, it was reported in 1897 that nearly all the children there 'seem[ed] to be tainted with scrofula and consumption' (quoted in Adams, 1995: 130). Overall, a 1908 study undertaken by the Smithsonian Institution concluded that by that year only one in every five students was likely to be 'entirely free' of tubercular symptoms (Hrdlicka, 1909: esp. 25, 32; Murphy, 1911: esp. 106–7).

Beginning in 1882, when the tuberculosis bacillus was first conclusively identified, a medical consensus rapidly formed holding that among the best defenses against the disease were 'strict hygiene, a nutritious diet ... and well-ventilated living quarters' (Adams, 1995: 130). Conditions in US boarding schools went in exactly the opposite direction, a circumstance greatly compounded by a gross underfunding of medical services (Szasz, 1999: 19). So blatant was the cause-and-effect relationship that, by 1899, even a BIA inspector, William McConnell, was openly denouncing the whole residential education system as embodying a policy of deliberate slaughter.

> The word 'murder' is a terrible word, but we are little less than murderers if we follow the course we are now following after the attention of those in charge has been called to its fatal results. Hundreds of boys and girls are sent home to die so that a sickly sentiment may be patronized and that institutions where brass bands, foot and base ball are the principal advertisements may be maintained. (quoted in Putney, 1980: 10–11)

'Those in charge,' repeatedly – although seldom so bluntly – informed of the silent holocaust occurring as a result of their methods and priorities, not only ignored it but, whenever possible, actively suppressed relevant information. More damning still is the pattern of promotion prevailing in the BIA throughout the entire period, a process which saw some of the most egregious offenders elevated to higher and broader realms of responsibility. On balance, then, there can be no reasonable dispute of the fact that responsible US officials knew *exactly* what they were doing when, during the half-century lasting from 1880 to 1930, they continued to feed other people's children like fodder into the maw of their residential facilities as fast as or faster than beds were vacated by dead or dying youngsters. Nor did the vaunted reforms marking America's 'New Deal' of the 1930s mean an abandonment of the system. In 1941, forty-nine schools were still operating, some 14,000 native youngsters were still consigned to them, and conditions, although noticeably improved, still produced rates of death by disease markedly higher than the norm (for statistics, see Szasz, 1999: 60; for health data, see, e.g., Wood, 1980: esp. 179–80). So it would remain, to one extent or another, until 1990, when the Phoenix Indian School finally closed its doors.

In Canada, where things have been rather better documented – albeit far from adequately – the full horror comes into clearer focus. This is in substantial part due to a study of fifteen residential schools undertaken in 1907 by Dr. P.H. Bryce, chief medical officer of the Indian Department. The Bryce Report, as it is usually called, revealed that of the 1,537 children who had attended the sample group of facilities since they'd opened – a period of ten years, on average – 42 per cent had died of 'consumption or tuberculosis,' either at the schools or shortly after being discharged. Extrapolating, Bryce's data indicated that of the 3,755 native children then under the 'care' of Canada's residential schools, 1,614 could be expected to have died a miserable death by the end of 1910 (Bryce, 1907: 17–20). In a follow-up survey conducted in 1909, Bryce collected additional information, all of it corroborating his initial report. At the Qu'Appelle School, the principal, a Father Hugonard, informed Bryce that his facility's record was 'something to be proud of' since 'only' 153 of the 795 youngsters who'd attended it between 1884 and 1905 had died in school or within two years of leaving it (Milloy, 1999: 92).

The reasons were neither hard to find, nor constrained to glaring dietary deficiencies. Press reports in the first decade of the twentieth century spoke of 'Indian boys and girls dying like flies' because of an 'absolute inattention to the bare necessities of [their] health' in 'schools that aid [the] white plague,' and noted how 'even war seldom shows as large a percentage of fatalities as does the education system imposed on our Indian wards.'[4]

The response of those in charge was to do nothing. Or, more accurately, they did nothing constructive. As in the US, they did continue to facilitate a steady *increase* in the number of native children lodged in the schools. Beyond that, their main effort appears to have been aimed at discrediting Bryce as a 'medical faddist' who had brought the system into 'undeserved disrepute' (S. Swinford, 4 December 1907). One ranking bureaucrat actually went on record describing the 'jolly, healthy children fairly bubbling over with vitality' supposedly inhabiting Manitoba's boarding schools (Manitoba Indian Commissioner David Laird, quoted in Milloy, 1999: 92). By 1914, the author of the Bryce Report had been pushed out of the Indian Service altogether, forced to watch from the sidelines in mounting rage and frustration as the business of 'educating' Indians went on as usual.

By 1922, Bryce had had enough, publishing a searing tract entitled *The Story of a National Crime* in which the mechanics of death in the schools were laid bare and responsibility placed squarely on Duncan Campbell Scott's conscious and undeviating blend of 'thrift' with ever greater numbers of compulsory enrollments (Bryce, 1922). Among other things revealed was that in several of the schools upon which Bryce had reported in 1907, conditions had grown demonstrably worse over the intervening decade and a half. At most residential schools, 'apparently robust children weakened shortly after admission,' and 'eventually became so sick' they had to be confined to sick bays where 'the dead, the dying, the sick and convalescent, were all [lumped] together in the same room' in order to hold down the cost of their 'care' (memo from W. Ditchburn, 12 October 1920; Rev. J. Woodsworth to Sec., 25 November 1918). Sometimes they were then 'buried two [or more] in a grave' to reduce the expense entailed in disposing of their corpses. Topping things off, Scott had ordered that departmental medical services be *cut back* in 1918 – the position of medical inspector was eliminated altogether – 'for reasons of economy' (Rev. J. Woodsworth to Sec., 25 November 1918).

The Indian Department mounted a vituperative defense of its policies and practices for public consumption. But privately, Scott himself conceded the substance of Bryce's charges. Writing behind a shroud of presumed confidentiality in a 1918 report to Superintendent General Arthur Meighan, he readily admitted that the buildings to which his minions were sending more and more native children were already seriously overcrowded and otherwise 'inadequate,' and that the resultant 'unsanitary [conditions therein] were undoubtedly chargeable with a very high death rate among pupils' (D.C. Scott to A. Meighan, January 1918). Thus informed, Meighan took no more corrective action than had his predecessors. Indeed, it would be another sixteen years before moneys were set aside to establish the first tuberculosis sanatorium for the ravaged youngsters, and even then no special funds were designated to improve conditions in the schools themselves. That would have to wait until 'comprehensive reforms' were finally undertaken in 1957. As late as 1969, reports on a number of schools revealed conditions were not especially different from those recorded by Bryce and others at the beginning of the century. So it would remain until the last of Canada's Indian residential facilities was closed in 1984.

Viewed in the whole, and especially in light of Scott's sharing of critical information with Arthur Meighan and other such highly placed officials, there can be no real question of the onus of blame resting upon the Indian Department alone. If it was not literally a policy consensus in Canada that residential schooling should be used as a handy medium through which to physically liquidate an appreciable segment of the country's aboriginal population, then their mass death was undeniably treated as an 'acceptable' by-product of the government's broader drive to annihilate them culturally. To refocus analyst John Milloy's apt assessment of the priorities displayed by the principal of Old Sun's School in 1922, Canadian officials as a group were plainly 'determined that, with slates and chalk in hand, the children would die on the road to civilization' (Milloy, 1999: 99).

As to Canada's 'general public,' leaving aside the transient and largely pro forma expressions of outraged 'concern' attending release first of the Bryce Report, and later of *The Story of a National Crime* – manifestations which in themselves prove that average settlers knew, or had reason to know, what was being done 'in their name' – 'the deaths, and the condition of the schools pricked no collective conscience, wrought no revolution,' nor even sustained pressure for a reformulation of policy. As in the US, the fate of native people, children included, was simply not discussed within the polite circles of Good Canadians. Instead, such issues, like those contemporaneously pertaining to Jews and other 'undesirables' in Germany, were swept, quietly and conveniently, 'into the darker reaches of the national consciousness' (Milloy, 1999: 102). A better illustration of 'the genocidal mentality' at work is impossible to conceive.

## The 'slow death measure' of forced labor

Amplifying the debilitating effects of continuous anxiety and stress, malnutrition, and the near-total absence of basic sanitation in the fostering of rampant disease among residential school students was the substantial work regimen imposed in most such institutions. A number of facilities were from the outset explicitly designated as 'industrial schools' – Pratt's prototype at Carlisle is a classic example; there were 25 such entities in the US and 22 in Canada by 1907 (Szasz, 1999: 10; Milloy, 1999: 55) – but those never endowed with that telltale descriptor ultimately functioned in much the same way. Overall, the situation in the US was such that in 1935 BIA employee Oliver LaFarge went on record describing the boarding school system as being composed of 'penal institutions – where little children [are] sentenced to hard labor for a term of years for the crime of being born of their mothers' (LaFarge, 1935: 233). In Canada, residential school survivors have also not infrequently compared their experience to imprisonment – in 1991, the Musqeam leader Wendy Grant-John referred to them as 'internment camps for children' (quoted in Fournier and Grey, 1997: 61) – although as those who had actually been incarcerated in both types of facility usually observed, 'the food was better in prison' (quoted in Miller, 1996: 387).

Whether or not they were formally designated as purveyors of 'industrial training,' virtually all residential facilities were, by design, 'frankly supported in part by the labor of their students,' who, by the time they reached fifth grade, 'work[ed] for half a day and [went] to school for half a day.' A US investigating commission found in 1928 that 'much of the work of Indian children in boarding schools would … be prohibited in most states under child labor laws' (Meriam et al., 1928: 13). The official justification in the US and Canada alike for exempting native children from such protections was that, in the course of their 'employment,' they were being prepared for future self-sufficiency by 'learning a trade.' The trades taught, however, often bore no relationship to the prospect of future employment. Plainly, production rather than 'education,' 'vocational' or otherwise, was at issue. As one analyst has put it, 'The student worked for the school rather than the school for the student' (Kizer, n.d.: 69).

The goal, openly and repeatedly stated on both sides of the border, was to make each school 'financially self-sufficient,' or even profit-making. Toward this end, where students were paid for their labor at all – some administrators apparently believed token 'wages' might provide incentive to greater productivity – the compensation was abysmally low. According to 1897 BIA guidelines, students new to a job should never be paid, but might receive 1 cent per hour after a few months. Children with two years' experience might receive a 'raise' to 1.5 cents per hour. Even these tiny sums did not go to the youngsters who earned them, however. Rather, they were deposited in no-interest 'savings accounts' (mis)managed by school administrators.

The labor demanded of children in residential institutions was not only dreary and demeaning, but often gut-bustingly difficult. In a single year, the thirty-eight 'working age' boys at the Fort Stevenson Indian Boarding School (North Dakota), 'in addition to cutting and hauling 300 posts, fencing in twenty acres of pasture, cutting over 200 cords of wood, and storing away 150 tons of ice … mined 150 tons of lignite coal. Proud of this accomplishment, the superintendent boasted that "a vast amount of hard labor" was required to extract the coal, partly because "about 9 feet of earth had to be removed before the vein was reached"' (Adams, 1995: 151). It is impossible to calculate with precision the extent to which the conditions of forced labor imposed upon residential school students, rather than the malnutrition and other adverse conditions to which they were all but universally subjected, proved decisive in lowering their resistance to the diseases that at times claimed half their number. Probably the best approach is, as historian David E. Stannard recommends, to treat the combination of factors as an inseparably interactive whole (Stannard, 1996: 177).

## Torture

To be sure, native children were not merely the passive victims of all that was being done to them. Virtually without exception, survivor narratives include accounts of subversion, both individual and collective, most commonly involving such activities as 'stealing' and/or foraging for food, possessing other 'contraband,' persistence in the speaking of native languages, and running away. In many – perhaps most – residential schools, such activities were so common and sustained as to comprise outright 'cultures of resistance' (for overviews, see Coleman, 1993: 146–61; Adams, 1995: 209–38; Miller, 1996: 343–74). And in most instances, the official response was to intensify the already harsh disciplinary regimen by which institutional life was defined, resorting to 'corrective measures' exceeding any reasonable limit or proportion. Many of the methods routinely employed not only went beyond the usual standards of 'cruel and unusual punishment' prohibited under Anglo-American law for application to convicted felons in penal facilities, but violated the prohibitions against torture found in international legal custom and convention.

Under guidelines promulgated in 1890, the schools were licensed to inflict corporal punishment, literal imprisonment in a 'guardhouse,' and other such penalties on students believed 'guilty of persistently using profane or obscene language; lewd conduct; stubborn insubordination; lying; fighting; wanton destruction of property; theft, or similar misbehavior' (*Annual Report of the Commissioner of Indian Affairs*, 56th Cong., 1st Sess., 1900: clii). 'In other words,' observes analyst David Wallace Adams, 'just about everything' the children did was subject to discretionary interpretation and punishment by their overseers (Adams, 1995: 121). The severity of such beatings, sometimes undertaken with fists, rubber hoses and even baseball bats, is attested by the case of a 13-year-old boy who in 1912 was 'held, handcuffed, and almost beaten into "insensibility" with a strap. The result was that "the boy collapsed, lay on the floor almost helpless, and … after sixteen days, twenty-six cruel scars remained on his body, and eleven upon his right arm" ' (Adams, 1995: 122). Such brutality, found by congressionally commissioned investigators to be endemic in 1928, was hardly the end of it. There are many accounts of children as young as 8 being shackled to posts, 'having a ball and chain tied to their ankle,' and so on (McBeth, 1983: 106).

Although in 1929 Indian Commissioner Burke made an ostentatious display of renewing the 1898 ban on the worst of such practices, his successor, Charles J. Rhodes, effectively gutted the constraints a year later. As had been the case with the 1898 constraints, Burke's 1929 ban was for the most part ignored anyway (almost invariably without discernible consequences to violators), and, irrespective of periodic official pronouncements to the contrary, 'harsh measures of discipline remained in use' at facilities like the Phoenix and St Francis (South Dakota) Indian schools into the mid-1980s (Trennert, 1988: 192). As always, things were no better in Canada, especially during the tenure of Duncan Campbell Scott as Indian Service director.

Those who physically resisted such abuse, usually but not always adolescent males, typically came in for still harsher treatment. One young man at the McKay School (Manitoba), who in 1924 fought back against a strapping after he was accused of 'slacking' at work – actually, his hands had become too blistered to hold the pitchfork he was assigned to use – ended up bruised 'black from his neck to his buttocks' (Milloy, 1999: 147). Another boy, upon being cracked across the skull with a cane by a staff thug named Skinner at the Red Deer School, seized the cane and hit his assailant back; shortly thereafter, the youngster was beaten so badly that he needed to undergo cranial surgery. Such atrocities were regularly reported to Scott, but, other than the release of a vacuous 1921 assertion that abuse would not be condoned, no action was taken. The torture continued on a system-wide basis, decade after decade, until the very end. During the late 1960s, for example, a staff member at the Oblates' St Philip's Residential School (Saskatchewan) regularly burned 'recalcitrant' children with his cigarette lighter, and developed a specialized punishment called 'whipping with five belts' in which a cluster of narrow straps resembling the infamous cat-o'-nine-tails – but embellished with metal studs – was used to induce a 'proper' degree of submissiveness in the unruly; 'It was not at all uncommon for this punishment to leave scabs that stuck to clothing and left scars' (Miller, 1996: 327). Another method of 'bringing unduly stubborn youngsters to their senses' during the same period was to place them in restraints and then apply electrical shocks (Chrisjohn and Young with Maraun, 1997: 32).

Native residential schoolchildren opted all too frequently to embrace the ultimate refusal of the conditions imposed upon them: suicide. In this connection, however, the record is sufficient to provide only occasional glimpses of what was happening. The first documented suicide at the Phoenix Indian School was that of a Pima boy in 1894, for instance; contemporaneous accounts strongly suggest that ending the burden of 'severe discipline and punishment' was likely his motive (Trennert, 1988: 50). At the Williams Lake School in 1920, 'in the aftermath of severe beatings' nine youngsters attempted mass suicide, one of them successfully, by eating water hemlock (Milloy, 1999: 148, 153–4).

'Cause of death' bookkeeping on both sides of the border was ultimately too shoddy – or deliberately misleading – to allow anything resembling a comprehensive and accurate appraisal of suicide rates in the schools. But even such fragmentary evidence as is available plainly belies apologistic screeds like Robert Havighurst's convenient – and therefore influential – 1971 study claiming that 'virtually no suicides occurred ... in boarding schools' during the first ninety years of their operation. There is, after all, a considerable distinction to be drawn between the number of suicides attempted on the one hand and the number of attempts recorded on the other, especially in a context where 'those in charge' at all levels preferred that things appear to be other than they actually were. Even without hard data on the number of child suicides claimed by the residential schools, the ghastly toll taken by the systematic torture practiced in those institutions for more than a century is quite clear.

## Predation

Throughout the entire period in which the residential schools were operating, in virtually every facility, and, perhaps most unspeakably, even as the children were mercilessly flogged for the slightest deviation from the supposed virtues of 'strict chastity' and other such aspects of 'Christian morality,' they were routinely subjected to the attentions of sexual predators among the staff members, quite prominently including priests, nuns, and Protestant clergy. So ubiquitous was the situation that in 1995 Douglas Hogarth, a Supreme Court judge for British Columbia, went on record describing his country's residential school system as having been 'nothing but a form of institutionalized pedophilia' and 'sexual terrorism' (quoted in Grant, 1996: 229).

Although they have adamantly denied it, 'those in charge,' both of the churches and of the Indian Service, knew about and defended this sexual predation as well. In numerous cases, when predation in a given school was discovered or suspected by native communities whose children were lodged there, the predator was simply moved to another institution and, at least in some instances, promoted.

Some indication of the scale of the predation is conveyed by a 1991 report of the Cariboo Tribal Council into the operations of the Oblates' St Joseph's [Mission] residential school in Williams Lake. The report

> produced shocking figures ... In answer to an interviewer's question to a group 187 people ... whether they had suffered sexual abuse as children [at the school], 89 answered in the affirmative, 38 in the negative, and 60 refused to answer. Depending on how the non-respondents are allocated between the 'yes' and 'no' categories, these data represent a reporting rate of from 48 to 70 per cent ... The chief investigators of a less scientific study of abuse at the Roman Catholic Kuper Island School in British Columbia found that more than half the [70] people interviewed had horrendous stories.... Mel H. Buffalo, an advisor to the Samson [Cree] band in Hobbema, Alberta, reported that 'every Indian person I've spoken to who attended these schools has a story of mental, physical or sexual abuse to relate.' (Miller, 1996: 329)

In 1993, three years after investigators for the Ministry of National Health and Welfare had also turned up – and publicly commented upon – evidence that '100% of the children at some schools were sexually abused' between 1950 and 1980 (quoted in *Globe and Mail*, 1 June 1990), the Indian Service, which had by then been merged into what is called the Department of Indian Affairs and Northern Development (DIAND), turned over the first thirty-five of its files on suspected molestation cases for further action by the RCMP. Meanwhile, conclusive proof was piling up in court, beginning in 1989, when Oblate priest Harold McIntee pled guilty to allegations that he'd molested more than a score of boys as young as 5 during his years at the St Joseph's Mission School. In 1995, Arthur Henry Plint, a career supervisor at the Alberni School, pled guilty to having committed serial sexual offenses against the children under his 'care' from the moment he was hired until his retirement twenty years later. His case is emblematic of the rest:

> Plint, then seventy-seven, cursed his accusers as he walked into court under the glare of television lights, hitting out with a cane in a final act of contempt and violence. Inside, he pled guilty to sixteen counts of indecent assault of aboriginal boys aged six to thirteen, between 1948 and 1968. Three of the boys were forcibly sodomized, others forced to perform oral sex ... often daily, for months and years. (Fournier and Grey, 1997: 71, 73–4)

As one official had already acknowledged, 'only the tip of the iceberg' appeared to have been revealed by such cases (quoted in Miller, 1996: 333). Under these circumstances, Canada's Aboriginal Rights Coalition requested in 1992 that the Indian Department initiate an official and comprehensive investigation of the extent to which sexual predation had prevailed in the schools. In December of that year, Duncan Campbell Scott's heir, Tom Siddon, continued his predecessor's tradition of hiding the truth by declaring that he did not 'believe a public inquiry [was] the best approach' to resolving the issue (quoted in Milloy, 1999: 301). Although 'by 1992, most of the churches had apologized' – the Presbyterians held out until late 1994 – Siddon also made it clear that the Indian Service had no intention of following suit: 'There would be no ministerial apology, no apology on behalf of Canadians, and no plans for [providing] compensation' to the victims (quoted in Milloy, 1999: 299, 301). The most the department was willing to offer was a carefully worded expression of 'regret' that bad things had happened in the schools, through no fault of its own.

The situation is even more putrid in the US. There, the wall of silence behind which much of what happened to the north was all too conveniently hidden prior to 1990 remains as towering as ever. Even amidst a burgeoning scandal concerning endemic sexual predations of priests and others operating in mainstream settings over the past thirty years, and of systematic cover-ups and protection of offenders, most prominently by the Catholic Church, there has been no exploration whatsoever of the probability that such abuse of native children was as pervasive in US residential schools as in Canada's. To the contrary, such efforts as have been made to 'explain' the much better-documented – and in that sense unavoidable – phenomena of forced labor and physical torture have been primarily of the sort designed to neutralize rather than elaborate the implications.

## Worlds of pain

It is true that in both Canada and the United States the imposition of residential schooling upon indigenous children ended some twenty years ago. It is *not* true, however, as DIAND's Tom Siddon was already claiming by 1991, that the effects are now 'in the past.' To the contrary, the ravages of a virulent cluster of psychological dysfunctions that has come to be known in Canada as 'Residential School Syndrome' (RSS) – there is no corresponding term in the US, although the symptomatologies involved are just as clearly present there – not only remains undiminished, but may in some respects have intensified during the decades since the last survivors were released from residential facilities. Given the proportion of the native population caught up in the residential school system during the last two generations of its operation, and the fact that the syndrome is demonstrably transmissible to children and others closely associated with or dependent upon survivors, the magnitude of its ongoing impact upon Native North America deserves exploration.

In its most common manifestations, RSS includes acutely conflicted self-concept and lowered self-esteem, emotional numbing (often described as 'inability to trust or form lasting bonds'), somatic disorder, chronic depression and anxiety (often phobic), insomnia and nightmares, dissociation, paranoia, sexual dysfunction, heightened irritability and tendency to fly into rages, strong tendencies towards alcoholism and drug addiction, and suicidal behavior. While the syndrome has been treated as if were something unprecedented and unique by most Canadian researchers – that is, as a 'clinical' phenomenon requiring extensive study before it can be either defined or effectively addressed – such posturing diverts attention from the fact that there is nothing at all new or especially different about RSS. Rather, it has a number of obvious and well-researched corollaries, including the entirely comparable sets of symptoms afflicting victims of rape, torture, hostage-taking, domestic violence and child abuse. Strong similarities also exist between the behaviors exhibited among those suffering RSS and the Post-Traumatic Stress Disorder (PTSD) often associated with soldiers who've undergone heavy combat. Perhaps most significantly, the symptomotologies of RSS are virtually interchangeable with those attending the so-called Concentration Camp Syndrome (CCS) manifested on a collective basis by survivors of both the nazi facilities and their counterparts in the Soviet Union and elsewhere.

One readily observable result of the residential schools, all but unremarked in discussions of RSS, is the existence of an entire stratum of native people in both Canada and the US who were, in what might be seen as a permanent variation of the so-called Stockholm Syndrome with which hostages are sometimes temporarily afflicted, 'ideologically converted' by their experience (see Symonds, 1982; Strentz, 1982). For the most part deeply Christianized, often just as deeply rejecting of their own peoples/traditions, and primally conditioned to identify their interests as coinciding with those of their oppressors, they have over the past fifty years been increasingly employed by the settler status quo – governmental, corporate and academic – as a sort of 'broker class,' willing to extend an appearance of 'native endorsement' to even the most objectively anti-Indian initiatives.[4] In exchange for their utility in perpetually subverting themselves and their peoples, the brokers typically receive incidental monetary compensation and appointments to prestigious – but invariably powerless – positions as Indian 'leaders.' The process steadily deepens their estrangement from native communities – wherein they are usually branded as 'sell-outs' – and furthers the process of sociopolitical fragmentation within the communities themselves.

A much larger group, which significantly overlaps with the first, consists of people among whom the 'neutralizing' symptomatologies of RSS predominate, either intermittently or continuously. Deculturated to the point of being unable to participate fully in their own societies (at least in their own minds), and congenitally barred by the race codes upon which North America's settler societies continue to function from fitting into them either, such people are trapped in a perpetual limbo of conflicted identity, personal unfulfillment, and despair. Seeking some sense of 'normalcy' in marriage and the forming of families, they typically discover that a combination of the psycho-emotional damage they've suffered in the schools, their all-but-total lack of experience in actual familial settings, and often their inability to secure the steady work necessary to provide for their dependants, generates catastrophic results. As a rule, they end up visiting upon their offspring some variation of the misery they themselves suffered as youngsters. Aware of this, but incapable of altering the destructive dynamics at play, most compound the problem by seeking the oblivion and self-nullification offered by alcohol and other substances. Ultimately – or alternatively – they seek the final 'closure' of suicide, at a rate more than five times the national average.

For the children of residential school survivors, childhood is often an experience worse than it was for one or both of their parents. Their suffering and witnessing of traumatic abuse begins much earlier – often at birth – and tends to be sustained longer and in a more intensive fashion. The tormentors of residential schoolchildren were at least the aliens who had displaced their parents; for the children of survivors, the tormentors all too frequently are their parents themselves. The record of the residential schools is filled to overflowing with poignant accounts of little boys and girls who cried themselves to sleep each night in loneliness for the warmth and affection of the homes from which they'd been torn; the children of survivors *are* home, and must shed their tears in desperate hunger for something they've never known. Children in the schools escaped in droves, almost always trying to return to the places whence they'd come; when the children of survivors run, as they often do, it is only 'away.'

It has been reasonably estimated that one in every two adult American Indians suffered acute alcoholism during the twentieth century. In some locales, the Grassy Narrows Reserve (Ontario), for example, as well as Alkali Lake (British Columbia), Norway House (Manitoba) and Cross Lake (Manitoba), the tally was at times 100 per cent (Shkilnyk, 1985; York, 1992: 175–200). Much verbiage – and untold research dollars – have been expended in trying not-so-subtly to affix blame to the victims themselves, a process of seeking and asserting 'proof' that native people are 'genetically predisposed to alcoholism' or that 'there is something in traditional cultures' that obtains the same result (Westermeyer, 1974; Leland, 1976; Maracle, 1993). No study has as yet attempted to correlate such obvious facts as that, while half of all native people have lately become alcoholics, an equal proportion were also processed through residential schools. In the same vein, although they share neither genetic nor cultural characteristics with Native North Americans, other peoples subjected to long-term colonization on the English model – the Irish, for instance – have been notoriously beset by comparable rates of alcoholism, 'schizo-phrenia,' and other such RSS-like maladies.

## Shaping the future

Native North Americans are by no means the only people who have been subjected to residential schooling, or something similar, by their colonizers. Certainly, the 'station' policy maintained by Australia with regard to the aboriginal populace of that subcontinent during the bulk of the twentieth century bears a more than passing resemblance, as do the results embodied in the Aborigines' 'lost generations.' Although residential facilities were not usually employed, the system of compulsory schooling imposed by Britain upon the Irish from the early nineteenth century onward entailed 'pedagogical' objectives identical to those pertaining to American Indians: destruction of linguistic and spiritual traditions, undermining of familial/ social structures, and so on. The same goals hallmark the modes of school-ing more selectively forced by the British upon their colonial subjects in India and West Africa. Occasionally, as with the British 'Home Child' program, some of the worst aspects of what was done to American Indian and Australian aboriginal young people have also been visited upon un-wanted or 'surplus' white youngsters. While the fate of the Home Children was an exceptionally ugly manifestation of the vicious class structure by which the 'English-speaking world' has organized itself internally, such phenomena have plainly been the rule in colonial settings.

Indeed, it has been observed that something akin to the residential school system is *inherent* to any successful order of colonialism. As Sartre noted in his preface to Frantz Fanon's monumental anti-colonialist tract, *The Wretched of the Earth*, and elsewhere, colonization can only be accom-plished by a violent subjugation 'internalized as Terror by the colonized':

> Colonial violence does not only aim to keep the enslaved people at a respectful distance, it also seeks to dehumanize them. No effort will be spared to liquidate their traditions, substitute our language for theirs, destroy their culture without [admitting them to] ours; they will be rendered stupid by exploitation. Mal-nourished and sick, if they continue to resist, fear will finish the job: the [natives] have guns pointed at them; along come civilians who settle [upon their] land and force them with the riding crop to farm it for them. If they resist, the soldiers [or police] will shoot and they are dead men; if they give in, they degrade themselves and they are no longer human beings; shame and fear fissure

their character and shatter their personality. The business is carried out briskly by experts: 'psychological services' are by no means a new invention. Neither is brainwashing. (Sartre, 2001a: 142–3)

Eventually, if the colonizers' system functions as intended, the colonized 'do not even need to be exterminated any more.... The body will be allowed to live on but the spirit will be destroyed' (Sartre, 2001b: 76). In effect, aside from the 'perpetual massacre' through which it is necessarily sustained, colonialism 'is by its very nature a [process] of cultural genocide. Colonization cannot take place without systematically liquidating all the [autochthonous] characteristics of the native society' (Sartre, 1968: 62–3). It follows that, for Sartre, colonialism, as such, *equals* genocide. It may be added, moreover, that there is nothing in his formulation, unlike those advanced from virtually every other quarter during the second half of the twentieth century, which is in the least inconsistent with Raphael Lemkin's original conception of the crime.

Sartre's percipience has been treated as controversial, especially among self-described 'genocide scholars.' For those not disposed to reject the formulation out of hand, there can be neither compromise nor equivocation. Given that residential schooling and its corollaries have all along served as cornerstones for the consolidation of colonial order, and that colonialism in itself amounts to genocide, there can be no hedging as to whether either the schools or their after-effects were and are 'really' genocidal. They were, and blatantly so. The 'something taking the place of this truth' remarked by Wittgenstein in the epigraph to this essay is thereby revealed as the aggregate of 'interpretations' holding that the Indian residential school systems maintained by the US and Canada were *anything but* instruments of genocide. The first task, then, is to 'uncover the source of the misrepresentation' and 'transform it into what is true.' Genocide, always and everywhere, must be called by its right name. So, too, must those who would camouflage or deny it be called by theirs.

Having thus 'defined the phenomenon' at hand in a fashion common to both Wittgenstein and Huey Newton, the question becomes how it might be caused 'to act in the desired manner' (that is, to cease and disappear). The answer, of course, resides in the 'source' of both the phenomenon and its misrepresentation. Insofar as the genocide embodied in residential schooling arises as an integral aspect of colonialism, then colonialism must be seen as constituting that source. It follows that the antidote will be found, exclusively so, in a thoroughgoing process of *decolonization*. To be consciously anti-genocidal, one must be actively anti-imperialist, and vice versa. To be in any way an apologist for colonialism is to be an active proponent of genocide. In this, given the dynamics of power at play, there are – indeed can be – no bystanders.

Rephrased in affirmative terms, decolonization in the context of Native North America means simply the assertion and realization by American Indians of the right to self-determination repeatedly confirmed in international law as being vested in *all* peoples, 'by virtue of [which], they freely determine their political status and freely pursue their economic, social and cultural development.'[5] More concretely, this means the extension of unfettered indigenous jurisdiction over the full extent of the territories explicitly reserved by native peoples for their own use and occupancy in their treaties with the US and Canada, as well as such territories as were expropriated from them through fraudulent or coerced treaties. Within these reconstituted homelands – an aggregate totaling perhaps half the continent – it follows that indigenous nations, *not* North America's settler state governments, will exercise complete control over everything from natural resource disposition, to their form(s) of government, to the criteria of citizenship. There can be none of the current US subterfuge of pretending that native people are already self-determining, or that they are entitled to exercise only a kind of 'internal self-determination' previously unknown to legal discourse.

Restitution in terms of property and jurisdiction are by no means the only elements involved in the decolonization of Native North America. The colonization itself occurred in flagrant violation of international law, not least through the systematic breach of some 400 ratified treaties in the US and scores more in Canada,[6] and has been maintained since 1945 in circumvention of provisions in the United Nations Charter making colonialism itself illegal. To this must be added the implications of sustained and multifaceted violations of the Genocide Convention and numerous other conventions, covenants and declarations by both North American settler states. Under international tort law, offending entities incur a liability with regard to each such breach of legality requiring that, to the extent possible, they repair all damages done as a result of their transgressions. In cases where reparation is not possible – for example, where land has been rendered uninhabitable by mining and/or contamination, or where the destruction of population is involved – they are obliged to make adequate compensation to the victims and survivors. Under no circumstances is an offending entity entitled to define adequacy of restitution, reparation or compensation; this is the prerogative/responsibility of a neutral third party such as the International Court of Justice ('World Court').

Finally, there is the matter of criminal culpability. Those who formulated and presided over, as well as those who carried out, criminal policies are subject to prosecution for their actions. Where domestic tribunals fail to mete out justice in such matters – as those of the US and Canada invariably have – the authority of the newly constituted International

Criminal Court may be invoked (despite an ongoing refusal on the part
of the US in particular to accept its jurisdiction). As to the matter of the
culpability lodged in the broader settler populations that have for so long
proven themselves accepting of what was and is being done to American
Indians, and who have gladly queued up to avail themselves of material
benefits plainly accruing at the expense of native people – a posture
adding up to complicity, if nothing else – a more metaphysical resolution
presents itself. In general, this would assume the form of penance explored quite eloquently by Karl Jaspers in his *The Question of German
Guilt*. At a minimum, providing an accurate account of Euro-American
history – thereby replacing national and cultural hubris with the sort of
humility accompanying all such admissions of criminal comportment –
would undoubtedly go far towards dissipating the attitudes which gave
rise to the residential school system and related atrocities, while giving no
small measure of psychic comfort to surviving victims.

The task is daunting. Yet, should those among North America's settler
societies who manage to see things clearly nonetheless shirk their responsibility to do that which is necessary, the agony of the Others who are
their countries' victims will continue, and even incrementally worsen to
the point of their long-prophesied extinction. Somewhere between this
point and that, those relegated a nullified existence will seize upon a
moment of cumulative anguish and do the job themselves – or try to –
in a manner both natural and far more horrific than if the defaulters had
done it themselves. If the resulting monumentality of violence would be
redeemed by the fact that it was 'no less than man reconstructing himself'
(to quote Sartre), far better that significant sectors of the colonizing populace joined hands with the colonized before the fact, eliminating colonialism in a common project that had the effect of reducing the magnitude
of violence experienced by *all* concerned.

Surely such a project is worthy by all conceivable moral, ethical, and
legal standards. Equally, we owe it to the survivors of the ongoing process
of genocide embodied in the residential schools – and to their children,
their grandchildren, and to our own humanity, if ever it is to be reclaimed
– that we shoulder the burden, *whatever* it may entail, of ensuring that the
order of colonialism is shattered at last, never to be restored. Most importantly, we owe it, all of us, to our coming generations, seven deep into the
future, to bequeath to them lives free of the nightmarish reality in which
we ourselves remain so mired. Should that prove to be the legacy of the
little ones who suffered so long and so terribly in the schools, then perhaps
their spirits may finally be at peace.

## Notes

Thanks are due to Shiinindio (John Peter Kelly) for his counsel and encouragement in my preparation of this essay, dedicated as it is to his late daughter – and my own much beloved wife – Kizhiibaabinisek (Leah Renae Kelly), who was among the myriad victims still being claimed by the genocide embodied in Canada's Indian residential schools.

1. For a seminal articulation of the 'settler state' concept and the especially virulent form of colonialism inherent to such entities, see Price, 1949.

2. Sheridan's actual statement was that 'the only good Indians I ever saw were dead'; quoted in Hutton, 1985: 180.

3. The quotations are assembled from articles in *Saturday Night* (23 November 1907) and the *Montreal Star* (15 November 1907), as well as a banner story titled 'Schools Aid White Plague – Startling Death Rolls Revealed Among Indians,' *The Ottawa Citizen*, 16 November 1907.

4. The term 'broker class' is borrowed from Rodolfo Acuña (1988: 377–86).

5. See, for example, the United Nations Declaration on the Granting of Independence to Colonial Countries and Peoples, UNGA Res. 1514 (XV), 15 UN GAOR, Supp. (No. 16) 66, UN Doc. A/4684 (1961) Pt. 2; the International Covenant on Economic, Social and Cultural Rights, UNGA Res. 2200 (XXI), 21 UN GAOR, Supp. (No. 16) 49, UN Doc. A/6316 (1967), *reprinted in* 6 I.L.M. 360 (1967) Art. 1 (1); the International Covenant on Civil and Political Rights, UNGA Res. 2200 (XXI), 21 UN GAOR, Supp. (No. 16) 52, UN Doc. A/6316 (1967), reprinted in 6 I.L.M. 368 (1967) Art. 1 (1); and the United Nations Declaration on the Right to Development, UNGA Res. 41/128, 41 UN GAOR, Supp. (No. 53) UN Doc. A/41/925 (1986).

6. For the texts of 371 treaties with Indians duly ratified by the US Senate, see Kappler, 1973.

## References

Acuña, A. (1988). *Occupied America: A history of the Chicanos* (3rd edition). New York: HarperCollins.

Adams, D.W. (1995). *Education for extinction: American Indians and the boarding school experience, 1875–1928*. Lawrence: University Press of Kansas.

Alexander, E. (1994), *The Holocaust and the war of ideas*. New Brunswick, NJ: Transaction Books.

Arad, Y., et al., eds (1989). *The Einsatzgruppen reports: Selections from the Nazi death squads' campaign against the Jews in occupied territories of the Soviet Union, July 1941– January 1943*. New York: Holocaust Library.

Bauer, Y. (1978). *The Holocaust in historical perspective*. Seattle: University of Washington Press.

Bauman, Z. (1989). *Modernity and the Holocaust*. Cambridge: Polity Press.

Brinkley, J. (2003). American Indians say documents show government has cheated them out of billions. *New York Times*, 7 January.

Bryce, P.H. (1922). *The story of a national crime: Being an appeal for justice for the Indians of Canada*. Ottawa: James Hope & Sons.

——— (1907). *Report on the Indian schools of Manitoba and the Northwest Territories* (The Bryce Report). Ottawa: Government Printing Bureau.

Burleigh, M. (1997). *Ethics and extermination: Reflections on the Nazi genocide.* Cambridge: Cambridge University Press.

Canadian Civil Liberties Association (1952). *Brief to the Senate standing committee on civil and constitutional affairs on hate propaganda.* Ottawa: Supplies and Services, 22 April.

Chrisjohn, R., and Young, S., with Maraun, M. (1997) *The circle game: Shadows and substance in the Indian residential school experience in Canada.* Penticton, BC: Theytus Books.

Churchill, W. (2003). Forbidding the G-word in Canada: Holocaust denial as judicial doctrine in Canada. In W. Churchill, *Perversions of justice: Indigenous peoples and Angloamerican law,* 247–61. San Francisco: City Lights.

Cleaver, E. (1969). Cleaver on Cleaver. *Ramparts,* 14–28 December.

Coleman, M.C. (1993). *American Indian children at school, 1850–1930.* Jackson: University of Mississippi Press.

Davis, R., and Zannis, M. (1973). *The genocide machine in Canada: The pacification of the North.* Montreal: Black Rose Books.

Department of Indian Affairs (Canada) (1889). *Annual report.* Ottawa: Supplies & Services.

Fournier, S., and Grey, E. (1997). *Stolen from our embrace: The abduction of First Nations children and the restoration of aboriginal communities.* Vancouver: Douglas & McIntyre.

*Globe and Mail* (1990). Reports of abuse may be low, expert says. *The Globe and Mail,* 1 June.

Goffman, E. (1961). The characteristics of total institutions. In A. Etzioni, ed., *Complex organizations: A sociological reader.* Chicago: Aldine.

Grant, A. (1996). *No end of grief: Indian residential schools in Canada.* Winnipeg: Pemmican Press.

Grinstead, E.P. (1914). The value of military drills. *Native American,* 21 March.

Hoig, S. (1961). *The Sand Creek massacre.* Norman: University of Oklahoma Press, 1961.

Horowitz, I.L. (1976). *Genocide: State power and mass murder.* New Brunswick, NJ: Transaction Books.

House of Commons, Canada (1952). *Report of the Special Committee on Hate Propaganda in Canada* (the Cohen Report). Ottawa: Supplies and Services.

Hrdlicka, A. (1909). *Tuberculosis among certain Indian tribes of the United States.* Washington, DC: Smithsonian Institution.

Hutton, P.A. (1985). *Phil Sheridan and his army.* Lincoln: University of Nebraska Press.

Johnson, B. (1989). *Indian school days.* Norman, OK: University of Oklahoma Press.

Kabotie, F. (1977). *Fred Kabotie, Hopi Indian artist: An autobiography told with Bill Belknap.* Flagstaff: Museum of Northern Arizona/Northland Press.

Kappler, C.J., ed. (1973). *Indian treaties, 1778–1883.* New York: Interland.

Kaywaykla, J. (1970). *In the days of Victorio: Recollections of a Warm Springs Apache.* Tucson: University of Arizona Press.

Kennedy, J.M. (2002). Truth and consequences on the reservation. *Los Angeles Times Magazine,* 7 July.

Kizer, W. (n.d.) History of the Flandreau Indian School, Flandreau, South Dakota. MA Thesis, University of South Dakota.

LaFarge, O. (1935). Revolution with reservations. *New Republic,* 9 October.

Leland, J. (1976). *Firewater myths: North American Indian drinking and alcohol addiction.* New Brunswick: Rutgers University Center for Alcohol Studies, No. 11.

Lemkin, R. (1944). *Axis rule in occupied Europe: Laws of occupation, analysis of government, proposals for redress.* Washington, DC: Carnegie Endowment for International Peace.

Leupp, F.E. (1910). *The Indian and his problem.* New York: Scribner's.

Lifton, R.J., and Markusen, E. (1988). *The genocidal mentality: Nazi holocaust and nuclear threat*. New York: Basic Books.

McBeth, S.J. (1983). *Ethnic identity and the boarding school experience of West-Central Oklahoma Indians*. Washington, DC: University Press of America.

Maracle, B. (1993). *Crazywater: Native voices on addiction and recovery*. New York: Penguin.

Meriam, L., et al. (1928). *The problem of Indian administration*. Baltimore: Johns Hopkins University Press.

Miller, J.R. (1996). *Shingwauk's vision: A history of the Indian residential schools*. Toronto: University of Toronto Press.

Milloy, J.S. (1999). '*A national crime': The Canadian government and the residential school system, 1879 to 1986*. Winnipeg: University of Manitoba Press.

Millward, M. (1992). Clean behind the ears: Micmac parents, Micmac children, and the Shubenacadie residential school. *New Maritimes*, March–April.

Murphy, J. (1911). Health problems of the Indians. *Annals of the Academy of Political Science*, no. 37 (March).

Nock, D.A. (1988). *A Victorian missionary and Canadian Indian policy: Cultural synthesis vs. cultural replacement*. Waterloo, ON: Wilfred Laurier University Press.

Pratt, R.H. (1895). The advantages of mingling Indians with Whites. *Proceedings and Addresses of the National Education Association, 1895*. Washington, DC: National Educational Association.

Price, A.G. (1949). *White settlers and native peoples*. Cambridge: Cambridge University Press.

Putney, D. (1980). Fighting the scourge: American Indian morbidity and federal policy, 1897–1928. Doctoral dissertation, Marquette University.

Sartre, J.-P. (2001a). Colonialism is a system. In J.-P. Sartre, *Colonialism and neocolonialism*. New York: Routledge.

———— (2001b). A victory. In J.-P. Sartre, *Colonialism and neocolonialism*. New York: Routledge.

———— (1968). On genocide. In J.-P. Sartre and A.E.K. Sartre, *On genocide and a summary of the evidence and the judgments of the International War Crimes Tribunal*. Boston: Beacon Press.

Scott, D.C. (1913). Indian affairs, 1867–1912. In A. Shortt and A.G. Doughty, eds., *Canada and its provinces*. Toronto: University of Edinburgh Press.

Sekaquaptewa, H., as told to Udall, L. (1962). *Me and mine: The life story of Helen Sekaquaptewa*. Tucson: University of Arizona Press.

Shkilnyk, A.M. (1985). *A poison stronger than love: The destruction of an Ojibwa community*. New Haven, CT: Yale University Press.

Simes, A.B. (1944). To Dir. of Indian Affairs. H. McGill, 19 October (N.A.C. RG 10, Vol. 6262, File 578–1 (4–5), MR C 8653) (The Simes Report).

Smith, R.W., Markusen, E., and Lifton, R.J. (1995). Professional ethics and the denial of the Armenian genocide. *Holocaust and Genocide Studies*, 9.

Stannard, D.E. (1996). Uniqueness as denial: The politics of Holocaust scholarship. In A.S. Rosenberg, ed., *Is the Holocaust unique? Perspectives on comparative genocide*, 163–208. Boulder, CO: Westview Press.

Stearn, E.W., and Stearn, A.E. (1945). *The effects of smallpox on the destiny of the Amerindian*. Boston: Bruce Humphries.

Strentz, T. (1982). The Stockholm syndrome: Law enforcement policy and victim behavior. In F.M. Ochberg and D.A. Soskis, eds., *Victims of terrorism*. Boulder, CO: Westview Press.

Strickland, R. (1997). *Tonto's revenge: Reflections on American Indian culture and policy.* Albuquerque: University of New Mexico Press.

———— (1991). Indian law and the miner's canary: The signs of poison gas. *Cleveland State Law Review* 39: 486–9.

Svaldi, D. (1989). *Sand Creek and the rhetoric of extermination: A case study in Indian–White relations.* Lanham, MD: University Press of America.

Symonds, M. (1982). Victim responses to terror: Understanding and treatment. In F.M. Ochberg and D.A. Soskis, eds, *Victims of terrorism.* Boulder, CO: Westview Press.

Szasz, M.C. (1999). *Education and the American Indian: The road to self-determination since 1928.* Albuquerque: University of New Mexico Press, 3rd edition.

Tennert, R.A., Jr. (1988). *The Phoenix Indian school: Forced assimilation in Arizona, 1891– 1935.* Norman: University of Oklahoma Press.

Titley, E.B. (1986). *A narrow vision: Duncan Campbell Scott and the administration of Indian affairs in Canada.* Vancouver: University of British Columbia Press.

Westermeyer, J. (1974). The drunken Indian: Myths and realities. *Psychiatric Annals* 4.

Wilbur, R.L., and DuPuy, W. (1931). *Conservation in the Department of Interior.* Washington, DC: US Dept of Interior.

Wood, R. (1980). Health problems facing American Indian women. Conference on the Educational and Occupational Needs of American Indian Women, October 1976. Washington, DC: US Dept of Education, Office of Educational Research and Improvement.

York, G. (1992). *The dispossessed: Life and death in native Canada.* Boston: Little, Brown.

# 5

# The Allies in World War II:
# The Anglo-American Bombardment
# of German Cities

## Eric Langenbacher

One of the most serious ethical dilemmas in modern warfare is the tension between *jus ad bellum* (just war) and *jus in bello* (justice in war) (Walzer, 1977: 21). Are any means justified in fighting a just war? What are legitimate targets in total or unconventional wars, where the distinction between combatant and civilian is blurred and where the entire economy and social life of an enemy power support its ability to fight and perpetrate crimes? Although such questions arise repeatedly in places like Vietnam, Afghanistan, and the Middle East, they continue to be posed most clearly in the bloodiest war of human history, World War II.

At a general level, however, there are no such dilemmas. In the European theater of that conflagration, the Nazi regime in Germany was a severe threat to all of the values democracies hold dear. It began the hostilities through naked aggression and conducted the war with unprecedented viciousness. Numerous soldiers, members of the party and its affiliated organizations (such as the SS and Gestapo), and many ordinary Germans planned and committed crimes against peace, war crimes and, above all, crimes against humanity, epitomized by the Holocaust (Bartov, 1991). Since the cessation of hostilities, the criminal nature of the regime, its wars, and the genocide it perpetrated have been assiduously documented, and unprecedented efforts were made to hold the criminals responsible, most notably at the Nuremberg Trials (Marrus, 1997). In the face of the Nazi evil, the justice of the Allied side in the struggle against the Third Reich and the necessity of defeating Nazism were and are beyond dispute: this was a quintessentially just war. The difficulty of the military effort is also undeniable, given the resources and power of the enemy and the brutality of the Nazi conduct of this 'total' war.

Given the overwhelming justice of the Allied side, relatively little attention has been devoted to the conduct and the actions of the Allies during the hostilities – that is, whether the means used to defeat Hitler's Germany were also just. A review of the historical record shows that neither the actual combat practice of the Western Allies in battle against the Wehrmacht, nor their treatment of prisoners of war, was questionable. Moreover, the Western occupation regime after 1945 was a paragon of restraint, generosity, and wisdom. What remains very much open to question, however, are the actions undertaken against German civilians during the war itself, specifically the aerial bombardment of Germany by the American (AAF) and British (RAF) Air Forces.[1]

This chapter explores the campaign of strategic, area, carpet or terror bombing against German cities and civilians between 1942 and 1945, with the intention of determining whether these actions were crimes of war. Such an assessment illuminates the fundamental questions of whether any means, even unjust ones, are acceptable in pursuit of a just end. I argue that these questions are still of utmost importance, because the very values and laws so central to the self-image of democracies, and which the West successfully defended against the Nazi threat, can be undermined and delegitimized if unethical or illegal acts are left unstudied, unacknowledged, and unpunished. I conclude by showing that many in the West acknowledged that excesses had been committed, and that the generous postwar policies toward Germany can be partly explained as an informal way to provide a form of redress and to make amends.

## Effects and effectiveness

To examine whether the aerial bombardment of cities was a crime of war, the material effects of the actions need to be investigated, as well as their intent, the questionable legal/ethical nature of the deeds, and knowledge of the consequences on the part of the relevant actors.[2]

The effects are clear and undisputed. By the end of the war in 1945, every large and medium-sized German city, as well as many smaller ones, had been destroyed or badly damaged by the Allied strategic-bombing offensive. Overall, 2.7 million tons of bombs were dropped, destroying 3.6 million homes (20 per cent of the country's total), leaving 7.5 million homeless (Kurowski, 1977: 356; USSBS, 1945: 1). Altogether, about 43 per cent of housing in the 61 cities with over 100,000 inhabitants (comprising 25 million people, or 32 per cent of the total population) and 50 per cent of the built-up area were completely destroyed. A further significant proportion of housing was damaged to various degrees (Kurowski, 1995: 204; USSBS, 1945: 72).

The most notable individual raids started with the 'Thousand Bomber Raid' against Cologne in 1942 that, in combination with other raids, destroyed 69.9 per cent of that city's housing (Sorge, 1986: 90). 'Operation Gomorrah' obliterated Hamburg in 1943, burning out 6 square miles of the city's core, destroying 49.2 per cent of housing, and damaging a further 30 per cent (Rumpf, 1963: 81; Diedendorf, 1993: 11; Markusen and Kopf, 1995: 158). Countless attacks on Berlin, the heaviest of which were the Battle of Berlin between November 1943 and March 1944 and 'Operation Thunderclap' in February 1945, annihilated 6,300 acres of the built-up area with 45,000 tons of bombs (Crane, 1993: 106–7; Rumpf, 1963: 125). Berlin lost about 40 per cent of its housing and the center of the city was over 70 per cent destroyed. The last great raid was the firebombing of Dresden in February 1945, which has become emblematic in postwar historical consciousness of the strategic-bombing offensive and the horrors of war (Schaffer, 1985: 97; see also Kurowski, 1995; Markusen and Kopf, 1995; Naumann, 1998). In other large cities, the percentage of housing completely lost ranged from 66 per cent in Dortmund and 50 per cent in Hanover to about 30 per cent in Munich (Kurowski, 1995: 204). Smaller cities were similarly affected, with overall destruction amounting to 89 per cent in Würzburg, 75 per cent in Wuppertal, and 83 per cent in Remscheid.[3] The loss of life was substantial. Estimates of deaths range from about 300,000 (USSBS, 1945: 1, 72) to 600,000 (Levine, 1992: 190; Rumpf, 1963: 162–4), and of injuries from 600,000 to over a million (Diedendorf, 1993: 11). The most lethal single raids were Hamburg and Dresden, with about 35,000 deaths each, and the 'Thunderclap' raid of 3 February 1945 on Berlin, which caused 25,000 deaths.[4]

Several other characteristics of the raids stand out. First, most of the destruction of German cities was to the central core, the most highly built-up areas and densely populated residential districts. Almost all historic buildings, including churches, former palaces, city halls and opera houses, and much of the social infrastructure like schools, universities, hospitals and stores were destroyed or greatly damaged.[5] Suburban and industrial areas were not as comprehensively damaged. The postwar United States Strategic Bombing Survey substantiates this, noting that 24 per cent of the total tonnage of bombs was dropped on residential or commercial parts of cities, 'almost twice the weight of bombs launched against all manufacturing targets together' (USSBS, 1945: 71). On the British side, approximately 75 per cent of the bombs dropped between early 1942 and 1945 were dropped in area raids (Garrett, 1993: 11–12). Second, most of the civilian victims were women, infants, and elderly people. Rumpf shows that for every 100 male casualties, there were 160 female casualties in Hamburg, 181 in Darmstadt, 136 in Kassel and 122 in Nuremberg (1963:

160). About 19 per cent of the victims were children under the age of 16, 5 per cent of whom were babies and children below school age, and about 20 per cent of the casualties were over the age of 60 (Rumpf, 1963: 161).[6] These groups suffered disproportionately because most adult males were away serving with the armed services or Nazi party organizations, and many adult women were working in factories (well defended and often not the main targets of attack). Adolescents and young adults were largely evacuated to rural or 'safe' urban areas, constituting a large portion of the approximately 6 million urban dwellers relocated as a response to the bombing campaign (Groehler, 1988: 292). Third, despite the destructive raids on Cologne and Hamburg earlier in the war, the vast majority of damage was inflicted at the very end of the conflict. Some 72 per cent of American bombs were dropped in the last ten months of the war (after 1 July 1944), that is to say, after the Luftwaffe was defeated (April 1944) and as the German armies were collapsing on all fronts (Werrell, 1986: 711).[7]

Already during the war, and continuing ever since, there has been intense debate over whether bombing was effective in weakening the Nazi German ability to fight and thus hastening the end of the war. Speaking for most scholars, Werrell (1986: 712) notes that 'it neither broke German morale nor deprived the German military of needed weapons.' Such sober views were shared by the official assessments of the Western Allies themselves. The United States Strategic Bombing Survey shows that German losses as a percentage of annual production were 2.5 per cent in 1942, 9 per cent in 1943, 17 per cent in 1944 and 19.5 per cent (at an annualized rate) in 1945 (USSBS, 1945: 74). However, total production increased until and peaked in 1944, revealing an underestimation of the German war economy's ability to increase production and divert resources from other non-essential areas.[8] Interestingly, 'throughout the period the losses inflicted by area attacks fell mostly on industries relatively unessential to the war effort' (74), mainly the consumer goods sector.[9] Moreover, civilian morale was not greatly affected. Instead of producing resistance to Hitler or a desire for peace, the most the bombing did was to destroy active enthusiasm for the regime and create apathetic, but not necessarily unproductive, workers (95–8). The amount of bombs dropped, and the extent of damage, actually produced diminishing returns, with inhabitants of the most bombed cities proving the least willing to surrender (96).

Others like Overy (1986) disagree, asserting that air power was a major component of the overall Allied strategy and success, and that it was more effective than is usually thought.[10] By 1944, the Germans were forced to divert substantial resources to fight the bombing, including 2 million soldiers and civilians engaged in air defense, 30 per cent of total gun output, and 20 per cent of heavy ammunition (122). Furthermore, despite the increase in production until 1944,

> Bombing placed a ceiling on German war production ... the amount of war material that Germany might have been able to produce for the crucial battles of 1944 and 1945 without bombing would have meant a longer and far more costly battle for the final defeat of fascism, and might have made necessary the use of atomic weapons in Europe as well. (123, 125)

However, he concludes that overall:

> Bombing was much more successful in interrupting production and bringing the military machine to a halt than in carrying out those tasks of terror and intimidation so publicized in the prewar period.... Despite the horror of bombing and the way in which it imposed a widespread and direct involvement in the war, the ordeal remained subsidiary to the contest over economic and military power with which the air war was primarily concerned. In terms of the effects of bomb destruction on the course of the war, it was the destruction of industrial resources, including labor, that determined a country's ability to continue the war, not the dislocation of community life itself ... such destruction (in Germany) became in Portal's unfortunate phrase, 'incidental.' (208)

John Keegan, referring to the campaign as terror bombing (as did Churchill shortly after the Dresden raid), concludes simply: 'it did not work' (Keegan, 1995: 27; see also Messerschmidt, 1988: 300).[11] In fact, most authors argue that precision attacks against military transportation or communication targets were much more important in weakening and defeating the enemy. More specifically, the campaign against German oil supplies and refineries (possible in late 1944, but not pursued until early 1945) is singled out as the crucial factor in shortening the war (Werrell, 1986; Levine, 1992).[12] Some authors go further, arguing that these policies, especially when continued after technological advances made alternatives possible, actually prolonged the war.[13] Levine (1992: 195) suggests that the British 'obsession with area attacks let oil production recover in the fall (of 1944) and probably prolonged the war into 1945.' He forcefully concludes that the air war did not 'measurably reduce the time it took to defeat the German armies in Europe' (192). Even the USSBS admits that the bombing produced highly effective fodder for Nazi propaganda, and may have actually created a greater sense of solidarity and desire to fight until the end.[14] Finally, many have speculated about the possible result if the massive resources devoted to indiscriminate strategic bombing had been invested elsewhere, such as in developing an effective fighter plane that could have accompanied precision-bombing missions much earlier in the war. Thus, it is questionable whether this lethal means actually shortened the war or decisively weakened the Nazi German war effort.

## Intent, international law and recognition

Even though the amount of destruction and number of civilian victims indicate explicit targeting, it remains possible that this was simply 'collateral damage' as a result of the bombing of legitimate military and economic targets.[15] This was not the case, particularly on the British side. The RAF started the war espousing a doctrine of precision attacks against military targets and for several years largely followed it. However, as a consequence of the 'erosion of mutual restraint' (Markusen and Kopf, 1995: 153),[16] in response to German attacks on Britain (the Battle of Britain, the London Blitz), as well as the heavy losses the air force encountered when attacking German targets, the policy was reappraised. By February 1942,[17] military and political leaders adopted a policy of area attacks conducted at night, and the shift was formalized by the appointment of Sir Arthur ('Bomber') Harris as head of the RAF Bomber Command. At the time, Churchill stated: 'the civilian population around the target areas must be made to feel the weight of war,' and even earlier, he thought defeating Hitler was possible only through 'an absolutely devastating, exterminating attack ... upon the Nazi homeland' (Garrett, 1993: 11). Sir Charles Portal, the Chief of Air Staff, provided detailed instructions regarding the new emphasis on targeting civilian morale and 'dehousing' German workers: 'the aiming points are to be built-up areas, not, for instance the dockyards or aircraft factories' (Garrett, 1993; see also Markusen and Kopf, 1995: 156).[18] Harris, who vehemently pursued area bombing until the very end of the war, deemed the latter to be 'panacea targets' and directed his crews to avoid them, even when ordered to attack them. The tactics employed included the use of incendiary bombs to create unmanageable fires (Hamburg, Dresden); waves of raids explicitly aimed at hitting fire and rescue crews responding to the first attacks; and later, when possible, low-level flights to strafe survivors and rescue crews. In late 1943, Harris summarized the aim of the campaign as 'the destruction of German cities, the killing of German workers and the disruption of civilized life throughout Germany' (Garrett, 1993: 33).

American policy and intent were more complicated. Until the end of the war, the official bombing doctrine espoused precision bombing, by day and at lower altitudes, of legitimate military targets. 'The primary purpose of American air power would be to disintegrate the enemy society by striking the most vital points in the web, such as oil refineries and power stations' (Schaffer, 1980: 320). Actual practice for most of the war corresponded to this rhetoric; what Werrell calls a surgical method stood in contrast to the British sledgehammer policy (705). Indeed, the AAF successfully resisted British pressure to shift to a coordinated policy of area attacks, notably at the Casablanca Conference of January 1943. American pressure led to the resulting 'Combined Bomber Offensive,' mandating 'the progressive destruction and dislocation of the German military, industrial and economic system, and the undermining of the morale of the German people to a point where their capacity for armed resistance is fatally weakened' (Levine, 1992: 77). At the time, AAF General Arnold called this 'a major victory, for we would bomb in accordance with American principles using methods for which our planes were designed' (Schaffer, 1985: 38).

Nevertheless, the precision-bombing doctrine eroded precipitously, and reality moved much closer to the British practice towards the end of the war. For example, in late 1943 the AAF began 'blind bombing' using radar to find targets. These inexact methods accounted for 80 per cent of American raids by the end of 1944, and 'depended for effectiveness upon drenching an area with bombs' (Markusen and Kopf, 1995: 167). Moreover, in the last months of the war, civilian morale was explicitly targeted, especially in the Clarion campaign against small towns and rural areas – even if only transportation facilities were officially targeted (Schaffer, 1980: 327). Finally, the famous Thunderclap operation explicitly attacked the working-class residential districts of Kreuzberg and Wedding in Berlin. Many argue that by this stage of the war there was little concern about the ethics of bombing. 'As their willingness to consider Thunderclap suggests, the Americans did not always inflexibly oppose area attacks, or bombing to undermine civilian morale, or even operations specifically aimed at killing civilians outright' (Levine, 1992: 176).[19] Schaffer concludes that there was a major difference between on-the-record policy, meant for domestic audiences (who presumably would have recoiled from indiscriminate bombing) and for posterity, and actual understanding and practice. Moreover, 'whatever restraints there were did not arise out of the consciences of the men who ran the AAF, for the record provides no indication that they objected on moral grounds ... they were expressing not personal repugnance to the bombing of non-combatants, but apprehension over the way others would regard the actions of the AAF' (Schaffer, 1980: 333).[20]

It is clear that civilians and cities were explicitly targeted, but was this acceptable conduct of war, given the international laws and conventions in force at the time? Again, experts are divided, given the novelty of the technology and the problematic status of civilians as non-combatants in modern wars. Groehler, for one, writes: 'the fact that strategic air raids were contrary to international law of the time is undisputed, and was also not denied in legal expert opinions sought internationally by the Royal Air Force, whose leadership, therefore, went to great lengths until late

1945 to conceal the true nature of the bombing campaign' (1992: 292). Messerschmidt notes that there was no specific ban, but argues that other conventions and agreements defined the practice as clearly unethical and illegal. In addition to certain relevant provisions in the Geneva Conventions of 1864, 1906, and 1929, banning (for example) attacks on enemy medical facilities or personnel engaged in search and rescue (Pictet, 1952: 14–15),[21] the most pertinent precedents include Articles 23 and 25 of the Hague Rules of Air Warfare from 1907. Article 23 states: 'aerial bombard-ment for the purpose of terrorizing the civilian population or destroying or damaging private property not of a military character, or of injuring non-combatants is prohibited' (Messerschmidt, 1992: 300). Article 25 proclaims: 'the attack or bombardment, by whatever means, of towns, villages, dwellings, or buildings which are undefended is prohibited' (324–5). The 1907 rules were never ratified, and other efforts in the 1920s and 1930s came to naught.[22] When war broke out in 1939, a murky legal situation pertained. Nevertheless,

> If it is possible to summarize the law of war as it existed at that time it could be reduced to two principles: a) indiscriminate (intentional) attack on the civilian population as such was prohibited; b) a legitimate military objective could be attacked wherever located so long as ordinary care was exercised in its attack ... collateral civilian casualties were not the concern of the attacker, but by state practice were regarded as an inevitable consequence of bombardment and a legitimate way to destroy an enemy's will to resist. (339)

What did leaders of belligerent nations think at the time? Messerschmidt shows (1992: 301) that 'the most important air powers in the European theatre of the Second World War assumed that there was a binding code for the conduct of the air war.' Both the British and American governments admitted as much at the outbreak of hostilities. In 1939, Chamberlain suggested three rules to govern bombing: that it was against international law to bomb civilians, that targets must be legitimate military targets, and that they must be capable of identification. These propositions were issued as guidelines to Bomber Command in 1938, and were even adopted as a non-binding League of Nations resolution (Garrett, 1993: 28–9; Hays Parks, 1992: 345). On the American side, Roosevelt proclaimed on 1 September 1939:

> I am ... addressing this urgent brief to every government which may be engaged in hostilities publicly to affirm its determination that its armed forces shall in no event, and under no circumstances, undertake the bombardment from the air of civilian populations or of unfortified cities. (Hays Parks, 1992: 345)

Garret (1993: 28) agrees that there was no formal ban on area bomb-ing, but contends that a war convention was in effect that 'the British government prior to World War Two seemed clearly to accept.' Hays Parks concludes that a legal vacuum existed, which was, however, not total: 'all nations agreed for humanitarian and utilitarian purposes that indiscriminate bombardment ... was prohibited' (Hays Parks, 1992: 352). In sum, explicit international laws were somewhat vague, but the 'war convention' (Walzer, 1977) clearly outlawed such practices, a position that almost all of the relevant military and political leaders – even Hitler – accepted.

## Ethics, conscience and recognition

It is already clear that the questionable legal and ethical nature of the bombing campaign against German cities was recognized by wartime policymakers. The very fact that the RAF and AAF disagreed over the practices is further evidence that these leaders knew it was wrong. On the American side, 'Spaatz (an AAF commander) repeatedly "raised the moral issue" involved in bombing enemy civilians,' while another high-level leader, Eaker, went so far as to state that 'we should never allow the history of this war to convict us of throwing the strategic bomber at the man in the street' (Schaffer, 1980: 318). When precision-bombing doctrines were being jettisoned in early 1945, another general characterized the raids as 'homicide and destruction' (Shaffer, 1985: 100).

There was also intense disagreement and debate in Britain among branches of the armed forces, within the political establishment, and among the general public. The writer Vera Brittain compared the bombings to Nazi treatment of prisoners in concentration camps; her voice was an isolated one, but not unique. A Labour MP publicly acknowledged the policy, stating in the House of Commons that 'no apologies are now offered for the indiscriminate bombing of women and children' (Garrett, 1993: 117). Many religious leaders also voiced concern. The Bishop of Chichester, for example, noted that 'the allies stand for something greater than power. The chief name inscribed on our banner is law' (Garrett, 1993: 113). Even Liddell Hart, a military historian who had defended strategic bombing earlier, came to oppose it, proclaiming: 'it will be ironical if the defenders of civilization depend for victory upon the most barbaric, and unskilled, way of winning a war' (Garrett, 1993: 105). Churchill, too, was well aware of what was being done. In 1935, he wrote: 'it is only in the 20th century that this hateful condition of inducing nations to surrender by massacring women and children has gained acceptance' (quoted in Garrett, 1993: 44). Yet during the war, he argued: 'it is absurd to consider morality on this topic ... In the last war the bombing of open cities was regarded as forbidden. Now everybody does it as a matter of course. It is simply a question of fashion changing as she does between long and short skirts for women' (Garrett, 1993: 45).[23]

There are additional pieces of evidence. The Americans and especially the British deceived their publics about the true nature of the policy, instructing military and political authorities to publicly (and sometimes even privately) proclaim the precision-bombing doctrine, even when presented with evidence to the contrary. Churchill's famous minute after the Dresden raid is illuminating: 'It seems to me that the moment has come when the question of bombing German cities simply for the sake of increasing the terror, though under other pretexts, should be reviewed ... the destruction of Dresden remains a serious query against the conduct of Allied bombing' (Walzer, 1977: 261). In fact, almost all defenses implicitly admit to the dubious legal and ethical nature of the policy. The 'supreme emergency,' which clearly obtained in 1940–41, had largely receded by 1944, when the bombing campaign peaked (261). This justification accepts the existence of rules, but argues that life-threatening circumstances warrant overriding them. Both the 'sliding scale' argument, 'the more justice the more right' (Walzer, 1977: 229), and what Markusen and Kopf call the 'healing–killing paradox' that 'efficient brutality hastens the end' (Markusen and Kopf, 1995: 201–90) assert that an unjust means is justified by the clear higher good of winning the just war. The injustice of the act used to achieve this end is admitted. Of course, as I argued above, whether the campaign hastened the end of the war is highly questionable, an issue raised by intelligence during the hostilities themselves (Webster and Frankland, 1961). Even the more general problematizing of the civilian–combatant distinction in modern total war revolves around how a civilian is to be defined, not the issue of whether persecuting or killing civilians is justified.[24] 'The just war tradition condemns indiscriminate bombing; the dilemma over the past century has been in identifying the line where military actions cease being permissible and become indiscriminate' (Hays Parks, 1992: 313). But the line still exists. Finally, the argument that the bombing campaign saved Allied lives, deployed even more readily to justify the attacks on Japan, is unacceptable. 'Neither the dropping of the atomic bombs nor the area bombardment of cities were a military necessity as defined in the rules of international law ... the end result of this strategy is the large-scale killing of non-combatants to spare soldiers. None of the above mentioned rules and provisions of international law permit such actions' (Messerschmidt, 1992: 306–7).

In retrospect, there was a rather clear, if unofficial, acknowledgment that the campaign was at least highly questionable. After issuing his minute on the firebombing of Dresden, Churchill, like other postwar leaders, consciously distanced himself from the strategic-bombing policy. It is germane that at the Nuremberg Trials, no Nazi or German was ever charged with crimes resulting from aerial bombardment. This was not because the Allies did not consider these acts to be crimes (see below), but because they did not want to attract criticism to their own policies.[25] More generally, in a process that Walzer (1977: 323) calls 'the dishonoring of Arthur Harris,' the head of Bomber Command was not promptly honored along with other wartime leaders. He was granted a baronetcy (not a peerage) only in 1953, when Churchill returned to power. Later, a leading military journal refused to review his memoirs, and the official history, highly critical toward him, declined to interview him.[26] Indeed, the history wrote that 'there had never been anything like the destruction produced in Germany by the area offensive of this period. The bomber crews themselves could see the holocausts of fire' (Webster and Frankland, 1961: 244). Westminster Abbey has no plaque to commemorate the casualties of Bomber Command (in contrast to the one for Fighter Command), and a statue to Harris was erected in London only in May 1992, by a private group of war veterans (the Bomber Command Association). That unveiling was highly contested at the time, with protests in Britain and Germany and highly critical coverage in the British press. The *Guardian*, for example, referred to the ceremony as 'the most acute diplomatic embarrassment of the past 12 years of international commemoration of the second world war,' and referred to the underlying issues as 'the longest-running controversy since the war ended' (Ezard, 1992). The mayor of Dresden spoke for most Germans when he stated that 'Nobody in history has ever erected a memorial to a hangman' (Weaver, 1992).

This lingering 'bad conscience,' and the desire to make amends, have been particularly evident in the postwar period in the case of the destruction of Dresden. Almost all discussions of the bombing campaign focus on the destruction of that city, which is widely recognized as a deplorable excess. 'Should Britain apologize for Dresden? The answer has to be yes, simply because it happened' (*Guardian*, 1995). The fiftieth anniversary of Dresden's destruction, in 1995, was the occasion of much soul-searching, and of ecumenical services aimed at reconciliation and atonement. Private organizations like the Dresden Trust are devoted to rebuilding the city (Clayton and Russell, 1999), and the British government even donated a new orb and cross to crown the reconstructed Frauenkirche (Church of Our Lady) when it is completed in 2006. There has been less soul-searching on the American side, but then the allegations against the AAF were never as far-reaching as those leveled against the RAF, at least with regard to the bombing of Germany. Nevertheless, in his examination of the controversy over the Smithsonian's Enola Gay exhibition in 1995, Kohn (1995) notes that air force veterans have felt slighted ever since the war, being incessantly criticized by 'liberal' pacifists. Like the British crews, they are also comparatively less well memorialized in Washington, DC. Finally, it can be argued that the generous postwar policies of the Western Allies, including the Marshall Plan and the rapid integration of the defeated enemy into West European and Atlanticist organizations, constituted a tacit recognition of the excesses that took place, and an indirect form of compensation and redress.

## Conclusion: was it a war crime?

Article 6(c) of the Charter of the International Military Tribunal at Nuremberg defines a war crime as

> violations of the laws or customs of war. Such violations shall include, but are not limited to, murder, ill-treatment or deportation to slave labor or for any other purpose of civilian population of or in occupied territory, murder or ill-treatment of prisoners of war or persons on the seas, killing of hostages, plunder or public or private property, wanton destruction of cities, towns or villages, or devastation not justified by military necessity. (United Nations, 1949, 93)

Was the Anglo-American bombing of Germany such a crime? The term is highly evocative, so a review of the facts is necessary before an assessment can be made. German cities were extensively destroyed during the war, and a minimum of 300,000 civilians, disproportionately women, children and the elderly, perished as a result of area bombing raids. Although most of these cities had some industry, the vast majority of destruction was to housing, historic buildings and social infrastructure. Such destruction was not 'collateral damage,' but was the result of explicit policies aimed at destroying civilian morale and lives, especially on the part of the British, but also by the Americans in the last months of the war. International law did not explicitly ban such policies, but many precedents and conventions pointed to the practice as being unacceptable. Moreover, numerous statements by Allied leaders revealed a clear recognition of the illegality of bombing civilians. Intensive efforts were made throughout the war to deceive the public (and other military leaders) regarding the true nature of the campaign. All of the possible attenuating circumstances that authors and policymakers cite in trying to justify the campaign implicitly admit to the illegality of the policy. It is also highly uncertain (and was at the time) that the policy hastened the end of the war. In the postwar period, recognition of excesses was apparent if unofficial, as exemplified by the treatment of Arthur Harris and a general guilty conscience, especially towards the destruction of Dresden.

Clearly, the aerial bombardment of German cities during World War II was a violation of international law, military ethics, and war convention. Walzer (1977: 261) concludes that 'the greater number by far of the German civilians killed by terror bombing were killed without moral (and probably also without military) reason.' Thus, especially on the British side, aerial bombardment was a crime of war, as defined above.[27] The wartime British military leaders – Harris, Portal, and even Churchill – were clearly responsible for the policy, and a good case could have been made against these men in the postwar period, if the political will had existed to mount prosecutions. Of course, there are many good reasons why this political will was lacking: these men, had, after all contributed to the necessary and just defeat of Nazism.

If anything good resulted from the carnage of the Second World War, it was the reaffirmation of the values of human and civil rights, freedom, and the rule of law that are fundamental to democracies. Moreover, the development of a corpus of international law that defined war crimes and crimes against humanity, and that established procedures to hold those guilty responsible, was a major step towards internationalizing these fundamental values. These values are universal, and are underpinned by non-arbitrary, equal, and fair applicability and implementation; they are undermined whenever they are not applied in such a fashion. Even-handed fidelity to these principles is necessary if we are not to destroy the principles themselves. This is the biggest supporting argument for prosecuting, or at least denouncing, the men responsible for orchestrating the aerial bombardment of German cities.

Finally, to return to the more general issue I began with – the dilemma of unjust means being used for a just end – democracy's representatives and defenders cannot advance such an argument if they truly seek to defend the values that define democracy. As the Marquess of Salisbury wrote during the war: 'Of course the Germans began it, but we do not take the devil as our example' (quoted in Ezard, 1992: 21). Lewis Mumford (1959: 39) was even clearer. He talked about the 'moral debacle' when

> both the United States and Britain adopted what was politely called 'obliteration bombing' ... these democratic governments sanctioned the dehumanized techniques of fascism. This was Nazidom's firmest victory and democracy's most servile surrender. That moral reversal undermined the eventual military triumph of the democracies.

Prosecuting the leaders who planned and implemented these policies over fifty years ago is impossible. Recognizing the crimes, and the need to prosecute their perpetrators, as fundamental to sustaining democratic values is not.

# Notes

1. I do not examine the possible crimes that the Soviet Union and Red Army perpetrated, including the mistreatment and murder of German prisoners of war, or the ethnic cleansing of Germans from Eastern Europe and the former eastern territories of the country, which included up to 2 million murders and tens of thousands of rapes.

2. I focus solely on Western policymakers and wartime military leaders and do not examine the role or responsibility of the actual soldiers, the bombing crews. Many of the same arguments made regarding German perpetrators of war crimes and crimes against humanity surface here, such as the wartime necessity of obeying orders and the (perceived) lack of choice. Garrett (1993: 75–85) discusses this dimension and argues that many crew members knew what they were doing and had ethical and moral difficulties carrying out the bombings.

3. Mention should also be made of the destruction of the German East as the Red Army advanced. Cities like Königsberg, Stettin and Breslau were literally obliterated, due to bombing, shelling and actual battle.

4. To contextualize these figures, the American bombing of Japan resulted in between 330,000 and 900,000 deaths and between 475,000 and 1,300,000 injuries, including 80–100,000 in the firebombing of Tokyo and 140,000 in the nuclear attack on Hiroshima. About 43 per cent of the built-up area of the major cities was destroyed (Schaffer, 1985: 148; Markusen and Kopf, 1995: 178–82; see also Dower, 1986). The Luftwaffe's bombing of Britain, including the London Blitz, and the Anglo-American bombing of France before the liberation resulted in about 60,000 deaths each (Kurowski, 1977: 356). The resources expended by the Allies in these campaigns were substantial. Combined, the USAF and the RAF lost 158,000 personnel and 21,914 bombers (USSBS, 1945: 1). Werrell (1986: 707) estimates that 40–50 per cent of the British war effort was devoted to the Royal Air Force (RAF) and as much as 30 per cent into the bombing offensive alone. The United States spent about 25 per cent of its total war-related expenditures on aviation, with some estimates ranging as high as 35 to 40 per cent.

5. Transportation (especially rail) and public utilities like electricity were also hit, which greatly affected civilian life. Nevertheless, these are legitimate and justifiable military targets.

6. Mention should also be made of the foreign slave laborers who were used in many factories, especially during the later phases of the war, many of whom also fell victim to the bombing. In addition, thousands of Allied prisoners of war died in the raids, the most notable example being Dresden.

7. Some authors argue that this is an exaggeration of the actual state of battle. The German defeat was not as rapid or as preordained as commonly thought. Fighting was fierce in Belgium (the Battle of the Bulge), and the Allies made various military 'errors' in the Low Countries (Macksey, 1987). Levine (1992: 176) writes: 'As the Ardennes offensive ended, there was intense gloom among the Western Allied leaders. It was not seen as a last-gasp effort but as evidence that the enemy was still strong. They feared the enemy would succeed in putting large numbers of jets and new-type submarines into action.' Neillands (2001: 382–405) notes that the Rhine had still not been crossed by the time of the Dresden raid in February 1945. This is to say, Allied leaders did not have the benefit of hindsight, and it was not clear until relatively late that the Nazi regime was utterly defeated.

8. The German ability to increase manpower by employing otherwise economically inactive segments of the population and slave labor were similarly overlooked. Most bombed cities needed between one month (Bremen) and five months (Hamburg)

to return to 80 per cent capacity, a much shorter time than predicted.

9. A similar set of conclusions emerged for the Royal Air Force (Webster and Frankland, 1961: 268).

10. Many Nazi leaders similarly disagreed with these Allied views. Albert Speer, the minister for armaments and munitions production, repeatedly singled out the bombing campaign as 'the greatest lost battle on the German side' and the 'cause of all our setbacks' (Neillands, 2001: 384).

11. Most authors conclude the opposite in the case of the bombing, conventional and nuclear, of Japan. Overy (1986: 126) writes: 'The "knockout blow," in all its horror and inhumanity, finally proved its point.' In general, 'Air power was more effective in the Far East than in the European theater' (100).

12. Macksey (1987: 177–8) highlights the little-known mining and blocking of the Danube river between April and September 1944, which halved oil deliveries from Romania at a minimal cost.

13. Early raids (which actually started on 4 September 1939) were exceedingly costly, given technological limitations and strong German defenses. There was no effective alternative to indiscriminate night bombing before 1943, short of not bombing at all. There have been several justifications for the decision to pursue this course of action, including bolstering British morale on the home front, fighting Nazism by the only means possible at the time, and providing a kind of second front years before an actual land invasion was possible.

14. Macksey (1987: 165) makes a similar point regarding Roosevelt's inopportune declaration of the unconditional-surrender policy. He also argues that a fundamental flaw of the area-bombing doctrine was that it did not take British experience during the Blitz into consideration, or exaggerated leading Nazis' apocalyptic responses to early raids such as Hamburg (168).

15. Several qualifications are necessary. Military operations in frontline sieges or battles caused some of the damage to the cities and civilian casualties. This kind of destruction is not under scrutiny because individual German military commanders had not surrendered when given the chance. Instead they engaged the enemy and risked what would come until the city under their command fell. Although numerous cities and towns in the West were destroyed in this way, due to fanatical SS or military commanders (Naumann, 1998), this was particularly pronounced on the Eastern front where battles with the Red Army were especially intense and uncompromising (e.g. Königsberg). Regarding Berlin, the USSBS could not determine how much destruction was caused by its bombing raids versus that done by the final ground battles. Second, the tactical use of bombing, accompanying and supporting a ground offensive, especially when used against a 'defended' city or against legitimate military or economic targets is also an acceptable practice. Civilian casualties as a consequence of such raids (e.g. workers in munitions plants) are considered acceptable collateral damage in international law. See Hays Parks, 1992.

16. In contrast to common perceptions of the Luftwaffe being the clear aggressor and pioneer of terror-bombing tactics (based on the bombings of Guernica during the Spanish Civil War, Rotterdam, Warsaw, and later Coventry), recent scholarship argues that terror tactics evolved dialectically and that excesses on the German side were mistakes that were contrary to official Luftwaffe policy. Rotterdam, for example, was bombed after it had surrendered, but the military authorities could not call back all of the bombers. See Boog, 1992.

17. Some authors argue that the decision was made much earlier, in late 1940 (Walzer, 1977: 255).

18. Many authors discuss the prewar doctrines associated with people like Douhet, Trenchard and Mitchell, who thought that bombing (seen as inevitable, given advances in technology) was a more humane way of waging war. It would minimize the casualties from trench warfare as experienced in World War I, and would have a massive effect on the enemy, delivering a quick 'knock-out' blow. Overall, the widely accepted belief was that strategic bombing could win the war alone. All of these premises, at least in Europe, proved false. See Garrett, 1993: 4–9, and Schaffer, 1985: 20–35, 80–106.

19. In August 1944, Roosevelt went so far as to state: 'We have got to be tough with Germany, and I mean the German people not just the Nazis. We either have to castrate the German people or you have got to treat them in such a manner so they can't just go on reproducing people who want to continue in the way they have in the past' (Markusen and Kopf, 1995: 168).

20. Some of Schaffer's views have been contested (see Mierzejewski et al., 1981). The record regarding Japan, and particularly the views of the architect of those campaigns, General Curtis LeMay, is very different, with no ambiguity as to the intent (burning cities and killing civilians). See Markusen and Kopf, 1995; and Dower, 1986. Note that most authors draw a connection between the strategic offensives against the two countries, with the bombings of Japan (in 1945) representing the culmination of trends begun with the bombing of Germany.

21. It was only in the 1949 revision to the Conventions that specific provisions were made to safeguard civilians during times of war.

22. Hays Parks notes, however (1992: 324), that the 1907 Hague Declaration 'is generally regarded as of no legal significance,' as almost all powers declined to sign it. Later efforts to stipulate and codify international law pertaining to bombing, such as the Washington Naval Conference (November 1921–February 1922) and the Hague Commission of Jurists (1923), were 'never adopted by any country' and were 'an immediate and total disaster' (339).

23. There has been a sustained assault on Churchill's reputation in recent years, emphasizing his incompetence and opportunism. See Hitchens, 2002.

24. Of course, this argument, carried to its logical conclusion, would justify genocide and the complete extermination of an enemy, given that almost anything an enemy does during hostilities supports the ability to make war. Even further, the obvious exception – the killing of children – can also be perversely justified, if such individuals are viewed as future soldiers or munitions producers, who, if the war does not end quickly, would become legitimate targets.

25. 'One item was not raised in the official proceedings: that of the air raids. All those taking part fought shy of this tricky problem … many years later Jackson admitted that the problem had in fact been discussed. The delegates, however, agreed to drop the controversial question because there would have been countercharges against the Allies' (Heydecker and Leeb, 1962: 62). See also Hays Parks, 1992: 346.

26. Harris returned embittered to his native South Africa in 1946. Numerous postwar writings attest to his awareness of, and bitterness towards, the official slights against him. Such attitudes are also evident among veterans today. For example, a massive campaign was mounted against a Canadian Broadcasting Company (CBC) television series, *The Valour and the Horror*, especially the episode entitled 'Death by Moonlight: Bomber Command,' which criticized the policy and actions of the RAF (including its many Canadian volunteers). Veterans and their organizations, such as the Bomber Harris Trust (www.blvl.igs.net/~jlynch/bharis29.htm), raised a considerable sum of money, forcing the CBC's ombudsman to apologize and prompting the Canadian Senate to hold hearings on the matter, but failing to get the Canadian Supreme Court to hear

the case. See Bercuson and Wise, 1994; and Hay, 1992. An official and independent military history later declared the series' depiction of events as historically accurate.

27. Markusen and Kopf (1995: 69, 244–58) go further still, contending that the strategic bombing was genocidal under the terms of the 1948 United Nations Convention on the Prevention and Punishment of the Crime of Genocide.

# References

Bartov, O. (1991). *Hitler's army: Soldiers, Nazis and war in the Third Reich*. New York: Oxford University Press.

Bercuson, D.J., and Wise, S.F., eds (1994). *The Valour and the Horror revisited*. Montreal: McGill-Queen's University Press.

Bohannan, C. and Valeriano, N. (1962). *Counterguerrilla operations*. New York: Praeger.

Boog, H. (1992). The Luftwaffe and indiscriminate bombing. In H. Boog, ed., *The conduct of the air war in the Second World War: An international comparison*. New York: Berg.

Clayton, A. and Russell, A., eds (1999). *Dresden: A city reborn*. Oxford: Berg.

Crane, C.C. (1993). *Bombs, cities and civilians: American airpower strategy in World War II*. Lawrence: University of Kansas Press.

Diefendorf, J.M. (1993). *In the wake of war: The reconstruction of German cities after World War Two*. New York: Oxford University Press.

Dower, J. (1986). *War without mercy: Race and power in the Pacific War*. New York: Pantheon Books.

Ezard, J. (1992). The firestorm rages on. *Guardian*, 18 May.

Garrett, S.A. (1993). *Ethics and airpower in World War II: The British bombing of German cities*. New York: St. Martin's Press.

Groehler, O. (1992). The Strategic Air War and its impact on the German civilian population. In H. Boog, ed., *The conduct of the air war in the Second World War: An international comparison*. New York: Berg.

*Guardian* (1995). Still, the slaughter of the innocents. *Guardian*, 14 February.

Hay, J. (1992). Bombing debate rubs a raw wound. *Citizen*, 15 November.

Hays Parks, W. (1992). Air war and the laws of war. In H. Boog, ed., *The conduct of the air war in the Second World War: An international comparison*. New York: Berg.

Heydecker, J. and Leeb, J. (1962). *The Nuremberg Trials*, trans. E.A. Downe. London: Heinemann.

Hitchens, C. (2002). The medals of his defeat. *Atlantic Monthly*, April: 118–37.

Keegan, J. (1995). *The battle for history: Re-fighting World War Two*. Toronto: Vintage Books.

Kohn, R.H. (1995). History and the culture wars: The case of the Smithsonian Institution's Enola Gay exhibition. *Journal of American History* 82, no. 3: 1036–63.

Kurowski, F. (1995). *Das Massaker von Dresden und der anglo-amerikanische Bombenterror, 1944–1945*. Berg: Druffel-Verlag.

———— (1977). *Der Luftkrieg über Deutschland*. Düsseldorf: Econ.

Levine, A.J. (1992). *The strategic bombing of Germany, 1940–1945*. Westport: Praeger.

Macksey, K. (1987). *Military errors of World War Two*. Poole: Arms and Armour Press.

Markusen, E. and Kopf, D. (1995). *The Holocaust and strategic bombing: Genocide and total war in the twentieth century*. Boulder: Westview Press.

Marrus, M. (1997). *The Nuremberg war crimes trial, 1945–6: A documentary history*. Boston: Bedford Books.

Messerschmidt, M. (1992). Strategic air war and international law. In H. Boog (ed.), *The conduct of the air war in the Second World War: An international comparison.* New York: Berg.

Mierzejewski, A.C., et al. (1981). American military ethics in World War II: An exchange. *Journal of American History* 68, no. 1: 85–92.

Mumford, L. (1959). The morals of extermination. *Atlantic Monthly*, October: 38–44.

Naumann, K. (1998). *Der Krieg als Text: Das Jahr 1945 im kulturellen Gedächtnis der Presse.* Hamburg: Hamburger Edition.

Neillands, R. (2001). *The bomber war: The allied air offensive against Nazi Germany.* Woodstock: The Overlook Press.

Overy, R. (1981). *The air war: 1939–1945.* New York: Stein & Day.

Pictet, Jean S., ed. (1952). *The Geneva Conventions of 12 August 1949: Commentary.* Geneva: International Committee of the Red Cross.

Rumpf, H. (1963). *The bombing of Germany,* trans. E. Fitzgerald. New York: Holt, Rinehart & Winston.

Schaffer, R. (1985). *Wings of judgment: American bombing in World War II.* New York: Oxford University Press.

——— (1980). American military ethics in World War II: The bombing of German civilians. *Journal of American History* 67, no. 2: 318–34.

Sorge, M.K. (1986). *The other price of Hitler's war: German military and civilian losses resulting from World War II.* New York: Greenwood Press.

United Nations (1949). *Charter and judgment of the Nürnberg Tribunal: History and analysis.* New York: United Nations General Assembly.

United States Strategic Bombing Survey (USSBS) (1945). *Overall report (European war).* Washington, DC: US Government Printing Office.

Walzer, Michael (1977). *Just and unjust wars: A moral argument with historical illustrations.* New York: Basic Books.

Weaver, M. (1992). Five days that hinge on one delicate hour. *Daily Telegraph*, 17 October.

Webster, Sir C., and Frankland, N. (1961). *The strategic air offensive against Germany, 1939–1945,* Vol. III. London: Her Majesty's Stationary Office.

Werrell, K.P. (1986). The strategic bombing of Germany in World War II: Costs and accomplishments. *Journal of American History* 73, no. 3: 702–13.

6

# Torture and Other Violations of the Law by the French Army during the Algerian War

## Raphaëlle Branche

Law is a historical entity; so, too, are its violations. Law has been used as an instrument to wage war while being subjected to extremely strong stresses. This sheds a powerful light on the contradiction whereby France – land of the Rights of Man, a democracy that strives to bring civilization and enlightenment to the world, especially to its colonies – has maintained, both verbally and (to a certain extent) practically, these fundamental precepts while radically contradicting them.

The study of violations of the law during wartime – of their reality as well as of the reasons for their use, of their oversight by the political authority and of their consequences for the political authority itself – provides a contradictory portrait of a democracy at war, engaged in combat with individuals who were neither full citizens nor foreigners. Colonial law was skilled at creating distinctions among 'Frenchmen.'

### 'Police operations' in Algeria

The first attacks that hit Algeria during the night of 1 November 1954 marked the beginning of armed confrontations that would eventually involve up to half a million French soldiers. Apart from fighting, these soldiers were assigned to carry out tasks as diverse as teaching, guarding crops, and patrolling the electric fences installed at frontiers – activities the goal of which was to preserve French Algeria in the face of the threat posed by a handful of armed nationalists. The nationalist forces were initially limited to eastern Algeria, until ideas first of autonomy, then of independence, gained ground among a majority of Algerians.

Since 1848, Algeria had been officially composed of French *départements*. For the French to recognize a state of war there was accordingly impossible. It would mean admitting the existence of a civil war within France – or, alternatively, the legitimacy of Algerians' nationalist claims. And so, for eight years, the French armed interventions in Algeria were officially referred to as 'police operations' aimed at 'maintaining order' on French territory. They were depicted, thus, as an internal matter.

This initial refusal to consider the 'Algerian events' as fundamentally political would have a bearing upon the manner in which the war was conducted, and how the French armed forces behaved on the ground. The normal peacetime framework would rapidly fail to provide adequate justification for repressive force. In the spring of 1955, the government succeeded in passing a law declaring a state of emergency that expanded the powers of the civil and military authorities in Algeria. The state of emergency contravened the law on two fronts, both by allowing exceptional police measures and by extending military authority. Thus, a prefect was granted the right to limit civil freedoms, and could go so far as to order house arrest or confinement in camps. As for the army, its legal powers were expanded with the aim of accelerating the course of justice, in a context described most often as 'the struggle against terrorism.'

The state of emergency originally decreed for certain Algerian wards was extended to the whole country on 20 August 1955. The killing of Europeans in Nord-Constantinois, followed by an unprecedented eruption of acts of violence against the Algerian population, rendered untenable the idea that this was merely a limited war. The harsh policies of those governing political life in Algeria gained wider support within metropolitan France, especially from Minister of the Interior Maurice Bourgès-Maunoury. In June 1955, Bourgès-Maunoury defended the state of emergency before representatives of the Interior Commission, declaring: 'If we had acted more forcefully at a certain moment, there would have been fewer people killed and mutilated. I do not believe that we will achieve anything by displaying weakness against people who have rejected our nation in a very clear fashion.'

This mindset was widespread among the state's top echelons. Some months later, those who defended a specific program of 'Peace in Algeria' gained a majority in the National Assembly. Guy Mollet, a socialist, was appointed chief executive. But the war was speedily reaffirmed as a priority, with victory on the ground viewed as a preliminary step – even if it were achieved by means other than all-out military victory. In March 1956, the government asked parliamentarians to grant it special powers to address the Algerian crisis. Unlike the state of emergency, this was not a question of granting *precise* powers, but rather of buttressing the principle of the executive's absolute power with regard to all matters concerning Algeria. These special powers were granted for a period of six months, whereupon the government decided to impose them on Algeria. The special powers were accompanied by the ceding of some prerogatives to the executive (i.e. the government in Paris). In fact, the powers frequently devolved to Robert Lacoste, resident Minister in Algeria, to use as he saw fit. Either through Lacoste's intervention, or directly through their delegation, these special powers signified the devolution of key powers to the army. This was presented as a temporary measure, but it would endure, and have grave consequences.

Indeed, the regulatory framework remained in place throughout the Algerian war. Maurice Bourgès-Maunoury, upon assuming chief executive powers, sought the extension of emergency measures to metropolitan France in summer 1957, and General de Gaulle later asked for their confirmation, as the law required. In October 1958, a statute repealed the requirement that each new government seek a renewal of the special powers. Never officially abrogated, they therefore continued in force even during the life of the Fifth Republic. Moreover, in February 1960 the government sought approval from the Assembly to assume full powers for one year. Thus, throughout the war, the conduct of Algerian affairs remained in the hands of the executive. It was this executive that, by issuing new regulations, redefined crimes and misdemeanors – though the penal code remained officially in force.

Another legislative framework existed alongside this national framework: international law and, as it happened, the 1949 Geneva Conventions.[1] This law placed new constraints on the legal conduct of war or 'armed conflict,' though it should be noted that the offences described – including rape and torture – were already prohibited under the peacetime French penal code. France adopted the conventions in 1951, and what we know today as 'the Algerian war' provided France with its first opportunity to implement them. In fact, viewed through the lens of international law, the conventions were highly pertinent in the Algerian case.[2] But French participants in the war, both civil and military, adamantly rejected such an approach.

The organization that claimed special custody of the Geneva Conventions was the International Committee of the Red Cross (ICRC). The general framework for its operations was established by France's chief executive, Pierre Mendès France. ICRC missions were allowed to enter Algerian territory, but were ordered to concern themselves with one matter only: the conditions under which prisoners were detained. This would demonstrate France's respect for the Third Geneva Convention, although this was never stated officially. France thus found herself in a paradoxical situation. The 'events' taking place in Algeria warranted the treatment of prisoners, under the Third Convention, as prisoners taken in armed conflict. However, these same 'events' did not justify the application of the First Convention to those wounded on the battlefield, or the Fourth to civilian populations. And so, as far as these other conventions were concerned, peace officially reigned in Algeria – although the tacit recognition of the Third Convention indicated a state of war. Inasmuch as the Third Convention was not officially recognized, however, it was still deemed permissible to turn a blind eye.

The political dimension of the law's application did not escape the notice of Algerian nationalists. As the self-styled Provisional Government for the Algerian Republic (GPRA), they agreed in 1960 to respect the conventions, in the context of negotiations with the French government. By adopting a position usually reserved for a state, the GPRA intended to affirm its own legitimacy and Algeria's proto-statehood.

Another consequence of the negotiations process was a certain improvement in France's application of the Geneva Conventions, at least insofar as the treatment of military prisoners was concerned. From March 1958, military internment centers were established to house 'rebels captured while armed.' This led, finally, to these men being accorded recognition as soldiers – even though they were not always considered prisoners of war, and though it was claimed that the Third Convention did not apply to them.

Thus, it seems that the acceptance of diplomatic intervention in the conflict prompted the emergence of an official enemy on the battlefield. Paradoxically, it was the prospect of peace between the two parties that rendered it necessary to depict the events in terms of war, of opposing 'sides' and 'enemy' soldiers. The history of the application of the Geneva Conventions during the Algerian war illustrates how an enemy originally considered a rebel against the state was transformed into an enemy that was both external and legitimate. Only with such an officially designated enemy could peace be concluded.

This brief explanation buttresses the idea that violations of the law in Algeria must be analyzed with reference to two separate legal codes. Moreover, the prevailing norms fluctuated according to the political context, leading to a similar flexibility in interpretations of violations – in particular whether emphasis was placed on written law or judicial practice. A nuanced presentation of violations by the French army thus requires not only a description of those violations, but analysis of their relationship to multiple and concurrent norms and processes. Only in this manner can we grasp how certain violent practices came to call into question not just the law, but the French state as a whole.

## Violence by the French army in Algeria: legality, legitimacy and violations of the law

The principal function of an army is to wage war. What, therefore, was the status of the acts of violence perpetrated by these agents during their mission, given that the framework in which the acts occurred had not been officially designated as a war? In particular, how did the acts derive their legitimacy, if we cannot speak of their legality? Perhaps the behavior of soldiers in the field provides the source of that legitimacy, independently of the 'laws of war.' If so, what were the practical and political ramifications?

During the Algerian war, these complex issues were debated vehemently. The unease evoked by acts of violence committed by a democratic army parallels the determined beating about the bush that characterized political debate in France in 2000–2001, when the use of torture by French soldiers again became the subject of fierce public controversy (see the Introduction to this volume).

Most acts of violence perpetrated by the French army targeted civilians. This was not surprising, in that the conditions in which the war was fought effectively blended combatants and civilian populations. At the outset of the conflict, French soldiers were obliged to report the deaths they caused to the *gendarmerie*, whose duty it was to make reports and conduct inquiries. Killing one's enemy on the battlefield, a legitimate action if a state of war exists, was not recognized as such. Nevertheless, in the light of subsequent and more prominent developments, we will set aside this particular act of violence for the remainder of the discussion.

From the first year of the war, two acts of violence grew exponentially: summary executions and internment in camps. The state of emergency authorizing house arrest underpinned the latter phenomenon, which expanded further over the course of the war, gradually escaping the control of the civil authority. In the French camps, where internment was theoretically supposed to be temporary, the military held some detainees for months or even years, sometimes submitting them to torture without the slightest qualm. These camps were signs both of the growing power of the military during the war, and of the inability of the civilian authorities, at least up to 1959–60, to ensure respect for certain elementary rights of prisoners.

As for summary executions, they were covered *a priori* by a lengthy directive from the Minister of National Defense and the Minister of the Interior. Dated 1 July 1955, it 'confirm[ed] the approach to be adopted vis-à-vis *rebels* in Algeria' (emphasis added). This directive required that military retaliation should be 'harsher, speedier, [and] total,' with each man asked 'to demonstrate creativity in applying the most appropriate means compatible with his conscience as a soldier.' But the directive also contained certain specific commands. Thus, 'every rebel bearing a weapon, or believed to be carrying one ... is to be shot immediately'; above all, soldiers 'must open fire on every suspect who attempts to flee.' This directive, relying as it did on a conception of the enemy that was already extremely vague ('rebels'), contributed to the development of an iconic figure of the war: the 'suspect.' Far from being directly involved in violent practices and organized in terrorist cells or armed bands (like standard 'rebels'), Algerian 'suspects' formed a huge group with notably blurred boundaries. The order made no distinction between civilian and military personnel, or even between armed and unarmed persons. Simply to take flight was to render one suspect: the authorization to shoot 'runaways' constituted the legalization *a priori* of summary executions.

In the early days of the war, regulatory leeway was granted to authorize prohibited acts. Summary executions were disguised as 'attempts to flee,' 'attempts to escape,' or 'the killing of escapers.' This offered one of the clearest indications of the exemptions from the laws of war that should have governed the use of force in Algeria. Other very ordinary acts of violence did not benefit quite so explicitly from this regulatory camouflage. They were authorized, but without direct approval being granted. The procedure allowed political and military authorities to obfuscate when distinguishing between the licit and illicit, and to speak only of 'screwups' or 'excesses' in the implementation of counterinsurgency policy. Two acts of violence that were expressly forbidden by the French penal code stand out in this category: the execution of hostages and torture.

The execution of hostages owed its genesis to colonial law, which assigned collective responsibility in the case of certain infractions, and authorized collective punishments, including forced labor. This principle was enforced in the spring of 1955: if an attack took place, the nearest village was considered collectively responsible. The reprisals that ensued might include executing hostages. Although this was officially prohibited, and condemned on several occasions in the French National Assembly, it was explicitly recommended by some military leaders, and tacitly implemented by others.

The practice of torture adds a significant dimension to this category of violence. Torture was used indiscriminately in the towns and in the mountains; in active operations or back in billets; against military prisoners or against civilians. Some prisoners were tortured immediately after their arrest, while others – or the same ones – languished in captivity for a period before more extreme measures were applied. The victims were fighters in the Algerian underground but also, and much more often, civilians suspected of providing the 'rebels' with supplies and money, or engaging in political organization and mobilization.

Even though torture was officially prohibited, a special group was established during the war to function as a secret service and specialize in the torture and eventual execution of prisoners. The organization – the Détachement Opérationnel de Protection (DOP) – was composed of all kinds of men, conscripts as well as career soldiers. This army-within-an-army comprised 2,000 men at its zenith. It actually took custody of a relatively small number of prisoners and 'suspects,' coming to specialize in the most difficult cases.

At the same time, torture was practiced by regular military units, notably by teams from the Deuxième Bureau, the office charged with gathering intelligence information. Alongside these teams, other soldiers might also be induced to torture prisoners, especially when the latter were to be interrogated immediately after capture – a process they were instructed to follow. From the beginning of the war, in fact, soldiers were pressured to view the search for information as their greatest priority. Torture, rarely explicitly recommended but often quietly suggested, was one way of obtaining it.

The historian should not, of course, focus only on the apparent goal of information-gathering. Whatever aims a torturer might set for himself, or believe to have been set for him, torture is characterized by the willingness of one or several persons to cause suffering to another human being. It is pain deliberately inflicted, carried out within a framework in which the victim is deprived of all rights while the executioner lacks none, including the right to put another human being to death. Torture aims to deprive the other of his or her ability to think, and has its psychological basis in the manipulation of the victim's fear of death or permanent injury.

During the Algerian war, torture was virtually always an act of violence inflicted by a group, under the command of a superior. It appeared to be subject to certain rules, and drew on a relatively limited array of violent acts. Torture sessions began with the systematic stripping of the victim. One method of torture was rarely used alone. It was more often combined with one of five separate tactics: beatings, hanging by the feet or hands, water torture, torture by electric shock, and rape.

The beatings were systematic; apart from them, electric shock was undeniably the most widely practised torture method. Indeed, technological developments allowed troops to transport an electric generator with them into combat – a machine also capable of providing electricity for the field telephone or radio. The functional aspect was clearly important, but this form of torture also held a great attraction for rational minds trying to convince themselves of the necessity of this violence in wartime. The generator permitted pain levels to be gradually increased, and adapted to the response of the victim. The use of a machine also allowed a soldier to distance himself from the violence inflicted, and from the body of the other person. We find inanimate objects similarly employed in the other torture methods (except beatings): a rope, a jerry can of water and funnel, objects for sexual violation. The use of these objects, and the accompanying desire for 'efficiency,' arose from the same impulse. They helped to entrench torture within a culture of supposedly 'civilized' and rational violence. In particular, it was imperative to differentiate the acts of violence from those employed by the Other, the enemy, which were characterized as 'barbarous' or 'savage.' Some authors eventually acknowledged the use of methods officially prohibited to, but regularly employed by, French troops. Through to the end of the war and until the present day, however, the term 'torture' was not used by French authorities, except to deny its existence or to minimize the scale of its use.

Matters are more straightforward when we turn to a final category of violent acts: those prohibited not just in theory, but explicitly and officially; those for which perpetrators were theoretically subject to punishment. One example is rape. Leaving aside rape as a tool of torture, wartime rapes did occur in Algeria. In most cases they were opportunistic, occurring especially during searches of 'suspect' villages. Mouloud Feraoun clearly understood this, writing of his native Kabylia: 'Once the soldiers have removed [the men] from their homes and have penned them up outside the village in order to ransack the houses, [the men] know that the sexual organs of their daughters and their wives will be ransacked as well.' Rapes were most often committed in a collective manner; other soldiers watched while the rapist was at work.

This particular act of violence struck a well-aimed blow at one of Algerian society's foundations: the virginity or 'purity' of women. It also attacked the manhood of Algerian men, which relied upon their ability to defend their women. Mouloud Feraoun echoes this when he writes: 'the *fellagha* [Algerian nationalists] have advised women not to talk about these things, to refuse to allow the enemy to believe that he has touched the Kabylian soul, as it were, and to bear themselves as true patriots who subordinate everything to the liberation of their enslaved homeland.'

If the effectiveness of rape in wartime can be questioned, its purpose – psychological destruction – cannot be contested. No attempt was ever made by French authorities to justify the use of such force. However viewed, it was to be condemned for its effects both on Algerian society and on military efficacy. In this respect, rape differed from torture, which found numerous defenders – political, military, and even religious.

Rape, then, was a prohibited use of violence. Was it ever penalized or condemned? No precise conclusion is possible based on archival study. Nonetheless, as far as one can judge, two trends emerged. On the one hand, cases of rape were judged and condemned at the instigation of superior officers, who demanded that guilty men be handed over to tribunals to be tried for their crimes. On the other hand, rape seems to have been considered as collateral war damage – not something on which one needed to dwell. Rapists did receive punishment, but not through the legal process – and not from some superior officers, who apparently encouraged their men to rape, although urging them to use discretion.

Clearly, then, it was not sufficient for an act of violence to be prohibited by French legal codes and statutes in order for it to be effectively punished. Did these clear and repeated prohibitions in fact set limits on soldiers' actions during the Algerian war? Torture was also prohibited theoretically, explicitly, and officially; its perpetrators, too, were liable in principle to be punished under the codes and statutes. In reality, however, torture enjoyed a much more ambiguous status; it was both prohibited and authorized. Depending upon the situation, a leader could seek refuge in these ambiguities. But once he had allowed torture to become entrenched, or had himself included it among the range of acceptable practices, it was impossible to step back. And the reality was that torture in Algeria went unpunished. If official texts condemned it, practice itself permitted and nurtured it, without any direct opposition being mounted by the high command or the broader political apparatus. The logic of war appeared to justify torture; thus, it would have been 'illogical' to punish it.

In fact, no trial of military torturers ever took place, with the exception of one trial held for inflicting death under torture. It concluded with the acquittal of the three officers who had admitted to their involvement. As long as torture was not subject to truly effective punishment, it was indeed – as Hans Kelsen defines it – an authorized practice. How, then, can we interpret the role of these acts of violence, especially torture, during the Algerian war?

## The role of torture

The soldiers who carried out the acts of violence described above (with the exception of rapes in the course of searches, which as noted were never justified by military necessity) committed them in the context of their perceived duties. Did this influence the nature of the violence and the interpretations of it that one might offer? The monopoly on legitimate violence that is normally asserted by state agents proved problematic when military and police agents were confronted with acts of violence that were manifestly unlawful and explicitly prohibited to them. Was it lawful to carry out an unlawful and prohibited act of violence within the context of one's duty as a soldier? If so, what were the implications of these practices for the state, a body whose legitimacy was perilously and closely tied to its legality?

These questions deserve special emphasis, since the Algerian events prompted a resort to specific acts of violence as basic weapons available to soldiers. In examining this violence, we touch precisely upon the domains of 'reasons of state': violence that is prohibited and officially denied, but authorized nonetheless to advance state interests.

The logic of reasons of state would normally entail limiting the violence to a small number of practitioners, such as members of the DOP. But instead, torture was widespread throughout the army, employed even by those who were not specialists in its application. These acts of violence, as I have already suggested, were both prohibited and authorized. This paradoxical state of affairs led the perpetrators to believe that their acts enjoyed a legitimacy founded in the requisites of war; the demands of the legal system, by contrast, seemed to them external, artificial, and perhaps unsuitable. Such a contrast gravely threatened a state seeking to reconcile, however tenuously, law and war. Operating outside the law had direct ramifications for the legitimacy of the French state. Soldiers who based their conceptions of legitimacy on military practice, and felt that the practice strengthened the army in the name of France, eventually sought to use force to influence the political direction of the country as a whole, through recurring attempts at military revolt. Examples here are numerous, from the hijacking of the aircraft transporting leaders of the FLN (National Liberation Front) in October 1956, to the bombardment of the Tunisian village of Sakiet in February 1958, to the creation of holding centers for prisoners in Algiers in 1957. (These last were totally clandestine centers that politicians felt obliged to legalize – to avoid losing complete control over them, or at least to maintain appearances.) It could also be argued that, as it transpired, the army had no need to stage a full-scale putsch. It had succeeded in imposing its will on the political system, a state of affairs that held as late as May 1958, when the French government fell and the military, under General Salan, finally succeeded in melding civil and military powers in Algeria.

It was only after General de Gaulle's speech on self-determination for Algerians, on 16 September 1959, that the political authority gradually regained control of the military effort, while conscious that it incurred great risks in doing so. The principal proponents of all-out war and the harshest methods were removed. The commander-in-chief General Challe had to leave Algeria; efforts were made to exercise greater control over the DOP; and so on. But this reclamation of powers was only partial. Moreover, it encountered profound hostility from the new commander-in-chief, who rejected the meddling of politicians in war operations. And it was partially responsible for the failed putsch mounted in April 1961, led by Generals Salan and Challe. At the same time, some officers joined the ranks of the Organisation Armée Secrète (OAS), which sought to establish itself as an alternative army advancing a distinct political project. Only with the end of the Algerian war were the authorities able to smash this opposition and take back firm control of the army.

These difficulties arose as the direct result of the sense of unity existing within army ranks during the war years. Whatever the differences among the various units and headquarters, this solidarity held firm when it came to the basic objective entrusted to the army by the political authorities: to make Algeria French, then negotiate independence from the strongest possible position. This goal was nourished by an amalgam of ideas, by particular views of the Algerians, and by an atmosphere of war that undoubtedly provided support for the acts of violence described above, in particular of torture. Beyond the direct victims – people executed, tortured and raped – these acts of violence formed part of a political lexicon, aimed at the Algerian population as a whole. The latter became the principal prize in the war – a war waged against the nationalists whom the Algerians allegedly sheltered, aided, or feared. The Algerian population thus became the chosen field of battle.

The central place of torture in the system of control was clear from that point on. The population was both a source of information and the target of psychological warfare. It was necessary for the French to keep the Algerian people off-balance, while confronting the nationalists operating in their midst. Torture was not, therefore, simply one means of obtaining information. It was an essential weapon, allowing the French to fulfill their fundamental war aims. Torture was used not only to force people to talk, but to make them understand – and remember – who wielded power. Torture was effectively adapted to the new form of warfare that the army faced in Algeria. This was not because the war demanded more intelligence-gathering than other conflicts, but because it required control over the civil population. In this sense, torture was above all a *political* form of violence. Meanwhile, the question of violations of the law – though never ignored – was considered a side-issue by all relevant decision-makers.

*Translated by Jo Jones*

# Notes

1. The first dealt with the condition of wounded and sick members of armed forces on the battlefield; the second with the wounded and sick at sea; the third with the treatment of prisoners; and the fourth with the protection of civilians in wartime. The emphasis on war was replaced by a wider emphasis on 'armed conflict.'

2. In fact, Article 3 (common to all four conventions) had taken great care to specify that there were non-international armed conflicts to which the conventions should equally apply.

# 7

# Atrocity and Its Discontents:
# US Double-mindedness about Massacre,
# from the Plains Wars to Indonesia

## Peter Dale Scott

One of the great needs of the twentieth century is a scientific study of atrocity and of the moral issues involved.

*Herbert Butterfield*[1]

What we're really doing in Vietnam is killing the *cause* of 'wars of liberation.' It's a testing ground – like Germany in Spain. It's an example to Central America and other guerrilla prone areas.

*Bernard Fall*[2]

### Atrocities, seminal and responsive

As any newspaper reader knows, we live in an age not just of atrocities, but of atrocities exploited to achieve political ends. This fact tends to be both underreported and underregistered in our minds. The whole topic of atrocity is so distasteful that we prefer to avert our eyes. And we comfort ourselves with the consolation that what cannot be helped – uncontrollable irrationality – need not really concern us.

Unfortunately, my research into atrocities has persuaded me that this consolation is not only false; it is part of the problem to be addressed. The most massive atrocities of this century have not arisen primarily from the spontaneous behavior of humans out of control. They have been managed atrocities, outrages provoked and exploited by state powers within the so-called civilized world. Our personal psychological denial of this basic fact facilitates and reinforces the large-scale political denial that allows the phenomenon of managed atrocity to continue.

The atrocities I address in this chapter are those committed on a personal level: mass rapes, mass murders, and torture. I do not mean to imply that we should be less concerned about impersonal atrocities, such as the in-discriminate slaughter inflicted by saturation bombings or nuclear weapons (see Langenbacher's discussion in this volume). The two phenomena are sometimes related, as when in Cambodia anti-Western killings on the ground followed years of American carpet-bombing from the air.

In the case of ground-level, hand-to-hand massacres, American media are quick to expose the personal atrocities of others – when they happen (not coincidentally) to be our enemies. We have heard much about the outrages committed by Nazi Germany and Japan during World War II; by Stalin; and by China through to the Cultural Revolution and Tienanmen Square. The massacres in Cambodia, with their pyramids of skulls, have been replaced in our media by the killing fields of East Africa, Bosnia, and Algeria. The massacres we do *not* hear about, at least at the time they are taking place, are those for which the United States itself is in large measure responsible. This ongoing, systematic suppression – from the Plains Wars of the nineteenth century to El Salvador in the 1980s – falsifies our understanding not just of our own history, but of all managed atrocities throughout the world.

For managed atrocities do not 'just happen'; they are not an inevitable consequence of human frailty and hatefulness. The more they are studied, the more they emerge as part of a single coherent narrative. Most of the bloody massacres today can be seen as part of the ongoing legacy of colonialism: a single narrative, whether the colonialism we speak of is capitalist, socialist, or Islamic. In many parts of the world the seminal acts of atrocity were connected to Western expansion, such as that of the British into India, the French into Indochina, the Spanish into Latin America, the Belgians into Central Africa, the Dutch into Indonesia. Indeed, one can reasonably wonder if the exertion of power over alien populations has ever been achieved without the use of atrocities to intimi-date the colonized into submission. Though many attempts have been made to link the commission of atrocities to the ethos of particular ex-pansionist nations, my studies suggest rather that atrocities are a feature of expansionist power itself.

These planned, state-sponsored atrocities may be declining in number, but they tend to be the largest in scale. And they continue to be signifi-cant: they are the atrocities that help most to explain the rest. For example, the atrocities of recent times in North Africa, Yugoslavia, and the Near East have gone on since before the imperial conquests of these areas, and are rooted ultimately in religious persecutions of a millennium or more ago. Nevertheless, the French scorched-earth campaign of the 1830s in Algeria and the ensuing repression can be considered seminal atrocities – quantum escalations in brutality whose consequences are seen in the responsive atrocities there today. Likewise, the history of Indonesia – the principal focus of this chapter – is a succession of invasions and atrocities. Nevertheless, the carefully planned and executed massacre of 1965, in which perhaps a million people were killed, can be called a seminal escalation, and one whose consequences are still being suffered.

Let me at this point clarify what I mean by managed atrocities. Atrocities can be used politically in different ways. They can be threatened (this practice is widespread). They can actually be committed. Or the commission of atrocity can be managed and exploited psychologically to induce further terror among survivors. This last-mentioned process, which I call managed atrocity, is known and taught at special US military schools as part of psychological warfare, or 'psywar.' A fully managed atrocity is one in which the pretext for the exploited atrocity is developed by the managers of the atrocity itself. Not all psywar by any means is managed atrocity. But all managed atrocity is psywar, and psywar is responsible for the seminal managed atrocities of today.[3]

This chapter began as a study into the theory and practice of US psywar as applied to the Indonesian archipelago. Here the case for US responsibility is more controversial than what has been conceded in Latin America. The scale of atrocity is also immensely larger, leading in the case of East Timor to the death of perhaps one-third of the population. As I proceeded with my research, however, I saw more and more clearly the relevance of US actions in Indonesia to superficially different massacres in Chile (1973), Cambodia (after 1975), and Algeria (in the 1990s). And I have come to appreciate better the difference between Cambodia and Algeria (which I see as responsive to earlier managed atrocities), and Chile (which at the level of massacre was unprovoked, seminal, and thoroughly 'ours').

The reader should understand that this narrative, though inevitably nasty, is in the end optimistic. It is difficult to address responsive atrocities, such as that in Bosnia. However, seminal atrocities, precisely because they are planned, can more easily be controlled. For this reason, I consider it imperative to examine the residue of the US's managed atrocities in the world today. I believe that terminating US management of atrocity is the best formula for ensuring that responsive atrocities diminish. For example, if public protest had deterred the US from its style of training and arming terrorists in Afghanistan after 1979, we might not have had the responsive atrocity of the World Trade Center by one of our own erstwhile terrorists in 1993, or the far more destructive attacks of 11 September 2001.

At least in theory, then, these processes are amenable to human control and amendment. We saw in the 1980s how the US-backed atrocities in El Salvador and Nicaragua could be limited or terminated by congressional action, especially after the long-denied massacre of hundreds of peasants at El Mozote in 1981 (by a US-trained battalion) was finally acknowledged. The delayed exposure of atrocities in East Timor led belatedly to US pressures on Indonesia, in the form of withholding military aid; and this in turn helped end the bloody Indonesian occupation of the territory.

The holding of a free and open referendum on self-determination for East Timor, and the subsequent ascension of East Timor to the ranks of the world's independent states, represented a great victory for the people of that small and sorry nation. Hopefully it will also strengthen a more general proposition: that where state authority can only be sustained by the continuous use of terror, that authority is illegitimate, and the international community should contemplate intervention for the restoration of peace. The example of East Timor should encourage us to believe that managed atrocity in this world is unacceptable, and can and should be eliminated.

## The two Indonesias and the two Americas

Before 1998, of all the Western nations, the one whose people knew least about the Indonesian army's record of atrocities was probably the United States. This was no accident. Despite deceptive public protestations about its support for human rights, the United States was also the major power with the greatest responsibility for those conditions of ongoing psychological warfare, which is to say terror.

US press silence about Indonesian atrocities in East Timor gradually lifted with the events leading to the fall of Suharto in late May 1998. In that conflict, two Indonesian traditions were evident, locked in a dramatic struggle to determine that country's future. One, representing one of the world's most tolerant Muslim cultures, sought a nonviolent return towards the democratic civil society that prevailed in the early 1950s. The other apparently hoped to maintain the army's ruthless domination of power, using violence and provocations reminiscent of Indonesia's violent bloodbath of 1965.

Yet there were also, and continue to be, two ongoing US traditions caught up in this struggle. One is humanitarian, represented by the millions of dollars that the US government has poured into Indonesian human rights groups and other non-governmental organizations. The other tradition, less recognized and trumpeted, believes in and teaches the use of repressive violence, in Indonesia and other parts of the Third World.

The conflicting goals of these two traditions have led to recurring showdowns in the US Congress. In March 1998, Congress learned that, despite its express prohibition in 1992, the Pentagon had continued to supply training to the Indonesian army unit, Kopassus, that had been most involved in massacres and torture over the last thirty-five years. On 8 May 1998, the Pentagon headed off congressional anger by suspending its controversial aid to the Indonesian Army (ABRI). It was, however, clear that Washington would not terminate the US–ABRI connection, which it regarded as its best hope to influence affairs in Indonesia.

The Kopassus Red Berets (then known as RPKAD) played a key role in the 1965 bloodbath that brought Suharto to power. The tactics taught Kopassus recently by US Green Berets – in 'Advanced Sniper Techniques,' 'Military Operations in Urban Terrain,' 'Psychological Operations,' and 'Close Quarters Combat' – suggest that in the 1990s the Pentagon was still improving the ability of Kopassus to use violence against Indonesian civilians. There were at least 41 such exercises between 1992 and 1997, and 20 more scheduled for 1998.[4]

On repeated occasions in the last four decades, the votes of the congressional majority to limit military aid have been similarly thwarted. (Only in the case of aid to Vietnam in 1974 was the limit respected, but that was because the Saigon regime fell before the limit was reached.) Congressional bans on aid to Contra death squads in Nicaragua in the mid-1980s were secretly and illegally subverted by Oliver North in the Reagan White House, with Pentagon and CIA support, provoking the Iran–Contra confrontation.

Indonesia's acute crisis in the late 1990s recalled in its details the political uncertainty at the end of the Sukarno era more than thirty years earlier. Political unrest was aggravated by economic disruption and inflation, so that protests mounted throughout Indonesia. Tensions built between the Suharto regime and the international community, above all the United States. They increased also between proponents of a nonviolent transition to a more democratic civil society, and provocations that in some cases appeared to be stage-managed by elements of the Indonesian army.

These same conditions in 1965 led to an army intervention and a change of leadership, accompanied by a military-backed massacre in which perhaps over a million civilians were murdered. That grim memory lends significance to another important similarity between 1965 and 1998 – one that has been generally ignored. Up until March 1998, as in 1965, though for different reasons, most members of the US Congress mistakenly believed that they had terminated US military training for Indonesian troops. In fact, in both periods, US training continued on the sly, and for obvious reasons of realpolitik.

In 1964–65, the US administration wished to maintain contact with the officer corps of the Indonesian army, which it regarded as a more secure ideological ally than the Indonesian head of state. On the other hand, it sought for the sake of appearances to distance itself publicly from the Indonesian army, as the latter prepared to eliminate its opponents by wholesale massacre. The first political motive was spelled out in a secret memo to President Johnson on 17 July 1964 (preceding the coup and massacre by one year):

> Our aid to Indonesia ... we are satisfied ... *is not helping Indonesia militarily*. It is, however, *permitting us to maintain some contact with key elements in Indonesia*, which are *interested in and capable of resisting Communist takeover*. We think this is of vital importance to the entire Free World.[5]

A Defense Department official reiterated in 1998 that the training program was designed to 'gain influence with successive generations of Indonesia officers.'[6] Meanwhile, the 1965 bloodbath was accompanied by US instructions to its officials to keep their distance. This appearance of distance was maintained in the 1990s as well.

Covert US aid and training before 1965 mostly took the innocuous-sounding form of 'civic action.' I have argued that in fact 'civic action' provided a cover, in Indonesia as in Vietnam, for psywar, and that psywar in turn had become a euphemism (used without translation by the key Red Beret organizers of the slaughter in Java) for techniques of terror, including massacre (Scott, 1985). I believe that through these links to the Indonesian army, US civilian and military advisors bear an important share of the responsibility for the 1965 killings.

In 1998 there was a risk that history might repeat itself. In February 1998, Admiral Joseph Prueher, US Commander-in-Chief, Pacific (CINCPAC), stated in London that trouble lay ahead in Indonesia: 'There is no economic and political stability. We're trying to work in an economic, political *and military* way, to be as supportive as we can to try to bring this back in line.'[7]

A number of prominent US visitors to Indonesia, such as Defense Secretary William Cohen, made a point of visiting Army General Prabowo, a US-trained general who graduated head of his class at Fort Benning, Georgia (Nairn, 1998). Prabowo was quite simply a murderer, having personally given the commands to shoot twenty civilians in East Timor in 1989. He had also headed the elite Kopassus Red Beret command, which was chiefly responsible for killings and torture in East Timor. It was a 1991 massacre in East Timor that led Congress to ban training in 1992, yet Kopassus was one of the chief groups the Pentagon continued to train.

Kopassus is also the successor unit to the RPKAD Red Berets, who were chiefly responsible for organizing the slaughter in 1965. Early in

1998, journalists reported that Prabowo was helping to instigate anti-Chinese rioting of the kind which, in 1965, preceded a more general massacre. In May 1998, Prabowo was demoted and later fired, after an investigation showed that elements of Kopassus had been involved in the torture and 'disappearances' of civilians. In 2000, he became the first person to be denied entry to the United States under the provisions of the United Nations Convention against Torture and other Cruel, Inhuman or Degrading Treatment or Punishment.[8]

The Pentagon certainly knew the implications of dealing with Prabowo and Kopassus, a unit notorious for terror, murder, rape, and torture. Yet when Congress banned training under the usual Pentagon program of International Military Education and Training (IMET), the Pentagon quietly kept on training Kopassus under a different program, that of Joint Combined Education and Training (J-CET).[9] A subsequent *New York Times* editorial specified that the Indonesians were trained under J-CET in 'riot-suppression,' and noted that 'it seems likely that the troops will be used to crush legitimate democratic protests.'[10]

The outcome of the Pentagon–Congress tussle over training troops is still a matter of concern, involving far more than the human rights violations in Indonesia. In Latin America and other parts of the world, the Pentagon has persisted, despite congressional concerns, in supplying training and aid to armies that are directly or indirectly involved in psywar massacres. Two recent examples are Colombia and Mexico, where officers accused of involvement in civilian massacres have been trained at the School of the Americas in Fort Benning. Even the Inspector-General of the Pentagon has conceded that execution and torture have been taught there in the past.[11] In December 2000 the US Army closed the school, but reopened it a month later under another name.[12]

## Developing psywar

The struggle to reduce US backing for state-supported violence will not be an easy one. For over two centuries, this nation has nourished conflicting attitudes towards atrocities. On the one hand is its humanitarian tradition, dating back to nineteenth-century concerns about the mistreatment of Indians and slaves. This has been the tradition most often given voice in Congress. On the other hand, as we shall see, is the tradition of explicitly defending the usefulness of atrocities, most recently in the service of counterinsurgency or 'low-intensity conflict.'

The result is an official schizophrenia with respect to state-sponsored violence. The two Americas are not in dialogue with each other; each simply proceeds as if the other were not worth taking seriously. Such schizoid divergence can break into violence at home, as we saw recently in the era of the Vietnam War.

East Timor is one victim of US-assisted atrocities that only recently have been addressed. I shall quote at this point from an eyewitness account by a Catholic missionary of a search-and-destroy mission in 1981, three years after the worst killings had ended.

> We saw with our own eyes the massacre of the people who were surrendering: all dead, even women and children, even the littlest ones ... not even pregnant women were spared: they were cut open.... They did what they had done to small children the previous year, grabbing them by the legs and smashing their heads against rocks.... All this was happening at a time when President Suharto of Indonesia had offered amnesty to all Timorese who surrendered.... The comments of Indonesian officers reveal the moral character of this army: 'We did the same thing in Java, in Borneo, in the Celebes, in Irian Jaya, and it worked.' That is, terror caused the people to submit. (Quoted in Barbedo de Magalhães, 1990: 52)[13]

Un-American as this conduct might seem, it is part of a counter-insurgency tradition that can be traced back to the US conquest of the Philippines, and before that to the wars against native Americans. Consider this observer's account of the 1864 massacre of an unsuspecting Indian encampment at Sand Creek, Colorado:

> They were scalped; their brains knocked out; the men used their knives, ripped open women, clubbed little children, knocked them in the head with their guns, beat their brains out, mutilated their bodies in every sense of the word.[14]

Like other atrocities, the Sand Creek massacre remains a focus of controversy a century and a half later, and has generated two parallel traditions of response, both American. An eastern-dominated Congress investigated and condemned the massacre as 'unprovoked and unwarranted' (as have most historians since), and voted substantial indemnities to relatives of the survivors.[15] But many whites in the region agreed with Colonel John Chivington, the commander, that the slaughter was the only way to bring peace.[16] To this day there are military historians who defend what happened at Sand Creek as an early example of pacification.[17]

Among those supporting atrocities against the Indian population were US Army Generals Sheridan and Sherman, whose explicit endorsement became a model for a later generation of commanders in the US–Philippine War in the 1900s (Churchill, 1997: 236–40; Miller, 1982: 94–5). We should therefore not be surprised to see much the same terrorist strategies exemplified in this latter conflict. For example, a contemporary news report stated that American soldiers killed 'men, women, children ... from lads of ten and up, an idea prevailing that the Filipino, as such, was little better than a dog.'

> Our soldiers have pumped salt water into men to 'make them talk,' have taken prisoner people who held up their hands and peacefully surrendered, and an hour later, without an atom of evidence to show they were even *insurrectos*, stood them on a bridge and shot them down one by one, to drop into the water below and float down as an example to those who found their bullet riddled corpses.

This testimony is the more credible because the correspondent approved of these tactics: 'It is not civilized warfare, but we are not dealing with a civilized people. The only thing they know and fear is force, violence, and brutality.'[18]

This sending of corpses downstream occurred under the command of General J. Franklin Bell, another commander who, like Colonel Chivington, has been remembered differently by civilian and military historians. Recently one of the latter, John Morgan Gates, has singled out General Bell for his 'excellent understanding of the role of benevolence in pacification'; and noted the consensus of 'both civil and military officials' in the Philippines that Bell's campaign in Batangas 'represented pacification in its most perfected form' (Gates, 1973: 258, 288).

Because of this, Gates claims, General Pershing's campaign against the Moros in 1908 greatly resembled Bell's, just as 'the campaign against the HUK movement in the Philippines following World War II greatly resembled the American campaign of almost fifty years earlier.... The American approach to the problem of pacification had been a studied one' (Gates, 1973: 288, 291). Thus, the motif of corpses dropped in rivers staged a comeback during the US-coordinated counterterrorism campaign in the Philippines in the 1950s:

> The special tactic of these squadrons was to cordon off areas; anyone they caught inside the cordon was considered an enemy.... almost daily you could find bodies floating in the river, many of them victims of [Major Napoleon] Valeriano's Nenita Unit.[19]

Valeriano went on to co-author an important American textbook on counterinsurgency, and to serve as part of the American pacification effort in Vietnam.[20]

Strikingly similar atrocities have been rife in other countries where the United States has played a decisive role in training and supplying troops. The following summarizes a survivor's account of a Guatemalan army raid on a village in Quiché:

The government troops came in, rounded up the population, and put them in the town building. They took all the men out and decapitated them. Then they raped and killed the women. Then they took the children and killed them by bashing their heads with rocks. (quoted in Peck, 1987: 329)

In nearby El Salvador, a sweep by the US-trained Atlacátl battalion was followed by the murder, one by one, of twenty-four women and children. 'Counterterror-style, the mutilated corpses were left behind as a warning to leftist guerrillas' (Valentine, 1990: 423–4). Likewise, a 1997 raid by uniformed paramilitaries in the Colombian village of Mapirapán resulted in dozens of decapitated corpses being thrown in a nearby river.[21] A recent RAND Corporation study confirms that the paramilitaries there 'routinely execute alleged guerrilla sympathizers to instill fear and compel support among the local population' (Rabasa and Chalk, n.d.: 56). Such horrors are intentional, meant to terrorize the rest of the population into submission.

## US psywar, Indonesia, and East Timor

There is no question that the US provided military materiel and training for the Indonesian invasion of East Timor, as well as a virtual green light. What has been long denied in America is the US role in preparing for a massacre by the Indonesian army of its own people in 1965. (It is symptomatic of this psychological denial that my own article on this subject has been published four times in Indonesia as well as in five other countries, but never in the United States.)

The key to US responsibility in 1965, as today, lay in special training for a key political paracommando battalion, the Red Berets. Later renamed Kopassus, this battalion was at the center of massacre and torture operations in the 1960s as in the 1990s. Its then-chief, Sarwo Edhie, appears to have been a CIA agent or contact.[22] It was he who, while giving orders in Indonesia for the elimination of the Indonesian Communist Party, used the American Army word 'psywar.' We learn from an official Indonesian account of the campaign to crush the Indonesian Communists ('the G30S/PKI') that Sarwo Edhie's meeting to plan this campaign in Surakarta on 26 October 1965 was organized according to the following principle (with the emphasized words not in Bahasa Indonesia but in English):

The G30S/PKI should be given no opportunity to concentrate/consolidate. It should be pushed back systematically by all means, including *psywar*, distribution of pamphlets and the spreading of information to achieve the goal of *slowing down* [G30S/PKI] activities.[23]

What followed this meeting is well known from other sources: not leaflet distribution, but the training of youths as death squads for civilian killings (Crouch, 1978: 151).

The psywar character of the 1965 massacres in Indonesia can be plainly seen in one of the first eyewitness accounts of the slaughter. The corpses choking the rivers of East Java were not just dumped there to dispose of them. They had been rigged to float, and thus to terrorize those living downstream:

> Stomachs torn open. The smell was unbelievable. To make sure they didn't sink, the carcasses were deliberately tied to, or impaled on, bamboo stakes. And the departure of corpses from the Kediri region down the Brantas achieved its golden age when bodies were stacked on rafts over which the PKI banner proudly flew. (Rochijat, 1985: 43–4)

This deliberate impaling on stakes, to ensure that the psychological message reached the maximum number of villages, hardly fits one scholar's description of it as 'unplanned brutality,' 'compounded by inexpert techniques and a desire to make the bodies unrecognizable' (Cribb, 1990: 15, 30). Rather, it seems to exemplify the practice of corpse mutilation and display used earlier in the Philippines, and codified in the 1962 US psywar handbook, *Counterguerrilla Operations* ('Few weapons have quite the same effect on guerrilla morale').[24]

The dispatching of Indonesian corpses downstream was supplemented by the display of decapitated heads and body parts, including male genitals, on highroads and in public places (Cribb, 1990: 140, 172, 175). This was earlier the practice of CT (Counter-Terror) teams in Vietnam, also re-cruited by the military from civilians. The teams would leave a Viet Cong head on a pole as they left a village, or a mutilated body, or ears nailed to houses ('The idea was that fear was a good weapon').[25] The CIA advisor who introduced this counter-terror to South Vietnam, Ralph Johnson, 'formulated his theory in the Philippines in the mid-1950s and as a police advisor in Indonesia in 1957 and 1958, prior to the failed Sukarno [*sic!*] coup.'[26]

Corpses and human heads were also displayed in East Timor after the Indonesian invasion of 1975, as part of a campaign of terror supported and supplied by the United States (see, e.g., Taylor, 1991: 102). But the core of the Indonesian pacification program in East Timor was the same as the core of General Bell's in Batangas: the forced resettlement of the popula-tion in villages which could be called concentration camps. (Forced relo-cation had, of course, earlier been the core of US pacification efforts against native Americans in the American West.)

For most Timorese, the focus of their lives became the strategic camps into which they were herded prior to being transported to new 'resettlement villages' in sites created away from their original homes.... As Mgr Costa Lopes, Apostolic Administrator of Dili until his dismissal in May 1983, noted: ... 'the problem is that people are forced to live in the settlements and are not allowed to travel outside.... This is the main reason why people cannot grow enough food.' ... An ICRC delegate, surveying the Hatolia camp where 80 per cent of its 8000 inhabitants were suffering from malnutrition, was reported as concluding that it was 'as bad as Biafra and potentially as serious as Kampuchea,' whilst the head of Catholic Relief Services commented that the problem was 'greater than anything I have seen in fourteen years of relief work in Asia.' (Taylor, 1991: 92, 93, 97)

Here is how General Bell's 'well-conceived' reconcentration plan was characterized by Professor Gates (writing in 1973, in the brief interval between the failure of such techniques in Vietnam and their introduction in East Timor):

A basic feature of General Bell's pacification policy was his plan for isolating the guerrillas from those supporting them.... He ordered each garrison commander to establish a plainly marked area. Unless they [the Filipinos] moved into them by December 25 their property would become liable to confiscation or destruction. Within the zones of protection, the Americans encouraged the Filipinos to erect new homes.... Schools were also provided, and all of the benevolent and humane actions that had characterized American operations in the Philippines were evident in the zones of reconcentration.... In the Philippines ... the [US governing] commission recognized the success of the army's approach to pacification, and it passed a reconcentration act in 1903, modeled on General Bell's techniques. (Gates, 1973: viii, 259–60, 288)

Like Professor Miller's book, Professor Gates's is clearly written as part of America's debate over Vietnam, where relocation was at the heart of the controversial US pacification program. The two books together illustrate an important division in American consciousness, antedating the Civil War. In response to books like those of Chomsky and Miller, Gates announced in his preface that he would concentrate 'on activities far removed from the already well-publicized and exaggerated atrocities of the Philippine campaign' (Gates, 1973: viii). Thus he omits aspects of Bell's 'perfected' campaign, which at the time caught the attention of US anti-imperialists, who objected in Congress:

When an American was 'murdered,' they were instructed to 'by lot select a P.O.W. – preferably one from the village in which the assassination took place – and execute him.'... The entire population outside of the major cities in Batangas was herded into concentration camps.... Everything outside of the camps was systematically destroyed....Bell's main target was the wealthier and better-educated classes.... Adding insult to injury, Bell made these people carry the petrol used to burn their own country homes. He compared such tactics to those of General Sherman in Georgia during the War Between the States and theorized that once the better elements were miserable enough they would persuade the others to stop fighting. (Miller, 1982: 207–8)

The same mix of terror, indiscriminate reprisals, and forced relocation shaped the American experiments in psychological warfare and counter-insurgency in Vietnam, culminating in Operation Phoenix. These were imitated in turn by Indonesia in East Timor, and today by paramilitaries in Colombia. Meanwhile, the atrocity business – given more polite titles, such as 'counterinsurgency' or 'low-intensity conflict' – remains a staple and a rationale for hard-headed Pentagon policymakers.

The culture of low-intensity conflict has spawned its own population of consultants, who defend death squads publicly in the same way that military historians defend Chivington and Gates. Thus, in 1986 death squads were cited as 'an extremely effective tool' by Neil Livingstone, who at the time was a counterterrorism consultant to Oliver North and the Reagan administration.[27] Four years later Michael Radu, a researcher at a formerly CIA-funded think-tank, justified the Salvadorean death squads for doing what they 'had to do,' and faulted the attempts of Congress to condition aid on respect for 'human rights' (his quotation marks) as a 'total misunderstanding of the situation' (Radu and Tismaneanu, 1990: 69–70). Radu also claimed that it was 'untenable' to treat the Salvadorean Archbishop Oscar Romero as a spiritual leader (17), presumably meaning that a death squad was quite right to murder him in 1980. Turning to a more timely topic, Radu attacked 'the absurd and artificial notion' in Latin America of university autonomy (15). This was shortly after the US-trained Atlacátl battalion had demonstrated its agreement with the thesis, in 1989, by murdering six Jesuit priests at San Salvador's principal university.

Congress responded to the Jesuit killings by attempting to terminate aid to the Salvadorean army, but the attempt was vetoed by President Bush in 1991 (Sharpe, 1991). Another split occurred at this time over aid to the Guatemalan army, after a colonel (who was also a CIA agent) was implicated in the murder of an American innkeeper, Michael DeVine. Citing this murder, the State Department 'cut off about $3 million a year in military aid to Guatemala.' But the CIA secretly continued 'liaison' support for Guatemala's military intelligence programs (which involved both murder and torture) to the tune of 'about $5 million to $7 million a year.'[28]

The Guatemala example showed the military–CIA mentality at odds not just with Congress, but with the civilian administration. Even presidential policies are regularly subverted by the military. The history of the Vietnam War was one of repeated violations of presidential guidelines by

US armed forces (see Scott, 1972: esp. 79–107). The problem has continued with US military aid, much of it also under JCET, to Colombia.[29]

## Conclusion

For generations, the United States has sustained two parallel but opposed
states of mind with respect to atrocities and human rights: that of most of
the public, and that of the majority of counterinsurgency specialists and
historians. There is nothing in history to suggest that the views of atrocity's proponents are destined to prevail. On the contrary, Congress should
recognize that atrocities have been and continue to be within its power to
control, at least in theory.

Vietnam provides an example of this. Congress contributed, however
belatedly, to the termination of that fatal experiment. Again, in the 1980s,
the US-backed atrocities in El Salvador and Nicaragua were scaled back
by congressional action, especially after the Atlacátl battalion's long-denied
1981 massacre at El Mozote was finally acknowledged.

Most recently, the atrocities in East Timor were finally acknowledged
by the US State Department and the *New York Times*, who had both
worked twenty years earlier to cover up Indonesia's genocidal campaign in
the territory. The breakthrough was soon followed by East Timor's belated
independence. This should serve as a reminder to cynics and faint-hearts
that America is capable of rising above the genocidal acts of its defenders
and allies.

What remains to be seen is whether Congress, which rebuked Colonel
Chivington in 1864 and exposed General Bell in 1901, can become an
agent to ensure that US-trained troops act to prevent massacres and other
atrocities, instead of (as at present) facilitating them. This will only happen
if the humanitarian forces in America rouse themselves yet again in opposition. We must bring the full force of publicity to bear on atrocities that
are tolerated only because of their relative obscurity.

Much progress has been made since 1965, when few people outside
Indonesia had any means of knowing what transpired there. Today, international organizations closely monitor human rights violations around the
world, and their work is supported by local monitors, who are sometimes
killed for their vigilance. A global consciousness is emerging that increasingly demands the prosecution and punishment of major human rights
violators at the international level. In general, I applaud these developments, including the establishment of international tribunals for accused
war criminals. But I think we must proceed very carefully down this path.

To begin with, the prosecution of human rights crimes should not
become a pretext for committing them. Many people, including this

author, were appalled by the way NATO, in the name of defending human rights, inflicted major civilian casualties on the nation of Yugoslavia (see MacDonald's chapter in this volume). We have not yet purged ourselves of the crusade mentality that killed in the name of Christianity; then in the name of enlightenment, progress, and development; and most recently in the name of human rights.

A related principle is that, even though peace requires justice, peace must precede justice; that is, justice should not become something that threatens an uncertain peace. I personally disagreed with my former allies in the international campaign for East Timorese independence who demanded *ex post facto* justice for East Timor via an international tribunal. This demand did not (in my view) take into account how such demands could further destabilize the already precarious, sometimes bloody status quo in Indonesia, as well as playing into the hands of military and Muslim extremists waiting in the wings.[30]

I believe that, ultimately, the best guardians of the new humanitarian consciousness are ordinary people, rather than any state apparatus, whether national or international. Just as past atrocities have endured through denial, so today the publicizing of atrocities and those who commit them is the most reliable antidote to their perpetuation. The consolidation of this new consciousness is a task too precious to be turned over to traditional state mechanisms of prosecution and punishment.

## Notes

1. Quoted in Cribb, 1990: 14. I want to express my debt to Cribb's important book, with which I shall sometimes take issue on particulars of interpretation. In general, Cribb's approach is phenomenological, mine is aetiological; he stresses irrationality where I also see rationality. I freely concede that there is merit to both approaches.

2. Fall quoted in Valentine, 1990: 89.

3. Obviously there will often be management and psychological exploitation of responsive atrocities as well.

4. Statement by Allan Nairn on the suspension of US military training aid to Indonesia, 9 May 1998.

5. *Declassified Documents Quarterly Catalogue*, 1982, 001786 (DOS Memo for President of 17 July 1964); emphasis in original.

6. *New York Times*, 17 March 1998: A3.

7. *International Herald Tribune*, 7 February 1998, emphasis added.

8. *Straits Times* (Singapore), 31 December 2000. As far as I can determine, this singular reversal of Prabowo's fortunes was not reported in the mainstream US press.

9. See Nairn, 1998; *New York Times*, 17 March 1998: A3.

10. *New York Times*, 23 March 1998: A18. The editorial attitude of the *Times* has shifted considerably since 1966, when its columnist James Reston described the Indonesian massacre and change of government as 'A Gleam of Light in Asia.'

11. *Washington Post*, 22 February 1997: 'The Pentagon's inspector general yesterday said repeated mistakes were made in the 1980s that caused descriptions of "objectionable" actions such as execution and torture to be included in US Army manuals' (A11).

12. *New York Times*, 24 June 2001. A bipartisan group of members of Congress has proposed House Resolution 1810, which would close the school permanently.

13. See also Dunn, 1996: 261: 'On the Indonesian side, there have been many reports that many soldiers viewed their operation as a further phase in the ongoing campaign to suppress communism that had followed the events of September 1965.'

14. John Smith, scout, quoted in Billington, 1974: 568. See also Churchill, 1997: 234. Smith's objectivity was challenged at the time, but today even defenders of the Sand Creek raid concede that most women and children there were killed, and their bodies mutilated (see, e.g., Dunn, 1985).

15. House of Representatives, 38th Cong., 2nd Sess., 'Massacre of Cheyenne Indians,' quoted in Hoig, 1977: 167. See also United States Congress, 1867a and 1867b.

16. See Churchill, 1997: 228–34. Silas Soule, one of the chief witnesses who testified against Chivington, was subsequently murdered by another soldier, who then escaped under mysterious circumstances. See Hoig, 1997: 172.

17. See Dunn, 1985 (an anthology).

18. *Philadelphia Ledger*, 19 November 1900, as quoted in US Cong., Senate, 57th Cong., 1st Sess., S. Doc. 166, 2. See also Miller, 1982; and Karnow, 1989: 188.

19. Interview with a pro-US Filipino colonel, as reported in Kerkvliet, 1979: 196; see also McClintock, 1992: 121.

20. See Bohannan and Valeriano, 1962. Valeriano was also employed to train the Cuban Task Force for the ill-fated Bay of Pigs invasion.

21. *San Francisco Chronicle*, 18 June 1998: A18.

22. Sarwo Edhie had allegedly been a CIA contact while serving at the Indonesian Embassy in Australia. See *Pacific*, May/June 1968.

23. In 'Pemberontakan G30S/PKI dan penumpasannya' (The revolt of the G30S/PKI and its suppression), trans. Robert Cribb, in Cribb, 1990: 164.

24. Charles Bohannon and Napoleon Valeriano, quoted in McClintock, 1992: 118.

25. Remark by CIA officer Pat McGarvey, quoted in Valentine, 1990: 62. Vietnam observer and counterinsurgency consultant Bernard Fall commented in 1965 that 'What we're really doing in Vietnam is killing the *cause* of "wars of liberation." It's a testing ground – like Germany in Spain. It's an example to Central America and other guerrilla prone areas.' Fall quoted in Valentine, 1990: 89.

26. Valentine, 1990: 44, 62–3. The term 'counter-terror' had more justification in Vietnam than in some other countries. Following French precedent, the NLF also, after summary trial of a selected victim before a 'people's court,' would then kill their victim in the center of the village, and leave the body on display with a death notice attached (Valentine, 1990: 43). There was no comparable PKI practice in Indonesia.

27. Neil C. Livingstone, quoted in McClintock, 1992: 429: 'In reality, death squads are an extremely effective tool, however odious, in combating terrorism and revolutionary challenges.' Commenting on the Argentine experience, Livingstone wrote: 'Too often the death of one family member at the hands of government security forces radicalized every brother, sister, and cousin, who then became terrorists in order to avenge the victim. Thus, when a terrorist was identified every member of his or her family was often killed to prevent blood feud.' For more on Livingstone, see Scott, 1989.

28. *New York Times*, 2 April 1995: 6. See also Nairn, 1995. Richard Nuccio, the State Department whistle-blower who revealed the CIA involvement to Congressional

Representative Torricelli, had his clearances revoked as a result by CIA Director John Deutch, backed ultimately by President Clinton (*New York Times*, 6 December 1996).

29. *New York Times*, 2 June 1998: A12: 'In March 1996, the Administration reacted to evidence that President Ernesto Samper had taken money from Cali traffickers by cutting off almost all American aid to Colombia except for what was designated to fight drugs.…Yet according to many officials, the Pentagon quietly distinguished itself by finding creative ways around the restrictions. "We refused to disengage," said a Pentagon official who spoke on the condition that he not be identified.'

30. For the same reason, I was even ambivalent about the 1999 cuts in US military aid to Indonesia, made in response to the army's sponsorship and protection of mayhem committed by pro-Indonesian militias. My position has been that the US, having trained the Indonesian army in terrorist psywar, should now accept responsibility for encouraging it in a more humanitarian direction.

# References

Barbedo de Magalhães, A., ed. (1990). *East Timor: Land of hope.* Oporto: Oporto University, President's Office.

Billington, R.A. (1974). *Westward expansion: A history of the American frontier.* New York: Macmillan.

Churchill, W. (1997). *A little matter of genocide: Holocaust and denial in the Americas, 1492 to the present.* San Francisco: City Lights Books.

Cribb, R. (1990). Introduction. In R. Cribb, ed., *The Indonesian killings of 1965–1966: Studies from Java and Bali.* Clayton, Victoria: Monash Papers on Southeast Asia, No. 21.

Crouch, H. (1978). *The army and politics in Indonesia.* Ithaca, NY: Cornell University Press.

Dunn, J. (1996). *Timor: A people betrayed.* Sydney: ABC Books.

Dunn, Lt.-Col.W.R. (1985). *'I stand by Sand Creek': A defense of Colonel John M. Chivington and the Third Colorado Cavalry.* Ft. Collins, CO: Old Army Press.

Gates, J.M. (1973). *Schoolbooks and Krags: The United States army in the Philippines, 1898–1902.* Westport, CT: Greenwood Press.

Hoig, S. (1977). *The Sand Creek massacre.* Norman, OK: University of Oklahoma Press.

Karnow, S. (1989). *In our image: America's empire in the Philippines.* New York: Random House.

Kerkvliet, B.J. (1979). *The Huk rebellion: A study of peasant revolt in the Philippines.* Quezon City: New Day Publishers.

McClintock, M. (1992). *Instruments of statecraft: U.S. guerrilla warfare, counterinsurgency, and counter-terrorism, 1940–1990.* New York: Pantheon.

Miller, S.C. (1982). *'Benevolent assimilation': The American conquest of the Philippines, 1899–1903.* New Haven: Yale University Press.

Nairn, A. (1998). Indonesia's killers. *The Nation*, 30 March.

——— (1995). CIA death squad. *The Nation*, 17 April.

Peck, J., ed. (1987). *The Chomsky reader.* New York: Pantheon.

Rabasa, A., and Chalk, P. (n.d.). *Colombian labyrnth: The synergy of drugs and insurgency and its implications for regional stability.* RAND publication MR-1339–AF; www.rand.org/publications/MR/MR1339/.

Radu, M., and Tismaneanu, V. (1990). *Latin American revolutionaries: Groups, goals, methods.* Washington: Pergamon–Brassey's International Defense Publishers.

Rochijat, P. (1985). Am I PKI or non-PKI? *Indonesia* 40 (October): 43–4.

Scott, P.D. (1989). Northwards without North. *Social Justice* (Summer): 1–30.

——— (1985). The United States and the overthrow of Sukarno, 1965–1967. *Pacific Affairs* 58, no. 2 (Summer): 239–64.

——— (1972). *The war conspiracy.* New York: Bobbs-Merrill.

Sharpe, K.E. (1991). U.S. holds to old habits in Salvador. *Christian Science Monitor,* 18 March.

Taylor, J.G. (1991). *Indonesia's forgotten war: The hidden history of East Timor.* London: Zed Books.

United States Congress (1867a). The Chivington massacre. *Reports of the committees.* Washington: GPO.

United States Congress (1867b). Sand Creek massacre. *Report of the Secretary of War.* Washington: GPO.

Valentine, D. (1990). *The Phoenix Program.* New York: William Morrow.

# 8

# Bob Kerrey's Atrocity, the Crime of Vietnam and the Historic Pattern of US Imperialism

## S. Brian Willson

### Mekong Delta, 1969

My US Air Force Combat Security unit was dispatched to Binh Thuy on 7 March 1969, to fortify a Vietnamese controlled airbase a few miles northwest of Can Tho City along the Bassac river. This was in Phong Dinh province, about 100 miles southwest of Saigon in the Mekong Delta. I was the First Lieutenant in charge of this unit of nearly forty men. Tet 1969, though far less intense than the devastating Tet offensive of 1968, had been launched by the Viet Cong (VC) less than two weeks earlier, on 23 February. Everybody was on edge. Two days later, on 25 February, then-Lieutenant and now ex-US senator Bob Kerrey and six other Navy Seals (Sea–Air–Land forces) under his command committed an atrocity at Thang Phong, where as many as twenty-four villagers were gunned down, at least half of whom were women and children (see also the Introduction to this volume). Thang Phong lies near the South China Sea in Kien Hoa province, about 50 miles directly east of Can Tho.

During Tet 1968, the Delta, like most of South Vietnam, had been hit hard. Thirteen of the sixteen provincial capitals had been seriously penetrated by the VC. Binh Thuy airbase had received eighteen different attacks in February and March 1968, far more than the other ten airbases in South Vietnam, with the exception of Tan Son Nhut in Saigon, which was also hit eighteen times. The US response had been furious, especially against VC operations in Can Tho City, and in My Tho and Ben Tre in Kien Hoa province to the east, not far from Thang Phong. At that time, the *New York Times* (6 February 1968) reported the infliction of at least 750 civilian casualties in My Tho, 350 in Can Tho, and 2,500 in Ben Tre. Ben Tre had been so pulverized by US firepower that a US major infamously explained, 'It became necessary to destroy the town to save it.'

Some months later, in December 1968, Operation 'Speedy Express,' conducted primarily by the Ninth Infantry Division, had begun sweeping missions designed to finish off VC units in the Delta, especially in the provinces of Kien Hoa and Vinh Binh. This operation was in full swing when I arrived. According to military historian, retired Col. Harry G. Summers, Jr., when Speedy Express had concluded operations in May 1969, there were nearly 11,000 'enemy' casualties.

As a combat security officer, I had to acquaint myself quickly with intelligence reports on 'enemy' activity, and locations and types of friendly resources. My job was, in essence, to protect airplanes in between their bombing missions. Since the villages they were bombing had been identified as being in a 'free fire zone,' it was easy to rationalize destroying everything. On occasion, through ground observations, I witnessed the horrific aftermath of these bombing missions – villages with bodies of mostly young women, many children, and a few elderly strewn on the ground. I never saw any weapons in these virtually defenseless villages. The bombing of civilian population centers, which at first I thought must be a mistake, I later concluded was deliberate and systematic.

I had been in Vietnam only a short time before I began to sense that virtually everybody, other than Vietnamese business, political, and military leaders, was at least secretly hostile to the US presence, and alternately sympathetic with the Vietnamese struggle for independence from *any* outside political/military force. Though at first I did not want to believe this, it was increasingly confirmed by other experiences: discussions with other US Air Force personnel and members of the Vietnamese military, interactions with members of the US Army's Ninth Infantry Division, conversations with numerous Vietnamese in the area, examination of Seventh Air Force bombing reports that conflicted with my own personal knowledge of bombings, and the reading of a history of US intervention written by two Cornell University professors (Kahin and Lewis, 1967).

After Tet 1968, the CIA Phoenix program had begun intense efforts to eliminate perceived political and military leadership in the VC. US air and ground forces had become much more indiscriminate in killing Vietnamese civilians while glibly designating most of them as VC. I had been briefed that three-quarters of South Vietnam had been designated by the US military command and local Vietnamese officials as a 'free fire zone,' meaning that virtually any villager in that vast area could be killed without question. Nonetheless – or perhaps as a result – in my continued visits to various villages northwest and northeast of Can Tho, there seemed little real support among villagers for the US and our South Vietnamese political/military ally.

Bob Kerrey, as leader of a Navy Seal team, was likely participating in Operation Speedy Express and/or the Phoenix assassination program. Many Navy Seal units were identified as 'hunter–killer' teams, and were especially skilled at infiltrating areas by sea in small boats or as frogmen. Their rigorous training explicitly prepared them for just such missions.

## 1954–65: US thwarts 1954 Geneva Accords, defies Vietnamese sovereignty and conducts illegal covert war

We in the US knew little or nothing about the Vietnamese people, their history, or their authentic sentiments. The Vietnamese had a long history of successfully resisting outside forces, no matter the numbers of their own losses. They fought the Chinese for nearly a thousand years, and then the French for a hundred. After the end of World War II, the French suffered nearly 175,000 casualties in their effort to restore their prewar colony, while the Vietnamese suffered perhaps more than a million dead in defending their independence.

The unilateral US intervention began in 1954, *immediately* following the humiliating French defeat. Our ignorance as US Americans, along with our intrinsic cultural racism and historic sense of superiority, produced a lawless, brutal use of force that knew virtually no limits when it came to violent assaults against the Vietnamese people and their culture. We troopers were simply guinea pigs! We did not realize the Vietnamese were prepared to defend their sacred independence at any cost. We did not even believe that the Vietnamese had the right to their independence.

The 21 July 1954 Geneva Agreement concluded the French war against the Vietnamese and legally promised them a unifying election, *mandated* to be held in July 1956. The US government knew that fair elections, in effect, meant a victory for revered Communist leader Ho Chi Minh. This was unacceptable. Thus, in June 1954, *prior* to the signing of the historic Agreement, the US began CIA-directed internal sabotage operations against the Vietnamese, while setting up puppet Ngo Dinh Diem (brought over to Vietnam from the US) as 'our' political leader. No elections were ever held. This set the stage for yet another war for Vietnamese independence – this time from unwanted US forces and their South Vietnamese puppets.

The extent of the US government's interference with independence movements in Asia should not be underestimated. US National Security Council documents from 1956 declared that our 'national security ...

would be endangered by Communist domination of mainland Southeast Asia.' Secret military plans stated that 'nuclear weapons will be used in general war and in military operations short of general war.' By March 1961, the Pentagon top brass recommended sending 60,000 soldiers to western Laos accompanied by air power that included, if necessary, use of nuclear weapons to ensure that the Royal Laotian government would prevail against the popular insurgency being waged against it.

The covert operations intended to destabilize the Vietnamese independence movement were in direct violation of the Geneva Agreements. They were also in violation of the United Nations Charter and other international laws. This covert war lasted nearly eleven years until the overt invasion by US forces commenced on 8 March 1965. This invasion was also in violation of international laws, as well as the US Constitution, which requires a declaration of war by Congress prior to initiating acts of war.

## 1965–75: US moves to illegal overt intervention

For the ten years 1965–75, the US continued its lawless behavior, unleashing forces that caused (and continue to cause) incomprehensible devastation in Vietnam:

- Eight million tons of bombs (four times the amount dropped by the US in all World War II) destroyed an area the size of the State of Maine, if laid crater to crater.
- US forces utilized 8 million additional tons of other kinds of ordnance.
- Nearly 400,000 tons of napalm, a totally indiscriminate incendiary weapon, was dropped on human targets.
- The callous identification of as much as three-quarters of South Vietnam as a 'free fire zone' justified the murder of virtually anyone found in thousands of villages in those vast areas.
- A historically unprecedented level of chemical warfare was practiced in the indiscriminate spraying of nearly 20 million gallons on one-seventh the area of South Vietnam. The lingering effects of chemical warfare poisoning continue to plague the health of adult Vietnamese (and ex-GIs) while causing increased birth defects. Samples of soil, water, food, and body fat of Vietnamese continues to the present day to reveal dangerously elevated levels of dioxin.
- Today Vietnamese officials estimate the continued dangerous presence of 3.5 million landmines and 300,000 tons of unexploded ordnance, leftovers from the war. Tragically, these munitions continue to explode when farmers and children accidentally detonate them in their work

and play activities, and kill or injure several thousand every year. The Vietnamese report 40,000 people killed since 1975 by landmines and buried bombs alone. That means that every day four or five Vietnamese are killed due to US ordnance. The war against the Vietnamese continues.

Examination of US conduct during the war indicates violation of the United Nations Charter prohibiting unilateral or bilateral military interventions not sanctioned by the UN, the US constitutional requirement of a declaration of war, and rules for war conduct as outlined in its own army field manuals (incorporating the Nuremberg Principles – see below). In addition, US conduct in the war regularly violated the 1907 Hague Convention in respect to land wars and bombardment by naval forces, the 1949 Geneva Convention relating to protection of civilians, prisoners of war, and the wounded and sick, and the Nuremberg Principles as formulated by the International Law Commission in 1950 proscribing war crimes and crimes against humanity. A massive number of civilian murders and destruction of civilian infrastructures were achieved through ground actions, indiscriminate bombings, chemical defoliation, use of incendiary weapons and napalm, scorched-earth campaigns, forced transfers of civilians, use of gas, and regular utilization of mutilation and torture, among other methods. This shameful litany of crimes violated virtually every rule of war ever formulated.

It is now believed that the US and its allies killed as many as 5 million Southeast Asian citizens during the active war years. The numbers of dead in Laos and Cambodia remain uncounted, but as of 1971 a Congressional Research Service report prepared for the US Senate Foreign Relations Committee indicated that over 1 million Laotians had been killed, wounded, and turned into refugees, with the figure for Cambodia estimated at 2 million. More than half a million 'secret' US bombing missions to Laos, beginning in late 1964, devastated entire populations and decimated ancient cultures. Estimates indicate that around 230,000 tons of bombs were dropped over northern Laos in 1968 and 1969 alone. Increasing numbers of US military personnel were added on Laotian ground in 1961. Land invasions of Laos occurred for two months in early 1969, and again for a week in early 1971. 'Secret' bombing of Cambodia had begun in March 1969. An outright land invasion of the country occurred from late April 1970 through the end of June, causing thousands of casualties. And the raging US covert wars in these countries did not finally cease until 14 August 1973, inflicting countless additional casualties. When the bombing in Cambodia finally ceased, the US Air Force had officially recorded dropping nearly 260,000 tons of bombs there. The total tonnage of bombs dropped in Laos over eight-and-a-half years exceeded 2 million.

The consensus now is that *more* than 3 million Vietnamese were killed (Herman and Chomsky, 2002; Karnow, 1984), with 300,000 additional missing in action and presumed dead (Mydans, 2000; Faas and Page, 1997; Franklin, 2000). In the process, the US lost nearly 59,000 of her own men and women, with about 2,000 additional missing, while four of her allies lost over 6,000 more. South Vietnamese military forces counted nearly 225,000 dead. All this carnage was inflicted to destroy the basic rights and capacity of the Vietnamese to construct their own independent, sovereign society. None of these people deserved to die in war. Vietnamese, Laotians, Cambodians, and US military grunts were all victims. All of these corpses were created because of a 'cause' that had been concocted by white male plutocrats in Washington, many of whom possessed Ph.D.s from prestigious universities. These politicians and their appointees, along with profit-making arms makers/dealers, desired, as did most of their predecessors extending far back in US history, to ensure the destruction of people's democratic movements that threatened US hegemony over markets and resources – in this case those located in East Asia – and the profits to be derived therefrom. But perhaps never did a small country suffer so much from an imperial nation as the Vietnamese did from the United States.

## Comparison of casualties

To grasp the nearly incomprehensible consequences to the Vietnamese society, it is instructive to reflect that during the US war against the Vietnamese, nearly one in ten, or *10 per cent* of Vietnam's population of approximately 35 million, was killed. In addition, vast areas of territory were devastated by bombing and chemical warfare, and Vietnam's infra-structure was largely destroyed.

This contrasts with one in 3,300, or 0.03 per cent of the US popu-lation, who needlessly died in the lawless intervention. What would be the effects on US society if we had suffered losses of 20 million, or 10 per cent of our population, in a war? Furthermore, how would it have affected us if vast regions of our country had been bombed and chemically de-foliated, simply because we insisted on the right to be free from a foreign power intending to dominate and control us?

## Vietnam was not an aberration

An honest examination of United States history shows that, unfortunately, violent intervention such as in Vietnam is not an aberration. The defining and enabling experience of US civilization was the holocaust perpetrated against millions of original inhabitants of the land (see Ward Churchill's and Peter Dale Scott's chapters in this volume). Native peoples living in thousands of villages and hunting regions were ruthlessly uprooted from their land base across the hemisphere. That act was followed by the kidnapping and transporting of millions of mostly Africans to the Americas to provide 'free' labor for building our original agricultural and mercantile system. Two-thirds of those originally seized in Africa perished while resisting arrest or during the deplorable conditions of transport to the coastal ports or across the Atlantic Ocean. This amounted to the second holocaust that underlies the foundation of US American civilization. This is an intrinsic part of our cultural ethos and karma, and is equally applicable to the other emergent Eurocentric nation-states in the Americas.

The historic record also reveals that the US has intervened militarily more than 400 times in more than 100 nations (Blechman and Kaplan, 1978; Congressional Research Service, 1993; Blum, 2000: chs 11, 17) to expand our control over global resources and markets – that is, expansion of resources and markets at gunpoint. In only five of those interventions did the Congress declare war as required by its constitution. As the body of international law unfolded, virtually all of these military incursions contravened its prohibitions. None of them (besides World War II) was predicated on any genuine concept of self-defense.[1] Additionally, it is now known that the US has covertly intervened in a variety of destabilizing actions *at least 6,000 times in over 100 countries* since the end of World War II alone.[2] All of these were gross criminal actions that violated a multitude of laws, both national and international.

How can we ignore this record? One of the principles now better understood is the perennial influence of the past. In other words, the past is always with us in the present. Lessons inherent in the history and evolving ecology of life's processes need to be honestly acknowledged and incorporated as part of today's wisdom. To mistakenly ignore these lessons risks almost certain repetition of previous injurious behaviors, with ever more severe consequences. As cultural historian Lewis Mumford has concluded, 'Without intuitions and memories, without ancient cultural landmarks, the intelligence is enfeebled' (Mumford, 1970: 75).

## Historical precedents of imperial behavior

Gruesome human behavior is not unique to US Americans. There are a number of historical precedents and cultural beliefs that have justified slavery and dehumanizing treatment of 'unfortunates.' The term 'civilization' first took form under kingship, which infused itself with divine power. Thus, centralized power became an end in itself, and emerged as the chief identifying mark of 'civilization.' Lewis Mumford has summarized its chief features as human sacrifice, war, arbitrary inequalities in wealth and privilege, and slavery and forced labor for industrial, agricultural and military purposes. Mesopotamia and Indus civilizations (4000–1800 BC), Egypt (3500–2180 BC), China (1700–1050 BC), Greece (750–400 BC) and Rome (500 BC-400 AD), all had slave economies to varying degrees. The Roman Empire required elaborate schemes of rationalized exploitation to maintain its grip over vast and distant territories. Notable Greek and Roman philosophers condoned the cataloguing of certain persons as inferior to others, in order to build a 'good' life. By the end of the 1400s, slavery was endemic in parts of medieval European, Islamic, and African societies. The Italians, Portuguese, and Spanish had well-established slave trades.

When Columbus stumbled into the populated Caribbean in October 1492, he launched what was to become perhaps the most egregious and systematic destruction of indigenous societies ever known. A handful of small 'advanced' nation-states at the western extremity of Eurasia in 400 years brought within their political control many of the diverse peoples of the earth across five continents. Though the western hemisphere became known as the 'New World,' the exploration, colonialization, and outright conquering of indigenous and emerging national societies touched virtually every region of the globe. The Europeans believed they were bringing 'blessings' – their Western science and Christian faith – to the 'savages' and 'subhumans.'

One of the most significant historic alterations of local economies and cultures occurred in the late Victorian period, especially the last quarter of the nineteenth century. This period saw many of the non-European peasant societies *involuntarily* integrated into a world economy. Essentially, European colonizers force-marched many of the world's indigenous into the emerging global capitalist economy. Widespread production and export of cash crops, and extraction and export of natural resources for the benefit of elites both domestic and foreign, replaced subsistence farming and decentralized village life. This marked the beginning of the 'Third' World, and an era in which dramatic income and wealth disparities (the 'development gap') created a deeply entrenched, nearly irrevocable division of humanity into classes. In effect, this was the foundation of the 'structural adjustment' program which today has become our political/economic religion, and the forerunner of what we now call globalization.[3]

## The special intensity and reach of Western and US imperialism

There is something striking about Western man, and the role the United States has played in asserting this Eurocentric model throughout the world. Novelist and historian Hans Koning has declared, 'What sets the West apart is its persistence, its capacity to stop at nothing' (Koning, 1991: 116). As Lewis Mumford summarizes, 'Wherever Western man went slavery, land robbery, lawlessness, culture-wrecking, and the outright extermination of both wild beasts and tame men went with him' (Mumford, 1970: 9).

Reading the accounts of early Puritans and white (male) settlers, founding fathers, US military officers, and countless politicians provides an explicit idea of the racist and arrogant thinking that possessed the founders of our 'civilization.' Captain John Smith of the Virginia colony in the early 1600s referred to the original inhabitants as 'subanimals' and 'beasts' worthy only of 'extermination' (Drinnon, 1990: 52, 55). Puritan leader John Endecott of the Massachusetts Bay Colony regularly ordered 'death' to the Pequot Indians (34, 51). The US founding document, the Declaration of Independence, refers to the original inhabitants as 'merciless savages,' and George Washington termed them 'beasts of prey' to be 'destroyed' (65, 99, 331). European settlers regularly called them 'brutes' or 'vermin' to be 'destroyed' (*200 Years*, 1973: 65). General William Tecumseh Sherman in the 1870s ordered 'extermination' as the 'final solution' to the 'Indian problem' (Fellman, 1995: 260; Drinnon, 1990: 329). It is highly interesting to note that Hitler's ideas of concentration camps and genocide were partly inspired by his study of the United States' policy of extermination of its indigenous population (Toland, 1976: 802).

The United States emerged as a world imperial power at the end of the Victorian period. This marked the beginning of an empire that would ultimately exceed all predecessors in scope, reach, and impact. The 'Spanish–American' war launched the US as a force in Latin America, the Caribbean, the Pacific, and parts of Asia. By this time, US agricultural and manufacturing production had begun seriously to exceed its capacity for domestic consumption. Maintenance of US capitalist profitability demanded identifying, then securing, overseas markets. The European powers had already established the model for colonization. The United States would refine and expand it.

In his message to Congress in 1904, President Roosevelt, after having seized Panama by force from Colombia in 1903 on the grounds of the latter being 'incapable of keeping order on the Isthmus,' maintained that in 'flagrant cases of wrongdoing' by Latin American republics, the US had the right to exercise an 'international police power' over them. This came to be known as the 'Big Stick' policy, and justified increased intervention into Latin American affairs. As a significant extension of the original Monroe Doctrine first declared in 1823, it also became known as the Roosevelt Corollary. All in all, the US sent in the Marines on more than a hundred occasions into twenty-three Latin American countries, starting as early as 1831, usually citing as justification the need 'to protect US interests and property.' The policy continues.

By the time the US entered World War I, 'progressive' President Wilson had Marines stationed in Haiti, Nicaragua, and the Dominican Republic. During his tenure, Marines landed in Mexico (eleven times), Cuba (1917), and Panama (1918). Furthermore, in 1918 Wilson sent 13,000 US troops to aid the 'White' side of the Russian civil war in seeking to overthrow the revolution. (Some say the Cold War really began at this point.) Wilson had earlier discussed the need for overseas expansion as the new frontier to replace the continent. He stressed the need for markets 'to which diplomacy and if need be power must make an open way.... Since trade ignores national boundaries and the manufacturer insists on having the world as a market, the flag of his nation must follow him, and the doors of the nations which are closed must be battered down' (Williams, 1972: 72). The Monroe Doctrine of 1823 had become a justification for belligerent US political, military and economic intervention as nations became increasingly economically dependent upon the United States and its profiteers.

With the advent of aerial bombings prior to and during World War I, the number of civilians murdered increased dramatically. The bombing of civilian targets is believed to have first ocurred with firebombs dropped by the Italians on Tripoli in 1911, where news accounts reported that 'Non-combatants, young and old, were slaughtered ruthlessly, without compunction and without shame.' This crime preceded similar, more systematic bombings by Italy in Ethiopia in 1936–37 and by Germany in Guernica, Spain, in 1937.

In September 1918, US Army Colonel William J. 'Billy' Mitchell led a mass bombing attack of some 1,500 aircraft employed in the first large-scale close air support of ground operations. This ultimately gave birth to the US love of air power, which, by the post-World War II period, would know no equal. The policy of mass extermination of civilians from the air had begun, and the US became active in such campaigns follow-ing the First World War. It used aerial bombings to support Marine ground actions in Haiti, 1919–20, and in Nicaragua, 1927–33, in efforts to rout native people resisting US occupation forces. In the process, it murdered countless civilians, always disregarding the cries of the people for due recognition. In 1920, the NAACP (National Association for the Advancement of Colored People) investigated US war crimes in Haiti and concluded that 3,000 Haitians had been killed by air power and Marines. A decade later, thousands of Nicaraguans were killed defending their country from an occupying force of 12,000 US Marines saved by the 'miracle of Marine air.'

The stage was set for the massive indiscriminate bombings of World War II, Korea, Vietnam, Iraq, and Serbia/Kosovo. Any genuine concern for civilians virtually disappeared by the end of World War II. The use of biological warfare in northern Korea and adjacent areas of China in 1952 (Endicott and Hagerman, 1998), and the unprecedented use of chemical warfare in Vietnam from 1962 to 1971, took a countless toll on civilian populations as well. (It is important to remind ourselves that a central provision of international law is clearly enshrined in the Geneva Conventions: 'The civilian population as such, as well as individual civilians, shall not be the object of attack.')

With the fall of the Berlin Wall in 1989 and consequent erosion of the serious 'threat' posed to capitalism by the socialist model, Pax Americana became a unipolar international order. Historic US racism and ethnocentrism were further entrenched. The United States, effectively a plutocracy under the guise of a constitutional democracy, now oversees the activities of the world's political and economic 'leaders' and profiteers. The result: a global economy that enriches a few at the expense of the vast majority and the health of the planet itself.

Tragically, we now face threats more serious than existed during the Cold War. The United States, as the world's only superpower, is virtually able to negate any effective power the United Nations might have to ensure compliance with its own Charter and other international laws. Thus, one bully, armed to the teeth, can pretty much do as its plutocrats dictate, with no effective checks from outside political forces or institutions designed to ensure compliance with international law.

The extent and depth of the horrendous record of US behavior and treatment toward foreign civilians remains unrecognized to this day. Perhaps this pattern differs little from that of previous empires or imperial wannabes, such as Great Britain, Japan, and Germany. However, the US record of marauding over the *past century*, in so many countries and against so many indigenous societies, distinguishes it from previous imperial nation-states. No one knows how many people have been murdered and maimed by these aggressive (and lawless) actions, but the figure is in multiples of millions – enough to constitute a third foundational holocaust for the modern global order. British playwright Harold Pinter describes US foreign policy with the phrase, 'Kiss my ass or I'll kick your head in' (Pinter,

1998: 216). This is a harsh description, but after a careful examination of the historic record it cannot be dispensed with as just crackpot talk.

## The American Way of Life

Addiction to the privileged American Way of Life (AWOL) motivates the exaction of heavy demands upon Mother Earth and her citizens. As a nation, the US has just 4.5 per cent of the world's population, yet insists on consuming anywhere from 25 per cent to nearly half of the world's resources, depending on which asset is examined. For example, the US consumes slightly more than 25 per cent of the world's oil production, but higher percentages of other critical resources. The US has nearly 500 passenger cars per 1,000 people, nearly six times the rate for the entire world's population, consuming high percentages of the globe's steel and rubber resources. People in the US consume paper at seventeen times the rate of those in the 'developing' world, and nearly six times the rate of the total world population.

In order to maintain, even expand, the luxuries of AWOL, and the profits derived therefrom, the United States must *continually* rationalize hegemonic measures to assure control over the globe's resources, markets, and pool of cheap labor. Thus, we espouse the religion of 'neoliberal' globalization, the goal of which is to extend unfettered capitalism to every nook and cranny of the earth, commodifying virtually every aspect of life, while privatizing and deregulating national economies, and threatening the skein of life as it has unfolded for millions of years.

## Healing as an antidote to our 'forever war'

An honest reckoning with the readily comprehensible, though deeply painful, lessons of Vietnam offers the American nation an opportunity to step back from its long imperial history. Vietnam is and will remain our 'forever war' – unless we choose to heed its lessons. It is important to recognize that our 'civilization' has been built on three holocausts, facilitated by racism and arrogant ethnocentrism. With powerful economic interests now located in every region of the world, and a military might that assures protection of the profits and resources necessary to maintain the privileged AWOL, it is virtually impossible for the US earnestly to seek peace. That would require commitment to a fair and just allocation of global resources. Such commitment can only be born out of a radically transformed consciousness, one that recognizes the sacred interconnectedness of all life and the need for respectful mutual aid. Yet when examined thoughtfully, this may be the only rational choice available to us.

The now unipolar, Pax Americana mindset, if not arrested soon, will almost certainly ensure the continued destruction of cultures, national sovereignties, and ecosystems. The rapid extinction of species that the world is now experiencing, unprecedented in recorded history, is likely a foreshadowing of our own extinction.

We veterans who understand this grotesquely unfair reality can courageously choose to take responsibility for our actions, especially since our cowardly government, which made the intervention decisions, is sadly unlikely to do so. Regularly forgotten, for example, is that the Paris Peace Accords signed by the United States and Vietnamese governments on 27 January 1973, complemented by the letter signed by President Nixon on 1 February, promised more than $4 billion for healing the wounds of war and postwar reconstruction. The US shamelessly reneged on this promise, and the aid was never provided.

The yearning for healing is so deeply felt that some veterans have returned to Southeast Asia, often in small groups, to participate in a variety of humanitarian missions, setting an example for our wider society. These missions range from building health clinics, orphanages, and schools, to the distribution of desperately needed materials and supplies, and removal of unexploded land mines and other ordnance. Atonement has been an important theme to these veterans, who now know that the war was wrong and our role in it was personally unfortunate, even if this can be ascribed to our ignorance. It has become important to assuage our pain and repair deep psychic wounds, and those of the Vietnamese as well, to feel whole once again. These acts of restoration help veterans experience a global citizenship, an antidote to the feeling of being an isolated 'American.' These individuals have chosen to avail themselves of the lessons of the Vietnam experience to salvage healthy lives through earnest truth-seeking and reconciliation. It is through healing that thinking and *feelings* undergo radical changes – changes that can give birth to alternative visions of a sustainable society, ecology, and polity. The alternatives may be so radically different as to be hardly recognizable when compared with today's pathological structures.

Bob Kerrey and his men killed for a massive Lie. I herewith offer a healing prescription for Senator Kerrey; other US souls still haunted by participation in that criminal war (or other wars) might consider something similar:

• First, Mr Kerrey, publicly return the Bronze Star you received for the killing of the civilians at Thang Phong. The medal needs to be renounced as drenched in the blood of the innocent people of that village.

- Second, travel to the village of Thang Phong in the Province of Kien Hoa to express your personal sorrow for the consequences of your actions, asking those people for forgiveness.
- Third, create a reparations or atonement fund, in cooperation with the Vietnamese people in that area, as a concrete and meaningful effort to repair in some way the harm done.
- And fourth, Mr Kerrey – perhaps the most important act for your own healing and for the healing of our entire nation – begin publicly teaching the authentic history of the Vietnam War and the Vietnamese people: how the US sabotaged the 1956 unifying elections mandated by the 1954 Geneva Agreements; how it fabricated a puppet government not supported by the vast majority of the Vietnamese people; how it maintained its imposture through a series of incredible lies that put Vietnamese, Cambodian, Laotian, and US men and women in harm's way, causing the needless death and maiming of millions. Thus you can educate US American society as to why so many civilians were murdered in confusion about who was VC or not, as the vast majority of Vietnamese were simply defending their rights to be free of unwanted outside forces. We US citizens would do no less if our own country was invaded.

It is true that every privileged power structure, extending back several millennia, has expended a large amount of resources to maintain its status, resisting any inkling of revolutionary ambitions to alter the formula of power. Cultural historians such as Lewis Mumford, Kirkpatrick Sale and the humane Russian anarchist Peter Kropotkin suggest that efforts at large-scale change have tended to support, perhaps naively, the very system they challenge – since they standardly accept the ideological premises of the prevailing power complex, no matter what its name. This merely transfers power from one ruling class to another, leaving the overall mechanism intact, with all its inherent defects.

It is my belief that humanity is on the verge of a new dynamic, where profound changes may arise from small groups and local communities that are able to withdraw from the traditional power complex and experiment with decentralized alternatives. What other power can effectively negate a bullying superpower, other than a transformation of heart and soul, from the very people throughout the hinterland whose complicity is required to sustain the bully? The alternative must be to create a new, decentralized society without repressive and impersonal manifestations of power. A new, empowering consciousness can liberate men and women from the official agencies of power, while resurrecting locally autonomous cultures and economies that adhere to the principles of sustainable bio-regions.

The Zapatista revolt that erupted in Chiapas, Mexico, in 1994 articulated something similar to this revived indigenous model, in response to 'neoliberalism.' The anti-globalization movement may also be showing signs of evolving in this way, promoting empowered localization as the alternative to grinding globalization. Not seeking to seize control of the power complex, which is viewed as increasingly suspect and unaccountable, the nonviolent radical model experiments with withdrawal from that complex, while quietly undermining it through lack of support. It seeks to restore empowerment to its more ancient source, the authority in humble human personalities and their intimate interaction with small, face-to-face communities and local ecosystems. Once this model becomes widespread, then a bio-regional model of federated cooperatives can emerge — one that abides by a truly sustainable, non-growth dynamic, respectful of the carrying capacity of Mother Earth.

## Conclusion

Veterans are in a unique position to initiate courageous leadership in a national healing process. This requires speaking the truth about what we know, including the fact that all people and the earth are intimately interconnected. Our souls, and the soul of our country, are at stake. Furthermore, the future of peace in the world may rest on a profound reckoning on the part of US Americans: one that acknowledges that our historical imperial policies have been deeply wrong, and that we now wish to make amends for our crimes, our arrogance, and our ignorance. I urge all citizens, especially veterans from Vietnam and other wars, to find the courage to reveal our own, and our country's, dark side; to disclose the incredible lies that our government has inflicted upon us, leading to the murder of millions of innocent human beings; and to experiment with a vision for life-affirming models that nurture small-scale, ecologically sustainable, truly democratic communities. The future of humankind may hinge on the results.

## Notes

1. When examining the larger context of the attack on 'our' Hawaiian property at Pearl Harbor in World War II, it is important to note that the indigenous peoples of Hawaii have never to this day consented to the involuntary annexation of their land by the United States in 1898. Furthermore, evidence now abounds that not only was there knowledge in advance at the highest levels within the US government of the Japanese attack, but that the latter was *deliberately provoked* to persuade an isolationist US popu-

lation to enter the war that it would not support unless attacked first (Stinnett, 2000).

2. On 18 June 1948, US President Harry Truman signed National Security Directive 10/2 (NSC-10/2), in which covert operations were specifically, and broadly, defined. The Central Intelligence Agency (CIA), created less than a year earlier, and directly answerable to the President through the newly established National Security Agency (NSC), was given primary responsibility for carrying out the covert actions as the NSC may from 'time to time direct.' There was an important stipulation, however, that 'the US government can plausibly disclaim any responsibility for them.'

This vaguely worded authority has been utilized thousands of times to carry out covert actions, from assassination attempts, government overthrows, and paramilitary operations, to concerted propaganda efforts, interference in free elections, and economic destabilization campaigns, in every corner of the world. The first indication of numbers of operations was revealed in 1976 when the Church Committee Report on CIA activities was published, and its chair, US Senator Frank Church (D-ID), stated that from 1961 to 1974 he had identified 900 major and 3,000 minor operations (Prados, 1996). If the period from 1947, when the CIA was first created, to 1960 witnessed covert actions at the same rate, one can estimate 1,800 major and 6,000 minor covert operations through 1974. Former CIA officer John Stockwell extrapolated in 1990 that the CIA likely had initiated and overseen about 3,000 major and over 10,000 minor covert operations up to that time (Stockwell, 1991).

Increasingly, the Special Operations components of the various military services work very closely, almost as associates, with the CIA. The Pentagon has acknowledged that Special Operations Forces have been deployed on thousands of missions to more than a hundred countries. In addition, the US has either an embassy or interests section in the vast majority of the world's 200-plus nations. At virtually all of these stations are assigned CIA case officers working under State Department cover.

The US government has historically provided military and/or economic aid to more than 150 countries, and regularly protects the assets and operations of thousands of transnational corporations, and trillions of dollars worth of investments, throughout the globe. This policy has regularly established the need for 'stable' economic climates, free of any 'threatening' insurgent activities by a nation's citizens – the majority of whom, more often than not, are aggrieved and suffering.

Identification of the nature and specific locations of the various secret US activities is made more difficult by the institution of 'plausible deniability.' However, by perusing various sources, one can identify more than a hundred countries from 1947 to the present where the CIA has chosen, from its vast menu of covert options, to interfere with the sovereignty of indigenous groups and nation-states. Almost without exception, every one of these actions has violated both domestic and international laws (Barnaby, 1988: 56–7, chart; Blum, 1995; Herman and Chomsky, 2002; *Third World Guide*, 1986: 489–96; Center For National Security Studies, 1977).

3. Modern, systematic structural adjustment was initiated in Chile following the 1973 military coup by General Augusto Pinochet, carried out at the insistence of the US, that overthrew the democratically elected government of President Salvador Allende. Chilean economists, trained at the conservative post-World War II University of Chicago School of Economics under the leadership of Milton Friedman and George Stigler, were able radically to transform the Chilean economy, using the junta's dictatorial power to establish what they viewed as the free-market paradise originally sketched out by Adam Smith in *The Wealth of Nations* (1776). The World Bank and the International Monetary Fund (IMF) enthusiastically contributed money to facilitate the socialization of the adjustment's benefits in favor of the rich, while the losses were thrust upon the

poor. The emerging democracy in Chile was destroyed, and the economic dominance of the Chilean upper class substantially increased. This effectively perpetuated the egregious effects of colonization in a different form.

# References

Barnaby, F. (1988). *The Gaia peace atlas.* New York: Doubleday.

Blechman, B.M., and Kaplan, S.S. (1978). *Force without war: U.S. armed forces as a political instrument*, Appendix B. Washington, D.C.: The Brookings Institution.

Blum, W. (2000). *Rogue state: A guide to the world's only superpower.* Monroe, ME: Common Courage Press.

——— (1995). *Killing hope: U.S. military and CIA interventions since World War II.* Monroe, ME: Common Courage Press.

Center For National Security Studies. (CNSS). (1977). *30 years of covert action.* Washington, DC: Center for National Security Studies.

Congressional Research Service (CRS) (Foreign Affairs and National Defense Division), Library of Congress (1993). *Instances of United States Armed Forces abroad, 1798–1993.* Washington, DC: Congressional Research Service.

Drinnon, R. (1990). *Facing west: The metaphysics of Indian hating and empire building.* New York: Schocken Books.

Endicott, S., and Hagerman, E. (1998). *The United States and biological warfare: Secrets from the early Cold War and Korea.* Bloomington, IN: Indiana University Press.

Faas, H., and Page, T., eds (1997). *Requiem: By the photographers who died in Vietnam and Indochina.* New York: Random House.

Fellman, M. (1995). *Citizen Sherman: A life of William Tecumseh Sherman.* New York: Random House.

Franklin, H.B. (2000). *Vietnam and other fantasies.* Amherst, MA: University of Massachusetts Press.

Herman, E.S., and Chomsky, N. (2002 [1988]). *Manufacturing consent: The political economy of the mass media.* New York: Pantheon.

Kahin, G.M., and Lewis, J.W. (1967). *The United States in Vietnam.* New York: Dial Press.

Karnow, S. (1984). *Vietnam: A history.* New York: Penguin Books.

Koning, H. (1991 [1976]). *Columbus: His enterprise – exploding the myth.* New York: Monthly Review Press.

Mumford, L. (1970). *The myth of the machine: The pentagon of power.* New York: Harcourt Brace Jovanovich.

Mydans, S. (2000). A war story's missing pages: Vietnam forgets those who lost. *The New York Times.* www.nytimes.com/library/world/asia/042400vietnam-graves.html.

Pinter, H. (1998). *Various voices: Prose, poetry, politics, 1948–1998.* New York: Grove Press.

Prados, J. (1996). *President's secret wars: CIA and Pentagon covert operations from World War II through the Persian Gulf.* Chicago: Elephant Paperbacks, Ivan R. Dee.

Stinnett, R.B. (2000). *Day of deceit: The truth about FDR and Pearl Harbor.* New York: The Free Press.

Stockwell, J. (1991). *The praetorian guard.* Cambridge, MA: South End Press.

Toland, J. (1976). *Adolf Hitler*, Vol. II. Garden City, NY: Doubleday.

*Third World Guide* (1986). New York: Grove Press.

*200 Years: A bicentennial illustrated history of the United States*, Vol 2. (1973). Washington, DC: US News & World Report.

Williams, W.A. (1972). *The tragedy of American diplomacy.* New York: W.W. Norton.

# Inaugural Statement to the Russell Vietnam War Crimes Tribunal (1966)

## Jean-Paul Sartre

Our Tribunal was formed, on the initiative of Lord Bertrand Russell, to decide whether the accusations of 'war crimes' levelled against the government of the United States as well as against those of South Korea, New Zealand and Australia, during the conflict in Vietnam, are justified.

During this inaugural session, the origin, function, aims and limits of the Tribunal must be clarified: the Tribunal means to explain itself, without sidetracking, on the question of what has been called its 'legitimacy.'

In 1945, something absolutely new in history appeared at Nuremberg with the first international Tribunal formed to pass judgement on crimes committed by a belligerent power. Until then there had been a few international agreements, for instance the Briand–Kellogg pact, which were aimed at limiting the *jus ad bellum*; but as no other body had been created to implement them, the relations between the powers continued to operate under the law of the jungle. It could not be otherwise: the nations which had built their wealth upon the conquest of great colonial empires would not have tolerated being judged upon their actions in Africa or Asia.

From 1939, the Hitlerian furies had endangered the world to such an extent that the horrified Allies decided, since they were to be the victors, to judge and condemn the wars of aggression and conquest, the maltreatment of prisoners and the tortures, as well as the racist practices known as 'genocide,' unaware that they were condemning themselves, in this way, for their own actions in the colonies.

For this reason, that is to say because they were recognizing the Nazi crimes, and because, in the more universal sense, they were opening the way to a real jurisdiction for the denunciation and condemnation of war crimes wherever committed, and whoever the culprits, the Tribunal of

Nuremberg is still the manifestation of a change of capital importance: the substitution of *jus ad bellum* by *jus contra bellum*.

Unfortunately, as is wont to happen whenever a new force is created by historical exigencies, this Tribunal was not free from serious faults. It has been said that it was a *diktat* of the victors to the vanquished and, which comes to the same thing, that it was not really being international: one group of nations was judging another. Would it have been more worthwhile to have taken the judges from neutral countries? I cannot say. What is certain, however, is that, although the decisions were perfectly just by ethical standards, they did not convince all Germans. The legitimacy of the magistrates and their sentences is contested to this day. Also, it has been declared that, if the fortunes of war had been otherwise, a tribunal of the Axis could have condemned the Allies for the bombing of Dresden or for that of Hiroshima.

Such a body would not have been difficult to set up. It would have sufficed that the body created for the judgement of the Nazis had continued after its original task, or that the United Nations, considering all the consequences of what had just been achieved, would, by a vote of the General Assembly, have consolidated it into a permanent tribunal, empowered to investigate and to judge all accusations of war crimes, even if the accused should be one of the countries that had been responsible for the sentencing at Nuremberg. In this way, the implicit universality of the original intention would have been clearly defined. However, we know what did happen: hardly had the last guilty German been sentenced than the Tribunal vanished and no one ever heard of it again.

Are we therefore so pure? Have there been no war crimes since 1945? Have we never had further resort to violence or to aggression? Have there been no more 'genocides'? Has no large country ever tried to break by force the sovereignty of a smaller one? Has there never been reason for denouncing more Oradours [Nazi 'reprisal' massacre in France in 1944 – Ed.] or Auschwitzes?

You know the truth: in the last twenty years, the great historical act has been the struggle of the underdeveloped nations for their freedom. The colonial empires have crumbled, and in their place independent nations have grown or have reclaimed ancient and traditional independence which had been eliminated by colonialism. All this has happened in suffering, sweat and blood. A tribunal such as that of Nuremberg has become a permanent necessity. I have already said that, before the Nazi trials, war was lawless. The Nuremberg Tribunal, an ambiguous reality, was created from the highest legal principles no doubt but, at the same time, it created a precedent, the embryo of a tradition. Nobody can go back, stop what has already existed, nor, when a small and poor country is the object of aggression, prevent one from thinking back to those trials and saying to oneself: it is this *very same thing* that was condemned then. In this way, the hasty and incomplete measures taken and then abandoned by the Allies in 1945 have created a real gap in international affairs. We sadly lack an organization which has been created and affirmed in its permanency and universality and which has irreversibly defined its rights and duties. It is a gap which *must* be filled and yet which no one will fill.

There are, in fact, two sources of power for such a body. The first is the state and its institutions. However, in this period of violence most governments, if they took such an initiative, would fear that it might one day be used against them and that they would find themselves in the dock with the accused.

And then, for many, the United States is a powerful ally: who would dare ask for the resurrection of a tribunal whose first action would be to demand an inquiry on the Vietnam conflict? The other source is the people, in a revolutionary period, when institutions are changing. But, although the struggle is implacable, how could the masses, divided by frontiers, unite and impose on the various governments an institution which would be a true *Court of the People?*

The Russell Tribunal was born of this doubly contradictory conclusion: the judgement of Nuremberg had necessitated the existence of an institution to inquire into war crimes and, if necessary, to sit in judgement; today neither governments nor the masses are capable of forming one. We are perfectly aware that we have not been given a mandate by anyone; but we took the initiative to meet, and we also know that nobody *could* have given us a mandate. It is true that our Tribunal is not an institution. But, it is not a substitute for any institution already in existence: it is, on the contrary, formed out of a void and for a real need. We were not recruited or invested with real powers by governments: but, as we have just seen, the investiture at Nuremberg was not enough to give the jurists un-questioned legality.... The Russell Tribunal believes, on the contrary, that its legality comes from both its absolute powerlessness and its universality.

We are powerless: that is the guarantee of our independence. There is nothing to help us except for the participation of the supporting commit-tees which are, like ourselves, meetings of private individuals. As we do not represent any government or party, we cannot receive orders. We will examine the facts 'in our souls and our consciences,' as we say, or, if one prefers, in the full liberty of our spirits. None of us can state, today, how the discussions will turn out and whether we answer yes or no to the accusations, or whether we will come to a conclusion at all, perhaps deciding that the evidence, though real, is insufficiently proven. What is certain, in any case, is that our weakness, even if we are convinced by the proof brought before us, would not enable us to condemn. What can even the lightest sentence mean if we do not have the means to put it into effect? We will therefore limit ourselves, should this arise, to declaring that this or that act does in fact fall under the jurisdiction of Nuremberg, and that it is therefore a war crime and that, if the law were applied, it would be appropriate for this or that sentence to be carried out. In this case, if possible, we will name the guilty. Thus, the Russell Tribunal will have no other function in this inquiry and its conclusions, but to make everybody understand the necessity for international jurisdiction – which it has neither the means nor the ambition to replace and the essence of which would be to resuscitate the *jus contra bellum*, stillborn at Nuremberg, and to substitute legal, ethical laws for the law of the jungle.

From the very fact that we are simple citizens, we have been able, in coopting ourselves from all over the world, to give our Tribunal a more universal structure than that which prevailed at Nuremberg. I do not only mean that a larger number of countries is represented; from this point of view there are still many gaps. But, most of all, whilst in 1945 the Germans were represented only in the dock, or sometimes as witnesses, here several members of the jury are from the USA. This means that they come from the country whose very policy is our subject and that they have, therefore, their own ways of understanding it. Whatever may be their conclusions, the intimate relation with their own country and its institutions and traditions will necessarily be reflected in this Tribunal's conclusions.

Whatever may be our wishes for impartiality and universality, we are very conscious that this does not legitimize our undertaking. What we would really like is that our legitimation would be in retrospect, or *a posteriori*. In fact we do not work for ourselves nor for our own edification, and we do not presume to impose our conclusions like a thunderbolt. In truth, we would wish, with press collaboration, to maintain constant contact between ourselves and the masses all over the world who are painfully watching the tragedy in Vietnam. We hope that they will be learning while we learn, that they will watch and understand, and come to their own conclusions. These conclusions, whatever they may be, we would wish to be reached individually and independently of those we come to ourselves. This session is a communal undertaking for which the final term should be, as a philosopher said, *une verité devenue*. If the masses agree with our judgement, it will become truth, and we, at the very moment when we step back so that they will become the guardians and powerful supporters of that truth, will then know that we have been legitimized. When the people show their agreement they will also show a greater need: that a real 'War Crimes Tribunal' be created on a permanent basis, that these crimes may be denounced and not sanctioned anywhere and at any time.

These last remarks reply to a critical comment made, without ill-feeling, in a Paris newspaper: 'What a strange Tribunal: jurymen but no judge!' It is true, we are only jurymen, we have no power to condemn, nor to acquit anyone. Therefore, we are not prosecutors. There will not even be a real accusation. Maître Matarasso, President of the Legal Commission, will read you a statement of the charges registered. The jurists, at the end of the session, will have to pronounce on these statements: are they justified or not? But judges exist everywhere. It is for the peoples of the world and, in particular, the American people that we are working.

# 9

# Charles Horman versus Henry Kissinger: US Intervention in 1970s Chile and the Case for Prosecutions

## Mario I. Aguilar

This chapter explores the role of Henry Kissinger and the US Government in the destruction of democracy in Chile. It analyses primary sources from the US National Security Archive Documents on Chile, along with Civil Action 77–1748, *Joyce Horman et al.* v. *Henry Kissinger et al.*, which clearly implicate Kissinger in fostering large-scale human rights violations.

Following the argument of Christopher Hitchens in *The Trial of Henry Kissinger* (Hitchens, 2001), I argue that the extensive killing of socialists and communists in Chile followed a policy, pushed by Kissinger in the name of democracy, under which not even US citizens were spared. In conclusion, I suggest that there is a case for international prosecution even though the US has not yet ratified the United Nations Convention on Torture.

The late twentieth century witnessed several events of international significance that changed our understanding of diplomacy as an interventionist policy and that catalyzed important legal investigations related to Chile. Prior to these events, the International Conventions on Human Rights and Torture were applied solely to those who had committed a material deed that was considered genocidal, as in the case of the Nazis tried in Nuremberg for crimes against humanity. The events in question were:

1. The arrest of Augusto Pinochet, the former Chilean dictator, in October 1998 in London, which brought to the forefront a number of issues pertaining to international law and the possible arrest of those accused of crimes against humanity by countries other than their own. Pinochet's arrest was followed by lengthy debates in the British Courts, the House

of Commons, and the House of Lords, regarding individual complicity in larger political conflicts, international law, and national state sovereignty, and the legal responsibility of those who did not prevent human rights abuses, such as kidnapping and torture, when they had the political power to do so.

2. The decision by the US government to declassify secret documents relating to Chile during the Pinochet regime in December 1998, followed by the subsequent declassification of thousands of other documents in the following years.[1]

3. The constitution of ad hoc International Tribunals in The Hague and Tanzania that received information, issued arrest warrants, and tried criminals involved in the mass extermination of ethnic groups in the former Yugoslavia and Rwanda.

Further investigations followed these developments, led by Spanish Judge Baltasar Garzón and related to the cooperation among several Latin American governments during the 1970s in arresting, torturing, killing, and disposing of the bodies of political opponents – the so-called Operation Condor. These legal investigations made it clear that the US State Department and the CIA had inside knowledge about Chilean events, and in some cases had been directly involved in undercover operations during the 1970s. Such knowledge and operations coincided with the years in which Henry Kissinger served as President Nixon's Assistant for National Security and as President Nixon's and President Ford's Secretary of State. This period in US foreign policy saw the US intervene in Vietnam and Indochina, Bangladesh, Chile, Cyprus, East Timor, as well as other regions of the world. Moreover, the release of declassified US security documents revealed Kissinger's role as a direct instigator of some of the human rights abuses perpetrated in other countries, including Chile.

In the wake of the publication of Hitchens's book, and the final delivery of declassified US documents in November 2001, this chapter considers Kissinger's involvement, and that of the US more generally, in the following events in Chile:

• The killing of army commander-in-chief René Schneider in 1970 in order to prevent President Salvador Allende from taking office.
• The generalised boycott of Chilean democracy by direct internal interference in the affairs of a foreign nation.
• The fostering of a military coup in September 1973.
• The killing of US citizens at the National Stadium in 1973.
• US involvement in supporting acts of kidnapping, torture and disappearance in cooperation with the security forces of Chile, Argentina, Uruguay, Paraguay, and Bolivia.

## The election of Salvador Allende

On 4 September 1970, Salvador Allende, a Chilean senator and founding member of the Chilean Socialist Party,[2] received the majority of votes in a presidential election contested by other two candidates: Jorge Alessandri, representing the right-wing coalition, and Radomiro Tomic, representing the Christian Democratic Party (PDC).

Allende did not achieve a majority of over 50 per cent of the votes, which would have sufficed to confirm him as the new president-elect. However, he won more votes than any other party – 36.2 per cent of the total. Following agreed-upon electoral procedures, the Chilean parliament confirmed Allende as President of Chile on 24 October 1970, as the Christian Democrat parliamentarians followed Chilean democratic tradition and supported the winner of an election plurality.[3] Allende took office on 4 November, and proceeded to implement what he called 'the Chilean road to socialism.'

The US State Department had supported the Christian Democrats during Eduardo Frei's administration, allegedly in order to prevent Soviet involvement in Chilean affairs during a historical period characterized both by Cold War tensions and by the US Alliance for Progress, which predicated aid upon support for the American way of life and US national security. William Colby, CIA Director (1973–75), denied providing any support for the National Party (PN) and the Christian Democrats in the elections. He wrote in a confidential memo to Kissinger that 'our role in the election was limited to an effort to denigrate Allende and his Popular Unity (UP) coalition during the campaign.'[4]

Even if this assertion were believable, by the time President Eduardo Frei had finished his stint in office and passed the presidential sash to Allende, the United States had grown enormously worried about the new Chilean government – the first democratically elected socialist government in the western hemisphere. The right-wing Chilean parties, international corporations such as the ITT, Pepsi-Cola, the Chase Manhattan Bank, and the CIA, were also deeply concerned.

Kissinger, who was at the center of US national-security policymaking, stated famously that he saw no reason why a country should be allowed to go Marxist simply because its people are irresponsible. The US ambassador to Chile, Edward Korry, reported in the following words the general feeling of the Nixon administration:

> It is a sad fact that Chile has taken the path to communism with only a little more than a third (36 per cent) of the nation approving this choice, but it is an immutable fact. It will have the most profound effect on Latin America and

beyond; we have suffered a grievous defeat; the consequences will be domestic and international; the repercussions will have immediate impact in some lands and delayed effect in others. (Korry quoted in Kissinger, 1979: 653)

Ambassador Korry was convinced that the Chilean military would not entertain the idea of a military coup, and he made his opinion clear to the US administration in a cable from Santiago, dated 7 September 1970. The following day, members of the so-called '40 Committee' met in Washington. In assessing Allende's victory, they realized that very little could be done from afar; Richard Helms, then director of the CIA, suggested that if a military coup were considered as an option, it would have little chance of success unless it was undertaken very rapidly. While other members had reservations about such a modus operandi, due to the risk of civil war in Chile, the chairman directed the US Embassy to produce an assessment on 'the pros and cons and problems and prospects involved should a Chilean military coup be organised now with US assistance, and the pros and cons and prospects involved in organizing an effective future Chilean opposition to Allende.'[5] A further meeting was scheduled for 14 September 1970.

The Chairman of the 40 Committee from 1969 to 1976 was Henry Kissinger. During that period, the 40 Committee supervised US covert operations abroad, and in some cases surveillance within the United States.[6]

Kissinger was unhappy with the idea of Allende taking over the Chilean presidency, and, after a series of meetings that took place in Washington eleven days after Allende's victory, it became clear that Nixon shared the same immediate concerns. Kissinger had briefed Nixon through a memorandum dated 17 September 1970, in which he shared his doubts about Korry's objectivity and analysis of the Chilean situation. He further suggested that the US administration was only reacting to events, rather than developing a clear plan of action. Kissinger advised Nixon to form a special task force that would meet daily and supervise the sending of a professional expert to take over the operation.[7]

The following day, Kissinger met with Donald Kendall (president of Pepsi-Cola) and with David Rockefeller of Chase Manhattan.[8] Later, he met with CIA director Richard Helms and President Nixon in the Oval Office. Ten million dollars was mustered for a secret operation built around a two-track strategy: a diplomatic track, and a covert operation that sought to encourage and catalyze a military coup, unbeknownst to the State Department, Congress, or Ambassador Korry in Santiago. A strategic group that met in Langley, Virginia, was to develop the two-track plan using the best men available; their immediate order was 'to make the [Chilean] economy scream.' The two-track policy as it emerged involved the following groups:

(a) A group in-charge of economic policies related to US investments, renegotiation of foreign debt, and economic aid to Chile; and,
(b) A group of CIA personnel, experts on covert operations, that without the knowledge of the US Congress and the US Ambassador in Chile was to make contact with those within the military and other sectors opposed to the election of Allende in Chile, with the aim of preventing his accession to power.

Group (b) proceeded to contact Chilean military that were open to the idea of a military coup. The instructions came from Kissinger as National Security Advisor, and were issued without the approval of the US Congress or the direct knowledge of the US ambassador in Chile.

The main obstacle for US plans for military intervention was the chief of the Chilean General Staff, René Schneider, who was completely opposed to any military intervention in the democratic process. In a 40 Committee meeting on 18 September 1970, it was decided that Schneider would have to be removed. The original plan was to convince some Chilean officers, with the help of interested civilians, to kidnap him before the meeting of the Chilean Congress on 24 October that was scheduled to decide on the confirmation of the new Chilean President.

The task of finding such officers was a difficult one. Chile had a tradition of military non-involvement in civilian matters – or such, at least, was the perception of political analysts at the time.[9] Richard Helms and his director of covert operations, Thomas Karamessines, warned Kissinger of the difficulties that confronted the plan. Nonetheless, Kissinger decided to push ahead. A sum of $50,000 was offered to any officer willing to kidnap Schneider in order to create chaos and panic and therefore impede Allende's confirmation as President.

Ambassador Korry had suggested to the US administration that it avoid any contact with members of Patria y Libertad (Fatherland and Freedom), a right-wing group with paramilitary members. However, General Roberto Viaux, a right-wing sympathizer of the movement, along with other members of Patria y Libertad, were approached and invited to kidnap Schneider. Kissinger's track-two group agreed to provide the guns and tear-gas grenades to be used in the operation. Meetings took place in Santiago from 16 to 18 October 1970, while Kissinger's group was dispatching the arms via special courier.

General Camilo Valenzuela, chief of the Santiago garrison, was also approached, and formed a separate group of sympathizers willing to kidnap Schneider. It was clear that Viaux, who had already attempted military action against President Frei in 1969, was not fully trusted by members of Kissinger's committees, and was perceived as an officer with little support among other Chilean officers.

Attempts to kidnap Schneider failed on 19–20 October; but Schneider was finally intercepted and killed on 2 October. Five cars blocked his Mercedes as he was being driven from the house of the army commander-in-chief to his offices at the Ministry of Defense. Schneider tried to resist by drawing a gun from his briefcase, and was shot several times. His death on 25 October at the Military Hospital produced a political uproar. President Frei declared a full national alert, with the army standing by, and three days of national mourning followed. At Schneider's requiem mass, former presidents of Chile and the newly elected president accompanied his coffin (see Alexander, 1978: 126–7; Nunn, 1976: 266–8; del Pozo, 1992: 362; Sigmund, 1977: 120–23; Valenzuela, 1978: 48–9). The day before, the Chilean Congress had ratified Allende's election by a substantial majority: 153 votes in favor and 35 against, with 7 abstentions.

## Obstructing Allende's road to socialism

The failure of the covert operation to provoke a reaction by the Chilean military via the kidnapping or killing of Schneider, followed by the ratification by the Chilean Congress of Allende as President of Chile, prompted the United States administration to intensify the work of group (a), based in Virginia. As early as 6 November 1970, the National Security Council met at the White House to discuss the Chilean situation. CIA director Helms emphasized that the composition of Allende's first cabinet was clearly tilted in favor of Marxists, and Kissinger expressed his conviction that Allende was trying to turn Chile into a socialist state (Kissinger, 1979: 653–83).

Different options were explored and strong opinions voiced. Nixon expressed his belief that the Latin American military, in particular the Chilean army, should be strongly supported throughout the coming period of Chilean socialism, stating:

> I will never agree with the policy of downgrading the military in Latin America. They are power centers subject to our influence. We want to give them some help. Brazil and Argentina particularly. Build them up with consultation. I want Defense to move on this. We'll go for more in the budget if necessary.[10]

Moreover, it was clear that harsh economic policies were to be followed in order to isolate Allende's government and render him unpopular with voters and even his own supporters. George A. Lincoln, Director of Emergency Preparedness, emphasized the possibility of manipulating the market for copper, Chile's main natural resource, in order to weaken the Allende regime. In the end, Nixon's proposed strategy became the basis for a consensus, when he told his advisors: 'On the economic side we want to give him [Allende] cold turkey. Make sure that EXIM [the Export–Import Bank] and the international organizations toughen up. If Allende can make it with Russian and Chinese help, so be it – but we do not want it to be with our help, either real or apparent.'[11]

Such economic policies resulted in a sharp downturn in US organizational involvement in Chile. One need only consult figures showing the marked disparity in US financial aid to the administrations of Frei, Allende and Pinochet. From 1964 to 1970, Frei received $1,176.8 million; Allende from 1971 to 1973, just $67.3 million; and Pinochet from 1974 to 1976, $628.1 million.[12]

Allende, meanwhile, pursued a program that stood in marked opposition to the US Alliance for Progress, which his government depicted as an unjust and neocolonial arrangement. In the words of the program of Allende's Popular Unity Coalition:

> Imperialist exploitation of backward economies takes many forms: it can take the form of investment in mines (copper, iron, etc.) and in industrial activities, both in banking and in commerce; it can mean technological control that forces us to pay the highest prices for equipment, licences and patents, or North American loans which stipulate that we must buy in the United States, and with the additional clause that the purchased goods are to be transported in American boats, etc.
>
> Let us quote a single instance: between 1952 and today the North Americans have invested $7,473,000,000 in Latin America. In the same period, they have taken $16,000,000,000 worth of profits away. (Allende 1973: 23)[13]

The alternative proposed by the Allende government became clearer in 1971, when the Chilean Congress approved the nationalization of the copper mines owned by US corporations.[14] Further policy initiatives established state ownership of banks,[15] promoted agrarian reform, and furthered cooperation with Cuba[16] and the Soviet Union.[17] All of these measures confirmed the initial worries of the US administration. The nationalization program extended to the Chilean branches of US corporations such as RCA Victor, Bethlehem Steel, US banks, Ford and ITT. In the case of Ford, the company was accused of boycotting the import of spare parts, while ITT became notorious for its support of the US economic boycott and attempted to enlist US intelligence in order to spy on Allende's supporters (Quimantú, 1972).[18]

President Nixon conveyed his concerns in writing to Allende, while nonetheless stressing that 'we are prepared to maintain the kind of relations with the Chilean government which they are inclined to maintain with us' (Allende, 1973: 104). Allende's response, in a public speech, suggested that Chile would follow the example of Mexico in maintaining links with all countries, and that his government could not equate the policies of the Organization of American States with the wishes of the US government.[19]

From 1971 to 1973, the CIA continued its covert operations in Chile, encouraging Allende's opponents with economic assistance and fomenting military distrust of governmental policies. By September 1972, Chile's trucker unions, an important sector given Chile's dramatic geographical length, staged a strike against the government that symbolized the concerns of Allende's opponents. The US administration helped to sustain the strike, which paralyzed Chile in an unprecedented fashion. This was a crucial moment in Chilean politics. Prior to the truckers' strike, all opposition to Allende's government had been channeled and expressed through the political parties. Instead, the truckers' strike triggered the 'direct mobilization by both big and small businessmen seeking to protect their stakes in the system' (Valenzuela, 1978: 78).

From 1971 onward, the CIA also conducted surveillance operations against liberal US citizens living and working in Chile. One of those citizens, Frank Teruggi, was later to be killed, along with Charles Horman, at Santiago's National Stadium following the military coup (see below). Throughout 1972, the CIA continued its efforts to foment discontent among the Chilean military. Some officers were seriously considering a military coup at the time of the truckers' strike; they were enthusiastically supported by CIA agents operating in Santiago.

The first signs of a possible military coup came on 29 June 1973, when a group of tanks from the Tacna Regiment made their way to the presidential palace, La Moneda, and installed themselves across from the building. By the time the mutiny had been brought under control by the military under the command of Augusto Pinochet, it was clear to political analysts and members of Allende's own government that a massive intervention could be forthcoming.

## The US diplomatic failure

The military coup took place on Tuesday, 11 September 1973. From key locations in Santiago, the commanders-in-chief of the armed forces directed the takeover of radio stations, factories, government buildings, and the presidential palace (Verdugo, 1997).

The US government welcomed the change of government, and quickly recognized the military junta as Chile's new legitimate authority. The Chilean navy, which had recently undertaken joint maneuvers with US ships, left the port of Valparaíso early in the morning of 11 September, and subsequently the marines and special naval forces took over the port and the main government buildings. What followed was the complete suppression of opposition forces and the formation of a centralized government in the hands of the Chilean armed forces. The US involvement in these events, which was sanctioned by Kissinger himself, became clearer with the arrest and murder of Charles Horman and Frank Teruggi at the National Stadium; other US citizens suspected of pro-Allende tendencies managed to go into hiding and flee the country (see, e.g., Cooper, 2001). While Horman and Teruggi were assassinated around the same time in the National Stadium, it was the case of Charles Horman that achieved the greatest prominence in subsequent years, becoming the subject of the book (Hauser, 1982) and film *Missing* and of a legal suit by the Horman family against Henry Kissinger and all those held responsible for his death.[20]

Charles and his wife Joyce had arrived in Chile in 1972 after touring other Latin American countries.[21] Together with other Americans, they formed the North American News Sources (FIN), a group that translated and disseminated pro-Allende articles in US newspapers. In April 1973, Horman joined others in a protest, in front of the US Consulate in Santiago, against the bombardment of Cambodia.[22]

When the military coup occurred, Horman was in Valparaíso, together with a US visitor, Terry Simon. Joyce remained in Santiago. Horman and Simon found it difficult to return to Santiago, and did so only because of an encounter at their hotel with a US Marine, Lieutenant Colonel Patrick Ryan. Ryan was at that time head of a five-man US Naval Group in Valparaíso, and held the title of Acting Chief of Navy Selection, US Military Group in Chile. Ryan had filed a situation report to the US administration stating that 'Chile's *coup d'état* was close to perfect.'[23] He was meeting at the hotel with another American, Arthur Creter, who identified himself as a retired naval engineer based in Panama. Creter told them that he had come to do a job, and the job had been done.[24]

On 15 September 1973, Navy Captain Ray Davis drove Horman and Simon back to Santiago in a car with Chilean navy identification. They stayed at the Carrera Hotel, as they could not reach Joyce by phone. The following day, they moved to the Horman home. After the decision was taken that they should all leave Chile, Horman and Simon went to the Braniff Airlines office on 17 September to buy tickets for the return to the United States. Braniff personnel told them to contact the US Consulate, as a list of Americans scheduled to leave Chile was being drawn up.

At the US Consulate, Marion Tipton, the vice-consul, told Horman and Simon that such a list did not exist. Tipton further commented to Simon that 'they never come in to visit us at normal times, but at times like this they come crawling out of the walls.'[25] It was clear that some young Americans had failed to register their names and addresses at the

US Consulate because they perceived the US Embassy as being the enemy of Allende's government.[26] In turn, the US Embassy and the State Department perceived such young Americans as being far too intimate in their relationship with enemies of the United States.[27]

On 17 September, shortly after he arrived home, Charles Horman was picked up by Chilean military personnel and taken to the National Stadium.[28] Only on 17 October did Horman's parents, Ed and Joyce, learn that Charles had been executed at the National Stadium (either on 18 or 20 September) and that his body had been found at the General Cemetery.[29] And only on 31 March was Horman's body released and flown to New York. By then, an autopsy was impossible. The Chileans had negotiated a deal with the US administration to return Horman's body in exchange for the sale of American-made missiles to the Pinochet administration.[30]

It is still unclear whether American personnel were present at Horman's execution or during his preceding torture sessions. What is clear, however, is that the US Embassy failed to provide protection for US citizens in Chile – their core diplomatic responsibility. Moreover, some Embassy officials, in direct communication with the US government, provided the new military authorities with information on US citizens living in Chile, apparently in the knowledge that the military would arrest and torture them. Investigations by US officials in 1976 indicated that 'US intelligence was aware the Government of Chile saw Horman in a rather serious light and US officials did nothing to discourage the logical outcome of the Government of Chile paranoia.'[31] It is possible, then, to argue that Kissinger and those following his directives in Santiago conspired to kidnap, torture, and murder US citizens in violation of Geneva Convention protections extended to civilians in time of 'war' (this was the term used by Pinochet to describe the military coup and its aftermath).

## Conclusion: The never-ending story

In 2001, the actions of Henry Kissinger and other US officials came under scrutiny yet again. Earlier, the US Senate had investigated covert operations related to Chile in the 1970s; while Kissinger's role had been questioned, he justified his overall actions on the grounds of the Cold War and US national security, and was not pressed further by the Senate committees.

Following Pinochet's 1998 arrest in London and revelations of US involvement in training Latin American officers accused of human rights abuses throughout Operation Condor, fingers were again pointed at Kissinger. It seemed scarcely credible that someone who was simultaneously chairman of the 40 Committee, National Security Advisor to the US President, and Secretary of State would be unaware of what had taken place in Chile and throughout the southern cone, or of the critical US role in the events. Kissinger's own writings make it clear that he saw his role as that of an agent for American foreign policy. He occasionally warned foreign governments (including Pinochet's) to preserve a good public image, but he fended off those who criticized human rights abuses in Chile and pressed for an end to military rule (see his report of a trip to Chile in June 1976: Kissinger, 1999: 749–60).

The accusations that can be levelled against Kissinger, based on the material presented in this chapter, are thus as follows:

1. He conspired with others to kidnap and to kill General Schneider in 1970, providing money and arms to facilitate the operation. He also conspired to deny the Chilean people the fruits of a fair and democratic election, intervening in the domestic political affairs of a sovereign state not at war with the United States, and in the case of an election where there was not even a hint of election fraud. In short, throughout 1970 he conspired to kidnap, to murder, and to suppress the functioning of democratic institutions.
2. Kissinger is responsible for conspiring to overthrow a democratic president and to assist security forces in kidnapping, torturing, and murdering political opponents. The direct agents of this conspiracy, on the US part, were US Navy personnel in Valparaíso and CIA agents at the National Stadium and possibly other detention centers.
3. Kissinger failed to instruct the US Ambassador in Chile to protect the lives of US citizens such as Charles Horman and Frank Teruggi, who were kidnapped, tortured and murdered while embassy staff offered assurances that they had no idea of these citizens' whereabouts.
4. Kissinger, as ex-Secretary of State, is responsible for extending US aid and military cooperation that greatly facilitated Operation Condor throughout the southern cone, notably in the case of Chilean prisoners transported from neighboring countries, who subsequently 'disappeared.'

As a result of the declassification of the secret US documents on Chile, parties involved in litigation against Kissinger have been able to file legal claims against him and others involved in the covert operations of the early 1970s. For example, on 11 September 2001, a criminal claim was filed before Judge Juan Guzmán Tapia in the Santiago courts, relating to Operation Condor (Ingreso Corte 2182–98). Those accused of involvement in kidnapping, torture and murder included Augusto Pinochet, Henry Kissinger, Richard Helms and Vernon Walters. Among those filing the case was Nobel prizewinner Rigoberta Menchú.

In addition, following the disclosure of the secret documents, the widow of General Schneider and his three children appeared on the US network CBS, together with Peter Kornbluh, a researcher and independent analyst at the National Security Archive. Kornbluh emphasized that this was the first time documentation had been procured relating to the Nixon administration's direct interference in the democratic institutions of other countries.[32]

As part of the National Security Archive's interest in Kissinger, the State Department announced on 9 August 2001 that Kissinger had turned over 10,000 pages of transcripts of his telephone conversations while in office from 1973 to January 1977. In December 1976 Kissinger had donated his telephone conversations transcripts to the Library of Congress, but with one proviso: that the transcripts were to be strictly controlled by himself and his lawyers until five years after his death.

In summary, the evidence for the prosecution in the Kissinger case is abundant, but Kissinger nonetheless remains a prominent and widely respected figure, a citizen above the law, both in the US and even in countries that suffered tremendously under his policies. For example, in February 2002, Brazilian President Fernando Henrique Cardoso proposed that the 'Ordem do Cruzeiro do Sul' be bestowed on Kissinger during his scheduled visit to Brazil the following month.

Against such traditional respect for the leading statesmen of friendly countries, we must set the evolution in international law towards the regulation of violent intervention in the affairs of sovereign states. Should this trend continue, and the effectiveness of such regulation increase, it is possible – and to be hoped – that political directives such as those issued by Kissinger and the administration he served will become anathema, and their criminal consequences in Latin America and throughout the world will be sharply reduced.

## Notes

1. In June 1999, 5,800 documents covering the period 1973–78 were declassified; in October 1999, 1,100 further documents covering the period 1968–73 were released; and finally, in November 2001, thousands of other documents covering mainly the period 1978–91 were declassified (State Department, 13,050; CIA, 1,550; FBI, 620; Pentagon, 370; National Security Council, 110; Justice Department, 50; and National Archives, 310).

2. The Chilean Socialist Party (PS) was founded in April 1933. Its declaration of principles stated: 'The Party adheres to Marxism as the method for interpreting reality and recognizes the class struggle as the motive force of history' (Socialist Party cited in Debray, 1971: 132–3). However, the Chilean Socialist Party refused to follow the international-ideological line pursued by the Chilean Communist Party (PC), supporting

instead a socialist movement conducted by popular forces at a purely Latin American level.

3. Kissinger himself was aware of these procedures, writing: 'The Chilean Congress would hold a runoff vote as required when no candidate received an electoral majority. Traditionally, it backed the candidate who received the plurality; it was expected to do so in this case and name Salvador Allende President of Chile' (Kissinger, 1979: 653).

4. W.E. Colby, Director Central Intelligence, Washington, D.C., 'CIA's [words deleted] Program in Chile [deleted],' Memorandum for Dr. Henry A. Kissinger, The Assistant to the President for National Security Affairs, 23 September 1973.

5. 'Minutes of the Meeting of the 40 Committee,' 8 September 1970, prepared by Frank M. Chapin, NSC Declassification Review [B.O. 12958] /X/ Release in full by L. Salvetti 7/28/2000.

6. After President Truman established the CIA at the beginning of the Cold War, and throughout the Eisenhower administration, it was deemed necessary that a trust-worthy body be appointed to supervise all covert operations. The Special Group was known as the 54/12 Group, after the National Security Directive that created it. Dur-ing the Johnson administration, it became known as the 303 Committee; subsequently, under Nixon and Ford, it was referred to as the 40 Committee. The numbers kept changing according to the rooms it occupied at the Old Executive Office, annexed to the White House, where the Departments of State, War and Navy functioned (Hitchens, 2001: 16–17).

7. In his memo, Kissinger reiterated his opinion that the State Department was unwilling to proceed with a covert operation. He further suggested that Ambassador Korry was the only one reporting on current developments in Santiago. However, Korry's reporting was considered 'inconsistent and contradictory,' and thus, Kissinger wrote, 'we cannot be sure of what the situation really is and how much Korry is justifying or camouflaging.' Henry A. Kissinger, 'Memorandum for the President,' The White House, 17 September 1970, non-log 10Z.

8. A few days before, Kissinger had met with Agustín Edwards, owner and pub-lisher of the conservative Chilean newspaper El Mercurio, who had come to Washington to warn the administration about the dangers of Allende's confirmation as Chilean president (Kissinger, 1979: 673).

9. In a recent study of civilian–military relations in Chile, Patricio Manns has shown that the military was involved in politics from the dawn of Chilean independence (Manns, 1999). Frederick Nunn, in his own historical work on the Chilean military, has suggested that 'the study of civil–military relations in Chile and Latin America (and elsewhere, for that matter) has a fruitful future because of the intricacies, exceptions, and contradictions involved' (Nunn, 1976: xii; cf. Burr, 1965). Relations with the military and the Chilean armed forces in general concerned Salvador Allende, who perceived them as an integral part of his economic and social policies. 'The Armed Forces and the Carabineros,' Allende interview with the foreign press, Santiago, 5 May 1971 (Allende, 1973: 135–7).

10. 'Memorandum of Conversation' – NSC Meeting – Chile (NSSM 97), Cabinet Room, The White House, Friday, 6 November 1970, 9.40 a.m.

11. Ibid.

12. 'Details of US Economic Assistance to Chile and from Multilateral Funds during the Government of Frei, Allende, and Pinochet', in Mares and Rojas Aravena, 2001: 11.

13. 'The Programme of Unidad Popular,' Programme approved by the Socialist Party, the Communist Party, the Radical Party, the Social Democratic Party, the Movement of Unitary Action (MAPU) and the Independent Popular Action, Santiago, 17 Decem-

ber 1969.

14. 'The Nationalization of Copper,' Allende speech in the Plaza de la Constitución, Santiago, 21 December 1970, in Allende, 1973: 78–83.

15. 'The Nationalization of the Banks,' Allende speech broadcast on radio and television, Santiago, 30 December 1970, in Allende, 1973: 84–9.

16. One of the first decisions taken by the Allende administration was the restoration of diplomatic ties with Cuba. See 'Relations with Cuba,' Allende speech broadcast on radio and television, Santiago, 11 November 1970, in Allende, 1973: 67–8.

17. In his first annual message to Congress, Allende compared the historical challenge of the Russian Revolution in 1917 with the challenges facing Chile: 'the opportunity has arisen to build a new model of society, not just where, in theory, it was to be expected, but where concrete conditions have arisen which favored its emergence. Chile is today the first nation in the world called upon to set up the second model for transition to a socialist society' (Allende, 1973: 140). See 'The Chilean Road to Socialism,' Allende's first annual message to Congress, Santiago, 21 May 1971, in Allende, 1973: 138–66.

18. See also US Senate, Subcommittee on Multinational Corporations, 'Report to the Committee on Foreign Relations: The International Telephone and Telegraph Company and Chile 1970–1971,' 21 June 1973, Washington, DC: Government Printing Office, 1973.

19. 'The United States of America,' Allende speech in response to a statement by President Nixon, Punta Arenas, 27 February 1971 (Allende, 1973: 103–8).

20. *Joyce Horman et al.* v. *Henry Kissinger et al.*, Civil Action 77–1748, 3 October 1977. This wrongful-death lawsuit against Kissinger and twelve other State Department official was dismissed without prejudice in 1981.

21. Charles Horman was born in New York City in 1942 and attended Phillips Exeter Academy. He later graduated from Harvard University with *magna cum laude* and Phi Beta Kappa honours. In 1964 Horman became a Fulbright Scholar. He was enlisted in the Air Force National Guard at the time of the Vietnam War, when he also served as a journalist.

22. Rhonda Copelon et al., Attorneys for the Plaintiffs, 'Complaint for Declaratory and Injunctive Relief and for Damages,' *Joyce Horman et al.* v. *Henry Kissinger et al.*

23. Patrick J. Ryan, US Military Group, 'Sitrep 2: Valparaiso, Chile,' 1 October 1973.

24. Commander-in-Chief of US Southern Command, Fort Amador, Panama Canal Zone, to Commander of US Military Group, Santiago, Chile, 21 November 1975.

25. Terry Simon, 'Statement of Terry Simon,' Horman Case in the US–Chile Declassification Project Documents.

26. Elmer B. Staats, Comptroller General of the United States, 'An Assessment of Selected US Embassy-Consular Efforts to Assist and Protect American Overseas During Crises and Emergencies,' Report of the General Accounting Office of the United States, 4 December 1975.

27. Richard R. Fagen, Stanford, California, to Senator J. William Fulbright, Washington, DC, 8 October 1973.

28. A neighbor had taken a taxi at the same time and by coincidence followed the same route as the military truck with Horman in it. See Nathaniel P. Davis, Santiago, Chile to Henry A. Kissinger, Washington, DC, 5 October 1973.

29. Rubenstein, 'Chronology of Information Received and Actions Taken Concerning Welfare and Whereabouts in Chile of Charles Edmund Horman.'

30. Smith to Shlaudeman, US–Chile Declassification Project Documents.

31. Government of Chile, Santiago, to Government of the United States, 30 October

1973, and Rudy V. Fimbres, Robert S. Driscoll and William V. Robertson to Harry W. Shlaudeman, Washington, DC, 25 August 1976.

    32. *Primera Línea*, 9 September 2001.


## References

Alexander, R.J. (1978). *The tragedy of Chile*. Westport, CT and London: Greenwood Press.

Allende, S. (1973). *Chile's road to socialism*, edited by Joan E. Garcés. Harmondsworth: Penguin.

Andrew, C. (1995). *For the President's eyes only: Secret intelligence and the American presidency from Washington to Bush*. New York: HarperCollins.

Buchwald, M.F. (2000). An American's wrongful death in Chile: Re-examining the Charles Horman case with documents declassified in 1999. Unpublished Senior Essay, Yale University.

Burr, R.N. (1965). *By reason or force: Chile and the balancing of power in South America, 1830–1905*. Berkeley and Los Angeles: University of California Press.

Cooper, M. (2001). *Pinochet and me*. London and New York: Verso.

Debray, R. (1971). *Conversations with Allende: Socialism in Chile*. London: New Left Review.

Hauser, T. (1982). *Missing*. Harmondsworth: Penguin.

——— (1978). *The execution of Charles Horman: An American sacrifice*. New York: Harcourt Brace Jovanovich.

Hitchens, C. (2001). *The trial of Henry Kissinger*. London and New York: Verso.

Ishay, M.R. (1997). *The human rights reader: Major political essays, speeches, and documents from the Bible to the present*. New York and London: Routledge.

Kissinger, H. (1999). *Years of renewal*. New York: Simon & Schuster.

——— (1994). *Diplomacy*. New York: Simon & Schuster.

——— (1982). *Years of upheaval*. Boston, MA: Little, Brown.

——— (1979). *White House years*. London: Weidenfeld & Nicolson.

Manns, P. (1999). *Chile: Una dictadura militar permanente (1811–1999)*. Santiago: Editorial Sudamericana.

Mares, D.R., and Rojas Aravena, F. (2001). *The United States and Chile: Coming in from the cold*. London and New York: Routledge.

Nunn, F.M. (1976). *The military in Chilean history: Essays on civil–military relations, 1810–1973*. Albuquerque, NM: University of New Mexico Press.

Pike, F.B. (1963). *Chile and the United States 1880–1962: The emergence of Chile's social crisis and the challenge to United States diplomacy*. Notre Dame, IN: University of Notre Dame Press.

del Pozo, J. (1992). *Rebeldes, reformistas y revolucionarios: Una historia oral de la izquierda chilena en la época de la Unidad Popular*. Santiago, Chile: Ediciones Documentas.

Quimantú (1972). *Documentos secretos de la ITT*. Santiago, Chile: Empresa Editora Nacional Quimantú.

Sigmund, P.E. (1977). *The overthrow of Allende and the politics of Chile, 1964–1976*. Pittsburgh, PA: University of Pittsburgh Press.

Valenzuela, A. (1978). *The breakdown of democratic regimes: Chile*. Baltimore and London: Johns Hopkins University Press.

Verdugo, P. (1998). *Interferencia secreta: 11 de septiembre de 1973*. Santiago: Editorial Sudamericana.

# 10

# The Wretched of the Nations:
# The West's Role in Human Rights Violations
# in the Bangladesh War of Independence

## Suhail Islam and Syed Hassan

### Human rights and their genesis in Eurocentrism

Prior to the American and French Revolutions of 1776 and 1789, the term 'the people' was merely an expression occasionally uttered by absolute monarchs. But following those great upheavals, 'the people' established their claims with such force that Western civilization thereafter acknowledged that sovereignty indeed belonged to the people.

In the wake of these two seminal events, the battles in the West were fought on cultural, political, and moral grounds. That is to say, the core of Western civilization and culture was based on the promotion of human rights and the concept of individual liberty. So it was that Abraham Lincoln, on the eve of the American Civil War, declared: 'They who deny freedom to others deserve it not for themselves, and under a just God cannot long retain it.' Staking out the same moral high ground, President Woodrow Wilson in the early twentieth century defined the nation he was leading as 'not a mere body of traders ... [but] a body of free men. Our greatness is built upon our freedom – [it] is moral, not material. We have a great ardor for gain; but we have a deep passion for the rights of man.'

And yet, in an ironic twist on Lincoln's and Wilson's fine words, the role of the West – including the United States – in international human rights violations was nothing short of abhorrent. Accordingly, 'human rights' was redefined as the new criterion by which the West, especially the US, declared itself to be civilized and other civilizations to be barbaric. The framework is reminiscent of that used by imperialists in colonial societies. More recently, during the Cold War rivalries between the super-powers, 'democracy' and 'freedom' were both used and abused to advance neocolonial agendas. Throughout Western history, the opponent and main target of propaganda has remained the same: the subaltern populace of the Third World, pitted against the ruling of what Edward W. Said calls the states of 'national security' (Said, 1990: 6). The briefest survey of human rights as a movement confirms this appraisal of its true meaning and role. The use of human rights as a pretext for Western political action dates back to the French occupation of Syria and Lebanon in August 1860, which was defined as necessary to protect Christian Maronite minorities. This strategy has only increased since the Second World War, with the current vogue for 'humanitarian interventions' only the latest variant.

Likewise, the formulation of human rights theory has also been politically motivated in large part, and led by advocates with their own narrow political agendas. The idea of a universal definition of human rights dates to the proposal of an International Bill of Rights of Man in 1945 by Hersch Lauterpecht, a leading Zionist. It was this proposal that led to the formulation of the Universal Declaration of Human Rights by the United Nations, adopted on 10 December 1948. This was drafted by a committee of fifteen experts from various countries; the debate was politically driven, and influenced by the ideological schism between socialism and capitalism. While the countries involved might appear to have formed a reasonable cross-section of the world community – they included Iran, the Soviet Union and India – a closer look at the terms of engagement and reference reveals this to be a fallacy. None of the representatives was nationally or culturally representative; in fact, it was a specific requirement of their engagement that they did *not* represent national or cultural interests, but rather were 'experts' in the narrow field of 'rights' discourse employed by the UN committee. Thus, all representatives adhered to a narrow concept of ethical theory hailing from such allegedly emancipatory texts as Thomas Paine's *Rights of Man* and the US Bill of Rights.

Nonetheless, the declaration was called 'universal' to provide it with an aura of authority and legitimacy. This declaration was then forced upon other countries, which, in a Western-dominated world, had little choice but to sign. In fact, not only is the UDHR not 'universal' in its origins, but the UN – largely controlled by the US – had, from the outset, no intention of implementing it. There were three subcommittees involved in drafting the UDHR, the third of which was charged with proposing mechanisms for its implementation. The findings of this subcommittee were rejected, and no other mechanism was subsequently approved.

The lessons of history, then, seem quite clear. Human rights, and the 'Universal' Declaration, have become tools of the West – used to further

Western influence and interests, while the West itself feels free to ignore their provisions. In the US invasion of Haiti or western support for the military takeover in Algeria, to cite just two recent examples, the West cited a need to 'preserve democracy.' In the last few years, the West has effectively supported aggressors like Slobodan Milosevic and Vladimir Putin in their respective campaigns against Muslims, while paying lip-service to their critics. We have seen the West supporting abuses of human rights in the Israeli–occupied terrorities, while at the same time bombing civilians in Iraq on the pretence of protecting Kuwait. The hypocrisy is truly impressive.

In this light, it is hardly surprising that the West in general, and the Anglo-American alliance in particular, have protected dictatorships and participated in rights violations whenever it is deemed in their interest to do so. The subject of this chapter, the disintegration of Pakistan as a result of the atrocities committed by its armed forces, is only one of many examples of Western double standards deepening the tragedy of the masses.

One aim of this study is to bring to wider attention Justice Hammodur Rahman's report, drafted after the disintegration of Pakistan, and to integrate its findings with the more recent perspective advanced by Christopher Hitchens on the Western role in that disintegration and the concomitant genocidal massacres of Bangladeshis. We will pay particular attention to the role of the US State Department, under President Nixon's Secretary of State, Henry Kissinger (see also the chapters by Steven Jacobs and Mario Aguilar in this volume).

## Elite conflict, Bengali Muslim nationalism and the creation of Bangladesh

The early 1970s witnessed a major transformation in the Muslim world's political systems. The Islamic republic of Pakistan, the largest Muslim country in terms of population, disintegrated, and two successor states emerged: Pakistan in the west, and Bangladesh in the east.

Why did this occur? The construction of this odd divide between East and West Pakistan is one of the legacies of imperialism. The British government partitioned British India into the dominions of India and Pakistan in 1947. British policy was based on the scheme embodied by the India Act of 1935, which developed a 'two-nation theory' and proposed that areas with a numerical majority of Hindus should constitute an independent India, while those with a majority of Muslims would constitute an independent Pakistan. Interestingly, the resolution for the partition of

India and Pakistan was moved by the great Bengali leader, A.K. Fazlul Haq, on 23 March 1940, at Lahore in present-day Pakistan. The partition duly took place, albeit at the cost of well over a million Muslim and Hindu lives. East Pakistan, present-day Bangladesh, was separated from the remainder of the state by 1,000 miles of hostile Indian territory.

In addition to this uniquely challenging geographical separation, 'united' Pakistan lacked either cultural or linguistic unity. The case for regional autonomy in economic and cultural affairs was therefore fairly strong (Wilcox, 1963). The conduct and attitude of the ostensibly all-Pakistan government towards East Pakistan made that case stronger still. Attempts by the central regime to deny Bengali (East Pakistani) demands, and to impose unitary rule, spawned a powerful Bengali autonomy movement (Westergaard, 1985).

Despite winning a majority in the Pakistani national assembly in the elections of 7 December 1970, the Bengali representatives under Sheikh Mujibur Rahman were prevented from taking office, even though their vote exceeded that of all other parties combined. (Mujibur's Awami League captured all but two of East Pakistan's 162 seats, while the Pakistan People's Party captured 81 of 138 seats in West Pakistan.) Indeed, the assembly never met.

The story of the secession of East Pakistan actually begins in 1947, when Pakistan came into existence as an independent dominion with a parliamentary and federal political system. The elites who dominated the Muslim League transferred their allegiance to Pakistan and became the ruling elite there, excluding all other movements and organizations. This elite's attempts to deny national status to Bengali language and culture, and to impose the Urdu language on Bengalis in the east, infuriated educated members of that group and further strengthened their ethnic identity (Ahmed, 1981). Support for regional autonomy mounted. As Rounaq Jahan writes in a new preface to her definitive analysis of Pakistan's disintegration:

> When I wrote this book twenty-five years ago [before the independence of Bangladesh], there was general consensus among the Bengalis that the policies and practices of successive regimes in Pakistan – suppression of fundamental rights, representative institutions and cultural freedom; economic disparity; misuse of religion in politics and monopoly of state power in the hands of a narrow civil–military bureaucratic elite were inevitably leading to the disintegration of the country. There was a general acknowledgment that the Bengalis were struggling not simply against Pakistani oppression and exploitation; [but] the nationalist movement was to establish a different vision of society and polity – a secular democratic state. (Jahan, 1994: preface)[1]

## The tragedy of 1971

Scores of books have been written addressing the darkest year in Greater Pakistan's history: the tragedy of 1971, which ultimately resulted in the dismemberment of the nation and the death of hundreds of thousands, perhaps as many as three million, Bengalis. Among the accounts that deserve particular attention is that of Lieutenant-General A.A.K. Niazi, who spearheaded military operations in Pakistan's eastern wing. In his book *The Betrayal of East Pakistan* (Niazi, 1998), this senior military figure exposed how superpower rivalries contributed to unnecessary bloodshed in the rapidly unfolding drama on the Indian subcontinent. This super-power role will be considered in greater detail later. However, it is indis-pensable to touch at this point on the actions of the West – in particular, those of the US, West Pakistan's power-broker – in encouraging atrocious violations of human rights and, eventually, the full-blown genocide that eventually gave rise to Bangladesh as an independent nation.

In Niazi's book, and his earlier declarations, we find reference to an 'enemy within.' The general had stated in November 1971 that

> In spite of spite of my shortages, difficulties, and handicaps, the step-motherly treatment by my high command, the knowledge that I was being used as a sacrificial lamb and that my troops were deemed an expendable commodity, and despite heavy pressure from a far superior enemy, I remained fighting till the end, and kept moving on the battlefield…. These were some of the handi-caps which were not encountered by our counterparts in West Pakistan, nor indeed by any other army during the war. (cited in Niazi, 1998: 115)

To be more specific, Niazi claimed that

> The so-called action on the political level was a farce. We had a number of friends in the UNO, but no one from our side showed any interest in raising the matter in the Security Council when India attacked East Pakistan [on] 21st November. If the aggrieved party itself was not interested, why should anyone have come to the rescue? (Niazi, 1998: 178)

This raises a critical question. If Pakistan itself was uninterested in raising the matter in the Security Council, how can the role of the West be considered influential or decisive? In the first place, Pakistan's leader, General Yahya, was fundamentally illegitimate. He could hardly be a spokes-person for Pakistan and a representative of its national interests – especially when Mujibur had received a majority in a free and fair national election. By supporting Yahya, therefore, the West – especially the US under President Nixon – not only chose to ignore the election results of 1970, but supported the military despot in his campaign to delay and indefinitely suspend a peaceful transfer of power to the democratically elected authority (see Kissinger, 1979).

Obviously, the US, and other Western countries who similarly turned a blind eye to Yahya's malfeasance, reasonably expected that the legal victor of the elections would resist such a political injustice. And when that resistance broke out, the governments of both the United States and Great Britain officially and fully supported General Yahya's regime. Also, both governments chose to conceal the widespread massacres in East Pakistan, which from their start represented a genocidal assault on the mass of the Bengali population.

At this critical juncture, it is ironic that Zulfikar Ali Bhutto – whose party, the Pakistan People's Party, had won the majority of seats in West Pakistan, and who was thus due to take his place in the political opposition – was appointed to represent Pakistan in the United Nations. The most prominent representative of the regime internationally was thus the figure who had *lost* national elections. Such an arrangement suited Bhutto's personal ambitions perfectly. It hardly mattered that, in this position, Bhutto was exposed to the manipulation of Western powers, rapidly becoming their pawn in the grand chess game of Cold War politics.

The historical record suggests, then, that Pakistan's dismemberment was the product of intersecting conspiracies. The forces of Mujibur, Bhutto, and the dozens of political parties in both East and West Pakistan each had its own cause to take up arms. Sociopolitical blunders were made on all sides. Nonetheless, the authors of genocide cannot be excused their crimes simply because others stumbled along the way. And chief among the external authors was the United States. Pakistan was led to believe that the United States would ultimately rescue its national integrity, regardless of the scale of the crimes it committed against predominantly Bengali citizens. In central respects, General Yahya Khan was led by the nose by President Nixon and his master diplomat, Henry Kissinger. Ordinary Pakistanis, and especially the Bengalis of East Pakistan, were invisible in the equation. As some of the most poverty-stricken and dispossessed people on earth, they could be annihilated in their hundreds of thousands – according to R.J. Rummel, the death toll in Bangladesh in 1970–71 very likely exceeded a million, and may have been as high as 3 million.[2] One is reminded of David Spurr's analysis in *The Rhetoric of Empire*:

> Under Western eyes, the body is that which is most proper to the primitive, the sign by which the primitive is represented. The body, rather than speech, law, or history, is the essential defining characteristic of primitive peoples. They live, according to this view, in their bodies and in natural space, but not in a body politic worthy of the name, nor in meaningful historical time. (Spurr, 1993: 22)

## Hitchens, Kissinger, and the case for a war-crimes trial

Christopher Hitchens's book *The Trial of Henry Kissinger* (Hitchens, 2001c) was first published in 2001 as a two-part series in *Harper's* magazine (Hitchens, 2001a, 2001b). Much of the work concentrates on Kissinger's role in the Vietnam War, in which the US deliberately targeted civilians for bombing and ground attacks 'as a matter of policy' (see also Brian Willson's chapter in this volume). Kissinger, Hitchens alleges, was the driving force in the expansion of the war to Laos and Cambodia, where US bombing killed an estimated 1,350,000 people, the vast majority civilians. Kissinger literally restructured the chain of command to allow him to take personal charge of bombing raids. He expressed happiness in his briefings to Nixon on the bombing, and seemed to be 'really having fun with it,' according to the President (quoted in Hitchens, 2001c: 37).

These actions provide some guide to the mindset of the man who turned, in 1970–71, to the unfolding events in Pakistan. With Kissinger at the helm, the US provided the Pakistani army with the arms, training, and military aid that enabled it to butcher up to 3 million people and spark the exodus of 10 million refugees to neighboring India. US diplomats in East Pakistan implored Kissinger to stop the killings and rein in its client. Instead, 'at the very height of the mass murder,' Kissinger sent a message to the Pakistani dictator, General Yahya Khan, thanking him for his 'delicacy and tact' (quoted in Hitchens, 2001c: 47). His general attitude to the military leader was approving and sympathetic (see Kissinger, 1979: 871).

What strategic considerations underlie the attitude of Kissinger and Nixon towards the Pakistani imbroglio? Clearly, Kissinger in particular disliked the non-aligned policy followed by India, which contrasted with Pakistan's eager military subservience to Washington. The emergence of an independent Bangladesh threatened a new addition to non-aligned ranks. There seems, as well, to have been a personality clash between Kissinger and Indira Gandhi, then prime minister of India (Kissinger, 1979: 880). Kissinger's grand policy, however, failed dismally when India invaded East Pakistan in December 1971 and defeated the Pakistani army in a week, seizing 90,000 prisoners of war. When Bangladesh achieved its independence, Kissinger's resentment was plain. He compared Sheikh Mujibur Rahman, Bangladesh's first president, to Chile's Salvador Allende – and appears to have prepared a similar fate for him. Among the significant new information unveiled by Hitchens is the US involvement in a military coup against Mujib in August 1975, leading to the murder of the nationalist leader and forty of his family members (Hitchens, 2001c: 51).

Another dimension to the story is Kissinger's head-over-heels enthusi-asm for 'opening up' the People's Republic of China. At the time of the Pakistan crisis, Romania was already working to ease US access to Bei-jing. For reasons that remain unexplained, Kissinger instead chose Islama-bad as the springboard for his secret trip to China. G.W. Choudhury, a member of the Pakistani cabinet from 1967 to 1971, writes that 'Nixon gave Yahya the special assignment to act as "courier" between Washington and Peking – an assignment which the latter carried out with the utmost secrecy and conscientiousness' (Choudhury, 1969: 68). As a reward to the general, Kissinger agreed to overlook Pakistan's political turmoil, and to designate it an 'internal affair.' The result was a crucial blind eye turned to the unfolding military atrocities in Pakistan's eastern wing.

Our own research shows that American diplomats in the Indian sub-continent, notably in Dhaka and Delhi, sent sufficient warnings of this turmoil, and details of the atrocities committed by the Pakistani central command after the 1970 elections. Hitchens supports this conclusion:

> On April 6, 1971, a cable of protest was written from the United States Con-sulate in what was then East Pakistan (the Bengali 'wing' of the Muslim state of Pakistan) … The cable's senior signatory, the Consul General in Dacca [Dhaka], was named Archer Blood, though it might have become known as the Blood Telegram in any case. Sent directly to Washington, its purpose was, quite simply, to denounce the complicity of the United States government in genocide. Its main section read:
>
>> 'Our government has failed to denounce the suppression of democracy [in Pakistan]. Our government has failed to denounce atrocities. Our govern-ment has failed to take forceful measures to protect its citizens while at the same time bending over backwards to placate the West Pak[istan] dominated government and to lessen any deservedly negative international public rela-tions impact against them. Our government has evidenced what many will consider moral bankruptcy, ironically at a time when the USSR sent Presi-dent Yahya Khan a message defending democracy, condemning the arrest of a leader of a democratially elected majority party incidentally pro-West, and calling for an end to repressive measures and bloodshed…. But we have chosen not to intervene, even morally, on the grounds that the Awami conflict, *in which unfortunately the overworked term genocide is applicable*, is purely an internal matter of a sovereign state. Private Americans have expressed dis-gust. We, as professional civil servants, express our dissent with current policy and fervently hope that our true and lasting interests here can be defined and our policies redirected.' (Hitchens, 2001c: 45, emphasis added)

The Blood Telegram was signed by twenty members of the United States diplomatic team in East Pakistan and, when it reached the State Depart-ment, also a further nine senior officers of the South Asia division. Hitchens contends that it was 'the most public and the most strongly worded démarche from State Department servants to the State Department that has ever been recorded' (Hitchens, 2001c: 45). But Blood's was not the only protest from a senior US diplomat in the region. Ambassador Kenneth Keating, the ranking US diplomat in New Delhi, added his protest to those of the dissentors.

Kissinger and Nixon reacted promptly and decisively to the unprecedented outburst of protest. As Hitchens writes, 'Archer Blood was immediately recalled from his post and Ambassador Keating was described by the President to Kissinger, with some contempt, as having been "taken over by the Indians".' It was at this point, too, that Kissinger notoriously praised General Yahya Khan for his 'delicacy and tact' (Hitchens, 2001c: 47).

The Blood Telegram and associated examples of diplomatic dissidence are a reminder that Hitchens's case against Kissinger and Nixon cannot be generalized into an accusation against the US diplomatic corps. US diplomats on the ground in fact did heroic work in reporting the atrocities. But their efforts were bound to be fruitless, given the amoral emphasis on power politics that Kissinger had raised to a fine, if murderous, art, and that Nixon enthusiastically endorsed.

## Kissinger responds

Henry Kissinger, whose status as an elder statesman is so apparently undiminished in the halls of US power that he can safely be appointed to a prestigious position as head of an independent inquiry into the terrorist attacks of 11 September 2001, has never responded directly to Hitchens's polemic or the other accusations of war crimes made against him. (He has, however, limited his international travels to avoid being seized and charged à la his protégé, Augusto Pinochet.) Perhaps, though, one can infer his views from an article published in *Foreign Affairs* a few months after Hitchens's book appeared (Kissinger, 2001b). Its title, 'The Pitfalls of Universal Jurisdiction,' is quite suggestive. It implies a kind of *a priori* skepticism towards a trend in international law that has gained significant ground in recent years, and has swept up Kissinger, however mildly, in its train. Kissinger contends that universal jurisdiction, designed to ensure that even the highest government official is liable to arrest and prosecution *anywhere in the world* for heinous crimes against humanity, is being pushed to extremes that risk substituting the tyranny of courts for the tyranny of governments. Referring to the landmark case against his old ally, Pinochet, Kissinger argues that any universal system must contain procedures not only to punish the wicked, but to control the righteous. Legal principles must not be used as weapons to settle political scores (Hussain, 2001–02).

At this point, certain questions arise. Does Kissinger believe that the Spanish magistrate who requested Pinochet's extradition (Baltasar Garzón), and the British authorities (particularly the House of Lords) who upheld it, should have been 'constrained' from doing so? Was the Pinochet case a matter of 'settling political scores'? Kissinger sidesteps such issues, focusing instead on the invalidity of universal jurisdiction as such, and the corresponding lack of fit between the new International Criminal Court and US national interests (Hussain, 2001–02). He writes in his recent book, *Does America Need a Foreign Policy?* (Kissinger, 2001a) that the statesman's ultimate dilemma is to strike a balance between values and interests, and occasionally between peace and justice. It seems not to occur to him that the wider world might prefer the value of peace *with* justice; that these elements are not contradictory, but mutually reinforcing. Such a perspective would, no doubt, be dismissed by Kissinger as 'idealistic.'

Ironically, Kissinger's book cautions that 'a deliberate quest for hegemony is the surest way to destroy the values that made the United States great,' and that 'America's ultimate challenge is to transform its power into moral consensus, promoting its values not by imposition but by their willing acceptance in a world that, for all its seeming resistance, desperately needs enlightened leadership' (Kissinger, 2001a: 281). Kissinger's own actions, in Bangladesh and elsewhere, could hardly be said to have revolved around 'willing' popular acceptance of US power and values, generating a broad 'moral consensus' among those unfortunates on the receiving end.

Fortunately, there seems little doubt that the arm of international law is growing longer, and the world smaller for national leaders and others accused of atrocities, from Augusto Pinochet to Kissinger himself. No longer are 'covert' US interventions immune from international scrutiny. In Chile itself, legal actions have been filed against Kissinger, together with extradition requests, both for his active involvement in the overthrow of the democratically elected Allende government, and support for the atrocious Pinochet regime that followed (Hussain, 2001–02).

If the analysis advanced at the outset of this chapter is correct, however, the regime of 'universal jurisdiction' cannot be viewed as the disinterested result of morally motivated global actors. The United States has, in effect, granted to itself the power of universal jurisdiction, while displaying a well-founded fear of its exercise by others. Its seizure of Manuel Noriega from Panama and his 1992 conviction for drug trafficking; its worldwide hunt for terrorists and campaigns against 'rogue' states; its pressuring of Yugoslavia to turn over Slobodan Milošević to the International Criminal Tribunal at the Hague – all demonstrate that the US can exploit and adapt humanitarian and human-rights standards for its own purposes, deforming them out of all recognition in the process. This is combined with an outright refusal to intervene where intervention, if valid anywhere, is most justified. Bangladesh during the genocide of 1971 provides a historical example. Chechnya today, for similar reasons of realpolitik, provides another.


## Postscript: Musharraf's visit, Pakistan's 'apology'

If Kissinger and other US leaders have never acknowledged their leading role in the atrocities inflicted on the Bengali population of East Pakistan, Pakistan's current leader, President Pervez Musharraf, has been slightly more forthcoming. On an August 2002 visit to Bangladesh, he expressed regret for the 'excesses' committed during the war of independence. But he called for 'bury[ing] the past in the spirit of magnanimity.' 'Your brothers and sisters in Pakistan share the pains of the events of 1971,' Musharraf wrote in the official visitors' book after laying a wreath at the National Martyrs Memorial outside Dhaka, dedicated to those killed in the war. 'The excesses committed during the unfortunate period are regrettable.... [But] let not the light of the future be dimmed. Let us move forward together.' Hailing Pakistan's 'Bangladeshi brothers and sisters,' he added that 'courage to compromise is greater than to confront.' With 'our joint resolve, the friendship between Pakistan and Bangladesh will flourish' (Habib, 2002).

Several Bangladeshi dailies ran editorials praising Musharraf for his statements, and characterizing his words as a 'good gesture' or a 'good beginning.' But did they really represent an acknowledgment or apology of substance? Other dailies termed Musharraf's apology 'cosmetic,' 'a cunning effort to sidetrack the historic crime against humanity.' The old Pakistani mindset, for these commentators, still dominated.

Normalization of relations between Bangladesh and Pakistan is crucial to a new beginning for the two countries. Healing the wounds of genocide, and truly burying history's most unpleasant legacies, is always extremely difficult. To the extent that it is achieved, though, it can provide important closure. Therefore, although public opinion in Bangladesh supports trials for West Pakistani war criminals (who were given safe passage from Bangladesh to Pakistan via India, under the terms of the Tripartite Agreement that concluded the war), the political mood leans towards reconciliation. Part of this vision of reconciliation, however, involves a genuine Pakistani acknowledgment of the scale of the human tragedy caused by its forces. President Musharraf's predecessors sought to shift the blame for barbaric acts onto the military or even a few generals. In this sense, Musharraf's expression of regret represents a real step forward (Kamaluddin, 2002). But an unconditional public apology is needed to begin truly to heal the wounds.

It is worth ending with the words of a joint statement issued by leaders of fifty-one civil rights organizations in Pakistan, a few days after Musharraf left Bangladesh, calling for such a public apology to the people of Bangladesh. 'We feel sad and burdened by what we know was a violation of the people's human rights,' the signatories wrote. 'The apology should have come a long time ago, and citizen groups did make attempts to do so.... We deeply feel that a message from us is necessary to acknowledge the historic wrongs, to express sincere apology and build a bond based on honest sentiments' (Kamaluddin, 2002).

## Notes

1. We agree with Jahan's comments about 'economic disparity,' 'misuse of religion in politics,' and 'the monopoly of state power in the hands of a narrow ... elite.' However, her assumption that the Bengali nationalist movement planned to create a different vision of society and polity, with the aim of establishing a 'secular democratic state,' in our view misrepresents the sociopolitical slant of the bulk of the ordinary population. Examined honestly, over 80 per cent of the Bangladeshi population is Muslim, and the Islamic heritage has been deeply rooted in the region for at least three centuries (Smith, 1957). Undeniably, atrocities have been committed in the name of religion, but these were flaws of individual rulers, not representative of the ideology of Islam. The Bangladeshi population is both highly tolerant and highly religious. The idea of secularism – that is, attempting to remove religion from people's lives and politics – likely did not animate the nationalist movement in the way that Jahan suggests.

2. Rummel writes: 'The human death toll over only 267 days was incredible. Just to give for five out of the eighteen districts some incomplete statistics published in Bangladesh newspapers or by an Inquiry Committee, the Pakistani army killed 100,000 Bengalis in Dacca, 150,000 in Khulna, 75,000 in Jessore, 95,000 in Comilla, and 100,000 in Chittagong. For eighteen districts the total is 1,247,000 killed. This was an incomplete toll, and to this day no one really knows the final toll. Some estimates of the democide [NB Rummel's 'death by government'] are much lower – one is of 300,000 dead – but most range from 1 million to 3 million.... The Pakistani army and allied paramilitary groups killed about one out of every sixty-one people in Pakistan overall; one out of every twenty-five Bengalis, Hindus, and others in East Pakistan. If the rate of killing for all of Pakistan is annualized over the years the Yahya martial law regime was in power (March 1969 to December 1971), then this one regime was more lethal than that of the Soviet Union, China under the communists, or Japan under the military (even through World War II)' (Rummel, 1994: 331).

## References

Ahmed, R. (1981). *The Bengal Muslims 1871–1906: A quest for identity*. New Delhi: Oxford University Press.

Bolander, D. (1987). *The new Webster quotation dictionary*. New York: Lexicon Publications.(Lincoln's quote is a speech to Henry L. Pierce & others at Springfield, IL, 6 April 1859).

Chatterjee, P. (1993). *Nationalist thought and the colonial world*. Minneapolis: University of Minnesota Press.

Choudhury, G.W. (1998). *The last days of united Pakistan*. Perth: University of Western Australia Press, 1998.

Habib, H. (2002). 'Regrets' for 1971. *Frontline* (India), 17–30 August.

Hitchens, C. (2001a). The case against Henry Kissinger. Part 1: The making of a war criminal *Harper's*, February.

——— (2001b). The case against Henry Kissinger. Part 2: Crimes against humanity. *Harper's*, March.

——— (2001c). *The trial of Henry Kissinger*. London and New York: Verso Books.

Hussain, S.M. (2001–02). Comments cited in *CCPA Monitor*, December–January. www.policyalternatives.ca.

Jahan, R. (1994). *Pakistan: Failure in national integration*. Dhaka: University Press.

Kamaluddin, S. (2002). Musharraf's Dhaka visit proves successful. *Daily Dawn*, 30 July.

Kissinger, H. (2001a). *Does America need a foreign policy?* New York: Simon & Schuster.

——— (2001b). The pitfalls of universal jurisdiction. *Foreign Affairs*, July/August.

——— (1979). *White House years*. Boston and Toronto: Little, Brown.

Niazi, A.A.K. (1998). *The betrayal of East Pakistan*. Oxford: Oxford University Press.

Rummel, R.J. (1994). *Death by government*. New Brunswick, NJ: Transaction Publishers.

Said, E. (1990). Figures, configurations, transfigurations. *Race and Class* 32, no. 1: 1–16.

Smith, W.C. (1957). *Islam in modern history*. Princeton: Princeton University Press.

Spurr, D. (1993). *The rhetoric of empire*. Durham, NC: Duke University Press.

Westergaard, K. (1985). *State and rural society in Bangladesh*. London and Malmo: Curzon Press.

Wilcox, W.A. (1963). *Pakistan: The consolation of nation*. New York: Columbia University Press.

# Indicting Henry Kissinger:
# The Response of Raphael Lemkin

## Steven L. Jacobs

### Salient facts regarding Raphael Lemkin

Raphael Lemkin was born in 1900 in the Polish village of Bezwodene, a rural farming area in eastern Poland. His family were themselves farmers whose relationship with their non-Jewish neighbors was reasonably harmonious, due, quite possibly, to their minority status and distance from the larger centers of Jewish life (notably Warsaw, which housed more than 50 per cent of all Polish Jews, and was home to the largest aggregate of both religious and secular Jews in the country). His own experiences growing up were relatively normal, as he wrote in his autobiography, *Unofficial Man: The Autobiography of Raphael Lemkin* (Totten and Jacobs, 2002).

Early in his adolescence, however, Lemkin 'discovered' the book *Quo Vadis* by the 1905 Polish Nobel laureate, Henryk Sienkiewicz (1846–1916), which tells the horrific story of the Roman Emperor Nero's near-genocidal treatment of the early Christians (54–68 AD) (Sienkiewicz, 1993). As Lemkin himself relates the tale, upon reading it he asked his mother why the Christians did not turn to the police for help. His mother responded by asking why he naively expected such help to be provided – a comment perhaps more accurately describing the reality of Jewish life in Poland than life in ancient Rome. Lemkin continues:

> I started to read about other attempts to destroy national, religious, and racial groups. Soon I understood that something more is required than the assistance of local police to stop this evil for which I have later coined the name 'Genocide.' The cases of Genocide in history caught my imagination. My thinking

was so intense that I have been almost seeing the events with my own eyes. I saw the French King, Charles XII, who enjoyed from the balcony of the royal castle the execution of the Huguenots and ordered more light to be thrown on their faces so they can better see the tortures. I saw the Catholics of 17th-century Japan being compelled to drink water, after which all openings of their bodies were cemented and heavy loads put upon their bodies until they exploded. I saw the Moslems of Spain crowded half-naked on the decks of boats under the murderous African sun, buying from the sailors the right to sit in the shade so that their miserable existence can be prolonged before their bodies are thrown into the sea. And I heard the screaming of Jews in pogroms, when their stomachs have been opened and filled with feathers, and tied with ropes.

I identified myself more and more with the sufferings of victims, whose numbers grew, and I continued my study of history. I understood that the function of memory is not only to register past events, but to stimulate human conscience. Soon contemporary examples of Genocide followed, such as the slaughter of the Armenians. It became clear to me that the diversity of nations, religious groups and races is essential to civilization because every one of these groups has a mission to fulfill and a contribution to make in terms of culture. To destroy these groups is to oppose the will of the Creator and to disturb the spiritual harmony of mankind. I decided to become a lawyer and work for the outlawing of Genocide and for its prevention through the cooperation of nations which must be made to understand that an attack on one of them is an attack on all of them.

My mature years I have devoted to this work. (Jacobs, 2002)

Further developing this early aptitude for law, Lemkin studied at the universities of Lwow, Poland, and Heidelberg, Germany, as well as in France. By 1927, he had become the Secretary of the Polish Court of Appeals in Warsaw, while still maintaining a private legal practice. From 1927 until 1935, he served as the Secretary of the Committee on the Codification of the Laws of the Polish Republic.

In 1933, Lemkin planned to attend the meeting of the League of Nations in Madrid, to present a proposal outlawing the twin crimes of 'vandalism' (for him, the destruction not only of property but of culture) and 'barbarism' (the destruction of persons). Though his material was sent on ahead, Lemkin himself was prevented from attending the meeting at the last moment, because his superiors viewed his intentions as a 'Jewish agenda item' – a reflection of the anti-Semitic editorials which had begun appearing in the leading newspaper, the *Warsaw Gazette*, directed toward him and his proposal.

With the outbreak of World War II, Lemkin joined the Polish underground, finally escaping to the United States in 1941. During the war years, he taught law first at Duke University and later at Yale University, served as an advisor to both the War Department and the Board of Economic Warfare, and later advised Supreme Court Justice Robert H. Jackson at the International Military Tribunal in Nuremberg, Germany.

Prior to this last service, he published what is ostensibly his *magnum opus*, *Axis Rule in Occupied Europe: Laws of Occupation, Analysis of Government, Proposals for Redress* (Lemkin, 1944).

When the war ended, Lemkin continued his academic work, but increasingly devoted himself to lobbying for the passage of a genocide resolution by the nascent United Nations.[1] With the help of then-president of the General Assembly, Herbert V. Evatt of Australia, and due to Lemkin's relentless letter-writing campaign, articles, speeches, and drafting of documents, the 'Genocide Convention,' as it is now popularly called, was passed in December 1948. Lemkin would then devote the remaining eleven years of his life seeking *unsuccessfully* to secure the Convention's passage and ratification by the United States (LeBlanc, 1991). Lemkin died in 1959 – alone, financially strapped, mourned by very few, and saddened by the failure of his beloved adopted country to ratify the Convention after the initial support offered it by then-President Harry S. Truman.

## Salient facts about *Axis Rule in Occupied Europe*

Other than *Axis Rule in Occupied Europe*, Lemkin's own efforts to secure publication of his several book-length manuscripts met with failure. The reason repeatedly given for such rejections was both a lack of interest in the topic itself and the absence of a large enough audience to make publication economically viable.[2] *Axis Rule in Occupied Europe* thus remains his masterwork. It is a massive tome of 674 pages, divided into three parts: I, German Techniques of Occupation; II, The Occupied Countries; and III, Laws of Occupation: Statutes, Decrees, and Other Documents. Of greatest relevance here is Chapter 9, 'Genocide,' which is discussed in detail below. In the preface to the volume, Lemkin draws his readers' attention to this central concept:

> The practice of extermination of nations and ethnic groups as carried out by the invaders is called by the author 'genocide,' a term deriving from the Greek word *genos* (tribe, race) and the Latin *cide* (by way of analogy, see homicide, fratricide) and is treated in a chapter under the same name.... Genocide is effected through a synchronized attack on different aspects of life of the captive peoples: in the political field (by destroying institutions of self-government, a German pattern of administration, and through colonization by Germans); in the social field (by disrupting the social cohesion of the nation involved and killing or removing elements such as the intelligentsia, which provide spiritual leadership – according to Hitler's statement in *Mein Kampf*, 'the greatest of spirits can be liquidated if its bearer is beaten to death with a rubber truncheon'); in the cultural field (by prohibiting or destroying cultural institutions and cultural activities; by substituting vocational education for education in the

liberal arts, in order to prevent humanistic thinking); in the economic field (by shifting the wealth to Germans and by prohibiting the exercise of trades and occupations by people who do not promote Germanism 'without reservations'); in the biological field (by a policy of depopulation and by promoting procreation by Germans in the occupied countries); in the field of physical existence (by introducing a starvation rationing system for non-Germans and by mass killings, mainly of Jews, Poles, Slovenes, and Russians); in the religious field (by interfering with the activities of the Church, which in many countries provides not only spiritual but also national leadership); in the field of morality (by attempts to create an atmosphere of moral debasement through promoting pornographic publications and motion pictures, and the excessive consumption of alcohol). (Lemkin, 1944: xi–xii)

In the chapter on 'Genocide,' Lemkin defends his deployment of 'A New Term and New Conception for Destruction of Nations':

By 'genocide' we mean the destruction of a nation or of an ethnic group.... Generally speaking, genocide does not necessarily mean the immediate destruction of a nation, except when accomplished by mass killings of all members of a nation. It is intended rather to signify a coordinated plan of different actions aiming at the destruction of essential foundations of the life of national groups, with the aim of annihilating the groups themselves. The objectives of such a plan would be disintegration of the political and social institutions of culture, language, national feelings, religion, and the economic existence of national groups, and the destruction of the personal security, liberty, health, dignity, and even the lives of the individuals belonging to such groups. Genocide is directed against the national group as an entity, and the actions involved are directed against individuals, not in their individual capacity, but as members of the national group.... Genocide has two phases: one, destruction of the national pattern of the oppressed group; the other the imposition of the national pattern of the oppressor. This imposition, in turn, may be made upon the oppressed population which is allowed to remain, or upon the territory alone, after removal of the population and the colonization of the area by the oppressor's own nationals. (Lemkin, 1944: 79)[3]

He then proceeds to explore 'Techniques of Genocide in Various Fields' (82–90): Political, Social, Cultural, Economic, Physical (Racial Discrimination in Feeding, Endangering of Health, Mass Killings), Religious, and Moral. He concludes the chapter with his 'Recommendations for the Future,' calling for 'an international multilateral treaty' to provide 'for the introduction, not only in the constitution but also in the criminal code of each country, of provisions protecting minority groups from oppression because of their nationhood, religion, or race. Each criminal code should have provisions inflicting penalties for genocide practice,' with the perpetrator of such genocidal crimes 'liable to trial not only in the country in which he committed the crime, but also, in the event of his escape therefrom, in any other country in which he might have taken refuge' (Lemkin, 1944: 93–4).

The remainder of this chapter will explore the application of Lemkin's theoretical and juridical framework to the case of Henry Kissinger. We first present the 'indictment' of Kissinger offered by Christopher Hitchens (Hitchens, 2001a, 2001b, 2001c), and then consider what Lemkin's response *might* have been to the evidence amassed against the former US diplomat.

## Indicting Henry Kissinger

The charges leveled at Henry Kissinger in Hitchens's book (and the two-part series in *Harper's* magazine that gave rise to it) can be summarized as follows:

- *Vietnam*   Political chicanery resulting in the unnecessary deaths of both military and civilian personnel, American and Vietnamese.
- *Chile*   Complicity in the assassinations of Army General René Schneider, President Salvador Allende, and diplomat Orlando Letelier.
- *Cyprus*   Complicity in the attempted assassination of President Archbishop Makarios.
- *Bangladesh*   Fostering the deaths of the Bangladeshi people at the hands of the West Pakistanis by explicit (if covert) support of military and governmental efforts which resulted in genocide.
- *East Timor*   Fostering the deaths of the East Timorese at the hands of the Indonesians by explicit (if covert) support of military and governmental efforts which resulted in genocide.
- *Greece*   Complicity in the death of reporter Elias Demetracopoulos.

In an insightful review of Hitchens's *The Trial of Henry Kissinger* in the London *Jewish Chronicle*, Lawrence Freedman, Professor of War Studies at King's College, London, speculates about the possible defense Kissinger *might* offer to the allegations against him. He concludes that Kissinger would stress the 'higher demands of foreign policy, especially at a time when the United States was reeling under the impact of Vietnam.' Freedman writes:

> Kissinger is a practitioner of the now-discredited art of *realpolitik*. This act was practiced in support of a higher purpose, to promote national interests while maintaining an orderly national system. *Realpolitik* had two tendencies. The first was to be conservative, in that radicalism was invariably disorderly. The second tendency was an antipathy to democratic processes to the extent that they interfered with deal-making. (Freedman, 2001: 33)

Kissinger, for his part, has hardly been forthcoming in his responses to questions about alleged war crimes. But he has been strident in defending his actions and vigorous in questioning the tactics and motivations of his attackers. Declaring his papers 'off-limits' to others – for security and other, seemingly personal, reasons – is one such example. Such stridency and vigor may bespeak a guilty conscience, or acknowledgment of deeds wrongly done by others with self-implication, or even serve as a psychological deflecting mechanism by someone whose power and ego needs dictate a refusal to confront accurate critiques, and constitute, in themselves, a form of psychosis.

This last possibility is strongly hinted at in Seymour Hersh's book, *The Price of Power: Kissinger in the Nixon White House* (Hersh, 1983). The hints are found in two places. First are the comments of Anthony Lake, reflecting on his resignation from the National Security Council in April 1970, and his failure at that time to call a news conference and reveal the more sordid realities of the Nixon White House:

> We didn't do so on the single calculation that it would destroy Henry. I knew the administration was squalid, but there was this enormous illusion about Henry. I clung to the delusion that the man was still rational and that even his own strong sense of self-survival would keep him out of real trouble. In effect, it was my theory of the ruthlessness of Henry Kissinger; in truth, there were no limits. (Hersh, 1983: 190)

Later on, Hersh cites the telling comment of a senior unnamed military official: 'Henry adores power, absolutely adores it ... To Henry, diplomacy is nothing without it' (quoted in Hersh, 1983: 239). One cannot but recall here Lord Acton's oft-quoted maxim: 'Power corrupts, and absolute power corrupts absolutely.' Indeed, Larry Berman consistently argues in his book *No Peace, No Honor: Nixon, Kissinger, and Betrayal in Vietnam* (Berman, 2001) that the corrosive results of power on both Nixon and Kissinger resulted in the tragic and needless deaths not only of American soldiers in Vietnam, but among the civilian population of that country as well.

Hitchens and Hersh are joined in their indictment of Kissinger by William Shawcross, who writes in his 1979 book *Sideshow: Kissinger, Nixon, and the Destruction of Cambodia*:

> It is a devastating portrait of Henry Kissinger – collaborator in the secret bombing of Cambodia begun in 1969 and later participant in a full-scale program of wiretapping designed to plug alleged leaks on the bombing – a man who built bridges and barricades all across Washington, extending his influence by cultivating the press, chosen leaders of Congress, and the Joint Chiefs; who waged a private war against the Secretaries of State and Defense; and reorganized the National Security System to consolidate his own power with no concern for the consequences of his actions. (Shawcross, 1979, jacket cover)

## Relevant international legislation

Relevant to the discussion of the charges cited above, from Lemkin's perspective, would be those salient passages of the (1948) United Nations Convention on the Prevention and Punishment of the Crime of Genocide, ratified by the United States in 1988. They read as follows:

ARTICLE I

... genocide whether committed in time of peace or in time of war is a crime under international law.

ARTICLE II

... genocide means any of the following acts committed with intent to destroy, in whole or in part, a national, ethnical, racial, or religious group, as such:

Killing members of the group;
Causing serious bodily harm to members of the group;
Deliberately inflicting on the group conditions of life calculated to bring about its physical destruction in whole or in part;
Imposing measures intended to prevent births within the group;
Forcibly transferring children of the group to another group.

ARTICLE III

The following acts shall be punishable:

Genocide;
Conspiracy to commit genocide;
Direct and public incitement to commit genocide;
Attempt to commit genocide;
Complicity in genocide.

ARTICLE IV

Persons committing genocide ... shall be punished, whether they are constitutionally responsible rulers, public officials, or private individuals.

ARTICLE VI

Persons charged with genocide ... shall be tried by a competent tribunal or the State in the territory of which the act was committed, or by such international penal tribunal as may have jurisdiction with respect to those Contracting Parties which shall have accepted its jurisdiction.

ARTICLE VII

The Contracting Parties pledge themselves in such cases to grant extradition in accordance with their laws and treaties in force.

Equally relevant are the indictments against the Nazi hierarchy associated with the International Military Tribunal (IMT) at Nuremberg, Germany, at the close of the Second World War. As Lemkin himself summarized them:

The Tribunal held its first public meeting in Berlin on October 18, 1945, and received the indictment, comprising more than 25,000 words. Four counts were

outlined. The four counts, on two or more of which each of the twenty-four
Nazi leaders were indicted, were as follows:

> 'The Common Plan' – or conspiracy to commit war crimes;
> 'Crimes Against Peace' – the planning, preparing, initiating, or waging of
> aggressive war;
> 'War Crimes' – violation of the laws and customs of war; and
> 'Crimes Against Humanity' …

For all these things go the words of which Justice Jackson said, thereby expressing the feelings of [a] shocked world: 'The wrongs which we seek to condemn
and punish have been so calculated, so malignant and so devastating that civilization cannot tolerate their being ignored because it cannot survive their being
repeated.' (Jacobs, 1992: 319–320)

## Raphael Lemkin's response?

Shawcross (1979), Hersh (1983), and Hitchens (2001) all arrive at the same
conclusion: Henry Kissinger is guilty of the same crimes for which defendants were prosecuted at Nuremberg, and those designated by the
United Nations Convention on the Prevention and Punishment of the
Crime of Genocide.[4] What, then, of Raphael Lemkin – lawyer and
professor of law, Polish-Jewish refugee from the Nazi carnage, present at
Nuremberg, and motivating presence behind the Genocide Convention?
The precision evident in Lemkin's work urges us to make some careful
distinctions in turn.

First, the crimes alleged against Henry Kissinger must be separated
into those related to genocide, those concerning crimes of war, and those
that fall into neither category. (The bridge between the first two, however, can be found in the fourth Nuremberg indictment, that which specifies
'crimes against humanity' as a precursor to a fuller understanding of
genocide, as evidenced by subsequent scholarship and commentary.) Thus,
the specific cases of Chile, Cyprus, and Greece, while reprehensible in
and of themselves, and the machinations of one willing to commit such
evil acts under the guise of American foreign policy (Freedman's 'realpolitik'), would, for Lemkin, better be addressed under other legislation,
specifically criminal indictments. To what degree Henry Kissinger is directly
or indirectly responsible for the deaths of René Schneider, Salvador
Allende, Orlando Letelier, and Elias Demetracopoulos – whether by
instigating, planning, or approving those acts – might constitute criminal
activity is a matter best determined in a criminal court. (That the governments of Chile and Greece have not sought this avenue of redress in
American courts, or asked for Kissinger's extradition to stand trial in their
own countries, suggests tellingly that political agendas supersede both legal
and moral ones.)

Second, the central focus of the crime of genocide is the element of *intentionality*: the verifiable desire on the perpetrator's part to destroy a given national, ethnic, racial or religious group, in whole or in part, through five specific means. In the cases of Vietnam, Bangladesh, and East Timor, whatever political motivations energized Henry Kissenger, there is no evidence of malicious hatred of the ethnic, racial or religious identities of those resident in those countries, or intent to destroy those groups as such. With regard to national identity, again – in the cases of Vietnam, Bangladesh, and East Timor – Kissinger's motivations do not seem to have lain in a desire to wipe these nation-states off the map. Nor is there any concrete evidence that Kissinger's (and Nixon's) support of the political and military activities of either the Pakistanis or Indonesians in the cases of the Bangladeshi or East Timorese which resulted in the genocidal decimation of both populations, and is now acknowledged as a seemingly obvious consequence of their policies, was either foreseen or endorsed by Kissinger and Nixon. Rather, they sought to answer to a supposedly higher calling: to ensure the dominance of the United States and its own interests throughout the world. Thus, an additionally stinging indictment of United States foreign policy under Nixon, the primary architect of which was Kissinger, is its myopic vision with regards to the United States' global interests at the expense of perceived lesser, unfortunate nations and populations. The critical question, then, specifically with regard to Kissinger, is this question of *genocidal intentionality* or *genocidal motivation* as a seemingly complicit bystander to such atrocities on the part of other nation-states with which the United States existed in relationship and sought to influence. Was Kissinger, in truth, a less-than-silent accomplice to others who committed such acts, or, as a result of his own contempt for perceived lesser beings, someone whose own unwillingness to address thoroughly the consequences of foreign policy decisions resulted in the genocide of those unfortunates? Documents recently released under the United States Freedom of Information Act with regard to East Timor, for example, reveal Kissinger's support of the Indonesian invasion, but no understanding that genocide as defined in the United Nations Convention was either an expected or a logical outcome, though the understanding was that the Indonesians would achieve military and political victory, and that the cost in death to the East Timorese would be substantial.

The fact, however, that genocide was implemented by others in these states – and in Cambodia as well – with the full knowledge and evident support of the Secretary of State under President Nixon and his National Security Advisor (Cambodia excepted) may warrant designating Kissinger (and Nixon) 'complicit bystanders.' This is a category worthy of condemnation and moral reproach, but one that incurs no *legal* consequences in the international arena. It may be morally repugnant that these other nations either practiced genocide internally (Cambodia under Pol Pot, Hun Sen, and Ieng Sary), or were the victims of genocide inflicted by others (Bangladesh by the West Pakistanis, East Timor by the Indonesians), while the United States had the power to intervene under Kissinger's watch, and did not. But it carries with it no legal indictment whatsoever. As heinous as the above-referenced genocidal acts remain, to find Kissinger (and Nixon) guilty of 'complicity to commit genocide' as specified in the United Nations Convention is questionable. At worst, they were *accidentally complicit*; at best, their foreign policy remains characterized by a flawed, limited understanding and by self-centered, self-promoting, and self-aggrandizing manipulation. Thus, Henry Kissinger is not, to use the French term associated with the genocide in Rwanda, a *génocidaire* – that is, one directly involved in the commission of such acts or one in a position of power to approve, sanction, or advocate such acts.

Complicating this discussion further, one must bear in mind that the United States in Vietnam was never officially engaged in a war as such – that is, one certified by Congress and executed by the president in his role as military commander-in-chief. Kissinger's crimes, to the degree that they are regarded as legally criminal acts, all occurred in so-called 'times of peace.'

Turning, then, to the first three charges against the defendants in the Nuremberg dock – 'conspiracy to commit war crimes;' 'the planning, preparing, initiating, or waging of aggressive war;' and/or 'violation of the laws and customs of war' – there should be no doubt whatsoever that Kissinger was himself committed to waging both a military and a political/diplomatic war in both Vietnam and Cambodia. The International Military Tribunal at the close of the Second World War, however, did not address these crimes in the context of a non-declared war, however well the criteria met those conditions. That is to say, acts of genocide committed outside of a declared war by two or more nation-states were not addressed by the IMT; brought to trial were those responsible for engaging in war, and the first three indictments, as such, all pertained to acts committed during the Second World War.

Even more specifically, however, neither Kissinger nor his boss Richard Nixon conspired to commit war crimes as such, though such crimes were, indeed, practiced by both South Vietnamese and American troops (e.g. at My Lai); nor did they intend to violate the laws and customs of war as they have been practiced in the modern period, though, equally, such violations did repeatedly occur. No commentary with which I am familiar with regard to the Nuremberg Trials, *at the time of their implementation*, addresses the indictments against those in the dock in times other than war, and, equally argues their applicability outside of that context. Thus, a stronger case could be mounted against Henry Kissinger with regard to the second charge – 'Crimes Against Peace: the planning, preparing, initiating, or waging of aggressive war' – but the legal status of the Vietnamese conflict as a 'non-war' makes such an indictment difficult. That American troops captured by the enemy were considered by them 'prisoners of war' reveals one additional absurdity of the so-called 'Vietnam conflict': one side understanding itself to be at war with the United States; and the United States refusing to acknowledge its involvement in a declared war. Thus, as the Nuremberg Tribunal understood it at the time, Henry Kissinger would *not* be classified as a 'war criminal,' though the acts he engaged in were certainly criminal. Thus, if Henry Kissinger could be classed as neither a *génocidaire* nor a war criminal, of what, precisely, is he guilty?

## Concluding thoughts

What, then, of the issue of 'retroactivity': could Kissinger be brought to trial these many years later for acts committed during his term of service? Initially, the answer would seem to be 'Yes.'

The International Law Commission of the United Nations, established in 1947 'to promote the progressive development of international law and its codification,' in 1950 recognized seven 'Principles of International Law Recognized in the Charter of the Nurnberg Tribunal and in the Judgment of the Tribunal':

I     Any person who commits an act which constitutes a crime under international law is responsible therefore and liable to punishment.

II    The fact that internal law does not impose a penalty for an act which constitutes a crime under international law does not relieve the person who committed the act from responsibility under international law.

III   The fact that a person who committed an act which constitutes a crime under international law acted as Head of State or responsible Governmental official does not relieve him from responsibility under international law.

IV    The fact that a person acted pursuant to order of his Government or of a superior does not relieve him from responsibility under international law, provided a moral choice was in fact possible to him.

V     Any person charged with a crime under international law has the right to a fair trial on the facts and law.

VI    The crimes hereinafter set out as crimes under international law:

(a)   Crimes against peace
(b)   War crimes
(c)   Crimes against humanity

VII Complicity in the commission of a crime against peace, a war crime, or crime against humanity as set forth in Principle VI is a crime under international law. (Principles of international law, n.d.)

Such a document is, in truth, little more than a restating of the arguments put forth at the International Military Tribunal at Nuremberg, already addressed. Significantly, however, the word 'genocide' appears nowhere in the document itself, specifically not in the extended enumeration of the crimes specified in Principle VI.

James Popple, in a 1989 article entitled 'The Right to Protection from Retroactive Criminal Law,' concluded:

> The right to protection from retroactive criminal law is well-recognized throughout the international community. Yet there are many examples, in communities which claim to espouse this right as being fundamental, where retroactive criminal laws have been made....
>
> The Nuremberg trials are generally said to have been fair, despite the demonstrably retrospective nature of the charges laid against the Nazi defendants. This is clearly due to society's abhorrence of the atrocities committed by the Nazis in World War II. Yet, regardless of the repugnant nature of what the Nazis did, it is clear that they were denied protection from retroactive criminal law....
>
> *In human rights conventions, the right to protection from retroactive criminal law is typically qualified by the proviso that the protection does not apply to acts or omissions which are criminal according to the general principles of law recognized by the community of nations ...*
>
> So, it can be seen that, despite the statement that the principle of non-retroactivity is a fundamental human right (in various statements of human rights), retroactive law has been made, and continues to be made, in societies which ostensibly accept that principle as being a right....
>
> Courts and legislatures have shown a willingness to adopt a retributive approach to punishment and to punish retrospectively. When judge-made law is taken into account, it is at least arguable that the human right is to be protected from retroactive criminal law is as much honoured in the breach as in the observance. Its application is limited, and that limitation is unpredictable. *Non-retroactivity is an important principle, but it does not deserve the status of a fundamental human right.* (Popple, 1989, emphasis added throughout)

Who, then, is to bring Kissinger to trial? Under which jurisdiction? In what country? Under what and whose laws, international or national?

It can be convincingly demonstrated that Henry Kissinger was guilty of the abuse of political power; an utter disregard of the democratic process; contempt not only for government but for the American people; and malign inattention to those who were themselves victims of genocide. One need only consider Kissinger's involvement in the assassination and attempted assassination of other government leaders (Cyprus and Chile); his standing by as others committed genocide and war crimes (Bangladesh and East Timor); and his callously aggressive activities during the Vietnam conflict are more than sufficient evidence of his corruption and criminal behavior. Realistically, however, the failure of succeeding United States administrations to address his acts, as well as the case of those countries who were specifically the beneficiaries or targets of his criminality, in all likelihood perpetuate Kissinger's status as a now-retired 'elder statesman' and media consultant – in short, as someone 'above the law.' Even the recently filed (2001) lawsuit by the family of the slain Chilean General René Schneider will, in all likelihood, go nowhere, given the reluctance of the United States government to bring to the bar of justice high-ranking administration officials for activities conducted and associated with the performance of their duties. Only the continuing and unrelenting glare of the public spotlight, and the unearthing of ever more documentary evidence, will tarnish his image in the eyes of the American people, and allow the truest portrait of him to be presented to the judgment of history.

The recent human rights victory of the extradition by a Spanish judge of former Chilean dictator Augusto Pinochet should, perhaps, signal another possibility and an indication of the initial success of the principle of universal jurisdiction in international law, the fourteen principles of which were enumerated at Princeton University, New Jersey, in 2001:

1 Fundamentals of Universal Jurisdiction
2 Serious Crimes Under International Law
3 Reliance on Universal Jurisdiction in the Absence of National Legislation
4 Obligation to Support Accountabilty
5 Immunities
6 Statutes of Limitations
7 Amnesties
8 Resolution of Competing National Jurisdictions
9 NON BIS IN IDEM/Double Jeopardy
10 Grounds for Refusal of Extradition
11 Adoption of National Legislation
12 Inclusion of Universal Jurisdiction in Future Treaties
13 Strengthening Accountability and Universal Jurisdiction
14 Settlement of Disputes.

These principles, which themselves are seemingly controversial and do not as yet have international standing or United Nations endorsement, go to the very heart of the sovereignty of a nation-state and those responsible for its leadership, whether elected, appointed or usurped. Significantly enough, Kissinger himself has addressed this concept of universal jurisdiction in a recent *Foreign Affairs* article entitled 'The Pitfalls of Universal Jurisdiction,' claiming that such jurisdiction poses 'extreme risks substituting the tyranny of judges for that of governments.' In this article, he also reveals his own political orientation with the comment: 'The role of the statesman is to choose the best option when seeking to advance the cause of peace and justice,' realizing that 'there is frequently a tension between the two and that any reconciliation is like to be partial' (Kissinger, 2001; see also the response of Kenneth Roth, executive director of Human Rights Watch, in the following issue of the journal).

Subsequent to this ongoing controversy, the recent (2002) decision of the Bush administration to pull out of the International Criminal Court would seem to ensure both immunity and impunity for Kissinger. Thus, in the aftermath of the forty-year struggle to ratify the 1948 UN Convention on the Prevention and Punishment of the Crime of Genocide, the US again opts to go it alone, and regards its own national state-sovereignty as above international law. As an extended consequence, those who were and are its leaders are guaranteed safety from prosecution for crimes committed while it office.

Who, then, is to bring Kissinger to trial? Under what jurisdiction? In what country? Under what and whose laws, international or national? While human rights advocates may cry correctly that Kissinger will end his days a free man, and jurists will debate the fine and finer points of international law, as well as Kissinger's guilt – however defined – all is by no means lost to those who continue to persevere in this area.

The broader trend perhaps induces more optimism. As these words are being written, Slobodan Milosevic, the ousted president of Serbia, stands in the dock at the International Criminal Tribunal for the former Yugoslavia (ICTY), indicted for war crimes and genocide. Rwandan political, military, and religious leaders continue to be brought to trial and convicted of genocidal crimes at the International Criminal Tribunal for Rwanda (ICTR). Both Tribunals are legacies not only of the International Military Tribunal (IMT) at Nuremberg, but of the 1948 United Nations Convention on the Prevention and Punishment of the Crime of Genocide. For Raphael Lemkin, Polish-Jewish émigré lawyer and refugee, the journey of a young boy reacting to an ancient massacre and its horrific repetition throughout history has, at long last, begun to bear fruit.

## Notes

1. As Lemkin wrote in *Axis Rule in Occupied Europe*: 'The alarming increase in barbarity typified with the advent of Hitler led the author to make a proposal to the Fifth International Conference for the Unification of Penal Law (held in Madrid in 1933, in cooperation with the Fifth Committee of the League of Nations) to the effect that an international treaty should be negotiated declaring that attacks upon national, religious, and ethnic groups should be made international crimes, and that *perpetrators of such crimes should not only be liable to trial in their own countries, but, in the event of escape, could also be tried in the place of refuge, or else extradited to the country where the crime was*

*committed*. His proposal not having been adopted at that time, he feels impelled to renew it now after the world has been faced with the tragic experiences of German rule. The negotiation of such a treaty at the present time by all nations of the civilized world, both belligerents and neutrals, would provide not only a more adequate basis for the punishment of war criminals but also the necessary procedural machinery for the extradition of such criminals by members of the United Nations and neutrals. More-over, it would also provide an adequate machinery for the international protection of national and ethnic groups against extermination attempts and oppression in time of peace' (Lemkin 1944: xiii, emphasis added).

2. Among Lemkin's manuscripts currently being edited and prepared for publica-tion by this author are: *Totally Unofficial: The Autobiography of Raphael Lemkin* (a manu-script of somewhere between 300 and 450 pages); *Introduction to the Study of Genocide* (an incomplete manuscript of nine chapters, comprising 140 pages, including a ration-ale for the project); *The Hitler Case* (only 60 pages of a five-chapter text have been found thus far – the project was evidently never completed); and *A History of Genocide: I. Antiquity; II. The Middle Ages; III. Modern Times* (62 chapters in total, but only one chapter of Volume I, three of Volume II, and 12 of Volume III have been found) (Jacobs, 1999: 109–11). To date, only one edited manuscript has been published: Lemkin's as-sessment of the International Military Tribunal (IMT) at Nuremberg, Germany, 1945, to which Lemkin served as a legal advisor. This has been given the title *Raphael Lemkin's Thoughts on Nazi Genocide: Not Guilty?* (Lewiston, NY: The Edwin Mellon Press, 1992, 375 pages). It is now out of print.

3. Parenthetically, what has been overlooked in the discussion of the use of Lemkin's invented word 'genocide' is his first footnote to this chapter: 'Another term could be used for the same idea, namely, *ethnocide*, consisting of the Greek word, "ethnos" – nation – and the Latin word "cide"' (Lemkin, 1944: 79).

4. See also Berman, 2001.

# References

Berman, L. (2001). *No peace, no honor: Nixon, Kissinger, and betrayal in Vietnam*. New York: The Free Press.

Forum: Regarding Henry Kissinger: A panel discussion on the making of a war crimi-nal. www.harpers.org/online/kissinger_forum.

Freedman, L. (2001). Cold war warmed up. *London Jewish Chronicle* 33.

Henry Kissinger on trial: A guide to the controversy surrounding the diplomat. www.britannica.com/kissinger.

Hersh, S.M. (1983). *The price of power: Kissinger in the Nixon White House*. New York: Summit Books.

Hitchens, C. (2001a). The case against Henry Kissinger. Part I: The making of a war criminal. *Harper's* 302, no. 1809, 33–58.

———— (2001b). The case against Henry Kissinger. Part II: Crimes against humanity. *Harper's* 302, no. 1810, 49–74.

———— (2001c). *The Trial of Henry Kissinger*. London: Verso.

Jacobs, S.L. (2002). Genesis of the concept of genocide according to its author from the original sources. *Human Rights Review* 3, no. 2, pp. 98–103.

———— (1999). The papers of Raphael Lemkin: a first look. *Journal of Genocide Research*, 1: 1, 105–114.

————, ed. (1992). *Raphael Lemkin's thoughts on Nazi genocide: Not guilty?* Lewiston, NY: The Edwin Mellen Press.

Kissinger, H. (2001). The pitfalls of universal jurisdiction. *Foreign Affairs*, July/August. www.thirdworldtraveler.com/Kissinger/Pitfalls_Univ_Juris_Kis.html.

LeBlanc, L.J. (1991). *The United States and the Genocide Convention*. Durham, NC: Duke University Press.

Lemkin, R. (1944). *Axis rule in occupied Europe: Laws of occupation, analysis of government, proposals for redress*. Washington, DC: Carnegie Endowment for International Peace.

Popple, J. (1989). The right to protection from retroactive criminal law. *Criminal Law Journal* 13, no. 4: 251–62; and *Australasian Law Students' Association Journal* 2: 5–18. www.cs.anu.edu.au/~James.Popple/publications/articles/retroactive.htm.

Principles of international law recognized in the Charter of the Nurnberg Tribunal and in the judgment of the tribunal (n.d.). www.un.org/law/ilc/texts/nurnberg.htm.

Shawcross, W. (1979). *Sideshow: Kissinger, Nixon and the destruction of Cambodia*. New York: Simon & Schuster.

Sienkiewicz, H. (1993). *Quo Vadis?*, trans. W.S. Kuniczak. New York: Hippocrene Books.

Totten, S., and Jacobs, S.L., eds (2002). *Pioneers of genocide studies*. Piscataway, NJ: Transaction Publishers.

# Crimes of the West in Democratic Congo: Reflections on Belgian Acceptance of 'Moral Responsibility' for the Death of Lumumba

## Thomas Turner

In February 2002, the Belgian government accepted 'moral responsibility' for the death of Congolese Prime Minister Patrice Lumumba forty-one years earlier. Louis Michel, Belgium's foreign minister, declared that 'In the light of criteria applicable today, certain members of the government of the time and certain Belgian actors of that period carry an irrefutable share of responsibility for the events that led to the death of Patrice Lumumba.' He went on to say that the government thought it appropriate 'to present to the family of Patrice Lumumba and to the Congolese people its deep and sincere regrets and apologies.' Brussels would contribute 3.75 million euros (over $3 million) to the Lumumba Foundation, created to promote democracy in the former Belgian colony (IRIN, 2002).

Too little, too late, some would say. Yet the Belgian statement is important in several respects. First, it is the result of a lengthy investigation by a parliamentary commission. In that sense, it represents a coming-to-terms with a major crime of the past.

Second, the statement of 'moral responsibility' is important also for what it does not say. The question of who, exactly, was involved on the Belgian side is avoided. 'Certain members of the government' share in the responsibility; but in a parliamentary government, ministers are collectively responsible. The expression 'certain Belgian actors of the period' is notably vague. Does it refer, perhaps, to the king and his court? The commission received from its panel of experts evidence of royal concern and involvement in the Lumumba question; but it toned down the matter in its final report (Péju, 2002). Did the 'certain actors' include corporate interests?

Third, the Belgian acceptance of responsibility was phrased so as to obscure the question of shared responsibility. To what extent was Belgium jointly responsible for the murder, together with its NATO ally, the United States, and with Congolese in positions of authority in Léopoldville (now Kinshasa) and in Elisabethville (now Lubumbashi)?

Analysis of the violence in Congo since 1960 poses several problems. There are many accusations that this or that Congolese has been a puppet of one outside force or another. In some cases, the accusations seem well founded. Some Congolese ministers, and other prominent members of the local elite, were being advised by Belgians. Further, a number of Congolese took money from foreign governments. However, it does not follow that such people were merely carrying out policies designed elsewhere.

The Belgians had assigned themselves the responsibility for leading the Congolese from savagery to civilization, or from childhood to adulthood. One wonders how long this process was supposed to take. According to a fact endlessly repeated in the press, Congo had only ten or twelve university graduates in 1960.

The inadequacy of this notion of the Congolese as childish individuals, merely carrying out policies elaborated elsewhere, is illustrated by the case of Moïse Tshombe, president of the secessionist State of Katanga, and later prime minister of Congo. Tshombe can be seen as serving the interests of Belgian mining capital, or as defending the interests of Katanga's African elite (as opposed to the Luba-Kasai, who held many jobs in the mining companies, and also to the central government in Léopoldville/Kinshasa, which was dependent on revenues from Katanga's mines). Tshombe has been described as a 'Florentine' – i.e. a master manipulator – by authors who seek to stress his autonomy (e.g. Brassine and Kestergat, 1991). Brian Urquhart of the United Nations described dealing with Tshombe as being like 'trying to get an eel into a bottle' (Power, 2000). Urquhart's UN colleague, the Irish scholar–diplomat Conor Cruise O'Brien, offered a more elegant interpretation, comparing Tshombe to the captain of the slave ship in Melville's *Benito Cereno*. The captain 'only appears to be the master of the ship; the real masters are the slaves themselves, who have revolted; the captain, who is, in fact, their prisoner, is serving to conceal the reality. It seemed to me that Tshombe was in a sense an inverted Benito Cereno, the slave who appears to have been made master of the ship, while the real masters are still the old slave-owners, now pretending to be simple passengers' (O'Brien, 1965). This is terrific writing, and of course O'Brien was there and looked Tshombe and his colleagues in the eye. But it seems to me that the simile is too simple.

The Belgian journalists Davister and Toussaint offer a better summary, according to which the 'prisoner' remained the same while those who held him prisoner changed over time. Tshombe was always someone's toy, 'and the importance of his role was always directly proportional to the importance of those who, one after another, took charge of him' (Davister and Toussaint, 1962).

Perhaps Tshombe was constantly being manipulated. But in my view, secessionist Katanga represented an alliance between European interests and fledgling African politicians including Tshombe. It is revealing that no one compared Godefroid Munongo, grandson of the legendary Msiri and pillar of the Katanga regime, to a prisoner. Decades later, it still is difficult to get a handle on Tshombe's role.

Joseph-Désiré Mobutu, later Mobutu Sese Seko, poses a similar problem. For some people in Washington, he was 'our man in Kinshasa' (Pachter, 1987; see also Schatzberg, 1991; Kelly, 1993). Yet it is difficult to imagine Americans supporting, let alone dreaming up, some of Mobutu's policies, such as breaking diplomatic relations with Israel in 1973. Mobutu is described as a 'political genius,' a master of divide-and-rule. Presumably, he acquired those skills over the years; but that leaves the observer with the problem of determining the degree of autonomy he possessed at a particular point in time.

Foreign governments intervened in Congo, notably the United States and Belgium; but here the level-of-analysis problem rears its head. One can assume that an ambassador speaks for his government. But 'bureaucratic analysis' (Allison, 1971; Allison and Zelikow, 1999) encourages us to look for distinctive organizational interests, and to the behavior of various agencies. The US State Department and the CIA, for example, might not always have been on the same page. Likewise, Belgium's prime minister and king may have had somewhat different interests and approaches.

Foreign governments did not act only through their own representatives and (perhaps) their Congolese agents. In the early 1960s, 'mercenaries' played prominent roles in Congo. These so-called mercenaries – white men who served in the gendarmerie (police/army) of Katanga, then as special forces of Congo under Tshombe – ostensibly were hired by the Katangan or Congolese authorities. By definition, a mercenary does not work for his own government. Thus, Colonel Mike Hoare, a South African, worked for Katanga and then for Congo. However, by his own admission, and according to the statement of Bob Denard, Hoare was paid by the CIA. Can one be sure that Hoare was not working for South Africa as well? And what of the Frenchman Denard: was he perhaps working for his own country, France?

In short, the problems of sorting out agency and responsibility are considerable. Let us turn to two undoubted instances of criminal action – the assassination of Lumumba and the kidnapping of Tshombe – to see what specific problems they pose.

## The murder of Lumumba

Any discussion of Western crimes in Congo must give priority to the murder of Patrice Lumumba, the first prime minister of Congo. A horrible event in itself, the murder set off waves of retaliation and counter-retaliation. The repercussions are being felt to this day.

Lumumba's party, the Lumumba wing of the Congolese National Movement (MNC-Lumumba), was almost unique among Congolese parties in being both national in orientation and radical in its opposition to colonialism (Weiss, 1967). By March 1960, three months prior to independence, Belgian authorities had concluded the necessity of 'eliminating' Lumumba, according to Professor Jean Omosombo, who is completing a study of Lumumba based in part on hitherto secret Belgian government documents.[1]

Lumumba's party did better than any other in pre-independence elections. He became prime minister despite Belgian attempts to find an alternative. The country attained independence on 30 June 1960, with Lumumba as prime minister and his rival, Joseph Kasavubu, as president. A week later, the Congo was plunged into chaos when the army mutinied against its Belgian officers. Belgium sent troops to protect its citizens, and mineral-rich Katanga seceded with Belgian backing. South Kasai, Congo's main source of diamonds, followed Katanga into secession.

Kasavubu and Lumumba initially cooperated to restore order, but relations between the two soon deteriorated. Brussels and Washington attempted to persuade Kasavubu to dismiss Lumumba. In September, after Lumumba had obtained Soviet aid for his attempt to recapture South Kasai, Kasavubu agreed. He dismissed Lumumba, who responded by dismissing the president. Mobutu, an aide to Lumumba who had been put in charge of the army in the aftermath of the mutiny, then 'neutralized' both Kasavubu and Lumumba.

Lumumba escaped from house arrest in Kinshasa, nearly reaching territory whose population was favorable to his party before being recaptured. To Mobutu, Kasavubu, and their foreign backers the lesson was clear. So long as Lumumba remained alive, there was a danger he could regain power. To prevent this, he was sent to secessionist Katanga, where he was tortured and murdered – apparently by Katangan soldiers under Belgian command.

The problem in assigning responsibility in the case is that there are too many potential culprits. Belgium began working to replace Lumumba almost immediately after its military intervention in July 1960. Foreign Minister Pierre Wigny sent a diplomat to Congo to sound out his counter-part, Congolese Foreign Minister Justin Bomboko, about a possible coup d'état. Minister without Portfolio W.J. Ganshof van der Meersch (who had supervised the pre-independence effort to find another prime minister instead of Lumumba) now sent an agent of the Belgian security police to Congo to conduct undercover destabilization efforts (Péju, 2002).

In October, the Belgian minister for African affairs, Count Harold d'Aspremont Linden, sent a telegram ordering the elimination of Lumumba. The African leader was to be kidnapped as part of the so-called 'Operation Barracuda.' It is unclear whether the eventual murder of Lumumba was perpetrated under the auspices of a revised 'Barracuda.'

The Americans launched their own covert action plan, 'Project Wizard,' in August 1960. Over the next few months, the CIA worked with and made payments to eight leading Congolese, including Kasavubu, Mobutu, Bomboko, Senate President Joseph Ileo, finance aide Albert Ndele, and labor leader Cyrille Adoula, 'who all played roles in Lumumba's downfall.' (Weissman, 2002). Weissman reports that the CIA joined Belgium in a plan for Ileo and Adoula to engineer a no-confidence vote in Lumumba's government, which would be followed by union-led demonstrations, the resignations of cabinet ministers (organized by Ndele) and Kasavubu's dismissal of Lumumba. The 'Special Group' of the US National Security Council authorized CIA payments to Kasavubu on 1 September, according to classified documents consulted by Weissman. Four days later, Kasavubu (by now 'persuaded') dismissed Lumumba.

When Mobutu 'neutralized' the president and the prime minister, he established a 'College of Commissioners' to act as a temporary govern-ment. Presented as an apolitical group of university students and derided by some as the 'student council' (Hempstone, 1962), the College was an illegal government headed by CIA allies Bomboko and Ndele. After the failure of repeated attempts to establish an anti-Lumumba government, and continued disorder in the capital, the 'College of Commissioners' asked Kasavubu to move Lumumba to a 'surer place.' Kasavubu told security chief Victor Nendaka (another Project Wizard participant) to transfer Lumumba to one of the secessionist provinces (Katanga or South Kasai). On 17 January, Nendaka sent Lumumba to Katanga, where he was killed. The specific objective of preventing a Lumumbist comeback was high-lighted by the identity of the two men killed with Lumumba. Joseph

Okito, the Senate vice-president, was a rival of Ileo, while Maurice Mpolo was a rival of Mobutu for control of the armed forces.

The US and Belgium were staunch NATO allies, but their views of the Congo were not identical. Belgian motivations seem to have centered on protection of their citizens and investments, especially in Katanga. Their goal was a neocolonial Congo, similar to the result achieved by the French in many of their former colonies. Lumumba, seen as the principal obstacle to such a plan, was demonized (Halen and Riesz, 1997). Often, he was depicted as an agent of communism.

The Americans' view was simpler. They focused on communism, as evidenced by a telegram sent by the CIA station in Léopoldville to its headquarters in Washington, early in August 1960:

> EMBASSY AND STATION BELIEVE CONGO EXPERIENCING CLASSIC COMMUNIST EFFORT TAKEOVER GOVERNMENT – WHETHER OR NOT LUMUMBA ACTUALLY COMMIE OR JUST PLAYING COMMIE GAME TO ASSIST HIS SOLIDIFYING POWER, ANTI-WEST FORCES RAPIDLY IN-CREASING POWER CONGO AND THERE MAY BE LITTLE TIME LEFT IN WHICH TAKE ACTION TO AVOID ANOTHER CUBA. (United States Senate, 1975: 57)

One cannot exclude the likely influence of economic interests. Indeed, the reference to Cuba could be interpreted to mean that such interests were threatened. But I find the 'business conflict' model proposed by David Gibbs unconvincing (Gibbs, 1991). The Americans interpreted the Congo in Cold War terms; economic interests, real or potential, were secondary.

These differences in orientation between Washington and Brussels showed up notably in Belgian promotion of, and American opposition to, the secession of Katanga. But the differences should not be overstated. Belgium and the US agreed on the need to replace Lumumba, and co-operated to some extent to attain this goal.

During the period 1961–65, Congo careened from crisis to crisis. Power in the capital was held by the so-called 'Binza Group,' named for the wealthy suburb where most of its members lived. The Binza Group comprised most of the veterans of the Americans' 'Operation Wizard,' including Mobutu, Bomboko, Ndele, and Nendaka. The Lumumbist opposition launched a series of insurrections, which took over about half of the country. These were put down thanks to coordinated efforts of the US and Belgium. A group of white mercenaries, at least some of them paid by the US, served as spearhead of the government counteroffensive. Late in 1965, when the tide had turned but the Lumumbist insurgents had not yet been completely defeated, President Kasavubu called for withdrawal of the mercenaries. This appears to have triggered the coup d'état of 25 November, which brought Mobutu to power.

Tshombe had been recalled from exile and named premier in 1964 to help President Kasavubu put down the Lumumbist insurgents. He was dismissed the following year as a result of his rivalry with Kasavubu, and returned to Spain. In 1967, after his return to the Congo was rumored, he was kidnapped and taken to Algeria, where he died of a heart attack in 1969. René Lemarchand points out the contradictory aspect of Mobutu's involvement in the elimination of his rival Tshombe:

> in an effort to allay suspicions that he was overwhelmingly dependent on the C.I.A. (a fact that had become patently clear during the 1964 rebellion, if not earlier), Mobutu decided to assume a more radical stance, and in order to give a substance of 'authenticity' to this new look, plans were made to bring Tshombe back from Spain and then stage a public execution of the 'neo-imperialist' stooge. For this primary reliance was placed on the C.I.A. The operation proved eminently successful, at least in its initial stage: on 30 June 1967, Tshombe's plane was hijacked over the Mediterranean, and after a forced landing in Algiers the leader of the Katanga secession was surrendered to the Algerian Government. At this point, however, it became apparent that Boumedienne was unwilling to deliver Tshombe unconditionally to Mobutu, a fact which the C.I.A. had failed to anticipate. (Lemarchand, 1976: 415)

Tshombe remained in an Algerian prison, where he died, allegedly of a heart attack. Mobutu's most dangerous rival disappeared, and in that sense the American government or the CIA can be considered to have achieved their objective of protecting 'their man.' But Mobutu was deprived of the public execution he had planned, according to Lemarchand. One could even argue that the kidnapping demonstrated Mobutu's dependency on his foreign backers, since his own operatives could not have executed such a plan.

## Complicity: the scholarship and the cable record

There can be little doubt that the West, and more specifically Belgium and the United States, were responsible for the death of the 'radical' nationalist Patrice Lumumba. The US bears the major responsibility for the death of the 'moderate,' regionalist Moïse Tshombe. These deaths, and the concomitant rise of Mobutu, reflect Western efforts to find an acceptable formula for decolonization, one in which Western political and economic interests would be protected.

What is not completely clear is the nature of the Americans' and Belgians' contributions, and the extent to which their efforts were coordinated. Part of the difficulty is that research on each side of the Atlantic has tended to incriminate or exculpate the individual government in question, rather than examining the question of shared responsibility.

The murder of Lumumba was a subject of intense interest in Belgium. However, in the absence of hard data, many early books on the subject were virtually works of fiction. Pierre De Vos's *Vie et mort de Lumumba* (De Vos, 1961) is an example. Other works used a documentary approach, based largely on published materials, such as the yearbooks published by CRISP (*Congo 1960*, *Congo 1961*, and so on). It was not until the 1990s that the murder of Lumumba was re-examined in Belgium. Professor Jean-Claude Willame (1990) 'revisited' the Congo crisis. Jacques Brassine, a minor actor in the Katanga secession, defended a doctoral dissertation at the Université Libre de Bruxelles that served as the basis for a non-scholarly publication, written in collaboration with the journalist and Congo specialist Jean Kestergat (Brassine and Kestergat, 1991). The main point of both the dissertation and the book was that Congolese (notably the 'Florentine' Tshombe) had killed Lumumba. Belgium, accordingly, was exonerated.

A Belgian sociologist, Ludo de Witte, took up the gauntlet thrown down by Brassine and Kestergat (De Witte, 1999, 2000, 2001). After several years of archival research and interviews, De Witte presented a detailed account of the assassination. He traced the links between Belgian policy and Belgian actions in Katanga. The book led to a parliamentary inquiry, which in turn led to the Belgian government statement accepting 'moral responsibility' for Lumumba's murder. De Witte, understandably, was interested mainly in establishing the responsibility of the Belgian government for Lumumba's death, which he felt had been played down by Brassine and Kestergat, as well as by conservative media such as the Brussels daily *La Libre Belgique*.

The parliamentary inquiry heard testimony from a wide variety of witnesses, including Belgians (such as Brassine) and Congolese. Among the latter were Victor Nendaka, head of the Sûreté in Kinshasa at the time of the murder; and Jean-Baptiste Kibwe, finance minister under Tshombe. Neither the Belgians nor the Congolese shed much new light on the issue of responsibility for the murder. Little attention was paid to the American connection, and next to none to the role of the late King Baudouin – still a very sensitive question in Belgium.

Early American treatments of the death of Lumumba were scarcely more serious than that of De Vos. Journalist Smith Hempstone published a pro-Katanga, anti-United Nations piece (Hempstone, 1962), but shed little light on the precise circumstances of Lumumba's death. Stephen Weissman's University of Chicago dissertation was eventually published by Cornell University Press (Weissman, 1974), apparently after being turned down by the University of Chicago Press for political reasons. In this work of high scholarly quality, the author laid out the contrasting versions of Cold War ideology that motivated the Eisenhower and Kennedy administrations. He was unable, at that point, to pinpoint American involvement in the death of Lumumba. However, the broad outline of Weissman's argument has stood the test of time.

American criticism of US Congo policy reached a peak in the 1970s, in the aftermath of the Vietnam War. The decolonization of Angola, with its Congo parallels, probably reinforced US interest in the Congo question. In this context, the Church Committee of the US Senate interviewed a minutes-taker for Eisenhower's National Security Council, who attested to the president's order to eliminate Lumumba. The committee also reported on several CIA attempts to kill Lumumba. However, the committee concluded that the US had not been involved in the actual murder. It should be noted that the Church Committee had no interest in diluting criticism of the US role by examining that of the Belgians.

In 1982, Madeline Kalb demonstrated the advances that could be made when detailed information became available. She made good use of 'Congo cables' sent from CIA and State Department representatives in Congo to their respective headquarters in Washington. These cables demonstrate American involvement in the death of Lumumba, well beyond what the Church Committee was willing to conclude (Kalb, 1982). And in 1992, on the basis of other documents obtained in Washington, Weissman was able to identify specific decisions and authorizations of payment to Kasavubu, Mobutu and other Congolese actors (Weissman, 2002a, 2002b).

The Americans and Belgians certainly shared an antipathy to Lumumba. They doubtless consulted with one another during 1959–60. A Belgian official who helped to engineer Lumumba's transfer to Katanga told Belgian researcher De Witte that he had kept CIA Kinshasa station chief Lawrence Devlin fully informed of the plan. 'The Americans were informed of the transfer because they actively discussed this thing for weeks,' De Witte reports (De Witte, 2001). Devlin denied any prior knowledge of the transfer, but this denial is implausible. Why should he and his agency not have concluded that the transfer of Lumumba and his colleagues to Katanga, where they certainly would be killed, was a suitable way of carrying out the task assigned by Eisenhower?

Circumstantial evidence of a joint American–Belgian role can be seen in two declassified American cables. On 13 January, apparently fearing that Lumumba would somehow manage to thwart American plans, Devlin or someone else in Kinshasa sent the following cable to Washington:

THE COMBINATION OF [LUMUMBA'S] POWERS AS DEMAGOGUE, HIS ABLE USE OF GOON SQUADS AND PROPAGANDA AND SPIRIT OF DEFEAT

WITHIN [GOVERNMENT] ... WOULD ALMOST CERTAINLY INSURE [LUMUMBA] VICTORY IN PARLIAMENT ... REFUSAL TAKE DRASTIC STEPS AT THIS TIME WILL LEAD DEFEAT OF [UNITED STATES] POLICY IN CONGO. (Kalb, 1982: 190)

Whether or not Washington was refusing to take 'drastic steps,' it appeared that *someone* was willing to take them. Just four days later, Mobutu and Kasavubu sent Lumumba, Okito, and Mpolo to Elisabethville, where they were killed. On 19 January, the CIA base chief in Elisabethville cabled headquarters:

THANKS FOR PATRICE. IF WE HAD KNOWN HE WAS COMING WE WOULD HAVE BAKED A SNAKE. (Kalb, 1982: 191)

'If we had known' might be interpreted as meaning that the CIA man in Katanga had not been told Lumumba was coming. But the cable-writer gives the game away by thanking his bosses (not Mobutu and Kasavubu, and not the Belgians) for sending Lumumba.

## Conclusion

The murder of Lumumba – a terrible crime in itself – has poisoned Congolese political life for decades. The 'Lumumbist' rebellions of 1964–67 were directed against the Kinshasa government of Kasavubu, Mobutu, and others, and of course against the US and Belgium. Lumumbist Laurent Kabila continued the struggle against Kinshasa into the 1980s. When then-Zaire began an abortive transition to democracy in the early 1990s, the National Conference held hearings on Lumumba's death. And when Kabila came to power in 1996, as successor to Mobutu, he called for a new investigation into the murder.

The main facts of the assassination are not in dispute. The work of Kalb, De Witte, Weissman and others has made it clear that the US and Belgium were active participants. In particular, Weissman's identification of American payments to major Congolese figures enables us to set aside earlier talk of 'puppets.' What is still needed is an inquiry focused on the specific question of the linkages between Belgium and the United States. Only when such an inquiry has published its results can Congo and the West begin to cooperate once again, on a healthier and more equitable basis.

## Note

1. Interview with Jean Omosombo, September 2002.

# References

Allison, G. (1971). *Essence of decision: Explaining the Cuban missile crisis*. Boston: Little, Brown.

Allison, G.T. and Zelikow, P. (1999). *Essence of decision: Explaining the Cuban missile crisis*. Baltimore, MD: Addison-Wesley.

Brassine, J. and Kestergat, J. (1991). *Qui a tué Patrice Lumumba?* Paris and Louvain-la-Neuve: Éditions Duculot.

Davister, P. and Toussaint, P. (1962). *Croisettes et casques bleus*. Brussels: Éditions Actuelles.

De Vos, P. (1961). *Vie et mort de Lumumba*. Paris: Calmann-Lévy.

De Witte, L. (2001). *The assassination of Lumumba*. London: Verso.

———— (2000). *L'assassinat de Lumumba*. Paris: Karthala.

———— (1999). *De moord op Lumumba*. Leuven: Van Halewyck.

Gérard-Libois, J. and Verhaegen, B. (1961). *Congo 1960*. Brussels: Centre de recherche et d'information socio-politiques.

Gibbs, D.N. (1991). *The political economy of Third World intervention: Mines, money, and U.S. policy in the Congo crisis*. Chicago: University of Chicago Press.

Halen, P. and Riesz, J., eds (1997). *Patrice Lumumba entre Dieu et Diable: Un héroe africain dans ses images*. Paris: Éditions l'Harmattan.

Hempstone, S. (1962). *Rebels, mercenaries, and dividends: The Katanga story*. New York: Praeger.

IRIN (2002). La Belgique présente ses excuses pour le rôle qu'elle a joué dans la mort, en 1961, du premier ministre congolais, Patrice Lumumba. Nairobi, 7 February.

Kalb, M.G. (1982). *Congo cables: The Cold War in Africa from Eisenhower to Kennedy*. New York: Macmillan.

Kelly, S. (1993). *America's tyrant: The CIA and Mobutu of Zaire*. Washington: The American University Press.

Lemarchand, R. (1976). The C.I.A. in Africa: How central? How intelligent? *The Journal of Modern African Studies* 14, no. 3: 401–26.

O'Brien, C.C. (1965). *To Katanga and back: A U.N. case history*. London: Four Square Books.

Pachter, E.F. (1987). *Our man in Kinshasa: U.S. relations with Mobutu, 1970–83: Patron–client relations in the international sphere*. Baltimore, MD: Johns Hopkins University, School of Advanced International Studies.

Péju, M. (2002). Le parlement belge à l'épreuve de Lumumba. *J.A./L'Intelligent*, 18–21.

Power, J. (2000). In Sierra Leone, the U.N. is battling for itself. 24 May. www.transnational.org/forum/power/2000/05sierraleone.html.

Schatzberg, M.G. (1991). *Mobutu or chaos? The United States and Zaire, 1960–1990*. Lanham, MD: University Press of America.

United States Senate (1975). *Alleged assassination plots involving foreign leaders*. Washington, DC: Government Printing Office.

Verhaegen, B., ed. (1962). *Congo 1961*. Brussels: CRISP.

Weiss, H. (1967). *Political protest in the Congo: the Parti Solidaire Africain during the independence struggle*. Princeton, NJ: Princeton University Press.

Weissman, S.R. (2002a). Opening the secret files on Lumumba's murder. *Washington Post*, 21 July.

———— (2002b). U.S. role in Lumumba murder revealed. *AllAfrica.com*, 22 July.

———— (1974). *American foreign policy in the Congo, 1960–64*. Ithaca: Cornell University Press.

Willame, J.-C. (1990). *Patrice Lumumba: La crise congolaise revisitée*. Paris: Karthala.

# 13

# In the Name of the Cold War: How the West Aided and Abetted the Barre Dictatorship of Somalia

## Mohamed Diriye Abdullahi

This chapter does not aim to provide details of the massacres committed by the US-supported Siad Barre dictatorship in Somalia. Rather, it attempts to review the Western assistance that enabled Barre to turn Somalia into a killing field for over a decade.

During the height of the Cold War, President Reagan had called the Soviets 'an evil empire.' It was true that the Soviets had a repressive regime in their own country, and supported some evil regimes elsewhere. However, granting the United States the moral high ground is untenable, given the US record of propping up its own evil regimes, including Siad Barre's, and anti-democratic guerrillas, such as Savimbi's in Angola.[1]

### American and Western complicity

The 1980s was the crucial decade that pushed Somalia over the precipice. During that time Somalia's role was that of a pawn on the superpower chessboard, a client state whose fascist dictator was useful to Washington in its global tussle with the Soviets.[2] It is certainly the case that prior to 1978, the Barre regime was allied with the Soviets, who supplied it with weapons and military training. However, during the period of Soviet-client status, Barre showed little of the beast he would later become under US patronage. In fact, his regime committed its most heinous crimes and massacres during the decade that it was allied with the West, not during the eight years it was allied with the Soviets. The latter period ended in 1978, when two things happened: (1) the Soviet Union decided to swap

Barre, a rustic dictator with little knowledge of communist social theories, for Colonel Mengistu of Ethiopia and his younger socialist officers, who appeared more inclined to implement communist ideals in their feudal country, notably in the area of land reform;[3] (2) Ethiopia, with the help of the Soviet Union, defeated the Somali army and drove it out of Somali-inhabited areas in Ethiopia.

These events, at the time, seemed to sound the death knell for the Barre regime. The public was overwhelmingly of the opinion that Siad Barre's policies had failed the country both internally and externally.[4] At last Somali democrats were showing their faces, hoping the time was right to change the country's course by sidelining Barre. But Barre, who had a sixth sense for opposition, saw the writing on the wall and frantically tried to find a solution to prolong his reign. Soon the miracle arrived: he was able to align the country with the West, and Washington moved in as the patron of his regime because of the strategic value of Somalia's northern coastline.[5]

For a brief period, this realignment of the country with the West took the wind out of the sails of Barre's critics, who were clamoring for democracy and a return to a free-market economy. People felt that the new alignment with the US, a country perceived as the champion of democracy, would not only force Barre to become more democratic but would also open up new avenues of trade and investment after years of Soviet-style austerity. As one Somali put it at the time, 'When the Russians were here … they only brought guns but no money. They were a bad people. But the Americans, they have money and will buy in our shops' (Girardet, 1981).

Taken as a whole, Somalis are a profoundly religious people, and most were happy to see their country extricated from an alliance with the disliked Communist bloc so much that instant celebrations erupted at the country's main university campus. But these hopes were to be more than dashed. Western assistance would reinforce Barre's regime further, and spur the dictator to commit massacres and other heinous deeds that most Somalis would never have imagined could be inflicted by their own government.

## Ignoring Barre's political orientation

When the US established its patron–client pact with the Barre regime in 1980, there were hardly any doubts about the true nature of the regime. Barre's Somalia was an absolute dictatorship, with no independent parliament, judiciary, unions, or media. There were half-a-dozen security agencies and a security court that dispatched political prisoners by firing squad on flimsy charges. It was evident that unless Somalis succeeded in curbing Barre's power or ousting him as rapidly as possible, he would use any available means to bolster his system, and his exit could only come at the price of bloodshed. In short, Barre's system was a monster that, if fed, would grow more monstrous still. On the other hand, if it were starved of financial and military resources for a few short years, there seemed little doubt the regime would crumble in the face of pressure from the outside, or domestic challenge.

Still, it could be argued that Somalia, as a nation-state, had legitimate military needs and deserved to be able to arm itself against an outside aggressor. However, it was no secret that, after the 1977–78 war with Ethiopia (itself instigated by the Barre regime), most of Barre's arms acquisitions from the West and proxy Third World countries were intended for internal repression rather than repulsing the Ethiopian army, itself bogged down in internal wars and hardly capable of invading Somalia. Thus, foreseeing the use to which Barre would put his vast array of weaponry was scarcely difficult. In fact, when Barre obtained eleven British-made Hawker Hunter fighter aircraft from Kuwait, obviously with British knowledge, Professor Robert Rotberg of MIT correctly claimed that they were intended for the suppression of internal dissidence (Rotberg, 1984). Piloted by white Rhodesians and South Africans, these same fighter aircraft would rain death upon refugees fleeing a genocidal campaign in the north in 1988. Unfortunately, despite the brutal nature of the Barre dictatorship, successive US administrations did not insist on any process of internal democratization; nor did they offer assistance to any of the democratic figures and forces in the country. Obviously, what counted for Washington above all was access to Somali ports and airports, and the right to install sophisticated surveillance and monitoring systems on Somali soil.

## The rationale for supporting the Barre dictatorship

The US presence in the Horn can be viewed as having had three main objectives: protecting pro-Western governments in the Middle East, meaning essentially autocracies such as Saudi Arabia and Kuwait; protecting the oil lanes from the Middle East to the Indian Ocean; and safeguarding Western access to Middle East oil (Lefebvre, 1991: 15). All three objectives can be summarized with one word – oil. Access to that single resource seemed to require guarding the 'maritime choke points' in the region, and rimming them with pro-Western regimes (Lefebvre, 1991: 20). The emphasis was thus placed on insuring a 'pro-Western' orientation among the regimes of the region, regardless of the internal repression or outright terror that those regimes practiced.

It was Somalia's bad luck to border the Bab-el-Mandeb 'choke point' on the Red Sea's southern entrance, and to be positioned as well within easy reach of the oil wells of the Gulf. The port city of Berbera in the north, where most of Barre's massacres occurred in the 1980s, lay at the epicenter of the Pentagon's desires. Berbera has an airport, modernized by the Soviets, with the longest runway in Africa, and a port that the Soviets also modernized as a fleet port when Somalia was in their camp.[6]

Further bad luck arose from the fact that the US administration would soon come to be headed by President Ronald Reagan and his cohort of gung-ho, Soviet-fighting cold warriors bent on curbing Soviet 'influence' in the Third World. The previous Carter administration had indeed signed a bases-for-arms pact with Barre, but was more cautious overall in providing support to his regime. Not so Reagan–Bush:[7]

> Under Ronald Reagan, arms transfers would not be restrained for the sake of restraint. Chester Crocker had argued that the Carter administration's active but disarmed diplomacy, because of its reluctance to commit resources at a time when African security issues had come to the fore, had resulted in missed opportunities to gain friends in Africa and win the respect of adversaries. Unaffected by the so-called Vietnam syndrome – reluctance to pledge American aid or put U. S. credibility on the line in the Third World – the Reagan administration was 'quite prepared to send arms to friendly governments.' (Lefebvre, 1991: 228)

Assistance other than arms was to flow to 'friendly governments,' including economic aid as well as moral and propaganda support. The man who, for almost ten years during the Reagan–Bush era, embodied all this assistance – to Somalia and other African countries – was Dr Chester Crocker. Crocker was then Assistant Secretary for African Affairs; today he is a professor of political science at Georgetown University, and a board member of the United States Institute for Peace (USIP), an institution created by Congress to promote democracy and peace worldwide. During his time as a political appointee, however, promoting democracy in Somalia was not Dr Crocker's priority. Rather, it was to solicit more funds from Congress for the Barre dictatorship, as well as to downplay reports from independent human rights groups about the brutalities of the Barre regime. The organization Africa Watch noted:

> In January 1989, the State Department not only failed to condemn flagrant human rights abuses, but instead rebuked Africa Watch for calling for an investigation of the problem. Numerous credible reports by the US and international media in 1988 and 1989 reported that Somalia had received shipments of chemical

weapons from Libya. One story, which was aired on January 12, 1989 on NBC News, reported that the Reagan Administration had information eight months earlier that Libyan President Qadafy gave Somalia chemical weapons. The State Department denied the account, but NBC stood by its story when questioned by a Congressional office. When Africa Watch raised concerns about the possible use of chemical weapons against the Isaaks with Assistant Secretary of State Chester Crocker, he rebuked our organization for making such a suggestion and indicated that the State Department was satisfied with the Somali government's categorical denials, stating that 'prudence and fairness warrant a heavy burden of proof with respect to charges against willful use of weapons of mass destruction by a government against its own people.' In view of the Somali government's campaign of destruction in the north, it is difficult to justify Mr. Crocker's confidence in the Somali government on this issue. (Africa Watch, 1990: 210–11)

## The destruction of the North

The regime whose version of the truth satisfied Dr Crocker had by then amassed a record of numerous massacres since aligning itself with the US, especially in northern Somalia. For example, in December 1984, forty-three men were summarily executed in Burao for no other reason than to cow the northern population and erode resistance to the regime (Africa Watch, 1990: 65). By 1988, the regime had committed a well-documented and genocidal 'ethnic cleansing' of large areas of Somalia, though this was a term that would gain currency in the media only later.

During the fateful year of 1988, which is the year that Somalia actually fell apart as a nation, guerrillas of the Somali National Movement (SNM), who had been engaged in hit-and-run attacks on the regime since 1982, decided to risk their lives in their homeland instead of being caught up in a squeeze between the Barre dictatorship and the Mengistu regime in Ethiopia, after the two dictators signed a peace treaty between them. (The SNM had rear bases in Ethiopian territory.) The insurgents, with the help of an open rebellion by a northern Somali population aggrieved by years of massacres, torture, ill-treatment, economic plunder, and social neglect, rapidly took control of the main cities and most of the countryside.

Ideologically, the SNM was a Western-leaning movement and 'one of the most democratic movements in the Horn of Africa,' even if it maintained a relationship with the Marxist regime of Mengistu Haile Mariam (see Dagne, 1992; Prunier, 1990–91). Its leaders were democrats as well: the movement had changed its leadership several times through congresses. The SNM was thus not a threat to the interests of the US or its allies. Its sole aim was to liberate its people from a murderous regime. But that regime's response was swift and vicious, constituting nothing less than a planned genocide.

Earlier, in 1986, Barre's viceroy in the north, General Said Hersi, alias General Morgan, or 'The Butcher of Hargeisa' (previously the dictator's bodyguard before marrying one of his daughters), had written a letter to his father-in-law, which subsequently become known as 'the letter of death.' In it, Hersi laid the foundations for a 'campaign of obliteration' against the northern population (Greenfield, 1987). The full implications of this policy would be felt in northern areas in 1988, as the regime's army directed its considerable firepower against the civilian population. Jet fighters would take off from Hargeisa airport, the northern capital, only to drop their deadly cargo a few miles away, in residential areas. Artillery units positioned on ridges around the city would direct round after round of shells onto the same residential quarters. Then soldiers would go door-to-door to eliminate any remaining residents and to loot homes. In a matter of days, the two largest cities in the north, Hargeisa and Burao, were reduced to rubble-strewn ghost towns.[8]

In two months, from May to July 1988, between 50,000 and 100,000 people were massacred by the regime's forces.[9] By then, any surviving urban Isaaks – that is to say, hundreds of thousands of members of the main northern clan community – had fled across the border into Ethiopia. They were pursued along the way by the British-made fighter-bombers piloted by mercenary South African and ex-Rhodesian pilots, paid $2,000 per sortie (see Simmons, 1989; House of Representatives, 1988). But this was a massacre that took place in obscurity – far from television cameras, since the regime refused to allow reporters into the region. Even the International Red Cross was denied the right to bring food and medicine to the civilian population (Brittain, 1988; see also Mather, 1988). The survivors of these genocidal strategies claim today that only the courage of the SNM fighters saved them from outright extermination, when the world stood by silent. In reality, however, it was more than that: every man and woman in the targeted population had become a freedom fighter, with nothing left to lose.

## Overall US assistance to Barre

The US was engaged in arming Barre long before 1988, the year of the genocidal massacres. According to some accounts, between 1980 and 1989 the US had provided Barre with about $35 million in lethal military assistance alone, while total military assistance amounted to $187 million from 1980 to 1987 (Beaver, 1992). The peak year was 1985, when military assistance totaled $75.8 million (National Academy of Sciences, 1988). These figures are hardly inconsiderable when it is borne in mind that at the time the Somali population was fewer than 6 million, and they represent a level of military assistance that has few parallels in military aid to African nations. In the first year following the 1988 slaughter, the US granted a further $41 million in military and economic assistance to the Barre regime (Feldman, 1988). The US also spent millions building or upgrading installations such as airports and ports for the benefit of both US forces and those of the Barre regime. Another barometer of the importance that the Reagan–Bush administrations attached to Somalia can be gleaned from the $38 million cost of the new US embassy in Mogadishu, completed in 1989. It was reportedly the most expensive embassy in Africa (Wells, 1992; Piles, 1991).

It is difficult to cite an exact figure for the total amount of US military and economic assistance to the Barre regime from 1979 to 1990. One estimate given for both types of assistance is roughly $1 billion (Hartung, 1993). The true sum is, however, probably far higher, since a large part of the assistance did not come in the form of price-tagged aid packages. For example, military assistance included technical assistance to repair the army's heavy weaponry, as well as the maintenance of airports and ports for use by US forces and Barre's army. This kind of assistance did not appear in the official aid packages.

Another way to comprehend the magnitude of the military aid provided to the Barre regime is to compare it with the rest of Africa. Between the years 1980 and 1989, the US supplied the Barre regime with 'the largest US security-assistance program ever provided to a sub-Saharan African state' (Menkhaus, 1997; see also Lefebvre, 1991: 199–200). In all of Africa, in fact, only Egypt received greater military assistance during this period.

In addition to the military-related assistance detailed above, the Pentagon provided the Barre army with military training through the IMED (International Military Education) program. Together with Barre's own highly selective military academy (selective not in the sense of merit, but in the sense of blind obedience to Barre), the regime produced an officer corps that would become the 'willing executioners' of the regime (see O'Sullivan, 1993; Canadian Broadcasting Corporation, 1992). It can be rightly said here that American taxpayers' money was used to pay for the education of would-be torturers and mass killers.

Even economic assistance to Somalia, in the form of food aid that such agencies as CARE provided, in the end contributed to Somalia's ruin. First, food aid provided the regime with the means to feed a huge standing army. Second, food aid killed off Somali food production – with the market full of food aid, especially cereals, farming did not make economic sense to Somali farmers, who were essentially cereal farmers. Third, by monetizing food aid – that is, selling it in the marketplace – the regime's top officials and friends grew richer, and saw little incentive to stop the flow of 'poison aid' coming into the country.[10]

## Assistance after the outbreak of the war in the north

The US provided critical assistance to Barre's army throughout the height of the fighting in 1988. This would contribute to prolonging both the war in the north and the regime's hold on power. For example, US communication specialists repaired the army's communications equipment during the fighting in Hargeisa, enabling its forces in the field to communicate with central command in Mogadishu. This undoubtedly raised the morale of Barre's forces and spurred them to further atrocities (Campbell, 1988). Also, a shipment of US weapons and munitions was delivered to the army, which promptly made use of it in the north. According to Colin Campbell, citing congressional sources: '[t]he weapons ... were of obvious and urgent value to the Siad government, and no one in the US doubted that they would be used to kill people.'[11] The shipment consisted of US$1.4 million worth of military equipment, including 1,200 M-16 automatic rifles and 2 million rounds of M-16 ammunition, 300,000 rounds of 30-caliber ammunition, and 500,000 rounds of 50-caliber ammunition (United States Department of the Army, 1993). The US Defense Department also provided a 220-bed field hospital to Barre's military, which was set up at Berbera in the north and was used to treat only wounded soldiers, not the civilians brutalized by the army. Finally, though we lack firm evidence, US intelligence information about the disposition of SNM troops was probably made available to Barre's commanding officers.

## Assistance from other Western countries

Other Western and pro-Western countries, in step with the United States, supplied arms and aid to the Barre regime. The most notable player was Italy, the former colonial power in the south. From 1978 to 1980, Italy provided about US$124 million in military assistance, consisting of light tanks and other weapons (United States Department of the Army, 1993). Additionally, between 1979 and 1982, the Barre regime bought with cash some $600 million in arms, mainly from Italy (Lefebvre, 1991: 208). The cash likely came from the US-allied Arab countries, such as Saudi Arabia – that is, from Third World proxies. There was no way the Somali economy, largely dependent on northern livestock exports, could have generated such resources for the regime in such a short time. Overall, during the crucial decade in question, the Italians spent more than $1 billion on the regime. The money went to armaments, corruption, and white-elephant projects (see Achtner, 1993). Italian cooperation continued until the fall of the regime in January 1991.

Key Third World proxies who provided either military or financial assistance to the Barre dictatorship include, in addition to Saudi Arabia, Egypt, Kuwait, Iraq, and Libya. The first three countries provided assistance designed to keep the Barre regime firmly in the 'pro-Western' camp (United States Department of the Army, 1993). In the case of Egypt, this meant mostly passing along Soviet military hardware, sometimes paid for by the Saudis. These were arms the Egyptians no longer needed in the wake of their alignment with the US. The Egyptians also provided training. The Saudis, for their part, continued their assistance until Barre's downfall; Saudi assistance was in the form of weapons such as armored and reconnaissance vehicles, small arms, and ammunition, as well as some training. Above all, however, the Saudis deserve special mention for their generous cash handouts to the regime. These included a donation of $70 million handed to Barre during his last month in power – money that went partly into the flight chest of the Barre family. Reportedly, the aim of this final donation was to secure the Barre regime's support for the war against Iraq (Le Monde, 1990).

Other important assistance, though not military in nature, came from the European Economic Commission (EEC), the IMF and the World Bank, based in the US and subject to US control in large measure, as well as the African Development Bank, subject also to Western shareholder control. Money from these alternative sources would come in handy for both the Barre regime and the top US officials supporting it. When Congress, acting on an initiative of a number of concerned members led by Howard Wolpe (D-Mich., then chairman of the House Subcommittee on Africa) and Sam Gejdensen (D-Conn.) blocked most of the direct bilateral aid to the Barre regime, the Bush administration supported multilateral aid in the form of a $70 million 'quick disbursing cash loan' from the World Bank, as well as $25 million from the African Development Bank (see Africa Watch, 1990: 212; Lefebvre, 1991: 252; Ottoway, 1988; Africa Report, 1990). A young Somali demonstrator outside the offices of the World Bank in Washington exclaimed: 'It is immoral madness! How can we, who must soon inherit our country's leadership, be expected to pay interest and back pay on monies that assuredly will be sidetracked to subsidize the murder of our fathers and mothers, our brothers and sisters?' (Greenfield, 1989: 10).

The attempt to keep assistance flowing to the Barre regime meant that during the Reagan–Bush era, even the rule that forbids US representatives to multilateral financial institutions from approving loans solicited by gross human rights violators (the International Financial Institutions Act) was waived. 'The Reagan and Bush Administrations ignored the application of this law to Somalia. Indeed, far from opposing loans to Barre, the executive branch ... actually promoted Somalia's cause within the banks' (Africa Watch, 1990: 213). Not only did these administrations ignore that particular rule, but 'close consultations between the Administration and Barre's military leaders continued well into 1989,' and as a sign of the importance attached to ties with the Barre regime, the US Central Command's new commander paid a visit to Somalia in March 1989. At a dinner in his honor, the US ambassador to Somalia, Frank Crigler, toasted 'the health of our distinguished visitor and his companions, as well as the strong ties of military cooperation between the United States and Somalia' (Africa Watch, 1990: 210).

This vouching for the Barre dictatorship permeated all levels of the Reagan and Bush administrations; it was not limited to Dr Crocker or to ambassadors such as Frank Crigler.[12] Refusing to give up on the regime until the very final moment, the Bush administration would trot out General Normal Schwarzkopf, would-be hero of the Gulf War, 'before the Senate Committee on Appropriations to request continuing military aid' to the Barre regime, even if by then Barre's massacres were well known, and open resistance to the regime had spread to the south and to the capital, Mogadishu (Shalom, 1993).

## US reactions to the 1988 massacres

As already noted, some concerned members of the US Congress had from an early date opposed aid to the Barre regime. This was even more true after 1988, following the publication of several detailed reports on the massacres and violations committed by the regime (see Amnesty International, 1988; Africa Watch, 1990). For example, Sam Gejdenson wrote: 'We are concerned about the reported suggestions that US military supplies or equipment service have been used to support the reported slaughter of civilians by Somali government troops' (Gejdenson, 1988). However, the US administration still wanted 'to prop up the faltering regime by asking Congress to grant $20 million in aid to Somalia ... [after] congressional outcry over human rights abuses ... led to the freezing of US funds' (Africa Report, 1989: 8). One State Department official offered the prevailing view in Washington on the Somali crisis: 'The sign that you give is that you stick by your friends' (see Feldman, 1988b). In a similarly laconic comment, a US official when asked about the massacres and destruction in the north, and the displacement of the majority of that region's population, said: 'in a situation of intense fighting, it would seem inevitable.... On the situation of human rights generally, we have conveyed our concerns privately from time to time' (see Feldman, 1988a). At one point, the right-wing Heritage Foundation joined in advocating continued aid to the Barre regime (Press, 1990).

## Bush abandons Somalia, then sends in the Marines

Eventually, Barre would be jettisoned by his Cold War sustainers, but only after he was ousted in 1991 from his southern capital by USC guerrillas, and Somalia would be abandoned as a derelict former Cold War pawn, torn apart by the bloodshed Barre had unleashed. After the fall of his dictatorship, the civil war would continue, this time pitting the main southern factions against each other, and a great famine would follow in its wake.

Unluckily for Somalia, big-power rivalry had ceased with the fall of the Soviet Union. Washington saw little use for Somali ports and airports, and thus no need to intervene in Somalia's factional fighting one way or the other. In fact, the value of Somalia in the eyes of the Bush administration fell so low that even a $20 million proposal to send a UN observer mission was rejected by the US – though this was peanuts compared to how much had been lavished on the Barre regime during the heyday of the Cold War. An editorialist from the Toronto *Globe and Mail*, noting the event, wrote:

> The United States, which supported sending 14,000 peacekeepers to the Balkans at a cost of $500-million, has opposed a UN move to send 500 troops to Somalia at a cost of $20-million. The Bush Administration excused this moral discrepancy by arguing that congress would not support another costly peacekeeping mission in an election. Instead of armed peacekeepers, the UN will send a squad of 47 pencil-toting observers to Somalia ... to 'monitor' the often-breached ceasefire arranged in March between Mogadishu's two most powerful warlords. (*Globe and Mail*, 1992)

A few months later, in November 1992, President Bush – flush from his Gulf War victory over Iraq – would try to correct that 'moral discrepancy' by announcing that the US would spearhead an international humanitarian intervention in Somalia, known as Operation Restore Hope. No one knows exactly why a huge contingent of Western troops (over 30,000 soldiers) was sent to Somalia. Some claim that the whole operation was linked to Bush's desire to improve his image before his departure from the White House (De la Gorge, 1992). Or was the operation designed as a combined PR campaign for Bush and the Pentagon (Brogan, 1992)? Or, better yet, was the departing Republican administration booby-trapping its Democratic successor, the Clinton administration (Simons, 1993)? Regardless of the mission's objectives, by the time Operation Restore Hope was launched, the worst of the famine (confined to the southwest region around Baidoa) was over. The weakest had already died, while food, through 'the tenacity of a handful of relief organizations, particularly the International Committee of the Red Cross,' had reached the survivors (see Perlez, 1992).

The operation, which later would be rebundled as a UN mission (UNOSOM), ended in fiasco mainly because of the arrogance of American leaders of the operation – in particular Admiral Jonathan Howe, previously a key figure in the capture of Manuel Noriega in Panama. Admiral Howe wrongly saw General Aidid, one of Mogadishu's two main militia leaders, as the mission's sole enemy and a candidate for a Noriega-style capture.[13] The arrogance arose in part from the presumption that African situations were easily solved with a show of might, rather than diplomacy. This mindset was evident in the words of General Lewis Mackenzie, a Canadian and one of the talking heads of the time: 'Unlike Bosnia, Somalia is a relatively easy military problem to deal with. They [UN] have to make the point … and this is the place to make it' (Bilski and Mackenzie, 1993).

In the first place, sending large Western contingents was misguided. Neither the thousands of young Western soldiers – whose knowledge of Africa was derived from the Tarzan films of their childhood or the famine documentaries of Western charities – nor the Somalis, a conservative Muslim society, had the cultural preparedness to deal with each other. As could only be expected, the mission soldiers killed and raped a great many Somalis. Subsequently, some Western countries, such as Canada, Belgium and Italy, held inquiries into the behavior of their armed personnel in Somalia. But the United States did not – even though it was the US forces, at the instigation of UNOSOM head Admiral Jonathan Howe, the Pentagon, and its commanders in Somalia, that committed the worst excesses, mostly through bombing raids. They also subsequently suffered the largest casualties, as a result of the 3 October raid that led to the death of eighteen US servicemen, as well as to the deaths of hundreds of Somalis, mostly civilians. Overall, the US-led intervention killed as many as 10,000 Somalis before international forces were withdrawn (see Ankomah, 2002).

## Avoiding responsibility for the Somalia mess

Eight years after the fact, the fatal October raid in Mogadishu has been fictionalized, with the help of the Pentagon, as an American war-heroism story in the film *Black Hawk Down*, whose premiere was attended by the

Pentagon's top brass as well as by Defense Secretary Donald Rumsfeld. It is a story that neatly eliminates the real context of the events, as well as the massacres committed by mission forces during the intervention, particularly the excesses of the US special forces who indiscriminately mowed down men, women, and children by the hundreds on that October day. In itself, the film symbolizes the US's ultimate self-exculpation of responsibility for Somalia's tragedy, and for the deaths of thousands of Somalis, at the hands of either the US-supported dictatorship or the predominantly Western forces that took part in the failed intervention.

Today, the major Western actors that aided and abetted the Barre regime view the current Somali situation as a mess entirely created by Somalis. No nation wants to be associated with what went wrong in Somalia in the 1980s. It is easier and more convenient to present the Somalis as 'barbarians' or uncivilized tribal people. Hence, America went to Somalia to do 'God's work' in a nation devastated by 'clan warfare' and famine (Monbiot, 2002). There might indeed have been elements of 'God's work' in the intervention, but it followed upon a great deal of 'Devil's aid' to Somalia, which Bush Senior knew all about but would not publicly own up to. Others have been outright dismissive of responsibility for the maintenance of Barre's regime, as evidenced by the following statement from a US diplomat previously stationed in Mogadishu: 'It's easy to blame us for all this.... This is a sovereign country we're talking about. They have chosen to spend [US military aid] that way, to hurt people and destroy their own economy' (Zeus, 2002). It apparently never occurred to this source that when the sovereignty of a people has been hijacked by a dictator, it makes no moral sense to prolong that people's agony by providing the dictator with the means – arms and money – to continue his dictatorship.[14]

However, while administration and State Department officials of the time are eager to disclaim all guilt for the Somali situation, some law-makers and members of the public in the US have rejected such views:

> There is widespread understanding among those familiar with Somalia that had the US government not supported the Barre regime with large amounts of military aid, he would have been forced to step down long before his misrule splintered the country. Prior to the dictator's downfall, former US Representative Howard Wolpe, then-chairman of the House Subcommittee on Africa, called on the State Department to encourage Barre to step down. His pleas were rejected. 'What you are seeing,' observed the congressman and former professor of African politics, 'is a general indifference to a disaster that we played a role in creating.' (Zeus, 2002)

## Conclusion

It is true that no Western leader specifically instructed Barre to use the arms provided to his regime to kill his own people. However, it remains a tenet of conventional jurisprudence that if someone aids and abets a person intent on killing, then that person can be considered an accessory to the crime. There is no doubt that the Barre regime was well known for the summary killing of civilians and for mass murders. With that knowledge, the military and financial support extended by successive US administrations and their allies to the Barre regime must be considered indefensible.

At this point, it is worth asking what, if anything, the West can do to offer redress for Somalia's fatal encounter with Cold War politics. It is unlikely that we can expect any reparations, or even meaningful apologies, from the great powers. After all, the deaths of Third World peoples are considered to lack 'political and media value in the West,' the victims being depicted as 'unpeople' (Pilger, 2002). And, as such, Somalis are probably one of the most significant 'unpeoples' of our time, as Afghans are today, or the Vietnamese were yesterday. Second, US administrations and their Western allies can always claim that they only helped to maintain the 'Somali Hitler' – they did not create him. Nonetheless, there are a number of things that the West, and in particular the US, could do for the sake of redress:

1. *Launch an inquiry*   The US Congress should inquire into the assumptions that led a great democracy to divert taxpayers' money to a murderous regime such as Barre's in order that, in the future, the earnings of the working mothers and fathers of America will not be used to bolster a dictatorship that engages in the wholesale murder of its citizens. This would also help avoid the need to send young Americans to die in foreign interventions that would have been unnecessary in the absence of such support for dictatorial figures.
2. *Help with mine clearance*   The north, where the Barre regime planted most of its mines, is Africa's most heavily mined region, laced with explosive devices from the score of nations that provided assistance to Barre's regime. International assistance could greatly reduce this enduring scourge (Press, 1993).
3. *Lift immediately the inhuman strangulation* that the Bush Junior administration has slapped on Somalia's economy through the freezing of the assets of its major banking enterprise and biggest private employer, Al-Bakarat – for no other reason than Al-Bakarat's alleged use as a conduit of money for a terror group based in Afghanistan. As is widely known,

American banking companies such as Western Union or City Bank may very well have been used for the same purposes – perhaps to an even greater extent, since they have a more substantial worldwide presence than Al-Barakat, a company that caters only to Somalis. Months later, proof of a terrorist link has still not been produced by the US administration. According to a statement by a senior American official, the whole aim of the assault on Al-Barakat and the impoverished Somali economy was to 'make a splash' in the US media (Golden, 2002), and hence in the minds of American voters. It did not matter to administration officials that this bank was a lifeline for thousands of destitute Somalis who depended on the remittances of relatives abroad.

4. *Bring to trial Somali war criminals*, some of whom received officer training in the US, along with the high officials of the Barre regime that currently reside in the United States. This latter group includes Barre's number two, General Samater, who now leads a cozy life in Virginia. Law-enforcement efforts might better be directed at such figures, rather than towards the arrest and deportation (on misdemeanor or immigration charges) of Somali immigrants working in the US.

5. *Erase the billions of dollars in loans* that were given to the Barre regime and used either to enrich its officials or to buy weapons to kill innocent Somalis. Should Somali families continue to pay for the bullets and shells that killed their loved ones?

It is hard to believe that any of these demands would be seriously entertained by Western administrations, least of all by the current Bush administration. President Bush and his team appear more concerned with threatening yet another intervention in Somalia, and many other places besides, all in the name of a new 'colder war' aimed at fuzzy and sometimes imaginary enemies in, mostly, Muslim countries of the Third World.[15] A more realistic idea might be for Somalis to appeal to the public in Western countries to head off another superpower intervention, and to encourage the provision of people-to-people assistance aimed at building, not destroying, a viable infrastructure for Somalis.

## Notes

1. Jonas Savimbi, the murderous guerrilla leader of UNITA, was hardly known for his commitment to democratic ideals, but was dubbed a 'freedom fighter' by the Reagan administration for his fight against the Soviet-supported (but somewhat more democratic) leaders of the MPLA government. President Reagan received Savimbi in 1986 and accorded him all the honors of a visiting head of government. The administration even cooperated with the apartheid regime in South Africa to arm Savimbi, as part of

its global policy that paid no heed whatsoever to the consequences for the civilian population of the targeted states. See Agence France-Presse, 2002; Weinrich, 1992.

2. In a similar fashion, the Afghan fundamentalist rebels, the precursors to the Taliban – now dubbed enemies of the US – were useful to Washington in its proxy war with the Soviets, designed to gain revenge for the debacle that was Vietnam.

3. Somalia is mostly a society of egalitarian nomads and small farmers who own the land they cultivate. When the element of Islam is added to the mix, one finds few people prepared to espouse the cause of revolutionary communism. The communist movement in Ethiopia was therefore more appealing to the Soviets. In addition, Ethiopia was the larger country, and thus a greater prize in terms of the East–West geopolitical struggle.

4. In a case that recalls the ambiguous messages sent by US Ambassador April Glaspie, alleged to have encouraged Saddam Hussein to invade Kuwait (Shalom, 1993), Barre received a message that he interpreted as meaning the US would provide him with arms if he went to war with Ethiopia. The message in question, from President Carter, was delivered by Barre's American doctor (see Lefebvre, 1991: 184). Incidentally, April Glaspie would go on to become a senior political advisor to Admiral Jonathan Howe, the man who bungled the US–UN humanitarian mission in Somalia in 1993.

5. In many ways, both the US and the USSR betrayed the democratic aspirations of Third World peoples by supporting atrocious and dictatorial regimes such as the Barre government in Somalia. One of the tragic consequences of that betrayal is the political stance, or trap, that some nascent Muslim intellectuals fell into during the 1980s and 1990s, expressed in the well-known slogan: 'no Easternisms, no Westernisms; this time it is Islamism.'

6. After Barre was overthrown in 1991, the north withdrew from its merger with the south, or Somalia proper, and reverted to its pre-1960 name of Somaliland. Before the 1960 merger between the two regions, Somalia was an Italian colony, while Somaliland was under British rule. Somaliland is now a de facto state that lacks international recognition but is otherwise a peaceful and stable country, while the civil war that overthrew the Barre regime still smolders in the south, depriving the country of a credible government.

7. Marion H. Smoak, a retired ambassador and chief of protocol during the Nixon administration, rebuked Howard Wolpe, then chairman of the Subcommittee on Africa in the House of Representatives, for expressing caution about arms deliveries to the Barre regime in 1982. Smoak argued: 'Red herrings from some members of the Congress and those of a defeatest [sic] belief must be recognized for what they are. No territory has been dragged behind the iron curtain thus far in this administration. Somalia must not be the first' (Smoak, 1982).

8. For a full account of the Barre regime's depredations, see Africa Watch, 1990. See also Amnesty International, 1988.

9. The estimates of the killings vary from 50,000 to 100,000. See, for example, *The Gazette*, 1990.

10. For a full treatment of the ravages of food aid in Somalia during Barre's years of alignment with the West, see Maren, 1996.

11. See Campbell, 1988. As someone who personally lost half his family during the 1988 massacres in Hargeisa, I have always wondered what part that critical assistance played in amplifying Barre's atrocities in the region.

12. Sometimes the relationships between American ambassadors and other high US officials, on the one hand, and officials of the Barre regime, on the other, went beyond the cordial to the truly personal. For example, Ambassador Crigler wrote a letter of

support for one former Barre official who was under investigation for war crimes in Canada. The letter stated that a certain Mohamed Sheikh Olow was 'someone of the highest integrity and moral conviction.' The man in question was an acting governor of the Northwest province when thousands of people were massacred and the regional capital, Hargeisa, reduced to rubble. See Magnish, 1997.

13. I have explored the background and failure of the US-led humanitarian intervention in Somalia in another work; see Abdullahi, 1995.

14. It is true that the Somalis were independent from their former colonial masters; but were they a free people or a subject people under the Barre regime? In the total absence of liberty and democracy, one may well say that under Barre the Somali people were a subject people who instead of a foreign colonial master had over them a native dictatorial master.

15. The term 'colder war' is drawn from Pilger, 2002.

# References

Abdullahi, M.D. (1995). *Fiasco in Somalia: US–UN intervention*. Pretoria: Africa Institute of South Africa.

Achtner, W. (1993). The Italian connection: How Rome helped ruin Somalia. *Washington Post*, 24 January.

*Africa Report* (1990). Somali government accused in 50,000 civilian deaths. March–April.

——— (1989). Support for Barre declines as Somali civil war intensifies. September–October.

Africa Watch (1990). *Somalia: A government at war with its own people*. London: Africa Watch.

Agence France-Presse (2002). One time 'freedom fighter' ditched by Washington. 23 February.

Amnesty International (1988). *Somalia: A long-term human rights crisis*. London: Amnesty International.

Ankomah, B. (1994). A great wrong. *New African*, May.

Beaver, P. (1992). Arms come full circle. *Globe and Mail*, 29 December.

Bilski, A., and Mackenzie, H. (1993). On the attack. *Maclean's*, 28 June.

Brittain, V. (1988). Somali troops in 'massacres and bombing.' *Guardian*, 3 July.

Brogan, P. (1992). The Waugh in Somalia goes on. *Ottawa Citizen*, 11 December.

Campbell, C. (1988). Libya, mercenaries aiding US-supported Somalia. *Atlanta Journal-Constitution*, 6 October.

Canadian Broadcasting Corporation (1992). Crimes against humanity. *The Fifth Estate* (television broadcast), 6 October.

Dagne, T. (1992). CRS report for Congress: Somalia: A country at war – prospects for peace and reconciliation. Washington, DC: Congressional Research Service, 15 June.

De la Gorge, P.-M. (1992). Figuration et gesticulation. *Jeune Afrique* 1667, 17–23 December.

Feldman, L. (1988a). Rebels create havoc for US-backed Somalia. *Christian Science Monitor*, 6 July.

——— (1988b). Critics charge U.S. policy fuels conflict in Somalia. *Christian Science Monitor*, 10 August.

*The Gazette* (1990) (Montreal). 50,000 Somali civilians reported killed. 18 January.

Gejdenson, S. (1988). Letter to the Honorable George Schultz, Secretary of State. Washington, 29 September.

Girardet, E. (1981). Somalia peeved about 'slow' pace of U.S. military aid. *Christian Science Monitor*, 7 December.

*Globe and Mail* (1992). If Sarajevo, why not Somalia? *Globe and Mail*, 22 July.

Greenfield, R. (1989). Somalia slides into chaos. *New African*, November.

———— (1987). Somalia's letter of death. *New African*, July.

Golden, Tim (2002). Second thoughts: was U.S. anti-terror move a wild shot? *New York Times*, 15 April.

Hartung, W.D. (1993). The U.S. has to control the spread of conventional arms to areas of conflict. *Christian Science Monitor*, 22 February.

House of Representatives, Committee on Foreign Affairs, Subcommittee on Africa (1988). Reported massacres and indiscriminate killings in Somalia. Washington, DC, 14 July.

Lefebvre, J.A. (1991). *Arms for the Horn: U.S. security policy in Ethiopia and Somalia, 1953–1991.* Pittsburgh: University of Pittsburgh Press.

Magnish, S. (1997). Ex-Somali official called a nice guy. *Toronto Sun*, 3 September.

Maren, M. (1996). *The road to hell: The ravaging effects of foreign aid and international charity.* New York: The Free Press.

Mather, I. (1988). Thousands flee as Somali soldiers massacre civilians. *Observer*, 3 July.

Menkhaus, K. (1997). U.S. foreign assistance to Somalia: Phoenix from the ashes? *Middle East Policy* 5, no. 1 (January): 124–6.

Monbiot, G. (2002). Both saviour and victim: Black Hawk Down creates a new and dangerous myth of American nationhood. *Guardian*, 29 January.

*Le Monde* (1990). Somalie: l'aggravation de la guerre civile. 27 December.

National Academy of Sciences (1988). Delegation urges Somalia to end human rights abuses (press release). Washington, DC, 14 January.

O'Sullivan, G. (1993). Another Cold War casualty. *The Humanist* 53, no. 1 (January): 36–7.

Ottaway, D.B. (1988). Congress blocking aid to Somalia. *Washington Post*, 26 October.

Perlez, J. (1992). Somalia 1992: Picking up pieces as famine subsides. *New York Times*, 31 December.

Piles, P. (1991). Somalia – starting from scratch. *Africa Report*, May–June.

Pilger, J. (2002). The colder war. *Mirror* (London), 29 January.

Press, R.M. (1993). Global effort grows to ban export and sale of land mines. *Christian Science Monitor*, 20 December.

———— (1990). Africa Watch sounds alarm on Somalia. *Christian Science Monitor*, 18 January.

Prunier, G. (1990–91). A candid view of the Somali National Movement. *Horn of Africa* 13, no. 3–4; 14, no. 1–2 (July–March).

Rotberg, R.I. (1984). Somalia and U.S. strategic interests. *Christian Science Monitor*, 24 December.

Shalom, S.R. (1993). Gravy train: Feeding the Pentagon by feeding Somalia. *ZMag.org*, November. www.zmag.org/zmag/articles/shalomsomalia.html.

Simons, A. (1992–93). Do we know what we're doing in Somalia? *Africa News*, 21 December–3 January.

Simmons, M. (1989). Hundreds of thousands hit by raids, aid workers say. *Guardian* (International Edition), 7 January.

Smoak, M.H. (1982). Correcting mistakes in the Horn of Africa. *Christian Science Monitor*, 16 August.

United States Department of the Army (1993). Chapter 5.05: Foreign Military Assistance, Army Area Handbook: Somalia. gopher://gopher.umsl.edu/11/library/govdocs/armyahbs/aahb3.

Wells, R. (1992). Somalia: Shell-shocked. *Focus on Africa* 3, no. 1 (January–March).

Windrich, E. (1992). *The Cold War guerrilla: Jonas Savimbi, the U.S. media and the Angolan war.* Greenwood Press.

Zeus, S. (2000). It didn't just start with Black Hawk Down: The long and hidden history of the United States in Somalia. *Foreign Policy in Focus*, 21 February. www.fpif.org/media/opeds/2002/0118zunesanet.html.

# 14

# The Security Council:
# Behind the Scenes in the
# Rwanda Genocide

## Linda R. Melvern

On 21 April 1994, the Security Council of the United Nations voted to pull out its peacekeepers from Rwanda. It was a milestone decision, today considered one of the most ignominious in the Council's history. Hundreds of thousands of Rwandans were being slaughtered in a planned, calculated, and organized campaign of genocide intended to eliminate a human group, the Tutsi. It was slaughter of a speed and on a scale not seen since the Nazi extermination program against the Jews.

The decision to evacuate the UN soldiers came after a long, acrimonious and agonizing Council debate held among ambassadors from fifteen member states in a small room adjacent to the Council chamber. It was an informal debate and it was intended to remain secret, with the policy of each government conveniently hidden from public scrutiny. This, it should be noted, is how the Security Council standardly conducts its business. In 1994, during three months of genocide in Rwanda, the Council was in almost constant secret session, meeting sometimes twice daily and long into the night. Yet in all the various international and national inquiries held into the circumstances of the genocide, not one has focused on what was said – and not said – in these secret Council meetings. The culture of secrecy is now so embedded in Council work that it is taken for granted both within and outside Council chambers.

It is hard to imagine now, but there was once a time when Security Council debates were held in open session. Nowadays, these crucial debates take place behind closed doors, and it is behind closed doors that the deals are done determining UN policy. The ambassadors only go into public session to vote on resolutions and make set speeches; all the important work is done elsewhere. Yet in the UN's first years the Council had operated in the full glare of publicity. It was possible to know the position of each government, and to hear the options discussed and the reasons given for decisions. In 1946, the then British ambassador, Sir Alexander Cadogan, had expressed his approval of open Council meetings. Cadogan was an advocate of public diplomacy, as exemplified in the debates in the Council, for it made it necessary for states to justify their national behavior in the eyes of the world. Every nation was amenable to some extent to world publicity. But over time the Council began to hold secret meetings, slowly in the 1960s, until by the 1980s closed-door debates had become a way of life.

The secret meetings of the Security Council held to discuss Rwanda while the genocide progressed would normally have remained secret, were it not for the fact that someone provided me with an account of them. This was an unprecedented leak of information, and this unique and valuable documentation revealed some shocking truths. Not least among them was the fact that during the first four weeks of the genocide, while most of the large-scale massacres of Tutsi took place, the systematic and continuing slaughter was not once debated at length by the Council. The mass killings were being conducted miles away from the fighting in a resumed civil war, and reports of mass murder had been sent to UN headquarters in cables sent from the field, from the headquarters of the peacekeeping mission (the UN Assistance Mission in Rwanda, UNAMIR) in the capital, Kigali. But in the Council the priority for discussion was the resumed civil war and whether or not a ceasefire could be arranged between the warring factions, the Hutu Power forces and the Rwanda Patriotic Front (RPF). On the killing of civilians and the threat to the thousands of refugees who had sought sanctuary in schools, churches and hospitals, the Council was virtually silent.

A plan to try to stop the mass slaughter, devised by the Force Commander of the UN peacekeepers in Rwanda, Canadian Lieutenant-General Romeo A. Dallaire, involved sending 5,500 troops as reinforcements. It was not discussed by the Council until it was almost too late. The majority of victims in Rwanda died in the first five weeks. A speedy reinforcement for the beleaguered peacekeepers would have sent the strongest possible signal to the extremist adherents of Hutu Power that the world was ready to back its promise of 'Never Again' – a promise enshrined in international law in the 1948 Convention on the Prevention and Punishment of the Crime of Genocide. But the main focus of the Council's secret discussions of Rwanda was very different.

Later, these agonizing meetings were described by one of the ambassadors occupying a non-permanent seat, Karel Kovanda of the Czech Republic: 'No one was sure what, if anything, needed to be done. Into this absolutely bizarre situation came the big powers ... who said they could do nothing.'

The debate in the Security Council is often shaped by recommendations from the Secretary-General, acting on advice from officials in the Secretariat, who in turn receive all cables from force commanders. When Rwanda's crisis spilled over into genocide in April 1994, no such recommendations were forthcoming. Some of the non-permanent members speculated that either the Secretariat had no options at all, in which case it was not up to the task of managing the conflict, or the body was overwhelmed to the point of paralysis. There was an assumption, actively encouraged by Belgium and supported by Britain and the US, that only a massive and dramatic intervention would succeed in Rwanda – and this was out of the question. Belgium, of course, had already unilaterally decided to withdraw its own troops from the peacekeeping mission. Along with two of the Council's most powerful members, the US and Britain, it had now decided that intervention in Rwanda was too dangerous. The Belgian ambassador at the UN conducted a concerted campaign to warn everyone – Secretariat officials and ambassadors – of the supposed danger. Little attention was paid to the humanitarian assistance that continued throughout the genocide, provided by a handful of volunteer peacekeepers who stayed on in Rwanda, and by the International Committee of the Red Cross and Médecins sans Frontières. Indeed, while the ICRC managed to send convoys of food and medical supplies to Rwanda throughout the three months of genocide, the UN failed even to resupply its own volunteer force. The 470 soldiers in the international force did all they could to help Rwandan victims. It was not for want of courage that they failed to rescue more people, but for want of petrol. At the UN headquarters in New York, a preoccupation with the renewed civil war meant that little attention was given to the contribution that peacekeepers in Rwanda could continue to make, even *without* reinforcements, in trying to alleviate the suffering.

## The crucial decisions

The importance of secrecy to the Council was dramatically illustrated on 29 April. The presidency of the Security Council changes monthly through alphabetic rotation, and in May it was New Zealand's turn. On that April day, the New Zealand ambassador, lawyer Colin Keating, tried to persuade Council members to recognize officially the fact of the Rwandan 'genocide.' But the British, Americans, and Chinese were strenuously against use of the word. Keating had prepared a Presidential Statement for Council approval recognizing the genocide. He believed that if recognition could be achieved, the Council would be faced with an obligation, under the 1948 Convention, to stop the killing. The debate over recognition went in circles, and long into the night. It was a Friday, and tempers were frayed.

For Keating this was brinkmanship. His term as president was ending, and so he decided to use the desperate measure of threatening public exposure. This would take the form of a draft resolution, tabled in Keating's national capacity, and requiring a vote. The vote would expose the position of every country to the glare of world opinion; and by now the wider world, at least the Western press, was beginning to take notice of the catastrophe unfolding in Rwanda. They followed on the heels of aid agencies like Oxfam and Human Rights Watch, which were calling the genocide a genocide, and lobbying for political actors to do the same. In the end, and only after threats of public exposure, a compromise was reached. The time-honored British ability for framing resolutions with mind-numbing ambiguity was called upon, and a watered-down presidential statement was issued. The statement quoted directly from the Genocide Convention, but did not itself use the word 'genocide.' It recognized the systematic nature of the massacres, and described attacks on defenceless civilians throughout the country, particularly in areas under control of the armed forces of the so-called 'interim government' of Rwanda. But the nature of the targets was not clearly specified.

No choices were presented and no risks taken as a result of these deliberations. In the first four weeks of genocide, when mass killings were occurring on a scale unprecedented in recorded history, the Western media failed to recognize that genocide was taking place. Journalists preferred to describe the killing in these first weeks as 'tribal' and anarchic, and this meant that public pressure could not be generated on domestic governments, contributing to the pervasive inaction at the level of the Security Council.

History will record the abject failure of the Council to act decisively in protecting civilian lives in Rwanda. The Council is the UN's most important body, empowered to determine threats to international peace and take corresponding enforcement action. Yet rarely are its actions and internal operations subject to challenge. The Council's method of working in secret and informal session is accompanied by a range of other institutional deficiencies: a lack of clear guidelines about peacekeeping management, no clear division of labor between ambassadors and the Secretariat, and a reliance on Secretariat officials for information on what is happening on the ground. As a result, the Council has served the world ill over in the last decade. Rwanda may be only one example of that broader failing, but in its genocidal consequences it towers over all others.

# 15

# US Policy and Iraq:
# A Case of Genocide?

## Denis J. Halliday

*This article,[1] based on a speech made in Spain to an international conference in November 1999 on the United Nations' regime of economic sanctions on the people of Iraq, briefly addresses the concern that those sanctions constitute genocide – a crime against humanity. It also touches on the incompatibility of such sanctions with the provisions of the United Nations Charter and similar instruments of international law calling out for the establishment of some means of oversight and control in regard to the work of the Security Council.*

During a visit to Paris in January 1999, to speak publicly about the terrible impact of United Nations economic sanctions on the people of Iraq, I used the term 'genocide' for the first time. This was done at a briefing for the press corps to describe the catastrophic situation that from direct personal experience of thirteen months in Baghdad I had come to consider nothing less than genocidal. The term was picked up by some journalists and used for headlines in the Paris newspapers and then similarly by one or two international wire services. Thereafter, during that visit, I was made to feel by some that I had crossed an invisible line of impropriety! I was criticized by a few for using the term in regard to the impact of economic sanctions themselves. It seemed also that it was deemed particularly inappropriate in respect of the Arab and Islamic people of Iraq. Since then I have observed that the term 'genocide' offends many in our Western media and establishment circles when it is used to describe the killing of others for which we are responsible, such as in Iraq. Perhaps for most, the term 'genocide' is too emotive and too intimate to our democratic obligation to accept responsibility for even the most disagreeable actions undertaken by our respective governments. For others, it was no more than overdue recognition of the crimes against innocent humanity ongoing throughout Iraq, including the 3 million Kurds of the three northern provinces.

Former US Attorney-General Ramsey Clark, the British author Geoff Simons, and a number of British Members of Parliament critical of British government economic sanctions and military policy have employed the term 'genocide' to convey their perception of the Iraq situation. Since the spring of 1999, the term has been used frequently by the establishment in the UK and the US together with mass media to describe the plight of Albanians in Kosovo and the killing of the people of East Timor. Clearly for these deadly situations, despite our historical involvement, the establishment spokespersons using the term 'genocide' did not feel in any way responsible. It seems that only others commit genocide, we Western democracies do not! How ironic coming from those nations that *inter alia* managed the transatlantic slave trade, the massacre of American Indians and the slaughter of the Aboriginal peoples of Australia.

In the fall semester of 1999, in a class I teach at Swarthmore College in Pennsylvania, we discussed the appropriateness of using the term 'genocide' to describe the human crisis in Iraq. We reviewed with some care the definition as set out by the Convention on the Prevention and Punishment of the Crime of Genocide of 1948. We noted the clear reference to the expression 'intent' as being essential in any determination of genocide. In considering UN Security Council Resolution 687, we did not find 'intent' spelled out in the text of 1991. Nevertheless, we noted the justification provided some years ago by the then ambassador to the UN and now Secretary of State for the sustained killing of some 500,000 Iraqi children.

Given the stark reality of death in Iraq under economic sanctions, the choice for the class in respect of the consequences of UN Resolution 687 was one between *de jure* and *de facto* genocide, or, as one student suggested, a choice between first-degree murder or manslaughter. The class looked between the lines of the Resolution, but the majority of students gave the original drafters the benefit of the doubt, and likewise to those member states that support the imposition of the uniquely comprehensive and devastating economic sanctions that Resolution 687 represents – sanctions that are particularly devastating, coming as they do on top of the illegal civilian-targeted bombing and missile attacks by the US and UK allies of the Gulf War. However, some including myself consider that by the deliberate continuation of the UN economic sanctions regime on Iraq, in full knowledge of their deadly impact as frequently reported by the Secretary-General and others, the member states of the Security Council are indeed guilty of intentionally sustaining a regime of genocide. It is this view that was supported overwhelmingly by international lawyers at the conference in Spain organized by the Spanish Campaign for the Lifting of Sanctions on Iraq.

The information provided by the various organizations of the United Nations system – FAO, WFP, UNICEF, and WHO – who have carried out surveys using international experts on infant and child mortality rates in Iraq under economic sanctions – underlines that we have *de facto* genocide. They have provided data showing the very significant increase in mortality rates over the years since Resolution 687 was imposed. We have also been given data by WHO showing significant increases in the deaths of adults, particularly among the aged in need of sophisticated drugs no long available in Iraq. We have figures showing extraordinary increases in the incidence of various cancers, including leukemia in children, since the use of depleted uranium by the UK and US during the Gulf War. We know the sad human cost today in Iraq of the *deliberate* destruction by Gulf War allies of the means for treatment and distribution of clean water, adequate electric power generation and effective urban sanitation systems. This damage was reported initially by the mission of then undersecretary-general and now president of Finland, Martti Ahtisaari, in 1991, and many times since by UNICEF and WHO.

The informally termed Oil-for-Food program, which is fully funded by Iraq through limited oil sales under UN auspices, was designed to prevent further deterioration, no more than that. The Security Council-approved but heavily constrained importation of limited and basic food-stuffs, medicines, and drugs into the country has done little more than maintain high mortality rates and massive malnutrition, as the recent UNICEF report has advised. Apart from considerable nutritional short-falls, including lack of adequate animal proteins, minerals and vitamins within that program, we have not seen the Security Council allow oil revenues substantially to repair the damage caused by the bombing of civilian infrastructure in 1991, 1996 and as recently as December 1998, in breach of the Geneva Conventions. By this denial and by controlling the ceiling on Iraqi oil revenues, the Security Council has determined with deliberation to block adequate repair of water, power and sewerage systems so critical in the battle to save the lives of countless infants and children. In other words, the Council has sustained a source for water-borne diseases leading to thousands of deaths monthly, particularly of infants and children. Likewise, adequate hard currency has not been available for re-equipping of hospitals and other healthcare facilities; and agricultural food production capacity remains starved of essential imported require-ments. In short, the Security Council has denied Iraq its right to import adequately, and at the same time its right to repair and rebuild that civilian infrastructure so critical for human well-being, indeed for life itself.

The Security Council has in effect illegally violated international law twice over. First, and contrary to the provisions of the Geneva Conventions, the targeting of men, women and children, noncombatants and civilians, via missile attacks and bombing of civilians and civilian infrastructure in 1991 and thereafter. And second, in an even more deadly, quiet and sustained manner of warfare, the killing of hundreds of thousands of Iraqi children, and adults, by the ongoing regime of comprehensive economic sanctions, an embargo backed up by the massive military presence of the USA throughout the Middle East. A military presence not only intimidating to the women and children of Iraq, but equally intimidating to many millions of peoples and their governments throughout the region. Whether one wishes to term economic sanctions on Iraq a form of warfare or not, crimes against humanity or not, the imposition of genocide or not, the sustained imposition of these sanctions constitutes the punishment of millions, and the deaths of hundreds of thousands of innocent human beings. Whatever the terminology, whatever the semantics used, the results are indisputably contrary to the spirit and the word of numerous international legal instruments.

With, or without original intent, the impact of economic sanctions constitutes genocide. Whether it is *de jure* or *de facto* genocide, the semantics are irrelevant to those people of Iraq who have seen their children die, their parents die, and their own health and the health of most deteriorate into a state of physical malnutrition, a condition of near national depression and an environment of social collapse.

The question, 'Does the genocidal impact of economic sanctions on Iraq represent first degree murder as in intent, or manslaughter as in negligence resulting nevertheless in death?', has been answered.

However, there remains another tragic consequence of the genocide in Iraq, and that is the irreparable damage it has done to the integrity and credibility of the United Nations itself. By sustaining economic sanctions on Iraq in full knowledge of the deadly consequences, the member states of the Security Council have undermined the very legal basis of the organization itself – the Charter. That is not to deny that the device of economic sanctions is provided for in Chapter 7 of the Charter – it is. One could query the intentions in the minds of the victors of World War II when these provisions were drafted in 1945, at a time when the infant UN was proportionally more heavily made up of large and powerful than small and weaker member states. Then, as today, the concept of economic sanctions, bilateral but also multilateral, is more attractive and viable to the powerful, the 'bully boy' states, than to the smaller potential victims.

Regardless of 1945 goals, the prolonged and uniquely comprehensive nature of the economic sanctions on Iraq, and economic sanctions regimes imposed elsewhere in the world, have undermined the very purposes and principles (Articles 1 and 2) of the United Nations Charter – the preamble of which calls *inter alia* for the well-being of all humanity. Likewise, prolonged economic sanctions neglect the rights spelled out in Articles 25 and 26 of the Universal Declaration of Human Rights. In reality, there are numerous international conventions neglected by the deliberate continuation of economic sanctions regardless of human cost, not least of which is the Convention on the Rights of the Child. These rights are intentionally denied every time an Iraqi child is without nutritious and plentiful food, a place in which to live decently, adequate medical attention, and a good education. A sanctions generation of deprivation has been created by the Security Council. The denial by the Security Council of the rights of an Iraqi child to have opportunities for the future, to life itself, destroys what the United Nations is mandated to enhance and sustain throughout the world.

The conventional Western response to the human crisis in Iraq is that it is solely the fault of their once convenient and former ally of the Iran–Iraq war era, President Saddam Hussein. This is simplistic, dishonest and irresponsible. Further, the history of the Ba'ath party (assisted into power by the CIA) shows that social welfare, including education and healthcare, are top priorities. The party certainly diminished political and civil rights, but basic human rights were enhanced between 1958 and 1990. Regardless of the illegal invasion of Kuwait, there is no possible justification for the murder of Iraqi children and adults, innocent of that invasion, by the US, UK and other powers simply because they cannot punish the leadership of Iraq. That is morally and legally unacceptable on all counts.

Combating this incompatibility between the Charter and instruments of international law with the impact of Security Council decisions such as Resolution 687 would appear to call for several actions. One might be an initiative by the larger, fully representative, and more democratic General Assembly to seek the advice of the International Court of Justice, and by so doing begin to assert meaningfully its oversight function in respect of the work of the powerful yet small and undemocratic Security Council. Another might be the establishment of an NGO to watch the impact of Security Council resolutions worldwide and to monitor their incompatibility with the Charter, the Universal Declaration of Human Rights, and other international legal instruments. Another might be radical reform of the Council so that it is no longer 'North' manipulated, but representative of the states and their peoples thoughout the world on whom its decisions impact.

In conclusion, the genocidal impact of the regime of economic sanctions on the people of Iraq violates the legal instruments that are fundamental to the credible continuation of the United Nations. The Organization urgently needs the protection of an oversight device or devices in regard to the output of the dangerously out-of-control Security Council. The Council is desperately in need of reform to introduce permanent North/ South balance and representation. The Council must begin to act in conformity with the essential provisions of the UN Charter itself. In the meantime, men and women of conscience, with moral posture and integrity, must continue to demand the termination of crimes against humanity committed by the member states of the present Security Council in respect to the people of Iraq.

## Note

1. Originally published in *AAUG Monitor* 15, no. 1, Spring 2000, under the title 'Economic Sanctions on the People of Iraq: First Degreee Murder or Manslaughter?'

# Criminal Complaint against the United States and Others for Crimes against the People of Iraq (1996) and Letter to the Security Council (2001)

## Ramsey Clark

### DOCUMENT 2

*Ramsey Clark's criminal charges against the US, Britain and leaders of the United Nations supplemented an earlier filing of 19 charges in 1991 pertaining to the Gulf War against Iraq. The charges were presented at the International Court on Crimes Against Humanity Committed by the UN Security Council on Iraq, in Madrid, Spain, 16–17 November 1996.*

**Criminal Complaint against the United States of America and Others for Crimes against the People of Iraq for Causing the Deaths of more than 1,500,000 People Including 750,000 Children under Five and Injury to the Entire Population by Genocidal Sanctions**
   **This Supplemental Complaint charges:**

The United States of America, President Bill Clinton, Secretary of State Warren Christopher, Secretary of Defense William Perry, US Ambassador to the United Nations Madeleine Albright, State Department Spokesman Nicholas Burns, the United Kingdom Prime Minister John Major; aided and abetted by United Nations Secretary General Boutros Boutros Ghali, Rolf Ekeus, Chairman of UN Special Commission on Iraq, and each Member Nation of the Security Council and its UN Ambassador from 1991 to date that failed to act affirmatively to relieve death and suffering caused by United Nations Sanctions against the People of Iraq; and others to be named;

**With genocide, crimes against humanity, the use of a weapon of mass destruction and other crimes specified herein.**

The criminal acts charged include the deliberate and intentional imposition, maintenance and enforcement of an economic blockade and sanctions against the people of Iraq from August 6, 1990 to this date with full knowledge constantly communicated that the blockade and sanctions were depriving the people of Iraq of essentials to support and protect human life. These essentials include medicines and medical supplies, safe drinking water, adequate food, insecticides, fertilizers, equipment and parts required for agriculture, food processing, storage and distribution, hospital and medical clinic procedures; a multitude of common items such as light bulbs and fluorescent tubes; equipment and parts for the generation and distribution of electricity, telephone and other communications, public transportation and other essential human services. Also denied the people of Iraq is knowledge of the existence of, and procedures and equipment to provide protection from, depleted uranium and dangerous chemical pollution released in the environment of Iraq by defendants. The United States has further subjected Iraq to random missile assaults which have killed civilians.

The direct consequence of such acts and others is direct physical injury to the majority of the population in Iraq, serious permanent injury to a substantial minority of the population and death to more than 1,500,000 people including 750,000 children under five years of age.

The formal criminal charges are:

1. The United States and its officials aided and abetted by others engaged in a continuing pattern of conduct from August 6, 1990 until this date to impose, maintain and enforce extreme economic sanctions and a strict military blockade on the people of Iraq for the purpose of injuring the entire population, killing its weakest members, infants, children, the elderly and the chronically ill, by depriving them of medicines, drinking water, food, and other essentials in order to maintain a large US military presence in the region and dominion and control over its people and resources including oil.

2. The United States, its President Bill Clinton and other officials, the United Kingdom and its Prime Minister John Major and other officials have committed a crime against humanity as defined in the Nuremberg Charter against the population of Iraq and engaged in a continuing and massive attack on the entire civilian population in violation of Articles 48, 51, 52, 54 and 55 of Protocol I Additional to the Geneva Convention 1977.

3. The United States, its President Bill Clinton and other officials, the United Kingdom and its Prime Minister John Major and other officials have committed genocide as defined in the Convention against Genocide against the population of Iraq including genocide by starvation and sickness

through use of sanctions as a weapon of mass destruction and violation of Article 54, Protection of Objects Indispensable to the Civilian Population, of Protocol I Additional to the Geneva Convention 1977.

4. The United States, its President Bill Clinton and other officials, the United Kingdom and its Prime Minister John Major and other officials have committed and engaged in a continuing course of conduct to prevent any interference with the long term criminal imposition of sanctions against the people of Iraq in order to support continuing US presence and domination of the region.

5. The United States, its President Bill Clinton and other officials, the United Kingdom and its Prime Minister John Major and other officials with US Ambassador Madeleine Albright as a principal agent have obstructed justice and corrupted United Nations functions, most prominently the Security Council, by political, economic and other coercions using systematic threats, manipulations and misinformation to silence protest and prevent votes or other acts to end sanctions against Iraq despite reports over a period of five years by every major UN agency concerned including UNICEF, UN World Food Program, UN Food and Agriculture Organization, which describe the deaths, injuries and suffering directly caused by the sanctions.

6. The United States, its President Bill Clinton and other officials have engaged in a continuing concealment and cover-up of the criminal assaults during January through March 1991 on nuclear reactors, chemical, fertilizer, insecticide plants, oil refineries, oil storage tanks, ammunition depots and bunkers in violation of humanitarian law including Article 56, Protecting Works and Installations Containing Dangerous Forces, exposing the civilian population of Iraq, and military personnel of Iraq, the United States and other countries to radiation and dangerous chemical pollution which continues for the population of Iraq causing deaths, sickness and permanent injuries including chemical and radiation poisoning, cancer, leukemia, tumors and diseased body organs.

7. The United States and its officers have concealed and failed to help protect the population of Iraq from the cover-up of the use by US forces of illegal weapons of a wide variety including rockets and missiles containing depleted uranium which have saturated soil, groundwater and other elements in Iraq and are a constant presence affecting large areas still undefined with deadly radiation causing death, illness and injury which will continue to harm the population with unforeseeable effects for thousands of years.

8. The United States and its officials have endeavored to extort money tribute from Iraq and institutionalize forced payments of money on a permanent basis by demanding [that] more than one half the value of all

oil sales taken from Iraq be paid as it directs as the price for reducing the sanctions to permit limited oil sales insufficient to feed the people and care for the sick. This is the functional and moral equivalent of holding a gun to the head of the children of Iraq and demanding of Iraq, pay half your income or we will shoot your children.

9. The United States has violated, and condoned violations of, human rights, civil liberties and the US Bill of Rights in the United States, in Kuwait, Saudi Arabia and elsewhere to achieve its purpose of complete domination of the region.

10. President Clinton, Ambassador Albright, Nicholas Burns and Rolf Ekeus have systematically manipulated, controlled, directed, misinformed, concealed from and restricted press and media coverage about conditions in Iraq, compliance with UN requirements, and the suffering of the people of Iraq to maintain overwhelming and consistent media support for genocide. This has been done in the face of their proclaiming that the deaths of more than half a million children are 'worth it' to control the region, that Saddam Hussein is responsible for all injury and could prevent this genocide by not putting 'his yacht on the Euphrates this winter,' or by shutting down his 'palace for the winter and using that money to buy food and medicine' and by insisting that the sanctions will be maintained until a government acceptable to the US is installed in Iraq.

Ramsey Clark
New York, 14 November 1996

## DOCUMENT 3

*The following letter was sent by Ramsey Clark to members of the UN Security Council on 28 February 2001.*

### RE: Security Council Action to End All Sanctions against Iraq and Prohibit US and UK Military Assaults Against Iraq.

Dear Members of the Security Council,

The genocide in Iraq caused by Security Council sanctions forced by the United States and the bombing of Iraq by US aircraft and missiles continues unabated. A nationwide survey by 50 US citizens in Iraq last month, my eleventh trip to Iraq since sanctions were imposed on August 6, 1990, confirmed that deaths caused by sanctions increased for the tenth consecutive year, though the rate of increase has declined. General health conditions continue to deteriorate though available food and medicine has increased slightly, apparently from the cumulative effects of decade long severe shortages.

Other health concerns include increasing cancer rates, greatest among the young, which the people of Iraq and the medical care system believe are caused by depleted uranium from the near one million depleted uranium shells fired into Iraq by the US in the first months of 1991 and the probable use of depleted uranium ammunition since. Among many examples of such concern we encountered was a statement made to me by the Roman Catholic Archbishop of Basra, Monsignor Djibrael Kassab, that the small Catholic population within his diocese has recently suffered three infant births with deformities never seen before including the absence of facial features and eyes, which he has reported to the Vatican.

Constant overflights with frequent aerial strikes against Iraq have continued, averaging several attacks a week with deaths and injuries nearly every week.

## The Genocidal Effect of Sanctions on Iraq to 20 January 2001

Infant mortality from selected illnesses caused by the UN sanctions against Iraq has increased from a monthly average of slightly less than 600 deaths in 1989 to more than 6700 in 2000, or eleven times. The percentage of total registered births under 2.5 kg in 1990 was 4.5 per cent. In 2000 it was nearly 25 per cent, up five times. For children under five years old the average number of reported cases of kwashiorkor, marasmus and other malnutrition illnesses caused by protein, calorie and/or vitamin deficiences rose from less than 8550 in 1990 to 190,000 in 2000, an increase of more than 22 times.

The sanctions must be completely removed immediately. Every day the sanctions continue adds to the death toll of the worst genocide of the last decade of the most violent century in human history.

The US, realizing that world opinion will no longer tolerate the sanctions, is seeking to take credit for modifying them while its purpose will be to continue to control their implementation and cause their reinstatement for alleged violations by Iraq. Under the ruse of arms inspections and false claims of arms violations, the US has systematically frustrated any easing of sanctions. The US has claimed, and failed to prove, a long series of violations by Iraq, including false claims that Iraq was withholding food and medicine from its own people, when Iraq's model system of food distribution and rationing has saved its people. I have repeatedly reported these US deceptions to the Security Council since the food for oil program was initiated. Combined with the failure of the Sanctions Committee to approve contracts by Iraq for purchases of urgently needed medicines, food and equipment, the US has succeeded in preventing the easing of sanctions and will continue to do so if they are not completely ended.

## Criminal Aerial Assaults on Iraq

The United States has bombed Iraq from aircraft and cruise missiles with impunity since the ceasefire in February 1991. In the week before the inauguration of William J. Clinton as President of the United States on January 20, 1993, President George Bush authorized a fierce campaign of bombing. President Clinton continued the aerial attacks and bombing on January 21, 1993 and throughout his eight years in office. On occasion large numbers of cruise missiles were launched, hitting among many civilian facilities the Al Rashid Hotel in Baghdad and the home of Iraq's most famous painter and the Director of its Museum of Modern Art, Leyla al Attar. Out of thousands of unlawful aerial sorties and hundreds of violent attacks on defenseless people in Iraq, including the passengers on a UN helicopter, the US did not suffer a single casualty. Still the US has insisted it must attack and kill Iraqis to protect its aircraft which had no right to fly over Iraq, though no US aircraft have been hit.

US aircraft joined occasionally by UK planes attacking targets in Iraq are engaged in criminal violence and crimes against peace. Those who ordered the flights and attacks, and the pilots who executed the orders committed criminal acts that have caused the deaths of hundreds of people.

The Security Council has condoned these continuing criminal assaults under pressure from the US and, tragically, has approved the genocidal sanctions against Iraq. It has ignored other illegal attacks by the US including the surprise attacks on Tripoli and Benghazi, Libya in April 1986 which killed hundreds of civilians, and the 20 cruise missile assault on the Al Shifa pharmaceutical plant in Khartoum, Sudan in August 1998 which provided half the medicine available to the people of Sudan. Nothing could be more dangerous to world peace.

The new US Administration has continued to make criminal aerial assaults on Iraq and threatened to increase them as an alternative to sanctions which it now suggests have failed.

The Security Council must proclaim the assaults on Iraq to be the crime they clearly are and demand they stop.

Widespread and growing anger at the genocidal sanctions and the criminal assaults against Iraq will turn into rage, violence and war unless they are stopped. The very first purpose of the UN is to prevent this scourge of war.

Sincerely,
Ramsey Clark

# 16

# The Fire in 1999?
# The United States, NATO
# and the Bombing of Yugoslavia

## David Bruce MacDonald

Since the end of the Cold War, the methods and objectives of United States foreign policy have come under increasing scrutiny. The Gulf War would produce Ramsey Clark's *The Fire this Time*, charging the United States with war crimes in Iraq (Clark, 1992). Christopher Hitchens's more recent *The Trial of Henry Kissinger* (Hitchens, 2001) accuses this former Nixonite hawk of a wide variety of atrocious crimes, giving new insight into Daniel Ellsberg's glib remark in 1972 that 'Henry has the best deal Faust ever made with Mephistopheles' (Vonnegut, 1974: 197).

This chapter will critically examine NATO's 1999 air campaign against Yugoslavia, Operation Allied Force. I will argue that while the United States did not commit war crimes in this case, they did break numerous international laws and conventions, causing untold 'collateral damage' in the process. Its humanitarian goals notwithstanding, NATO's operation was found wanting on numerous counts. We can cite NATO's haste in rushing into an underprepared military solution; its unwillingness to endanger the lives of its own soldiers to protect Yugoslavia's civilians; its use of highly questionable weaponry on civilian targets; and its seeming ignorance of the region's specific features. The chapter begins by looking at some of the background to NATO intervention, including members' conceptions of strategy and where these went wrong. We will then examine the consequences wrought by the air campaign, and examine what international laws and conventions were broken. A final section considers the question of blame, and how much of it should be borne by the United States. However, I will also argue that there are important mitigating factors that must be taken into consideration when analyzing Allied Force and its aftermath.

## Precedents

The Allied campaign in Yugoslavia in 1999 was not without its precedents. The 1990 Gulf War reinforced US enthusiasm about the use of advanced technology to win a conflict quickly and efficiently. It took under six weeks for a force of some 800,000 troops to decimate the Iraqi army, with a US fatality rate of less than one per 3,000 soldiers. This, according to Stephen Biddle, 'made the Gulf War a shaping event for defense planning in the 1990s ... a Gulf War yardstick' (Biddle, 1996: 142–43). Of importance here was the belief that the world's problems could now be solved using high-altitude bombing and the latest military technology. However, the Gulf War also involved highly questionable tactics against civilians. Former US Attorney General Ramsey Clark would accuse the United States of no fewer than nineteen separate war crimes, including breaches of the Hague and Geneva Conventions, the Nuremberg and UN Charters, and the US Constitution, for the dropping of over 80 thousand tons of bombs, and the deaths of between 125,000 and 150,000 Iraqi soldiers and civilians (Clark, 1992: xvii–xviii, 38, 40).[1]

A second precedent was to be found in the 1995 NATO air-strikes in Bosnia-Herzegovina. After sixteen months of failing to get Bosnian Serb leaders to negotiate over the Contact Group Plan, the US launched Operation Deliberate Force on 30 August – the largest military action in NATO's history. Bosnian Serb positions around Sarajevo were pounded by US planes, coupled with French and British artillery from the Rapid Reaction Forces operating in Bosnia (Holbrooke, 1998: 101–2). Certainly there was a predecent for the 1999 air strikes – the airstrikes of 1995. These produced exactly the result the Americans intended, and with surprising speed. After 16 months of failing to get Bosnian Serb leaders to negotiate over the Contact Group Plan, US military and political staff concluded that more forceful means would be required to bring the Bosnian Serbs to the bargaining table. Within hours, Slobodan Milosevic secured the signatures of all the relevant high-ranking Serbian and Bosnian-Serb leaders to a document creating a joint delegation to participate in negotiations. This document, later referred to as the 'Patriarch Paper' by US Chief Negotiator Richard Holbrooke, gave Milosevic 'virtually total power over the fate of the Bosnian Serbs' (Holbrooke, 1998: 105–6). Holbrooke's analysis of this state of affairs was as arrogant as it was representative of US views at the time:

> I was beginning to get the sense of the Pale Serbs: headstrong, given to empty theatrical statements, but in the end, essentially bullies when their bluff was called. The Western mistake over the previous four years had been to treat the

Serbs as rational people, with whom one could argue, negotiate, compromise, and agree. In fact, they respected only force or an unambiguous and credible threat to use it. (Holbrooke, 1998: 152)

These two precedents yielded a number of lessons: first, the UN was a useful tool of US foreign policy; second, air power could achieve quick and effective results; third, the Serbs were bullies who understood force and little else; and fourth, the United States had the right (even perhaps the duty) to intervene in Yugoslavia.

However, Kosovo was not 'a second Bosnia.' In Bosnia, the Serbs formed roughly one-third of the population, but in Kosovo they accounted for just 10 per cent. While there were few real cultural and linguistic differences between Bosnian Serbs, Croats, and Moslems, Serbs and Albanians spoke different languages, and were of different (and historically antagonistic) ethnic groups. Another difference was the nature of the conflict. The Bosnian conflict was largely confined to the region; Kosovo had enormous potential for spillover, making it potentially far more destabilizing. The military strategy, too, was dissimilar. While a combination of air strikes and ground forces had succeeded in Bosnia, Clinton hobbled his administration early in the Kosovo debacle when he announced: 'I do not intend to put our troops in Kosovo to fight a war' (quoted in Daalder and O'Hanlon, 2000: 130). Without 'crucial land-based reinforcements,' Deliberate Force would not have succeeded. This military reality, along with others, seems to have been ignored (Shawcross, 2001: 332).

More important, perhaps, was the alliance's underestimation of Kosovo's significance in Serbian politics. While Milosevic happily sold out the Bosnian Serbs during the Dayton peace process, he was not prepared to give up Kosovo, which was seen to be historically Serbian. Bosnia was never as important to the Serbs as Kosovo – the 'Serbian Jerusalem,' site of the Battle of Kosovo of 1389, and location of some of Serbia's most revered churches and monasteries. Additionally, the reaction against Kosovar nationalism in the mid-1980s was key to Milosevic's rise to power. Kosovo made his reputation, and its loss would clearly be his undoing – something US strategists failed to take into account (Hyland, 1999: 44–5).

## The war begins

In 1998, an asymmetrical civil war was taking place in Kosovo, pitting a ragtag but determined Kosovo Liberation Army (created in 1996) against units of the Yugoslav armed forces, loosely allied with a variety of Serbian paramilitary groups – among them the infamous 'Tigers' of Zeljko Raz-natovic ('Arkan'), and Vojislav Seselj's 'White Eagles'. In 1998, the conflict produced some 300,000 refugees and hundreds of dead, but hopes were raised when a ceasefire agreement was signed in October, calling for the reduction of Yugoslav military and police units in Kosovo and the creation of a 2,000-strong 'Kosovo Verification Mission' to monitor the situation. However, neither side appeared to have had any intention of honoring the agreement. By January 1999, the fighting had resumed (Bardos, 1999). Yugoslavia would soon be denounced in the eyes of the world after Serbian paramilitary forces massacred Albanian civilians in the village of Racak on 15 January. Three weeks later, on 6 February, the European Union, Russia and the United States launched a series of negotiations at the palace of Rambouillet, just outside Paris (Bardos, 1999).

The question of whether war could have been averted is an important one. It seems clear, in hindsight, that the 90-page 'Rambouillet Peace Agreement' was designed to be unacceptable to the Serbs. Under the agreement, a NATO-appointed Civilian Implementation Mission (CIM) would have had direct control over Kosovo, including 'the authority to issue binding directives to the Parties on all important matters he saw fit, including appointing and removing officials and curtailing institutions' (quoted in Parenti, 2000: 110). Of particular concern was the unpublicized 'Appendix B,' which would have allowed NATO personnel complete and unrestricted access throughout the region, including airspace and water-ways.[2] Even Henry Kissinger called the Rambouillet text 'a provocation, an excuse to start bombing ... a terrible document that should not have been presented in that form' (Shawcross, 2001: 329).

But the messenger as well as the message was provocative. As Allan Little argued, 'The Americans knew that because it had to be Nato [making the demands], the chances of the Serbs accepting the deal were very small' (Little, 2000). It seems clear from a reading of the events leading to the conflict, and an analysis of US calculations, that the US believed Milosevic would respond only to force or the threat of force. The sooner such force could be brought to bear, the sooner the conflict would be resolved and the US could pull out of the region. By 22 March, in a last-ditch attempt to convince Milosevic to sign, Holbrooke led a mission to Belgrade, but this effort was ultimately unsuccessful. So on 24 March, NATO began Operation Allied Force (Bardos, 1999). Some 51 targets had been hastily drawn up, and within a short time, 40 had been hit. The first targets included a military academy in the suburbs of Belgrade, the Batajnica airbase, a major communications mast on Mount Avala, and Yugoslavia's air-defence systems (Judah, 2000: 237–8). As Clinton argued, NATO had three primary goals: 'To demonstrate the seriousness of NATO's purpose so that the Serbian leaders understand the imperative of reversing course, [to] deter an even bloodier offensive against innocent civilians in Kosovo, and, if necessary, to seriously damage the Serb military's capacity to harm the people of Kosovo' (Daalder and O'Hanlon, 2000: 101).

Operation Allied Force lasted seventy-eight days. In the first month, NATO flew an average of 300 sorties a day, about 100 of these being bombing runs (or 'strike sorties'). This was then increased as the conflict progressed to 500 sorties daily with 150 bombing runs. By the end of May, the daily rate had increased to between 600 and 700, with almost 300 daily bombing runs. Altogether, nearly 40,000 aircraft sorties were flown during the course of the conflict (Greenberg, 2000: 212; Daalder and O'Hanlon, 2000: 143–4, 209). The campaign would end on 2 June, when Finnish President Maarti Ahtisaari and Boris Yeltsin's personal envoy Viktor Chernomyrdin finally persuaded Milosevic to sign a somewhat modified version of the Rambouillet Agreement, later codified as UN Security Council Resolution 1244. Kosovo would remain legally a part of Yugoslavia, but would be subject to a separate international administration known as the United Nations Mission in Kosovo, or UNMIK. On 9 June, a Military-Technical Agreement paved the way for withdrawal of Yugoslav forces, and the entry of KFOR troops (Bardos, 1999).

In hindsight, the US severely miscalculated the duration of the war. Believing that Milosevic would buckle at the first display of high-tech military power, the CIA argued in January 1999 that 'Milosevic doesn't want a war he can't win.... After enough of a defence to sustain his honour and assuage his backers he will quickly sue for peace' (see Borger and Taylor-Norton, 1999; Borger, 1999). Milosevic, too, was convinced that NATO would back off after a token bombing campaign, which he jokingly called 'bombing lite' (Judah, 2000: 229). As Michael Ignatieff paraphrases the 'cynically cheerful scenario': 'we would pretend to bomb Milosevic, and he would pretend to resist and then a deal would be done, dropping a province he could no longer control into the lap of the international community.' However, the truth turned out to be otherwise: 'In his cynicism, Milosevic gambled that NATO would never go to war for its values. In our innocence, we gambled that he would never risk destruction for his' (Ignatieff, 2000: 48–9; see also Bardos, 1999).

In their enthusiasm to finish the war quickly, washing their hands of what they saw as a bloody and intractable situation, the United States and its allies engaged in a wide variety of breaches of international law, many of which involved the targeting of civilians and civilian infrastructure, and the use of weapons and tactics which had no legitimate place on any battlefield.

## Unintended civilian consequences?

If the situation prevailing in Kosovo before Allied Force was serious, it would pale next to the full-scale catastrophe that the bombing campaign produced. By mid-April, after only two weeks of bombing, some 350,000 refugees had poured out of Kosovo, fleeing south to Macedonia and Albania (Chomsky, 2000: 34). By the end of the campaign, the refugee total stood at 850,000, with an additional 500,000 people internally displaced within Kosovo (Daalder and O'Hanlon, 2000: 108–9; also Crace, 1999). The bombing soon became a backdrop for a program of systematic ethnic cleansing, as the number of Serbian troops and police in Kosovo increased by 25 per cent to 40,000 men (Norton-Taylor, 1999). Almost from day one, Serbian forces began rounding up ethnic Albanians from Pristina, Qirez, and other cities (Black and Borger, 1999).

Forced expulsions took place at gunpoint, with Serbian militia groups going door to door. In some instances, heavy weapons such as tanks, artillery, helicopters and aircraft were used to promote an exodus. During the conflict, over 100,000 homes in 500 villages, towns and cities were damaged or destroyed, most looted beforehand. Horrific crimes, such as shooting, burning people alive, amputation, rape, and even the hacking-off of nipples, were reported throughout this period (Daalder and O'Hanlon, 2000: 109–11). Estimates of the death toll hover around 10,000 Albanian casualties (mostly at Serb hands), along with thousands of Yugoslav soldiers and civilians (Greenberg, 2000: 212).

Western policymakers, it seemed, had seriously miscalculated the effects of the bombing – Milosevic had not backed down. James Rubin, Albright's State Department spokesman described an 'escalating pattern of Serbian attacks,' while former National Security Advisor Carnes Lord argued: 'although western officials continue to deny it, there can be little doubt that the bombing campaign has provided both motive and opportunity for a wider and more savage Serbian operation than what was first envisioned' (quoted in Chomsky, 2000: 35). As one journalist wrote forcefully: 'At bottom there remains the terrible truth that the volcanic catastrophe of the sudden Kosovo population displacements were triggered by the Nato bombing, and by the decision of Western governments to impose impossible conditions on the Serbian sovereign state. We knew it would happen, the Serbs said it would happen, and it did happen' (quoted in Gott, 1999).

While the creation of hundreds of thousands of refugees was certainly an unintended consequence of NATO's air war, it was not entirely unpredictable. While Serbia drove people out, the indiscriminate nature of NATO's high-altitude bombing also triggered massive population shifts.

Other factors included the lack of power supplies, telephone lines, and clean water, coupled with a more general fear of violence. This included the fear of getting caught in the middle of KLA and Yugoslav crossfire, the fear of a NATO ground war (which the KLA predicted), and an un-willingness to join the KLA 'general mobilization' that was taking place throughout Kosovo. That 70–100,000 Serbs also fled Kosovo during the bombing suggests that the campaign itself and the fear it generated were driving everybody out (Parenti, 2000: 131, 135).

## Civilian deaths

According to Human Rights Watch, NATO was directly responsible for the deaths of between 488 and 527 civilians in 90 separate incidents. In breaking down the causes of these deaths, HRW charged that NATO had pursued a range of questionable tactics. It had

> conducted air attacks using cluster bombs near populated areas; attacked targets of questionable military legitimacy, including Serb Radio and Television, heat-ing plants, and bridges; did not take adequate precautions in warning civilians of attacks; took insufficient precautions identifying the presence of civilians when attacking convoys and mobile targets; and caused excessive civilian casu-alties by not taking sufficient measures to verify that military targets did not have concentrations of civilians (such as at Korisa). (Human Rights Watch, 2000a)

The organization also noted that 43 of the attacks took place during daylight hours, when civilians were most likely to be working in targeted buildings or using roads and bridges that were scheduled for attack (Human Rights Watch, 2000a). Had NATO given adequate warning to civilians that an attack was coming; had they attacked at night; had they been more careful with target selection; and had they bombed from a lower altitude, casualty rates could have been reduced by as much as 50 per cent (Parenti, 2000: 122; Daalder and O'Hanlon, 2000: 122–3).

Three of the most catastrophic attacks occurred in mid-April. On 12 April, at least ten people died and sixteen were injured after NATO pilots targeted a passenger train going over a bridge in mid-morning. NATO first denied the bombing, then later dismissed it as an 'uncanny accident' (Helm, 1999). The next day, NATO bombed the Belgrade suburb of Banjica, intending to hit a military barracks. It also hit the Military Medical Academy hospital some 50 metres away, putting both injured soldiers and civilians at risk (Fisk, 1999). On 14 April, a refugee convoy coming from Djakovica in southwestern Kosovo was struck with nine 500-pound laser-guided bombs launched by US F-16 fighter planes. Up to 80 civilians were killed in this attack, which NATO leaders later admitted was an accident – they thought that they were firing on military vehicles, not tractors (Walker et al., 1999). Even during the first three weeks of the assault, it was clear that NATO's air campaign was not targeting only military installations. As Maggie O'Kane concluded, 'After 17 days of bombing it is clear that Nato's targets are as much politically motivated against Mr. Milosevic personally, as they are strategically driven' (O'Kane, 1999a).

Classified under the amorphous military heading 'lines of communication,' 70 per cent of Danube road bridges were destroyed, 50 per cent of Danube rail bridges and 50 per cent of Kosovo's road corridors. By the end of May, electrical grids and transformers were also being destroyed. Cigarette factories, fertilizer plants, chemical factories, even the homes and offices of Milosevic's political allies were attacked, as well as his party headquarters (Daalder and O'Hanlon, 2000: 200–201). Of the obviously non-military targets, the bombing of the Serbian Radio and Television headquarters in Belgrade on 23 April was one of the most dubious, and resulted in 14 deaths. There was certainly no military or strategic value in the raid, leading Human Rights Watch to conclude: 'In this case, the purpose of the attack again seems to have been more psychological harassment of the civilian population than to obtain direct military effect. The risks involved to the civilian population in undertaking this urban attack grossly outweigh any perceived military benefit' (Human Rights Watch, 2000a). Other inexplicable targets included the Dubrava Penitentiary in Kosovo, which was subject to two attacks, on 19 and 21 May. The first bombing resulted in the deaths of 3 prisoners and 1 guard, the second resulted in the deaths of some 19 prisoners (Human Rights Watch, 2000a).

In Montenegro, where Milo Djukanovic's anti-Milosevic government had been steering a neutral course, bombs rained down on Podgorica and Danilograd – ostensibly, it was argued, to knock out Yugoslav radar defences (Dinmore, 1999). On 9 April, a residential suburb of Pristina was attacked, when a bomb was 'seduced off the target' (Crace, 1999). Peripheral regions such as Vojvodina were also hit. The mayor of Novi Sad noted that by 20 April, 7 bridges, 50 businesses, and some 20 schools had been hit, together with 1 museum, 2 monasteries and the university. The total damage, he estimated, already ran to 7 billion deutschmarks. The Danube, which had carried some 10 million tons of shipping annually, was paralysed during the conflict, blocking off the main transportation route for Balkan countries to the West (O'Kane, 1999b). During this period, NATO dropped white propaganda leaflets assuring the population that not they but their government was being targeted.

Another key concern was the environmental degradation and destruction that occurred as a corollary to Operation Allied Force. On 18 April, NATO forces bombed the Pancevo combined fertilizer factory and oil refinery. The immediate result was 'a huge toxic, carcinogenic cloud of gas phosgene, chlorine and hydrochloric acid over Belgrade … as well as 15–20 kilometer long slicks in the Danube.' Other bombing targets included the Prva Iskra detergent plant in Baritz, led to a discharge of toxic gases. The bombing of a Nis tobacco plant led to an explosion of chemical additives, discharging cadmium into the atmosphere. The repeated bombing of the Zaztava plant in Kragujevac resulted in poisonous piralena liquid flows into the Lepenitsa river. Repeat bombing of the Milan Blagojevic plastic manufacturing plant in Lucani brought about severe petrochemical explosions. In other regions, including Belgrade, Pristina, Pancevo, Lipovic, and Novi Sad, the targeting of refineries and fuel depots led to uncontrollable fires and serious problems of air pollution (Lykourezos, 1999).

A large number of cultural, religious and educational buildings and monuments also appear to have been destroyed during the campaign. According to UNESCO, 12 historical monuments in Kosovo, central Serbia and Vojvodina were completely demolished by NATO attacks, and another 39 suffered substantial damage. Many of these were on UNESCO's World Heritage list, including the fourteenth-century Gracanica Monastery, which was bombed twice, and the thirteenth-century Pec Patriarchate. Additionally, NATO air strikes purportedly hit more than 2,000 schools. On 10 April alone, NATO attacked and destroyed village schools in the towns of Bogutova, Raska, Lacevci, Tavnik and Lozno, the first having been targeted with no fewer than six missiles (Lykourezos, 1999). What exactly NATO was hoping to accomplish with such attacks is unclear.

Whether it was the result of faulty intelligence or sabotage, the Chinese Embassy attack will count as one of the worst blunders of modern warfare. Targeting the wrong side of Belgrade's Lenjinov Boulevard, NATO bombed the embassy on 7 May, rather than the Federal Directorate of Supply and Procurement on the opposite side, provoking violent anti-US protests in China. The CIA claimed to have been using maps dated from 1992 (Evans, 1999). In the end, one employee was fired and several officials were disciplined after the attack, in which three Chinese lost their lives (Dalder and O'Hanlon, 2000: 147). Coming at a time when a diplomatic breakthrough seemed to be on the horizon, its political effects were devastating. Lawrence Freedman argues that, '[w]hile [it is] impossible to prove, this attack may have added a couple of weeks to the length of the war' (quoted in Daalder and O'Hanlon, 2000: 147).

Many of these tactical errors were the result of a lack of long-range strategic planning. At the beginning of Operation Allied Force, NATO had drawn up only 51 targets for its sketchy battle plans; by 28 March, these were expanded to include a target list 'aimed at demoralizing Serbia's population.' In practice, some 60 per cent of NATO targets were of questionable 'dual use' (Judah, 2000: 256–7; for a further discussion, see Ignatieff, 2000: 170). Rather than encouraging the Serbs to rise up against Milosevic, attacks on civilians and civilian infrastructure, recalled one analyst, 'played directly into Milosevic's hands and, appeared to contradict the claim that the enemy was Milosevic and not the Serbian people' (Judah, 2000: 239). In this respect, Operation Allied Force was a dismal failure.

## Depleted uranium

The highly controversial use of depleted uranium (DU) ammunition has also raised serious concerns. Depleted uranium – what is left over when natural uranium has been enriched – is an extremely effective material for anti-tank weaponry, since it is 70 per cent denser than lead, and can easily punch through armor (Kirby, 2001). In all, NATO launched 112 strikes with depleted uranium ammunition, with 84 targets in Kosovo (Kroeger, 2001). Most of these weapons fell in civilian areas, among the very civilian populations NATO was supposed to be defending. Many European governments have also expressed concern about higher-than-normal rates of leukemia and radiation poisoning among their peacekeeping troops. Soldiers from Italy, Belgium, Holland, Spain, Portugal, the Czech Republic, and France have all died of suspicious causes after six-month tours in the Balkans (BBC News, 2001b).

DU ammunition was widely used during the Gulf War, where an estimated 940,000 DU projectiles were dropped on Iraq by Coalition forces (BBC News, 2001e). Between 1994 and 1995, NATO warplanes also dropped some 10,000 rounds of DU ammunition in Bosnia, creating what NATO peacekeeping troops have called 'Balkan Syndrome' – little different from 'Gulf War Syndrome' (Kroeger, 2001). Both syndromes appear to have identical symptoms that include 'increases in birth defects, stillbirths, childhood leukemia and other cancers' (Lykourezos, 1999; see also Kirby, 1999). While various oblique statements concerning the use of these weapons were made during Operation Allied Force, only in June 2000 did NATO finally admit it had used 'approximately 31,000 rounds of DU' during the campaign (BBC News, 2000a). NATO denies any link between DU weapons and leukemia or other radiation illnesses. It does acknowledge that the burning clouds of vapor produced by DU weapons are radioactive, but claims these are short-lived and localized (Kirby, 2001).

However, radiation physicists at the University of Maryland submitted a report to the US Department of Energy in April 1999, concluding that 'DU should never be used in a battlefield scenario, because of its hazards to health.' British biologist Roger Coghill has argued that while DU in its inert form is relatively safe, it poses a serious threat when it hits a target. At this stage, 'DU catches fire, and much of the round is turned into burning dust. The particles are extremely small, they can travel up to 300 kilometers. They are also beta-emitters, which are dangerous if inhaled.' According to Coghill, 'The particles can then lodge in the lungs, resisting the body's attempts to flush them out, and can wreak havoc with the immune system' (quoted in Kirby, 1999). Some 43 per cent of DU is also water-soluble, which means it can enter the bloodstream and move anywhere in the body (BBC News, 1999d). A recent study by Middlesex University examined urine samples from people in Bosnia and Kosovo, and found DU in every sample collected, suggesting 'it was likely that the metal was present in the food chain' (BBC News, 2001d).

The effects of DU weaponry were certainly not confined to Yugoslavia. By mid-June 1999, scientists in northern Greece reported 25 per cent increases in radiation levels whenever the wind blew from Kosovo. Bulgarian researchers also reported increases in radiation levels of as much as 800 per cent during and after the conflict (Kirby, 1999). As of 2001, there had been no attempts by NATO to clean up the debris from DU weapons. In January, a United Nations monitoring team found 'parts of DU weapons lying about in villages and graveyards where they could easily be picked up' (BBC News, 2001a).

## Cluster bombs

Another evil during the air campaign was the use of cluster bombs, many of which caused civilian casualties. Cluster bombs have been around since the 1960s, and were widely used in Vietnam and Iraq. Unlike typical bombs, cluster bombs contain 150 to 250 submunitions or 'bomblets' that are designed to explode over a large area once the bomb has been dropped from an aircraft (Marcus, 2000). What makes cluster bombs extremely dangerous is their high dud ratio; about 10 per cent of bomblets do not explode on impact, leaving large amounts of unexploded ordnance. Cluster bombs can easily drift from a designated target to civilian areas if dropped from high altitude, and their brightly colored casings are often attractive to children. This has contributed to numerous child fatalities (BBC News, 2001c).

During the Gulf War, an estimated 62,000 cluster bombs were dropped on Iraq, leaving behind a minimum of 1.2 to 1.5 million unexploded bomblets (Human Rights Watch, 1999). More than 1,600 civilians (400 Iraqis and 1,200 Kuwaitis) were killed, and over 2,500 injured, in the first two years after the Gulf War from accidents involving submunitions (Human Rights Watch, 1999). During Operation Allied Force, cluster bombs were also a weapon of choice, and approximately 1,400 were dropped on Kosovo by British and US forces, resulting in the deaths of some 200 Kosovar civilians and two Nepalese Gurkha peacekeepers (Wood, 2000; BBC News, 1999a).

## The KLA and regional instability

There is no doubt that the NATO campaign wrought horrific devastation. Whether or not its actions constitute war crimes as such, Yugoslavia's infrastructure and economy will not soon recover from the pounding. Independent estimates indicate that the NATO campaign caused $30–40 billion in damage to the Yugoslav economy. The conflict also left Serbia awash with refugees. Before the campaign, the province was already struggling to absorb between 500,000 and 550,000 refugees from the Croatian and Bosnian conflicts. To these were added another 230,000, mostly Kosovar Serbs, during and after the campaign. By the end of 1999, Yugoslavia had the dubious distinction of supporting the largest refugee population of any country in Europe, while also being among the poorest (Bardos, 1999; Human Rights Watch, 2000b).

Added to these refugee problems were serious problems of instability in Kosovo itself. Another unintended consequence of Operation Allied Force was the massive increase of KLA power, coterminous with Milosevic's ethnic cleansing activities. It appears that the rapid growth of the KLA by 1999 to a '30,000 strong force equipped with grenade launchers, anti-tank weapons, and AK47s' was closely linked to Kosovars' increasing involvement in the heroin trade in Switzerland, Germany, and Scandinavia. One intelligence source claimed in the *Berliner Zeitung* that some DM 900 million had reached Kosovo since 1997, half of it from illegal drugs money (Boyes and Wright, 1999).[3] In the West, the KLA were first denounced as terrorists, but this position later changed, and Holbrooke was sent in to negotiate with several different KLA factions (Hyland, 1999: 45). After the bombing campaign ended in early June, the KLA agreed to disband, and a 3,000-member Kosovo Protection Corps was created. However, the real goal of the KPC, according to its leader Agim Ceku, was to retain some form of Kosovar military organisation while continuing to train Albanians in military techniques (Daalder and O'Hanlon, 2000: 178). Though they had been officially disbanded, many KLA units remained intact, and managed to hide the majority of their weaponry (Bardos, 1999).

Once the peace accord was signed, KFOR forces began slowly moving into the region. By September, 49,000 of the 50,000 force were moved in, and due to their efforts nearly all of the Albanian refugees were able to return home by the end of June. However, while this force was described as 'creating a secure environment for refugees and internally displaced persons to the return to their homes,' this was not true for all (Daalder and O'Hanlon, 2000: 176). As Yugoslav troops were withdrawn and NATO forces moved in, a dangerous power vacuum developed, leading inexorably to the rise of extremist factions which rapidly became the key power bases in the province (Bardos, 1999).

The first targets were Serbs and Romani, both of whom were subjected to revenge attacks. Human rights violations against Serbs, such as executions, abductions and intimidation, increased after the bombing. Romani left *en masse* after intimidation, killings, and house-burning by Kosovar militia groups. The OSCE blamed members of the KLA and the Kosovo Protection Corps for much of the damage (BBC News, 1999c). Half of all murders in the five months after the bombing were of Serbian civilians, even though Albanians now made up 95 per cent of the population, prompting the BBC to report: 'Though on a much smaller scale, the revenge attacks on Kosovar Serbs have taken on the form of ethnic cleansing in reverse' (BBC News, 1999b). By the end of the year, the International Red Cross estimated that some 247,000 Serbs and Romani had fled the province. Pristine's Serbian population was reduced from 20,000 to 1,000 (Judah, 2000: 287, 289).[4] Attacks on Serbian Orthodox religious sites also became commonplace, with claims that some eighty churches and monasteries were destroyed after June 1999 (Bardos, 1999). By 2000, international officials were arguing that the wave of violence against Serbs and other minorities was 'orchestrated' and 'systematic' (Human Rights Watch, 2000b).

This situation was not helped by the power struggles within the KLA. By the end of 1999, the KLA was splitting into several competing factions, and politically motivated assassinations began among rival groups for control of territory and resources (Bardos, 1999). By 2000, UN agencies reported that the rates of theft, blackmail, and kidnapping had risen 70 per cent (Bardos, 1999). In their 2000 report, Human Rights Watch argued: 'Despite an ongoing security gap for minorities, political violence, and growing crime, with elements of former KLA and Kosovo Protection Corps clearly implicated, NATO and the UN remained unable or unwilling to confront the perpetrators in a decisive and consistent manner' (Human Rights

Watch, 2000b). While assistance to Kosovo was but a small fraction of the costs of waging war, Western governments were reluctant to donate the $25 million needed to bridge the financial gap for 1999, and would not even consider the $125 million gap for 2000. In the words of one reporter, the UN administration was being 'starved of funds by the countries that had fought and won the war.' By the end of 1999, there was 'no justice, no police, no power, no water, not even new identity documents to replace those the Serbs had stolen in the spring.' Bernard Kouchner rightly called it 'a scandal' (quoted in Shawcross, 2001: 366–7). Human Rights Watch (2000b) has tactfully called US policy a 'laissez-faire approach.'

## Regional instability

One of the West's avowed aims in launching this campaign was to prevent regional instability. Yet, such instability became, insidiously and inexorably, a part of Operation Allied Force. Economically, both Romania and Bulgaria paid a heavy price for their support of the NATO air campaign. In Romania, President Emil Constantinescu hoped that by obediently granting NATO full access to Romanian air space, and joining the embargo against Yugoslavia, a 'second Marshall plan' would be forthcoming. It was not. Romania's foreign debt of $2.8 billion was not written off, nor was there compensation for the estimated $1 billion of losses resulting from the conflict. Romanian shipping companies alone claimed losses of $1.3 million a month due to the blockage of the Danube river, formerly used to transport 67 per cent of its exports (Guruita, 1999).

In Bulgaria, the Ministry of Trade and Tourism estimated that nearly 168.7 million leva ($90.7 million) had been lost as a result of 'forfeited profits, spoiled produce, and breached contracts.' The blockage of the Danube resulted in transportation company losses of 67.9 million leva, prompting one leading politician to remark that Bulgaria was 'seduced and left, or will be left, as a pregnant bride at the altar' (quoted in Karadjov, 1999). Hungary, which had only been a NATO member for twelve days prior to Operation Allied Force, estimated that it too had lost hundreds of millions of dollars in trade because of the conflict (Hartung and Kaufman, 2000: 207). Yugoslavia's neighbors, it seemed, have paid an unreasonably high price for their cooperation and compliance.

Sadly, the worst punishment was reserved for Macedonia. Here, Albanians comprised 23 per cent of the country's entire population, and with the bombing campaign they became an increasingly vocal and militant minority (Bassett, 1999). Tens of thousands of refugees flooded into Macedonia during Operation Allied Force, with few resources to accommodate them.

By 2000, radical elements within the KLA formed a National Liberation Army, and began to provoke violent insurrections in Macedonia (Bardos, 2001). In the wake of regional instability in 2001, this country, which had enjoyed eight years of relative peace, was forced to call on NATO for assistance, and within a few months 3,500 NATO MFOR (Macedonian Forces) were stationed throughout the country as part of Operation Essential Harvest (see Reuters, 2001a, 2001b, 2001c; also Jovanovski, 2001). While NATO (primarily British peacekeepers) did help to defuse the situation in Macedonia, the increased militancy and size of the KLA and its successors were almost certainly a legacy of the bombing campaign and Milosevic's brutal reaction to it.

## Assigning blame

There is little doubt that the United States bears primary responsibility for Operation Allied Force and its consequences. US allies had few precision-guided munitions in their arsenals, and some countries, like France, constantly questioned the legitimacy of almost every dual-use target. While Britain was arguably the US's strongest ally, the British too did comparatively little. A Commons Defence Select Committee report in 2000 stated that Britain's air forces were 'badly equipped,' and were responsible for fewer than 5 per cent of NATO sorties. 'Britain's major contribution to the campaign,' the report claimed, 'was to drop unguided 1,000 lb. cluster bombs,' these being 'of limited military value and questionable legitimacy' (BBC News, 2000b).

For those on the ground, it was clear that the United States was in charge. NATO pilot Captain Martin de la Hoz argued that 'All the missions that we flew, all and every one, were planned by US high military authorities. Even more, they were all planned in detail, including attacking planes, targets and types of ammunition that we would have to throw' (quoted and discussed in Parenti, 2000: 122–3). Towards the end of the campaign, the possibility even arose that the United States would have continued in Kosovo without its NATO allies. As Sandy Berger declared in a speech on 2 June, there would be a victory in Kosovo, 'in or outside NATO.... A consensus in NATO is valuable. But it is not [a] sine qua non. We want to move with NATO, but it can't prevent us from moving' (quoted in Daalder and O'Hanlon, 2000: 160). It was thus clear that the US was using NATO as an instrument of its own foreign policy, and was willing to do what it thought right irrespective of its allies.

Did the United States commit war crimes during Operation Allied Force? I believe not. But it did break numerous domestic and international conventions in its quest for 'justice.' The US and its NATO allies clearly violated the UN Charter, which prohibits nations from attacking other states for claimed violations of human rights. This is covered by Article 2(4), which prevents 'threat or use of force against' another state. There are only two exceptions: Article 51, which allows a nation to use force in 'self defence if an armed attack occurs against' it or an allied country; the Charter also authorizes the Security Council to employ force to counter threats to or breaches of international peace, but only with its explicit permission (Lobel and Ratner, 2000: 113). For its part, NATO claims that it based its attacks on several UN Security Council resolutions, in particular Resolution 1199 (September 1998) and Resolution 1203 (October 1998), both of which imposed strict limitations on Serbian military activities and troop deployments in Kosovo – limits ignored by the Milosevic regime. Daalder and O'Hanlon (2000: 102–3) argue, 'the international legal basis for NATO's action was admittedly ambiguous – but certainly not altogether lacking.'

While this 'ambiguous' basis seemed sufficient for NATO, this fact alone confers no real legitimacy. As Alexander Lykourezos has countered: 'When the Security Council intends to sanction the use of force, it has always done so in its resolutions, in a clear and unequivocal fashion. The Security Council had no intention to authorize the use of force, since it was clear that such a resolution would raise vetoes from China and Russia who have been vocal in their opposition to the exercise of force against Yugoslavia.... NATO ... unilaterally and unlawfully, decided to circumvent the UN and take matters into its own hands' (Lykourezos, 1999; see Sections 3.1.2 and 3.2.1).[5]

Loebel and Ratner have also argued that bypassing the Security Council meant the United Nations was unable to open real negotiations with the Serbs: 'It is possible that the settlement that ended the war would have been achieved without the use of force. The Security Council might have required a deletion of several of the most objectionable aspects of the so-called Rambouillet Agreement that mandated that other peaceful means to resolve the crisis be attempted' (Lobel and Ratner, 2000: 114). However unlikely, the Council might have broken through Milosevic's intransigence and brokered some sort of compromise. However, by forcing his hand, NATO insured that Milosevic would act ruthlessly to safeguard his own self-preservation.

The United States also violated NATO's 1949 founding treaty, which obliges member nations to act only in accordance with the principles and procedures of the United Nations. Force is only authorized for mutual self-defense when a member state is under attack; NATO may only resort to force to defend a non-member state if the government of that state specifically requests NATO assistance. The exception to this rule is if force is authorized by the UN Security Council. In this case, it clearly was not (Lykourezos, 1999, Section 3.3.1; also discussed in Valasek, 2000: 50–51).

Even the United States Constitution was violated. Article 1, Section 8 obliges Congress to declare war before troops can be deployed against a sovereign state. This was not done, even though Undersecretary of State Thomas Pickering testified before the House Committee on International Relations that the bombing campaign was indeed an act of war. The US's War Powers Act was also violated during the bombing. This requires the president to seek approval from Congress for any military action lasting over sixty days, something Clinton failed to do. No one, however, seemed to mind. The War Powers Resolution allows the president, as Commander in Chief of the armed forces, to deploy US troops, but only if one of three conditions prevails: there is a declaration of war; there is specific authorization from Congress; or there is a national emergency as a result of an attack on US soil, including its territories, possessions and armed forces.[6] In the case of Kosovo, none of these conditions was fulfilled.

The most damning violations concern breaches of the 1949 Geneva Conventions, incidentally adopted as Article 2 (a) and (c) of the Statute for the International Criminal Tribunal for the former Yugoslavia (Lykourezos, 1999). Protocol I (1977) is meant to afford general protection for civilians in times of war against hostile military operations. Combatants are required to take great care in discriminating between military and civilian targets, and they must take all necessary precautions to avoid or minimize harm to civilians. As Human Rights Watch argues, 'Attacks which may be expected to cause incidental loss of life or injuries to civilians, or to cause damage to civilian objectives *are indiscriminate* if this harm to civilians is excessive in relation to the concrete and direct military advantage anticipated (Protocol I, article 57 (2))' (Human Rights Watch, 2000a). By failing to take adequate steps to minimize civilian casualties, by their attacks on ambiguous 'dual-use' targets and their assault on civilian infrastructure, including passenger trains, hospitals, monuments and prisons, the United States and its allies did indeed violate Protocol I of the Geneva Conventions through *indiscriminate* attacks.

## US 'war crimes'?

During the bombing campaign, Yugoslavia in fact took the ten NATO countries to the International Court of Justice, claiming that Operation Allied Force was a violation of Yugoslavia's sovereignty. In opening Yugoslavia's case, Rodoljub Etinski accused NATO not just of committing 'illegal acts,' but also of committing crimes against peace and 'the crime of genocide.' In Greece, thousands of well-known personalities, including high court judges, signed on to a suit to indict NATO leaders for crimes against humanity at the ICTY (Wolf and Smith, 1999). Yugoslav authorities would buttress this with a two-volume 'white book' entitled *NATO Crimes in Yugoslavia*, complete with an array of lurid pictures (Judah, 2000: 259).

By November, two Canadian lawyers had filed three thick volumes of evidence against some 67 NATO leaders, with ICTY chief prosecutor Carla Del Ponte. The charges included causing billions of dollars in property damage and maiming and/or killing thousands of civilians. Two months later, Del Ponte made it clear that it was unlikely that any formal investigation into NATO wartime activities would take place. For many, this was hardly surprising, given that the ICTY was established in 1993 by the UN Security Council at the behest of the United States, and has been primarily supported, both financially and militarily, by the same country (Parenti, 2000: 127–8). In the end, it is doubtful that the United States will ever be brought to account for its actions in Kosovo. While a moratorium may someday be issued on DU weapons and cluster bombs, such moratoria are unlikely to lead to any charges against the United States. As Christopher Hitchens has argued in *The Trial of Henry Kissinger*, 'The United States is the most generous in granting immunity to itself and partial immunity to its servants, and the most laggard in adhering to international treaties' (Hitchens, 2001: 128).

While the United States broke a variety of domestic and international conventions, it is doubtful that this will result in legal repercussions. While the US should be brought to task for violating the Geneva Conventions, the other charges are more contentious. I would argue that there are a number of mitigating factors in favor of the United States and its NATO allies that make claims of NATO war crimes somewhat untenable. The first issue is Serbia's own culpability in war crimes, and perhaps even genocide. Milosevic and his paramilitaries, not NATO, were to blame for the deaths of an estimated 10,000 Albanians during the campaign, and for the ethnic cleansing of 850,000 civilians. Serbian leaders have also been convicted of genocide. On 2 August 2001, the ICTY found Bosnian Serb General Radislav Krstic guilty of genocide, for his role in the execution of some 7,000 Bosnian Muslim men and boys near Srebrenica in July 1995 (Transitions Online, 2001b).

More recently, Milosevic himself was turned over to the Tribunal to stand trial for genocide in Bosnia. While Milosevic and his colleagues may well be guilty of such atrocities, it was no coincidence that on 27 May 1999, during the bombing campaign, Milosevic was indicted along with four senior colleagues. As William Shawcross reports (2001: 347), the

Tribunal had long been demanding Allied intelligence intercepts, which had hitherto been withheld. Certainly, a cynical double game is evident here. NATO members were happy to 'play ball' with a 'genocidal' dictator when it suited their own ends. When he was no longer useful, he was abandoned. But nevertheless the fact remains that Milosevic's machinations over the past ten years have resulted in hundreds of thousands of civilians either killed or turned into refugees.

Also, there were real crimes committed in Kosovo, and these should not be ignored. In June 2001, mass graves were uncovered around Yugoslavia: six near Belgrade, and others close to an army training site near Petrovo Selo, a village in eastern Serbia. Altogether, an estimated 1,000 bodies had been transported out of Kosovo and hidden during the war (Graham, 2001). In March 1999, according to the Serbian Crime Investigation Department, Milosevic ordered the Serbian interior minister to 'eliminate all the traces that could lead to any evidence of crimes' (Transitions Online, 2001a). He was also alleged to have ordered a cover-up of any graves 'that could be a subject of interest to the Hague officials' (Stojkovic, 2001). Milosevic's own activities, combined with those of such paramilitary groups as the Tigers and White Eagles, prove that there was a real need for military intervention, even if Western claims of genocide later proved to be exaggerated.

A second issue concerns NATO's humanitarian assistance and efforts to deal with the refugee problems. While perhaps too little, too late, NATO did try to mitigate the refugee crisis brought about by the bombing campaign. By early April, NATO responded to requests by the UN High Commissioner for Refugees, and began a relief operation for Albanian refugees. By the end of May, NATO had flown some 4,500 tons of food and water and 8,500 tons of medical supplies and other equipment to the refugee camps. This humanitarian relief prevented epidemics from breaking out in the camps and resulted in fewer lives lost (Daalder and O'Hanlon, 2000: 124–5). Also, NATO efforts to resettle Kosovar Albanians after the conflict were surprisingly effective, with 808,913 refugees of 848,100 returning by November 1999. Certainly, the revenge attacks and the ethnic cleansing of Serbs and Romani demonstrate reluctance and a certain cynicism after the fact, but it remains true that NATO succeeded in re-establishing peace for Kosovars, in what Tim Judah (2000: 286) has called 'the quickest and biggest refugee return in modern history.'

A final point concerns the United Nations' tacit approval of the campaign, even if it violated the UN Charter. When Russia introduced a draft UN resolution on 26 March 1999, backed by India, China, Belarus and Namibia and calling for an end to the bombing, Secretary General Kofi Annan refused to condemn NATO's actions. Rather, he tacitly supported the organization, arguing that 'there are times when the use of force may be legitimate in the pursuit of peace' (quoted in Daalder and O'Hanlon, 2000: 127). In his keynote speech in September 1999, Annan would again justify Operation Allied Force, forcefully contending: 'If, in those dark days and hours leading up to the genocide [in Rwanda], a coalition of states had been prepared to act in defence of the Tutsi population, but did not receive prompt Council authorization, should a coalition have stood aside and allowed a horror to unfold?' (Wheeler, 2001: 114). The UN also played a key role in bringing about the ceasefire which ended the conflict, approving both a Chapter IV resolution recognising a peace accord, and implementation procedures for an open-ended KFOR mission under Security Council control (Daalder and O'Hanlon, 2000: 174–5).

One could certainly argue that the UN is a tool of the Western powers, and that the five permanent members of the Security Council hold the rest of the world in check. There is no doubt that the structure of the UN, and its funding methods, are imperfect and in need of reform.[7] However, if one is to condemn the US based on UN conventions and articles, Annan's tacit approval of the campaign, and his use of the offices of the UN to end the conflict, do demonstrate a degree of cooperation and good will between these two organizations – like it or not.

I also find myself in agreement with Nicholas Wheeler's assessment: that while NATO should be brought to task for bypassing the Security Council, the Council, by its own inaction, equally undermined the legitimacy of the UN as a force for peace and security in the world. Three Security Council resolutions (1160, 1199, and 1203) were adopted recognizing human rights abuses in Kosovo. 'Consequently,' argues Wheeler, 'having willed the ends of policy, the Security Council was failing in its duty by not willing the military means to implement the demands in the face of persistent non-compliance' (Wheeler, 2001: 119). The international system is not perfect, and while one does not want to see an out-of-control United States wreaking havoc on the world stage, NATO is – rightly or wrongly – filling gaps in the UN's international security framework. Rather than condemn it, we should applaud its goals, but continue to express concern (and outrage if need be) over its more objectionable methods.

## Conclusion

The United States committed many abhorrent acts during Operation Allied Force, and bore a greater part of the responsibility for NATO's activities in the campaign, some of which stood in violation of the Geneva

Conventions. Nevertheless, there was a very real humanitarian catastrophe in Kosovo which the UN was unwilling to solve, due largely to Chinese and Russian objections. NATO spent billions of dollars attempting to defuse a conflict which had little strategic import for the United States. While the use of DU weapons and cluster bombs should be denounced, as well as the destruction of civilian infrastructure and the killing of civilians, the situation could have been much worse than it was. We can be thankful that the atrocities of the first Gulf War were not repeated in Kosovo and Yugoslavia as a whole. Clinton's fire in 1999 – fortunately – did not mirror that ignited by George H.W. Bush nine years earlier.

## Notes

1. The 19 specific charges can be found in Appendix III of Clark, 1992: 264–5.
2. For a summation of Parenti's case see, Parenti, 2000: 110–13.
3. The figure of 30,000 was first claimed by Hashim Thaci at Rambouillet. See Daalder and O'Hanlon, 2000: 151.
4. Estimates vary, however. Parenti gives a figure of 200,000 (2000, 157, 161); Daalder and O'Hanlon claim 100,000 (2000: 177).
5. Mason (1999) also argues that the United Nations Security Council had to be bypassed, because for domestic reasons (namely Chechnya, Tibet, and Taiwan) neither Russia nor China would have agreed to the campaign.
6. For a more complete discussion, see Parenti, 2000: 116–17.
7. This was an argument made recently by former National Security Advisor Anthony Lake in his 6 Nightmares: Real Threats in a Dangerous World and How America Can Meet Them (Lake, 2000: 162–3).

## References

Bardos, G. (2001). Country files: Yugoslavia: Annual report 2000: The end of the Milo-sevic regime. *Transitions Online*, 16 August. http://archive.tol.cz/frartic/yugar00.html.
——— (1999). Country files: Yugoslavia: Annual report 1999: War, intervention, and anarchy. *Transitions Online*. http://archive.tol.cz/countries/yugar99.html.
Bassett, R. (1999). Balkan endgame? *Jane's Defence Weekly*, 31 March.
BBC News (2001a). Depleted uranium: EU concern grows. 6 January.
——— (2001b). NI Balkan vets offered health tests. 9 January.
——— (2001c). Call for cluster bomb ban. 8 August.
——— (2001d). Fresh fears over depleted uranium. 12 April.
——— (2001e). WHO studies depleted uranium in Iraq. 23 August.
——— (2000a). Nato reveals Kosovo depleted uranium use. 22 March.
——— (2000b). UK Kosovo role slammed: The contribution of air strikes was 'at best marginal.' 24 October.
——— (1999a). Nato bomb caused Gurkha deaths. 22 June.
——— (1999b). Q&A: Counting Kosovo's dead. 12 November.

———— (1999c). Horrors of Kosovo revealed: Mass graves containing the bodies of Kosovo Albanians have been discovered. 6 December.

———— (1999d). Depleted uranium ban demanded. 17 December.

Biddle, S. (1996). Victory misunderstood: What the Gulf War tells us about the future of conflict. *International Security* 21, no. 2 (Fall): 142–3.

Black, I., and Borger, J. (1999). Serbs remain defiant as the missile attacks go on. *The Guardian*, 26 March.

Borger, J. (1999). Misjudging Milosevic. *Guardian*, 19 April.

Borger, J., and Taylor-Norton, R. (1999). Belgrade in week four of the war they thought would be over in four days. *Guardian*, 19 April.

Boyes, R., and Wright, E. (1999). Drugs money linked to the Kosovo rebels. *The Times*, 24 March.

Chomsky, N. (2000). *Rogue states: The rule of force in world affairs*. London: Pluto Press.

Clark, R. (1992). *The fire this time: U.S. war crimes in the Gulf*. New York: Thunder's Mouth Press.

Crace, J. (1999). Fifty years and counting. *Guardian* Education, 20 April.

Daalder, I., and O'Hanlon, M. (2000). *Winning ugly: NATO's war to save Kosovo*. Washington, DC: Brookings Institution Press.

Dinmore, G. (1999). Federal republic at risk of splitting. *Financial Times*, 25 March.

Evans, M.(1999). CIA planners failed to check the phone book. *The Times*, 10 May.

Fisk, R. (1999). 'Collateral damage' lies dying in a shattered Belgrade hospital. *Independent*, 14 April.

Freedman, L. (1999). The future of international politics in the wake of Kosovo. *Jane's Defence Weekly*, 21 July.

Gott, R. (1999). Stop the war. Nato should lose. *Guardian*, 10 April.

Graham, B. (2001). Mass grave trail leads to Milosevic. *Sunday Times*, 17 June.

Greenberg, R. (2000). U.S. policy in the Balkans. In M. Honey and T. Barry, eds, *Global focus: U.S. foreign policy at the turn of the millennium*. London: Palgrave Macmillan.

Guruita, B. (1999). The price of acquiescence. *Transitions Online*, 7 October. http://archive.tol.cz/oct99/theprice.html.

Hartung, W., and Kaufman, R. (2000). NATO expands east. In M. Honey et al., eds, *Global Focus*. London: Palgrave Macmillan.

Helm, T. (1999). Pilot knew he had hit train on bridge but fired again. *Daily Telegraph*, 14 April.

Hitchens, C. (2001). *The trial of Henry Kissinger*. London: Verso.

Holbrooke, R. (1998). *To end a war*. New York: Random House.

Human Rights Watch (2000a). Civilian deaths in the Nato air campaign. *Human Rights Watch Reports* 12, no. 1 (February). www.hrw.org/reports/2000/nato/.

———— (2000b). World report 2000: Federal Republic of Yugoslavia. www.hrw.org/wr2k/Eca-26.htm.

———— (1999). NATO's use of cluster munitions in Yugoslavia. Human Rights Watch Backgrounder, 11 May. www.hrw.org/reports/1999/nato2/index.htm#TopOfPage.

Hyland, W. (1999). *Clinton's world: Remaking American foreign policy*. London: Praeger.

Ignatieff, M. (2000). *Virtual war: Kosovo and beyond*. London: Vintage.

Jovanovski, V. (2001). Macedonia: NATO deploys. *Transitions Online*, 16 August. www.tol.cz.week.html.

Judah, T. (2000). *Kosovo: War and revenge*. New Haven, CT: Yale University Press.

Karadjov, C. (1999). Cashing in on cooperation. *Transitions Online*, 9 October. http://archive.tol.cz/oct99/cashing.html.

Kirby, A. (2001). Q&A: Depleted uranium weapons. *BBC News*, 4 January.

———— (1999). Depleted uranium 'threatens Balkan cancer epidemic.' *BBC News*, 30 July.

Kroeger, A. (2001). Depleted uranium: Bosnia tests start. *BBC News*, 25 January.

Lake, A. (2000). *6 nightmares: Real threats in a dangerous world and how Americans can meet them*. Boston: Little, Brown.

Little, A. (2000). Behind the Kosovo crisis. BBC News, 12 March.

Lobel, J., and Ratner, M. (2000). Humanitarian intervention: A dangerous doctrine. In M. Honey et al., eds, *Global Focus*. London: Palgrave Macmillan.

Lykourezos, A. (1999). Before the prosecutor of the International Criminal Tribunal for the former Yugoslavia: Complaint charging NATO's political and military leaders and all responsible NATO personnel with grave breaches of the Geneva Convention of 1949 and violations of the laws and customs of war. Athens, 3 May. www.nato-warcrimes.gr/html/eng/readit.html#.

Marcus, J. (2000). Analysis: Why use cluster bombs? *BBC News*, 8 August.

Mason, B. (1999). Kosovo: The lessons and the winners. *BBC News*, 11 June.

Norton-Taylor, R. (1999). Weighing the military options. *Guardian*, 11 May.

O'Kane, M. (1999a). One man in the bullseye. *Guardian*, 10 April.

———— (1999b). Bitter view in eye of storm. *Guardian*, 20 April.

Parenti, M. (2000). *To kill a nation: The attack on Yugoslavia*. London: Verso.

Reuters (2001a). Macedonian peace plan announced. *The Press*, 14 August.

———— (2001b). Rebels agree to disarm to Nato. *The Press*, 16 August.

———— (2001c). Nato mulls wider Macedonia role. *The Press*, 20 August.

Shawcross, W. (2001). *Deliver us from evil: Warlords and peacekeepers in a world of endless conflict*. London: Bloomsbury.

Stojkovic, D. (2001). Unearthing the recent past. *Transitions Online*, 19 June. http://balkanreport.tol.cz/look/BRR/article.

Transitions Online (2001a). Sinking evidence. 28 May. http://balkanreport.tol.cz/look/BRR/article.

———— (2001b). Guilty of genocide. 7 August. http://balkanreport.tol.cz/look/BRR/article.

Valasek, T. (2000). Nato at 50. In M. Honey et al., eds, *Global Focus*. London: Palgrave Macmillan.

Vonnegut, K. (1974). *Wampeters, Foma & Granfalloons: Opinions*. New York: Dell.

Walker, M., et al. (1999). The moment a pilot had to decide. *Guardian*, 20 April.

Wheeler, N.J. (2001). Humanitarian intervention after Kosovo: Emergent norm, moral duty or the coming anarchy? *International Affairs* 77, no. 1: 113–28.

Wolf, J., and Smith, H. (1999). Yugoslavia takes Nato to court for genocide. *Guardian*, 11 May.

Wood, N. (2000). Kosovo mine expert criticises NATO. *BBC News*, 23 May.

# 17

# Collateral Damage:
# The Human Cost of Structural Violence

## Peter G. Prontzos

If poverty is not a result of nature, then great is our sin.

*Charles Darwin*

When almost 3,000 people were killed in the criminal attacks on the World Trade Center and the Pentagon, the United States mobilized immense resources in the name of fighting terrorism. On top of an initial $396.1 billion allocated for the military in fiscal year 2003 (Council for a Livable World, 2002: 1), Washington added $40 billion in additional spending after 11 September. In July 2002, Congress authorized another $28.9 billion 'to fight terrorism' (*Vancouver Sun*, 2002b).[1]

Other governments followed the US lead. The justification offered for these expenditures was the need to prevent the unnecessary deaths of more innocent people. However, as United Nations Secretary-General Kofi Annan points out, *every year* 'more than 10 million children still die from mostly preventable diseases' – over 27,000 per day, more than nine times the number of victims of September 11 (UNICEF, 2002: 6). And *every day*, more than 16,000 children under the age of 5 die from lack of food alone – a figure that is more than five times the number of victims of the terrorism of September 11. To be precise:

> Every five seconds, somewhere in the world, a child dies as a result of malnutrition. That is 700 every hour ... 6 million every year. The world has enough food to nourish these children and enough income to afford to nourish them, but their own families or states do not have enough income. *They die, ultimately, from poverty*. Consider that in the same five seconds in which another child dies this way, the world spends $125,000 on military forces. A thousandth of that amount would save the child's life. (Goldstein, 2003: 457, emphasis added)

In other words, in the year following the attacks of 9/11, another 16 million children perished from *easily preventable* diseases and hunger – but there was no global mobilization to prevent this holocaust. The word 'holocaust,' with its echo of the Nazi genocide against Jews and others, is appropriate for many reasons, not the least of which is the number of victims. Every year, as many children die from lack of food as the total number of Jews exterminated by the Nazis. And this silent 'kindercide' is repeated incessantly, year in and year out.

These deaths, however, are the result not of war or of nature, but of *structural violence*, deleterious conditions that derive from economic and political structures of power, created and maintained by human actions and institutions. Like the use of military force which results in un-intentional death and injury to civilians, the 'collateral damage' to people and the natural world that is inflicted by structural violence is an un-intentional side-effect of specific policies designed to increase the wealth of transnational financial institutions and corporations. While less dramatic than military violence, structural violence actually accounts for far more deaths than does war.[2] The number of deaths in an average year from all structural causes is a matter of conjecture, but it probably totals over 50 million – the total in almost six years of combat in the Second World War. And just as in armed conflict, the cost of structural violence must be measured not only by the death count, but by the number and severity of all its casualties.

Structural violence can be both political and economic, lethal and non-lethal. Political examples include discrimination on the basis of race, reli-gion, and gender (e.g. against blacks in apartheid-era South Africa and Kurds in Turkey today; towards Catholics in Northern Ireland; and against women everywhere). The forms of economic structural violence, how-ever, are even more varied and destructive than the political kind. For instance, 'the number of people living on less than $1 per day – about 1.2 billion – has grown since the mid-1980s.' These people 'live in utter, abject poverty, without access to basic nutrition or health care…. [And over 3 billion human beings,] half of all people globally have incomes of less than $2 a day' (Goldstein, 2003: 456–7). They often suffer a range of injurious conditions, such as overwork (or, conversely, unemployment); lack of clean water; vulnerability to disease; inadequate housing; little or no medical care; and limited or no access to education. A human being who dies from hunger is just as much a casualty as a soldier felled by enemy fire.

People living in the rich countries are also often victims of economic structural violence, even if it is not always as flagrant as in the developing world. To take one example more or less at random, an analysis of fifteen studies, all from the United States, examined 26,000 hospitals and 38 million patients. The result: private for-profit ownership of hospitals, in comparison with not-for-profit ownership, results in a *higher risk of death for patients*' (Devereaux, 2002: 1399, emphasis added). One might also point to the thousands of workers who are injured or killed on the job each year; the millions of people who die annually from air pollution in both developed and underdeveloped countries; and the number of people who succumb every year to such preventable scourges as malaria and tuberculosis (1.7 million each) (Results Canada, 2002: 2).

This chapter will explore the nature and scope of some of the most significant problems associated with structural violence, along with the relatively minor costs that would be necessary to address and reduce them. It then considers the forces, especially the Western-dominated global economic structure of neoliberal capitalism, that have both created the sources of structural violence and now resist their reduction. The conclusion briefly considers possible strategies to reduce the damage that structural violence inflicts on both human beings and our environment.

It is impossible to overemphasize one fundamental truth: there are no longer any material reasons for scarcity in the modern world. As I hope to show, we have had the knowledge, resources, and technology for decades (at least) to construct a rational and humane world order in which no one goes hungry; is denied medical care; suffers harm or death from poisons in his or her environment and food; lacks clean water, decent housing, and education – and so on. Structural violence, then, more than anything results from decisions made by people in power. The suffering and death that result are neither natural nor inevitable.

## Examples of structural violence

The lives of billions of human beings can fairly be described as 'nasty, brutish, and short.' Consider the kind of desperate circumstances, so alien to the world of privilege, described in this report:

> a pipeline explosion and fire killed 250 villagers in southern Nigeria, as they were scooping up spilled gasoline with buckets ... Villagers hurriedly organized a mass burial for 50 of the charred victims, including many who dived into a nearby river with their clothes on fire ... Piles of scorched bodies lay near the pipeline in this village ... close to the Niger Delta town of Jesse, where about 1,000 people died in a similar disaster in 1998. (Reuters, 2000)

Extreme poverty drove people to take these chances in order to make a few extra dollars, even though they were well aware of the horrible fate that had befallen their neighbors just two years previously. (A similar catastrophe occurred in 2003.)

Or consider the story of Bangon Phallak, a Thai woman who had to confront a terrible dilemma: 'What does her four-year-old daughter need more, food or a mother?' As the *New York Times* reported:

> Mrs. Bangon, a gentle woman whose soft face is framed by thick black hair, explained that the family cannot afford both ... her husband has lost his job as a construction worker, and so the family earns only a trickle of cash through odd jobs in this tiny village in northeastern Thailand. That money can be used to buy rice and milk for the little girl, Saiyamon, who has become anemic and malnourished. Or Mrs. Bangon can try to save the tattered small-denomination bills for a stomach operation that she needs to save her own life. For now, Mrs. Bangon has chosen to spend the money on Saiyamon. She herself has already lived for 32 years, she reasons, and what would be the point of preserving a mother at the cost of a child? (Kristof, 1998)

These vignettes are, tragically, not exceptional. Rather, they are indicative of the common dilemma of the majority of humanity who, through no fault of their own, cannot earn enough money to meet basic needs. Again, this is not a dilemma limited to the poor. Even in the wealthiest country on earth, the United States, which is 'the only Western country without universal health care, nearly 12 million ... children have no medical coverage' (*Globe and Mail*, 2002). (Over 30 million adults are also not covered by health insurance in the US.)

While it is difficult to grasp the enormity of this problem, the following sample conveys some sense of the human dimensions of structural violence. (All figures are in US dollars unless otherwise noted; some of the statistics overlap.)

- The number of human beings who try to live on less than $1 per day has risen to more than 1.2 billion (*CCPA Monitor*, 2002b: 3).
- The number of human beings who try to live on less than $2 per day has risen to over 2.8 billion (Results Canada, 2002: 1).
- The number of people in the majority ['third'] world who are chronically malnourished stands at over 800 million (Results Canada, 2002: 3). Meanwhile, 'Despite a decade-long economic boom, every fifth child in the United States still lives in poverty' (Koring, 2000). (Washington has refused to ratify the UN Convention on the Rights of the Child.)
- 'Breathing polluted air in major cities is as dangerous as long-term exposure to second-hand cigarette smoke.' Air pollution in major cities, primarily from the burning of fossil fuels, is linked to such killers as lung cancer, heart disease, strokes, and childhood asthma (Mittelstaedt, 2002).

- Over 2.4 billion people lack access to basic sanitation (Results Canada, 2002: 3).
- 'More than one billion people have no access to clean water,' according to the World Health Organization (2001a).
- Every year, 5.3 million people die from unsafe water (Results Canada, 2002: 3).
- The global supply of water is also threatened: 'the US intelligence community concludes that, by 2015, nearly half of the world's population − more than three billion people − will be in countries lacking sufficient water' (*Globe and Mail*, 2001).
- Every day, 1,600 women die giving birth, a form of gendercide that totals almost 600,000 each year. 'For every woman who dies, approximately 30 more incur injuries, infections, and disabilities.' Poverty alone does not explain this problem. The Cuban medical system has reduced maternal mortality to 2.4 per 10,000 births, almost the rate in North America. Adam Jones notes that the total cost of funding 'Cuba's grass-roots approach' on a global scale 'would be US $200 million, about the price of a half dozen jet fighters' (Jones, 1999−2000).
- More than 40 million people have HIV/AIDS, and 22 million have already died from this preventable disease − 3 million in 2001 alone (Results Canada, 2002: 2).
- 'World-wide, some 50,000 people die *every day* as a result of poor shelter, polluted water, and inadequate sanitation' (*CCPA Monitor*, 2002b: 3, emphasis added).
- 'Tobacco use in all forms is responsible for about 30% of all cancer deaths in developed countries and a rapidly rising proportion in developing countries ... and cigarette smoking in particular is encouraged by the marketing activities of national and multinational tobacco companies' (World Health Organization, 2002). WHO reports that the death toll from smoking is 'now 4.9 million a year' (*Vancouver Sun*, 2002a).
- 'Most of the Earth's people will be on the losing side' of the effects of global warming, according to a UN panel on climate change (Canadian Broadcasting Corporation, 2001). The results of increasing greenhouse gas emissions will include: rising sea levels, threatening densely populated coastal areas with massive flooding; the melting of polar icecaps, perhaps in as little as twenty-five years; reduced crop yields leading to rising malnutrition; huge economic costs; disruption of natural ecosystems, promoting the spread of 'infectious diseases like malaria and yellow fever as the mosquito and other insect vectors move north and south from the tropics' (Recer, 2002); and large-scale loss of life. 'Global warming may have killed between 50,000 and 100,000 people in the past three years and made up to 300 million people homeless.... The

extreme weather ... has had its greatest impact in developing nations, which produce only 20% of the world's carbon dioxide.' (Canadian Broadcasting Corporation, 2001).

These scenarios, diverse as they are, present only a partial picture of the toll of structural violence. Such violence also wreaks havoc, for example, when people are too exhausted from overwork to care for their families; when they are too poor to purchase medical care; when children are neglected; when stress leads to heart attacks and other illnesses; when rising unemployment increases family violence; when more people find themselves homeless; when family farms disappear due to competition with agribusiness; and when people die because the pharmaceuticals they need are not properly tested, or are too expensive.[3] Also, when 'natural' disasters such as hurricanes and earthquakes strike, they are much more devastating to people in poor countries and poor communities, which disproportionately lack both the wealth and the infrastructure (health services, communications, well-built housing, and so on) to withstand nature's assault. And there is another, more subtle connection between the violence we inflict on the environment and the effects on human health: 'Almost one-third of the global burden of disease can be attributed to environmental risk factors' (World Health Organization, 2001b).

The connections between structural violence and state violence also merit consideration. James K. Galbraith and George Purcell reviewed 'the relationship between various forms of state violence – including war, revolution, civil violence, and *coups d'état* – and a measure of inequality'. They found, among other things, 'a connection between two phenomena that intuitively and theoretically should be connected' (Galbraith and Purcell, 2001: 211). One particularly striking example of the connection between increasing inequality and poverty on the one hand, and violence on the other, was the genocide in the former Yugoslavia. Harvard economic historian Robert Allen contends that:

> The International Monetary Fund (IMF) and World Bank imposed various macro-economic reforms and structural adjustment programs on the country that first checked economic expansion and after 1990 led to widespread collapse and unemployment. (Allen, 1999: 5)

Allen holds that the violence in Yugoslavia (and later in Kosovo, which served as the excuse for the subsequent US/NATO bombing of Serbia in 1999), was the result, to a significant extent, of the insecurity, fear, and nationalism that followed in the wake of the economic implosion.[4]

## Addressing the crisis

The problems wholly or partly due to structural violence are legion, and the sheer scope of the effort required to tackle them might seem over-whelming. There are, however, important signs of progress in a number of areas. One example is the number of children who die annually from preventable diseases. This figure dropped from 12.7 million in 1990 to about 10 million in 2000 (UNICEF, 2002). Child mortality in developing countries similarly fell, from 168 per thousand live births in 1980 to 93 per thousand in 2001 (Results Canada, 2002: 4). 'More than 175 countries are polio-free' (UNICEF, 2002), and, while 'in 1950 about 55% of the world's population lived on less than US$1 a day.... By 1992, only 24% of the world's population had to make do with that tiny amount' (Cienski, 2002). At the same time, however, more people are poor now than at any other time, and there is no reason to expect the numbers to decrease.

Given the massive global wealth that already exists, the amount of additional resources needed to sharply reduce levels of structural violence worldwide is only a small percentage of what is available today. The un-precedented rise in productivity in the twentieth century means that 'we are now producing almost five times per person what our ancestors pro-duced in 1900' (Little, 2000). Another way to view this opportunity is to examine the growth of per capita gross domestic product (GDP) over the last thirty years. By 1998, the per capita GDP of the richest countries had increased significantly compared with 1973. In this period alone, the wealth of Western Europe was up over 55 per cent; Canada, the United States, Australia, and New Zealand averaged growth of over 61 per cent; while Japan's average wealth per person increased by over 78 per cent. For the world as a whole, the increase in wealth measured by per capita GDP grew from $4,104 to $5,709 (in 1990 dollars) – an increase of almost 40 per cent (Lee, 2002: 2, Table 1). These rapid rises prompt serious questions about the rationalizations offered by neoliberal governments for the dramatic reductions in foreign aid to poor countries, especially since the end of the Cold War (whatever happened to the 'peace dividend'?). They also reduce the credibility of claims by diverse governments that they are no longer wealthy enough to finance the wide-ranging domestic social programs established after the Second World War, such as old-age pensions, public health programs, unemployment insurance, and low-cost post-secondary education.

Paradoxically, increased productivity and wealth have coincided with increased inequality. The years 1973–98, for instance, witnessed growing economic differences among the world's regions. The difference in per capita GDP between the regions with highest income and those with the lowest increased from 13:1 to 19:1 (Lee, 2002). More dramatically, the United Nations *Human Development Report* for 1999 showed that, while in 1960 'the top 20% of the world's people in the richest countries had 30 times the income (in terms of total GDP) of the poorest 20% ... By 1997, the top 20% received 74 times the income of the bottom 20%' (Lee, 2002). One of the more striking inequalities shows up in figures for 1997: the income of the richest 1 per cent of the earth's population was equal to the total income of the poorest 57 per cent – about 3.5 billion people (Rees, 2002).

Even China, which has boasted high economic growth rates for many years, has witnessed a dramatic increase in inequality between the lucky minority and the great majority of citizens, such as the astonishing 200 million Chinese who are either unemployed or underemployed, including 'the approximately 100 million dispossessed known in China as the "floating population"' (Cernetig, 2000).

These growing disparities are found *within* the most developed nations as well. The gap between the rich and almost everyone else in the G7 countries, even the US, Britain, and Canada, has been widening for years. US government studies found that, in the richest country on earth, 'the rich are getting richer and the poor are getting poorer,' especially low-income families. But the middle class is falling behind as well. 'By the "mid-1990s, there were 40 states where the gap between the highest-income 20 per cent and of families and the middle 20 per cent of families with children was larger than it has been"' since the 1970s. 'The long term trend towards increasing inequality has continued over the past decade *despite the sustained economic growth* ... [and] the widening income gap may get worse' (Koring, 1997, emphasis added). Indeed, by 2002, the Census Bureau confirmed that the situation had deteriorated, and that another '1.3 million Americans slipped below the government's official poverty line ... the first increase since 1993.' Perhaps coincidentally, the Bureau noted that, 'In terms of class breakdown, only households with incomes above $150,000 were able to post gains, with the greatest losses ... occurring at the bottom of the income ladder' (Pearlstein, 2002). Moreover,

- 'The financial wealth of the top 1% of US households now exceeds the combined household financial wealth of the bottom 95%. The share of the nation's after-tax income received by the top 1 per cent nearly doubled from 1979–1997. *By 1998, the top 1% had as much combined income as the 100 million Americans with the lowest earnings*' (Gates, 2002: 19, emphasis added).
- Conditions in the UK have also deteriorated since the introduction of the neoliberal economic policies of Margaret Thatcher (and continuing

under Tony Blair's 'New Labour'). 'More than five million people in Britain are living in conditions of absolute poverty,' with single parents the worst off, according to a 2001 study. 'Two million Britons reported going without food over the past 12 months' (Goodspeed, 2001).

- At the same time, the average worker is spending more time on the job than his or her counterpart did thirty or forty years ago, with the inevitable damage to family life and child-rearing associated with longer hours and greater stress. Health Canada reports that 50-hour work weeks are becoming 'the standard' and that one in four Canadians now has to work more than 50 hours each week, a load which approaches that found 'in the 19th century' (Jones, 2002).
- Meanwhile, in the year 2000, 'the net worth of the world's wealthiest people grew 6 per cent to a total of $27 trillion (US)' (Dixon, 2001).
- 'According to the UN, the assets of the three richest people in 1998 were larger than the combined GDP of all least developed countries' (Lee, 2002: 3).

Since there exists far more wealth in the world than is necessary to address the main economic causes of structural violence, the real problem is one of priorities and power. Consider that in the year 2000, before the increased allocations that followed the attacks of 11 September, governments around the world chose to spend $798 billion on their militaries (Results Canada, 2002; the US spends about as much as the rest of the world combined). The US/NATO bombing of Yugoslavia alone in 1999 cost approximately $50 billion, and it is likely that the war against Iraq, and the occupation that followed, will cost much more. The amount spent around the world to prevent the so-called 'Y2K bug' was in excess of $500 billion – while over $413 billion was spent on advertising in 1998 alone (*CCPA Monitor*, 1999: 9). Tens of billions of dollars have flooded into what President Eisenhower called the US 'military–industrial complex' for work on 'Star Wars' ballistic missile defense systems. The world's richest individual, Bill Gates, was worth over $58 billion in 2001.

Contrast these expenditures with the relatively tiny amounts that would be required to reduce levels of structural violence drastically. For instance, the annual additional cost of providing basic education, healthcare, food, and safe water for all of the world's people by 2015 is estimated at a paltry $38 billion. The annual cost to provide reproductive care for all women is less than a third of that sum – $12 billion. The total cost of providing vaccines to every child and preventing the 3 million 'children who die from vaccine-preventable deaths each year' would be $1.3 billion (Results Canada, 2002: 1, 4). In the real world of globalizing neoliberalism, however, between 1982 and 1999, there was 'a net transfer of $1.5 *trillion* from South to North.' (McQuaig, 1999: 9, emphasis in original). 'Meanwhile, in the year 2000, the total value of goods and services produced globally was measured at a staggering $44 trillion (Goldstein, 2003: 19). Finally, British biologists estimate that, while the money 'needed to protect and preserve the world's natural ecosystems' is around US$300 billion per year, the amount spent by governments subsidizing environmentally hazardous activities is 'up to $1,450 billion per year' (*Report on Business*, 2000).

## What is to be done?

For supporters of capitalist 'globalization,' the key to reducing inequality is for governments to get out of the way and allow market forces to create greater economic growth. This, in turn, will lead to rising prosperity for all classes and nations through 'free trade' and exercise of the principle of comparative advantage. As one recent front-page headline in the *National Post* boldly proclaimed: 'Globalization cures poverty' (Cienski, 2002).

While there are, of course, many definitions of 'globalization,' the dominant ideological paradigm is neoliberalism. 'At its core, the neoliberal approach is straightforward: simply let the market operate, get the state out of the way, privatize all the institutions you can, and leave everything to corporations and individuals interacting through the marketplace' (Langdon, 1999: 39). In this view, neo-liberal capitalism and 'free trade' are the ingredients not only for economic development, but for the establishment of freedom and democracy. Many years ago, the Nobel prizewinning US economist (and 'father' of neoliberalism), Milton Friedman, wrote that the 'kind of economic organization that provides economic freedom directly, namely, competitive capitalism, also promotes political freedom.' Friedman argued that there is no alternative to 'market democracies' (Bill Clinton's phrase), since, in his view:

> Fundamentally, there are only two ways of co-ordinating the economic activities of millions. One is central direction involving the use of coercion – the technique of the army and the modern totalitarian state. The other is voluntary co-operation of individuals – the technique of the market place. (Friedman, 1962: 13)

If it is true that the only alternative to capitalism is the 'modern totalitarian state' (e.g. the former Soviet Union and present-day North Korea), then there is no real choice at all, and perhaps we truly have arrived at the 'end of history.' To back up these claims, neoliberals point to significant improvements in human welfare, noted above. There are, however, a number of reasons, both historical and theoretical, to doubt the core propositions of global capitalism. The starting point for any honest evaluation of the system of private ownership of the means of production is the *world* capitalist system. It would be a distortion, for example, only to consider the prosperity of the wealthy core areas of the 'North,' while ignoring the less congenial conditions in the poor periphery of the South. The persistence of the extreme and growing inequalities outlined above, as well as the grinding poverty that afflicts the majority people in the world, cast serious and perhaps fatal doubt on the efficacy of the market as a long-term solution. Thus, while the percentage of the world's population who try to survive on less than US$1 per day has decreased, the total number of people living in absolute poverty has continued to rise. Given the failure of global capitalism over the past two hundred years to fulfill its promise of prosperity for most people under its domination, it takes a monumental leap of faith to believe that the future will bring a profound change for the better. More importantly, one might question whether it is right for those of us who are relatively well off to expect today's victims of structural violence to wait patiently in the hope that, decades from now, prosperity might at long last 'trickle down' to them; that their grandchildren might not die from malnutrition or preventable disease, and might live long enough to enjoy the 'privileges' (safe and sufficient food, medical care, education) that only a minority now enjoys. James Laxer has pointed out that

> The defenders of today's predatory capitalism have to contort themselves to make the claim that the system they advocate is the best way to meet the needs and aspirations of humanity.... Capitalism works best for a small minority of the world's people, condemns hundreds of millions to exploitation and a stunted existence, and leaves billions, particularly in the Third World, in a state of poverty or near-poverty. (Laxer, 1998: 249)

The capitalist imperative to reap profit at almost any cost is reinforced by the necessity to grow or die. Any business that cannot expand and compete will eventually succumb to other corporate sharks that are more single-minded and powerful. These twin imperatives of profit and competition are constant and essential features of the private sector, and account for the growing inequality in the world. Businesses that ignore the market imperatives of putting competition and growth ahead of all social and environmental considerations will not survive. Milton Friedman, for instance, denounced concern for 'any social responsibility other than to make as much money as possible' (Winter, 1992: 106). As Frank Stronach, CEO of Magna International, admitted: 'Profit means money. Money has no heart, no soul, no conscience, no homeland' (Hurtig, 1991: 196).

Canadian philosopher John McMurtry sums up this central contradiction of neoliberal capitalism as follows:

However many millions or billions of society's or the world's human population are misemployed, underemployed, or starvation-waged with not enough to live on, and however life-destructive and chronically debilitating their hours and conditions of work are – a majority of the world altogether – there is no principle, norm or standard in neo-classical market theory or global market practice which recognizes or can recognize any of these depredations of human life as an issue or a problem.... This is because only humans with sufficient money-demand to purchase corporate products are recognized by this global system as possessing any right to access any good – from food to water to housing, health care, or whatever else. (McMurtry, 2002: 2–3)

It is obvious that structural violence could be significantly reduced if production were primarily oriented towards products and services that met human needs. As mentioned, the potential to establish the conditions for a more humane and egalitarian society has existed for a long time. Almost one hundred years ago, Bertrand Russell observed that:

with the help of science, and by the elimination of the vast amount of un-productive work involved in internal and international competition, the whole community could be kept in comfort by means of four hours work a day.... We may assume that there would no longer be unproductive labour spent on arma-ments ... advertisements, [and] costly luxuries for the very rich. (Russell, 1977: 143, 152)

In other words, poverty, the loss of opportunity for individual develop-ment, and the lack of free time, in both richer and poorer countries, are utterly unnecessary. The problem of global hunger exemplifies the paradox: 'food production is not determined necessarily by the global *need* for food, it is determined by the market for food, that is how many people have the means to pay for it,' in the words of Richard Robbins. He concludes 'that the poverty that causes hunger is a consequence of global economic forces, such as the financial debt that peripheral countries ac-cumulated' (Robbins, 2002: 172, 193). Hunger and poverty, then, result from the choices that some people have the power to make. They are neither natural nor necessary. Instead, as Murray Bookchin pointed out in 1971, we have the potential to become a 'post-scarcity' global community: .

Until very recently, human society developed around the brute issues posed by unavoidable material scarcity.... The great historic splits that destroyed early organic societies ... had their origins in the problems of survival, in problems that involved the mere maintenance of human existence. Material scarcity pro-vided the historic rationale for the development of the patriarchal family, pri-vate property, class domination, and the state.... We in this century have finally opened the prospect of material abundance for all to enjoy – sufficiency in the means of life without the need for grinding, day-to-day toil.... [However] ... the word 'post-scarcity' means fundamentally more than a mere abundance of the means of life: it decidedly includes the kind of life these means support.

The human relationships and psyche of the individual in a post-scarcity society must fully reflect the freedom, security and self-expression that this abundance makes possible. (Bookchin, 1977: 9–10)

Such a social reconstruction will not happen, in Bookchin's view, as long as the great majority of people have little or no power – political, social, and economic – to ensure that their needs are met. As long as political and economic elites are allowed to set priorities that protect and enhance their own profits and power, significant change to remedy problems with both the global political economy and the environment will be impossible. The alternative to elite domination is authentic democracy embracing all aspects of social, political, and *economic* life. I stress economic democracy because, without control of the means of production, of their own labor power, and of the means to sustain themselves and their communities, a majority of citizens will find it difficult to resist those who do control the means of life. The power that flows directly from this wealth, such as backing for friendly politicians and political parties and control over the mass media, gives the 'power elite' an undemocratic advantage in ensuring that their ambitions for even greater wealth and power receive priority. That is why the struggle for democracy has always been a struggle against the power of wealth. Looked at in another way, 'Democracy is the most powerful tool for social change history has ever seen' (Rebick, 2000: 43).

The same lack of substantial democracy confronts those seeking to protect our natural environment. Is there a fundamental flaw in an economic system, the only goal of which is the accumulation of private profit, while objectives like protecting the biosphere must always be secondary and derivative? Is it a coincidence that those interests that most strongly oppose meaningful attempts to reduce global warming through the reduction of greenhouse gases are the very same businesses that profit the most from the wasteful burning of fossil fuels? The global water supply is the next major target of transnationals. This essential resource, according to *Fortune* magazine, 'promises to be to the 21st century what oil was to the 20th century: the precious commodity that determines the wealth of nations' (Barlow and Clarke, 2002: 104). Seizing control of water supplies in both industrial countries (e.g. Britain) and poor countries (e.g. Bolivia) is already causing massive problems and even deaths, as residents fight to preserve their access to water (Palast, 2002). Meanwhile, the accelerating destruction of the earth's natural habitat is one reason why '[o]ne in eight of the world's bird species and one in four of its mammals are threatened with extinction' (Read, 2002). In particular, '[e]very single species and subspecies of great ape on the planet now teeters on the edge of dying out, part of the acceleration of the dinosaur-style mass extinction now under way' (Mitchell, 2002).

The major sources of these problems, once again, are the neoliberal dogmas that now dominate the global economy. Peter Victor of York University writes:

> Conventional economics either ignores the environment or treats it as an appendage to the economy.... In ecological economics, the economy is seen as a subsystem of society, which, in turn, is a subsystem of the biosphere. Climate change is just one example of what happens when economies operate as if the other systems to which they are related do not matter. (Victor, 2002)

Dr William Rees of the University of British Columbia argues that two unsustainable economic myths are driving us towards social and environmental disaster. One is the belief that we can achieve unlimited economic expansion through liberalized trade without irrevocably damaging the biosphere. Rees contends that it is logically impossible to have infinite economic growth in a finite environment, and that orthodox neoliberal economic theory fails to factor in both the economic contribution to economies that derive from the natural world, on the one hand, and the harm being inflicted upon the environment, on the other. Capitalism treats nature as an infinite resource and an infinite garbage dump. Its only value, as Locke wrote, is as a source of economic utility. The late Ralph Miliband summed up the reasons for capitalism's obsession with profit and lack of concern for any other values: 'Capitalism is above all about private profit; and this ... is not compatible with a good life for all. For capitalism is essentially driven by the *micro-rationality* of the firm, not by the *macro-rationality* required by society' (Miliband, 1994: 12–13). Paradoxically, the micro-rationality of the firm and of the market can only be sustained by its supposed nemesis, the state. For instance, the Earth Council recently estimated that 'in four sectors alone – water, energy, transport and agriculture – more than $700 billion dollars a year is spent on subsidizing practices that are environmentally and socially damaging' (Strong, 2000). Merely ending such illiberal practices would benefit humanity and the environment, while a fraction of that wealth, redirected to human needs, could fuel progress that would border on the miraculous.

Rees also takes issue with the liberal notion that maximizing one's utilities – that is, owning more things and acquiring more wealth – is the only measure of personal well-being. In his view, once a certain point of material satisfaction is reached, the focus on amassing greater wealth results in diminishing returns. In addition, the pathological drive to have more and more 'stuff' undermines other values that contribute significantly to one's well-being, such as clean air, time for family and friends, safe streets, lower stress, learning, enjoying the natural world, and so on.

For Bookchin, 'the idea of dominating nature is not inherent in the human species' but springs largely from the 'domination of human by human,' which developed in conditions of economic scarcity even before the rise of distinct economic classes (Bookchin, 1999, Overview). Specifically, he believes that any

> attempt to solve the environmental crisis within a bourgeois framework must be dismissed as chimerical. Capitalism is inherently anti-ecological. Competition and accumulation constitute its very law of life, a law which Marx pungently summarized in the phrase, 'production for the sake of production.' (Bookchin, 1971: 16)

James O'Connor is a socialist who has written extensively on the connections between the global political economy and the environment, and the intimate connections between crises in both spheres. He points out that

> the vitality of Western capitalism since World War II has been based on the massive externalization of the social and ecological costs of production. Since the slowdown of world economic growth in the mid-1970s, the concerns of both socialism and ecology have become more pressing than ever before.... The accumulation of global capital ... has produced ever more devastating effects, not only on wealth and income distribution ... but also on the environment.... Given the relatively slow rate of growth of worldwide market demand since the mid-1970s, capitalist enterprises have been less able to defend or restore profits by expanding their markets and selling more commodities.... Instead, global capitalism has attempted to rescue itself from its deepening crisis by cutting costs, raising the rate of exploitation of labour, and depleting and exhausting resources. (O'Connor, 1993: 20–21)

While Adam Smith could not foresee, in the late 1700s, the degree to which the natural world would be threatened by industrial capitalism, he did object to the negative effects that unrestrained economic greed, and especially the division of labor, were already having on most workers:

> The understandings of the greater part of men are necessarily formed by their ordinary employments [so that] the man whose life is spent performing a few simple operations ... has no occasion to exert his understanding ... and generally becomes as stupid and ignorant as it is possible for a human creature to be.... But in every improved and civilized society this is the state into which the laboring poor, that is, the great body of the people, must necessarily fall unless government takes pains to prevent it. (Cited in Chomsky, 1993)

Smith had it right, even for poor countries. For instance, in 2001, Kofi Annan praised the Cuban model, saying that it 'demonstrates how much nations can do with the resources they have if they focus on the right priorities – health, education and literacy' (quoted in Deen, 2000). Looking north, a study in the *British Medical Journal* that compared death rates in Canada and the US 'found that income inequality was a significant explanatory variable ... that lead[s] to lower mortality rates [in Canada] than in the United States' (Koch, 2000). A more recent report by Statistics Canada confirmed this important conclusion, finding 'that the difference in lifespan between low-income and high-income Canadians has declined significantly since 1971 ... the year universal medicare ... was put into place across the country.... Analysts said other programs aimed at creating income equity and improving early childhood development have also helped.' Interestingly, one of the authors pointed out that 'the life expectancy in our *poorest* neighbourhoods is still higher than the *average* life expectancy in the US' (Mickleburgh, 2002, emphasis added).

In the wake of 11 September 2001, we have read and heard a great deal about the supposed 'root causes' of terrorism. Several points need to be stressed. First, the self-serving position of the Bush administration, that the source of terror is simply 'evildoers' who hate freedom and democracy, is too farcical to merit serious comment. Second, religious fanaticism, inequality, poverty, and misery are not the only sources of terror. The frequent and bloody use of military force by the United States not only outrages many throughout the world; Washington's resort to force is seen as a model – a way for terrorists to 'justify' their own depredations. As 'unrealistic' as it sounds, suppose that the United States (and the other G7 nations), in the aftermath of 11 September, had honestly pledged to provide additional billions of dollars in real development aid to the world's poor, to open up their markets, and to take other steps to tackle poverty, instead of increasing military spending and attacking other countries. Which course would most likely reduce future terrorist atrocities and needless killings? Which course would be more ethical?

Third, as many of the case studies in this book demonstrate, the United States itself has been one of the most significant perpetrators of terrorism – from the crimes against native peoples in the republic's early days, through to more contemporary actions, such as its ardent support for a host of brutal client states and allies (including, until 1990, Saddam Hussein); its terrorist attacks and economic embargo against Cuba ('economic genocide,' according to Pope John Paul II); the slaughter of over 3 million people in Vietnam; the bombing of Yugoslavia, and so on. Such policies, along with the Bush doctrine of permanent US global military dominance and unilateral 'preventive' war, more than justify Nelson Mandela's claim that 'the attitude of the United States of America is a threat to world peace' (*Globe and Mail*, 2002). As US policy towards Iran,

Guatemala, Vietnam, Chile, Nicaragua, and many other nations has demonstrated, Washington will not tolerate independent governments which put the needs of their own citizens ahead of US corporate and political interests.

## Globalizing greed

Today, 'globalization' is 'largely about establishing global rules that act as a constitution for investor rights, and which are beyond any parliamentary challenges' (Gindin, 2002: 1). These rules are embodied in the neoliberal institutions of the World Trade Organization, the International Monetary Fund, the World Bank, and scores of similar bodies. 'They are,' in the opinion of Greg Palast, 'interchangeable masks of a single governance system' (Palast, 2002: 53). While other rich nations exert influence in these forums, it is indisputable that the United States dominates them, and uses them to proclaim and reinforce the ideology appropriately known as the 'Washington Consensus.' The result has been the fortifying of a global economic system that is in essence an international casino, wherein a relative handful of gamblers (investors) undermine economies and destroy environments in their ceaseless quest for profit. For all the talk about democracy and human rights, there is only one right that is sacred to global investors: 'to put it crudely but accurately ... the primary concern of US foreign policy is to guarantee the freedom to rob and to exploit' (Chomsky, 1987: 7). Workers are robbed of the value that they have created with their own time and sweat and talent in order to enrich foreign (and sometimes domestic) investors. Thus, every dollar that goes to a Nike stockholder is a dollar not paid to a Nike worker in Indonesia or China, and this zero-sum relationship dooms the worker to a life with little opportunity or hope.

This sort of economic relationship, that of appropriating the wealth produced by the labor of others, is elemental to the concept of 'imperialism,' a term the use of which appears to be undergoing a revival these days. Parenti defines imperialism as 'the process whereby the dominant politico-economic interests of one nation expropriate for their own enrichment the land, labor, raw materials, and markets of another people' (Parenti, 1995: 1). Two central techniques of extracting wealth from poor countries should be stressed. One is the system of global debt, which has two particularly deleterious effects. First and most obviously, it drains tens of billions of dollars from poor countries every year, so that money is unavailable for health and education, food subsidies, or even encouraging economic growth and development. Thus, 'Tanzania's debt service payments are nine times what it spends on primary health care and four times what it spends on primary education' (UNDP, 1999). As Palast has documented, when the IMF/World Bank 'ordered Tanzania to charge fees for school attendance ... enrollment dropped from 80 per cent to 66 per cent.' Even worse,

> in that African state, 1.3 million people are getting ready to die of AIDS. The IMF and World Bank have come to the rescue with a brilliant neoliberal solution: require Tanzania to charge for hospital appointments, previously free. Since the Bank imposed this requirement, the number of patients treated in Dar Es Salaam's three big public hospitals has dropped by 53 per cent. The Bank's cure must be working. (Palast, 2002: 47)

Overall, 15 years of IMF/World Bank management of Tanzania's economy saw its per capita GDP drop 'from $309 to $210 ... and the rate of abject poverty jumped to 51 per cent of the population' (47).

The second major effect of debt is that the rich states, operating through the international financial institutions, use the need for loans to service debt to force underdeveloped nations to adopt policies that favor transnational corporations over the needs of their own populations. This often seriously exacerbates domestic problems, as is widely acknowledged even by advocates. Structural adjustment policies (SAPs) are imposed as a condition for loans and/or renegotiating debts, and on condition that the recipient country accepts privatization, capital market liberalization, 'market-based pricing' (i.e. higher prices), a reduction in subsidies for public services (water, food, utilities), and increased liberalization of capital for foreign trade and investment (Palast, 2002: 51–2). The results are often disastrous; the collapse of the Argentine economy is only the most recent spectacular failure. Conn Hallinan, a journalist and lecturer at the University of California, wrote that 'Latin America's third largest economy has been derailed by IMF policies that ... were made right here in the USA,' and that resulted in devastation to Argentina's industrial base, skyrocketing unemployment, higher prices, and an unsupportable debt – while foreign speculators made windfall profits (Hallinan, 2002).

The Argentine case is hardly unique. The situation in the former Soviet bloc nations is, in general, even worse under the austerity regime that has ruled since 1991. Poverty has skyrocketed and life expectancy, especially for men, has plunged. One of the leading architects of the introduction of a market system in those countries is Harvard economist Jeffery Sachs, who acknowledged in 2002: 'We have squeezed these countries to the point where their health systems are absolutely unable to function. Education systems are broken down, and *there's a lot of death associated with the collapse of public health and the lack of access to medicine*' (quoted in Tyrangiel,

2002, emphasis added). It appears that the toll in foreshortened lives may number in the *tens of millions in Russia alone*. In a scathing indictment of the policies of 'savage capitalism' imposed on Russia by the 'nihilistic zealotry' of 'reformers,' both domestic and in the United States, Stephen Cohen notes that

> the lives lost of perhaps 100 million Russians seem not to matter, only American investments, loans, and reputations.... So great is Russia's economic and thus social catastrophe that we must now speak of another unprecedented development: the literal demodernization of a twentieth-century country. When the infrastructures of production, distribution, technology, science, transportation, heating, and sewage disposal disintegrate; when tens of millions of people do not receive their salaries, some 75 per cent of society lives below or barely above the subsistence level, and millions of them are actually starving; when male life expectancy has plunged as low as fifty-eight years, malnutrition has become the norm among schoolchildren, once-eradicated diseases are again becoming epidemics, and basic welfare provisions are disappearing; when even highly educated professionals must grow their own food in order to survive and well over half the nation's economic transactions are barter – all this, and more, is indisputable evidence of a tragic 'transition' backward to a premodern era. (Cohen, 2000: 38, 50, 159)

After a detailed study of World Bank policies, Bruce Rich concluded that 'the poor in most of its borrowing countries are in worse shape than they were a decade and a half before. The poorest fifth of the world's population has seen its share of global income fall from 2.3% to 1.4% over the past 30 years' (*CCPA Monitor*, 2002a: 19). Unequal economic and political power explain this outcome: Hallinan points out that 'the United States and its allies make all the decisions. The Netherlands ... has more voting power than China and India,' whose populations include over one-third of all humanity (Hallinan, 2002). The situation is much the same at the International Monetary Fund. Nobel prizewinning economist Joseph Stiglitz, who served as chief economist at the World Bank, recently specified the interests represented by the IMF: 'Finance ministers and central bank governors have seats at the table, not labor unions ... so they push policies that reflect the ... interests of the financial community.' When it comes to the beneficiaries of structural adjustment, Stiglitz is clear that the bailouts are designed for rich investors: 'These policies protect foreign creditors,' not workers, the poor, or the general population (Komisar, 2000: 35, 36).

Moreover, every day, over $1.5 trillion changes hands in international financial transactions, the vast majority of which – between 90 and 95 per cent – is pure speculation (gambling on currencies, stocks, and bonds) rather than productive investment. These capital flows not only undermine the ability of all governments to control their own economies and currencies, but the 'capital flight' from poor countries robs them of desperately needed funds for productive investment, healthcare, and so on. With this increased capital mobility, and as 'corporations move their operations around the world, they pit workers, communities, and entire countries off against each other to see who will provide the lowest wages and cheapest environmental and social costs,' resulting in a 'race to the bottom' for the majority of people (Smith and Brecher, 2000).

Rees points out that the neoliberal 'terms of trade and of the structural adjustment programs forced on Third World countries are *exactly opposite* to the policies under which the wealthy nations developed.' All of them – including Britain, the US, and Japan – initially followed mercantile, protectionist policies, and only accepted 'free trade' (in certain sectors; see below) when they were developed enough to benefit from such liberal policies. Rees says that 'the power brokers of developed countries know exactly what they are doing,' and quotes economist J.W. Smith: 'Their grand strategy is to impose unequal trades upon the world so as to lay claim to the natural wealth and labors of the weak nations.' This strategy is remarkably consistent with Parenti's definition of 'imperialism,' cited above. The effect, in Rees's view, is that 'the poor countries are actually financing the rich through low pay for equally productive labor, investment in commodity production for the wealthy world, and other dimensions of unequal trade. In the 1960s 'only' three dollars flowed North for every dollar flowing South; by the late 1990s, the ratio was seven to one' (Rees, 2002).

Ironically, too, for states that claim 'free trade' as their ideal, the G7 nations use high tariff and non-tariff barriers to trade, such as agricultural subsidies, depriving poor states of tens of billions of dollars in income every year. The industrialized countries spend $350 billion every year subsidizing their agricultural sectors, 'more than the economic output for all of Africa ... "Reducing agricultural subsidies is the single most important area where rich countries can do something",' according to the World Bank. These subsidies cost poor countries billions of dollars per year (MacGregor, 2002), and even IMF Director Horst Kohler has condemned rich industrialized countries which refuse 'to drop "selfish" trade protectionist policies that hurt poorer nations' (Canadian Broadcasting Corporation, 2002). The underdeveloped world is rarely allowed to compete when it has a comparative advantage.

Rich states promote neoliberalism because it works – for the rich. Consider that, in the two decades before neoliberalism was put into practice on a global scale, 'per capita income grew 73 per cent in Latin America and 34 per cent in Africa' between 1960 and 1980, while in the ensuing twenty years, Latin American growth was only 6 per cent 'and

African incomes have *declined* by 23 percent' (Palast, 2002: 48). If the government of an underdeveloped country does try to improve the life of its people rather than the profits of transnational corporations, 'the market' will make it as difficult as possible to succeed. When Luis Ignacio 'Lula' da Silva, the socialist leader of the Workers Party in Brazil, was leading in the race for the Brazilian presidency in 2002, investors 'drove down the value of Brazil's currency, stocks and bonds.' After Lula still received a landslide 61 per cent of the vote, investors were again threatening to hammer Brazil's economy over his 'unrealistic' priority: to end 'hunger among the country's 170 million people ... in a [nation] blessed with abundant natural wealth' (Knox, 2002).

What such neoliberal practices primarily accomplish, unsurprisingly, is the transfer of more wealth to the rich at the expense of everyone else, especially the poor. One result is that the 'combined wealth of the world's 200 richest people hit $1 trillion in 1999; the combined income of the 582 million people living in the 43 least developed countries is $146 billion,' according to the United Nations (UNDP, 2000: 82). Again, the phenomenon of appropriating surplus labor value is not limited to the working class of poor nations. In the United States, rising productivity in the manufacturing sector has not resulted in proportionately better wages for workers. While productivity has continued its increase since the early 1980s, hourly compensation per worker has fallen behind. Hence, 'almost the entire gain from increasing productivity since 1980 has been appropriated as surplus by capital' (*Monthly Review*, 2002: 7).[5]

With extreme inequalities in wealth go extreme inequalities in power. This concentration of economic and political power in the hands of a few is *inevitably* in inverse proportion to the poverty and powerlessness of the majority, especially on a global scale. Those who have such economic power seek not only to hold on to it at almost any cost, but to increase their domination, driven by the imperatives of competition and profit-maximization. Their hold on political power is one key element in maintaining their domination. These dynamics are the most important underlying causes of structural violence, and the most powerful obstacles to significant amelioration of the phenomenon.

## Conclusion

Ultimately, the only way in which structural violence will be significantly reduced is if the political economy of each nation, and of the world as a whole, is effectively democratized. This will be difficult, especially if McMurtry is correct in his view that the 'ultimate subject and sovereign ruler of the world is the transnational corporation' (McMurtry, 2002: 1), and as 'meaningful ... decision-making is vested in private institutions and the quasi-governmental structures that are coalescing into what the *Financial Times* calls a "de facto world government" that operates in secret and without accountability' (cited in Chomsky, 1994: 17). Rather, the economy – and the rest of society – must be democratized through a movement of the great majority, in the interests of the great majority, rather than in the interests of a few. Such a transformation is impossible within the parameters of the present system, as Takis Fotopoulos has pointed out in framing his vision of 'inclusive democracy':

> Within the present institutional framework, the policy options of the elites (either of the neoliberal of social-democratic variety) are severely restricted. Within an internationalized market economy, the introduction of effective social controls to protect the underclass and the marginalized, or to preserve the environment, will create serious comparative disadvantages for the nation-state or economic bloc that will embark on such policies ... In other words, *within the constraints imposed by the institutional framework* of the international market economy, the elites are right in stressing that 'there is no alternative.' (Fotopoulos, 1997: 358, emphasis in original)

Dryzek elaborates on the 'institutional framework' that constrains any attempt to make meaningful changes within a corporate-dominated society. In an insightful and nuanced examination of the possibility of democracy in 'capitalist times,' he argues that, 'once in place, the market is a constraining mechanism of remarkable power and persistence. Governments in market systems are constrained by the need to induce enterprises to invest.' In other words, business domination of the economy – hence control of the means of life, employment, and so on – can check most challenges to its rule by its threat to damage or at least limit the production and distribution of essentials. Dryzek explains that 'governments typically do not dare pursue policies with a significant negative impact on business profitability ... for fear of precipitating a "capital strike".' In such cases, 'it is not parliament or public opinion that constitutes the most important sounding board for government policy but, rather, markets, and especially financial ones' (Dryzek, 1996: 25–6).

Is there any realistic alternative to such elite domination, the entrenched structural violence that it oversees, and the ecocatastrophe that looms on the horizon? Perhaps. In discussing the global movement for democracy (mistakenly termed 'anti-globalization'), Naomi Klein points out that while 'neoliberalism is the common target, there is also an emerging consensus that participatory democracy at the local level – whether through unions, neighborhoods, farms, villages, anarchist collectives, or aboriginal self-government' lies at the heart of the new vision of development. Freedom, empowerment, capacity-building, democracy, respect, and solidarity are among this model's other features (Klein, 2002: 442). Many forms of local democracy have been proposed, and some are in the process of being implemented. Some are informal and ad hoc, while some – like 'inclusive democracy' and the 'libertarian municipalism' outlined by Bookchin – have a more extensive theoretical underpinning. What they tend to have in common, as Klein notes, is a focus on broad citizen participation. This emphasis on participatory democracy has recently been summarized by the eminent US economic historian Robert Heilbroner, who contends that it might be possible to construct

> a society whose mode of cooperation is neither custom and tradition, nor centralized command, nor subservient to market pressures and incentives. Its integrating principle would be participation – the engagement of all citizens in the mutual determination of every phase of their economic lives through discussion and voting. This principle would touch on the determination of the tasks each person performs, the goods and services produced in the enterprise in which each person works, the share that each is entitled to take from the common flow of goods. Participation thus envisages a world in which widely shared decision-making by discussion and vote displaces decision-making by self-interest alone, or by persons privileged by wealth or position to make unilateral determinations. It assumes that social and economic equality has replaced social and economic inequality as the widely endorsed norm of the society, because equality seems best suited to enable individuals to lead the most rewarding lives they can. (Heilbroner, 1992: 116–17)

Heilbroner does not expect his vision to be realized for decades, if ever. However, should such a political and economic system eventually come into being, it could well spell the end of the worst forms of structural violence. The democratic and egalitarian aspects of a participatory social order would act to promote a just outcome. They are also the most likely paths to achieving an ecologically sustainable economy, since the capitalist imperative of putting profit before all other values would cease to be the operative principle.

Ultimately, people of all countries will need to unite and work towards common goals. Perhaps Chomsky best sums up the role that can be played by those living in the privileged countries of the West:

> The struggle for freedom is never over. The people of the Third World need our sympathetic understanding and, much more than that, they need our help. … Whether they can succeed against the kind of brutality we impose on them depends in large part on what happens here…. And that's just part of the task that lies before us. There's a growing Third World at home. There are systems of illegitimate authority in every corner of the social, political, economic, and cultural worlds. For the first time in human history, we have to face the problem of protecting an environment that can sustain a decent human existence. We don't know that honest and dedicated effort will be enough to solve or even mitigate such problems as these. We can be quite confident, however, that the lack of such efforts will spell disaster. (Chomsky, 1997: 100–101)

## Notes

1. 'While the budget is being touted for fighting terrorism, the bulk of the funding goes for buying weapons and a force structure designed during the Cold War,' such as for twelve new Trident II (D-5) submarine-launched nuclear missiles (Council for a Livable World, 2002).

2. Since 'the wars of the 20th century alone have killed over 100 million' people (Nester, 2001: 285), the yearly average is about one million. For most years, however, this figure is much lower since the total includes major anomalies, such as the 50 million killed in the Second World War. It should be noted, however, that between 1990 and 2000, around 200,000 children were killed in armed conflicts (*CCPA Monitor*, 2002b: 3).

3. Or, more subtly, when life-saving drugs are not developed in the first place because those needing them are so poor that there is little effective demand – and little profit to be made.

4. Another major factor, according to James Bissett, former Canadian ambassador to Yugoslavia, was that, 'as early as 1998, the [US] Central Intelligence Agency, assisted by the British Special Armed Services, were arming and training Kosovo Liberation Army members in Albania to foment armed rebellion in Kosovo' (Bissett, 2001).

5. Upon closer inspection, many of the development gains since the Second World War were registered in the first three decades. As the global economic system was liberalized, economic growth slowed, and not just in poor countries. For instance, 'the American economy has actually been declining on a decade-by-decade basis since the 1960s. The trend has been absolutely consistent for four decades, and the direction is down' (Martin, 2000). As goes the US economy, so goes the world. The 'annual growth in global business productivity between 1947 and 1973 equaled 2.85%. But from 1973 to 1997, it only amounted to 1.1%' (*Report on Business*, 1999). In effect, the greatest promise of neoliberalism, that it will create the conditions for economic growth, is contradicted by the higher growth rates that generally were found under less liberal conditions from 1945 to 1973.

## References

Allen, R. (1999). IMF's structural reform set stage for Kosovo conflict. *CCPA Monitor*, September.

Barlow, M. and Clarke, T. (2002). Blue gold: The battle against corporate theft of the world's water. Toronto: Stoddart.

Bissett, J. (2001). We created a monster. *Globe and Mail*, July 31.

Bookchin, M. (1999) Overview of Social Ecology. http://homepages.together.net/~jbiehl/overview.htm.

———— (1977). *Post scarcity anarchism*. Montreal: Black Rose.

Canadian Broadcasting Corporation (2001). Scientists spell out risks from global warming. 19 February. http://cbc.ca/cgi-bin/templates/view.cgi?/news/2001/02/19/climate010219.

*CCPA Monitor* (2002a). Bank's poverty 'alleviation' policy making poverty worse. Ottawa: Canadian Centre for Policy Alternatives, June. www.policyalternatives.ca.

———— (2002b). Enduring terrors and world poverty. February.

———— (1999). Advertising. September.

Cernetig, M. (2000). China's new peasant army toils on Garbage Mountain. *Globe and Mail*, 10 February.

Chomsky, N. (1997). *What Uncle Sam really wants*. Tucson: Odonian Press.

────── (1994). Time bombs. *In These Times*. 21 February.

────── (1993). *Year 501: The conquest continues.* Montreal: Black Rose.

────── (1987). *On power and ideology: The Managua lectures.* Boston: South End Press.

Cienski, J. (2002). Globalization cures poverty. *National Post*, 9 July.

Cohen, S.F. (2000). *Failed crusade: America and the tragedy of post-communist Russia.* New York: W.W. Norton.

Council for a Livable World (2002). Fiscal year 2003 military budget at a glance. Washington. www.clw.org/milspend/dodbud03.html.

Deen, T. (2000). 'Development: Annan praises Cuba for its social achievements.' *Interpress Service*, 12 April.

Devereaux, P.J., et al. (2002). A systematic review and meta-analysis of studies comparing mortality rates of private for-profit and private not-for-profit hospitals. *Canadian Medical Association Journal* 166, no. 11: 1399–406.

Dixon, G. (2001). Richest get richer in 2000. *Globe and Mail*, 15 May.

Dryzek, J. (1996). *Democracy in capitalist times: Ideals, limits, and struggles.* New York: Oxford University Press.

Fotopoulos, T. (1997). *Towards an inclusive democracy.* London: Cassell.

Friedman, M. (1962). *Capitalism and freedom.* Chicago: University of Chicago Press.

Galbraith, J., and Purcell, G. (2001). Inequality and state violence. In J. Galbraith and M. Berner, eds, *Inequality and industrial change.* Cambridge: Cambridge University Press.

Gates, J. (2002). 21 ways neoliberalism is redistributing wealth worldwide. *CCPA Monitor* 8, no. 9 (April).

Gindin, S. (2002). Social justice and globalization. *Monthly Review*, June.

*Globe and Mail* (2002). U.S. threat to world peace, Mandela says. 12 September.

────── (2001). A thirsty world? 4 January.

Goldstein, J. (2003). *International relations*, 5th edn. New York: Longman.

Goodspeed, P. (2001). Severe poverty grips million in Britain. *National Post*, 9 March.

Hallinan, C. (2002). The global goodfellas at the IMF. *San Francisco Examiner*, 11 January. www.zmag.org/content/GlobalEconomics/hallinanifm.cfm.

Heilbroner, R. (1992). *Twenty-first century capitalism.* Concord, ON: Anansi.

Hurtig, M. (1991). *The betrayal of Canada.* Toronto: Stoddart.

Jones, A. (1999–2000). Case study: Maternal mortality. www.gendercide.org/case_maternal.html.

Jones, D. (2002). Canadian family values. *Vancouver Sun*, 31 August.

Klein, N. (2002). Farewell to the end of history. In P. Prontzos, ed., *Readings on Democratic Socialism.* Vancouver: Langara College.

Knox, P. (2002). Brazil's president-elect to tackle hunger first. *Globe and Mail*, 29 October.

Koch, T. (2000). Distributing Canada's wealth across the country saves lives. *Globe and Mail*, 2 August.

Komisar, L. (2000). Joseph Stiglitz. *The Progressive*, June.

Koring, P. (2000). One in five U.S. children in poverty. *Globe and Mail*, 25 March.

────── (1997). U.S. economic inequality grows. *Globe and Mail*, 23 December.

Kristof, N. (1998). Those who had nothing have even less. *Globe and Mail*, 13 June.

Langdon, S. (1999). *Global poverty, democracy, and North–South change.* Toronto: Garamond.

Laxer, J. (1998). *The undeclared war: Class conflict in the age of cyber capitalism.* Toronto: Penguin.

Lee, M. (2002). The global divide. In *Behind the numbers*. Ottawa: Canadian Centre for Policy Alternatives. www.policyalternatives.ca.

Little, B. (2000). Century of productivity, inequality. *Globe and Mail*, 17 April.

MacGregor, K. (2002). Agricultural subsidies must be cut, nations say. *Globe and Mail*, 28 August.

Martin, J. (2000). Boom? What boom? *Financial Post*, 30 March.

McMurtry, J. (2002). The FTAA and the WTO: meta-program for corporate rule. http://zmag.org/CrisesCurEvts?Globalism/mcmurtry.htm.

McQuaig, L. (1999). 'Debt relief for poor countries comes with strings attached,' *CCPA Monitor*, September.

Mickleburgh, R. (2002). Poor are living longer. *Globe and Mail*, 27 September.

Miliband, R. (1994). *Socialism for a sceptical age*. Cambridge: Polity Press.

Mitchell, A. (2002). Great apes fall victim in headlong drives to mass extinction. *Globe and Mail*, 8 October.

Mittelstaedt, M. (2002). Dirty air as lethal as second-hand smoke, study says. *Globe and Mail*, 2 March.

*Monthly Review* (2002). The new face of capitalism. April.

O'Connor, J. (1993). Red–green politics. *Socialist Studies* 9.

Palast, G. (2002). *The best democracy that money can buy*. London: Pluto Press.

Parenti, M. (1995). *Against empire*. San Francisco: City Lights.

Pearlstein, S. (2002). U.S. poverty, wage gaps increased by recession. *Vancouver Sun*, 25 September.

Read, N. (2002). 1 in 4 mammals face extinction. *Vancouver Sun*, 9 October.

Rebick, J. (2000). *Imagine democracy*. Toronto: Stoddart.

Recer, P. (2002). New, dangerous diseases thrive in global warming. *Vancouver Sun*, 21 June.

Rees, W. (2002). Human nature: An impediment to sustainability? Lecture, Langara College, Vancouver, BC, 15 March.

*Report on Business* (2000). Spectrum, January.

——— (1999). Spectrum. July.

Results Canada (2002). Resources – Facts and figures 2001. Ottawa. www.results.ca/resources/2001–facts-and-figures-en.html.

Reuters (2000). 250 Nigerians die scooping up spilled gasoline. *Vancouver Sun*, 15 July.

Robbins, R. (2002). *Global problems and the culture of capitalism*, 2nd edn. Boston: Allyn & Bacon.

Russell, B. (1977). *Roads to freedom*. London: Unwin.

Smith, B., and Brecher, J. (2000). What's next in debate on globalization? *Advertising Age*, 20 March.

Strong, M. (2000). Cry the beloved planet. *Globe and Mail*, 22 May.

Tyrangiel, J. (2002). Bono. *Time* (Latin American Edition), 4 March.

UNICEF (2002). The state of the world's children. New York: UNICEF.

*Vancouver Sun* (2002a). Death toll from smoking now 4.9 million a year. 12 October.

——— (2002b). $28–billion U.S. anti-terror package okayed. 25 July.

Victor, P. (2002). Green economics (letter). *Globe and Mail*, 5 September.

Winter, J. (1992). *Common cents: Media portrayal of the Gulf War and other events*. Montreal: Black Rose.

World Health Organization (2002). Gateway to children's environmental health. www.who.int/peh/ceh/ondex.htm.

——— (2001a). Death toll from dirty water 3.4 million a year, WHO says. *Globe and Mail*, 22 March.

——— (2001b). Cancer. www.who.int/cancer/main.cfm.

# PART III

# Truth and Restitution

# 18

# Institutional Responses to Genocide and Mass Atrocity

## Ernesto Verdeja

The twentieth century enjoys the macabre distinction of having experienced the highest number of state-sponsored murders and mass killings in the history of humanity. The numbers are sobering: nearly 170 million dead by genocide, massacres, extrajudicial killings and other state actions not including warfare, and about 40 million directly through war (Rummel, 1997). Perhaps in response, during the last century a global human rights discourse has developed and matured, espousing fundamental ideals of human dignity and respect not subject to the whims of state actors. Yet its development has been neither even nor incremental. The Nuremberg and Tokyo trials and the UN Genocide Convention established the principle that perpetrators of crimes against humanity should be tried and punished for their actions, but the Cold War put human rights concerns in a deep freeze for nearly forty years. In the Soviet–American bipolar world, human rights rhetoric was manipulated for political purposes, and was rarely if ever the motivating force behind foreign policy (Ball, 1999).

Human rights law is today the weakest component of international jurisprudence, certainly much weaker than international business or trade law. Still, there is no doubt that with the end of the Cold War, human rights discourse has gained strength. The 1990s witnessed the establishment of two international war crimes tribunals, for Rwanda and the former Yugoslavia, followed by tribunals for Sierra Leone, Congo, East Timor and an International Criminal Court. 'Retributive' justice has become a guiding norm for human rights supporters around the world.

Yet tribunals have not been the only institutional response offered by human rights advocates. Over the past twenty years there have been increasing calls for the establishment of truth commissions to compile official histories of oppression and to offer forums for survivors to recount their personal stories. Nations in South America, Asia, Africa and Eastern Europe have adopted truth commissions as a way of coming to terms with painful pasts. Generally eschewing formal trials (because of political constraints), commissions have focused on restoring the dignity of victims and survivors and producing a definitive account of the past, espousing what advocates call 'restorative' justice.

This chapter will consider how nations moving in a positive normative direction – that is, from a repressive to a more democratic state of affairs – have attempted to come to terms with their violent history. Specifically, it will consider the viability of tribunals and truth commissions (TCs). The chapter is divided into two sections. The first part, 'Theoretical Issues,' briefly discusses the normative underpinnings of tribunals and truth commissions, retributive and restorative justice, respectively. I will consider the justifications, promises and limits of both models. The second part, 'Empirical Considerations,' identifies factors that affect the viability of commissions and tribunals, and emphasizes the importance of contextual constraints on their implementation and use.

## Theoretical issues

There are at least four normative criteria that any complete theory of post-atrocity justice must address:

1. How are perpetrators held accountable?
2. How are the needs of victims addressed?
3. How much emphasis does each theory place on constructing an accurate report of past crimes?
4. How does each theory further the rule of law, democratic politics and reconciliation?

These four normative criteria will guide my assessment of the strengths and weaknesses of restorative and retributive justice, and commissions and tribunals. I will refer to these criteria throughout this initial section, using them as a measuring stick to evaluate the viability of both forms of justice.

### Retributive justice and tribunals

Proponents of retributive justice privilege the importance of trying and punishing perpetrators. This approach, rooted in classical notions of justice, is the moving force behind criminal prosecution in domestic courts and the establishment of international tribunals. Nevertheless, retributive justice is sometimes considered no more than an excuse for vengeance. Vengeance may imply proportionality in punishment, but runs the risk of degenerating into reciprocal and unending violence. Retributive justice distances itself from vengeance by tempering the demand for swift retaliation with substantive and procedural protections for the accused, and replacing the victim's desire for immediate reprisal with the rule of law. Retribution in this chapter will be used in this sense, as a type of institutionalized, punitive response based on the rule of law. This formulation serves as an important heuristic device and moral ideal to orient our discussion of post-atrocity justice.

Following Minow (1998: 25), there are at least three criteria that retribution must satisfy if it is to remain within the bounds of the rule of law and not degenerate into vengeance: (i) a commitment to redress past abuses using generalized, codified, preexisting standards; (ii) the use of a formal system characterized by impartiality and transparency with due process protections; and (iii) the power to impose a binding sentence on the defendant which amounts to more than public censure lacking coercive force.

Advocates of retributive justice offer several justifications for trials, ranging from non-consequentialist to fully consequentialist. I will address each of these in turn.

- *Following severe social trauma, basic notions of justice demand that violators be punished for their actions.* This notion of retribution is non-consequentialist; it places no emphasis on the social consequences of its actualization and appeals instead to notions of 'just desserts' (Nozick, 1981: 363–99; Kant, 1980: 102–18).
- *Victims regain self esteem and dignity* by seeing their violators punished publicly for their crimes. Trials acknowledge victims by showing the world that their demands for justice are legitimate and compelling (Neier, 1998).
- *Identifying and punishing leaders of crimes against humanity places individual guilt on key actors, organizers and institutions.* By identifying individual leaders as perpetrators, claims of collective guilt that associate crimes with an entire ethnic or national group are avoided (Prunier, 1997: 342).
- Trials may also *temper and reroute demands for vengeance into institutionalized and fair proceedings for assessing guilt,* reducing the likelihood that victims will 'take justice into their own hands' and engage in vigilantism (Shklar, 1986: 158).
- A *public record* of crimes is established by amassing and interrogating evidence in a procedurally fair setting (Bass, 2000: 302–304).

- Tribunals *foster the domestic rule of law*, the basis for a democratically stable and peaceful society (Robertson, 2000: 243–285).
- There exists *a duty deriving from international law* (both treaty-based and customary) to prosecute grave breaches of fundamental human rights (Orentlicher, 1991).
- *Tribunals deter future tyrants*, serving as a warning about what may befall leaders who terrorize their populations (Roth, 1999).

Employing the four normative criteria listed above, we can identify the strengths and weaknesses of tribunals and their justifications.

*Accountability*    Trials are created first and foremost to assess and assign culpability. Tribunals focus on punishing perpetrators rather than recognizing victims, and thus are driven by the importance of establishing accountability. They achieve a decision of culpability based on higher standards of evidence and due process protections for defendants than TCs (which are not, after all, judicial organs). Furthermore, by identifying specific persons and agencies as violators, tribunals avoid indicting an entire ethnic group (for example, all Serbs or Germans). Nevertheless, tribunals suffer from the opposite problem: the issue of *selectivity*. At best, they can prosecute only a select number of violators, a significant problem in the face of massive human rights violations like genocide, crimes against humanity, and similar abuses that depend on the participation of a large number of perpetrators and coordinated efforts by the state. Confronted by this limitation, they are best used to prosecute high-level intellectual authors of crimes and their immediate subordinates.

*Victim recognition*    Though powerful agents of accountability, trials are not as successful as commissions when it comes to acknowledging the suffering of victims. Certainly, trials provide a public forum for victims to recount their stories, and following a successful prosecution it becomes more difficult to dismiss past crimes as hyperbole or fabrication. Nonetheless, victim recognition is not the primary goal of tribunals, and most tribunals allow testimony only as a means of furthering prosecution, not of directly acknowledging victims. To the extent that victims may regain their dignity through the trial of their tormentors, this is achieved through the satisfaction of seeing them punished; but trials do not directly address the psychological and material needs of victims. In this sense, a public truth commission designed specifically with their interests in mind becomes an invaluable complement to the work of trials.

*Truth*    Trial records also serve as a public record of past atrocity. The Eichmann trial produced a wealth of information on the organization of the Final Solution, and the Auschwitz trials identified the gruesome process of extermination that was paradigmatic of the Holocaust (Douglas, 2001). More recently, the Raboteau trial in Haiti unearthed significant information on the internal organization and operation of the US-backed FRAPH death squad (Concannon, 2001). Prosecutions of intellectual authors of crimes must include investigations of the bureaucracies and agencies they head, and this, in turn, provides a window into the hierarchical organization of state terror. In this way, tribunals contribute to the larger project of creating a factual account of the past. Still, it is important to note that tribunals (ideally) seek evidence to prosecute individuals, not entire collectives or institutions. Thus, it is not categorically the case that tribunals will identify the systemic dimension of repression and terror. Because truth commissions are not procedurally limited to individual prosecutions, their capacity to investigate past atrocities may be broader in scope, offering another important complement to trials.

*Rule of law*   Trials offer a means of publicly condemning past violence and, consequently, promoting the rule of law and consolidation of democracy. Transitional regimes that fail to prosecute or purge human rights abusers inherit a political arrangement with potentially dangerous authoritarian enclaves which may undermine a fragile transitional democracy. Holding perpetrators accountable for their actions eliminates these enclaves of impunity – a crucial goal if societies are to rebuild on solidly democratic grounds.

Nevertheless, transitional regimes are often constrained by amnesties. Consequently, the ideal of the 'rule of law' is best expressed in international human rights law, where amnesties are not recognized and the retributive impulse is most clearly articulated. The UN tribunals for the former Yugoslavia and Rwanda and the International Criminal Court are the best expressions of this. With a mandate to prosecute the most heinous violations of human rights law, these courts are not shackled by the exigencies of domestic politics, and can focus on holding perpetrators accountable for genocide, war crimes and crimes against humanity (Deschenes, 2000).

In general, then, we can say that retributive justice, as actualized in trials, focuses on accountability and creating an accurate and credible record of past violations, as well as contributing to the rule of law through a fundamental rejection of impunity. Restorative justice, articulated through truth commissions, shifts the focus to victims and offers a broader account of the past than that found in trials, providing an important complement to the retributive impulse driving prosecutions.

*Restorative justice and truth commissions*

In the past three decades, outgoing elites have sought amnesties to protect themselves from prosecution for human rights violations. In Latin America alone, numerous amnesties have been enacted: Chile (1978), Brazil (1979), Guatemala (1982, 1996), Argentina (1983), Uruguay (1986), El Salvador (1993), Nicaragua (1990), and Peru (1995). Where amnesties were passed, truth commissions have been established as viable moral alternatives to prosecutions.

Commissions construct an official account of past abuses over a certain period of time in a specific country or in a particular conflict. They encourage victims, relatives, bystanders and perpetrators to participate, and in some instances offer them a public forum to do so. Furthermore, commissions may include a series of institutional reform and reparations recommendations. Behind all of these measures is a commitment to acknowledging victims and restoring their sense of dignity and moral worth. Thus, truth commissions are seen as paradigmatic examples of restorative justice.

There are several differences between truth commissions and tribunals. First, truth commissions generally, though not always, lack subpoena powers. Second, commissions do not follow proof of guilt with a sentence for the guilty. In this sense, justice understood as state-authored punishment is eschewed for the production of an accurate account of the past, seeking to explain human rights violations against the backdrop of broader social and political processes. Third, truth commissions operate for a specific period of time (normally six months to two-and-a-half years), at the end of which they produce a report of their findings for public dissemination. The commission is then dissolved.

Over the past two decades, truth commissions have become respected alternatives to traditional criminal trials. Over twenty commissions have been established. The more successful commissions are composed of prestigious citizens (authors, public intellectuals, lawyers, and so forth) not holding public office and representing a wide range of the political spectrum. Truth commissions occupy a unique space between the state and civil society. Although they are sponsored by the state, the inclusion of non-governmental members as well as broad relations with the NGO community result in a body that, optimally, is open to greater input from civil society actors than tribunals.

Supporters offer several justifications for assembling truth commissions and pursuing restorative justice. The primary purpose of such commissions is *to produce an accurate public record of a country's past crimes*, through archival and forensic truth-seeking complemented by interviewing survivors and perpetrators (Boraine, 2000). Advocates also point to the *therapeutic benefits* of truth commissions. By providing victims with a sympathetic public platform to present their stories, commissions contribute to their personal healing, and offer a phenomenological or experiential truth that complements archival and forensic truth (Krog, 1998). Concomitantly, the public airing of survivors' stories *incriminates perpetrators*, offering a kind of punishment akin to that found in a trial and achieving a powerful symbolic punishment through the shaming and public stigmatization of violators (Kiss, 2001). Public testimonies contribute to societal reflection and, ideally, *healing in society itself*, helping restore and affirm the democratic values of respect and tolerance, and repair the torn social fabric (Tutu, 1999). Lastly, because of their unique position in cataloguing and analyzing systemic abuse and violence, commissions are well situated to *provide policy recommendations for institutional reform and restructuring, and reparations programs for victims* (Crocker, 2000).

*Truth*   Truth commissions aim at constructing an accurate report of past crimes. Argentina's truth commission documented the disappearances of nearly 9,000 persons, providing a fuller picture of the atrocities committed during that country's 'dirty war' (Argentine National Commission on the Disappeared, 1986). These reports complement tribunal records by identifying broader patterns of violence and abuse that may fall outside the purview of prosecutions. In some instances, commissions do not uncover crimes so much as *publicize* what is known but considered taboo for public discussion, and thus play a critical role in breaking the discourse of denial, contributing to the public's knowledge of human rights abuses and helping undermine the culture of impunity – itself based on secrecy – of the armed forces.

*Accountability*   Because truth commissions are not juridical bodies with the capacity to formally punish human rights violators, they use symbolic forms of punishment, namely shaming and humiliating perpetrators publicly by identifying them in the course of the commission's work. Shaming, particularly in conjunction with a report which identifies actual violations (thus implicitly connecting the individual to specific actions, rather than merely to a political ideology), should not be underestimated. South Africa's final report not only gave incontrovertible evidence of the state's machinations to protect apartheid; it also morally condemned those persons associated with the abuses, providing a kind of accountability that resonated deeply with the public. Moreover, commissions can contribute to accountability by forwarding their files to tribunals (international or domestic) and recommending prosecution.

*Victim recognition*   Recent scholarship emphasizes the social healing dimension of victim testimony, both for victims and for society as a whole. A key component of the South African commission's work, advocates argue that testimony achieves 'restorative justice,' the restoration of personal dignity to survivors by publicly acknowledging their suffering, and contributes to general societal reconciliation by reviving social bonds that were destroyed during the period the violence (Krog, 1998).

Commissions may also recommend reparations for victims and their dependants, including personal and familial *rehabilitation* through access to medical, psychological and legal services, *compensation* for financially calculable losses, *restitution* of lost or stolen property, and remedies aimed at the *prevention* of future violations (Van Boven, 1990). Though reparations cannot return lost loved ones or erase the traumas of torture, they can have a positive impact on destitute victims, and, more broadly, serve as an acknowledgement by the state of its responsibility for past crimes. In Argentina and Chile, reparations were provided with precisely these goals in mind (Hayner, 2001: 170–83; Kritz, 1995, Vol. 3: 683–95; Loveman and Lira, 2000: 525–8). Nevertheless, to be considered legitimate, reparations must be tailored and put forth as truly moral responses to the past, and must find some resonance with the psychological and material needs of victims in order to contribute to their recognition.

*Rule of law, democracy, and reconciliation*   Commissions can contribute to the rule of law through policy recommendations on institutional reform of the armed forces, national police, judiciary, and other state actors. They may recommend prosecution – domestic or even international – for perpetrators; removal of military, police or judges from active duty; social and educational programs fostering human rights principles; and constitutional safeguards against impunity.

More broadly, truth commissions seek to foster reconciliation. Advocates argue that unearthing the past is the initial step to social reconciliation, for erstwhile enemies cannot repair broken bonds without first knowing what happened *to whom* and *at whose hands*. The past must be openly discussed before a nation can move on, lest resentments and tensions continue to poison social relations. The strength of this argument is difficult to gauge, since reconciliation is a long, uneven process that may benefit from a truth commission, but also requires reconciliatory efforts at political, social, and personal levels. Nevertheless, the position between the state and civil society that most commissions enjoy may allow them to function as facilitators for long-term reconciliation.

Tribunals and truth commissions, and retributive and restorative justice more generally, share a number of goals: they seek to uncover past atrocities, hold perpetrators accountable, acknowledge victims, and promote the rule of law and reconciliation. They differ, however, in emphasis: the retributive approach promotes accountability over victim acknowledgment, while restorative justice endorses the importance of recognizing victims rather than prosecuting perpetrators. This difference is also manifested in empirical terms, as discussed below. The following section highlights a number of factors that constrain the use of commissions and tribunals.

## Empirical considerations

The previous section identified the theoretical issues at stake in employing truth commissions and tribunals in post-atrocity societies. But the options available to transition architects are not so extensive; they must work within specific political, social and economic parameters that constrain their choices (Zalaquett, 1992). In this section, I discuss seven factors that play a critical role in assessing the viability of commissions and tribunals.

1. *Degree of institutionalization and legitimacy of previous regime* The degree of institutionalization and legitimacy of the perpetrating regime affects the likely success of efforts to seek legal recourse for political crimes. Institutionalization means at least three things: the regime rules through the use of formal and bureaucratic mechanisms, so that different aspects of governance are managed and coordinated by various departments; it has penetrated civil and political society systematically and deeply; and it seems stable and durable.[1] Institutionalized perpetrator regimes are essentially Janus-faced: they assemble complex legal justifications for their actions, bureaucratize violence, and generally rationalize all forms of repression, yet also engage in extra-legal terror against political opponents and the broader population, particularly through the use of secret police, death squads, disappearances and massacres.

Institutionalization is normally accompanied by an increase in legal justifications for crimes through the emergence of a large body of state-security law, and in this sense we can say that a perverted 'rule of law' exists. Here, rules, edicts, statutes, executive orders, administrative decrees and legislation all work to justify what is essentially a terroristic regime, giving a kind of legal patina to an otherwise despotic state. Concomitantly, the state employs its military and security apparatus to violent ends, often working outside (but in harmony with) the established legal framework. The upshot is a large body of law and archival evidence identifying the organization ·and systematization of state-sponsored violence. The more institutionalized and centralized the terror, the more likely it is that a significant body of documentation delineating the coordination of bureau-cracies and security forces will exist. Of course, the peculiarities of a negotiated transition may make acquiring this information difficult, par-ticularly if the perpetrating institutions manage to retain some degree of autonomy. In Chile and Argentina, the armed forces were fairly successful at retaining control of records on their 'dirty wars,' though what has emerged indicates that in both instances the state's violence was highly rationalized and bureaucratized. In South Africa, the armed forces and national police destroyed many of their records of death-squad activity, and the militaries of Central America have simply refused to hand over damning internal documents.

Nevertheless, systematized state terror complemented by a robust body of documentation can facilitate the truth-seeking and prosecutorial goals of tribunals, and thus institutionalized regimes make good candidates for trials of lead perpetrators. The more rigorous a link that can be made between superiors and material authors of crimes, the greater the likeli-hood of successful prosecution because a strong hierarchy of legal (and moral) responsibility can be identified (Osiel, 1999).

Yet institutionalization poses obstacles as well. Where a regime has promulgated a wide array of laws condoning state violence, prosecution of perpetrators must deal with *ex post facto* considerations (Hart, 1958; Fuller, 1958; Rosenberg, 1996). Following the collapse of communism, Hungary passed legislation allowing prosecutions for crimes related to the brutal Soviet suppression of the 1956 uprising, extending the statute of limita-tions for serious crimes and treason and thus justifying its investigation of the past. The Constitutional Court, however, ruled that the treason law was unconstitutional because it violated retroactivity protections. Only after parliament passed legislation permitting the prosecution of 'war crimes' (not subject to retroactivity claims because of the Nuremberg precedent) did trials begin (Teitel, 2001: 35–51). Retroactivity poses a problem in a strictly legal sense, since prosecuting someone for an abuse that was tech-nically legal when committed is a violation of due process. Nevertheless, crimes against humanity, war crimes and genocide are all violations of international law and thus non-derogable, so the salience of the retro-activity problem is somewhat dulled. Though domestic legislation may have existed permitting, or at least not condemning, certain forms of violations (under a state security doctrine, for example), retroactivity will become less of an issue as international human rights norms gain greater traction, trumping its legitimacy (Robertson, 2000: 243–84).

An additional difficulty arises with complex, multilayered systems of repression, which complicate the criminal-legal understanding of res-ponsibility (normally understood as predicated on individuals, not institutions). If the perpetrator regime was highly institutionalized, with a wide web of repression implicating numerous bureaucracies and agencies (as in South Africa and Eastern Europe) and enjoying widespread support or at least acquiescence – and thus arguably legitimacy – then prosecution of individuals can be vulnerable to charges of selectivity: only some violators face prosecution, while the majority (normally the higher-echelon violators) will escape justice. Where these considerations hold, truth commissions offer an important complement to prosecutions by illuminating how repression entails the cooperation of numerous institutional actors coordinated and directed from above.

2. *Independence and fairness of the judiciary*   In some transitions, the judiciary remains an enclave of the past regime, significantly limiting the ability of victims to obtain redress. In these instances, trials are unfeasible, and truth commissions may be the only viable domestic institutional response. Nevertheless, there are alternatives: regional or international fora, such as the Inter-American Court of Human Rights and the permanent International Criminal Court (ICC), and, under certain conditions, case-specific tribunals assembled by the United Nations. This latter approach requires UN Security Council support, which in turn poses numerous practical obstacles. The apprehension of some major powers, particularly the US, towards the expansion of universal criminal jurisdiction impedes the proliferation of UN tribunals.

Victims may also turn to foreign national courts to seek redress. The US Torture Victim Protection Act (1991) has served as a vehicle to prosecute foreigners domestically for violations of 'the law of nations,' and this manner of tort redress is gaining popularity as universal jurisdiction becomes more widely accepted in national jurisprudence (*Filartiga* v. *Pena Ilara*, 1980; *Kadic* v. *Karadzic*, 1995; *Doe* v. *Karadzic*, 1995). Criminal trials in foreign courts are also gaining acceptance; Belgium recently sentenced four Rwandans (including two nuns) for their role in genocidal killings.

Nevertheless, the reconstruction of the national judiciary remains the best hope for domestic accountability and a crucial prophylactic against future impunity.

3. *Extent of perpetrator population*   In some instances, there exist relatively few overt perpetrators and many 'beneficiaries,' or persons who benefit from the political circumstances without actively participating politically. In South Africa, for example, apartheid benefited all white South Africans, regardless of their political affiliations or relations to the state. The apartheid government enjoyed the tacit support of much of the (Afrikaner) white population, but many were not active oppressors.

Other cases are markedly different. The political terror of the Hutu Power regime in Rwanda included the active participation of many Hutu civilians; thus, the perpetrator population was high relative to the number of beneficiaries. The same can be said of Cambodia. Although the Khmer Rouge ruled through terror and did not enjoy wide-ranging support outside its own ranks, there were few beneficiaries of the regime who were not implicated directly in gross human rights violations.

In all of these cases, tribunals can offer an important, though limited, contribution to accountability. Where there are relatively few overt perpetrators and many beneficiaries, the latter cannot be held legally accountable; however, it would be misguided to simply ignore their moral responsibility. A truth commission can serve as an important complement to trials by highlighting that complicity and responsibility go well beyond the narrowly understood notions of criminal liability characteristic of criminal prosecutions. In South Africa the commission investigated the role that business, legal, medical, religious and other professional communities played in supporting the apartheid regime. Investigations of this sort underscore the wide support that some terroristic states enjoy, morally implicating beneficiaries and countering claims that the latter were ignorant of the state's violence.

Where the perpetrator population is large, resource restrictions make it unlikely that every violator can be tried. Rwanda holds upward of 110,000 alleged *génocidaires* in its prisons, but does not have the resources to try them all fairly. A useful institutional complement to the prosecution of elites, such as a truth commission, would help to clarify the broader issues of responsibility and collaboration that are characteristic of large-scale political violence.

Truth commissions can also identify key accomplices and collaborators abroad, delineating the role *foreign* governments play in supporting oppressive regimes. The Guatemalan Commission for Historical Clarification (1999) obtained numerous documents from the US government through Freedom of Information Act requests, in conjunction with the National Security Archive, an American NGO. The declassified documents helped identify US support for the military regime, highlighting the otherwise obscure connections between the two governments. The 1992 Commission of Inquiry in Chad provided detailed assessments of the US role in training and funding dictator Hisian Habré's security forces, who murdered at least 40,000 civilians and tortured countless others. An Angolan truth commission, called for after the death of rebel leader Jonas Savimbi, could supply valuable information on the role played by the Soviet Union, Cuba, the United States and South Africa in that country's brutal civil war. These are all broad, systemic issues surrounding perpetrator populations which cannot be addressed solely in trials. Of course, such processes can similarly be constrained by a foreign power's failure to turn over relevant documents and individuals. The US withholding of documents seized from Haitian FRAPH headquarters and its refusal to extradite FRAPH paramilitary leader Emmanuel Constant for trial, as well as Russia's refusal to open its files on its war in Afghanistan, are illustrative of the myriad ways in which foreign powers can undermine domestic efforts at obtaining justice.

4. *Mode of transition*    A key element in assessing what type of institutional response to pursue is the mode of political transition between regimes. Where the transition is achieved through a victory in war or other sharp break with the past, the new government has the political capital to punish defeated elites through trials, with little concern for the opposition's power. The Tokyo and Nuremberg tribunals, as well as the domestic successor trials in Rwanda, underscore the wide latitude that victors have in pursuing retribution. However, where the transition is tightly 'pacted,' or negotiated, trials are rarely politically feasible. Previous elites may still enjoy significant political or military power, and can threaten to undermine the new political order if they feel their privileges are in jeopardy. Here, truth commissions may offer an alternative response to the past, investigating elites' actions and shaming them through publication of a truth report identifying their crimes.

Even this, however, can prove difficult. Often, elites will demand severe and debilitating restrictions on the operation of commissions. In Chile, the military maintained sufficient political clout after the transition to demand that the commission's final report not name perpetrators, and the 1978 amnesty – covering violations from 1973 through to the time of its passage – effectively ensured that the most egregious abuses would be protected from prosecution. The greater the power of entrenched elites, the greater the political constraints on the moral response. Nevertheless, the gradual expansion of democratic values and practices, combined with the erosion of the authoritarian enclaves' power, may allow for future prosecutions. Chile is currently undergoing a reappraisal of the Pinochet era, and there is now more support for trials than there was only a few years ago. A large part of this can be traced to the 1998 detention of General Pinochet in London, an example of how international events can redefine domestic political contours and permit a reconsideration of what negotiated pacts portend for the future.

The UN-backed Sierra Leone Truth and Reconciliation Commission must negotiate its way around the 1999 Lomé peace agreement, which granted a blanket amnesty for all human rights violations committed during the nine-year civil war leading up to the peace accord. At the time of signing, government forces fighting Foday Sankoh's Revolutionary United Front – infamous for butchering and mutilating civilians – were in a weak bargaining position, and amnesty was seen as the only way of ending hostilities. The commission is nevertheless faced with a difficult task: identifying and possibly recommending for prosecution major war criminals against the backdrop of a legal system that already recognizes protection for crimes committed before 1999. The UN has indicated that it will ignore the amnesty for genocide, war crimes, and crimes against humanity, and has established a tribunal to deal with these cases.

This is the proper course to take. International law does not recognize amnesties for grave human rights violations, so amnesties are essentially void and the crimes subject to prosecution in international fora or, through the emerging principle of universal jurisdiction, in foreign national courts. Tightly pacted transitions which include some form of amnesty may be necessary to remove a despotic regime. But international courts are under no obligation to recognize them; furthermore, amnesties do not in principle protect major foreign accomplices and co-perpetrators from prosecution.

5. *Material, financial and personnel resources*    The financial resources that commissions and tribunals require make it unlikely that a poor nation undergoing substantial political transformation could provide the necessary funding without significant outside assistance. Tribunals, in particular, are especially costly. A *fair* trial of a high-level perpetrator can cost millions of dollars, making numerous trials difficult to justify from a strictly budgetary perspective, particularly when a country is faced with myriad other pressing humanitarian concerns and some of those funds could be used to alleviate the plight of victims and others. International funding is often difficult to secure, and qualified personnel such as lawyers, judges and legal experts may be in short supply. The Rwandan genocide left only a handful of lawyers in the country, creating a seemingly insurmountable obstacle to formal domestic prosecutions. With hardly any attorneys to prosecute – much less defend – suspects, the likelihood of fair trials is seriously diminished. It would be a mistake, of course, to choose a commission over widespread trials simply on budgetary grounds. To do so would make a mockery of the principle of a moral response, delegating the moral calculus to the rather profane level of bean-counting and penny-pinching. Nevertheless, budgetary constraints *are* constraints. South Africa spent approximately $18 million a year on its commission, a sum unmatched by any other similar body, and commissioners never-

theless felt their work was underfunded. So, too, with the UN-sponsored truth commissions in El Salvador and Guatemala (Lester, 2000: 78–110).

Closely related to the above resource factors is political will. Does the successor regime have the will and commitment actually to pursue and sustain a rigorous, institutional response? Human rights advocates have often found a great deal of rhetorical governmental support for their ambitious projects, only to realize later that the regime has no interest whatsoever in matching its words with deeds. The lack of interest is, unsurprisingly, reflected in the lack of money and resources available for commissions and tribunals. Uganda assembled two commissions – in 1974 and 1986 – that were duly ignored by the state, and Ecuador's 1996 commission folded after five months, producing no final report on police and military abuses. Zimbabwe's 1985 state-sanctioned commission, investigating state repression in Matabeleland, never released its report; the government quashed its publication, claiming the findings would unleash 'ethnic conflict' (Hayner, 2001: 55). Similarly, post–World War I trials to prosecute Turkish perpetrators quickly foundered after the Allies lost interest, and the architects of the Armenian genocide were thus never held accountable. Political will and sufficient resources are crucial if institutional responses to the past are to succeed. Otherwise, they will remain token gestures and a further insult to the victims.

*6. Salience of specific domestic, cultural, political and religious discourses available for furthering the causes of justice and reconciliation* Truth commissions and tribunals should draw from domestic discourses that can strengthen their legitimacy. Archbishop Tutu, chairman of the South African commission, has often turned to Christian notions of forgiveness as an important virtue in dealing with perpetrators (an admittedly controversial proposition), and local leaders have called for *ubuntu*, roughly translated from Zulu as 'humanness,' to underscore the importance of rebuilding interpersonal relationships in the construction of a new moral and political order. These notions and others offer a rich discursive fund which can feed broader efforts at reconciliation and coming to terms with the past.

Prosecutions have also taken a decidedly autochthonous turn. In Rwanda, the state has supplemented formal trials with *gacacas* – essentially popular tribunals rooted in local customs – for lower-level perpetrators. Though the state has outlined formal criteria for their operation, *gacacas* gain much of their legitimacy from their identification with tradition and their basis on customary notions of responsibility and accountability (Vandeginste, 2001). This and similar cases point to the salience of local and national discourses on justice and reconciliation, for only if the population at large can identify with these institutions will they have any deep and transformative impact.

7. *Possibility of future social unrest through the use of truth commissions and trials*    Finally, there exists the very subjective factor of predicting – reckoning may be a more appropriate term – whether commissions or tribunals will contribute to the resumption of violence, be it through coup, civil war or revolution. Political elites must engage in a delicate calculus to ascertain whether certain kinds of institutional responses may lead to a renewal of violence. An assessment of factors 2, 3 and 4 above offers some direction in ascertaining whether and what type of institutional responses should be employed. Highly pacted transitions leave authoritarian enclaves in politics, the economy, and occasionally the armed forces, creating significant obstacles to the use of trials. This was the case in El Salvador, Guatemala and South Africa, though in the last instance the government employed a novel form of selective prosecution. In general, truth commissions may offer the only possibility of moral response without resulting in renewed conflict, and retributive efforts will have to be pursued in the international arena, with all of the great-power pitfalls that entails.

## Conclusion

Institutional responses are an important, though by no means sufficient, element of larger societal efforts to confront the past. Political elites must discuss past violence publicly and frankly by acknowledging injustices and responsibility as a step toward the reconstruction of society, and civil society actors should contribute to reconciliation by providing critical interpretations of past violence more nuanced than elite historical narratives. Individuals, too, must find ways of addressing complex personal issues of responsibility, revenge, forgiveness and moral transformation. All of these concerns point to the fundamentally *disjunctured* and *uneven* nature of reconciliation. Nevertheless, institutional mechanisms *can* make a difference, particularly when the retributive elements of tribunals are paired with the restorative dimension of truth commissions. Rather than seeing them as separate, incompatible bodies, they should be understood as complementing one another. The emphasis in retribution satisfies moral demands for accountability, and through reparations and public survivor testimony commissions acknowledge victims in ways tribunals cannot. Both institutional responses, moreover, help unearth the truth about atrocities. Though a transition to a more just society will always be fraught with difficulty and pain, institutional responses can serve as important first steps by helping mend a tattered social fabric.

Additionally, we should not lose sight of foreign complicity in human rights abuses; most modern cases of state-sponsored human rights violations have occurred with the support of foreign governments, often the United States or the Soviet Union. Current international law makes it difficult to prosecute leaders for actions committed in other states, though as the ongoing trial of Milosevic indicates, this may be changing. Nevertheless, there is no doubt that political power often trumps law, and justice will not be achieved if foreign accomplices remain unaccountable. Domestic justice will remain stunted if only national actors are investigated and prosecuted. Because of the crucial element of foreign involvement in modern civil wars and domestic atrocities – a phenomenon best captured in the Cold War term 'proxy war' – robust international justice mechanisms are required as well. UN ad hoc tribunals and the ICC, as well as regional human rights courts, point in this direction, though all are hampered to differing degrees by the machinations of realpolitik. The balance, then, between domestic imperatives for justice and the international reluctance toward universal jurisdiction will remain the fundamental cleavage in future human rights discourse.

## Notes

1. Precisely how long is an issue for case study, and cannot be ascertained *a priori*. In large part, it concerns the degree to which the state has succeeded in convincing the population as a whole that it is institutionalized and permanent, and thus not likely to disappear anytime soon.

## References

Argentine National Commission on the Disappeared (1986). *Nunca Más: Report of the Argentine National Commission on the Disappeared.* New York: Farrar Straus & Giroux.

Ball, H. (1999). *Prosecuting war crimes and genocide: The twentieth century experience.* Lawrence: University of Kansas Press.

Bass, G. (2000). *Stay the hand of vengeance: The politics of war crimes tribunals.* Princeton, NJ: Princeton University Press.

Boraine, A. (2000). Truth and reconciliation in South Africa: The third way. In R. Rotberg and D. Thompson, eds, *Truth v. Justice*, 141–57. Princeton: Princeton University Press.

Chilean National Commission on Truth and Reconciliation (1993). *Report of the Chilean National Commission on Truth and Reconciliation*, 2 vols. Southbend, IN: University of Notre Dame Press.

Concannon, B., Jr. (2001). Justice for Haiti: The Raboteau trial. *The International Lawyer* 35, no. 2 (Summer): 613–48.

Crocker, D. (2000). Truth commissions, transitional justice, and civil society. In R.

Rotberg and D. Thompson, eds, *Truth v. Justice*, 99–121. Princeton: Princeton University Press.

Deschenes, J. (2000). Justice and crimes against humanity. In G. Bahtia et al., eds, *Peace, Justice and Freedom*, 90–140. Edmonton, AB: University of Alberta Press.

Douglas, L. (2001). *The memory of judgment*. New Haven, CT: Yale University Press.

*Filartiga* v. *Pena Ilara*, 630 F2d 876, 890. Second Circuit 1980.

Fuller, L.L. (1958). Positivism and fidelity to law – A reply to Professor Hart. *Harvard Law Review* 71: 630–49.

Green, L. (2000). Crimes against humanity and the law. In G. Bahtia et al., eds, *Peace, Justice and Freedom*, 91–120. Edmonton, AB: University of Alberta Press.

Commission for Historical Clarification (1999). *Memoria del Silencio: Informe de la Comisión de Esclarecimiento Histórico de Guatemala*. Guatemala: CEH Press.

Hart, H.L.A. (1958). Positivism and the separation of law and morals. *Harvard Law Review* 71: 593–629.

Hayner, P. (2001). *Unspeakable truths: Confronting state terror and atrocity*. New York: Routledge.

Herman, J. (1997). *Trauma and recovery: The aftermath of violence: From domestic abuse to political terror*. New York: Basic Books.

*Kadic* v. *Karadzic*; *Doe* v. *Karadzic* 60 F3d 232. Second Circuit 1995.

Kant, I. (1980). On punishment. In *The philosophy of law*, 90–134. London: Hill Press.

Kiss, E. (2001). Moral ambition within and beyond political constraints. In R. Rotberg and D. Thompson, eds, *Truth v. Justice*, 68–98. Princeton: Princeton University Press.

Kritz, N., ed. (1995). *Transitional justice: How emerging democracies reckon with former regimes*, 3 vols. Washington: US Peace Institute.

Krog, A. (1998). *Country of my skull: Guilt, sorrow, and the limits of forgiveness in the new South Africa*. New York: Random House.

Lester, I. (2002). *Comisiones de la Verdad y la Reconciliación Nacional*. Santiago: Esperanza.

Loveman, B. and Lira, E. (2000). *Las Ardientes Cenizas del Olvido*. Santiago: LOM.

Minow, M. (1998). *Between vengeance and forgiveness: Facing history after genocide and mass violence*. Boston: Beacon Press.

Neier, A. (1998). *War crimes: Brutality, genocide, terror, and the struggle for justice*. New York: Times Books.

Nozick, R. (1981). Retribution and revenge. In *Philosophical explanations*, 81–123. Cambridge, MA: Harvard University Press.

Orentlicher, D. (1991). Settling accounts: The duty to prosecute human rights violations of a prior regime. *Yale Law Journal* 100, no. 2537: 2537–614.

Osiel, M. J. (1999). *Obeying orders: Atrocity, military discipline and the law of war*. New Brunswick, NJ: Transaction Publishers.

Prunier, G. (1997). *The Rwanda crisis*. New York: Columbia University Press.

Robertson, G. (2000). *Crimes against humanity: The struggle for global justice*. New York: The New Press.

Roht-Arriaza, N., ed. (1995). *Impunity and human rights in international law and practice*. Oxford: Oxford University Press.

Rosenberg, T. (1996). *The haunted land: Facing Europe's ghosts after communism*. Boston: Vintage Books.

Roth, K. (1999). Human rights in the Haitian transition to democracy. In C. Hesse and R. Post, eds, *Human rights in political transition: Gettysburg to Bosnia*, 93–134. New York: Zone Books.

Rummel, R.J. (1997). *Statistics of democide, genocide, and mass murder since 1900*. Charlottesville, VA: Center for National Security Law, University of Virginia.

Schwartz, H. (1994). Lustration in Eastern Europe. *Parker School of Eastern European Law* 1, no. 2: 141–8.

Shklar, J. (1986). *Legalism*. Cambridge, MA: Harvard University Press.

Soyinka, W. (2000). Memory, truth and healing. In I. Amadaiume and A. An-Na'im, eds, *The politics of memory in Africa*. London: Zed Books.

Strang, H. and Braithwaite, J. (2000). *Restorative justice: Philosophy to practice*. Burlington, VT: Ashgate.

Teitel, R. (2001). *Transitional justice*. Oxford: Oxford University Press.

Torture Victim Protection Act of 1991, U.S. Code, vol. 28, secs. 1602–1611 (1994).

Truth and Reconciliation Commission of South Africa (1999). *Truth and Reconciliation Commission of South Africa report*, 5 vols. New York: Grove.

Tutu, D. (1999). *No future without forgiveness*. New York: Doubleday.

United Nations (1993). *From madness to hope: The 12-year war in El Salvador: Report of the Commission on the Truth for El Salvador*. New York: United Nations Doc. S/25500/ Annex.

Van Boven, T. (1990). *United Nations Commission on Human Rights: Study concerning the right to restitution, compensation, and rehabilitation for victims of gross human rights violations and fundamental freedoms*. New York: United Nations doc. E/CN.4/1990/10.

Vandeginste, S. (2001). Rwanda: Dealing with genocide and crimes against humanity in the context of armed conflict and failed political transition. In N. Biggar, ed., *Burying the past: Making peace and doing justice after civil conflict*, 223–53. Washington: Georgetown University Press.

Van der Merwe, H. (2001). National and community reconciliation: Competing agendas in the South African Truth and Reconciliation Commission. In N. Biggar, ed., *Burying the past: Making peace and doing justice after civil conflict*, 85–106. Washington: Georgetown University Press.

Zalaquett, J. (2002). Balancing ethical imperatives and political constraints: The dilemma of new democracies confronting past human rights violations. *Hastings Law Journal* 43, no. 6: 1425–38.

# 19

# International Citizens' Tribunals on Human Rights

## Arthur Jay Klinghoffer

International citizens' tribunals, often labeled 'commissions of inquiry' or 'international people's tribunals,' attempt to rally public opinion in order to effect governmental policy changes or influence the judicial process while human rights violations are still being committed. The aim is to apply moral standards to the internationalization of justice, but these tribunals are composed of public intellectuals rather than representatives of the state, so their decisions are extrajudicial and have no legal standing. Perhaps this is why such tribunals have been largely neglected in the literature on international law. Nevertheless, it is evident that their emphasis on the role of concerned citizens is striking an increasingly responsive chord among publics attuned to current trends in the advancement of human rights.[1] Furthermore, international citizens' tribunals often confront major world powers, such as the United States and Russia, which have been able to avoid prosecution under the existing legal regime for their alleged human rights abuses.

Unfortunately, international citizens' tribunals are not as effective as they should be, because of their overly aggressive procedures and their biased ideological slant. Too often they adopt the trappings of formal legal structures by issuing verdicts rather than concentrating on the gathering of evidence. Their saliency would be enhanced were they to emulate grand juries rather than courts, and use their inquiries to arrive at indictments. In addition, these tribunals should strive for greater ideological diversity when selecting panelists. They tend to lose credibility with the media when they are seen to act only as agents of the left, and when their verdicts are unanimous. Inclusion of dissenting opinions would therefore be beneficial to their public image.

## Conceptual foundations

If the absence of permanent legal structures prepared to condemn the powerful is the problem, then international citizens' tribunals are proposed as the solution. They are intrinsic to 'transnational democracy' and 'globalization from below,' and are an integral component of an 'emerging global society.' As explained by international law specialist Richard Falk, 'law belongs to all of us,' and 'we must reclaim it from the destructive forces that are crystallized in imperial power politics at this time' (see International People's Tribunal, 1994: 4–5; Dixon, ed., 1985: 20). Most tribunal proponents contend that citizens have the secondary responsibility to act against injustice if states and international organizations neglect to carry out their primary responsibility. Falk writes that 'the peoples of the world enjoy ultimate sovereignty, including the right to appropriate legal forms, and to establish legitimate institutions and procedures as needed,' while Nobel Peace Prize laureate José Ramos Horta of East Timor declares that if governments do not defend the people's rights, 'we will have to find new forms of action that will' (International People's Tribunal, 1994: 4; 1997 People's Summit on APEC, n.d.).

International citizens' tribunals cannot impose their decisions upon transgressing states, but this apparent weakness may be turned into an advantage, at least in theory. Such tribunals are not indebted to states, and are not influenced by them. Powerlessness may thus prove to be a virtue, and contribute to tribunals' legitimacy.

Tribunals are assembled by self-appointed organizing committees, thereby tainting their impartiality. However, preconceived opinions could possibly be altered once confronted with evidence and, as philosopher Bertrand Russell argued, panelists of solid character may be just despite their strong convictions. You don't have to be indifferent, noted Russell, to be impartial, nor have an empty mind in order to assure an open mind (Russell, 1967: 126).

Moral equivalence is often problematic at tribunals, and is usually rejected because of an aversion to giving equal status to the crimes of those identified as victims. Tribunal advocates maintain that those who are weak may resort to sporadic acts of resistance, but any war crimes committed in so doing are not deemed morally equivalent to the acts of those with superior force who violate international legal norms systematically (Untitled document, 1967).

Tribunals are not formal legal bodies, and defendants are not necessarily present. The latter are often invited, but choose not to appear before what they consider to be a biased forum. Sometimes the tribunal appoints an expert to present testimony on behalf of the defense – but surely the prosecution side of the case predominates. *In absentia* defendants thus tend to be the norm rather than the exception.

Tribunals are proliferating, and their scope is broadening to include women's rights, indigenous rights, and workers' rights. Miscarriages of justice against specific individuals are to a great extent being replaced by indictments of the system, generally labeled 'global capitalism.' Defects and inequities are portrayed as institutional, and a movement from below generated by the people is advanced as the antidote. The prime aim is to transform international law so that justice will be based on giving voice to those considered weak and oppressed. According to Richard Falk's interpretation of international law, sovereignty of the people has gradually been expanded to include collective group rights of 'peoples.' Falk further maintains that law is a 'progressive' weapon, a 'political tool' used to facilitate change. It incorporates undertones of class warfare, and should be used as a means of empowerment (International People's Tribunal, 1994: 4; Falk, 2001).

The Martens clause in the 1907 Hague Conventions, according to which states are bound by usages deriving from 'the laws of humanity and the dictates of the public conscience,' is an important precedent justifying citizens' power. Also pertinent are Articles 1 and 55 of the UN Charter and General Assembly Resolution 1514 (1960), which declares that all peoples are entitled to self-determination. The key document setting forth the countertraditional position in international law is the Universal Declaration of the Rights of Peoples, formulated in Algiers in 1976 (Lewy, 1978: 224–5; Basso, 1975: 5; Bowring, n.d.).[2]

Note that international citizens' tribunals differ from truth commissions. Whereas the former are unofficial and have no state sponsorship, the latter are state funded, panelists are appointed by their governments, and monetary reparations are sometimes assessed.

## The Reichstag fire trial case

After World War I, the new Wilsonian order featured an upsurge in attention paid to international law, ethics, public opinion and the role of public intellectuals (see Lippmann, 1925: 55, 69–70, 197). On the ideological front, a struggle developed between Bolshevism and Nazism, and it is this confrontation that set the stage for the world's first international citizens' tribunal. Adolf Hitler became the chancellor of Germany on 30 January 1933. On 27 February, a Dutchman named Marinus van der Lubbe caused considerable damage to the Reichstag building through an act of arson. He was quickly arrested, but so were three Bulgarian communists and the leader of the communist delegation in the Reichstag, Ernst Torgler. They were not perpetrators of the crime, but had been detained as part of a scenario in which the Nazis blamed the communists for the blaze and depicted it as the first phase of a communist insurrection. Most civil liberties were suspended on 28 February as the Nazi government began a roundup of thousands of communists. The communists claimed, in turn, that the Nazis were using the pretext of a supposed plot to increase their votes in the 5 March Reichstag election. In fact, the Nazis did greatly enhance their parliamentary representation, and then proceeded on 29 March to pass a retroactive death-penalty law that included a crime of 'revolutionary arson.' On 1 April, the Communist Party was banned.

Willi Muenzenberg, an important tactician in the Communist International, orchestrated a campaign to counter the Nazis. One element was preparation of the *Brown Book of the Hitler Terror*, which accused the Nazis of being van der Lubbe's accomplices (*Brown Book of the Hitler Terror*, 1933). Another was to campaign against the German indictment of four communists and use public relations as a counterweight to the planned Reichstag fire trial. This resulted in the establishment of an international citizens' tribunal, organized in the form of a commission of inquiry. With the support of many British Labourites, the tribunal convened in London on 14 September. This was one week before the scheduled German trial, and was an intentional effort to turn world opinion against the Nazi court process. The tribunal panel was composed of lawyers from several countries, including the noted American civil libertarian Arthur Garfield Hays and the British Labour parliamentarian and King's Counsel Denis Nowell (D.N.) Pritt. Although communists worked behind the scenes to create the tribunal, they were careful not to select any communists as panelists.

Stafford Cripps, a former Solicitor-General and future Chancellor of the Exchequer, gave the opening address. Basically, supporters maintained that the tribunal was justified because the German trial would be politically influenced by the Nazis, the defendants would not be permitted to use the services of foreign lawyers, and refugee witnesses would not be able to testify due to the lack of a German guarantee for their security. On 20 September, the day before the official trial was to begin in Leipzig, the tribunal issued 'final conclusions' asserting the innocence of the four communist defendants and strongly suggesting that the Nazis had conspired with van der Lubbe. Copies of the tribunal transcript were forwarded to the judges and prosecutor in Leipzig, but not placed into evidence. However, the materials were well publicized, and had an impact through the international media. In addition, Hays received approval from the German judiciary to serve as an assistant to Torgler's attorney, Alfons Sack.

The *New York Times* correctly predicted that the tribunal in London would force the court to respond to its findings (Tolischus, 1933). Indeed, the Nazis were on the defensive at Leipzig, attempting to refute transcript evidence and the *Brown Book*. The courtroom tactics of Bulgarian defendant Georgi Dimitrov were crucial in this regard, as he constantly accused the Nazis of the arson. Eventually, even chief prosecutor Karl Werner called for the acquittal of the three Bulgarians – but not of Torgler, who was a German – on the grounds that the evidence was insufficient to convict them. On the other hand, he continued to deny Nazi guilt for the fire.

The international citizens' tribunal helped to organize rallies calling for the acquittal of the four communists, heard additional witnesses in Paris on 4–5 October while the Leipzig trial was in progress, and convened in London on 18–20 December once Werner had withdrawn his request for the conviction of the Bulgarians. At this latter session, the emphasis was on pressing for the acquittal of Torgler. Arthur Garfield Hays encouraged the Leipzig court by declaring: 'If these men are acquitted, the world will realize that at best one court in Germany is objective and independent and that even in the midst of terror instituted by the Nazis, you judges have shown the courage of your convictions' (Hays, 1942: 386).

On 23 December, the Leipzig court proclaimed the Nazis innocent of arson, and cited a purported communist plan for insurrection. But it also acquitted the four communists. Van der Lubbe was sentenced to death, and guillotined on 10 January. Despite their victory in court, the communist defendants were not released. The German media clamored for a new trial, and the defendants were placed in 'protective custody.' Minister of the Interior Hermann Goering had threatened precisely this in his testimony at Leipzig, claiming that the four communists had 'reason to be afraid' should they be freed after the trial (quoted in *New York Times*, 5 November 1933). The international citizens' tribunal again generated publicity over the plight of the detained communists, and a deal was soon worked out between Germany and the Soviet Union in which Moscow would grant citizenship to the three Bulgarians, who had been stripped of citizenship by their own homeland. Germany would then repatriate them to the Soviet Union. On 27 February, the anniversary of the Reichstag fire, the Bulgarians arrived in the Soviet capital. Torgler remained in jail until June 1935. Goering had opposed the release of the Bulgarians, claiming that had the communists triumphed over the Nazis 'they would have hung us up.' He declared: 'I see no reason why we should be more considerate' (quoted in *The Times*, 21 February 1934). Nonetheless, Goering was forced to acquiesce to Hitler's deal with Stalin.

The first international citizens' tribunal had taken on Nazi Germany, and had won. Without its efforts, it is unlikely that the German court would have acquitted the four communists. Intellectuals had confronted a totalitarian state, and had successfully used public opinion as a weapon to further their cause. Contributing to the tribunal's efficacy was its ability to project a moderate image by hiding the Communist International's role in its formation. At the same time, the non-communist lawyers who served as panelists were indeed upholders of liberal democracy. Hays, who was neither a Marxist nor a Leninist, endeavored to limit communist influence over the proceedings. In fact, he soon became involved with the organization of the second international citizens' tribunal, which was directed against the Soviet Union.

## The Moscow show trials case

At the first Moscow show trial of August 1936, prominent leaders of the Communist Party were charged with counterrevolutionary acts purportedly carried out in collusion with the exiled former commissar of both war and foreign affairs, Leon Trotsky. Tellingly, the Soviet Union did not attempt to extradite the fiery anti-Stalinist from exile in Norway, because he would then have had an opportunity to challenge the Soviet system in court, as Dimitrov had challenged Nazism at Leipzig. Trotsky was willing to testify in Moscow, but as this was not possible he called for the establishment of an international citizens' tribunal where he could defend himself from Soviet charges and expose the Moscow show trial as a sham.

In October, proponents of Trotsky's right to a fair hearing began to organize in New York. Many were surely Trotskyists, but socialists and liberals were also included. The Trotskyist role was not hidden, but there were also supporters who did not proclaim Trotsky's innocence, and whose main concern was the application of democratic procedures. All agreed that there should be a tribunal, and that a new place of asylum would have to be found for Trotsky because Norway would not permit him to participate in a tribunal as long as he was an exile in that country. In December, a somewhat misnamed 'defense committee' was founded in New York, and similar committees were formed in Britain, France and Czechoslovakia.

Efforts to relocate Trotsky were successful, and he settled into Mexican exile in January 1937. That same month featured a second Moscow show trial, and another call by Trotsky for a tribunal where he could defend himself against Soviet charges. In February and March, the 'defense committee' in New York put together a commission to investigate the show trials, and called upon noted pragmatist philosopher John Dewey to serve as its chairman. The commission accordingly came to be known as the 'Dewey Commission.' Members of the 'defense committee' were included, but there was a careful effort to project an image of impartiality by excluding committed Trotskyists. In contrast to the Reichstag fire tribunal, hardly any of the members were lawyers, since it was maintained that the main issue was not Trotsky's guilt or innocence but the show trials themselves, and members should therefore be able to place them in appropriate historical and social context. The defense committee financed the Dewey Commission, and even provided a lawyer for Trotsky, but it did gradually gain public acceptance as not strictly partisan through John Dewey's considerable efforts.

Dewey, a defense committee member, had retired as a professor at Columbia University in 1930. He was not a Trotskyist, but had become active on the defense committee because he sought justice for Trotsky and believed that the exiled revolutionary had a right to defend himself against Soviet charges. Dewey was deeply concerned about democratic modes of inquiry, and warned that many Americans were becoming attracted to a Soviet model that he believed was excessively based on ends rather than means. For him, democracy was a process, not an end in itself; it was an educational means of arriving at truth (Dewey, 1922: 223, 229, 236–7; Bullert, 1983: 135; Meyer, 1938: 53, 55; Farrell, 1965; Zeldin, 1991: 388–9, 392–3). Dewey was likewise highly critical of Trotskyism, which he saw as based on absolutes, and he disagreed with Trotsky on the essence of Stalinism. From Dewey's perspective, Stalinism had evolved out of Bolshevism; from Trotsky's, it was a perversion of the Leninist course.

The Dewey Commission planned hearings in Mexico, with Trotsky as the star witness. Presiding over these sessions was to be a subcommission drawn from the membership of the larger commission. It turned out that none of the five panelists was a lawyer. Arthur Garfield Hays was invited to serve, but he preferred to serve as counsel to the subcommission rather than as a member. He tried to establish a legal framework that included the presentation of evidence by Stalinists. Dewey agreed, but Hays had to drop out due to a scheduled court date in the United States. Rather belatedly, invitations to participate in the hearings were sent to prominent communists, including the Soviet ambassador to the US, Alexander Troyanovsky; but all failed to respond owing to their expectation that the international citizens' tribunal would be biased in favor of Trotsky.

The April 1937 tribunal that convened in Coyoacán, just outside Mexico City, provided a forum for the eloquent Trotsky to refute Soviet charges against him and to expose the trumped-up nature of the Moscow show-trial process.[3] At the conclusion of the testimony, the subcommission declined to issue any findings or verdict. As had been arranged in advance, all testimony and documents were to be submitted to the full Dewey Commission in New York. The latter was then to compile the hearings transcript, take evidence from additional witnesses, add documents supplied by other defense committees in Europe, and then issue a final report. In the meantime, the tribunal in Coyoacán still managed to exert an influence on public opinion, as Trotsky's presentation of evidence encouraged public skepticism about the validity of confessions made by the defendants in Moscow. Nevertheless, many liberal democrats and partisans of the left were still reluctant to criticize the Soviet Union, believing that its role in a 'united front' against fascism was crucial. Dewey would have none of this. After the tribunal, he described purported Soviet democracy as a 'farce,' and maintained that 'we must stop looking to the Soviet Union as a model for solving our own economic difficulties and as a source of defense for democracy against fascism.' At the same time, he declared that he had come to disagree with Trotsky even more than previously (Meyer, 1938: 55–9).

In September 1937, the Dewey Commission released the full transcript of the Coyoacán hearings, along with a summary of findings. The final report and verdict, labeling the Moscow show trials as 'frame-ups' and concluding that Trotsky was not party to a conspiracy with the defendants, was issued in December (Commission of Inquiry, 1972). By this time, the Dewey Commission had significantly influenced the world's media, which were now more prepared to accept Trotsky's innocence.

The Dewey Commission's success was tempered by the fact that its hearings in Mexico could not attract media attention similar to that garnered in London by the Reichstag fire international citizens' tribunal. Furthermore, a third Moscow show trial took place in March 1938 – after the publication of the Commission's final report. The Commission therefore had not influenced the tragic course of Soviet injustice. It had helped secure a form of exoneration for Trotsky, but had not saved any show trial defendants from execution. Although the original impetus for the international citizens' tribunal had come from Trotskyists, liberals had seized control of the process, and had demonstrated the centrality of a focus on means as fundamental to democracy.

## The Vietnam war crimes case

Bertrand Russell, exploiting his prestige as a leading philosopher, was the guiding force behind the creation of the International War Crimes Tribunal – which came to be known as the 'Russell Tribunal.' He did not attend the hearings, but provided logistical assistance and funding through his Bertrand Russell Peace Foundation in London, and attracted many prominent intellectuals to the cause. He was instrumental in planning the sessions held in Stockholm in May 1967 and in Roskilde (Denmark) in November 1967 to consider alleged American crimes in Vietnam, including aggression, usage of banned weapons, bombing of civilian targets, inhumane treatment of prisoners, resort to forced labor and deportation, and genocide. Among the panelists were French philosophers Jean-Paul Sartre (see Document 1) and Simone de Beauvoir, Yugoslav international law expert Vladimir Dedijer, and American peace activists Dave Dellinger and Carl Oglesby. Stokely Carmichael was also a member, but he rarely attended, and did not participate in the final verdict.

Many potential tribunal panelists rejected invitations to participate in what they viewed as a stacked procedure. One concern was that the defendants would not be present. Lyndon Johnson, Dean Rusk, Robert McNamara and other US officials were invited, but refused to attend. Another was that no defense would be presented. The US would not defend itself before what it saw as a kangaroo court, and tribunal organizers would not accept any defense not authorized by the US government. Most damaging to the tribunal was the objection voiced by Yale history professor Staughton Lynd, who had actually gone to North Vietnam on the tribunal's behalf to investigate American war crimes. He argued that there must be equal readiness to condemn all crimes, whether committed by the US or its enemies. No double standard could be tolerated (Lynd, 1967–68: 76; Lynd, 1967).

Organizational difficulties marred preparations for the tribunal. The headquarters were in London, and tribunal members in France such as Sartre and de Beauvoir were left out of the loop on many matters. Rivalry set in between London and Paris, in part caused by friction between Russell's private secretary Ralph Schoenman and the Paris group. Contrasting procedural methodologies were also evident. Russell and Schoenman publicly declared American guilt. The Paris group was more legalistic, wanting to judge American actions on the basis of international law, and seeking to avoid issuing a verdict prior to presentation of evidence.

The Stockholm hearings focused on the use of fragmentation bombs, the targeting of civilians, and the destruction of dykes. Medical, scientific and legal evidence was introduced. Cross-examination was carried out mainly by Sartre and Dedijer. Delegates from North Vietnam and the Vietcong were in attendance, and Ho Chi Minh sent a telegram of support. The verdict was that the US was guilty of violating international law through acts of aggression. The argument that it was defending South Vietnam from the North was rejected because Vietnam was one country and could not aggress against itself. South Korea, Australia and New

Zealand were found to be accomplices, and the US, Thailand and South Vietnam were found guilty (with one abstention) of aggression against Cambodia. The US was also found guilty on the charge of war crimes through its targeting of civilians and usage of prohibited weapons.

Overall, the tribunal failed to capture the media's imagination. Attention was diverted by the Arab–Israeli crisis in the Middle East, and Western states were disturbed by the tribunal's partisanship. The Soviet Union and its allies paid little heed to proceedings, considering many of the tribunal organizers to be Trotskyists. US national security adviser Walt Rostow and the consul-general in Stockholm, Turner Cameron, Jr., informed Washington that world press reaction was negative, and that there was no need for the US to consider a countertrial or economic sanctions against Sweden (Rostow, 1967; Logevall, 1993: 430).

The Roskilde hearings concentrated on napalm and chemical warfare; the treatment of prisoners and civilians; military action against Laos; the roles of Thailand, the Philippines and Japan; and, most importantly, the allegation of genocide. At first de Beauvoir, Oglesby and some other panelists were skeptical about applying the Genocide Convention, while Dedijer led the charge to condemn the US for such behavior. Eventually, Dedijer won out as the panel was swayed by evidence of chemical defoliation, the bombing of civilian targets (especially with cluster bombs), and the forcing of Vietnamese into strategic hamlets where sanitary conditions were poor and health problems rife.

The Roskilde verdict was unanimous in finding the US guilty for using illegal weapons, maltreating prisoners of war and civilians, and aggressing against Laos. There were also unanimous decisions on Thai and Filipino complicity in American aggression, but three negative votes were registered in regard to Japanese responsibility on the grounds that while Japan provided assistance, it did not directly participate in the aggression. There was a unanimous vote of guilty on the genocide charge.

As at Stockholm, the North Vietnamese viewed the verdict as encouraging their military struggle. Their delegates gave tribunal members rings made from downed American aircraft, and the chief Vietcong delegate presented his movement's flag. Simone de Beauvoir expressed displeasure about the public-relations impact of Roskilde, commenting: 'The distressing side of it all was that because of the negligence of the press there were so few of us to profit from this impressive collection of documents, evidence and explanations' (de Beauvoir, 1993: 363). This assessment was indeed accurate. The tribunal had shot itself in the foot due to excessive stridency and partisanship, and had undermined its excellent accumulation of crucial evidence.

## The tribunal movement

The number of international citizens' tribunals proliferated after the Russell Tribunal, as the Bertrand Russell Peace Foundation and several panelists tried to establish an ongoing institutionalized process. Vladimir Dedijer and the Italian socialist lawyer and parliamentarian Lelio Basso played major roles in a series of hearings known as 'Russell II,' and Basso was also a guiding force in the formulation of the July 1976 Universal Declaration of the Rights of Peoples. That same year, Basso established the Lelio Basso International Foundation for the Rights and Liberation of Peoples, and in June 1979 he founded the Permanent People's Tribunal (PPT). He recognized that the term 'people's' had communist connotations that could negatively affect the public image of the PPT, but rejected use of the word 'citizens' because it was too 'bourgeois' (Falk, 2001).

The PPT asserts that it serves the 'dispossessed' and provides a forum for 'marginalized voices.' It seeks to expose injustices not addressed by governments or the United Nations, and accentuates international human rights laws – portrayed as superseding state sovereignty.[4] Exploring the causes of crimes is deemed as appropriate as gathering evidence about their perpetration. The PPT maintains an institutional home in Italy, and has a roster of panelists willing to serve on tribunals. Potential plaintiffs approach the PPT with requests, and sometimes agree to cover the costs involved. Twenty-seven hearings have been completed, and many non-PPT tribunals select experienced panelists from the PPT roster.

One area covered by international citizens' tribunals is group rights pertaining to women, indigenous peoples, psychiatric patients, asylum seekers, and immigrants. A December 2000 Tokyo tribunal on the Japanese military's use of 'comfort women' during World War II was particularly effective in focusing world attention on a neglected issue. The Japanese government had stonewalled on an apology, and was unwilling to pay financial compensation. Both North and South Korea pressed for the tribunal, which concluded that former Japanese military leaders and the late Emperor Hirohito were guilty of crimes against humanity (Cho, 2000).[5]

Tribunals on internal political repression have covered cases as diverse as Guatemala, Chile, Tibet and the retroactive 1915–16 Turkish genocide against the Armenians. A 1980 Antwerp tribunal on the Philippines is particularly noteworthy for its attempt to apply the 1976 Algiers declaration's interpretation of self-determination. Armed struggle aimed at toppling the Marcos government was justified in accordance with the 'collective rights of peoples,' and the Filipino government was delegitimized on the basis of alleged fraudulent elections, the imposition of martial law, neocolonial dominance by the United States, and economic subservience to the World Bank and International Monetary Fund. The tribunal was highly publicized in the Philippines, and may have contributed to the 'people's power' revolution of 1986 (Permanent People's Tribunal, 1981: 4, 275–9, and 290–91).

Tribunals dealing with external aggression, such as those on Nicaragua, Panama and the Gulf War, have tended to focus on the United States as the perpetrator. Once the Cold War ended, critics of the US switched their emphasis to 'global capitalism.' The first major hearings were in Tokyo in 1993, where structural adjustment programs (SAPs), the World Bank, and the International Monetary Fund were lambasted for their roles in extending American economic hegemony. Pointedly, the sessions were held just prior to a Group of Seven (G7) summit, and called for the exercise of 'transnational democracy' to counter 'oppressive patterns and practices emanating from the geopolitical centers of power in the North.' Basically, the tribunal was portrayed as an effort by non-governmental organizations (NGOs) to challenge the G7 structure established by the industrialized states (International People's Tribunal, 1994: iii, 7, 121–5, 151). Later tribunals on specific aspects of 'global capitalism' covered workers' rights, consumers' rights, environmental damage, safety standards, and industrial hazards.[6]

Justice for specific individuals, as in the case of Trotsky and the fire-trial defendants, has not been the purpose of most recent tribunals. The main exception was the 1997 tribunal for Mumia Abu-Jamal, a black radical convicted of the 1981 murder of Philadelphia police officer Daniel Faulkner. The Mumia tribunal called for 'his immediate release, exoneration and compensation,' and found many government officials and prosecutors guilty of 'criminal conspiracy to deny Mumia Abu-Jamal's human rights.' Although the pro-Mumia movement has been successful in delaying application of the death penalty, the tribunal was not effective in its immediate aim: overturning the verdict passed by the Philadephia Common Pleas Court. In 1998, the Pennsylvania Supreme Court denied Mumia's request for a new trial (see People's International Tribunal for Justice for Mumia Abu-Jamal, n.d. a, b, c).[7]

Tribunals have investigated many important cases, and uncovered much pertinent evidence. Nevertheless, they have undercut their effectiveness and limited media attention through their questionable procedures. One problem is that verdicts are almost always unanimous, creating the impression that the tribunals are kangaroo courts. Second, concern for the Third World is not mirrored in the venues selected or the composition of panels. Tribunals are generally held in Europe, even if their subject matter pertains to the Third World, and the panelists tend to be Europeans or

Americans. Third, tribunals are often viewed by the media as partisan toward the political left. (This concern has been addressed to some extent with sessions criticizing the Soviet role in Afghanistan and Chinese policy in Tibet. At the time of writing, sessions are under way in Lithuania to investigate abuses perpetrated during the Soviet period.) Lastly, tribunals have failed to attract the involvement of major public intellectuals of the caliber of Dewey and Russell, further limiting media interest in their proceedings.

## Suggestions for reform

International citizens' tribunals help to enhance participatory democracy and universal jurisdiction, and are an effective means of holding major powers to account. Tribunals established by the United Nations, such as those for the former Yugoslavia and Rwanda, are unlikely to take on members of the 'Big Five' countries, which can also protect themselves under an International Criminal Court (ICC) regime via the dilatory authority granted to the Security Council. In particular, the United States has been working hard to exclude itself from ICC jurisdiction.

Tribunals should have a permanent institutional base, a common set of procedures, and a pool of qualified panelists available to serve. In addition, transcripts of hearings and documentary material should be placed on the Internet. Using the existing Permanent People's Tribunal as a base, with some important modifications, would be a practical solution.

Tribunals should convene in major media centers in order to garner attention, and they should be better timed to coincide with pending court deliberations or governmental policy decisions. Panels should be given ample time to arrive at their findings. Too often, verdicts are issued very quickly – and sometimes have even been written prior to the presentation of testimony. Such practices undermine the legitimacy of tribunals in the eyes of the public.

Activist groups, often NGOs, play a crucial role in organizing tribunals, but their participation should be separated from the hearings they sponsor. Members of the organizing committee should not be panelists. Additionally, ideological rhetoric should be eschewed, because it vastly reduces media coverage and public support. Democratic techniques of jurisprudence should take precedence over ideological ends. There should also be less fear of perceived moral equivalence – a problem that can be remedied by including a representative for the defense even if actual defendants refuse to take part in the tribunal. Admitting that crimes may be committed by both sides in conflict situations would surely help to refute charges of excessive partisanship.

International citizens' tribunals should operate less like quasi-legal courts, and more like grand juries. They should determine whether an indictment should be issued, not render a verdict. Further, they should incorporate a mechanism to challenge the composition of the panel, and institute a process by which an enlarged majority (perhaps three-quarters) is needed to sustain an indictment. As with a grand jury, the defense must be represented. There should, however, be one significant departure from grand-jury practice: namely, open hearings. Secrecy is certainly not compatible with public relations, and revealing the votes of individual panelists may also be publicly instructive. In such cases, dissenting panelists would be able to issue their own findings. An image of fairness would thus be projected, as freedom to arrive at countervailing opinions would buttress a tribunal's democratic credentials.

International citizens' tribunals demonstrate that non-official actors may perform crucial roles in confronting criminal behavior and furthering the cause of human rights. Sovereignty should not be the sole preserve of the state, and justice should at least in part emanate from the people. Effective tribunals are critical here, but reforms must be implemented if tribunals are to realize their full potential.

## Notes

1. For a closer examination of international citizens' tribunals, see Klinghoffer and Klinghoffer, 2002.

2. The text of the Universal Declaration of the Rights of Peoples appears in Permanent People's Tribunal, 1981: 282–4.

3. Division within the subcommission became problematic when Carleton Beals walked out prior to the conclusion of the hearings. He had procedural and personal differences with other subcommission members, and also felt that they were too deferential to Trotsky.

4. See the PPT website at www.grisnet.T/filb/tribu.eng.html.

5. See also http://srd.yahoo.com/srst/27768279/japan+sexual+slavery/1/5/http://witness.peacenet.or.

6. For example, the 1984 Bhopal disaster in India was dealt with retroactively by a 1992 tribunal.

7. The judgment of the Pennsylvania Supreme Court can be found at www.mastalk.com.

## References

1997 People's Summit on APEC. n.d. www.vcn.bc.co/summit/popindex.htm.

Basso, L. (1975). Inaugural discourse. In W. Jerman, ed., *Repression in Latin America*, 3–9. Nottingham: Spokesman Books.

De Beauvoir, S. (1993). *All said and done.* New York: Paragon House.

Bowring, B. (n.d.). Socialism, liberation struggles and the law. http://members. netscapeonline.co.uk/suzyboyce1/files/book1/3_9.htm.

*The Brown Book of the Hitler terror* (1933). New York: Knopf.

Bullert, G. (1983). *The politics of John Dewey.* Buffalo: Prometheus.

Cho, S.-Y. (2000). On the constitution and the procedure of the Women's International War Crimes Tribunal on Japan's military sexual slavery in 2000. http://witness. peacenet.or.kr/symek2000.htm.

Commission of Inquiry into the Charges Made Against Leon Trotsky in the Moscow Trials (1972). *Not guilty.* New York: Monad Press.

Dewey, J. (1922). *Human nature and conduct.* New York: Modern Library.

Dixon, Marlene, ed. (1985). *On trial: Reagan's war against Nicaragua.* San Francisco: Synthesis.

Falk, R. (2001). Interview by Judith Klinghoffer, 6 March.

Farrell, J. (1965). Memories of John Dewey. Tape 13, John Dewey Papers, Morris Library, Southern Illinois University, 102/81, 5 November.

Hays, A.G. (1942). *City lawyer.* New York: Simon & Schuster.

International People's Tribunal (1994). *The people vs. global capital.* New York: Apex.

Klinghoffer, A. and Klinghoffer, J. (2002). *International citizens' tribunals: Mobilizing public opinion to advance human rights.* New York: Palgrave.

Lewy, G. (1978). *America in Vietnam.* Oxford: Oxford University Press.

Lippmann, W. (1925). *The phantom public.* New York: Harcourt, Brace.

Logevall, F. (1993). The Swedish conflict over Vietnam. *Diplomatic History* 17, no. 3 (Summer): 421–45.

Lynd, S. (1967). Letter to B. Russell in Bertrand Russell Archives, McMaster University, 10.3/372, 13 January.

——— (1967–68). The War Crimes Tribunal: A dissent. *Liberation* 12, no. 9–10 (December–January).

Meyer, A. (1938). Significance of the Trotsky trial: Interview with John Dewey. *International Conciliation* 337: 53–60.

*New York Times* (1933). Promises to punish guilty. Associated Press dispatch, 5 November.

People's International Tribunal for Justice for Mumia Abu-Jamal (n.d. a). Findings of fact and conclusions of law. www.geocities.com/CapitolHill/4167/tribunal.html.

——— (n.d. b). Findings of the judges. www.iacenter.org/Tribunal.htm.

——— (n.d. c). Tribunal verdict. www.mumia.org/fns405.html.

Permanent People's Tribunal (1981). *Philippines: Repression and resistance.* Manila: Komite ng Sambayanang Pilipino.

Rostow, W.W. (1967). Letter to L.B. Johnson, National Security File, Memos to the President, Vol. 27, Box 16, LBJ Library, Austin, Texas, 5 May.

Russell, B. (1967). *War crimes in Vietnam.* London: Allen & Unwin.

——— (1968). *The autobiography of Bertrand Russell,* Vol. III, *1944–1967.* London: Allen & Unwin.

Tolischus, Otto (1933). Nazis offer alibis in Reichstag fire. *New York Times,* 23 September.

Untitled document (1967). Bertrand Russell Archives, McMaster University, Hamilton, ON, Canada, 10.5/384.

Zeldin, X. (1991). John Dewey's role in the 1937 Trotsky Commission. *Public Affairs Quarterly* 5, no. 4 (October): 387–94.

# 20

# Coming to Terms with the Past: The Case for a Truth and Reparations Commission on Slavery, Segregation and Colonialism

## Francis Njubi Nesbitt

Today we lay claim to our right to redress from the banks and businesses that enabled gross violations of our human rights.

This is the only route left open to us to ensure that the truth is known about the extent of corporate complicity in apartheid abuses and that justice is delivered to those who suffered. The victims cannot be left to pay for their own suffering. Multinational corporations must be put on notice that complicity in crimes against humanity does not pay.

*Khulumani Support Group, 12 November 2002*

Does the West owe reparations to Africans and people of African descent for 500 years of slavery, colonialism, Jim Crow laws, and apartheid? This is a question that places most black and white people on opposite sides of a familiar divide. Yet, like the anti-apartheid movement of the 1980s, which forced the West to acknowledge that apartheid was a 'crime against humanity,' the reparations campaign is gaining momentum and transforming human rights discourse in the global public sphere. Western recalcitrance was demonstrated once again at the World Conference Against Racism, Racial Discrimination, Xenophobia, and Related Intolerance (WCAR) held in Durban, South Africa from 31 August to 7 September 2001 (UNHCHR, 2002) (see Document 4 following this chapter). At the conference, delegates from Africa and the Diaspora came together to demand that the West acknowledge that slavery and colonialism were crimes against humanity with serious contemporary effects that require reparatory compensation. The United States walked out of the conference, refusing to acknowledge that slavery and the slave trade were crimes. The US argued that the atrocities were legal at the time, and that accepting responsibility would open the door to lawsuits. Nevertheless, on 8

September 2001, the conference adopted a declaration acknowledging that slavery and the slave trade were 'crimes against humanity' and 'should always have been so.' The resolution also acknowledged the wrongs of slavery and colonialism, and recommended that the international community take measures to alleviate the impact of these crimes. Yet the declaration fell far short of the African demand for an explicit apology and reparations for the enslavement of millions of Africans and the bloody colonization of the continent; for a cancellation of illegitimate debt; and for the return of Africa's material and cultural treasures. Nevertheless, the acknowledgment that slavery and colonialism are crimes provides the international reparations movement with a foundation on which to build its case.

## Three strategies: legal, political and mass movement

Since the WCAR, the black reparations movement has gained considerable momentum. Activists have adopted legal, political and mass-movement strategies. A follow-up conference, the African and African Descendants' World Conference Against Racism, held in Barbados in October 2002, demonstrates the strength of the mass-movement strategy. The conference, which attracted over 500 participants, discussed a plethora of issues including lawsuits against France, England, Portugal and Germany, AIDS and affirmative action. The conference resulted in the formation of a Pan African Movement to deal with issues ranging from racial profiling to poverty and reparations for slavery, colonialism and apartheid (Wilkinson, 2002). Participants agreed to initiate lawsuits against Britain, Germany, France, and Belgium, to be followed by suits against Portugal, Spain, and the Netherlands.

The movement showed both its strengths and weaknesses at the Bridgetown conference. On the plus side was its mobilization of hundreds of participants from all parts of the world to discuss the issue of reparations. This mobilization and formation of a pan-African organization to facilitate communication and collaboration among activists in different parts of the world demonstrates the growing maturity of the movement. On the minus side was the tendency of activists to indulge in tangential gestures that had little practical value. This was evident in the majority floor vote calling for the expulsion of non-Africans from the conference. The vocal and organized Afro-British and African-American delegations demanded the vote, but the motion was carried at an unacceptable cost, resulting in the loss of delegates from Cuba, South Africa and Colombia, who could not accept the decision despite their African heritage. Given the minuscule presence of non-Africans at the conference, this vote was self-indulgent at best.

The legal strategy has been the most successful in obtaining reparations for people of African descent in the short run. These lawsuits have spread from the United States to Haiti, Kenya and Jamaica. In 1999, lawyer Alexander Pires won $1 billion for 24,000 black families who charged discrimination by the Department of Agriculture. The US Department of Agriculture provided no loans to African-American farmers until 1997. 'Ninety-five per cent of all farm loans went to white farmers. And until the 1960s, the USDA had a special section called Negro Loans, which ensured that black applicants were rejected. It's amazing' (*Harper's*, 2000). In March 2002, a reparations lawsuit was filed against Aetna, CSI and Providence Bank, along with a hundred other companies, charging that they had profited from slavery (Cox, 2002). Also planning class-action lawsuits is a group of high-powered lawyers led by civil rights attorney Johnnie Cochran and Harvard University law professor Charles Ogletree. The precedent for these lawsuits is the $6 billion settlement won by the World Jewish Congress on behalf of Holocaust slave laborers.

In Kenya, survivors of the War of Independence and concentration camps established by the British have sued the British government for war crimes. Among incidents likely to be at the top of the agenda are the Hola massacre, where seventy detainees were beaten to death; castrations at Nyangwethu Screening Camp; and the Lari massacre, in which civilians – mostly women and children – were allegedly killed by colonial and loyalist forces. Colonial officials estimated that 10,527 LFA fighters were killed and 2,633 captured by the British forces between 1952 and 1956, when the insurgency against colonialism peaked. About 1,826 'loyal African' soldiers were killed and 918 wounded. At least 2,000 innocent black people were also killed. After failing to track down the freedom fighters effectively, the colonial government turned on the African population, arresting thousands and detaining about 77,000 in what was called 'Operation Anvil.' When the state of emergency was lifted, about 38,449 Kenyans were still in detention, convicted of either being 'Mau Mau' or their sympathizers.

In Jamaica, lawyers served a writ on Queen Elizabeth II when she visited Kingston in February 2002 (Wilkinson, 2002). France is also being targeted because it forced Haiti to pay 150 million francs as compensation for French property lost during the slave uprising that led to the first black republic in the West. Although these reparations lawsuits are critical components of the movement, they need to be placed in perspective. Single-issue class action lawsuits only benefit the parties affected by the particular crime against humanity. While it is critical that the Kenyan victims of detention, torture, castration and confiscation receive compensation, their case would be immeasurably strengthened by a formal association with similar suits in Jamaica, the United States and Namibia. This collaboration would allow the aggrieved to share experiences and collaborate on the broader challenge of restoring Africa to its rightful place as an equal in global affairs.

A third strategy is the political campaign for reparations that seeks to convince governments to acknowledge their role in human rights violations and provide compensation for property and lives lost. The role of government has been prominent during periods of reconstruction after major wars, genocide, and other mass human rights violations. Union Army General William Tecumseh Sherman's Field Order #15, for instance, required military officers to provide black families with 40-acre plots on former slave plantations as compensation for unpaid labor. On 11 March 1867 Thaddeus Stevens of Pennsylvania introduced H.R. 29, which called for redistribution of former slave plantations among the freed slaves. President Andrew Johnson reversed Sherman's field order and vetoed H.R. 29. One hundred and nineteen years later, Representative John Conyers of Michigan introduced H.R. 891 in the 104th Congress, calling for a commission to be established to study the question of reparations. Despite the conservative tenor of its request, by contrast with Stevens's call for redistribution of property, Conyers's mild proposal received little support, and as a result has yet to make it out of committee.

On 4 May 1994, the State of Florida passed the Rosewood Compensation Act, acknowledging the state's responsibility for failing to prevent a massacre of the town's black residents in a white rampage in 1923 (Brooks, 1999). The pogrom lasted for days, leading to charges that the state of Florida could have intervened and saved lives and property. The Act provided compensation of up to $150,000 for victims and their families (a total of $7 million), and established scholarships for minority students with preference given to Rosewood residents (Brooks, 1999).

Reconstruction after colonial rule in Africa sometimes involved land-redistribution schemes that resembled General Sherman's field order. In Kenya, British settlers were forced to vacate Kikuyuland after a ten-year guerrilla war, but not before they had been 'compensated' for land taken by force from African peasants. The British also secured a promise from Kenya's first African president, Jomo Kenyatta, that he would not pursue compensation claims for war crimes. A similar agreement between Zimbabwe's Robert Mugabe and the British in 1980 failed to materialize, leading to the current crisis as war veterans attempt to take back their lands from settlers.

In Brazil and Colombia, people of African descent continue to seek title to lands they have occupied for hundreds of years. In 2000, Brazil's

Congress voted that residents of Quilombos in northeastern Brazil should receive title deeds to lands they had occupied – in some cases since the fifteenth century, when Africans created independent communities of fugitive slaves. Afro-Colombians also received title to lands occupied by former slaves, but have been displaced by right-wing paramilitary gangs linked to the Colombian military. The Afro-Colombians had the misfortune to occupy land near oilfields and mineral deposits. Massacres and forced displacement are pulling the population out by the roots. According to Mary Jo McConahay, the Chocó province on the Pacific, home to 400,000 people, has been hard-hit by the Colombian war. The area is the source of mineral deposits critical to the aerospace and nuclear industries; of oil, gold, and silver; and of most of the timber felled in Colombia. In 1998, Afro-Colombian Governor Luis Murillo declared Chocó off-limits to all armed groups, including the army. Within months, courts stripped him of office, and he was kidnapped and held by a death-squad in Bogota. He escaped, and is now living in exile in Washington, DC (McConahay, 2002).

The biggest challenge for the growing movement is to develop a global structure that will bring together different parts of the movement for dialogue and development of a global vision and strategy for reparations. There is no doubt, for instance, that the mass kidnapping and deportation of millions from the African continent is at the core of the reparations claims of all parties, be they from the Caribbean, South America, the United States, or even the African continent itself. This global trade in Africans and the products of their labor also underpins the second pillar of the reparations campaign, which is the claim that the West received unjust riches from the centuries of unpaid labor of Africans and their descendants in the Diaspora. Africans and people of African descent in the Diaspora were and continue to be targeted as a racial group, not as individuals. Slavery, Jim Crow laws, apartheid, and colonialism created a racial caste system that continues to determine the life-chances of people of African descent, based primarily on their color. Thus a pan-African effort is imperative if the campaign is to encompass the global implications of slavery and its legacies of segregation, colonialism, and global apartheid.

To meet this challenge, this chapter proposes the formation of a truth and reparations commission that would provide a global vision and a forum for the coordination of the movement's different parts. The 'truth commission' model would provide the movement with a structure to coordinate the activities of regional tribunals and case-specific committees to be charged with establishing as clear a picture as possible of the impact of slavery, colonialism and segregation. The regional tribunals would identify the perpetrators of these crimes, assess damages, and make specific recommendations on compensatory measures. Accordingly, the remainder of this chapter examines the emergence of truth commissions as tools of conflict resolution, before making detailed recommendations for the establishment of a pan-African truth and reparations commission.

## Truth commissions

Since the mid-1970s, nineteen 'truth commissions' have been established in sixteen countries to investigate human rights violations. These commissions have explored the disappearances and assassinations of individuals, massacres, and the activities of specific leaders and regimes. They have become significant tools of conflict resolution in societies wracked by communal, racial and ethnic violence. They reflect a commitment to reconciliation and the development of cultural values stressing the rule of law and a culture of human rights. The commissions have generally been successful in establishing facts about the disappearance, torture and death of thousands of persons, allowing families the consolation of at least knowing how their relatives met their fate (Boraine and Levy, 1995; Ignatieff, 1995; Asmal and Roberts, 1996). They are also linked by their examination of human rights abuses by government officials and other public and private institutions. Truth commissions explore the circumstances under which crimes against humanity were committed, and recommend measures to restore material and human resources taken from the victims. Some, like the South African Truth and Reconciliation Commission, are authorized to recommend reparations and compensatory damages. The truth commissions examined in this study have the following characteristics. They:

- focus on the past;
- investigate violations that occurred in the midst of racial, ethnic or other civil strife;
- examine human rights violations perpetrated by government officials;
- exist only for a brief period of time, and dissolve after issuing their reports;
- secure access to information held by both the regime under investigation and the new government;
- have the power to subpoena sensitive documents;
- publish the names of perpetrators;
- are open to the public and media;
- have the authority to call for reparations or compensatory damages.

The commissions have had mixed results. In some cases, like that of Chile's 1990 National Commission on Truth and Reconciliation, they have met their limited goal of investigating 'disappearances.' The Chilean commission provided details of 2,920 cases of disappearance, but was criticized for providing truth without justice (Human Rights Watch, 1993). General amnesty has marred many of the Latin American commissions. Critics say the amnesty provisions allow the perpetrators to continue to hold public office with impunity. The truth commission for El Salvador, for instance, investigated a twelve-year civil war in 1993, naming those it deemed responsible for wartime atrocities (Human Rights Watch, 1993). After the report was issued, however, the government passed legislation granting general amnesty to perpetrators, some of whom retained powerful positions in the regime.

The South African Truth and Reconciliation Commission (TRC), which drew on the experiences on El Salvador, Chile and Argentina, is notable for granting amnesty only to individuals (that is, not a general amnesty). These individuals had to convince the committee that their crimes were politically motivated. The TRC also decided to give the media and public full access to the hearings, and to publish the names of the perpetrators of atrocities. As Dr Alexander Boraine, co-chair of the TRC, put it at an international conference on mass violence in Belgium in 1996:

> South Africa's experience is very similar to many other countries in that witness after witness at the Human Rights Violations Committee hearings have emphasized their deep fundamental need to know the truth surrounding the loss of their loved one. Over and over again people have pleaded to know what happened to the father or the mother, the sister, the brother, the son or the daughter. Where is he or she buried? Why did they do this? This is a common refrain at almost every public hearing. In other words, knowing the details and circumstances of the human rights violation in itself is part of the healing process. (Boraine and Levy, 1995)

This need to know the truth about human rights violations and the fate of family and community members is universal. In the case considered in this chapter, we are talking about the mass kidnapping of African men, women and children; their forced deportation to a foreign land, with millions killed en route, followed by enslavement for 444 years and an ensuing century of segregation, colonialism and apartheid. The descendants' need to know the truth about the circumstances of this horrific crime, and the desire for justice and restitution, is not only understandable, but involves a fundamental right. The truth about the impact of slavery, colonialism and apartheid on people of African descent today is also critical if the West is to come to terms with its past. The experience of the last thirty years has shown that the quest for truth cannot raise the dead. But it can provide compensation and dignified closure for survivors and solidify the democratic process by making perpetrators accountable for their actions.

The South African TRC was established by the country's Interim Constitution, which stated that,

> In order to advance such reconciliation and reconstruction, amnesty shall be granted in respect of acts, omissions and offenses associated with political ob- jectives and committed in the course of conflicts of the past. To this end Par- liament under this constitution shall adopt a law determining … and providing for mechanisms, criteria and procedures, including tribunals, if any through which such amnesty shall be dealt with.

According to Mr Dullar Omar, South Africa's Minister of Justice, the Truth and Reconciliation Commission was established to help South Africans come to terms with the past on a morally acceptable basis while advancing the cause of reconciliation. Omar argues that the commission is based on the belief that 'the truth concerning human rights violations in our country cannot be suppressed or simply forgotten. They ought to be investigated, recorded and made known.' The victims of the apartheid system need to know the truth as a part of the healing process. 'It is the search for truth which can create a moral climate in which reconciliation and peace will flourish.'

The TRC produced a mountain of evidence on the complicity of the apartheid regime in human rights violations. The National Party, police and military voluntarily released secret documents to avoid subpoena and the amnesty provision encouraged former police and army officials to detail their roles in the harassment, torture and assassination of anti-apartheid activists. In its December 1996 report, issued one year into the TRC's sessions, Pumla Godobo-Madikizela, a member of the Human Rights Violations Committee, argued that 'survivors and families of victims of past atrocities reclaimed their stories from apartheid politicians.' She contended that the TRC had effectively investigated the facts about the torture and death of many individuals, including the student leader Steve Biko. Through its investigations, it had debunked the myth of black-on-black violence and exposed the existence of a 'Third Force' within the state that carried out the assassinations and massacres in the black townships. Although the TRC has been criticized for its amnesty provisions, Alexander Boraine argues that its mandate was limited, and that it was never designed as a substitute for criminal justice (Boraine and Levy, 1995).

Like the Latin American commissions, the South African TRC proved effective in investigating crimes against humanity. But it did not take the next logical step and recommend reparations in the form of compensation from the government and the beneficiaries of the violations. The South African TRC also suffered from a number of well-known missteps. One was the focus on gross human rights violations that were illegal under apartheid laws, but not on the victims of forced removals and the millions who suffered under racial laws. Another was the lack of accountability displayed by the National Party and corporations that profited from apartheid. Also controversial are the TRC's measures regarding reconciliation. While some argue that the objective of the TRC was to promote reconciliation, not to achieve it, and that significant strides had been made in that direction, others contend that it failed dismally to achieve that mandate.

## The Pan-African Truth and Reparations Commission

The greatest weakness of the truth commission model to this point is its failure to focus on economic and social rights, and to recommend reparations for groups dispossessed of their land and resources. Thus, the South African model is useful both for its structure and (in part) its outcome. But the model must be transformed to accommodate the needs of the twenty-first-century reparations movement. A pan-African truth and reparations commission, therefore, should seek to replicate the South African experience in discussing and documenting the truth about slavery, colonialism, and apartheid, while also recommending reparations and the restoration of natural and cultural resources as necessary.

The truth commission structure would allow Africans and African Americans from the Caribbean, the United States, and South America to seek collective redress for 500 years of slavery, colonialism, and neocolonialism. The model also provides an opportunity for people of African descent to learn the truth about human rights violations from perpetrators and governments and corporations responsible for such acts.

The need for a united pan-Africanist reparations movement is critical to avoid divide-and-rule tactics that are already evident in the anti-reparations campaign (Horowitz et al., 2002). These forces have revived the nineteenth-century myth of African and Arab involvement in the slave trade, as though this absolves Europeans from responsibility for five hundred years of involvement in the enslaving, colonizing, and dehumanizing of people of African descent. Only a united pan-African movement can counter such tactics. The precedent for such a global analysis is found in pan-Africanist scholarship, which has long argued that slavery, colonialism and neocolonialism are part of the same capitalist system that enriched the

West at the expense of Africans. In *Capitalism and Slavery*, Eric Williams (1961) argued that Africans provided the unpaid labor that made it possible for the West to accumulate the financial resources that fueled the emergence of the global capitalist system – a system that has enriched the West, at the expense of the rest, for the last half-millennium. Williams also claimed that the ideology of white supremacy and black inferiority emerged to justify the enslavement of millions of African people.

Williams's intervention in the slavery debate was followed by Walter Rodney's detailed analysis of Europe's role in the underdevelopment of Africa. In *How Europe Underdeveloped Africa* (1974), Rodney argued that the slave trade and colonialism were responsible for the poverty and underdevelopment of postcolonial African countries. His analysis of the role of slavery in the development of European corporations and of port cities like Liverpool would be critical in identifying those companies and governments that benefited from slavery and colonialism (Rodney, 1974). Rodney's analysis was extended and refined by Kwame Nkrumah in *Neocolonialism: The Last Stage of Imperialism* (1966), which argued that the global corporations, along with international financial institutions like the World Bank, were built on the backs of African slaves and forced-labor camps in the colonies. More recently, Ali Mazrui (2001) has argued that the global capitalist system has evolved into a caste system that resembles the South African system of apartheid, with its gross racial inequalities based on exploitation of African labor. Randall Robinson's *The Debt: What America Owes Blacks* (2000) builds on this tradition, arguing that the prosperity of the United States is based on the equity amassed through 246 years of unpaid labor coerced from African Americans. Robinson argues that the reparations movement is the logical extension of the pan-Africanist impulse in the African Diaspora. (Robinson has deep roots in the pan-Africanist movement. As president of TransAfrica, the African-American lobby for Africa, he led a highly successful campaign urging Congress to pass economic sanctions against South Africa. He has now taken on a leading role in the reparations campaign, joining forces with Charles Ogletree, Johnnie Cochran and Alexander Pires in a Reparations Coordinating Committee charged with preparing lawsuits against governments and corporations that benefited from slavery.)

These efforts at the national and international levels are commendable, but they require a more developed critique of capitalism, and thus a strategy to tie the campaigns to the global anti-capitalist movements. These movements would be natural allies of the reparations movement, if the issue were framed as part of a multifaceted attack on race and class oppression, instead of centering itself on calls for an apology and a paycheck. Reparations must be seen not as an end, but as a means to achieve a more equitable distribution of wealth and power, the creation of a democratic culture, and the dismantling of structures of global apartheid. As Robin Kelley puts it:

> The reparations campaign, despite its potential contribution to eliminating racism and remaking the world, can never be an end in itself. Money and resources are always important, but a new vision and new values cannot be bought. And without at least a rudimentary criticism of the capitalist culture that consumes us, even reparations can have disastrous consequences. (Kelley, 2002: 133)

Progressive pan-Africanists' goal of reparations in addition to structural transformation can best be achieved by adopting a modified truth commission model, one that would expose the ways in which slavery, colonialism and globalization have produced the obscene inequalities known aptly as global apartheid. The truth commission model also provides an opportunity for scholars and other experts to document and publish credible information on age-old questions about the impact of slavery and colonialism on African, European, and American societies, and its legacy in current social, political and interracial relations.

The 2001 Durban Conference designation of slavery and colonialism as crimes against humanity settled one of the most contentious points in the reparations debate. This international consensus, adopted by 168 countries, provides the legal basis for a claim under international law. This can be combined with the findings of the Nuremberg Tribunal, which defined crimes against humanity as 'murder, extermination, enslavement, deportation, and other inhuman acts committed against any civilian population … whether or not in violation of the domestic law of the country here perpetrated.'

It is also a tenet of international law that those who commit crimes against humanity must pay reparations, including compensation for lives and property. They must also acknowledge that a crime was committed and pledge to end ongoing abuses (Human Rights Watch, 2001). After World War II, the Allies agreed to provide the Jewish people with reparations in the form of a homeland (now the State of Israel) and compensation for lives lost and property destroyed. The Federal Republic of Germany reached an agreement with the State of Israel in which Germany agreed to pay the costs of resettling 500,000 Jews who had fled from Europe. Since then, Germany has paid more than $50 billion in reparations for the Holocaust. More recently, corporations involved in the enslavement of Jews during World War II paid over $5 billion to establish the Holocaust Slave Fund. The United States and Canada, for their part, have paid monetary compensation and returned land to numerous Native American groups. In 1998, the United States Congress passed the Civil

Liberties Act to make reparation to Japanese Americans interned in concentration camps during World War II (Maki et al., 1999). A total of $1.2 billion was disbursed in $20,000 portions to victims and descendants of Japanese internees in the United States (Maki et al., 1999).

## Regional panels

Our proposed commission should be divided into regional panels and subdivided into thematic groups that will discuss specific types of violations (such as slavery, colonialism, and neocolonialism) and their impact on both victims and perpetrators. The regional panels should be charged with:

1. establishing as complete a picture as possible of the causes, nature and extent of the gross violations of human rights committed during the period, including the perspectives of the victims and the motives and perspectives of the persons responsible for committing the violations, to be accomplished through investigations and public hearings;
2. establishing and publicizing the fate or whereabouts of victims, and restoring the human and civil dignity of such victims;
3. compiling reports that will provide as comprehensive an account as possible of the commission's activities and findings, and containing recommendations for the prevention of future human rights violations;
4. recommending reparations for unpaid labor, damages and restitution of stolen resources such as land and cultural artefacts, based on the evidence collected. The commission as a whole should recommend measures to counter the effect of global inequalities engendered by a system of white supremacy.

Accordingly, the first task of the truth commission's regional panels should be to determine the extent of the crimes committed, and how they contributed to the destitution of specific groups of Africans and their latter-day descendants. It should not be difficult to show that 500 years of systematic depopulation of the African continent, its colonization by European powers, and the continued exploitation of African resources by Western corporations have exacerbated the poverty, instability and destitution of African peoples today. In addition to the destitution of the continent, people of African descent in the Diaspora have historically faced genocide, racial pogroms, and lynching, and continue to grapple with systematic discrimination in employment, healthcare, and government services throughout Europe and the Americas. The enduring impact of these crimes against the African peoples is thus amply evident in their political, economic and social marginalization the world over.

In addition to determining the extent of the crime, the panels would need to identify the claimants and defendants. On the African continent, for instance, claimants could range from countries to specific ethnic groups, like the Herero of Namibia, who are currently making the case for genocide against the Germans (see Jan-Bart Gewald's chapter in this volume), or the Kikuyu of Kenya, who are planning to sue the British government for war crimes. If, for example, it is found that Afro-Brazilians continue to suffer from discrimination and structural exclusions established during the era of slavery, the present-day leaders of those governments responsible for the original crimes must make reparations. In the Afro-Brazilian case, this would mean both the Portuguese, who were deeply involved in the slave trade, and the Brazilian government, which is responsible for the perpetuation of subsequent racist structures and practices.

Among the most contentious issues that the commissions will have to deal with is the form that reparations should take. Lawsuits seeking compensation for specific acts of violence or loss of property focus on direct payment of cash settlements to individuals and groups. This is the precedent set in the Jewish and Japanese cases, in which cash settlements formed the bulk of reparations, but were accompanied by official acknowledgment of atrocities and explicit apologies. In the case of Native Americans, both the United States and Canada have paid reparations in the form of land, cash and legal autonomy, for example in allowing Native groups special rights to run casinos in the United States.

To avoid reparations being seen as just a paycheck or apologetic rhetoric, the movement needs to build on the last three decades of transformation of human rights norms, in particular the increasing focus on economic and social rights. The movement must also seek allies outside African communities, particularly in the emerging anti-capitalist and anti-globalization movements of both South and North. The structure for discussion of a global reparations and transformation movement exists. The recommendations advanced in the 1993 Abuja Declaration of the Organization of African Unity (now the African Union), for instance, provide an excellent foundation. The declaration argued that reparations should include the transfer of capital, skills and power to African communities. This transfer of power could be effected through the cancellation of 'odious debt' carried by African and Caribbean countries; the equitable provision of health services, including AIDS medication; and the end of racial discrimination in the United States, Europe and North and South America. The Abuja Declaration has become a reference point for activists across the globe. The WCAR follow-up conference in Barbados contended that reparations should seek to rebuild black communities through the reconstruction of key development institutions: education, healthcare, the economy, and the environment (Clarke, 2002: 2). This focus on the political and economic infrastructure in black communities around the world provides a transformative vision that would make reparations a catalyst for the redistribution of power in the global financial and political system.

## Afterword

As I write, it is reported that the Apartheid Debt and Reparations Campaign has filed suit in New York Eastern District Court against banks and other companies in six Western countries, seeking redress for 'aiding and abetting a crime against humanity' (Apartheid Debt, 2002). Eight Western banks and twelve oil, transport, communications technology, and armaments companies are named, and called upon to contribute to healing the damage caused by their profiteering from apartheid. The contribution would take the form of compensation to the victims, and reparations to be used for reconstruction and development programs. The class action suit, *Khulumani et al. v. Barclays et al.*, was filed on behalf of 32,000 members of an apartheid victims' rights organization called the Khulumani Support Group (KSG). Lawyers for KSG argued the suit based on common-law principles of liability and the Alien Tort Claim Act (28 USC 1350), which grants US courts jurisdiction over some violations of international law, regardless of where the violations occur. Thus the claim argues that US-based manufacturers of arms, computers, and vehicles provided the computers that enabled South African whites to create the hated passbook system; the armored cars that patrolled black townships; and the weapons used to maim and kill Africans. Arms manufacturers and oil companies continued to reap profits from sales to South Africa, despite international sanctions. Meanwhile, the banks provided the funding for South Africa's military and police infrastructure.

The Khulumani Support Group's lawsuit displays the strength of the legal strategy in the broad reparations movement. It has served notice to the global financial and political elite in New York and Washington that they will be held to account for their rapacious profiteering. The KSG's class-action suit in New York builds brilliantly on the precedent set by the Holocaust Slave Reparations Fund by using the Alien Tort Claim Act to seek compensation for crimes against humanity. (The HSRF suit set the ball rolling by winning $6 billion for victims and descendants of Holocaust slave laborers.)

Yet the KSG's strategy, like the Kenyan independence war victims' suits against Britain, would benefit greatly from association with a unified pan-African reparations movement, one whose agenda would extend beyond one-time compensation to include transformation of the global political economy and international human rights norms. Without this critical normative perspective, the reparations movement will likely go the way of South Africa's Truth and Reconciliation Commission, the civil rights movement in the United States, affirmative action, and the Highly Indebted Poor Countries initiative. The limited goals of these poverty-alleviation strategies were laudable in themselves, but failed to take into account the systemic nature of global apartheid. Dramatic court victories are important. But they need to be linked to efforts to eliminate the crushing debt burden on African and Caribbean countries; to secure equal access to healthcare and life-saving drugs; to gain equal access to education and information technology; and to achieve the democratization of the United Nations, the Bretton Woods institutions, and the World Trade Organization.

## References

Allen, R.L. (1998). Past due: The African American quest for reparations. *Black Scholar* 28, no. 2: 2–17.

Apartheid Debt and Reparations Campaign (2002). Major apartheid reparations suit filed in US court. Media statement, 12 November. www.cmht.com/casewatch/civil/apartheid.html.

Asmal, A., and Roberts, R., eds (1996). *Reconciliation through truth: A reckoning of apartheid's criminal governance.* Cape Town: David Phillips.

Boraine, A. and Levy, J., eds (1995). *The healing of a nation?* Cape Town: Justice in Transition Project.

Brooks, R.L., ed. (1999). *When sorry isn't enough.* New York: New York University Press.

Clarke, B. (2002). We must touch on the real issues. *Barbados Advocate,* 17 October. www.barbadosadvocate.com/NewViewNewsleft.cfm?Record=10273.

Cox, J. (2002). Corporations challenged by reparations activists. *USA Today,* 21 February.

*Harper's* magazine (2000). Making the case for slave reparations. *Harper's,* November.

Horowitz, D., et al. (2001). David Horowitz's 'ten reasons why reparations for slavery is a bad idea for blacks – and racist too.' *Black Scholar* 31, no. 2: 48–55.

Human Rights Watch (2001). *An approach to reparations.* New York: Human Rights Watch, 19 May.

——— (1993). *Accountability and human rights: The report of the United Nations Commussion on the Truth for El Salvador.* New York: Human Rights Watch, August.

Ignatieff, M. (1996). Articles of faith. *Index on Censorship,* May.

Kelley, R. (2002). *Freedom dreams: The black radical imagination.* New York: Free Press.

McConahay, M. (2002). For Afro-Colombians, the war is not about drugs. *NCM Online,* 12 June.

Maga, T.P. (1998). Ronald Reagan and redress for Japanese American internment, 1983–88. *Presidential Studies Quarterly* 28, no. 3: 606–19.

Maki, M.T., et al. (1999). *Achieving the impossible dream: How Japanese-Americans obtained redress.* Chicago: University of Illinois Press.

Mazrui, A.A. (1994). Global Africa: From abolitionists to reparationists. *African Studies Review* 37, no. 3: 1–18.

Munford, C. (1996). *Race and reparations: A black perspective for the 21st century.* Trenton: Africa World Press.

Nkrumah, K. (1966). *Neo-colonialism: The last stage of imperialism.* New York: International Publishers.

Robinson, R. (2000). *The debt: What America owes to blacks.* New York: Penguin Putnam.

Rodney, W. (1974). *How Europe underdeveloped Africa.* Washington: Howard University Press.

UNHCR (2002). Declaration of the World Conference against Racism, Racial Discrimination, Xenophobia and Related Intolerance. Durban, South Africa, 31 August– 8 September 2001. www.unhchr.ch/huridocda/huridoca.nsf/(Symbol)/A.Conf. 189.12.En?Opendocument.

Westley, R. (1998). Many billions gone: Is it time to consider the case for Black reparations? *Boston College Law Review* 40, no. 429 (December).

Williams, E.E. (1961). *Capitalism and slavery.* New York: Russell & Russell.

Wilkinson, B. (2002). Blacks consider suing France for wrongdoings in Haiti. *IPS*, 27 September.

# The World Conference against Racism: Declarations on the Transatlantic Slave Trade

**From the final declaration of the UN-sponsored World Conference against Racism, Durban, September 2002**

[Paragraph] 10. We acknowledge that slavery and the slave trade, including the transatlantic slave trade, were appalling tragedies in the history of humanity not only because of their abhorrent barbarism but also in terms of their magnitude, organised nature and especially their negation of the essence of victims, and further acknowledge that slavery and the slave trade are a crime against humanity and should always have been so, especially the transatlantic slave trade, and are among the major sources and manifestations of racism, racial discrimination, xenophobia and related intolerance, and that Africans and people of African descent, Asians and people of Asian descent and indigenous peoples were victims of these acts and continue to be victims of their consequences.

11. The World Conference recognises that colonialism has led to racism, racial discrimination, xenophobia and related intolerance, and that Africans and people of African descent, and people of Asian descent and indigenous peoples were victims of colonialism and continue to be victims of its consequences. We acknowledge the suffering caused by colonialism and affirm that, whatever and wherever it occurred, it must be condemned and its recurrence prevented. We further regret that the effects and persistence of these structures and practices have been among the factors contributing to lasting social and economic inequalities in many parts of the world today.

119. The World Conference, aware of the moral obligation on the part of all concerned States, calls on these states to take appropriate and effective measures to halt and reverse the lasting consequences of those practices.

124. The World Conference recognises the efforts of developing countries, in particular, the commitment and the determination of the African leaders to seriously address the challenges of poverty, underdevelopment, marginalisation, social exclusion, economic disparities, instability and insecurity, through initiatives such as the New African Initiative and other innovative mechanisms such as the World Solidarity Fund for the Eradication of Poverty, and calls upon developed countries, the United Nations, and its specialised agencies as well as international financial institutions to provide, through their operational programs, new and additional financial resources as appropriate to support these initiatives.

125. The World Conference recognises that these historical injustices have undeniably contributed to poverty, underdevelopment, marginalisation, social exclusion, economic disparities, instability and insecurity that affect many people in different parts of the world, in particular in developing countries. The World Conference recognises the need to develop programs for the social and economic development of these societies and the Diaspora within the framework of a new partnership based on the spirit of solidarity and mutual respect in the following areas.

- Debt relief
- Poverty eradication
- Building or strengthening democratic institutions
- Promotion of foreign direct investment
- Market access
- Intensify efforts to meet the internationally agreed targets for Official Development Assistance (ODA) transfers to developing countries
- New Information and Communication Technologies (ICT) bridging the digital divide
- Agriculture and food security
- Transfer of technology
- Transparent and accountable governance
- Investment in health infrastructure in tackling HIV/Aids, TB and malaria, including among others through the Global Aids and Health Fund
- Infrastructure development
- Human resource development including capacity building
- Education, training and cultural development
- Mutual legal assistance in the repatriation of illegally obtained and illegally transferred (stashed) funds in accordance with national and international instruments
- Illicit traffic in arms and light weapons

- Restitution of art objects, historical artifacts and documents to their countries of origin in accordance with bilateral agreements or international instruments
- Trafficking in persons, particularly, women and children
- Facilitation of welcomed return and resettlement of the descendants of enslaved Africans.

# PART IV

# Closing Observations

# 21

# Afghanistan and Beyond

## Adam Jones

An accounting of the sheer scale and continuity and consequences of American imperial violence is our elite's most enduring taboo.

*John Pilger* (2001)

On 11 September 2001, terrorism and mass murder struck the West as never before. The destruction of the World Trade Center and the attack on the Pentagon constituted a symbolic as well as substantive assault on US power and Western-dominated global capitalism. This chapter argues that the attacks came as a boon to the Bush administration, permitting the most uninhibited campaign of geopolitical expansion and military build-up in decades. The goal, according to Breyten Breytenbach, 'is obvious: subjugating the world ... to U.S. power for the sake of America's interests' (Breytenbach, 2002). Anatol Lieven of Washington's Carnegie Endowment is equally blunt: the Bush administration's goal is nothing short of 'unilateral domination through absolute military superiority' (cited in Chomsky, 2002).[1] William Pfaff points to the 'attempt to impose a new order on international society through military force and political and economic pressures' (Pfaff, 2002). For Susan Sontag, the 'war against terror' has 'no foreseeable end.... That is one sign that it is not a war but, rather, a mandate for expanding the use of American power' indefinitely (Sontag, 2002).[2]

An early step along the path to the new Pax Americana was the ferocious assault, in October and November 2001, upon the ramshackle, almost defenseless country of Afghanistan, its armed forces, and its civilian population. Thousands of civilians were likely killed directly by US forces during the extensive bombing campaign. Those same forces may also have been complicit – or at the very least criminally negligent – in one of the worst genocidal massacres of recent years, that of Taliban (mostly non-Afghan) prisoners captured by the Northern Alliance after the fall of Mazar-i-Sharif. In addition, many thousands – possibly tens of thousands – of Afghans died unknown and unrecorded during the winter of 2001–02. A focus on humanitarian assistance, such as aid organizations were pleading for, might well have saved them. The fighting and massive population movements further disrupted harvests in 2002, leading aid agencies to warn of a renewed crisis for the winter of 2002–03, as this book went into production.

Postwar reports from Afghanistan speak of fragile or nonexistent security for the vast majority of the population, with only Kabul an island of relative calm. Even the lot of that sector of the Afghan population used above all others to justify the 'humanitarian' intervention, Afghan women, has hardly changed for the overwhelming majority (Constable, 2002). Politically, the brutal and reactionary centralized rule of the Taliban has been replaced by the brutal and reactionary decentralized rule of the warlords, with the US taking sides and sending in B-52s as deemed necessary. Back to the future we may be headed: 'the last time [the warlords] were in charge the country slipped into a horrid civil war to which the hand-chopping, head-chopping Taliban were the puritanical solution.' So noted Peter Maass in the *New York Times* Magazine (Maass, 2002), adding that while 'the destruction of the Taliban has made the United States a safer country, … the same cannot be said for Afghanistan.' Whether even the security of ordinary Americans has benefited, as Maass claims, is highly questionable. Americans now must concern themselves not just with al-Qaeda's machinations, but with the ardent desire of their own government to strip them of constitutional protections and expose them to an apparatus of surveillance and snooping that makes Orwell's *Nineteen Eighty-Four* read more and more like today's news dispatches.

## Targeting Afghanistan

It is unfortunate but probably true that we will never know the full scale of the deaths from starvation and disease that have occurred in Afghanistan since the Allied attack was launched. What evidence there is, though, suggests deaths almost certainly in the thousands, and very likely the tens of thousands:

> [From the BBC:] Tens of thousands of people face starvation this winter in western Afghanistan – despite a huge international aid effort. About seven million people depend on aid in Afghanistan – but the disruption to supplies during last

year's fighting broke a vulnerable food chain. The worst affected area is the mountainous province of Badghis, in western Afghanistan.... Some villagers ... have died of hunger or related diseases ... families have resorted to selling their own daughters for grain.... The only answer for Oxfam is to pump in more food to fill the backlog. They lost three months during the fighting and in that vacuum people·died. (Lyon, 2002)

While the West celebrates the surrender of Kandahar and the collapse of the Taliban, here in Maslakh camp in western Afghanistan there is no celebratory slaughtering of goats or distribution of sweets, but only weeping and funerals.... Every night as the temperature dips well below zero, as many as 40 people die from cold and starvation [about the death-toll of the World Trade Center attacks every two-and-a-half months; other media sources claimed up to 100 a day were dying]. In the six cemeteries scattered through the camp, many of the piles of stones marking graves are so tiny that it is clear most victims are children and babies.... 'The world made us lots of promises,' Ismail Khan, the Governor of Herat, told *The Telegraph*. 'Now people are dying and it has no excuse not to act.' (Lamb, 2001; see also *The Economist*, 2001; Fassihi, 2001; Waldman, 2001)

Starvation was no longer a threat − it was a daily reality. Every week, through the month of November [2001] and into December ... more than a hundred people in [the district of] Abdulgan died of malnutrition.... They died because they were trapped by nature and politics and war.... Eventually, through a massive effort that included some 400 donkeys, several of whom froze to death during the journey, the International Relief [*sic*: Rescue] Committee brought supplies of wheat to the people of Abdulgan. When the relief workers arrived, they found a scene of complete devastation, village after village filled with the dead and dying.... The total number of dead over the last few months [in Abdulgan district alone] has to run into the thousands. (Finkel, 2002)

A recent assessment of the population in the Sar-e-Pol camp in Afghanistan shows a dramatic situation. There are more children in feeding centers than ever before. The number of severely malnourished have increased. Mortality rates have doubled ... The food crisis in northern Afghanistan is reaching alarming proportions [February 2002].... [A] concerted effort is needed from the international community to avert a disaster.... 'We are getting increasingly frustrated with the promises of the international community,' concludes MSF's [Médecins Sans Frontières's] Christopher Stokes. 'All the talk of world leaders, donor countries and international organizations of their commitment to the Afghan people, translate into little for many people in remote areas. In northern Afghanistan, a new disaster is in the making and can only be averted by immediate and unrestrained action.' (Médecins Sans Frontières, 2002)

The link between the problems of aid supply and the bombing campaign against Afghanistan is a truism. As early as 8 October 2001, 'leading British aid agencies' warned that 'the launching of military attacks on Afghanistan will worsen the humanitarian crisis in the country'; a representative of Christian aid, Daleep Mukherjee, noted that 'any offensive military action or threat of military action makes it impossible to deliver' the necessary security conditions for aid supplies; a spokesperson for the Catholic charity Cafod emphasized (in the reporter's paraphrase) that 'launching air strikes while the borders were still closed would leave people who were already starving stranded without access to aid' (Steele and Lawrence, 2001).[3] On 12 October 2001, the *Guardian* reported that 'aid agencies face a race against time to get sufficient stockpiles of food into the country. *It is a race they look almost certain to lose as long as the bombing continues*' (Kelso and McCarthy, 2001, emphasis added). A few days later, a representative of Oxfam stated that 'It is now evident that we cannot, in reasonable safety, get food to hungry Afghan people. We've reached the point where it is simply unrealistic for us to do our job in Afghanistan. We've run out of food, the borders are closed, we can't reach our staff, and time's running out' (Oxfam, 2001).

One of the most cynical assaults on the humanitarian well-being of the Afghan population was the US decision, a scant five days after the 11 September attacks, to demand that Pakistan 'eliminat[e] … truck convoys that provide much of the food and other supplies to Afghanistan's civilian population.' Meanwhile, 'the threat of military strikes … forced the removal of international aid workers that crippled the assistance program.' This according to Noam Chomsky, who added that it 'looks like what's happening is some sort of silent genocide' (Chomsky, 2001).[4]

A key additional factor in the suffering was the willful destruction of what political stability existed in Afghanistan under the Taliban – a grim and repressive stability, to be sure, but one that in key respects was preferable to the chaotic situation that ensued during and after the Taliban's fall from power. With the central government destroyed and the writ of its interim replacement barely extending beyond Kabul, the ancient phenomenon of warlordism reasserted itself, with Allied acquiescence and often enthusiastic assistance. According to Norah Niland, a worker at the UN coordinating office for Afghanistan, 'continuing volatility and insecurity have drastically curtailed aid agency plans to redeploy international staff and scale up outreach programs before winter generates its own set of problems' (quoted in Karacs, 2001). Mark Bartolini of the International Rescue Committee claimed that 'we're probably operating at 20 per cent of what we could be, due to security problems' (quoted in Bowman and Gamerman, 2001). Typical was the situation in the predominantly Pashtun areas of Afghanistan seized by the victorious Northern Alliance, which proceeded to inflict 'serious abuse, including beatings, killings, rapes, and widespread looting' on the civilian population,[5] without any known efforts by the Allies to restrain their surrogates. The *Baltimore Sun* quoted Kenneth Bacon of Refugees International as saying that 'The Taliban didn't interfere with efforts to deliver food to the neediest people. In a strange way, food delivery to parts of the country is more difficult now than it was under the Taliban, and there's no excuse for that' (quoted in Bowman and Gamerman, 2001). A story in the *Denver Post* stated that 'since the warlords took over Jalalabad ... many homes are being raided by mysterious gunmen ... [who] grab every penny and every scrap of food.' 'At least under the Taliban there was no robbery,' an Afghan told the *Post*'s reporter. 'People were feeling hopeful when the US bombed,' another commented. 'But it's gotten even worse. If Bush wants to remove terrorists, why does he not remove them from this place?' (quoted in Seibert, 2001).

Aside from the intentional exacerbation of the humanitarian crisis, a range of criminal actions, either direct or indirect, can be imputed to Allied (notably US) forces in the Afghanistan campaign:

*State terrorism*    The US Federal Bureau of Investigation defines terrorism as 'the unlawful use of force or violence against persons or property to intimidate or coerce a government, the civilian population, or any segment thereof, in furtherance of political or social objectives' (cited in Cryan, 2001). In this light, what is one to make of the following report, issued prior to the fall of Kandahar to Northern Alliance forces?

> Around-the-clock bombing raids *designed to shatter the nerves and morale* of the people of Kandahar have produced *a kind of mass nervous breakdown*, according to refugees fleeing the besieged Taliban stronghold. 'It was like being inside a nightmare,' said a man who arrived at the Pakistan border yesterday. 'Everyone was crying. There were dead people everywhere.' ... Most terrifying of all ... have been the Daisy Cutter bombs, which produce colossal, bone-shaking explosions and level everything around with a lethal hail of explosive shrapnel. The refugees said they had no idea how many people have been killed in the raids, except that the number was extremely high. *The relentless bombing raids have had a devastating psychological effect.* Many refugees said people in Kandahar were reduced to a state of panic, frantically trying to find a place where they would be safe, or fleeing to the Pakistan border. (Cheney, 2001, emphases added)

Marc Herold's 'accounting' of civilian victims of the assault on Afghanistan (see below) also notes that the bombing campaign 'contributed to wholesale panic amongst residents of villages and cities, leading to floods of refugees seeking to escape' – up to 80 per cent of the population of Kabul and Kandahar, for example (Herold, 2001). It is hard not to agree with Mahajan, who calls the protracted bombing of Afghanistan 'one of the most shameful spectacles in modern history, [as] the richest and most powerful nation on earth pounded one of the poorest, most desolate nations on earth for months while proclaiming its virtue to the world' (Mahajan, 2002: 98).

*Large-scale killing of civilians*   There is little doubt, at the time of writing, that more – perhaps many more – civilians have been directly killed in the 'war on terror' than died in the World Trade Center and Pentagon attacks combined. The most substantial single exploration of the issue is the 'Dossier on Civilian Victims of United States' Aerial Bombing of Afghanistan' prepared by Professor Marc Herold of the Whittemore School of Business and Economics at the University of New Hampshire. Herold at first documented a total of 3,767 civilians deaths in the first two-and-a-half months of the US air campaign against Afghanistan, later revising his total slightly downwards, to '3000 to 3600' (Mahajan, 2002: 48). The toll could be ascribed, according to Herold, to 'the apparent willingness of US military strategists to fire missiles into, and drop bombs upon, heavily populated areas of Afghanistan.... [T]he critical element remains the very low value put upon Afghan civilian lives by US military planners and the political elite.' In Herold's view, 'There is no difference between the attacks upon the WTC whose primary goal was the destruction of a symbol, and the US–UK revenge coalition bombing of military targets located in populated urban areas. Both are criminal. Slaughter is slaughter' (Herold, 2001).[6]

Attempts to establish accurately the scale of civilian deaths in the campaign have been hampered by the deliberate obstruction of the US government, which decided, in October 2001, to 'spen[d] millions of dollars to prevent western media from seeing highly accurate civilian satellite pictures of the effects of bombing in Afghanistan.' The decision was taken 'after reports of heavy civilian casualties from the overnight bombing of training camps near Darunta, north-west of Jalalabad' (Campbell, 2001).

*Attacks on civilian infrastructure*   In November 2001, the UK *Independent* reported UN warnings of a 'disaster of tremendous proportions' following the US bombing (in seven separate raids) of a hydroelectric plant near the Kajakai dam in South Afghanistan:

> UN officials say that the loss of electricity will increase the suffering of civilians in southern Afghanistan, which has already suffered massive damage from American air raids. They fear that further air raids risk destroying the dam itself, with catastrophic consequences for the region.... [According to a UN report,] 'If the dam collapses the whole Helmand valley would be flooded, risking the life of tens of thousands of people in addition to destroying the lands benefiting around 500,000 people (and feeding around 1,000,000 people).' (Parry 2001)

Fortunately for the civilian population, the dam was never breached; but unless total incompetence reigned, the repeated attacks close to the barrier were carried out in the knowledge that they *could*, and perhaps in the expectation that they *would*, lead to a humanitarian disaster (which in a domestic setting would qualify as criminal negligence, if not attempted murder), and that the obliteration of electrical power for an entire region would cause large-scale civilian suffering. It is worth remembering that the Nazi stooge Arthur Seyss-Inquhart was tried and executed after World War II for atrocities that included breaching dykes in the Netherlands.

Other examples of attacks on civilian infrastructure are cited by Herold in his accounting of civilian deaths in Afghanistan. Certain 'US bombing target hits are impossible to "explain" in terms other than the US seeking to inflict maximum pain upon Afghan society and perceived "enemies" ... [these include] the Kabul telephone exchange, the Al Jazeera Kabul office, trucks and buses filled with fleeing refugees, and the numerous attacks upon civilian trucks carrying fuel oil. Indeed, the bombing of Afghan civilian infrastructure parallels that of the Afghan civilian' (Herold, 2001).

*Mistreatment of prisoners-of-war*  Reports of abuses against prisoners-of-war, including mass killings (discussed further below), circulated in the final days of the war and continued to emerge in 2002. In late December 2001, the *Guardian* reported that 'Afghanistan's new authorities are brutalising Taliban and al-Qaida prisoners to soften them up before handing them to American forces'; guards 'admitted ... that they routinely tortured inmates during interrogations to extract information, which was given to American officials trying to identify suspects to be prosecuted in the US' (Carroll, 2001). Almost exactly a year later, evidence surfaced that prisoners held at the Bagram air base for transfer to detention facilities at the US naval base in Guantánamo Bay, Cuba, were being exposed to CIA 'stress and duress' techniques similar to the techniques inflicted upon Irish detainees and prisoners in the UK during the torture controversy of the 1970s (see Conroy, 2001). In a letter to President Bush, Kenneth Roth, executive director of Human Rights Watch, described prisoners kept 'standing or kneeling for hours,' held in 'awkward, painful positions' and deprived of sleep – methods that in the view of Roth's organization 'would place the United States in violation of some of the most fundamental prohibitions of international human rights law.' The US was also accused of turning prisoners over to the intelligence services of countries notorious for their routine use of torture – another 'violation of international law,' this time 'complicit[y] in torture committed by other governments,' according to Roth (see Cooperman, 2002). At the Afghan jail of Shebarghan, meanwhile, the US was 'accused of openly flouting the Geneva Conventions' by 'washing its hands' of responsibility for conditions at the jail, which the US originally 'helped to operate' and then turned over to one of its favorite warlords, General Abdul Rashid Dostum. The US was now expressing hopes that 'humanitarian groups and charities will step in and improve the conditions at the jail, where 3,300 prisoners are squeezed together in grossly overcrowded, unsanitary cells, and where many have already died from disease.' Leonard Rubinstein, a representative of a Physicians for Human Rights (PHR) delegation that toured the prison, stated: 'The information is that the Pentagon is doing nothing for the conditions at the prison. That is a decision that has been taken at four-star general level.' Under the Geneva Convention, the PHR claimed, the US was still responsible for the appalling conditions: 'This obligation exists irrespective [of] whether the US physically captured the prisoners, whether it currently has custody of them, or whether the detained individuals are considered prisoners of war of the US.' Another member of the delegation, Dr Jennifer Leaning, said: 'We are dealing with a quiet atrocity. These men are ordinary Taliban soldiers. The US has led, controlled and organized this war – [it] understands the situation and is responsible' (quoted in Buncombe, 2002).[7]

*Srebrenica in Afghanistan?*   Only subsequently, however, did it become clear that those who survived to endure the horrors of Shebarghan were the lucky ones, at least temporarily. There is now little doubt that massive atrocities occurred against prisoners who were supposedly being transferred to the prison. A combination of murder through asphyxiation and extra-judicial execution seems to have resulted in a slaughter of defenseless detainees that, if it did not match the 7,000 Bosnian men and boys exterminated at Srebrenica in July 1995, was of a similar order of magnitude. According to Jamie Doran, producer of a shocking documentary titled *Massacre at Mazar*, thousands of Taliban prisoners – 'young men who had expected the protection of the Geneva conventions' after surrendering to US and US-backed forces – had 'instead died horribly, either from suffocation [in container trucks] or by summary execution.' Thousands more were missing after the surrender of the fortress of Kunduz. 'Over 5,000 are missing. A few may have escaped; others may have bought their freedom while more may have been sold to the security agencies of their countries, to return to a terrible fate. But according to a number of eyewitnesses found during a six-month investigation, most lie in the sand' at Dasht Leili, a site only ten minutes' drive from Shebarghan's gates (Doran, 2002).

Doran goes further still, claiming that US soldiers were present when the death containers were opened, and ordered the destruction of the ghastly evidence:

> When the containers were finally opened, a mess of urine, blood, faeces, vomit and rotting flesh was all that remained.... As the containers were lined up outside the prison, a soldier accompanying the convoy was present when the

prison commanders received orders to dispose of the evidence quickly: 'Most of the containers had bullet holes. In each container maybe 150–160 had been killed. Some were still breathing, but most were dead. *The Americans told the Shebarghan people to get them outside the city before they were filmed by satellite.*' (Doran, 2002, emphasis added)

As Doran notes, 'This accusation about US involvement will be crucial to any inquiry: international, and national, civil and military law relies on establishing the chain of command under which crimes took place. It is a matter of determining who was running the show at Shebarghan' (Doran, 2002, emphasis added). There is strong *prima facie* evidence that the US was in fact 'running the show' – at least in the sense that Israeli forces were directing events when they ushered their Christian Phalangist allies into the Palestinian refugee camps of Sabra and Shatila in 1982, with consequences that are both widely known and still emerging (see Fisk, 2001). *Newsweek's* detailed investigation of 'The Death Convoy of Afghanistan' stated straightforwardly that 'American forces were working intimately with "allies" who committed what could well qualify as war crimes' (Dehghanpisheh et al., 2002).

Witness testimony has also alleged that '600 Taliban PoWs who survived the containers' shipment to the Shebarghan prison ... were taken to a spot in the desert and executed *in the presence of about 30 to 40 US special-forces soldiers*' (Kirschbaum, 2002, emphasis added), while others involved themselves enthusiastically and directly in the 'dirty work' of prisoner torture and disposal of corpses:

> Even for those who survived the journey ... to Shiberghan prison, *their fate at the hands of American soldiers was hardly more merciful than death in the desert*, according to eyewitnesses. One soldier recounted an incident when a US soldier murdered a Taliban prisoner in order to frighten the others into talking: 'When I was a soldier at Shebarghan, I saw an American soldier breaking a prisoner's neck. Another time, they poured acid or something on them. The Americans did whatever they wanted; we had no power to stop them. *Everything was under the control of the American commander.*' A general in the Northern Alliance, also stationed at Shebarghan at the time, claimed: 'I was a witness. I saw them [US soldiers] stab their legs, cut their tongues, cut their hair and cut their beards. Sometimes it looked as if they were doing it for pleasure. They would take a prisoner outside, beat him up and return him to the jail. But sometimes they were never returned and they disappeared, the prisoner disappeared.' (Doran, 2002, emphasis added)

An integral part of any investigation into these mass killings and other atrocities ought to be the contemporaneous statements of US officials, notably Defense Secretary Donald Rumsfeld, who in the waning days of the war appeared to be cheerleading for the slaughter of prisoners. Rumsfeld originally announced that the US was 'not inclined to negotiate surrenders,' later 'clarifying' his statement by claiming that while Afghan Taliban should be allowed out of the net that was closing around Kunduz, no such treatment could be accorded to foreign fighters: 'My hope is that they will either be killed or taken prisoner' (quoted in Mahajan, 2002: 51). In the end, Rumsfeld had the best of both worlds: thousands of men were *first* taken prisoner and *then* killed. Something similar appears to have held for the hundreds killed in the alleged 'uprising' at Qala-i-Jangi fort near Mazar-i-Sharif. 'Some reports indicated that hundreds of the dead had their hands tied behind their backs,' while indiscriminate aerial bombing claimed many more lives (Mahajan, 2002: 52).

## 'Operation Endless Deployment'

For the Bush administration, the terrorist attacks on American soil were a godsend. They bolstered the president's legitimacy in the wake of the chaotic 2000 elections; pushed his approval ratings to unheard-of levels; fueled Republican success in the 2002 congressional elections; masked the usual massive tax cuts for the rich; and spurred $600 billion in added military spending – read: subsidies for high-tech and security-related industries – over the next ten years (the US *increase* in military spending in 2002 was greater than the *total* military spending of any other state). In global perspective, the 11 September attacks permitted the most ambitious expansion of US imperial power since at least the early 1980s, and perhaps since the 1950s.[8] Hartung et al. refer to it as 'Operation Endless Deployment':

> Since September 2001 U.S. forces have built, upgraded or expanded military facilities in Bahrain, Qatar, Kuwait, Saudi Arabia, Oman, Turkey, Bulgaria, Pakistan, Afghanistan, Uzbekistan and Kyrgyzstan; authorized extended training missions or open-ended troop deployments in Djibouti, the Philippines and the former Soviet republic of Georgia; negotiated access to airfields in Kazakhstan; and engaged in major military exercises, involving thousands of US personnel, in Jordan, Kuwait and India.... These forward bases, many of which have been arranged through secretive, ad hoc arrangements, currently house an estimated 60,000 personnel [as of October 2002].... Funds for training and military aid, which are often used to grease the wheels of U.S. access to overseas military facilities, have been increased substantially since the start of the Administration's war on terrorism. The budget request for training foreign military personnel is up by 27 per cent in the fiscal-year 2003 budget, while funding for the government's largest military aid program, Foreign Military Financing, is slated to top $4 billion. The bulk of this additional funding is going to countries like Uzbekistan, Pakistan and India [and Colombia], which had previously been under restrictions on what they could receive from the United States because of records of systematic human rights abuses, antidemocratic practices or develop-

ment of nuclear weapons. Now these same nations are viewed as indispensable allies in the Administration's war on terrorism.... In a mid-August [2002] briefing, Gen. Tommy Franks, the head of the Central Command, suggested that the length of the U.S. military presence in Afghanistan could end up rivaling the fifty-year U.S. presence in South Korea. And if the Bush Administration is not dissuaded from moving full-speed ahead with its plans to invade Iraq, several independent military experts have suggested that an occupying force of 75,000–100,000 troops may be needed to stabilize that country, giving rise to the need for additional formal or informal bases to house U.S. troops. (Hartung et al., 2002)

Who, a decade ago, would have imagined US and Allied troops on the territory of the republics of former Soviet Central Asia? What other pretext than the 'war on terror' could have been found to extend weaponry and training to countries as diverse as the Philippines, Georgia, Yemen, Indonesia, and Colombia – in fact, just about any country that asks for such 'aid' or can be pressured into accepting it? It seems every week brings news of a fresh element in the equation. In December 2002, the United States announced a beefed-up alliance with Algeria, consistently one of the world's leading purveyors of domestic terrorism over the last two decades (100–150,000 killed in its civil war, very likely two-thirds of them by the state). 'Washington has much to learn from Algeria on ways to fight terrorism,' William Burns, the Assistant Secretary of State for Near East Affairs, announced sagely. Thus, 'We are putting the finishing touches to an agreement to sell Algeria military equipment to fight terrorism. These steps aim at intensifying the security cooperation between the two countries.' The aid will go primarily to an army which one prominent defector charges with 'killing indiscriminately' and 'exterminat[ing] anyone who supports the Islamists, not just terrorists' (Tremlett, 2002). Once again, then, a Western power has become a supporter of state terrorism in Algeria – reminding us of an earlier generation of battles against 'rebels' and 'terrorists,' detailed in this volume by Raphaëlle Branche.[9] And another country receives a blank cheque for any future repression, so long as it can be justified by the fight against terror – and what cannot be?

Although it is secondary to this volume's focus, the domestic implications of the post-September 11 period are central to the overall US project of domination. In the wake of the collapse of the Soviet bogey, what but a devastating terrorist attack could have allowed 'a demented Caesarism' to take hold in the American republic, 'such as one would once have found among the Soviets, or as one finds today in places like Zimbabwe, North Korea, Cuba (and Iraq)' (Miller, 2002)?[10] What could have permitted truly 'astonishing assertion[s]' of presidential authority like 'President Bush's claim of a right to hold any American citizen whom he designates as an "enemy combatant" in military prison indefinitely, without trial and without the right to speak with a lawyer' (Lewis, 2002)? What could have justified the creation and introduction, 'with no public notice or debate,' of 'the world's largest computer system and database, one with the ability to track every credit card purchase, travel reservation, medical treatment and common transaction by every citizen in the United States'?

This last reference is to the 'Total Information Awareness' system, which professor of constitutional law Jonathan Turley describes as the realization of 'the dream of every petty despot in history: the ability to track citizens in real time and to reconstruct their associations and interests.' The system is to be run by an 'Information Awareness Office' (a masterpiece of Newspeak: 'who could be against greater awareness of information?,' asks Turley), headed by none other than John Poindexter, a key figure in the 1980s' conspiracy to ship arms to Iran, a designated terrorist state. Poindexter 'is the perfect Orwellian figure for the perfect Orwellian project. As a man convicted of falsifying and destroying information [about the Iran–Contra conspiracy], he now will be put in charge of gathering information on every citizen' (Turley, 2002). Poindexter joined an almost surreal procession of disreputable figures from the Reagan era (Elliot Abrams, John Negroponte, Otto Reich), revived for a new era whose imperial swagger and contempt for the rule of law was doubtless familiar to them (Welch, 2002).[11]

## Targeting Iraq... and Cuba

The September 11 attacks were followed by a tightening of the regime of economic sanctions against Iraq, which, as Denis Halliday argues in this volume, have probably been genocidal in their character and in their impact on the Iraqi population. The conservative *Economist* reported in January 2002 that

> America's prickly mood has already led to a surge in the number of 'holds' put on contracts under the UN's oil for food program. Some $5 billion in orders, *all but a fraction of them intended for humanitarian purposes*, now languish undelivered due to American fears that they may serve some military purpose. Meantime, oil prices have fallen 30% since September, and the stringent new mechanism the UN now imposes, whereby prices for Iraqi oil are set retroactively every 15 days, is frightening off customers. The Iraqis' meagre income, already less than a quarter of pre-Gulf war levels, looks set to shrink even further. (*The Economist* 2002a, emphasis added)

The *San Francisco Chronicle* notes that 'U.N. sources who would not speak for attribution complain that the United States has stood by the strict sanctions in the hope that the Iraqi people will one day rise up against Hussein for causing their suffering' (Ditmars, 2002). (Article 54 of the

1949 Geneva Convention states that 'Starvation of civilians as a method of warfare is prohibited.')

As work on this chapter was completed, Washington appeared poised to invade Iraq regardless of the outcome of investigations by the UN inspectors ushered back into Iraq in November 2002. It was even possible that the war (or a subsequent campaign against North Korea) could feature the first use of nuclear weapons since 1945. A report by Michael Gordon of the *New York Times* described 'the Pentagon's new blueprint on nuclear forces' as 'cit[ing] the need for new nuclear arms that could have a lower yield and produce less nuclear fallout.... The targets might be situated in Iraq, Iran, Syria, Libya or North Korea.... Critics fear that by calling for the development of more effective nuclear weapons, the Pentagon is making the unthinkable thinkable, blurring the distinction between nuclear weapons and conventional arms' (Gordon, 2002).[12]

It can at least be said that if nuclear weapons are used in the war on (of?) terror, there will be no shortage of pundits in the United States willing to praise the decision. In a hair-raising compendium of media commentary after the September 11 attacks, FAIR (Fairness and Accuracy in Reporting) cited statements like the following:

> The response to this unimaginable 21st-century Pearl Harbor should be as simple as it is swift – kill the bastards. A gunshot between the eyes, blow them to smithereens, poison them if you have to. As for cities or countries that host these worms, bomb them into basketball courts. (Steve Dunleavy of the *New York Post*)

> If we flatten part of Damascus or Tehran or whatever it takes, that is part of the solution. (Rich Lowry, editor of the *National Review*)

> TIME TO TAKE NAMES AND NUKE AFGHANISTAN. (Caption to Gary Brookins' cartoon in the *Richmond Times–Dispatch*)

> At a bare minimum, tactical nuclear capabilities should be used against the bin Laden camps in the desert of Afghanistan. To do less would be rightly seen by the poisoned minds that orchestrated these attacks as cowardice on the part of the United States and the current administration. (Thomas Woodrow, formerly of the Defense Intelligence Agency)

> This is no time to be precious about locating the exact individuals directly involved in this particular terrorist attack.... We should invade their countries, kill their leaders and convert them to Christianity [!]. We weren't punctilious about locating and punishing only Hitler and his top officers. We carpet-bombed German cities; we killed civilians. That's war. (Ann Coulter, syndicated columnist; see Fairness and Accuracy in Reporting 2002)

Other countries were in the gunsights, including most obviously Iraq, as well as North Korea, Iran, and another longtime US irritant – Fidel

Castro's Cuba. In a blinding flash of hypocrisy, Cuba was added to the US list of states supporting terrorism – after decades in which Cuba was on the receiving end of probably the most sustained international terrorist campaign of the twentieth century, at US hands. In a March 2002 speech, President Castro stated:

> The government of the United States should ask Cuba for forgiveness for the thousands of acts of aggression, sabotage and terrorism committed against our country for 43 years.... The US government will never have the moral authority to combat terrorism while it continues to use such practices against nations like Cuba ... when thousands of Cubans have died as victims of terrorism from the US and not one US citizen has suffered the least scratch nor has one screw even been affected by any action of such a nature by Cuba.

The ban on shipments of food and medicine under the economic embargo constituted, Castro argued, 'acts of genocide' against the Cuban people. The US, he added, 'should renounce its policy of world domination, stop intervening in other countries, respect the United Nations' authority and comply with international treaties it signed.' The Associated Press dispatch from which these quotations are drawn was headlined, 'Castro Oozes Anti-US Rhetoric...' (Cawthorne, 2002). (Oozes like a slug, perhaps?) A more apt title would have been, 'Castro Makes Some Telling Points.'

While the propaganda campaign against Cuba swelled, a more practical campaign of many years' standing was further expanded. It aimed to secure the release from prison and/or the pardon of a host of 'militant Cuban exiles convicted of terrorist offenses.' As detailed in *Cuba Confidential* by Ann Louise Bardach (Bardach, 2002), George W., his brother Jeb, and George Bush Sr. have all played roles in releasing notorious terrorist individuals. For example,

> at the request of Jeb, Mr. Bush Sr. intervened to release the convicted Cuban terrorist Orlando Bosch from prison and then granted him U.S. residency. According to the Justice Department in George Bush Sr.'s administration, Bosch had participated in more than 30 terrorist acts. He was convicted of firing a rocket into a Polish ship which was on passage to Cuba. He was also implicated in the 1976 blowing-up of a Cubana plane flying to Havana from Venezuela in which all 73 civilians on board were killed.

George W., for his part, supplemented his 'sweep of terrorist suspects' by approving the freeing from jail of other convicted terrorists (Campbell, 2001). They were released into a South Florida society that surely counts as one of the world's leading terrorist states-within-a-state. 'There is no war on terrorism,' John Pilger wrote contemptuously. 'If there was, the Royal Marines and the SAS would be storming the beaches of Florida, where more CIA-funded terrorists, ex-Latin American dictators and torturers, are given refuge than anywhere on earth' (Pilger, n.d.).

## Conclusion

This chapter has argued that the US campaign against Afghanistan, far from being motivated by a desire to 'fight terror,' was conducted for the principal purpose of expanding US geostrategic and economic power. Despite claims that the interests of Afghan civilians were paramount, they were killed directly and indirectly in their thousands or tens of thousands. Postwar Afghanistan has been left shattered and fragmented, with no indication that the US and its allies are interested in bringing meaningful security to the mass of the population. The campaign will likely serve as a rough guide to its successors. As the gunsights turn to Iraq, for example, there is no hint that negotiations will be preferred to war, or that multilateral mechanisms will exercise effective constraints on US and British policy, or that the consequences for the Iraqi population will be any less devastating than for their Afghan counterparts.

## Afterword: censored on H-Genocide

On purely moral grounds, the scale of the humanitarian crisis in Afghanistan, and the possible destructive impact of the Allied bombing campaign on attempts to ameliorate it, should have been the leading 'story' in the news media, and the primary policy consideration for Allied governments. No one not clinically deranged would have expected this to be the case, however. Indeed, the humanitarian equation was shunted to the realm of public-relations operations, such as the US's derisory dropping of food packets in Northern Alliance-controlled areas as a storm of bombs rained down on Taliban positions and civilian areas. Coverage of the humanitarian crisis was minimal in the US press, though far more extensive in British media. And critics who raised the idea that conditions were grave and the bombing a serious impediment to aid efforts were prone to be ridiculed or silenced outright – as I discovered in October 2001, when I sought on three separate occasions to post messages about the humanitarian situation in Afghanistan to the H-Genocide academic mailing list.

In the first post (12 October 2001), I cited testimony from humanitarian organizations and United Nations staffers to the effect that the bombing campaign against Afghanistan was the major obstacle to the delivery of desperately needed food aid to the Afghan civilian population. I asked: 'If coalition leaders are aware of the present situation, as most of the major humanitarian agencies and international media appear to be, and choose to continue the bombing in coming weeks … could any resulting large-scale mortality legitimately be termed genocidal?'[13] I did not myself offer an answer to the question, but no matter: all three posts were rejected by the H–Genocide editorial board. As the list editor stated in response to the second attempted post (22 October), the 'overwhelming opinion' of the board 'was that we were not going to publish a message that escalated the human tragedy that is developing to the status of genocide. This was seen … [as] a rather large error', despite the mandate of the mailing list to 'make every effort to encourage a free exchange of ideas,' and the fact that the state's role in committing genocide through famine has been a regular theme of the recent genocide literature, in the context of Stalin's USSR, Mao's China, and Mengistu's Ethiopia (see, e.g., Conquest, 1986; Dolot, 1985). 'There seems to me a fundamental question to be asked here,' I wrote in the third and last of the rejected posts. 'Is it up to the list editors to decide what can legitimately be considered a genocide and which interpretations are "erroneous," and to accept or reject posts on this basis? Is not the appropriate place to discuss and debate this issue the list itself?'

Apparently not. In my third post, I explicitly requested that the H–Genocide board provide me with their reasons for rejecting the posts. Excerpts from correspondence from the board members to the list editor were subsequently forwarded to me. In them, board members referred to me as 'a loose cannon' whose writings were 'libelous and disgraceful' and evoked 'anger and revulsion'; and as someone who taught at a 'hot-bed of anti-American and anti-Western thought' (a patently absurd description of my current institution, CIDE, in Mexico City). One board member accused me of 'terrorist apologism [of the type] that is unfortunately be-coming popular among the enemies of this great country' (i.e. the United States, where eight out of nine members of the editorial board were based); another claimed that I was 'simply sophomoric or … intentionally manipulative.' The extraordinary venom and *ad hominem* character of these responses, I wrote at the time, testified to 'the politically-inspired censor-ship of alternative views' and 'the "chill" that has descended over political discussion and debate in the United States, and elsewhere, since the atrocities of September 11.' In my case, the chill only deepened: in February 2002, I was banned from posting to the H–Genocide list, an editorial-board decision that was formalized (and made permanent) in September of the same year. Subsequently even my right to receive postings by other list members was withdrawn.

In the introduction to this book, I suggested that the genocide-studies community has generally been more willing than others in the social sciences to acknowledge, or at least explore, the Western role in genocide and crimes against humanity. The actions of the H-Genocide editorial board, however – to the limited but not insignificant extent that they can be considered representative of the genocide-studies community as a whole – suggest that constraints remain, and may in fact have increased in the wake of 11 September. The community may still be less prone than others to substitute unthinking patriotism or outright jingoism for reasoned analysis. But it is hardly immune to the temptation.

## Notes

1. Chomsky adds: 'September 11 provided an opportunity and pretext to implement long-standing plans to take control of Iraq's immense oil wealth, a central component of the Persian Gulf resources that the State Department in 1945 described as a "stupendous source of strategic power, and one of the greatest material prizes in world history"' (Chomsky, 2002).

2. For a fine overview of the conflict in Afghanistan and its wider role in US imperial expansion, see Mahajan, 2002. He considers that the United States has adopted 'an overwhelming, overweening unilateralism that has the rest of the world aghast' (Mahajan, 2002: 143).

3. Cafod further noted: 'We would remind the international community that international law obliges those who have taken armed action to make sure that civilians have access to humanitarian aid.'

4. Mahajan charges the US with 'several acts that were highly suggestive of an attempt to impose starvation and suffering selectively as a means of political coercion,' including the repeated and supposedly 'accidental' bombing of the Red Cross warehouse in Kabul, which high-level military sources allegedly considered 'both deliberate and justified,' because it was (mistakenly) believed that the Taliban had commandeered the food supply. Mahajan adds: 'Of course, the first principle of humanitarian relief is that it be impartial, that aid be given on the basis of need without any consideration of political agenda. In fact, tampering with aid on political grounds violates international law. Unfortunately, the United States government has quite a record of doing exactly that' (Mahajan, 2002: 37–8).

5. 'Afghanistan: Stop Abuse in Northern Afghanistan,' Human Rights Watch press release, 7 March 2002.

6. Herold cites Tim Wise's apt comment: 'Even though civilian deaths have not been the deliberate goal of the current bombing – as they were for the attackers of 9/11 – the end result has been a distinction without a difference. Dead is dead, and when one's actions have entirely foreseeable consequences, it is little more than a precious and empty platitude to argue that those consequences were merely accidental.'

7. For PHR's press release on the prison visit, see Physicians for Human Rights, 2002. See also Leaning and Heffernan, 2002: 'In our visit to the prison ... we found cell blocks designed for 20 prisoners holding up to 100 men; 8 to 10 toilets for each 1,000 men; bathing facilities outdoor in the mud; and grossly inadequate food and medical care. Dysentery is epidemic. The prison's commander, General Jarobak, told us that "many, many, many men" had already died.'

8. President Bush's foreign policy advisor Condoleezza Rice, speaking in April 2002,

noted: 'The international system has been in flux since the collapse of Soviet power. Now it is possible – indeed probable – that that transition is coming to an end. If that is right, then … this is a period not just of grave danger, but of enormous opportunity … *a period akin to 1945 to 1947*, when American leadership expanded the number of free and democratic states – Japan and Germany among the greater powers – to create a new balance of power that favored freedom.' Cited in FitzGerald, 2002, emphasis added.

9. At first sight anomalously, the present-day Algerian government pays little heed to the renewed debate over the French use of torture on Algerian territory in the dying years of its colonial rule. An influential military figure referred to it as exclusively an 'internal French affair.' The reason, according to the dissident historian Mohammed Harbi, that government officials 'aren't interested in the debate on torture [is] because they're doing the very same thing today' (Shatz, 2002).

10. US Vice-President Dick Cheney stated in February 2002: 'When America's great enemy suddenly disappeared, many wondered what new direction our foreign policy would take. We spoke, as always, of long-term problems and regional crises throughout the world, but there was no single, immediate, global threat that any roomful of experts could agree upon. All of that changed five months ago [on 11 September]. The threat is known and our role is clear now.' Cited in FitzGerald, 2002.

11. Welch notes that 'In eight of the 50 states, being convicted of any felony is enough to forfeit the very right to vote, for life.' No such forfeiture or other penalty applies, however, if 'the criminal is a Republican politician.… The appointments [of Iran–Contra figures] amount to a declaration that the "rule of law" is no more than a political slogan, hardly worth heeding as long as the government believes its crusade is noble' (Welch, 2002).

12. Robert Scheer has pointed to 'the absurdity … [of] risk[ing] escalating a world-wide nuclear arms race to nuke a shadow terrorist enemy whose most effective military action to date was begun with box cutters.' 'What we need instead,' Scheer argues, 'is a US-led world-wide campaign to shun nuclear weapons as inherently genocidal.… It is we who have defined rogue nations as those bent on developing weapons of mass destruction. How then can we so cavalierly entertain the idea of again leading the world down the path to nuclear Armageddon?' (Scheer, 2002).

13. For the text of all three posts, and the related correspondence referred to here, see Jones, 2002a.

# References

Bardach, A.L. (2002). *Cuba confidential: Love and vengeance in Miami and Havana*. New York: Random House.

Blum, W. (2001). *Rogue state: A guide to the world's only superpower*. London: Zed Books.

Bowman, T. and Gamerman, E. (2001). Aid distribution in Afghanistan deteriorates. *Baltimore Sun*, 5 December.

Breytenbach, B. (2002). Letter to America. *The Nation*, 23 September.

Buncombe, A. (2002). US held responsible for conditions in Afghan jail. *Independent*, 29 January.

Campbell, D. (2001). US buys up all satellite war images. *Guardian*, 17 October.

Carroll, R. (2001). Afghan jailers beat confessions from men. *Guardian*, 28 December.

Cawthorne, A. (2002). Castro oozes anti-U.S. rhetoric, slams war on terror. Associated Press dispatch in *The News* (Mexico City), 10 March.

Cheney, P. (2001). U.S. attacks on Taliban stronghold 'a nightmare.' *Globe and Mail*, December.

Chomsky, N. (2002) *Necessary illusions: Thought control in democratic societies*. Toronto: CBC Enterprises.

———— (2001). The new war against terror. Speech at the Massachusetts Institute of Technology, 18 October. www.zmag.org/GlobalWatch/chomskymit.htm.

Cohne, S.F. (2000). *Failed crusade: America and the tragedy of post-communist Russia*. New York: W.W. Norton.

Conquest, R. (1986). *The harvest of sorrow: Soviet collectivization and the terror-famine*. New York: Oxford University Press.

Conroy, J. (2001) *Unspeakable acts, ordinary people: The dynamics of torture*. Berkeley: University of California Press.

Constable, P. (2002). Afghan women are still policed. *Washington Post*, 28 December.

Cooperman, A. (2002). CIA interrogation under fire: Human rights groups say techniques could be torture. *Washington Post*, 28 December.

Cryan, P. (2001, November). Defining terrorism. *Counterpunch*, 29 November. www.counterpunch.org/cryan1.html.

Dehghanpisheh, B., et al. (2002). The death convoy of Afghanistan. *Newsweek*, 26 August.

Ditmars, H. (2002). Iraqis fear it can only get worse. *San Francisco Chronicle*, 14 February.

Dolot, M. (1985). *Execution by hunger: The hidden holocaust*. New York: W.W. Norton.

Doran, J. (2002). Afghanistan's secret graves: A drive to death in the desert. *Le Monde diplomatique*, September.

*The Economist* (2002a). Greed, fear and confusion to Saddam's rescue. 26 January.

———— (2002b). Who needs whom? 9 March.

———— (2002c). Counter-offensive. 9 March.

———— (2001). Death by bureaucracy. 8 December.

Elliott, L. and Denny, C. (2002). 6m face death if West fails to provide aid. *Guardian*, 13 March.

Elliott, M. (2002). Right man, right time. *Time*, 4 March.

Fairness and Accuracy in Reporting (2001). Media advisory: Media march to war. 17 September. www.fair.org/press-releases/wtc-war-punditry.html.

Fassihi, F. (2001). Afghan refugees' plight may reach epic proportions. Newhouse News Service dispatch in *The News* (Mexico City), 2 December.

Finkel, M. (2002). To wait or flee. *New York Times* Magazine, 17 February.

Fisk, R. (2001). Another war on terror. Another proxy army. Another mysterious massacre. And now, after 19 years, perhaps the truth at last... *Independent*, 4 November.

FitzGerald, F. (2002). How hawks captured the White House. *Guardian* (UK), 24 September.

Gordon, M.R. (2002). Nuclear arms for deterrence or fighting? *New York Times*, 11 March.

Hartung, William D., et al. (2002). Operation endless deployment. *The Nation*, 21 October. www.thenation.com/doc.mhtml?i=20021021&s=hartung.

Herold, M.W. (2001). A dossier on civilian victims of United States' aerial bombing of Afghanistan: A comprehensive accounting. www.zmag.org/herold.htm.

Human Rights Watch (2002). Afghanistan: Stop abuse in northern Afghanistan. Press release, 7 March. www.hrw.org/press/2002/03/pashtest030702.htm.

Italie, H. (2002). Educators aim to make sense of Sept. 11. Associated Press dispatch, 6 March.

Jones, A. (2002a). Censored on H-Genocide. http://adamjones.freeservers.com/h-genocide.html.

———— (2002b). Genocide and humanitarian intervention: Incorporating the gender variable. *Journal of Humanitarian Assistance*, February. www.jha.ac/articles/a080.htm.

Karacs, I. (2001). Humanitarian crisis 'anarchy' leaves 1m without food. *Independent on Sunday*, 9 December.

Kelso, P. and McCarthy, R. (2001). Millions will die unless food convoys resume soon. *Guardian*, 12 October.

Kirschbaum, E. (2002). U.S. role in deaths alleged. *Globe and Mail*, 19 December.

Lamb, C. (2001). They call this 'the slaughterhouse.' *Sunday Telegraph*, 9 December.

Leaning, J. and Heffernan, J. (2002). Forgotten prisoners of war. *New York Times*, 2 February.

Lewis, A. (2002). Bush and Iraq. *New York Review of Books*, 7 November.

Lyon, D. (2002). Hunger and death in Afghan villages. *BBC Online*, 4 February. http://news.bbc.co.uk/hi/english/world/south_asia/newsid_1800000/1800440.stm.

Maass, P. (2002). Gul Agha gets his province back. *New York Times* Magazine, 6 January.

Mahajan, R. (2002). *The new crusade: America's war on terrorism*. New York: Monthly Review Press.

Médecins Sans Frontières (2002). MSF report: Alarming food crisis in northern Afghanistan. 21 February. www.doctorswithoutborders.org/pr/2002/02212002.shtml.

Miller, M.C. (2002). In the wake of 9–11, the American press has embraced a 'demented caesarism.' *ZNet*, 13 September.

New York Times News Service (2002). Attack plan. In *The News* (Mexico City), 10 March.

Oxfam (2001). Aid agency calls for pause in bombing. 17 October. www.caa.org.au/pr/2001/afghanistan5.html.

Parry, R.L. (2001). UN fears 'disaster' over strikes near huge dam. *Independent*, 8 November.

Pfaff, W. (2002). U.S. policies will produce disorder in 2003. *The News* (Mexico City), 28 December.

Pilger, J. (n.d. [November 2001?]). Hidden agenda behind war on terror. www.zmag.org/hiddenpilger.htm.

———— (2001). A war in the American tradition. *New Statesman*, 15 October. www.zmag.org/pilgerwar.htm.

Physicians for Human Rights (2002). Physicians for Human Rights reveals appalling conditions at Shebarghan prison in Afghanistan. 28 January. www.phrusa.org/research/afghanistan/report_release.html.

Scheer, R. (2002). The fallout of desperation: When in doubt, nuke 'em. *ZNet*, 13 March. www.zmag.org/content/TerrorWar/scheernukes.cfm.

Seibert, T. (2001). Warlords waylay aid, sources say. *Denver Post*, 23 November.

Shatz, A. (2002). The torture of Algiers. *New York Review of Books*, 21 November.

Sontag, S. (2002). Real battles and empty metaphors. *New York Times*, 10 September.

Steele, J. and Lawrence, F. (2001). Main aid agencies reject US air drops. *Guardian*, 8 October.

Tremlett, G. (2002). U.S. arms Algeria for fight against Islamic terror. *Guardian*, 10 December.

Turley, J. (2002). Orwellian echoes in U.S. should create outcry. *The News* (Mexico City) (from *Los Angeles Times*), 26 November.

Waldman, A. (2001). Where thousands of drought refugees wait for food or death. *New York Times*, 26 November.

Washington Post Foreign Service (2002). Afghan about-face: U.S. military takes a softer tack. *Washington Post*, 1 October.

Welch, M. (2002). Rubbing salt in old wounds: Bush's appointments of Iran-Contra scandal alumni add insult to unhealed injuries of the Cold War. *National Post*, 14 December.

Wise, T. (2001). Consistently inconsistent: Rhetoric meets reality in the war on terrorism. *ZNet*, 15 November. www.zmag.org/wiseconsist.htm.

# 22

# Letter to America

## Breyten Breytenbach

Dear Jack,

This is an extraordinarily difficult letter to write, and it may even be a perilous exercise. Dangerous because your present Administration and its specialized agencies by all accounts know no restraint in hitting out at any perceived enemy of America, and nobody or nothing can protect one from their vindictiveness. Not even American courts are any longer a bulwark against arbitrary exactions. Take the people being kept in that concentration camp in Guantánamo: They are literally extraterritorial, by force made anonymous and stateless so that no law, domestic or international, is habilitated to protect them. It may be an extreme example brought about by abnormal circumstances – but the criteria of human rights kick in, surely, precisely when the conditions are extreme and the situation is abnormal. The predominant yardstick of your government is not human rights but national interests. (Your President keeps repeating the mantra.) In what way is this order of priorities any different from those of the defunct Soviet Union or other totalitarian regimes?

The war against terror is an all-purpose fig leaf for violating or ignoring local laws and international agreements and treaties. So, talking to America is like dealing with a very aggressive beast: One must do so softly, not make any brusque moves or run off at the mouth if you wish to survive. In dancing with the enemy one follows his steps even if counting under one's breath. But do be careful not to dance too close to containers intended for transporting war prisoners in Afghanistan: One risks finding one's face blackened by a premature death.

Why is it difficult? Because the United States is a complex entity despite the gung-ho slogans and simplistic posturing in moments of national hysteria. Your political system is resilient and well tested; it has always harbored counterforces; it allows quite effectively for alternation: for a swing-back of the pendulum whenever policies have strayed too far from middle-class interests – with the result that you have a large middle ground of acceptable political practices. Why, through the role of elected representatives, the people who vote even have a rudimentary democratic control over public affairs! Except maybe in Florida. Better still – your history has shown how powerful a moral catharsis expressed through popular resistance to injustice can sometimes be; I have in mind the grassroots opposition to the Vietnam War. And all along there was no dearth of strong voices speaking firm convictions and enunciating sure ethical standards.

Where are they now? What happened to the influential intellectuals and the trustworthy journalists explaining the ineluctable consequences of your present policies? Where are the clergy calling for humility and some compassion for the rest of the world? Are there no ordinary folk pointing out that the President and his cronies are naked, cynical, morally reprehensible and very, very dangerous not only for the world but also for American interests – and by now probably out of control? Are these voices stifled? Has the public arena of freely debated expressions of concern been sapped of all influence? Are people indifferent to the havoc wreaked all over the world by America's diktat policies, destroying the underpinnings of decent international coexistence? Or are they perhaps secretly and shamefully gleeful, as closet supporters of this Showdown at OK Corral approach? They (and you and I) are most likely hunkered down, waiting for the storm of imbecility to pass. How deadened we have become!

In reality the workings of your governing system are opaque and covert, while hiding in the chattering spotlight of an ostensible transparency, even though the ultimate objective is clear. Who really makes the policy decisions? Sure, the respective functions are well identified: The elected representatives bluster and raise money, the lobbyists buy and sell favors, the media spin and purr patriotically, the intellectuals wring their soft hands, the minorities duck and dive and hang out flags ... But who and what are the forces shaping America's role in the world?

The goal, I submit, is obvious: subjugating the world (which is barbarian, dangerous, envious and ungrateful) to US power for the sake of America's interests. That is, to the benefit of America's rich. It's as simple as that. Oh, there was a moment of high camp when it was suggested that the aim was to make the world safe for democracy! That particular fig leaf went up in cigar smoke and now all the other excuses are just so much bullshit, even the charlatan pretense of being a nation under siege. This last one, I further submit, was a sustained Orson Wellesian campaign to stampede the nation in order to better facilitate what was in effect a right-wing coup carried out by cracker fundamentalists, desk warriors proposing to 'terminate' the states that they don't like, warmed up Dr Strangeloves and oil-greedy conservative capitalists.

I do not want to equate your glorious nation with the deplorable image of a President who, at best, appears to be a bar-room braggart smirking and winking to his mates as he holds forth his hand-me-down platitudes and insights and naïve solutions. Because I know you have many faces and I realize how rich you are in diversity. Would I be writing this way if I had in mind a black or Hispanic or Asian-American, members of those vastly silent components of your society? It would be a tragic mistake for us out here to imagine that Bush represents the hearts and the minds of the majority of your countrymen. Many of your black and other compatriots must be just as anguished as we are.

Still, Jack, certain things need to be said and repeated. I realize it is difficult for you to know what's happening in the world, since your entertainment media have by now totally blurred the distinctions between information and propaganda, and banal psychological and commercial manipulation must be the least effective way of disseminating understanding. You need to know that your country has made the world a much more dangerous place for the rest of us. International treaties to limit the destruction of our shared natural environment, to stop the manufacture of maiming personnel mines, to outlaw torture, to bring war criminals to international justice, to do something about the murderous and growing gulf between rich and poor, to guarantee natural food for the humble of the earth, to allow for local economic solutions to specific conditions of injustice, for that matter to permit local products to have access to American markets, to mobilize the world against hunger, have all been gutted by the USA. Your government is blackmailing every single miserable and corrupt mother's son in power in the world to do things your way. It has forced itself on the rest of us in its support and abetment of corrupt and tyrannical regimes. It has lost all ethical credibility in its one-sided and unequivocal support of the Israeli government campaign that must ultimately lead to the ethnocide of the Palestinians. And in this it has promoted – sponsored? – the bringing about of a deleterious international climate, since state terrorism can now be carried out with arrogance, disdain and impunity. As far as the Arab nations are concerned, America, giving unquestioned legitimacy to despotic regimes, refusing any recognition of home-grown alternative democratic forces, favored the emergence of a bearded opposition who in time must become radicalized and fanaticized to the point where they can be exterminated as vermin. And the oilfields will be safe.

I'm too harsh. I'm cutting corners. I'm pontificating. But my friend, if you were to look around the world you would see that America is largely perceived as a rogue state.

Can there be a turn-back? Have things gone too far, beyond a point of possible return? Can it be that some of the core and founding assumptions (it is said) of your culture are ultimately dangerous to the survival of the world? I'm referring to your propensity for patriotism (to me it's an attitude, not a value), to the fervent belief in a capitalist free-market system with the concomitant conviction that progress is infinite, that one can eternally remake and invent the self, that it is more important to be self-made than to collectively husband the planet's diminishing resources, that the instant gratification of the desire for goods is the substance of the right to happiness, that the world and life and all its manifestations can be apprehended and described in terms of good and evil, finally that you can flare for a while in samsara, the world of illusions (and desperately make it last with artificial means and Californian hocus-pocus before taking all your prostheses to heaven).

If this is so, what then? With whom? You see, the most detestable effect is that so many of us have to drink this poison, to look at you as a threat, to live with the knowledge of cultural and economic and military danger in our veins, and to be obliged to either submit or resist.

I don't want to pass the buck. Don't imagine it is necessarily any better elsewhere. We, in this elsewhere, have to look for our own solutions. Europe is pusillanimous, carefully though hypocritically hostile and closed to foreigners, particularly those from the South; the EU is by now little more than a convenience for its citizens and politically and culturally much less than the contents of any of its constituent parts.

And Africa? As a part-time South African (the other parts are French and Spanish and Senegalese and New Yorker), I've always wondered whether Thabo Mbeki would be America's thin globalizing wedge (at the time of Clinton and Gore it certainly seemed so) or whether he was ultimately going to be the leader who can strategically lead Africa against America. But the question is hypothetical. Thabo Mbeki is no alternative to the world economic system squeezing the poor for the sustainable enrichment of the rich; as in countries like Indonesia and your own (see the role of the oil companies), he too has opted for crony capitalism. Africa's leading establishments are rotten to the core. Mbeki is no different. His elocution is more suave and his prancing more Western, that's all.

What do we do, then? As we move into the chronicle of a war foretold (against Iraq), it is going to be difficult to stay cool. Certainly, we must continue fighting globalization as it exists now, reject the article of faith that postulates a limitless and lawless progress and expansion of greed, subvert the acceptance of might is right, spike the murderous folly of One God. And do so cautiously and patiently, counting our steps. It is going to be a long dance.

Let us find and respect one another.

Your friend,
    Breyten Breytenbach

## Note

Originally published in *The Nation*, 23 September 2002.

# About the Contributors

**Mohamed Diriye Abdullahi** is a linguist specializing in the languages, cultures, and history of the Horn of Africa. He holds a Ph.D. in linguistics from Université de Montréal. He has been variously a teacher of French, a translator, and a press and radio journalist in Somalia. He is currently an independent researcher. He is the author of *Parlons Somali* (L'Harmattan, 1996); *The Culture and Customs of Somalia* (Greenwood Press, 2001); and *Fiasco in Somalia: The US–UN Intervention* (Africa Institute of South Africa, 1995). *Email*: mdiriye@hotmail.com

**Mario I. Aguilar** is Dean of the Faculty of Divinity at the University of St Andrews, Scotland, and author of several books, including *The Rwanda Genocide* (AMECEA Gaba Publications, 1998). *Email*: mia2@stand.ac.uk

**Raphaëlle Branche** teaches Contemporary History at the University of Rennes. She is also an Associate Researcher at the Contemporary History Institute (CNRS), where she jointly conducts a seminar on Repression, Administration and Supervision in the Colonial World in the Twentieth Century. She has published *La Torture et l'armée pendant la guerre d'Algérie, 1954–1962* (Gallimard, 2001). *Email*: raphaell@club-internet.fr

**Breyten Breytenbach** is one of the leading figures in modern South African arts. He was jailed by the apartheid regime on terrorism charges in 1975, and moved to Paris upon his release in 1982. His prison memoir, *The True Confessions of an Albino Terrorist*, appeared the following year. His paintings have been exhibited in many countries since the early 1960s. Among his many prizes and awards are the Alan Paton Award for Literature (South Africa) and the Prix d'Ivry pour la Peinture (France). He is a faculty member of the Graduate School of Creative Writing at New York University, and from 2000 to 2003 was Visiting Professor in the Graduate School of Humanities at the University of Cape Town.

**Ward Churchill** (Keetoowah Band Cherokee) is Professor of American Indian Studies and Chair of the Department of Ethnic Studies at the University of Colorado/Boulder. Among his more than twenty books are *A Little Matter of Genocide: Holocaust and Denial in the Americas, 1492 to the Present* (1997), *Struggle for the Land:*

*Native North American Resistance to Genocide, Ecocide and Colonization* (1999), and *Acts of Rebellion: The Ward Churchill Reader* (2003). *Email*: Ward.Churchill@ Colorado.edu

**Ramsey Clark** was Attorney General of the United States from 1967 to 1969, when he gained renown for his commitment to civil liberties and civil rights. He was also the first Attorney General to support abolition of the death penalty. He subsequently taught law and became prominent in the movement against the Vietnam War. He convened the Commission of Inquiry for the International War Crimes Tribunal investigating crimes against the Iraqi people during the 1990–91 Gulf War and the era of economic sanctions that followed.

**Jan-Bart Gewald** works at the African Studies Centre in Leiden, the Netherlands, and has taught at the University of Leiden and the Institute for African Studies at the University of Cologne, Germany. He has studied African History and African Political Studies at Rhodes University, South Africa, and holds a Ph.D. in History from the University of Leiden in the Netherlands. He has published two books on Herero history: *Herero Heroes: A Socio-Political History of the Herero of Namibia, 1890–1923* (Oxford, 1999) and *We Thought We Would Be Free: Socio-cultural Aspects of Herero History in Namibia* (Cologne, 2000); has coedited a volume on Herero society with Michael Bollig, *People, Cattle and Land: The Herero Speaking People of Southern Africa* (Cologne, 2001); and, together with Jeremy Silvester, has published an annotated new edition of the British government 'Blue Book' dealing with the Herero genocide in Namibia. Apart from a number of book contributions, his articles have appeared in the *Journal of African History*, the *Journal of African Cultural Studies*, *African Affairs* and other publications. *Email*: gewald@fsw.leidenuniv.nl

**Denis J. Halliday** worked with the United Nations for three-and-a-half decades, including as Assistant Secretary General for Human Resources Management and UN Humanitarian Coordinator for Iraq. He resigned in November 1998 in protest over sanctions against Iraq. He is presently Lang Visiting Professor for Social Change at Swarthmore College in Pennsylvania.

**Syed Hassan** is an Associate Professor in the Department of English and Foreign Languages at Claflin University in Orangeburg, South Carolina. He holds a Master's degree in English Literature and another in History from the University of Dhaka, Bangladesh. Dr Hassan has completed his Ph.D. in Modern English Poetry at Purdue University, Indiana. *Email*: Syedkmhassan@sc.rr.com

**Suhail Mohiul Islam** is Assistant Professor of English at the Nazareth College of Rochester, New York. Currently, his main research field is postcolonial discourse analysis, sociolinguistics and rhetoric and technical communication, with particular reference to United States and South Asia. He has written on empire and literacy, and is currently working on socio-political themes in South Asian languages and literature. *Email*: smislam@naz.edu

**Steven L. Jacobs** holds the Aaron Aronov Chair of Judaic Studies at the University of Alabama, Tuscaloosa, AL, where he is an Associate Professor of Religious Studies. His primary fields of interest are Holocaust and Genocide Studies as well as post-biblical Jewish and Christian religious thought and re-interpretation. Among his books are *Contemporary Jewish and Contemporary Christian Religious Responses to the Holocaust* (1992); *Raphael Lemkin's Thoughts on Nazi Genocide* (1992); *Rethinking*

*Jewish Faith: The Child of a Survivor Responds* (1994); *The Holocaust Now: Contemporary Christian and Jewish Thought* (1996); and *Pioneers of Genocide Studies* (2002, with Samuel Totten). He also served as Associate Editor of the *Encyclopedia of Genocide* (1999), and is the Secretary-Treasurer of the International Association of Genocide Scholars. *Email*: sjacobs@bama.ua.edu

**Adam Jones** is currently Professor of International Studies at the Center for Research and Teaching in Economics (CIDE) in Mexico City. He is author *of Beyond the Barricades: Nicaragua and the Struggle for the Sandinista Press, 1979–1998* (Ohio University Press, 2002), and editor of *Gendercide and Genocide* (Vanderbilt University Press, forthcoming). His scholarly articles have appeared in *Review of International Studies, Ethnic and Racial Studies, Journal of Genocide Research, Journal of Human Rights*, and other publications. He is Executive Director of Gendercide Watch (www.gendercide.org), a Web-based educational initiative. *Personal website*: adamjones.freeservers.com. *Email*: adamj_jones@hotmail.com

**Arthur Jay Klinghoffer** is a Professor of Political Science at Rutgers University. His two most recent books are *The International Dimension of Genocide in Rwanda* (New York University Press, 1998) and, as coauthor, *International Citizens' Tribunals: Mobilizing Public Opinion to Advance Human Rights* (Palgrave, 2002). Dr Klinghoffer has been a Senior Fellow at the Nobel Institute in Oslo, and a Fulbright Professor in China and Israel.

**Eric Langenbacher** is a Visiting Assistant Professor at the Department of Government, Georgetown University. His dissertation, defended with distinction in September 2002, is titled 'Memory Regimes in Contemporary Germany,' and is currently being turned into a book manuscript. His next research project will look at at the degree to which ethnic minorities in Germany and Europe accept dominant collective memories. *Email*: langenbe@georgetown.edu

**David Bruce MacDonald** holds a Ph.D. in International Relations from the London School of Economics and Political Science. His first book, *Balkan Holocausts? Serbian and Croatian Victim Centred Propaganda and the War in Yugoslavia* was published in 2003 by Manchester University Press. From 1999 to 2003 he was Assistant Visiting Professor in the social sciences at the École Supérieur de Commerce de Paris (ESCP-EAP). He is currently a Lecturer in Political Studies at the University of Otago in Dunedin, New Zealand. *Email*: david.macdonald@stonebow.otago.ac.nz

**Linda R. Melvern** is one of Britain's leading investigative journalists. Since leaving the *Sunday Times* she has published four books, including, in 1995, a fifty-year history of the UN. Her book on the genocide in Rwanda, *A People Betrayed: The Role of the West in Rwanda's Genocide*, (Zed Books/St. Martin's Palgrave) was published in 2000, and is in its third printing. She is an Honorary Fellow of the University of Wales, Aberystwyth, in the Department of International Politics. An archive of the documents used in the research for *A People Betrayed* is in a special collection at the Hugh Owen Library, University of Wales, Aberystwyth. *Email*: linda@melvern.co.uk

**Francis Njubi Nesbitt** is an Assistant Professor of Africana Studies at San Diego State University in San Diego, California. He teaches African American politics, black political thought and race and public policy. He is the author of *Race for Sanctions: African Americans against Apartheid, 1946–1994* (Indiana University Press,

2003). For 2003–04, Dr Nesbitt is a Visiting Professor at the University of California, Los Angeles, where he is completing his second book, *African Intellectuals in the Belly of the Beast: Migration, Identity and the Politics of Exile*. email: fnesbitt@mail.sdsu.edu

**Peter G. Prontzos** teaches Political Science at Langara College in Vancouver, Canada. Born in San Francisco, he has been a writer and activist in movements for democracy, peace, and social justice since the US attack on Vietnam, when he moved to Canada to resist Indochina service with the Marine corps. His dishonourable discharge holds pride of place on his office wall. He has three wonderful children, Rachael, Eleni, and Yeorgios. *Email*: pprontzo@langara.bc.ca

**Jean-Paul Sartre** (1905–1980) was one of France's leading twentieth-century philosophers, novelists, and playwrights. He was also a vocal opponent of the French war against Algeria and the US war against Indochina. Among his numerous essays is 'On Genocide,' prepared for the Russell Tribunal on war crimes in Vietnam (1967).

**Peter Dale Scott** is a former Canadian diplomat and Professor of English at the University of California, Berkeley. His latest book is *Drugs, Oil, and War: The United States in Afghanistan, Colombia, and Indochina* (Rowman & Littlefield, 2003). In 2000, he published *Minding the Darkness*, the final volume of his poetic trilogy *Seculum*. In 2002 he received the Lannan Poetry Award. *Email*: pdscottweb@hotmail.com

**Peter Stoett** is an Associate Professor of Political Science at Concordia University in Montreal. His research and publications focus on human rights and environmental issues, and international relations theory. His recent books include *Human and Global Security: An Exploration of Terms* (University of Toronto Press, 2000) and, with Allen Sens, *Global Politics: Origins, Currents, Directions* (ITP Nelson, 2001). *Email*: pstoett@vax2.concordia.ca

**Thomas Turner** is Professor of Political Science at the National University of Rwanda. He is the author of *Ethnogenèse et nationalisme en Afrique centrale: les racines de Lumumba* (Harmattan, 2000), and co-author (with Crawford Young) of *The Rise and Decline of the Zairian State* (University of Wisconsin Press, 1985). *Email*: tommyagain@yahoo.com

**Ernesto Verdeja** is a Ph.D. candidate in Political Science at the Graduate Faculty of the New School University in New York City. His dissertation examines the normative underpinnings of truth commissions and tribunals, and their contributions to larger processes of reconciliation in post-atrocity societies. *Email*: ven8202@mindspring.com

**S. Brian Willson**, a former US Air Force Captain, directed a combat security unit in Vietnam in 1969. His global travels as a civilian continue to document US violations of international laws committed with almost total impunity. He was nearly killed in 1987 during a peaceful protest of US Central American policies, losing both legs and suffering a skull fracture and severe brain injury. His essays are available at www.brianwillson.com; he has also published a book, *On Third World Legs* (Charles Kerr, 1992). Willson holds two honorary Ph.D.s, an M.S. in correctional administration, and a Juris Doctor. *Email*: bw@brianwillson.com

# Index